SOMETHING ABOUT THE AUTHOR

SOMETHING ABOUT THE AUTHOR

Facts and Pictures about Authors
and Illustrators of Books for Young People

Anne Commire

VOLUME 16

GALE RESEARCH
BOOK TOWER
DETROIT, MICHIGAN
48226

Also Published by Gale

CONTEMPORARY AUTHORS

*A Bio-Bibliographical Guide to Current Writers in
Fiction, General Nonfiction, Poetry, Journalism,
Drama, Motion Pictures, Television,
and Other Fields*

(Now Covers Nearly 56,000 Authors)

Associate Editors: Agnes Garrett, Helga McCue

Assistant Editor: Linda Shedd

Consultant: Adele Sarkissian

Sketchwriters: Dianne H. Anderson, Rosemary DeAngelis Bridges,
Catherine Coray, D. Jayne Higo, Gail Schermer,
Susan L. Stetler

Research Assistant: Kathleen Betsko

Editorial Assistant: Elisa Ann Sawchuk

Table of Contents

Introduction

Beginning with Volume 15, the time span covered by *Something about the Author* was broadened to include major children's writers who died before 1961, which was the former cut-off point for writers covered in this series. This change will make *SATA* even more helpful to its many thousands of student and professional users.

Authors who did not come within the scope of *SATA* have formerly been included in *Yesterday's Authors of Books for Children,* of which Gale has published two volumes.

It has been pointed out by users, however, that it is inconvenient to have a body of related materials broken up by an arbitrary criterion such as the date of a person's death. Also, some libraries are not able to afford both series, and are therefore denied access to material on some of the most important writers in the juvenile field.

It has been decided, therefore, to discontinue the *YABC* series, and to include in *SATA* at least the most outstanding among the older writers who had been selected for listing in *YABC*. Volumes 1 and 2 of *YABC* will be kept in print, and the listings in those two volumes will be included in the cumulative *SATA* index.

GRATEFUL ACKNOWLEDGEMENT

is made to the following publishers, authors, and artists, for their kind permission to reproduce copyrighted material. ■ **W. H. ALLEN & CO., LTD.** Illustration by Miroslav Sasek from *This is Edinburgh* by Miroslav Sasek. Copyright © 1968 by Miroslav Sasek./ Illustration by Miroslav Sasek from *This is Ireland* by Miroslav Sasek. Copyright © 1969 Miroslav Sasek./ Illustration by Miroslav Sasek from *This is London* by Miroslav Sasek. Copyright © 1969 by Miroslav Sasek./ Illustration by Miroslav Sasek from *This is San Francisco* by Miroslav Sasek. Copyright © 1962 by Miroslav Sasek. All reprinted by permission of W. H. Allen & Co., Ltd. ■ **AMERICAN LIBRARY ASSOCIATION.** Sidelight excerpts from an article "Of Life, Love, Death, Kids, and Inhalation Therapy: An Interview with Paul Zindel," Winter, 1968, *Top of the News.*/ Sidelight excerpts from *British Children's Authors* by Cornelia Jones and Olivia R. Way. Copyright © 1976 by the American Library Association. Both reprinted by permission of American Library Association. ■ **ARTEMIS VERLAG.** Illustration from *Celestino Piatti's Animal ABC*, text by Jon Reid. Copyright © 1965 by Artemis Verlag (Zurich). Reprinted by permission of Artemis Verlag. ■ **ATHENEUM PUBLISHERS.** Illustration by Harold Little from *A Flag at the Pole* by Paxton Davis. Copyright © 1976 by Paxton Davis./ Illustration from *Celestino Piatti's Animal ABC*, text by Jon Reid. Copyright © 1965 by Artemis Verlag (Zurich)./ Illustration by Haig and Regina Shekerjian from *The Boy, The Rat, and The Butterfly* by Beatrice de Regniers. Drawings copyright © 1971 by Haig and Regina Shekerjian. All reprinted by permission of Atheneum Publishers. ■ **ATLANTIC MONTHLY PRESS.** Illustration by Walter Lorraine from *McBroom and the Beanstalk* by Sid Fleishman. Text copyright © 1978 by Albert S. Fleishman. Illustrations copyright © 1978 by Walter H. Lorraine. Reprinted by permission of Atlantic Monthly Press. ■ **THE BOBBS-MERRILL CO.** Illustration by Nathan Goldstein from *Allen Pinkerton, Young Detective* by Kathryn Kilby Borland and Helen Ross Speicher. Copyright © 1962 by The Bobbs-Merrill Co./ Illustration by Rafaello Busoni from *Why the Chimes Rang* by Raymond MacDonald Alden. Copyright 1954 by The Bobbs-Merrill Co. Both reprinted by permission of the Bobbs-Merrill Co. ■ **THE BODLEY HEAD.** Illustration by Shirley Hughes from *Dogger* by Shirley Hughes. Copyright © 1977 by Shirley Hughes./ Sidelight excerpts from Andrew Lang by Roger Lancelyn Green. Copyright © 1962 by The Bodley Head./ Sidelight excerpts from *The Bodley Head Monographs: Walter de la Mare* by Leonard Clark. All reprinted by permission of The Bodley Head. ■ **R. R. BOWKER CO.** Sidelight excerpts from an article "Monjo's Manifest Destiny," May 15, 1974, *Library Journal.* Reprinted by permission of R. R. Bowker Co. ■ **JONATHAN CAPE, LTD.** Illustration by Kay Nielsen from *Red Magic: A Collection of the World's Best Fairy Tales*, edited by R. Wilson. Reprinted by permission of Jonathan Cape, Ltd. ■ **CHILTON BOOK CO.** Sidelight excerpts from *Horatio's Boys* by Edwin Hoyt. Copyright © 1974 by Edwin Hoyt. Reprinted by permission of Chilton Book Co. ■ **CHRISTIAN SCIENCE PUBLISHING SOCIETY.** Sidelight excerpts from an article "You Plant a Way of Looking . . .," by Pamela Marsh, Nov. 6, 1969, *Christian Science Monitor.* Reprinted by permission of Christian Science Publishing Society. ■ **WILLIAM COLLINS SONS, LTD.** Illustration by Will Nickless from *King Solomon's Mines* by Henry Rider Haggard. Reprinted by permission of William Collins Sons, Ltd. ■ **COWARD, McCANN AND GEOGHEGAN, INC.** Illustration by Cyndy Szekeres from *Four-Ring Three* by Miriam Anne Bourne. Illustrations copyright © 1973 by Cyndy Szekeres./ Illustration by Joel Schick from *The 17 Gerbils of Class 4A* by William H. Hooks. Illustrations copyright © 1976 by Pongid Productions./ Illustration by Margot Tomes from *The Secrets of the Sachem's Tree* by F. N. Monjo. Copyright © 1972 by F. N. Mongo and Margot Tomes./ Illustration by Arabelle Wheatley from *Cracks and Crannies — What Lives There* by Wilda Ross. Illustrations copyright © 1975 by Arabelle Wheatley. All reprinted by permission of Coward, McCann and Geoghegan, Inc. ■ **CREATION HOUSE.** Sidelight excerpts from *Maria* by Maria von Trapp. Reprinted by permission of Creation House. ■ **THOMAS Y. CROWELL CO.** Illustration by John Burningham from *The Blanket* by John Burningham. Copyright © 1975 by John Burningham./ Illustration by Moneta Barnett from *James Weldon Johnson* by Ophelia Settle Egypt. Illustrations copyright © 1974 by Moneta Barnett./ Illustration by Janet Archer from *A Question of Courage* by Marjorie Darke. All reprinted by permission of Thomas Y. Crowell Co. ■ **T. S. DENISON AND CO.** Illustration by Howard E. Lindberg from "The Adventures of Sinbad the Sailor" in *Folk Tales of Arabia* by L. E. Leipold. Copyright MCMLXXIII by T. S. Denison and Co. Reprinted by permission of T. S. Denison and Co. ■ **J. M. DENT AND SONS, LTD.** Illustration by Babs Van Wely from *The Seven-Times Search*, English version by Gillian Hume and Paul Biegel. Copyright © 1971, English translation, J. M. Dent and Sons Ltd./ Illustration by E. H. Shepard from *The Brownies and Other Stories* by J. H. Ewing. First published in this edition 1964./ Illustration by Randolph Caldecott from *Lob Lie by the Fire* in *Lob Lie-by-the Fire [and] The Story of a Short Life* by Mrs. Ewing. First published in this edition 1964./ All reprinted by permission of J. M. Dent and Sons, Ltd. ■ **ANDRÉ DEUTSCH, LTD.** Wood engravings by Joseph Sloan from *Faraway World* by W. Towrie Cutt. Copyright © 1977 by W. Towrie Cutt. Illustrations copyright © 1977 by Joseph Sloan. Reprinted by permission of André Deutsch, Ltd. ■ **THE DIAL PRESS.** Illustrations by Tom Feelings from *Moja Means One* by Muriel Feelings. Illustrations copyright © 1971 by Tom Feelings./ Illustrations by Mercer Mayer from *Ah-Choo* by Mercer Mayer. Copyright © 1976 by Mercer Mayer./ Illustration by Mercer Mayer from *Frog Goes to Dinner* by Mercer Mayer. Copyright © 1974 by Mercer Mayer. All reprinted by permission of The Dial Press. ■ **DOUBLEDAY & CO., INC.** Jacket illustration by Howard Berelson from *The Quest for Atlantis* by John S. Bowman. Copyright © 1971 by John S. Bowman./ Illustration by Kay Nielsen from *Twelve Dancing Princesses and Other Fairy Tales* by A. T. Quiller-Couch. Both reprinted by permission of Doubleday & Co., Inc. ■ **E. P. DUTTON CO.** Illustration by E. H. Shepard from *The Brownies and Other Stories* by J. H. Ewing. First published in this edition 1964./ Illustration by Randolph Caldecott from *Lob Lie by the Fire* in *Lob Lie-by-the-Fire [and] The Story of a Short Life* by Mrs. Ewing. First published in this edition 1964./ Sidelight excerpts taken from the introduction to *When I Was a Child: An Anthology*, edited by Edward Wagenknecht. Copyright © 1946 by Edward Wagenknecht. All reprinted by permission of E. P. Dutton Co. ■ **FABER AND FABER, LTD.** Illustration by Rex Whistler from *The Lord Fish* by Walter de la Mare./ Sidelight excerpts from *Tea With Walter de la Mare* by Russell Brain. Both reprinted by permission of Faber. ■ **FOUR WINDS PRESS.** Woodcut by Nonny Hogrogian from *Country Cat, City Cat* by David Kherdian. Copyright © 1979 by David Kherdian and Nonny H. Kherdian. Reprinted by permission of Four Winds Press, a division of Scholastic Book Services, Inc. ■ **GROSSET AND DUNLAP, INC.** Illustration by Rafaello Busoni from *A Tale of Two Cities* by Charles Dickens. Copyright © 1948 by Grosset and Dunlap, Inc. Reprinted by permission of Grosset and Dunlap, Inc. ■ **HARCOURT BRACE JOVANOVICH, INC.** Illustration by Pamela Johnson from *Nothing Rhymes with April* by Naomi J. Karp. Illustrations copyright © 1974 Harcourt Brace Jovanovich, Inc./ Illustration by Paul Nussbaumer from *William Tell and His Son* By Bettina Hürlimann./ Copyright © 1965 Atlantis Verlag (AG Zurich). Both reprinted by permission of Harcourt Brace Jovanovich, Inc. ■ **HARPER AND ROW, PUBLISHERS, INC.** Illustration by Harry Bertschmann from *The Other Side of a Poem* by Barbara Abercrombie. Copyright © 1977 by Barbara Mattes Abercrombie./ Sidelight excerpts from *Harper's Weekly*, Volume 53, June 12, 1909./ Illustration by Howard Pyle from *Howard Pyle's Book of Pirates* by Howard Pyle. Copyright 1921 by Harper & Bros./ Illustration by Ben Schecter from *A Summer Secret* by Ben Shecter. Copyright © 1977 by Ben Schecter./ Illustrations by Doug Kingman from *The Effect of Gamma Rays on Man in the Moon Marigolds* by Paul Zindel. Copyright © 1970, 1971 by Paul Zindel./ Illustrations by John Melo from *I Love My Mother* by Paul Zindel. Illustrations copyright © 1975 by John Melo. All reprinted by permission of Harper and Row, Publishers, Inc. ■ **HARVEY HOUSE, INC.** Illustration by William Sauts Bock from *Malcolm Yucca Seed* by Lynne Gessner. Copyright © 1977 by Harvey House. Reprinted by permission of Harvey House, Inc. ■ **HASTINGS HOUSE, PUBLISHERS, INC.** Illustration by Barbara Cooney from *Wynken, Blynken and Nod* by Eugene Field. Copyright © 1964 by Barbara Cooney Porter./ Illustration by Sonia O. Lisker from *The House on Pendleton Block* by Ann Waldron. Copyright © 1975 by Ann Waldron. Both reprinted by permission of Hastings House, Publishers, Inc. ■ **HEARST MAGAZINES.** Sidelight excerpts from an article "You've Never Seen Anything Like Her," by Rex Reed, November, 1972, *Harper's Bazaar*. Reprinted by permission of Hearst Magazine. ■ **HODDER & STROUGHTON, LTD.** Illustrations by Kay Nielsen from *East of the Sun, West of the Moon: Old Tales from the North* by Peter Christen Asbjörnsen and Jörgen Engebretsen./ Illustration by Kay Nielsen from *Hansel and Gretel and Other Stories* by Jacob Ludwig Karl and Wilhelm Karl Grimm./ Sidelight excerpts from *The Cloak That I Left* by Lilias Rider Haggard. All reprinted by permission of Hodder and Stoughton, Ltd. ■ **HOLIDAY HOUSE.** Illustration by Joseph Cellini from *The First Days of Life* by Russell Freedman. Text copyright © 1974 by Russell Freedman. Illustrations copyright © 1974 by Holiday House. Reprinted by permission of Holiday House. ■ **HOLT, RINEHART AND WINSTON.** Illustration by Sandra E. Case from *Let's Do Yoga* by Ruth Richards and Joy Abrams. Copyright © 1975 by Holt, Rinehart and Winston, Inc./ Illustration by Dorothy Lathrop from *Mr. Bumps and His Monkey* by Walter de la Mare. Copyright 1942 by the John C. Winston Co./ Illustration from *This Year: Next Year* by Walter de la Mare and Harold Jones./ Illustration by H. M. Brock from *The Mahatma and the Hare* by H. Rider Haggard. Copyright 1911 by Henry Holt and Co./ Illustration by Adrienne Adams from *The Twelve Dancing Princesses* by Andrew Lang. Illustrations copyright © 1966 by Adrienne Adams./ Illustration by Gerald McDermott from *Anan-*

si the Spider, adapted by Gerald McDermott. Copyright © 1972 by Landmark Production, Inc./ Illustration by Brinton Turkle from *Poor Richard in France* by F. N. Monjo. Copyright © 1973 by Ferdinand Monjo and Lousie L. Monjo and Brinton Turkle./ Sidelight excerpts from *Lessons of a Lifetime* by Lord Baden-Powell. All reprinted by permission of Holt, Rinehart and Winston. ■ **THE HORN BOOK, INC.** Sidelight excerpts from *Illustrators of Children's Books: 1946-1956,* compiled by Bertha Mahony Miller and others. Copyright © 1958 by The Horn Book, Inc./ Sidelight excerpts from an article "Great Men, Melodies, Experiments, Plots, Predictability, and Surprises," October, 1975, *Horn Book.*/ Sidelight excerpts from an article "On the Rainbow Trail," April, 1975, *Horn Book.*/ Sidelight excerpt from an article "New Approaches to Writing and Illustrating Children's Books," edited by Bertha Miller and Elinor Whitney Field, *Caldecott Medal Books: 1938-1957.* All reprinted by permission of The Horn Book, Inc. ■ **HOUGHTON MIFFLIN CO.** Illustration by Arnold Edwin Bare from *Mauis' Summer* by Arnold Edwin Bare. Reprinted by permission of Houghton Mifflin Co. ■ **ALFRED A. KNOPF, INC.** Illustration by Barbara Cooney from *Peacock Pie* by Walter de la Mare. Copyright © 1961 by Barbara Cooney./ Illustration by Alan Howard from *Tales Told Again* by Walter de la Mare. Copyright 1927 & renewed 1955 by Walter de la Mare./ Illustration by Lady McCrady from *An Umbrella Named Umbrella* by Tobi Tobias. Text copyright © 1976 by Tobi Tobias. Illustrations copyright © 1976 by Lady McCrady./ Illustration by Mai Vo-Dinh from *First Snow* by Helen Coutant. Text copyright © 1974 by Helen Coutant. Illustrations copyright © 1974 by Vo-Dinh./ Sidelight excerpts from the introduction to *Tom Tiddler's Ground,* edited by Walter de la Mare./ Sidelight excerpts from the introduction to *Stories from the Bible,* edited by Walter de la Mare./ Illustration by Eva Hülsmann from *The Giant Panda at Home* by Margaret Rau. Text copyright © 1977 by Margaret Rau. Illustrations copyright © 1977 by Alfred A. Knopf. All reprinted by permission of Alfred A. Knopf, Inc., a division of Random House, Inc. ■ **LITTLE, BROWN AND CO.** Illustration by Robert Lawson from *Mr. Popper's Penguins* by Richard and Florence Atwater. Copyright © 1938 by Florence Atwater, Doris Atwater and Carroll Atwater Bishop./ Illustration by Frank T. Merrill from *The Man Without a Country.*/ Illustration by Trina Schart Hyman from *King Stork* by Howard Pyle. Illustrations copyright © 1973 by Trina Schart Hyman./ Photograph by Henry Humphrey from *The Sights and Sounds of Flying,* text by Henry Humphrey. Text, illustrations and sound recordings copyright © 1973 by Henry Humphrey./ Sidelight excerpts from *The Life and Letters of Edward Everett Hale* by Edward E. Hale, Jr., Volume I./ Sidelight excerpts from *The Life and Letters of Edward Everett Hale* by Edward E. Hale, Jr. Volume II./ Sidelight excerpts from *A New England Boyhood* by Edward Everett Hale. All reprinted by permission of Little, Brown and Co. ■ **LONGMANS, GREEN & CO.** Illustration by Maurice Greiffenhagen from *She: A History of Adventure* by H. Rider Haggard. Illustrations by Marc Simont from *Red Fairy Book,* edited by Andrew Lang. Copyright 1948 by Longmans, Green and Co./ Sidelight excerpts from *The Days of My Life: An Autobiography,* edited by C. J. Longman, Volume I./ Sidelight excerpts from *The Days of My Life: An Autobiography,* edited by C. J. Longman, Volume II. All reprinted by permission of Longmans, Green & Co. ■ **MACMILLAN PUBLISHING CO.** Illustration by Garth Williams from *Amigo* by Byrd Baylor Schweitzer. Text copyright © 1963 by Byrd Baylor Schweitzer. Illustrations copyright © 1963 by Garth Williams./ Illustrations from *Spunky* by Berta and Elmer Hader. Copyright 1933 by Macmillan Publishing Co., Inc., renewed 1961 by Berta and Elmer Hader./ Illustration by Berta H. and Elmer S. Hader from *Little Antelope* by Berta H. and Elmer S. Hader. Copyright © by Berta H. and Elmer S. Hader./ Illustration from *The Big Snow* by Berta and Elmer Hader. Copyright 1948 by Berta Hader and Elmer Hader, renewed 1976 by Berta Hader./ Illustration by Diane Redfield Massie from *The Komodo Dragon's Jewels* by Diane Redfield Massie. Copyright © 1975 by Diane Redfield Massie./ Illustration by Miroslav Sasek from *This is Edinburgh* by Miroslav Sasek. Copyright © 1968 by Miroslav Sasek./ Illustration by Miroslav Sasek from *This is Ireland* Miroslav Sasek. Copyright © 1969 Miroslav Sasek. Illustration by Miroslav Sasek from *This is London* by Miroslav Sasek. Copyright © 1969 by Miroslav Sasek./ Illustration by Miroslav Sasek from *This is San Francisco* by Miroslav Sasek. Copyright © 1962 by Miroslav Sasek./ Sidelight excerpts from *From Rags to Riches* by John Tebble. All reprinted by permission of Macmillan Publishing Co. ■ **DAVID McKAY CO., INC.** Sidelight excerpts from *The Third Door: An Autobiography of an American Negro* by Ellen Tarry./ Sidelight excerpts from *Memories of India* by Sir Robert Baden-Powell. Both reprinted by permission of David McKay Co., Inc. ■ **NORTHLAND PRESS.** Illustration by Joel Rodriguez from *High Country Canvas* by Vada F. Carlson. Reprinted by permission of Northland Press. ■ **OPEN COURT PUBLISHING CO.** Sidelight excerpts from an article "Meet Your Author — F. N. Monjo." September, 1925, *Cricket Magazine.* Reprinted by permission of Open Court Publishing Co. ■ **OXFORD UNIVERSITY PRESS.** Sidelight excerpts and illustrations by Thomas Bewick from *Thomas Bewick: A Memoir Written by Himself,* edited by Iain Bain. Copyright © 1975 Oxford University Press./ Sidelight excerpts from *Thomas Bewick* by Montague Weekly. © 1953 Oxford University Press. All reprinted by permission of Oxford University Press. ■ **PADDINGTON PRESS, LTD.** Illustrations by Thomas Bewick from *The Fables of Aesop.* Copyright © 1975 by Paddington Press, Ltd. Reprinted by permission of Paddington Press, Ltd. ■ **PANTHEON BOOKS.** Illustration by Prudence Seward from *A Truckload of Rice* by Paul Berna. Translated by John Buchanon-Brown. Copyright © 1968 by The Bodley Head, Ltd. Reprinted by permission of Pantheon Books, a division of Random House,

Inc. ■ **PARENTS' MAGAZINE PRESS.** Illustration by Cyndy Szekeres from *What Can You Do Without a Place to Play?* by Kathryn Hitte. Text copyright ©1971 by Kathryn Hitte. Illustrations copyright © 1971 by Cyndy Szekeres. Reprinted by permission of Parents' Magazine Press. ■ **PRENTICE-HALL, INC.** Sidelight excerpts from *Life of Eugene Field* by Slason Thompson. Reprinted by permission of Prentice-Hall. ■ **G. P. PUTNAM'S SONS.** Illustration by Charles Dougherty from *Let's Go to Europe* by Charles Mercer. Copyright © 1968 by Charles Mercer./ Sidelight excerpts from *Baden-Powell: The Two Lives of a Hero* by William Hillcourt with Olave, Lady Baden-Powell. Copyright © 1964 by William Hillcourt with Olave, Lady Baden-Powell. Both reprinted by permission of G. P. Putnam's Sons. ■ **RANDOM HOUSE, INC.** Illustration by John Burningham from *Borka* by John Burningham. Copyright ©1963 by John Burningham./ Illustration by Everett Shinn from *The Man Without a Country* by Edward Everett Hale. Both reprinted by permission of Random House, Inc. ■ **SAAFIELD PUBLISHERS.** Illustration by Fern B. Peat from *The Sugar Plum Tree and Other Verses* by Eugene Field. Reprinted by permission of Saafield Publishers. ■ **SCHOLASTIC MAGAZINES, INC.** Illustration from *My Brother Sam is Dead* by James Lincoln Collier and Christopher Collier. Copyright © 1974 by James Lincoln Collier and Christopher Collier./ Sidelight excerpts from *Books are by People* by Lee Bennett Hopkins./ Sidelight excerpts from an article "Voice Talks With Paul Zindel," April 27, 1970, *Scholastic Voice.* Reprinted by permission of Scholastic Magazines, Inc. ■ **CHARLES SCRIBNER'S SONS.** Illustration by Maxfield Parrish from *Poems of Childhood* by Eugene Field. Copyright 1904 by Charles Scribner. Copyright 1932 by Julia S. Field./ Illustration by Peter Parnall from *A Dog's Book of Birds* by Peter Parnall. Copyright © 1977 by Peter Parnall./ Illustration by Howard Pyle from *The Story of King Arthur and His Knights.* Copyright 1903 by Charles Scribner's Sons. Copyright 1931 by Anne Poole Pyle. Copyright 1933 by Charles Scribner's Sons./ Sidelight excerpts from *Field Days: The Life, Times and Reputation of Eugene Field* by Robert Conrow./ Sidelight excerpts from *The Eugene Field I Knew* by Francis Wilson./ Illustration by Claire and George Lauden, Jr. from *The Defender* by Nicholas Kalashnikoff. Copyright 1951 by Nicholas Kalashnikoff. All reprinted by permission of Charles Scribner's Sons. ■ **SIMON AND SCHUSTER, INC.** Illustration by Laszlo Kubinyi from *Perplexing Puzzles and Tantalizing Teasers* by Martin Gardner. Text copyright © 1969 by Martin Gardner. Illustrations copyright © 1969 by Laszlo Kubinyi./ Illustrations by Hilary Knight from *Eloise* by Kay Thompson. Copyright © 1955 by Kay Thompson and Hilary Knight. Both reprinted by permission of Simon and Schuster, Inc. ■ **TUNDRA BOOKS.** Illustration by Ann Blades from *Mary of Mile 18* by Ann Blades. Copyright © 1971 by Ann Blades. Reprinted by permission of Tundra Books. ■ **UNIVERSITY OF TEXAS PRESS.** Sidelights excerpts from *Edward Everett Hale: A Biography* by Jean Holloway. Copyright © 1956 by Jean Holloway. Reprinted by permission of University of Texas Press. ■ **THE VIKING PRESS.** Illustration by Don Miller from *Searchers of the Sea* by Charles Michael Daugherty. Copyright © 1961 by Charles Michael Daugherty./ Illustrations by Dorothy P. Lathrop and sidelight excerpts from *Bells and Grass* by Walter de la Mare. Copyright 1942 by Walter de la Mare./ Drawing by Richard Egielski from *The Porcelain Pagoda* by F. N. Monjo. Copyright © 1976 by Ferdinand Monjo. Illustrations copyright © 1976 by Viking Penguin, Inc./ Illustration by Alexander and Alexandra Allan from *My Dog Rinty* by Ellen Tarry and Marie Hall Ets. Copyright 1946 by Marie Hall Ets and Ellen Tarry. All reprinted by permission of The Viking Press. ■ **HENRY Z. WALCK, INC.** Sidelight excerpts from *Mrs. Ewing* by Gillian Avery./ Illustration by Ingrid Fetz from *Where The Good Luck Was* by Osmond Molarsky. Text copyright © 1970 by Osmond Molarsky. Illustrations copyright © 1970 by Ingrid Fetz. Both reprinted by permission of Henry Z. Walck, Inc. ■ **FREDERICK WARNE AND CO.** Illustration by Paul Galdone from *Dance of the Animals* by Pura Belpré. Illustration copyright © 1972 by Paul Galdone./ Illustration by Georgette Bordier from *A Young Person's Guide to Ballet* by Noel Streatfeild. Copyright © 1975 by The Felix Gluck Press, Ltd. Both reprinted by permission of Frederick Warne and Co. ■ **FRANKLIN WATTS, INC.** Illustrations by Leonard Everett Fisher from *The Man Without a Country* by Edward Everett Hale. Copyright © 1960 by Franklin Watts, Inc./ Illustration by Brian Wildsmith from *Brian Wildsmith's ABC.* Copyright © 1962 by Brian Wildsmith./ Illustration by Brian Wildsmith from *The Twelve Days of Christmas*, adapted by Brian Wildsmith. Copyright © 1972 Brian Wildsmith. All reprinted by permission of Franklin Watts, Inc. ■ **WAYSIDE PRESS.** Sidelight excerpts from *Horatio Alger or American Hero Era* by Ralph Gardner. Reprinted by permission of Wayside Press. ■ **ALBERT WHITMAN AND CO.** Illustrated by Charles Lynch from *Busy Office, Busy People* by Jene Barr. Copyright © 1968 by Albert Whitman. Reprinted by permission of Albert Whitman and Co. ■

Sidelight excerpts from an article "An Interview with David Kherdian," by Ara Baliozian in *The Armenian Post*, January 12, 1978. Reprinted by permission of *The Armenian Post.*/ Sidelight excerpts from *W. W. Denslow* by Douglas Greene and Michael P. Hearn. Copyright © 1976 by Clarke Historical Library. Reprinted by permission of the Clarke Historical Library and Douglas Greene./ Photograph from *If You Could See What I Hear* by Tom Sullivan and Derek Gill. Copyright © 1975 by Thomas J. Sullivan and Derek L. T. Gill. Reprinted by permission of Derek Gill./ Illustration by Barbara Latham from *Hurdy-Gurdy Holiday* by Leah Gale. Reprinted by permission of Barbara Latham./ Sidelight excerpts from an article "On Illustrators — My View," by Walter Lorraine in *The Calendar*, March-August, 1975. Reprinted by permission of *The Calendar Magazine*, Ltd./ Poster Advertisement from *To Have and To Hold* by Howard Pyle. Reprinted by permission of the Delaware Art Museum./ Sidelight excerpts from *Harper's Weekly*, Volume 53, June 12, 1909. Reprinted by permission of Harper's Magazine Co./ Sidelight excerpts from an article "McCall's Visits Kay Thompson," by Cynthia Lindsay, January, 1957, *McCall's.* Reprinted by permission of McCall Publishing Co./ Illustration by Hilary Knight from *Eloise* by Kay Thompson. Copyright © 1955 by Kay Thompson and Hilary Knight. Reprinted by permission of Kay Thompson./ Sidelight excerpts from *Women's Home Companion*, Volume 39, April, 1912. Reprinted by permission of *Women's Home Companion.*/ Sidelight excerpts from an article "The Problem of Maria Solved, Almost," by Frederick John Pratson, April, 1978, *Saturday Evening Post.* Reprinted by permission of the *Saturday Evening Post.*/ Illustration by John Gretzer from *Jim Thorpe* by Thomas Fall. Text copyright © 1970 by Donald Snow. Illustrations copyright © 1970 by John Gretzer. Reprinted with permission of "Crowell Biographies."

PHOTO CREDITS

Lord Baden-Powell (painting by Shirley Slocum): National Portrait Gallery, London; Ralph Henry Barbour: Underwood & Underwood; Christopher Collier: Norman Y. Lono; Paxton Davis: W. Patrick Hinely; W. W. Denslow (1899): Courtesy of Nancy Hubbard Brady, (1859) and courtesy of Patricia Denslow Eykyn; Walter de la Mare: Mark Gerson, John Gay, London; Lynne Gessner: Woodward; Edward Everett Hale (Hale the patriarch): Library of Congress; Kathryn Hitte: Richard Leach Photo; William Hooks: Norman Galinsky; Naomi J. Karp: Ferenz Fedor Studio; Barbara Land: Toni-Gerard; Gerald McDermott: Barbara Bordnick; Howard Pyle: Library of Congress; Regina Shekerjian: Haig Shekerjian; Kay Thompson: James J. Kriegsman; Paul Zindel: Martha Swope.

SOMETHING ABOUT THE AUTHOR

A poem can tell a story that makes you ask "What happens next?" A poem can make you smile or giggle or even laugh out loud. ■ (From *The Other Side of a Poem* by Barbara Abercrombie. Illustrated by Harry Bertschmann.)

ABERCROMBIE, Barbara (Mattes) 1939-

PERSONAL: Born April 6, 1939, in Evanston, Ill.; daughter of William F. (a businessman and writer) and Grace (a pianist; maiden name, Mann) Mattes; married Gordon E. Abercrombie (a stockbroker), March 8, 1964; children: Brooke Louise, Gillan Grace. *Education:* Attended Briarcliff College, 1957-58, and Los Angeles Harbor College, 1971—. *Residence:* Palos Verdes Estates, Calif. *Agent:* Aaron M. Priest Literary Agency, 150 East 35th St., New York, N.Y. 10016.

CAREER: Actress, 1959-64 (on Broadway, in summer stock, on tour, and on television, including appearances on "Ironside" and "Route 66"); free-lance writer. Teacher of creative writing to children.

WRITINGS: (Editor) *The Other Side of a Poem,* Harper, 1977; (with Norma Almquist and Jeanne Nichols) *Traveling Without a Camera,* The Peck Street Press, 1978; *Good Riddance* (adult novel), Harper, 1979; *Amanda And Heather and Company* (juvenile), Dandelion Press, 1979. Contributor of poems to little magazines.

WORK IN PROGRESS: A book for children.

SIDELIGHTS: "When I was little my favorite past time was making up stories for my paper dolls. I had whole families of dolls—their clothes, houses, towns, pets, all the details of their lives carefully worked out. I find it rather amaz-

BARBARA ABERCROMBIE

ing that I get paid for doing more or less the same thing as an adult.

"I like writing for both children and adults and find that the stories all come from the same place—trying to make sense of life. For both it's a matter of trying to dig for something meaningful or universal through the ordinary. That's why I like writing novels. Everything can go in. Habits, meals, clothes, weather—all the details that add up to real life."

ABRAMS, Joy   1941-

PERSONAL: Born March 17, 1941, in New York; daughter of Martin and Pearl Rudnick; married Kenneth L. Abrams (an attorney), April 7, 1962; children: Nancy Gayle, David Robert, Michael Joseph. *Education:* Brooklyn College of the City University of New York, B.A., 1961; Arizona State University, M.A., 1962. *Religion:* Jewish. *Residence:* Phoenix, Ariz.

CAREER: Elementary school teacher in Glendale, Ariz., 1961-62; nursery school teacher in Phoenix, Ariz., 1962-63; substitute elementary school teacher in Phoenix, Ariz., 1963—. Owner of Yoga Studio, 1975—. Worked at Good Samaritan Learning Disability School, and Kivel Nursing Home. Also worked as photographic model. *Member:* Alan Foss Leukemia Society, B'nai B'rith.

WRITINGS: (With Ruth Richards) *Let's Do Yoga* (juvenile; Child Study Association book list), Holt, 1975. Also author of *Look Good, Feel Good* with Pam Gray and Ruth Richards, 1978.

WORK IN PROGRESS: Who Do I Turn To?: Learning Disabilities and Your Child, publication expected in 1981.

SIDELIGHTS: "From age six I've written poems to my mother and father. I loved to write and read as a youngster. At age twelve, I was ill with polio. The compassion and love shown by friends and relatives was helpful to my recovery. I always had great compassion for others, but from that time on I knew that my work someday would involve helping others. Throughout my years of high school and college, although studying to be a teacher, I voraciously read books on health and nutrition and took courses on the subject when time allowed. I also kept writing poetry and children's books and helped fellow classmates with school reports.

"I attended Brooklyn College and got a vacation playground license. During the summers I worked with deprived children in Manhattan. In 1961, I got a B.A. in early childhood education.

"I moved to Arizona in that year and worked on my M.A. in elementary education and taught first grade and later kindergarten and nursery school. During that time I devoted all my spare time to Kivel Nursing Home, working with an aphasia victim. I also did some photographic modeling.

"In 1962 I married Kenneth Abrams and subsequently had three children. I devoted my spare time to working with disabled youngsters at Samuel Gompers Rehabilitation Center and Good Samaritan Learning Disabilities School, as well as studying yoga.

"In 1972 I got my Masters in elementary education and began tutoring children with learning problems incorporating some yoga techniques.

Good habits are formed in early childhood. ■ (From *Let's Do Yoga* by Ruth Richards and Joy Abrams. Illustrated by Sandra E. Case.)

JOY ABRAMS

"From that, the book, *Let's Do Yoga* was born. In 1975 I opened my own yoga studio which is a Japanese tea house, where I teach yoga, beauty and nutrition tips to all ages. I recently co-authored a book called, *Look Good, Feel Good*, dealing with beauty and grooming, nutrition and yoga. I am also working on another M.A. in learning disabilities. I also speak Spanish fluently.

"To have a career as well as a young family requires great discipline, as well as support and understanding from your family. My husband and children are proud of my efforts and have given me encouragement. Most people believe that you write a book and that's the end of it. They are not aware of the rewrites and the regular work hours writing entails."

HOBBIES AND OTHER INTERESTS: Travel (Macao, Hong Kong, Spain, Germany, France, Italy, Switzerland, the Caribbean).

ALGER, Horatio, Jr.   1832-1899
(Arthur Lee Putnam)

PERSONAL: Born January 13, 1832, in Revere, Massachusetts; died July 18, 1899, in Natick, Massachusetts; son of Horatio (a Unitarian minister) and Olive (Fenno) Alger. *Education:* Graduated from Harvard University, 1852, and from Harvard Divinity School, 1856.

CAREER: Author of books for young people. Worked as a private tutor; ordained a Unitarian minister, 1864, and be-

came pastor of the Unitarian Church in Brewster, Massachusetts; left the ministry to become chaplain of Newsboy's Lodging House in Manhattan, 1866-96. *Awards, honors:* The American Schools and Colleges Association presents "Horatio Alger Awards" each year to those Americans, who in their estimation, have become successful in spite of earlier handicaps.

WRITINGS—All novels, except as noted: *Bertha's Christmas Vision*, Brown, Bazin, 1856; *Nothing to Do: A Tilt at Our Best Society*, J. French, 1857; *Frank's Campaign; or, What Boys Can Do on the Farm for the Camp*, Loring, 1864; *Paul Prescott's Charge*, Loring, 1865; *Helen Ford*, Loring, 1866; *Ragged Dick; or, Street Life in New York with the Bootblacks*, Loring, 1868, reissued, Collier Books, 1962; *Fame and Fortune; or, The Progress of Richard Hunter*, Loring, 1868; *Charlie Codman's Cruise*, Loring, 1866; *Mark, the Match Boy; or, Richard Hunter's Ward*, Loring, 1869, reissued, Collier Books, 1962; *Rough and Ready; or, Life among the New York Newsboys*, Loring, 1869; *Luck and Pluck; or, J. Oakley's Inheritance*, Loring, 1869.

Sink or Swim; or, Harry Raymond's Resolve, Loring, 1870; *Rufus and Rose; or, The Fortunes of Rough and Ready*, Loring, 1870; *Ben, the Luggage Boy*, Loring, 1870; *Tattered Tom*, Loring, 1871; *Strong and Steady; or, Paddle Your Own Canoe*, Loring, 1871, reissued, Major Books, 1975; *Paul the Peddler; or, The Adventures of a Young Street Merchant*, Loring, 1871; *Slow and Sure; or, From the Street to the Shop*, W. L. Allison, 1872; *Strive and Succeed; or, The Progress of Walter Conrad*, Loring, 1872, reissued, Media Books, 1972; *Phil the Fiddler; or, The Story of a Young Street Musician*, reprinted, Aeonian Press, 1976; *Bound to Rise*, Porter & Coates, 1873, also published as *Try and Trust; or, The Story of a Bound Boy*, Loring, 1873; *Ju-*

Horatio Alger, Harvard days.

(From *Brave and Bold: The Fortunes of a Factory Boy* by Horatio Alger, Jr.)

lius; or, The Street Boy Out West, Loring, 1874, reissued, Holt, 1967; *Risen from the Ranks; or Harry Walton's Success,* Loring, 1874, reissued, Media Books, 1972; *Brave and Bold; or, The Fortunes of a Factory Boy,* Loring, 1874, reprinted, Aeonian Press, 1976.

Jack's Ward; or, The Boy Guardian, J. C. Winston, 1875, reprinted, Aeonian Press, 1976; *The Young Outlaw; or, Adrift in the Streets,* Loring, 1875, reissued, Major Books, 1975; (with sister, O. Augusta Cheney) *Seeking His Fortune, and Other Dialogues,* Loring, 1875; *Sam's Chance, and How He Proved It,* Loring, 1876; *Shifting for Himself; or, Gilbert Grayson's Fortunes,* Loring, 1876; *Wait and Hope; or, Ben Bradford's Motto,* Loring, 1877; *Herbert Carter's Legacy; or, The Inventor's Son,* Loring, 1877; *Grand'ther Baldwin's Thanksgiving, with Other Ballads and Poems,* Loring, 1879; *The Young Miner; or, Tom Nelson in California,* Loring, 1879, reprinted, Book Club of California, 1965; *The Young Adventurer; or, Tom's Trip Across the Plains,* Loring, 1879.

The Young Explorer; or Among the Sierras, Loring, 1880; *Tony the Hero; or, A Brave Boy's Adventures with a Tramp,* Ogilvie, 1880; *Tom the Bootblack; or, The Road to Success,* Ogilvie, 1880, reprinted, Aeonian Press, 1976; *From Canal Boy to President; or, The Boyhood and Manhood of James A. Garfield* (biography), J. R. Anderson, 1881, reprinted, Scholarly Press, 1976; *Telegraph Boy,* Porter & Coates, 1882, also published as *Mark Mason's Victory: The Trials and Triumphs of a Telegraph Boy,* Burt, 1899; *From Farm Boy to Senator, being the History of the Boyhood and Manhood of Daniel Webster* (biography),

Ogilvie, 1882; *Ben's Nugget; or, A Boy's Search for Fortune,* Porter & Coates, 1882; *Young Circus Rider; or, The Mystery of Robert Rudd,* Porter & Coates, 1883; *The Train Boy,* G. W. Carleton, 1883, reprinted, Aeonian Press, 1975; *Dan, the Detective,* G. W. Carleton, 1883; *Abraham Lincoln, the Backwoods Boy; or, How a Young Rail-Splitter Became President* (biography), Anderson & Allen, 1883, also published as *The Backwoods Boy; or, The Boyhood and Manhood of Abraham Lincoln,* Street & Smith, 1883; *Do and Dare; or, A Brave Boy's Fight for Fortune,* Porter & Coates, 1884.

The Western Boy; or, The Road to Success, [New York], 1885; *Hector's Inheritance; or, The Boys of Smith Institute,* Porter & Coates, 1885; *Helping Himself; or, Grant Thornton's Ambition,* Porter & Coates, 1886; *Store Boy; or, The Fortunes of Ben Barclay,* Porter & Coates, 1887, reissued, Holt, 1967; *Joe's Luck,* Burt, 1887; *Frank Fowler, the Cash Boy,* Burt, 1887; (under pseudonym Arthur Lee Putnam) *The Adventures of a New York Telegraph Boy,* F. A. Munsey, 1887; *The Errand Boy; or, How Phil Brent Won Success,* Burt, 1888; *The Young Acrobat of the Great North American Circus,* F. A. Munsey, 1888; (under pseudonym Arthur Lee Putnam) *Tom Tracy; or, the Trials of a New York Newsboy,* F. F. Lovell, 1888; *Tom Thatcher's Fortune,* Burt, 1888; *Tom Temple's Career,* Burt, 1888; *Bob Burton; or, The Young Ranchman of the Missouri,* J. C. Winston, 1888; *Luke Walton; or, The Chicago Newsboy,* Porter & Coates, 1889, reprinted, Aeonian Press, 1976.

Victor Dane, the Young Secretary, Porter & Coates, 1890; *Struggling Upward,* Porter & Coates, 1890, reissued, Nauti-

Alger (right), his brother-in-law Cheney (left), and a friend.

lus Books, 1971; (under pseudonym Arthur Lee Putnam) *Ned Newton,* American Publishers, 1890; *Odds against Him; or, Carl Crawford's Experience,* Penn Publishing, 1890; *Five Hundred Dollars; or, Jacob Marlowe's Secret,* U.S. Book Co., 1890; *Both Sides of the Continent; or, Mark Stanton,* Street & Smith, 1890; *Five Hundred Dollar Check,* U.S. Book Co., 1891; *Erie Train-Boy,* U.S. Book Co., 1891, reprinted, Aeonian Press, 1974; *Dean Dunham; or, The Waterford Mystery,* U.S. Book Co., 1891, reprinted, Aeonian Press, 1974; (under pseudonym Arthur Lee Putnam) *A New York Boy,* Lovell, 1891; *Young Boatman of Pine Point,* Penn Publishing, 1892; *Ralph Raymond's Heir,* F. M. Lupton, 1892, reprinted, Aeonian Press, 1974; *Digging for Gold: A Story of California,* Porter & Coates, 1892, reprinted, Aeonian Press, 1976; *Facing the World; or, The Haps and Mishaps of Harry Vane,* Porter & Coates, 1893; *Dan, the Newsboy,* Burt, 1893; *In a New World; or, Among the Gold-Fields of Australia,* J. C. Winston, 1893, reissued, Media Books, 1972; *Only an Irish Boy; or, Andy Burke's Fortunes and Misfortunes,* Porter & Coates, 1894.

Adrift in the City; or Oliver Conrad's Plucky Flight, J. C. Winston, 1895, reprinted, Aeonian Press, 1976; *Frank Hunter's Peril,* J. C. Winston, 1896; *The Young Salesman,* H. T. Coates, 1896; *Frank and Fearless; or, The Fortunes of Jasper Kent,* H. T. Coates, 1897, reprinted, Aeonian Press, 1974; *Walter Sherwood's Probation,* H. T. Coates, 1897; *A Boy's Fortune; or, The Strange Adventures of Ben Baker,* H. T. Coates, 1898; *The Young Bank Messenger,* J. C. Winston, 1898; *Rupert's Ambition,* H. T. Coates, 1899; *Jed, the Poorhouse Boy,* J. C. Winston, 1899, reprinted, Aeonian Press, 1976.

Falling in with Fortune; or, The Experiences of a Young Secretary, Mershon, 1900; *A Debt of Honor: The Story of Gerald Lane's Success in the Far West* (illustrated by J. Watson Davis), Burt, 1900; *Out for Business; or, Robert Frost's Strange Career,* Mershon, 1900; *Ben Bruce: Scenes in the Life of Bowery Newsboy* (illustrated by J. W. Davis), Burt, 1901; *Making His Mark* (illustrated by Robert L. Mason), Penn Publishing, 1901; *Nelson the Newsboy; or, Afloat in New York,* Mershon, 1901; *Lost at Sea; or, Robert Roscoe's Strange Cruise,* Mershon, 1901; *Lester's Luck,* T. H. Coates, 1901; *Tom Brace, Who He Was and How He Fared,* Street & Smith, 1901; *Young Captain Jack; or, The Son of a Soldier,* Mershon, 1901, reprinted, Aeonian Press, 1974; *Walter Griffith,* Smith & Street, 1901; *Andy Grant's Pluck,* H. T. Coates, 1902; *A Rolling Stone; or, The Adventures of a Wanderer,* Thompson & Thomas, 1902, reprinted, Aeonian Press, 1974; *Tom Turner's Legacy: The Story of How He Secured It* (illustrated by J. W. Davis), Burt, 1902; *World before Him,* Penn Publishing, 1902, reissued, Odyssey Press, 1966; *Striving for Fortune; or, Walter Griffith's Trials and Successes,* Street & Smith, 1902.

Bernard Brook's Adventures: The Story of a Brave Boy's Trials (illustrated by J. W. Davis), Burt, 1903; *Chester Rand; or, A New Path to Fortune,* H. T. Coates, 1903; *Forging Ahead,* Penn Publishing, 1903; *Finding a Fortune* (illustrated by W. S. Lukens), Penn Publishing, 1904; *Jerry, the Backwoods Boy; or, The Parkhurst Treasure,* Mershon, 1904; *Fairy in the Wold,* Hurst, 1905; *Driven from Home: or Carl Crawford's Experience,* Hurst, 1905; *From Farm to Fortune; or, Nat Nason's Strange Experience,* Stitt Publishing, 1905; *Mark Manning's Mission: The Story of a Shoe*

Factory Boy (illustrated by J. W. Davis), Burt, 1905, reprinted, Aeonian Press, 1974; *The Young Book Agent; or, Frank Hardy's Road to Success,* Stitt Publishing, 1905.

Joe the Hotel Boy; or, Winning Out by Pluck, Cupples & Leon, 1906; *Trials and Triumphs of Mark Mason,* Street & Smith, 1906; *Randy of the River; or, The Adventures of a Young Deckhand,* Chatterton-Park, 1906; *The Young Musician* (illustrated by Clyde O. Deland), Penn Publishing, 1906; *Grit; or, The Young Boatman of Pine Point,* Hurst, 1907; *A Cousin's Conspiracy,* Hurst, 1907; *In Search of Treasure: The Story of Guy's Eventful Voyage* (illustrated by J. W. Davis), Burt, 1907; *Wait and Win: The Story of Jack Drummond's Pluck* (illustrated by J. W. Davis), Burt, 1908; *Ben Logan's Triumph; or The Boys of Boxwood Academy,* Cupples & Leon, 1908; *Making His Way; or, Frank Courtney's Struggle Upward,* New York Book Co., 1911, reprinted, Arno, 1975; *Alger Street: The Poetry of Horatio Alger, Jr.* (edited by Gilbert K. Westgard, II), J. S. Canner, 1964; *Silas Snobden's Office Boy,* Doubleday, 1973; *Cast upon the Breakers,* Doubleday, 1974; *The Disagreeable Woman,* Aeonian Press, 1976.

Also author of *The Nugget Finders: A Tale of the Gold Fields of Australia, The Tin Box, and What It Contained, Tony the Tramp; or, Right is Might, Work and Win; or, A Hard-Earned Reward, Andy Gordon,* and *Robert Coverdale's Struggle; or, On the Wave of Success.* Contributor of stories to W. T. Adams' periodical, *Student and Schoolmate.*

ADAPTATIONS—Plays: *Rags to Riches* (a musical melodrama; based on *Ragged Dick* and *Mark the Match Boy;* lyrics by Aurand Harris and Eva Franklin and music by E. Franklin), Anchorage Press, 1966.

SIDELIGHTS: **January 13, 1832.** Born in Revere, Massachusetts, Alger's father was a minister who indoctrinated his son with strict religious preparation. He was often ridiculed by his classmates at school. "I cannot go back to school, mother. They laugh at my clothes and call me 'Holy Horatio, the parson's son.' I want to be like other boys!" [Ralph Gardner, *Horatio Alger; or, American Hero Era,* Wayside Press, 1964.[1]]

His father expected him to follow in his footsteps. "I shall be a teacher of the ways of God, a preacher of His commandments, a liberal thinker, a loyal citizen." [John Tebble, *From Rags to Riches: Horatio Alger, Jr. and the American Dream,* Macmillan, 1963.[2]]

1844. Family moved to Marlborough, Massachusetts when Horatio Alger, Sr. received a new pastorate. Horatio Jr. was enrolled at the Gates Academy and despite some misgivings, joined the debating society. "I'm not fond of speaking in class if I don't have to . . . because I stutter and the others laugh."[1]

1847. Accepted to Harvard University, still confused about career plans. "Maybe I would prefer to teach or become a journalist. However, if I'm to be a minister, I'll try to be a good one."[1]

He employed him, though it may have been at a later period, to chop wood, and take care of his garden, and do chores about the house, and years afterward, as we shall see, it was he who enabled James to enter Williams College, and pursue his studies there until he graduated, and was ready to do the work of an educated man in the world. ■ (From *From Canal Boy to President* by Horatio Alger, Jr.)

(From the American Conservatory Theatre production of "Horatio," with Daniel Davis and Charles Lanyer, 1974-75 season in San Francisco.)

June 20, 1849. Received $2 payment for poem and short story sold to *Pictorial National Library,* a Boston monthly.

1852. Graduated Harvard. Attempted to earn his living as a writer instead of going to Divinity School. "No period of my life has been one of such unmixed happiness as the four years which have been spent within college walls. Whatever may be the course of my life hereafter, I shall never cease to regard it with mingled feelings of pleasure and regret—pleasure which the recollection of past happiness never fails to excite—regret that it is gone forever." [Edwin Hoyt, *Horatio's Boys: The Life and Works of Horatio Alger, Jr.,* Chilton Book Co., 1974.[3]]

1853. Writing career stalled, entered Harvard Divinity School. "... And I shall become a minister. However I mean to keep writing at the same time."[1]

1854. Accepted teaching position at a boys' boarding school in East Greenwich, Rhode Island. Seventeen prose pieces published in magazines.

1856. A friend who wrote juvenile books under the pen name, "Oliver Optic," guided Alger to the publication of his first book, *Bertha's Christmas Vision.*

1860. Graduated from Harvard Divinity School.

1860-1861. Embarked on "the grand tour" of Europe, especially enjoyed his trip to Italy. "I have the impression that I've been here before. All is familiar and, from the moment we arrived, I believe I could have given accurate directions to a stranger. ..."

"Foreign-looking people were engaged in various occupations which they freely pursued out of doors, while others had no earthly business but to stare at passersby. The villagers are so different from our own. The varied landscape, with Vesuvius smoking menacingly in the background, possesses beauty that has not been overrated, and every foot of it is classic ground.

"In coming down the mountain, [my friend] Charley and myself were some distance in advance of the rest of the party. We kept on, not suspecting we lost the way, until we came to the edge of a ravine we hadn't seen before. Turning the donkeys about, we retraced our course nearly a mile. Here three paths branched off, but we were uncertain which to take. Charley suggested we trust to the donkeys' instinct, but they were firmly determined to offer us no help whatever.

"What time is it?" asked Dick.

"Seven o'clock."

"Seven o'clock. I ougter've been up an hour ago. I know what 'twas made me so precious sleepy. I went to the Old Bowery last night and didn't turn in till past twelve." ■ (From *Ragged Dick: Or Street Life in New York* by Horatio Alger, Jr.)

"At last we guessed at the road, and after a time overtook a priest. I summoned up sufficient Italian to ask him the direction but, unfortunately, couldn't understand his voluble answer. In perplexity, I switched to Latin, and then my early devotion to Andrews and Stoddard's Latin Grammar served me in a way I could hardly have dreamed of in my schoolboy days."[1]

1862. Returned to Harvard to tutor, after being turned down for Civil War service due to asthmatic condition. "I've been feeling so rotten—not being able to get into the fight—that I had no mind for writing, nor for that matter, teaching or preaching."[1]

1864. Launched as writer of boys books when A. K. Loring of Boston agreed to publish *Frank's Campaign*. "I'm so keen to know what you think of my novel [Mr. Loring] I'd have pushed through snow twice as deep."[1]

December 8, 1864. Ordained as pastor of Brewster Church on Cape Cod. "My people are kindly and good, but in character more austere than any I've known. I believe they would prefer a parson of their own cut; one who was a seaman before becoming a man of God. I keep trying to understand their ways, but they say I am 'a purely Boston preacher,' meaning, I suppose, better suited to a city parish than to their needs."[1]

1866. Charged with "gross immorality," dismissed by Brewster congregation, slipped out of town fearing repercussions of allegations involving him and some young boys. Horatio Alger, Jr. remarked, "I was imprudent."[3]

March, 1866. Left for New York to pursue writing career in earnest. "I'm on my way to New York. I'm quite positive I can support myself as a writer and in those exhilarating surroundings, I can produce better than ever before. I feel it already and ideas keep popping about, within, just calling out to me to get them on paper."[1]

January, 1867. *Ragged Dick* became bestseller—the New York Street boy, who through an act of daring, places his first foot on the shaky ladder to success. "Frankly, this tale

A promotion piece by one of Alger's publishers.

of life in the streets almost writes itself, as there exists in New York today an unruly horde of boys in straits so desperate as to seem unbelievable.

"Their plight first attracted me some years since, during a brief visit here. But now, with the Rebellion ended, their number increases daily. Most of them are homeless orphans, sleeping in cellars or alleyways. They support themselves as best they can, mainly as newsboys or bootblacks. Some engage as baggage carriers around the piers or run errands. Also, I'm sorry to tell you, many live by begging or by stealing, imposing upon smaller boys of their class, and other despicable ways. Still, there are enough good ones among them, given half a chance.

"There appears to be an endless supply of material here, for there also are newsboys, luggage carriers and messengers who exist by wits and initiative in a dozen different ways."[1]

1867. Joined philanthropist, Charles Bruce, in fight to improve newsboy's living conditions. Moved into the Newsboys Lodging House, where he became a generous and popular figure. "Their increased ranks are greatly a result of the war. Their parents may have been killed or simply took the opportunity to abandon them. Some, apparently, were left where their mothers had them.

"Among the older boys are a number who ran away from farm homes to serve as drummers and foragers with the troops, and many of the children—there are girls among them—followed the armies, becoming mascots or begging or stealing to live. At any rate, they somehow made their way to the city, and now accept constant struggle as a part of their daily lives."[1]

1870-1873. Wrote series of "street boy" books which became enormously popular. "[I have] endeavored to show that even a street boy, by enterprise, industry, and integrity, may hope to become a useful and respected citizen."[3]

1871. Exposed the "padrone" system, in which young street musicians and beggars were exploited by unscrupulous adults. "The evidence of malicious treatment which I have

Alger house, Marlborough, Massachusetts.

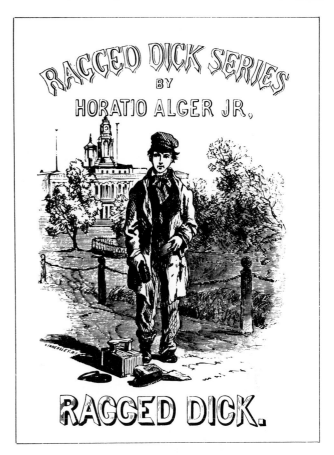

An illustrator's view of Alger's young hero, Ragged Dick. ■ (From *Ragged Dick: Or Street Life in New York* by Horatio Alger, Jr.)

seen so far, if it is a fair sample, is unholy and must be stopped. The leaders must be punished. Why, I saw a boy fourteen years old, weighing fifty pounds, starved and weak, also mentally deficient. I met him at ten o'clock at night, afraid to go home. He only had collected sixty cents. . . . Let me find further evidence of this padrone business and I swear to you that if more of it is like what I know now, I will not rest until the curse is wiped away and until every right minded man and woman screams in protest at this foul thing whose stench makes me sick. Let me uncover other facts of like import and I will not rest until New York is purged and every mishandled child set free."[2]

1873. Made second "grand tour" of Europe accompanied by members of his family. "After having visited, for a second time, some of the leading countries of Europe, I am able to confirm what has so often been asserted, that nowhere here not even in the Swiss republic, of which I am a temporary resident, are such opportunities afforded to those who wish to rise, as in America. We hear, indeed, occasional stories of prominent men who have risen from the ranks; but what is rare and occasional in Europe is the rule with us."[3]

1875. Gave up dream of writing "the great American novel," decided to devote himself to boys books. "These stories have been intended to illustrate the proverb that 'God helps those who are willing to help themselves.' Those who sit down and wait passively for fortune to shower her gifts upon them are likely to wait a long time."[3]

Horatio Alger, drawing by Stevan Dohanos.

1877. Visited the western part of U.S.A. to find new material for stories. "Why, they swapped bigger lies than Bret Harte claimed he and Sam Clemens used to concoct while sitting around a barroom stove."[1]

1882. Wrote biography of recently assassinated President Garfield, followed by a biography of Lincoln.

Fall, 1882. Father, Horatio Alger Sr., died.

1883. Tutored Benjamin Cardozo, future Supreme Court justice.

1886. Adopted pen name of Arthur Lee Putnam, so that readers of Alger serializations would not become confused as to which story they were following.

1890. Contracted bronchial infection, travelled West for health reasons.

1892. Visited family in Natick, Massachusetts accompanied by young Oren Trott, a boy he was attempting to help. "It appears that a boy named Hunt—a very bad boy, as [Oren] Trott's [father] writes—followed him around persistently and as Oren is of easy disposition, managed to induce him to

go about with him. This boy, *alone,* broke into some place and stole two watches and a ring. He prevailed upon Oren to sell the watches for him by offering him part of the proceeds. The sum realized was only a dollar and a quarter, but the fact that Oren sold them makes him an accomplice in the eyes of the law.

"Both boys were arrested. Hunt is in jail now but Oren is at home going to school as usual. Still, he as well as Hunt will have to stand trial in January. A lawyer will be employed but whether the court will discriminate between Hunt and the boy whom he led into mischief is uncertain. Mr. and Mrs. Trott, who are excellent people, are very anxious and sad, and find the suspense hard to bear. If Oren knew the watches were stolen he was very weak and foolish to consent to sell them, and he realizes this now. I hope his previous good character will help him. He told me when he went home that he wished he had some boy companions at Peale's Island like the Natick boys. . . .

"Of course I shall stand by him whatever happens. I always do stand by a friend in time of trouble. I should like to have you show this letter to your uncle, as I want Oren's friends in Natick to think as well of him as they can. I should also like to have you say as little as possible about his trouble.

"I don't know if you have heard that one of the boys who used to frequent my room—not to my satisfaction—is now at Sing Sing prison. Confined for burglary. I interested myself to obtain a mitigation of his sentence and was very successful. His prison term is two years, while it might have been ten or even more. I don't know the circumstances but he is not of the desperate type of which burglars are made. I don't think he realized what he was doing. I have sent him an autoharp to fill up his time as the prisoners are not now employed. I am on friendly terms with the warden, who is an admirable man."[3]

1896. Began to come to terms with criticism of his writing and the similarity of all his stories. "As to the notice of my own books there is undoubtedly a family resemblance between them but I find this does not seem an objection to readers."[3]

1897. Spent more time in Natick in ill health. Began lecturing and became less prolific. "The country is still pleasant. Looking out the window I see on the lot adjoining the house a hundred oak and walnut trees. The leaves are beginning to change color. Every day a few children appear whom we allow to pick the nuts that have fallen. They are not of very good quality but the trees probably average 50 feet in height."[3]

"I have twice attended the Boston theatre, delivered a poem before the Women's Suffrage League and went to two entertainments in Natick.... On Monday night, in Waltham, I gave a talk, interspersed with readings from *Ragged Dick,* on 'The Street Boys of New York.' Among the audience were about 100 boys. One met me in the street the next day and said, 'Yer done good last evenin'. When are you goin' to lecture agin?' What gratifies me most is that boys, though strangers, seem to regard me as a personal friend.

"... A new game called 'Authors' will be issued by the U.S. Playing Card Company, in Cincinnati, in the fall. I am in it. I have sent them my photograph, which will appear.... A boy writes me from a Georgia college that they have my books in the library."[1]

"I wonder ... how it would seem to be ... young and full of life and enthusiasm.... I shouldn't dare to go back to 19 again, lest my share of success prove to be less than it has been.... If I could come back 50 years from now probably I should feel bewildered in reading the New York *Tribune* of 1947."[3]

July 18, 1899. Died in Natick, Massachusetts. He had written his own epitaph, employing titles of his stories. "Six feet underground reposes Horatio Alger, *Helping Himself* to a part of the earth, not *Digging for Gold* or *In Search of Treasure,* but *Struggling Upward* and *Bound to Rise* at last *In a New World* where it shall be said he is *Risen from the Ranks.*"[2]

In 1928, Herbert Mayes wrote *Alger, a Biography Without a Hero,* which for many years served as the chief reference source for the life of Horatio Alger Jr. It has since been shown that much of the material in the Mayes book was "fictional."

FOR MORE INFORMATION SEE: John A. Beckwith and Geoffrey G. Coope, editors, "Horatio Alger, Jr.," in *Contemporary American Biography,* Harper, 1941; Stewart H. Holbrook, *Lost Men of American History,* Macmillan,

1946; George Allison Phelps, *Holidays and Philosophical Biographies,* House-Warven, 1951; F. L. Allen, "Horatio Alger, Jr.," in *Perspectives,* edited by Leonard F. Dean, Harcourt, 1954; M. Fishwick, "Rise and Fall of Horatio Alger," *Saturday Review,* November 17, 1956; Clifton Fadiman, "Horatio Alger, Fare Thee Well; or, The Road to Success," in his *Any Number Can Play,* World Publishing, 1957; F. L. Allen, "Horatio Alger, Jr.," in *Saturday Review Gallery,* Simon & Schuster, 1959.

Frank Gruber, *Horatio Alger, Jr.: A Biography and Bibliography,* Grover Jones Press, 1961; John W. Tebbel, *From Rags to Riches: Horatio Alger, Jr., and the American Dream,* Macmillan, 1963; Ralph D. Gardner, *Horatio Alger; or, The American Hero Era,* Wayside Press, 1964; J. G. Cawelti, "From Rags to Respectability: Horatio Alger," in his *Apostles of the Self-Made Man,* University of Chicago Press, 1965; Frederic C. Jaher, editor, "Horatio Alger, Jr., and the Response to Industrialism," in *The Age of Industrialism in America,* Free Press, 1968; Brian Doyle, editor, *Who's Who of Children's Literature,* Schocken Books, 1968; Malcolm Cowley, "Horatio Alger: Failure," *Horizon,* Summer, 1970; M. Cowley, *Many-Windowed House,* Southern Illinois University Press, 1970; Edwin P. Hoyt, *Horatio's Boys: The Life and Works of Horatio Alger, Jr.,* Chilton, 1974.

ATWATER, Florence (Hasseltine Carroll)

PERSONAL: Married Richard Tupper Atwater (a writer), 1921; children: two daughters. *Education:* Attended University of Chicago.

CAREER: Completed writing *Mr. Popper's Penguins* for her husband after he became ill. *Awards, honors:* Newbery Medal runner up, 1939, for *Mr. Popper's Penguins;* Young Reader's Choice Award, 1941, for *Mr. Popper's Penguins.*

WRITINGS: (With Richard Tupper Atwater, husband), *Mr. Popper's Penguins* (illustrated by Robert Lawson), Little, Brown, 1938.

FOR MORE INFORMATION SEE: Muriel Fuller, editor, *More Junior Authors,* H. W. Wilson, 1963.

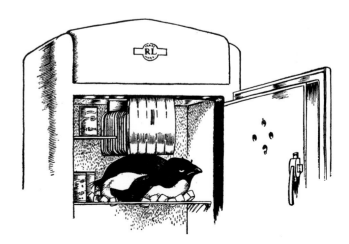

All day he would sit with his little white-circled eyes staring out sadly from the refrigerator. ■ (From *Mr. Popper's Penguins* by Richard and Florence Atwater. Illustrated by Robert Lawson.)

Lieutenant Baden-Powell, age 21.

BADEN-POWELL, Robert (Stephenson Smyth) 1857-1941

PERSONAL: Born February 22, 1857, in London, England; died January 8, 1941; son of the Reverend Baden-Powell (a minister and professor of geometry) and Henrietta Grace (Smyth) Baden-Powell; married Olave Soames, 1912; children: one son, two daughters. *Education:* Attended Charterhouse.

CAREER: British Army, 1876-1910. Served as a staff officer, 13th Hussars, in India, Afghanistan, and South Africa, 1876; assistant military secretary, South Africa, 1887-89, Malta, 1890-93; special service in command of Native Levies, Ashanti, 1895; Chief Staff Officer, Matabeleland campaign, 1896-97; Commander of 5th Dragoon Guards, 1897-99; defense of Mafeking, 1899-1900; operations in Transvaal, 1900-01; organized South African Constabulary and served as its Inspector-General, 1900-03; Inspector-General of Cavalry, 1903-07; commanded Northumbrian Territorial Division, 1908; retired, 1910, as Colonel-in-Chief of 13/18th Hussars. Exhibited sculpture in the Royal Academy, 1907. Founded the Boy Scouts and Girl Scouts, 1908, and established the periodical, *The Scout,* April, 1908. *Member:* Cavalry Club, Beefsteak Club.

AWARDS, HONORS—Military: Mentioned in dispatches for operations in Zululand, 1888; campaign of Matabeleland, 1896-97; defense of Mafeking, 1899-1900; operations in Transvaal, 1900-01. Civilian: Companion of the Bath, 1900; Knighted, 1909; Commander of the Royal Victorian Order, 1909; Knight Commander of the Royal Victorian Order, 1909; Knight Commander of the Bath, 1909; Baronet, 1922;

Knight Grand Cross of the Royal Victorian Order, 1923; Knight Grand Cross of St. Michael and St. George, 1927; first Baron, 1929; Order of Merit, 1937; Chevalier Order of Christ of Portugal; Cross of Commander of Legion of Honor; Fellow of Royal Geographic Society; Grand Cross of Alfonso XII; Grand Cross of Gedeminus (Lithuania); Grand Cross of Orange of Nassau (Holland); Grand Cross of Order of the Sword (Sweden); Grand Cross of Three Stars (Latvia); Grand Cross Order of Dannebrog; Grand Cross Order of Merit (Austria); Grand Cross of the Order of the Redeemer of Greece; Knight of Grace, St. John Order; Order of the Crown of Belgium; Order of Merit (Chile); Order of Merit, first class (Hungary); Order of Phoenix (Greece); Order of Polonia Restituta (Poland); Order of White Lion (Czechoslovakia).

WRITINGS—Military: *Aids to Scouting for NCO's and Men,* Gale & Polden, 1883; *On Vedette: An Easy Aide Memoire to Vedettes on Outpost Duty,* Gale & Polden, 1883; *Reconnaissance and Scouting: A Practical Course of Instruction,* Clowes, 1884; *Cavalry Instruction* (lectures), Harrison, 1885; *The Downfall of Prempeh: A Diary of Life with the Native Levy in Ashanti, 1895-96,* Methuen, 1896, reprinted, Scholarly Press, 1976; *The Matabele Campaign: Being a Narrative of the Campaign in Suppressing the Native Rising in Matabeleland and Mashonaland,* Methuen, 1897, reprinted, Scholarly Press, 1976; (author of introduction) Fletcher Smythe Baden-Powell, *War in Practice: Some Tactical and Other Lessons of the Campaign of South Africa, 1899-1902,* Isbister, 1903; *Sketches in Mafeking and East Africa,* Smith, Elder, 1907; *Quick Training for War: A Few Practical Suggestions* (illustrated by the author), H. Jenkins, 1914; *Memories of India* (illustrated by the author), D. McKay, 1915 (published in England as *Indian Memories,* H. Jenkins, 1915); *The Reminiscences of a Spy,* C. Brown, 1915; *My Adventures as a Spy* (illustrated by the author), C. A. Pearson, 1915.

Scouting: *Scouting for Boys: A Handbook for Instruction in Good Citizenship,* H. Cox, 1908, reissued, C. A. Pearson, 1961; *Yarns for Boy Scouts Told Round the Camp Fire,* C. A. Pearson, 1909; (with Agnes Baden-Powell) *Girl Guides: A Suggestion for Character Training for Girls,* Bishopsgate Press, 1909; *Scouting Games,* C. A. Pearson, 1909; (author of preface) Victor Bridges, *Camping Out, for Boy Scouts and Others,* C. A. Pearson, 1910; *Sea Scouting for Boys,* J. Brown, 1911; *The Canadian Boy Scout: A Handbook for Instruction in Good Citizenship,* G. Morang, 1911; (editor) *B-P's Books for Boys,* Bennett, 1912; *Boy Scouts beyond the Seas: My World Tour* (illustrated by the author), C. A. Pearson, 1913; (author of introduction) *Boy Scouts and What They Do,* Oldfields, 1914, published in America as *What Scouts Can Do: More Yarns,* Lippincott, 1921; *Marksmanship for Boys: The Red Feather and How to Win It,* C. A. Pearson, 1915.

Young Knights of the Empire, Their Code, and Further Scout Yarns, C. A. Pearson, 1916, Lippincott, 1917; *The Wolf Cub's Handbook,* C. A. Pearson, 1916, reissued, 1962, Boy Scouts of America, 1918; *Girl Guiding: A Handbook,* C. A. Pearson, 1918, reissued, 1957; *Handbook for Canada,* adapted by Gerald H. Brown, McClelland & Stewart, 1919; *Brownies or Blue Birds: A Handbook for Young Girl Guides,* C. A. Pearson, 1920; *Scoutmastership: A Handbook for Scoutmasters on the Theory of Scout Training,* Putnam, 1920; *Rovering to Success: A Book of Life-Sport for Young Men* (illustrated by the author), H. Jenkins, 1922; *Blazing the Trail: Being Wise Saws and Modern Instances from the Works of the Chief Scout,* edited by Laura Holt, C.

A. Pearson, 1923; *Report on the Boy Scouts and Girl Guides in South Africa,* [London], 1927; *Scouting and Youth Movements,* Cape & Smith, 1931; *Scouting Round the World* (illustrated by the author), H. Jenkins, 1935; *Adventuring to Manhood,* C. A. Pearson, 1936; *African Adventures,* C. A. Pearson, 1937; *Paddle Your Own Canoe; or, Tips for Boys from the Jungle and Elsewhere,* Macmillan, 1939; *B-P's Outlook* (selections from the author's contributions to *The Scout*), C. A. Pearson, 1941.

Other: *Pigsticking; or, Hoghunting: A Complete Account for Sportsmen and Others* (illustrated by the author), Harrison, 1889; *The Sport of Rajahs,* G. Morang, 1900; *Sport in War* (illustrated by the author), F. A. Stokes, 1900; (author of introduction) John Jackson, *Ambidexterity,* K. Paul, 1905; (author of introduction) Caroline Kirkland, *Some African Highways,* D. Estes, 1908; *An Old Wolf's Favorites: Animals I Have Known,* C. A. Pearson, 1921, Lippincott, 1922; *Life's Snags and How to Meet Them: Talks to Young Men,* C. A. Pearson, 1927; *My Hat,* B. Blackwell, 1929; *Lessons of a Lifetime* (autobiography), Holt, 1933; *Lessons from the Varsity of Life* (illustrated by the author), C. A. Pearson, 1933; *Adventures and Accidents,* Methuen, 1934; (with Stanley Baldwin and others) *Happiness and Success,* F. Muller, 1936; *Birds and Beasts in Africa,* Macmillan, 1938; *More Sketches of Kenya,* Macmillan, 1940.

Contributor to periodicals, including *The Scout, Marvel,* and *Boy's Journal.*

ADAPTATIONS—Play: Mary Constance Hill, *The Story of the Brownies* (two-act; adaptation of a story in *The Handbook for Brownies or Blue Birds),* Epworth, 1935.

SIDELIGHTS: **February 22, 1857.** Born, in London, to Professor Baden-Powell and Henrietta Grace Smyth Powell. Early education was informal, but for a few years at a private school in London. "When your father is a clergyman with fourteen children, and you are the last but two, there is not much money flying around for you." [Lord Baden-Powell, *Lessons of a Lifetime,* Henry Holt and Co., 1933.[1]]

1860. Father died. "From my father I derived but little in the way of education for he died when I was but three years old. This was a great loss to me for he was a man of many parts.

"Fortunately for me my father's character was attacked some nine years after his death, by Dr. Pusey, who wrote such imputations against his Christianity as drew a chorus of indignation and refutation from those who had known him and admired his broad-minded views.

"If these were in advance of their time (for he was a scientist as well as a preacher) they were views which are freely discussed and generally accepted to-day.

"Had it not been for this defence of him I might never have known his qualities."[1]

1865. Articulated an early philosophy to his grandfather:

"Law's For Me When I Am Old

"I will have the poor people to be as rich as we are, and they ought by rights to be as happy as we are, and all who go across the crossings shall give the poor crossing sweepers some money and you ought to thank God for what he has given us and he has made the poor people to be poor and the rich people to be rich, and I can tell you how to be good, now

The hero of Mafeking.

I will tell you. You must pray to God whenever you can but you cannot be good with only praying but you must also try very hard to be good.

By R.S.S. Powell 26 February 1865''

[William Hillcourt with Olave, Lady Baden-Powell, *Baden-Powell:The Two Lives of a Hero,* G. P. Putnam's, 1964.[2]]

1868. Left home for his first formal schooling at the Rose Hill School of Tunbridge Wells.

1870. Won a scholarship to the Charterhouse School in London. ''When I was thirteen I went up to Edinburgh and tried for a scholarship at Fettes College. I was lucky enough to get a scholarship as one of the original foundationers.

''But I did not after all avail myself of it, for my luck went further. Only a week or two later I was granted a foundation scholarship at Charterhouse. This I accepted.

''I was not a clever boy, nor, I grieve to say, was I as industrious a boy as I ought to have been. According to the school reports I began fairly well in my conduct but deteriorated as I went on. . . .

''I have been comforted to find that greater men than I have also shown that they were no geniuses in school subjects. Winston Churchill, in his delightful book, *My Early Life,* confesses that he could not grasp either classics or mathematics when at school.''[1]

At the Charterhouse School the opportunities for new and exciting experiences were abundant. ''My first bombshell fell upon me when, as a small boy at Charterhouse, I suddenly found myself ordered to play the leading part, Bob Nettles, in a comedy called—'To Parents and Guardians.'

''Dr. Haigh Brown, who had very far-sighted views, looked upon play-acting as a useful means of education for certain intellects among the boys, and so he encouraged, in fact almost ordered, theatricals among us. . . .''[1]

And there were many lessons to be learned. ''When I was a small boy at Charterhouse, outside the school walls was 'The Copse,' a long stretch of woodland on a steep hillside, extending for a mile or so round the playing fields.

''It was here that I used to imagine myself a backwoodsman, trapper, and scout. I used to creep about warily looking for 'sign' and getting 'close up' observation of rabbits, squirrels, rats and birds.

''As a trapper I set my snares, and when I caught a rabbit or hare (which wasn't often) I learned by painful experiment to skin, clean and cook him. But knowing that the Redskins were about, in the shape of masters looking for boys out of bounds, I used a very small non-smoky fire for fear of giving away my whereabouts.

''Incidentally also I gained sufficient cunning to hide up in trees when danger of this kind was toward, since experience told me that masters hunting for boys seldom looked upward. The Greeks made a blooper when they styled man 'anthropos,' or 'he who looks up,' since in practice he generally fails to look above his own level.

''Thus, without knowing it, I was gaining an education that was to be of infinite value to me later.''[1]

1876. Baden-Powell was turned down for entrance at Oxford University, but tested for, and was accepted by the Army. ''The second bombshell of my life burst upon me some four months after leaving school. I was on board the 'Gertrude,' a yacht belonging to Professor Acland, a professor at Oxford, an old friend of my father's, who was his 'opposite number' as Savilian professor of geometry.

''One of the guests on board was the Dean of Christchurch, the celebrated and handsome old divine, Dr. Liddell.

''The dean accosted me one morning with the news that, according to the newspaper, a namesake of mine had passed his exam for the army. And there, in black and white, was my own name!

''Well, the army council cannot well turn me out now, so I may as well confess that I practically got into the army by fraud; that is, I got in by examination, but examination is by no means a fair test of a fellow's abilities.

''When I went up for the army exam it was naturally without much hope of passing. Indeed I took the whole thing airily as a trial canter over the course. . . .

''Early in my army career I committed myself to authorship by writing a little handbook for the use of my men called *Reconnaissance and Scouting.* Later on when I came up for examination for promotion in the subject of reconnaissance the examiner asked whether I was the author of the handbook on the subject, and he had the decency to pass me without any further question.

''So to any candidate for examination who is doubtful about his ability to pass in any particular subject, my advice is to write a book about it and let it be known to the examiner that you are the author. Material for the book can of course be obtained from the many other existing books on the subject.''[1]

December 6, 1876. Assigned to the 13th Hussars at Lucknow, India, landing first at Bombay. ''I can remember to this day the smell of India which assailed our nostrils before we had set foot ashore at the Apollo Bunder, and, though it is very many years ago, I can well remember the bother which my companion and I had in getting our baggage safely ·ashore, loaded on a bullock-wagon and conveyed from the docks to Watson's Hotel. We had donned our best uniforms and were not a little proud of ourselves in the early part of the day; but as hour followed hour in that soggy heat we seemed to melt into the thick tight-bound cloth, and we wished we had something more seasonable to wear. By nightfall we were dog tired and our pride had all leaked out, and under the cover of darkness we all willingly climbed up on to the pile of baggage on our bullock-cart and allowed ourselves to be ignominiously carried through the back streets of Bombay to the great hotel.

''Then followed a long journey by train up country via Jubbulpore to Lucknow, where the regiment was stationed. . . .

''Lucknow still showed the marks of the Mutiny of twenty years before. The palace at Dilkoosha near the cantonments, and the Residency in Lucknow itself still stood in ruins as they were left after the fight, knocked to pieces by shell fire, and thickly pitted with bullet marks. Naturally they were of intense interest to us as invisible reminders of the struggle which had taken place for the maintenance of British supremacy in India.

"My first night at Lucknow was spent at the hotel, for we arrived about eleven p.m. and were told that the cantonments were five miles away. Next morning we started off and found the mess and the adjutant's house, but everybody was out. Later we met the adjutant riding along the road. It was odd to see a fellow and his horse all decked out in the things I knew so well by sight but whose fitting-on I did not understand. He soon showed us an unoccupied bungalow. We sent a bullock-cart to fetch our luggage from the station and returned to the hotel for our light luggage. When we returned to the bungalow we found it filled with natives; we thought at first they meant to stop us from entering, but we found they were servants in want of places.

"It is very different nowadays, when the natives are put on a higher standing with the Europeans. In some quarters it is complained that they are allowed to become too familiar: in a native state under native rule they still carry out the practice of saluting their own rajahs and any white man who comes there, but in British India they now treat a white man merely as an equal. Theoretically this is as it should be, but practically, until they are fit to govern themselves, it is a danger—to themselves.

"It is generally acknowledged that to be able to rule a man must first have learnt how to obey. In the training of the average Indian boy there is not as yet any discipline nor any attempt to inculcate in him a sense of honour, of fair play, of honesty, truth, and self discipline and other attributes which go to make a reliable man of character.

"Without a healthy foundation in these a scholastic education is apt to develop the microbe of priggishness, and swelled head." [Sir Robert Baden-Powell, *Memories of India,* David McKay, 1915.[3]]

Physical health was frequently threatened in this strange new land. "During my first year in India it seemed to me that I was being plugged full of medicine almost every day, sometimes for liver, sometimes for fever, and sometimes for my inside. When I had fever I would proceed to treat it in a way that will make many smile. My way was at dinner to eat very little, drink some good champagne, and before going to bed to have for twenty minutes a boiling hot bath with a cold stream on one's head, then a dose of castor oil then to bed in flannel clothes. Next day I would lie down and take quinine and then the fever went. But my old liver hurt sometimes, especially after jogging about on duty or in the riding-school, and I became so wretchedly thin that I had to have my pantaloons taken in and I could put three fingers between my legs and my top boots, which once were quite tight."[3]

Had a marvelous example to follow in his Commanding Officer, Colonel Sir Baker Russell. "Sir Baker was beloved of the men. The regiment, being the 13th Hussars, was nicknamed, 'The Baker's Dozen.' He practised many things which in those days were looked upon as heresy, but are recognised to-day as producing the highest efficiency, that is, regard for and development of the human side and the individuality of the men themselves. Thus when we paraded for a field-day we generally did so at a rendezvous some two or three miles from barracks, and each man made his own way to the spot individually, instead of being marched there, and one of the standing orders in the regiment was this: 'It is as great a crime for a hussar to be before his time as after it.' This entailed strict punctuality on the part of the men in being at the appointed place at the appointed time. They had to judge for themselves how long it would take them to get there without hustling their horses, and they took their own line of country and used their own senses in arriving at the place properly and up to time.

"On one occasion the Colonel had to lecture one of his men for some minor misbehaviour. The man was a splendid type of old soldier, a wonderful boxer, swordsman, rider, and marksman, but he was very fond of his mug of ale. When he was brought up for having had a drop too much, the Colonel remarked to him: 'My good man, I only wish I could drink as much as you do and keep as good a nerve. Tell me how you manage it and I will let you off.' Ben Hagan, for that was the fellow's name, explained his secret. It was to fill a handbasin with beer every night before turning in and to place it underneath his bed. Then his first act on waking in the morning was to pour it down his throat. He believed that the only way to preserve health and nerve was to take big doses of really stale beer the first thing in the morning.

"It is curious, looking back on those days, to see what an enormous change has come over the men with respect to temperance and sobriety. It was the natural thing for every man to go to bed 'half cocked,' as they called it, and it was not entirely unknown amongst the officers too! When a regiment went on service from England, it was usual for a certain number of men to be retained or to be borrowed from another regiment to collect all the drunken ones for transhipment to the train or ship on the morning of embarkation. Even then there was generally a large number of deserters who did not turn up at all to go abroad. Nowadays a regiment goes off for foreign service just as if it were going off to a review or to manoeuvres: not an absentee, not a man the worse for liquor. The men are of a better class and tone, and facilities are given them for keeping up their sober habits. In barracks they have proper supper-rooms where they can get moderate refreshments of all kinds at moderate prices. Formerly they were not allowed to have beer with their dinners, and they naturally adjourned as soon as dinner was over to the canteen to get their beer, remaining there, being treated or standing treat, for the rest of the afternoon, until they were full. . . .

"That idea of Sir Baker Russell's of letting men make their own way to parade, etc., was acted upon by me in after years by making it imperative for every man to go [for] a ride by himself of about one hundred and twenty miles, and to take a week in doing it. This tended to make men self-reliant, reliable, intelligent, and smart. At first it was feared that many of them, finding themselves away from all regimental restraint, would break out and make an orgy of it; but I have never heard a single complaint of the men on this head. They knew they were trusted to carry out this duty of riding off to report on some distant object, whether a railway station, a bridge, or a piece of country, and they took a pride in themselves and their horses while away, because they knew that the good name of the regiment was in their hands. We found it in practice the very best reformer for a stupid man that could be devised. He had no one to lean upon for advice or direction, he merely had his plain, simple orders, which he had to exercise his intelligence in carrying out."[3]

Not all was hard work and responsibility. "One of the main pleasures of life in India for the young officer is polo. The game is indigenous to the country and has for centuries been played in Persia. The first record of its introduction into British notice was in 1862, when a team of Manipuris played an exhibition game on the racecourse at Calcutta. It was afterwards taken up by the 11th Bengal Lancers and eventually by the 9th Lancers and 10th Hussars. It first made its appearance in England in 1874, when the 5th Lancers took it up as a game. It was particularly popular among the Manipuri tribes in Upper Bengal. There the polo ground is the village street, the ponies are little rats of twelve hands high, and the players play with short mallets which they use indiscriminately with either hand. When I first joined, a large number of players played on either side, and the rules were not very strict about the size of ponies, or as to crossing, off-side and the like. But as regiment began to play against regiment, and eventually tournaments developed, the rules crystallised and the game became more and more one of skill and discipline. . . .

"One team against which we had often to play possessed a back with an infernally bad temper, and once his feelings were aroused he was quite useless as a player; and thus our aim was to bump him or catch his stick as early as possible in the game, since it put him out of conceit with himself and with everybody else. . . .

"Part of the pleasure attaching to polo was that involved in getting a raw pony and training it for the game. It was a real satisfaction to a poor man to pick up ponies in all sorts of out-of-the-way places, such as country villages, fairs, etc., and then to break them in, make them handy, balance them, and educate them into playing the game. This training was not only a pastime of itself but incidentally an education to the rider as well. We felt almost inclined to pity the millionaire who bought his ready-made polo ponies, since he could not know the satisfaction of using the instruments made by his own hand for the purpose. . . .

"The ponies themselves seem to enter truly into the game and really to enjoy it. My ponies were at all times pets and companions; indeed, my last two in India, handsome grey Arabs, were as tame as dogs, and used to go out for walks with me, running with me, stopping and turning as I did, and coming to hand when whistled for, as sensible and as jolly as could be. I had reason to judge of the keenness of ponies for the game when on one occasion I was racing with another player for the ball. As my pony was gradually inch by inch passing his, it suddenly turned its head and, gripping hold of my fore-arm, dragged me off my mount and held me firmly, refusing to let me go in spite of the efforts of its rider, and only a smashing blow on the nose caused it to relax its grip and release me. My arm was black and blue for a week afterwards.

"The inter-regimental polo tournament is the great event of the year for all regiments in India, and on one occasion it was held at Meerut while my regiment was stationed there. All the teams visiting the place for the occasion naturally made use of our mess, and we formed a very large and happy family. On the night after the final tie had been decided, we had a grand dinner to signalise the event. The health of the winning team was drunk collectively and individually with all honours, and each member of it in turn tendered his thanks to the assembled company. Then the winning team proposed the health of the losers, and they naturally returned their thanks in a similar way, and proceeded to propose the toast of the runners-up, and so it went on during the greater part of the evening until every team in the place had had its health proposed, and speeches had been made without number, all harping on the one topic of polo.

"When all was over and a sigh of relief was going round, there suddenly sprang to his feet one of the members of the 4th Hussars' team, who said: 'Now, gentleman, you would probably like to hear me address you on the subject of polo!' It was Mr. Winston Churchill. Naturally there were cries of:

'No, we don't! Sit down!' and so on, but disregarding all their objections, with a genial smile he proceeded to discourse on the subject, and before long all opposition dropped as his honied words flowed upon their ears, and in a short time he was hard at it expounding the beauties and the possibilities of this wonderful game. He proceeded to show how it was not merely the finest game in the world but the most noble and soul-inspiring contest in the whole universe, and having made his point he wound up with a peroration which brought us all cheering to our feet. When the cheering and applause had died down one in authority arose and gave voice to the feelings of all when he said: 'Well, that is enough of Winston for this evening,' and the orator was taken in hand by some lusty subalterns and placed underneath an overturned sofa upon which two of the heaviest were then seated, with orders not to allow him out for the rest of the evening."[3]

Daily life in the India Regiment held unique challenges. "There is no doubt that the best preventative of disease in India is plenty of work, occupation and exercise. It is the ennui that kills. The difficulty is to make the work interesting so that it does not become a treadmill of drudgery. For the officers shooting, pigsticking, and polo all offer their attractions and make them far more healthy as a rule than are the men. Our Colonel was so fully impressed with the value of keeping up the health of his officers that, instead of keeping the weekly holiday as determined by regulations on Thursday, he moved it to Friday, and thus made the week-end into an outing by removing the mess into the jungle and leaving only the orderly officer to take charge of the regiment during Friday, Saturday, and Sunday. Those of the men who were good shots and capable of looking after themselves were also encouraged, during the hot weather, to go and live out in camp for several days at a time. The Government allowed a certain number of sporting guns for this purpose, and a large number of the men availed themselves of the privilege and made themselves into self-reliant, capable bushmen.

"There was too much of a tendency to coddle the men during the hot weather. Native syces, or grooms, were supplied by Government to look after their horses; but we made the men groom and feed their horses regularly, as it gave them exercise and occupation. At least once a week we had all-night field-days.

"Then also a great deal of our drill and instruction was competitive between squads, sections or troops. Latterly the system of teaching the men to be scouts came in as an additional form of training, which appealed to the men and gave them plenty of outdoor exercise by day and by night.

"It was reported to me *sub rosa* that one of the men when in hospital confided to his nurse: 'This new Colonel is the devil to work us; but the worst of it is, the more we work the more healthy we are.'"[3]

Began to formulate ideas for the Boy Scout Movement. "A new occupation also has lately started, fortunately for me, in a direction in which I have a say personally, and that is in the development of the Boy Scout Movement. This at first glance would appear to be entirely men's work; but, as we find in England, there are many centres in which there are plenty of boys but no men to take them in hand. The ladies have come forward and proved themselves most able organisers and instructors of scouting work, and their field in this direction is now enlarged by the institution of the Wolf Cubs, or branch of Junior Scouts for small boys of from nine to eleven, who are more particularly amenable to instruction by ladies. Also the Girl Guides have now made a great start in India, and promise to exercise a most valuable influence in the education of girls in that country. The principles on which they are trained are very much the same as those which guide the education of the Boy Scouts, but the details are those which apply to womanhood, in the shape of nursing and housekeeping, and the many details connected therewith."[3]

On the necessity of the India Regiment: "We as a nation are exceptionally fortunate in having a valuable training ground for our officers in the North-West Frontier of India, with real live enemies always ready to oblige in giving us practical instruction in the field in tactics and strategy, transport and supply, sanitation and ambulance work, and general staff duties. If Waterloo was won on the playing-fields of Eton, there are many victories before us that will have been won in the more practical fields of the North-West Frontier.

"Half of our good soldiers have made their names in the first instance in this arena. Critics love to disparage our 'Sepoy Generals'; but though their tactics may not be suitable to European warfare, they have at any rate learnt to handle men in difficult circumstances. They have had to adapt their common-sense to the situation; they have been faced with intricate problems of organisation and supply, and above all they have learnt to know themselves under the ordeal of war, which cannot be imitated even in the best manoeuvres. Those that have stood the test must *ipso facto* be the more valuable soldiers for any field. Scarcely a single year has passed during the last century in which there has not been some fighting on this frontier.

"A peace advocate has suggested that, in order to stop the numerous little wars in which we indulge so frequently in different parts of our Empire, every officer should on joining the service be awarded half a dozen war medals, and that one should then be taken from him for every campaign in which he subsequently takes part. The idea in the promoter's mind was that wars are brought about by officers on the hunt for medals."[3]

November, 1884. The 13th Hussars were transferred to South Africa. He soon acquired a staff position. "In due course I got a footing on the staff in a humble capacity, as A.D.C. to General H. A. Smyth, commander-in-chief in South Africa.

"Life on the staff at the Cape, under a well-loved general and popular lady, was a very happy and enjoyable experience. It was hardly what one would call soldiering, but there was lots of headquarters work, more especially as the post of military secretary being temporarily vacant, I was told off to act in that capacity in addition to my duties as A.D.C. This gave me most valuable training and experience in staff work.

"In my spare time I had plenty of occupation since I was the honorary secretary of the Polo Club, for which I got up fêtes and gymkhanas in order to raise funds for making our ground and pavilion.

"Then, in addition to lending a hand in theatricals, Pierrette minstrels, drawing society, &c., I was second whip and, for one short season, master of the Cape Foxhounds.

"Altogether I was now in a very different kind of atmosphere from that of soldiering, and for a time it was a pleasant change. Indeed it was great fun, a regular beano, when . . . bang came a bombshell!

Sir Robert, Chief Scout of the British Empire.

"An alarming telegram came through from Zululand to say that the Zulus were up. They had defied the police; some troops from Natal had been sent to back up the civil force and been driven back with loss. Generally the fat was in the fire.

"The governor of Natal (and incidentally of Zululand) was disturbed in his mind. He wanted more troops as a backing, but being by title 'Commander in Chief' of Natal he did not want military generals butting in. However, General Smyth saw that if there were to be troops there must be transport and supplies and organisation and hospitals and remounts, and that every hour's delay meant wider outbreak, so without ado he despatched all necessary orders and promptly embarked with his staff for Natal and Zululand.

"Here again my luck was in. The post of military secretary was just then vacant, waiting for a field officer to be appointed from England. I was gazetted to act as such in the interim although I was below the rank of field officer.

"Different small columns were sent through the country so soon as all organised resistance was at an end, to clear up and collect surrenders and arms. Here and there there were little scraps but as a rule that Usutus gave in readily.

"When accompanying one of these reconnaissances for rounding up cattle I came to the edge of a high cliff overgrown with thick bush.

"While peering down into the valley below to see what had become of some enemy scouts whom we were following up, my orderly suddenly called out—'Look out, sir, behind you.'

"I jumped round and there stood a splendid figure of a Zulu warrior, in all the glory of glistening brown skin and the white plumed head-dress from which the Usutu had their nickname of 'Tyokobais.'

"With his great shield of ox-side and his bright assegais he made a fine picture. He had popped up from under the brow of the cliff to get me, but finding another with me he did not stop to argue but sprang down into cover again. I could see him and another running and scrambling along a sort of track on the face of the bluff, and I kept along above them with my pistol ready, and before long they crossed a bit of open rock-face, giving me a chance.

"But I didn't take it. I wanted to see where they were making for, and very soon they disappeared into what was evidently the mouth of a cave. My particular friend caught his shield in a bush in the course of his flight and rather than be delayed left it there.

"So, accompanied by my orderly, I went down the path and got the shield.

"Following the path along I presently found that in place of a cave there was a deep crevice or gully in the cliff face which ran right down to the plain below.

"As I looked down into this a strange sight met my eyes. The gully was packed with the brown faces with rolling eyes and white teeth of hundreds of women and children, refugees hiding from us. Down below, nearest to the plain, were crowds of warriors, evidently waiting for an attack from that direction. I had come in at the back door!

"I made my Basuto orderly call to the Usutus that fighting was all over now and that no harm would be done to them if they surrendered quietly, and in my heart of hearts I warmly hoped they would. Just then our flanking party turned up, moving along the base of the cliff, and this helped them to make up their minds, which had been pretty well joggled up by our unexpected appearance also at the back door. So they called 'Pax.'

"Then I made my way down through them. The women seemed to think that this was the beginning of the slaughter and began screaming and pushing to get out of my reach. In the struggle a small brown imp fell off a rock on which he had been put, so I naturally picked him up and replaced him, giving him something to play with. This had a miraculous effect; the hub-bub died down; remarks were passed from mouth to mouth and I was able to squeeze down among them without further trouble.

"One of my fellows below, seeing me doing this shouted, 'What is it like there?' To which I replied—'Just like the squash at a London ball'; from which bright remark the gully came to be known as the Ballroom Staircase.

"Eventually Dinizulu took refuge in his stronghold the Ceza Bush. Had he held out there we should have had a tough job in taking it, consisting as it did of a mass of boulders, bush and caves, all over a steep mountain side.

"As it was he decamped, and a few days later came in and surrendered."[1]

April 29, 1896. "After the ashanti show I was quartered with my squadron of the 13th Hussars at Belfast.

"One day I received a telegram from General Sir Frederick Carrington, to the effect that he was ordered on service to South Africa and was starting in three days' time; if I could join him he would take me as his chief staff officer.

"This was the 29th April and he was sailing on the 2nd May.

"I left at once and while on the journey I sent a telegram to my colonel at Regimental Headquarters at Dundalk, saying that I was off to South Africa and asking his leave—not quite the orthodox procedure but excusable—at least I thought so—under the circumstances.

"The colonel did not recall me so I went; and I have owed a debt of gratitude to that colonel ever since, for without knowing it I went then for the best adventure of my life.

"The reason for the sudden call for General Carrington was that the Matabele tribe in South Africa had broken out, and its warriors were murdering the white settlers there.

"The Matabele were originally Zulus who under the leadership of 'Msilikatsi, son of Matshobane, had been sent on a raiding expedition by the Zulu king, Tshaka, in 1817.

"Their attack having failed they were expected to return, according to custom, and to be disarmed and then to have their necks broken by the women of the tribe. On this occasion they did not see it in the same light, and elected not to return home but to go off, on their own, with unbroken necks, to the northward, until they could discover a suitable country to settle in.

''This they eventually found in what is now known as Southern Rhodesia where, having wiped out the unwarlike Makalaka inhabitants, and having bagged their women and cattle, they settled down at Gubulawayo and formed a new tribe. . . .

''We now come to 1896, when the Matabele had settled down and had been hoping that the British invasion of the country was merely a temporary raid, such as they were in the habit of dealing themselves.

''Finding that the British intended remaining there they turned in their dilemma to the 'Mlimo'—their god—whom for generations past they had been wont to consult for advise on national emergencies.

''This oracle gave out his instructions in a certain cave in the Matropos and also in two or three other places in Mashonaland.

''On this occasion his advice was that the Matabele warriors should make their way to Bulawayo on a certain night and massacre the white people in the place, and after that should go out and kill the individual white settlers on their farms.

''This plan miscarried owing to the impatience of the warriors when making their way to the rendezvous, as they could not resist the temptation of killing some of the farmers as they passed near their homesteads. Several of these men, however, managed to escape and to get away into Bulawayo and to give warning of the impending attack. Among those who escaped was Selous, the celebrated big game hunter, who had a farm some thirty miles out of Bulawayo. . . .

''Meantime the settlers organised themselves into fighting units mounted and dismounted, and carried out bold attacks on the enemy when and where they found it possible. . . .

''From Mafeking the general, with his staff (consisting of Colonel Vyvyan, as assistant adjutant general, and Captain Ferguson as A.D.C., Colonel Bridge as quartermaster general, and myself as chief staff officer), proceeded by coach, a regular old 'Deadwood' affair, with eight mules, on our long trek.

''It took us ten days and nights to get there, the most unrestful journey I have ever endured. We picked up fresh mules at the mail stations every fifteen miles or so. The marvel was that, though in the enemy's country, the Matabele never interfered with the traffic on this roadway. The reason which they afterwards gave for this was that they supposed that if they left open a way of retreat the people of Bulawayo would be glad to avail themselves of it and escape out of the country.

''It was not in their programme that we should use it the other way on!

''Immediately on arrival at Bulawayo we fixed up our office and started to organise.

''There were a few fights about the district and the Matabele eventually retired to their great stronghold in the Matopo Hills.

''These hills consisted of a tract of country, broken up into piles of granite boulders, mounting in many places to eight or nine hundred feet in height, full of caves and deep ravines

Baden-Powell, Chief Scout of the world.

Baden-Powell and the Prince of Wales, Imperial Jamboree, 1924.

half hidden in vegetation of cactus, Mahobahoba, and baobab trees.

"The district extended for some fifty miles in length and twenty in depth and was the most damnable country that could be imagined for fighting over. . . .

"One job for my column was to capture if possible one of the two "Mlimos' who were urging the people to go on fighting against us. Major Watts had succeeded in getting one of these, Makoni, and the man was tried and executed.

"About the same time my column came across the other, named Uwini, who with about a thousand men, was holding a number of strong kopjes. These we proposed to attack severally, and in taking the first one we lost four men, but after an exciting scrap, in dark tunnels and underground, our men captured the chief himself, wounded but defiant.

"There were various crimes against him including the murder of at least two white men. We tried him by court-martial and he was found guilty and sentenced to death.

"A few days later the surprising order came from the governor of South Africa indicating that I should be tried by court-martial as being responsible for the execution of Uwini, since I had signed his death warrant, and directing that I should be placed under arrest.

"Sir Frederick Carrington telegraphed to the governor in reply requesting that 'Colonel Baden-Powell should be spared the indignity of arrest as an officer who had done so much excellent service,' but that a court of enquiry should be held.

"This came off in due course at Gwelo. The charge against me was to the effect that, having arrested a malefactor, I should have handed him over to the nearest police station to be tried by civil authorities.

"In my defence I rather confined myself to the legal point that according to military law I had the power to exercise my own judgment if I was over a hundred miles from a superior authority.

"I was over a hundred miles from my general and over a thousand miles from the governor, though had I been only fifty miles away I should have acted in the same way since summary punishment in the presence of his own people had given one the exceptional opportunity of smashing their belief in the "Mlimo.'

"It also gained their surrender and thereby saved the many lives which would have been lost, both among our own men and amongst the enemy, if we had had to continue our attack on the eight successive kopjes forming their stronghold.

"Of course the court found me 'not guilty' and I was released without a stain on my character, as it were.

"When I got home from the Matabele campaign I rejoined my regiment, the 13th Hussars, in Dublin. I arrived there in the early morning, had a tub, and in stripping for the purpose I took from my neck a little amulet which had been given me by my Irish groom, Martin Dillon, when I started out for the campaign the year before. He had begged me so earnestly to wear it because it had received special blessing from his priest that I did so in order to humour him.

"I took this off, as I said, in going to my tub, and on proceeding to dress again I could not find it anywhere.

"That morning when I met old Dillon I told him of its mysterious disappearance, and he was not in the least surprised but merely remarked that that was quite natural. It had only been given to me to ensure the preservation of my life during the campaign and having performed that duty it had now naturally disappeared.

"Anyhow I never saw it again, though a thorough search was made."[1]

'1897. "I had been with the regiment just long enough to buy myself a new outfit when suddenly, bang, came another bombshell.

"I had been awarded a brevet lieutenant colonelcy for the Ashanti campaign, and a further brevet of full colonel for the Matabele campaign, so although I figured as major in the regiment, below the lieutenant-colonel in command and the senior major, second in command, I was actually senior to both of these in rank which was a bit of an anomaly.

"This had not occurred to me until the colonel sent for me one day and informed that I was appointed to command the 5th Dragoon Guards.

"This was indeed a bombshell but I waved it off by saying to him—'I don't want to go. I would rather stop in the regiment.'

"However he then explained to me that as a full colonel it was impossible for me to remain where I was, and so I had to go.

"Leaving my old regiment was perhaps one of the bitterest moments of my life.

"I had served in it for twenty-one years, the very best years of my life, and the going away was a big wrench especially in the actual departure which was worse than I expected.

"I arranged with my servant that I would slip away in the early morning before breakfast; and, so that it should not be noticed, he was to have a cab round at the back door of my quarters and get it all loaded up with my luggage so that I could nip away unseen.

"When all was ready I sneaked out of the back door, there to find my cab, with the regimental sergeant major sitting on the box conducting the band which was also in attendance, every man of my squadron harnessed in on long ropes, and the whole regiment there to see me out of the barrack gate!

"And off we went, the most choky experience I ever had.

"My last glimpse of the barracks showed blankets being waved from every window, and all through the slums and streets of Dublin went this mad procession which finally landed me at the station with a farewell cheer.

"Thank God I was allowed to come back to the regiment again a few years later, as its colonel in chief, which I still remain, and have thus completed over fifty-five years' connection with the old 'Lillywhites.' "[1]

August 29, 1900. Received new orders. "I want you to see me without delay regarding formation of police force for Transvaal, Orange River Colony, and Swaziland.

"Such was the bombshell which, on the 29th of August, 1900, was burst upon me in a telegram from Lord Roberts at Belfast (Transvaal) just as I had taken over command at Nylstrom of a force of all arms with which I was to operate in the northern districts. . . .

"A few days later I was on my way down country to see Lord Milner, the high commissioner, at Cape Town, since the police as a civil force would be under his direction.

"It was a long railway journey in those days of blown-up bridges, all night stoppage, broken lines and 'deviations'; but I utilised the time in planning out my scheme in fuller detail on several sheets of paper, with estimates of personnel, ranks, equipment, food, horses, transport, training, distribution, duties, finance, medical staff, housing, etc., etc.

"For passing the time on a long journey try planning a police force; it beats jigsaws and crossword puzzles all to fits.

"On the journey down country I met with a wonderful experience. At several places where the train stopped there were large lines of communication camps, and the men crowded around the train to cheer. At one place they swarmed into the carriage itself to shake hands and then that happened similar to what happened to me later on in Russia.

"A sudden mania seemed to break out among the crowd and every man seemed to want to give me something as a memento. It might be a pipe or a matchbox, an old knife, money, anything the man happened to have about him, and one dear fellow, finding his pockets empty, tore from his breast his only possession, a medal ribbon. I have it still—a great treasure—bless him, whoever he was!

Baden-Powell, painting a water-colour.

"The day before I was due to reach Cape Town I got wind of an unnerving ordeal which I should have to go through. The mayor and corporation were going to meet me at the station. In order to avoid this I telegraphed on to Government House, where I was to report myself, that I was unfortunately delayed and might not arrive until a day or two later.

"This, I knew, would be passed on to the mayor, who would then postpone the reception till at least the following day, and meantime I should slip in unnoticed and 'unreceived.'

"So, when my train drew into Cape Town station, I happily rolled up all my small kit, ready to walk to Government House, with an eager eye to bath and breakfast. But—Goodness, what was this? The platform was a swaying mass of humanity, overflowing on to the roofs of neighbouring trains, all cheering and waving.

"I have but a confused memory of what followed. I believe that a tiny space was cleared in which the mayor was able to greet me with a short speech, and then I was bundled off, on the heads of a roaring mass, out of the station into the sunlight of Adderley Street. I do remember that two excellent fellows seized hold of my breeches pockets on either side to prevent my money from falling out, and in this way I was marched—more or less upside down—through Cape Town, all the way to Government House. There I was carried past the bewildered sentry and was at last deposited with a flop in the hall.

"The butler, hastily summoned from his pantry, appeared on the scene to find a dishevelled, dirty, khaki-clad figure standing there, with a roaring mob outside the door. He, naturally, looked upon me for the time as a truculent leader of a revolution.

"But a British butler is nothing if he cannot be dignified, even in the worst crisis, so he sternly demanded what I wanted. I was at a loss. I realised that I was not expected there until the following day and that Government House had not passed on my message to the town. All I could think of to blurt out at the moment was—'Could I have a bath, please?'"[1]

October 2, 1909. Invited by His Majesty, King Edward, to stay at the palace at Balmoral to discuss the future of Boy Scouting. "But about this time another bombshell fell upon me. This was the outbreak of Boy Scouting, on a suggestion which I had made, but which produced such a crop of Boy Scouts all over the country that the demands upon my time and energies grew to such an extent that I had to consider whether I was justified in continuing my soldiering or whether to take up this new growth and organise it.

"King Edward had invited me to Balmoral, and there he talked over the question of the Boy Scouts with me at great length, and though it was all in embryo he showed a strong belief in its possibilities and urged me to go on with it. So later, when the question rose in my mind as to whether I could do both works adequately, it came to the ears of the King that I was contemplating retiring from the army, and he at once sent word to ask whether this was the case, saying he considered that it would be unwise of me to leave the service when, as he expressed it, I had just got my footing on the ladder.

"But the next day, having thought it over more fully, he agreed that seeing the possibilities that lay before the Scout movement, and that its organisation could not be put into other hands, it would after all be right on my part to resign from the army and devote myself to this other work.

"Apropos of my visit to Balmoral, I had gone there to receive from His Majesty the honour of knighthood as a Knight Commander of the Victorian Order. I had arrived in the late afternoon and was told that the investiture would take place the following day, but just as I was dressing for dinner, Legge, the King's equerry, came rushing into my room and said that His Majesty wanted to decorate me *at once* and hurried me off to his dressing room.

"My diary records: While outside the door Col. Legge took off my miniature medals and pinned on two safety pins outside my coat, calling at the same time to a footman to bring a cushion and another a sword.

"It was like preparation for an execution.

"Then we walked in.

"The King, in Highland dress, shook hands smiling most genially and kept hold of my hand while he told me that for my many services in the past and especially for my present one of organising the Boy Scouts for the country he proposed to make me a Knight Commander of the Victorian Order.

"He then sat down and I knelt on the cushion in front of him, the equerry handed him the sword and he tapped me on each shoulder and hung the cross round my neck and hooked the star of the Order on my coat, and gave me his hand to kiss. Then he laughingly told me that his valet would put the ribbon right for me, and out I went.

"(Oddly enough the other day when I went to hang up my hat for the first time in the House of Lords, the usher who received me reminded me that he was that same valet who had helped me and he also told me that I had slept that night in the room next to the King.)

"This operation delayed me for a few minutes and when I got down to the drawing-room I found all the party were awaiting me, and those who possessed the Victorian Order formed a sort of little guard of honour inside the door waiting to shake me by the hand. It was all very embarrassing, and very jolly.

"Later I found that the reason for this undue haste was that the dinner cards were already printed beforehand, and the staff officer in charge of this job had supposed I would be knighted that day instead of the next and had therefore put me down as 'Sir Robert,' and it was in order to make the card correct that the King had had to do the knighting without delay!

"After dinner King Edward called me aside and sat me down on the sofa beside him and talked for half an hour about my Boy Scouts.

"The movement was not two years old then, but it had spread rapidly. The previous day I had been at Glasgow for a rally at which 5,640 boys were present, and the previous month 11,000 were present at the Crystal Palace gathering.

"His Majesty asked me all about our aims and methods and expressed his great belief that the movement was just what the country needed. He said that it would grow into a big valuable institution and that he would like to review the Scouts the following year in Windsor Park. He agreed to my suggestion that boys who worked hard and passed special tests for efficiency should be ranked as 'King's Scouts.'

"I went to bed a happy man that night.

"On my sending in my request to retire from the army there arose the question of my pension. To my horror I was told that the royal warrant did not allow of a pension for one of my age.

"My promotion had been so rapid that I was a lieutenant-general at fifty, whereas the warrant did not allow for anybody holding that rank under sixty-two.

"I had had exceptional luck, of course, in getting brevet promotion at every step in rank; thus: I had got a direct commission instead of two years at Sandhurst. Two years' ante-date was granted to me as sub-lieutenant on passing exam with honours for lieutenant.

"As lieutenant and adjutant I had promotion to supernumerary captain, as captain I acted as military secretary in the field and so was promoted to brevet major, as major in Ashanti awarded brevet colonel, as lieutenant-colonel in Matabeleland awarded brevet full colonel, as full colonel in the Boer War special promotion to major-general at the comparatively early age of forty-three, thus becoming lieutenant-general before I was fifty.

"Arrangements, however, were eventually made for my pension. I was further granted the Reward for Meritorious Service.

"I was appointed colonel in chief to my old regiment, the 13th Hussars, and in addition to the K.C.V.O. the King then conferred on me the honour of the K.C.B.

"Ian Hamilton, in congratulating me, wrote: 'It never rains but it pours and on you it has poured to the extent of giving you a Bath.'

"It was a big wrench to take this last step out of the service that I had loved so well, though at the same time I did not mind taking my foot off the ladder for I had no wish to do any further climbing up it. I was not built for a general. I liked being a regimental officer in personal touch with my men.

"It was no small consolation to receive from the Secretary of State for War the letter which he sent me, expressing his kindly regret in losing me from the army, in which he added: '. . . But I feel that the organisation of your Boy Scouts has so important a bearing on the future that probably the greatest service you can render to the country is to devote yourself to it.'

"And so ended my Life Number One."[1]

1912. "I now started on my second life in this world.

"I had definitely left the army, in 1910. I was now settling down to be a good citizen as a warden of the Mercers' Company (N.B. A mercer, like a poet, is born, not made); and the Boy Scout movement had started itself and was finding its feet far and wide.

"This, though it promised to be the biggest job of my life, was at the same time the easiest, since everybody connected with it met me half-way with their keenness.

"In 1912 all was going smoothly and well when out of the blue an entirely new kind of bomb suddenly caught me in the midriff!

"It was in this way. During my first life I had had my time fairly fully occupied, with little leisure for thinking of such extraneous matters as marriage; indeed I had been rallied by my best friend, 'Ginger' Gordon, 15th Hussars, on being a confirmed old bachelor; and when I said that I had no desire to get married and I felt sure that nobody would desire to marry me, he looked at me quizzically for a space and then remarked, with the laugh of one who knew: 'You'll get it in the neck one day when you least expect it, old boy!'

"And I did.

"In the course of following up the science of tracking I had practised the art of deducing people's character from their footprints and gait. Native trackers the world over read the character as well as the actions or intentions of the footprinter, e.g., toes turned out imply a liar, outside heel depression means adventurous, and so on.

"In this research I came to the conclusion, for instance, that about 46 per cent of women were very adventurous with one leg and hesitant on the other, i.e., liable to act on impulse.

"So when I came to an exception it caught my attention.

"One such I noted where a girl—a total stranger to me and whose face I had not seen—trod in a way that showed her to be possessed of honesty of purpose and commonsense as well as of the spirit of adventure.

"I happened to notice that she had a spaniel with her.

"This was while I was still in the army and I was going into Knightsbridge Barracks at the time. I thought no more of it.

"Two years later, on board my ship for the West Indies, I recognised the same gait in a fellow-passenger. When introduced I charged her with living in London. Wrong. My sleuthing was at fault; she lived in Dorsetshire! 'But have you not a brown and white spaniel?' 'Yes.' (Surprise registered.)

"'Were you never in London? Near Knightsbridge Barracks?' 'Yes, two years ago.'

"So we married—and lived happily ever after.

"Thus began my second life, and with it the Boy Scouts and the Girl Guides."[1]

1914-1919. "The movement was still very young, only six years old, when war broke out. But it was sound. The boys had developed the right spirit and were all keen to do service for the country. Men and women came forward to take the places of Scoutmasters who had gone to the front, and, where these were not forthcoming, the senior boys themselves took command and carried on the Troops.

"After the War, in 1919, we made a start with the senior branch of the movement for Scouts over 17½, whom we called Rovers. This branch gradually took shape under the direction of Colonel Ulick de Burgh, and promised to meet a great need. I therefore wrote a book called *Rovering to Success,* in which I said . . . 'It always seems to me so odd that when a man dies he takes out with him all the knowledge that he has acquired in his life-time while sowing his wild oats or winning his successes. He leaves his sons or younger brothers to go through all the work of learning it over again from their own experience.

"'Why can't he pass it on so that they start with his amount of knowledge to the good to begin with, and so get on to a higher stage of efficiency and sense right away?'

"In the book I warn the young men of the various rocks against which they are likely to come up in their voyage through life, and these rocks may be summed up generally as Horses, Wine, Women, Humbugs, and Irreligion.

"The book then goes on to describe the organisation of the Rovers as a Brotherhood of cheerful Service for others.

"That book, *Rovering to Success,* has brought me as great a return, if not a greater than *Scouting for Boys,* seeing that it has induced a very large number of young men to write to me personally and privately seeking further advice.

"These letters I have treated entirely in confidence and have answered them myself to the best of my ability. It has been an eye-opener to realise how great is the need for some such advice for the adolescent lad, when so very many of them explained that they had been left in ignorance and were shy of asking their parents or pastors, but having read the book had come to me for sympathy.

"These many human documents appealed directly to one's heart for it is so astounding to find that they will adopt me as a father-confessor when in person I was a total stranger to them. But I accepted their trust."[1]

August, 1920. The first Boy Scout Jamboree held in London. "After the War a great meeting of scouts from all countries was organised in London to bring the nations together through Scouting and to signalise the peace.

"It was something bigger than a rally so we called it a jamboree. I have often been asked—'Why call it by that name?' and my reply has been—'What else could you call it?'

"This took place in Olympia and lasted for ten days. Some twelve thousand boys were present, representative groups coming from a large number of foreign countries for the occasion.

"The show proved popular beyond our expectations. Not having foreseen this our accommodation for the public was too limited and we lost money, but at the same time gained a reputation.

"On the final day representatives of all the foreign countries met and selected me to be Chief Scout of the World and this was enunciated by a wonderful procession of the nations in their national dress and bearing the colours of their countries. It was a very marvellous procession, to which dramatic effect was given by two majestic ladies, representing Britannia and Columbia. I was told to march along behind these.

"In the midst of the procession round the arena an American boy came forward bringing me a carved chair. I asked him what it was for, and he said it was to sit down on, so I sat down then and there.

"The master of ceremonies and marshals rushed at me from various sides and ejected the boy with his chair, as I was upsetting the whole show. It turned out to be an unauthorised presentation by the boy himself, who had carved this chair for me and thought this an opportune moment for presenting it! . . .

"In the same year we received a cablegram from Lord Chelmsford, Viceroy of India, inviting my wife, who was Chief of the Girl Guides, and myself to visit that country and to help to establish the Scouts and Guides on a proper footing.

"We stayed not upon the order of our going but went, and had a wonderfully interesting and successful time. We found about six different organisations calling themselves Scouts, working on very sketchy lines, and many of them strongly impregnated with politics, and all agreeing to differ from one another.

"We visited most parts of the country and saw great promise if only they could be brought together and consolidated into one general body.

"Many of the leaders had totally mistaken notions as to the aims of the movement, and when one came to talk matters over with them they proved amenable to reason.

"Eventually Mrs. Annie Besant, who headed a very considerable contingent, agreed to join up with the parent movement, and as she commanded the respect of the Indians generally, there was little doubt that her action in doing so would prove a very persuasive example to the remainder.

"So it was arranged that we should have a great rally of all the sections of the movement, and Mrs. Besant would come out into the centre and take from me the Scout Promise.

"With all the dramatic force at my command I called upon her, in my most impressive manner, to repeat after me the words of the Scout Promise.

"At that moment my mind wandered. I thought of other things, and for the life of me I could not myself remember the words of the Scout Promise! There was an awkward pause. I felt a perfect fool; I swallowed once or twice and tried to begin; but the actual words had vanished.

"However, Mrs. Besant recognised my dilemma and rose nobly to the occasion. With all the ability of a trained theatrical prompter she gave me the cue, whispered my words to me, which I then roared out in ringing tones, with as much confidence as if I had never faltered.

"Thanks to this initiation by Mrs. Besant, the diverse sections joined in amalgamating into one movement for All India, and from that day it has gone on and prospered even under the abnormally difficult times through which that country has been passing.

"We further visited Burma, and Ceylon, and on our homeward voyage called in at Egypt and Palestine."[1]

1925-1927. Boy Scout work brought opportunities for travel and honor. "In 1925, my wife and I again visited the United States of America to attend the Girl Guide World Conference, at which was inaugurated the World Bureau.

"In the autumn we sailed for South Africa for a tour of inspection of Scouts and Guides. This took us seven months and was in itself a pilgrimage of intense interest, both in reviving memories and in realising future possibilities.

"On our return home in 1927 I was surprised by the King conferring upon me the high honour of the Grand Cross of St. Michael and St. George.

"As I have shown elsewhere I had more than once—in fact three times I believe—been recommended for the C.M.G. (Companion of St. Michael and St. George, or nicknamed 'Colonial Made Gentleman') for services in Ashanti, Swaziland, and Matabeleland respectively. These having been denied naturally provoked the desire for this Order, though as a rule I have no liking for Orders (and consequently find myself plastered with them). But the C.M.G. I did covet. And here I found myself suddenly invested with the Grand Cross.

"I wrote very badly to the King's private secretary, who was a personal friend, telling my delight and my reason for it—and I believe he went and showed my letter to His Majesty. This was scarcely fair on me but at any rate it told truthfully my appreciation."[1]

1928. The Girl Guide movement came into prominence. "The following year my wife and I visited the Scouts and Guides in New Zealand and Australasia and, on our way home, in South Africa again. This was a most interesting if somewhat strenuous tour but at the same time well worth the effort.

"Rapid as has been the rise of the Scout Movement, and surprising as has been the measure of its adoption by foreign countries, the Girl Guide movement has surpassed it in both the particulars.

"'We are the Girl Scouts' was the announcement made with a certain air of confident self-assertion by a pert little person of some eleven years at the first rally of the Boy Scouts. This was at the Crystal Palace in 1909.

"She was the spokeswoman of a small group of girls dressed as nearly as possible in imitation of their brothers, the Scouts.

"The presence and the quite evident keenness of these girls opened one's eyes to the feeling that here lay an opening for a public application of the Scout method of character-training and self-development.

At this time, over twenty years ago, women were only just coming into their own in the work of the world. Character development was actually more needed by them than by their brothers since they had had less opportunity of forming it in their comparatively more secluded life.

"They needed it for their growing responsibilities in social life, they needed it also in their capacity as mothers for imparting it to their offspring.

"The school education of girls had been put on a higher and steadily improving footing, but the problem of their character training was as yet unsolved.

"Character cannot be taught in a class. It has, necessarily, to be expanded in the individual, and largely by effort on the part of the pupil herself.

"With the Boy Scouts we aimed to help them to develop their character by sporting activities and outdoor adventures with which a moral code of chivalry was carefully linked. One had long realised that girls generally preferred to read boys' literature, that stories of Wild West dramas appealed to them far more than those about heroines in academies for young ladies.

"Now the girls were coming forward of their own volition to get the same adventure as their brothers.

"With much spirit, however, meeting one halfway, it was not a difficult task to devise a scheme similar in principle to that of the Scouts while differing in detail to meet the requirements of the girl's life.

"Miss Charlotte Mason, the founder of the House of Education for training women teachers, had to some extent foreseen this when she adopted as a text book for their instruction a little book called *Aids to Scouting* which I had written for young soldiers. She found in it something educative, so after my encounter with these self-assertive 'Girls Scouts' I was not without hope in suggesting a sister movement to that of the Boy Scouts. To this we gave the name 'Girl Guides.'

"The term 'Guides' was intended to give an idea of romance and adventure while it indicated also their future responsibilities for directing their menfolk and bringing up their children on right lines.

"The general aim of its training was similar to that of the Scouts, namely to develop character and health and sense of service to others, while in particular it would give them practical instruction in home-making, mother-craft, etc.

"This aim was to be pursued largely by self-education through outdoor recreation in good companionship. The training would be under the direction of a 'Guide,' that is, one who in relationship was neither a schoolmistress nor a martinet, but, rather, an elder sister.

"The Guides, like the Scouts, were organised in small companies not exceeding thirty-two in number so that each individual temperament could be studied and educated.

"Then the girls are grouped progressively according to age, as Brownies, Guides, and Rangers.

"In the first two or three years little could be done in the way of organising the Guides since one was fairly snowed under by the phenomenal growth of the Scout movement; but in the hands of a committee of energetic women things then began to take shape and before long the movement had its own headquarters, its uniform, and its handbook and rules.

"The uniform was an important item, not merely as an attraction, as it undoubtedly was to the girls but because under it all differences of social standing were hidden and forgotten.

"One of our tenets is to extend our good will and toleration so that we pay no regard to differences of class or country or creed. All are accepted in the sisterhood who can subscribe to our religious policy which is on the simple basic foundation of most of the beliefs in the world, namely, love of God and love for one's neighbour. The actual form in which these are expressed is left to their pastors and parents; it is immaterial to us so long as they *are* expressed."[1]

1932. Looked back on seventy-five years of activity. "When one has passed the 75th milestone and has got to that stage of life when he thinks twice before deciding whether it is now worth while to order a new evening coat, it is allowable to look back along the road one has travelled.

"Your natural inclination is to preach and to warn other travellers of snags in the path, but isn't it better to signal to them some of the joys by the way which they might otherwise miss?

"The great thing that strikes you on looking back is how quickly you have come—how very brief is the span of life on this earth. The warning that one would give therefore is that it is well not to fritter it away on things that don't count in the end; nor on the other hand is it good to take life too seriously as some seem to do. Make it a *happy* life while you have it. *That is where success is possible to every man.*

"Varied are the ideas of what constitutes 'success,' e.g., money, position, power, achievement, honours, and the like. But these are not open to every man—nor do they bring what is real success, namely, happiness.

Painting of Lord Baden-Powell by Shirley Slocombe, 1916.

"Happiness is open to all, since when you boil it down it merely consists of contentment with what you have got and doing what you can for other people.

"As Sir Henry Newbolt sums it up—'The real test of success is whether a life has been a happy one and a *happy-giving one.*'

"I believe that the Devil Worshippers of the East hold the belief that for 6,000 years the Devil will rule the world and that Christ will rule for a similar period. Just now the Devil is having his reign, and the Devil is best described by the term 'Selfulness,' or lack of wide and sympathetic outlook.

"This can be seen in every individual, class, sect, or nation to-day.

"Individually we all of us stick in our respective ruts, be they the army, or club life, or sport, or other line.

"Similarly we see only our own social class.

"Education has no wider outlook than making scholars.

"Religion has no wider outlook than making churchmen.

"Nationalism has no wider outlook than the self-determination of its own country.

"Christianity or broad-minded love-practice does not as yet prevail in this world.

"In the Boy Scout and Girl Guide movement we are making the attempt to oust selfulness by inculcating in the young a wider vision and mutual good will and service. We do not pretend that scouting will do the trick but since it has caught on as a brotherhood with such an extraordinary rapidity in so many different countries irrespective of class, creed or race, one may hope that at any rate it is a definite step in the desired direction. . . .

"Looking back over my own 'narrow span,' two bright spots among many which at once instinctively spring to mind are:

"In Life Number 1 the rough time among good companions on the sunbaked veldt in the Matabele campaign; and in life Number 2 a little warm hand dragging me down till her two little arms can reach round my neck, when with a soft moist kiss she whispers, 'Just one more good-night story, Daddy.'

"I write this sitting in my garden at the close of a perfect day in late September, with the ruddy afterglow of sunset giving a new tone to the lights and shadows across the woodlands stretched below, and a violet haze upon the distant heights where I have wandered.

"There is the scent of roses in the air—and sweetbriar. A rook caws sleepily in the elms near by in answer to the distant crooning of a dove. A bee hums drowsily by, hive-ward bound. All is peace in the home at dusk, ere night closes down.

"She sits by me, in the silence of comradeship, who has shared some of the toil of the afternoon—and the joy of it. It is good to laze, honestly half-tired, and to look back and feel that though one has had one's day it has, in spite of one's limitations, not been an idle one, that one has enjoyed it to the full and that one is lucky in being rich through having few wants and fewer regrets.

"Through an upper window comes the laughing chatter of the young folk going to bed.

"To-morrow *their* day will come.

"May it be as happy a one as mine has been, God bless them!

"As for me—it will be my bedtime soon.

"Good night."[1]

January 8, 1941. Died in his home at The Outspan, Nyeri, Kenya.

FOR MORE INFORMATION SEE: Esse V. Hathaway, "Fair Play," in her *Partners in Progress,* McGraw, 1935; Reginald H. Kiernan, *Baden-Powell,* D. McKay, 1939, reprinted, Argosy, 1970; Robert Lynd, "Happiness Again," in his *Life's Little Oddities,* W. Salloch, 1941; Eileen Kirkpatrick Wade, *27 Years with Baden-Powell,* Blandford, 1957; Duncan W. Grinnell-Milne, *Baden-Powell at Mafeking,* Bodley Head, 1957; "Honor to an Old Scout," *Life,* March 11, 1957; Ernest E. Reynolds, *Baden-Powell: A Biography of Lord Baden-Powell of Gilwell,* Oxford University Press, 1957; Brian Doyle, editor, *Who's Who of Children's Literature,* Schocken Books, 1968; Ronald Seth, *Some of My Favorite Spies,* Chilton, 1968; John Canning, editor, *100 Great Adventures,* Taplinger, 1969; E. K. Wade, *Olave Baden-Powell: The Authorized Biography of the World Chief Guide,* Verry, 1971; Cyril Davey, *Fifty Lives for God,* Judson, 1973.

For children: Roy Burnham, *B-P's Life in Pictures: The Story of Lord Baden-Powell of Gilwell,* Boy Scouts Association, 1952; Patrick Pringle, *When They Were Boys,* Roy, 1954; David W. Walters, *Modern Lives,* Collins, 1954; Geoffrey Bond, *Baden-Powell Story: The Boy's Life of Lord Baden-Powell of Gilwell,* Staples, 1955; Maude Elsie Carter, *Life of Baden-Powell,* Longmans, 1956; G. Bond, *Adventures of Baden-Powell,* Staples, 1957; Arthur Catherall, "Robert Baden-Powell: Chief Scout of the World," in *Children's Book of Famous Lives,* edited by Eric Duthie, Odhams, 1958; Catherall, *Young Baden-Powell,* Roy, 1962; William Hillcourt and Olave Baden-Powell, *Baden-Powell: Two Lives of a Hero,* Putnam, 1964; Wyatt Blassingame, *Baden-Powell: Chief Scout of the World,* Garrard, 1966; R. J. Unstead, *Men and Women in History,* Black, 1967; Russell Freedman, *Scouting with Baden-Powell,* Holiday House, 1967; I. O. Evans, *Benefactors of the World,* F. Warne, 1968; Wyndham Charles, *Chief Scout of the World: Robert Baden-Powell,* Blackie & Son, 1969.

BARBOUR, Ralph Henry 1870-1944
(Richard Stillman Powell)

PERSONAL: Born November 13, 1870, in Cambridge, Massachusetts; died February 19, 1944, in Pass Christian, Mississippi; son of James Henry and Elizabeth Middleton (Morgan) Barbour. *Education:* Attended Highland Military Academy, Worcester, Massachusetts. *Home:* Pass Christian, Mississippi.

CAREER: Author. Worked on newspapers in Boston, Denver, Chicago, and Philadelphia as a leg-man, court reporter, literary editor, columnist, correspondent, and rewrite man. Was a rancher for four years in Grand Valley, Colorado.

RALPH HENRY BARBOUR

WRITINGS—Fiction: *The Half-Back: A Story of School, Football, and Golf* (illustrated by B. West Clinedinst), D. Appleton, 1899; *For the Honor of the School* (illustrated by Charles M. Relyea), D. Appleton, 1900; *Captain of the Crew* (illustrated by C. M. Relyea), D. Appleton, 1901; *Behind the Line: A Story of College Life and Football* (illustrated by C. M. Relyea), D. Appleton, 1902; *The Land of Joy*, Doubleday, Page, 1903; *Weatherby's Inning: A Story of College Life and Baseball* (illustrated by C. M. Relyea), D. Appleton, 1903; *The Arrival of Jimpson, and Other Stories*, D. Appleton, 1904; *Kitty of the Roses* (illustrated by Frederic J. von Rapp), Lippincott, 1904; *On Your Mark! A Story of College Life and Athletics* (illustrated by C. M. Relyea), D. Appleton, 1904; *Four in Camp: A Story of Summer Adventures in the New Hampshire Woods*, D. Appleton, 1905; *An Orchard Princess* (illustrated by James Montgomery Flagg), Lippincott, 1905.

The Crimson Sweater (illustrated by C. M. Relyea), Century, 1906; *Four Afoot: Being the Adventures of the Big Four on the Highway*, D. Appleton, 1906; *A Maid in Arcady* (illustrated by F. J. von Rapp), Lippincott, 1906; *Four Afloat: Being the Adventures of the Big Four on the Water*, D. Appleton, 1907; *Holly: The Romance of a Southern Girl* (illustrated by Edwin F. Bayha), Lippincott, 1907; *The Spirit of the School*, D. Appleton, 1907; *Tom, Dick, and Harriet* (illustrated by C. M. Relyea), Century, 1907; *Foreward Pass: A Story of the "New Football"*, D. Appleton, 1908; *Harry's Island* (illustrated by C. M. Relyea), Century, 1908; *My Lady of the Fog* (illustrated by Clarence F. Underwood), Lippincott, 1908; *Captain Chub* (illustrated by C. M. Relyea), Century, 1909; *Double Play: A Story of School and Baseball*, D. Appleton, 1909; *The Lilac Girl* (illustrated by C. F. Underwood), Lippincott, 1909; *The Golden Heart* (illustrated by C. F. Underwood), Lippincott, 1910; *Kingsford, Quarter* (illustrated by C. M. Re-

lyea), Century, 1910; *The New Boy at Hiltop, and Other Stories*, D. Appleton, 1910; *Winning His "Y": A Story of School Athletics*, D. Appleton, 1910; *Finkler's Field: A Story of School and Baseball*, D. Appleton, 1911; *The House in the Hedge* (illustrated by Gertrude A. Kay), Moffat, Yard, 1911; *Joyce of the Jasmines* (illustrated by C. F. Underwood), Lippincott, 1911; *Team-Mates* (illustrated by C. M. Relyea), Century, 1911; *For Yardley: A Story of Track and Field*, D. Appleton, 1911; *Change Signals: A Story of the New Football*, D. Appleton, 1912; *Crofton Chums* (illustrated by C. M. Relyea), Century, 1912; *Cupid en Route* (illustrated by F. Foster Lincoln), R. G. Badger, 1912; *The Harbor of Love* (illustrated by George W. Plank), Lippincott, 1912; *Around the End*, D. Appleton, 1913; *The Junior Trophy*, D. Appleton, 1913; *Lady Laughter* (illustrated by Gayle Hoskins), Lippincott, 1913; *Partners Three* (illustrated by C. M. Relyea), M. A. Donohue, 1913; *Peggy in the Rain*, D. Appleton, 1913; *Benton's Venture*, D. Appleton, 1914; *The Brother of a Hero* (illustrated by C. M. Relyea), D. Appleton, 1914; *Left End Edwards* (illustrated by C. M. Relyea), Dodd, 1914; *The Story My Doggie Told to Me* (illustrated by John Rae), Dodd, 1914.

Danforth Plays the Game: Stories for Boys Little and Big (illustrated by John A. Coughlin), D. Appleton, 1915;

At the top of the sandy road he turned and waved farewell. ■ (From *Four Afloat* by Ralph Henry Barbour. Illustrated by August Spaenkuch.)

Heart's Content (illustrated by H. Weston Taylor), Lippincott, 1915; *Left Tackle Thayer* (illustrated by C. M. Relyea), Dodd, 1915; *The Lucky Seventh* (illustrated by Norman P. Rockwell), D. Appleton, 1915; *The Secret Play* (illustrated by N. P. Rockwell), D. Appleton, 1915; *Left Guard Gilbert* (illustrated by Edward C. Caswell), Dodd, 1916; *The Purple Pennant* (illustrated by N. P. Rockwell), D. Appleton, 1916; *Rivals for the Team: A Story of School Life and Football* (illustrated by C. M. Relyea), D. Appleton, 1916; *The Adventure Club Afloat* (illustrated by E. C. Caswell), Dodd, 1917; *Center Rush Rowland* (illustrated by E. C. Caswell), Dodd, 1917; *Hitting the Line* (illustrated by N. P. Rockwell), D. Appleton, 1917; *Winning His Game* (illustrated by Walt Louderback), D. Appleton, 1917; *The Adventure Club with the Fleet* (illustrated by E. C. Caswell), Dodd, 1918; *For the Freedom of the Seas* (illustrated by Charles L. Wrenn), D. Appleton, 1918; *Keeping His Course* (illustrated by W. Louderback), D. Appleton, 1918; (with H. P. Holt) *Lost Island* (illustrated by C. M. Relyea), Century, 1918; (with H. P. Holt) *Fortunes of War* (illustrated by C. M. Relyea), Century, 1919; *Full-Back Foster* (illustrated by E. C. Caswell), Dodd, 1919; *Guarding His Goal* (illustrated by George Avison), D. Appleton, 1919; *The Play That Won*, D. Appleton, 1919; *Under the Yankee Ensign*, D. Appleton, 1919.

Fourth Down!, D. Appleton, 1920; (with H. P. Holt) *Joan of the Island*, Small, Maynard, 1920; *The Lost Dirigible*,

Beside Sandy tripped the Obnoxious Kid, waving triumphantly her red and white banner. ■ (From *Team-Mates* by Ralph Henry Barbour. Illustrated by C.M. Relyea.)

D. Appleton, 1920; (with H. P. Holt) *The Mystery of the Sea-Lark* (illustrated by C. M. Relyea), Century, 1920; *Quarter-Back Bates* (illustrated by Frank J. Rigney), Dodd, 1920; *Kick Formation*, D. Appleton, 1921; *Left Half Harmon* (illustrated by Leslie Crump), Dodd, 1921; *Metipom's Hostage*, Houghton, 1921; *Three-Base Benson*, D. Appleton, 1921; *Coxswain of the Eight*, D. Appleton, 1922; (with H. P. Holt) *Over Two Seas*, D. Appleton, 1922; *Right End Emerson* (illustrated by L. Crump), Dodd, 1922; *The Turner Twins* (illustrated by C. M. Relyea), Century, 1922; *For the Good of the Team*, D. Appleton, 1923; *Nid and Nod* (illustrated by C. M. Relyea), Century, 1923; *Right Guard Grant* (illustrated by L. Crump), Dodd, 1923; *The Fighting Scrub*, D. Appleton, 1924; *Follow the Ball*, D. Appleton, 1924; *Infield Rivals*, D. Appleton, 1924; *Right Tackle Todd* (illustrated by L. Crump), Dodd, 1924; *Spaniard's Cave* (illustrated by C. M. Relyea), Century, 1924.

Barry Locke: Half-Back (illustrated by C. M. Relyea), Century, 1925; *Bases Full!*, D. Appleton, 1925; *Hold 'em Wyndham*, D. Appleton, 1925; *Right Half Hollins* (illustrated by L. Crump), Dodd, 1925; *The Last Play*, D. Appleton, 1926; *Pud Pringle: Pirate*, Houghton, 1926; *Tod Hale with the Crew*, Dodd, 1926; *The Winning Year*, D. Appleton, 1926; *Heading North: Automobile Adventures*, Revell, 1927; *Tod Hale at Camp* (illustrated by L. Crump), Dodd, 1927; *Adventures of Tom Marvel* (illustrated by A. G. Peck), D. Appleton, 1928; *Comrades of the Key*, Cen-

Hiding his face as best he could, he lifted his voice in loud cries for help. ■ (From *Behind the Line* by Ralph Henry Barbour. Illustrated by C.M. Relyea.)

"I am looking for Bert Middleton," he announced. ■ (From *The Spirit of the School* by Ralph Henry Barbour.)

tury, 1928; *Danger Ahead: More Automobile Adventures,* Revell, 1928; *The Fortunes of the Team,* Houghton, 1928; *Hunt Holds the Center,* D. Appleton, 1928; *Lovell Leads Off,* D. Appleton, 1928; *Substitute Jimmy* (illustrated by Charles Lassell), Century, 1928; *Tod Hale on the Scrub* (illustrated by L. Crump), Dodd, 1928; *Giles of the Mayflower* (illustrated by A. O. Scott), D. Appleton, 1929; *Grantham Gets On,* D. Appleton, 1929; *Tod Hale on the Nine* (illustrated by L. Crump), Dodd, 1929.

Candidate for the Line (illustrated by A. O. Scott), D. Appleton, 1930; *Flashing Oars,* D. Appleton, 1930; *The Fumbled Pass* (illustrated by G. Avison), D. Appleton, 1931; *Danby's Error,* Cosmopolitan Book, 1931; *Mystery Island* (illustrated by John D. Whiting), Century, 1931; *Squeeze Play* (illustrated by G. Avison), D. Appleton, 1931; *The Club Battery* (illustrated by G. Avison), D. Appleton, 1932; *Hero of the Camp* (illustrated by William Meilink), D. Appleton, 1932; *Pirates of the Shoals,* Farrar & Rinehart, 1932; *Skate, Glendale!,* Farrar & Rinehart, 1932; *Beaton Runs the Mile* (illustrated by Neil O'Keeffe), D. Appleton, 1933; *The Crew of the "Casco": An Adventure of the Maine Coast,* Farrar & Rinehart, 1933; *Goal to Go* (illustrated by N. O'Keeffe), D. Appleton, 1933; *Peril in the Swamp,* Farrar & Rinehart, 1934; *The Scoring Play* (illustrated by N. O'Keeffe), Appleton-Century, 1934; *Southworth Scores* (illustrated by N. O'Keeffe), Appleton-Century, 1934.

The Five-Dollar Dog (illustrated by E. C. Caswell), Appleton-Century, 1935; *Five Points Service* (illustrated by E. C. Caswell), Appleton-Century, 1935; *The Glendale Five,* Farrar & Rinehart, 1935; *Merritt Leads the Nine* (illustrated by George M. Richards), Appleton-Century, 1936; *Watch that Pass!* (illustrated by G. M. Richards), Appleton-Century, 1936; *The School That Didn't Care* (illustrated by Inglewood Smith), Appleton-Century, 1937; *The Score Is Tied* (illustrated by Robert A. Graef), Appleton-Century, 1937; *Three in a Trailer* (illustrated by E. C. Caswell), Appleton-Century, 1937; *Fighting Guard* (illustrated by R. A. Graef), Appleton-Century, 1938; *Rivals on the Mound* (illustrated by Charles Czap), Appleton-Century, 1938; *The Last Quarter* (illustrated by Edwin Earle), Appleton-Century, 1939; *The Three-Cornered Dog* (illustrated by R. M. Brinkerhoff), Appleton-Century, 1939.

Death in the Virgins, Appleton-Century, 1940; *Hurricane Sands* (illustrated by James Reid), Appleton-Century, 1940; *Ninth Inning Rally* (illustrated by R. A. Graef), Appleton-Century, 1940; *The Infield Twins* (illustrated by Robert S. Robinson), Appleton-Century, 1941; *The Target Pass* (illustrated by N. O'Keeffe), Appleton-Century, 1941; *All Hands Stand By!* (illustrated by Manning de Villeneuve Lee), Appleton-Century, 1942; *Barclay Back* (illustrated by I. B. Hazelton), Appleton-Century, 1942; *Thad and the G-Man* (illustrated by N. O'Keeffe), Appleton-Century, 1942; *Mystery on the Bayou* (illustrated by Thomas McGowan),

Appleton-Century, 1943; *The Mystery of the Rubber Boat* (illustrated by E. C. Caswell), Appleton-Century, 1943.

Nonfiction: *The Book of School and College Sports,* D. Appleton, 1904; *Let's Go to Florida!,* Dodd, 1926; *The Boy's Book of Dogs* (illustrated by Morgan Dennis), Dodd, 1928; (with La Mar Sarra) *Football Plays for Boys,* Appleton-Century, 1923; (with L. M. Sarra) *How to Play Better Baseball,* Appleton-Century, 1935; *For Safety!* (illustrated by E. C. Caswell), Appleton-Century, 1936; *Good Manners for Boys,* Appleton-Century, 1937; (with L. M. Sarra) *How to Play Six-Man Football,* Appleton-Century, 1939; (with L. M. Sarra) *How to Play Better Basketball,* Appleton-Century, 1941.

Also contributor (sometimes under pseudonym Richard Stillman Powell) to various periodicals, including *Life, Puck, Truth,* and *St. Nicholas.*

ADAPTATIONS: "The Half-Back" (motion picture), Thomas A. Edison, Inc., 1917.

SIDELIGHTS: "I was born in Cambridge, Massachusetts, **November 13, 1870.** My father, James Henry Barbour, was of Colonial and Revolutionary stock, his forebears having been, I gather, an extremely Puritanical lot with morbid consciences, painfully honest, and opposed to all frivolities of the flesh or spirit. Those qualities, however, waned somewhat short of me.

"My mother was Elizabeth Middleton Morgan, whose parents arrived from Derbyshire, England, just in time for her to be born in Massachusetts. She was a painter of considerable talent and that fact provided a distinctly artistic atmosphere for my boyhood. I was educated in public schools of Cambridge, the New Church School at Waltham, and the Highland Military Academy at Worcester, Massachusetts.

"At about the age of seventeen, in spite of earlier inclination to become an artist, I broke out with rhymes and jests which, over the *nom de plume* of Richard Stillman Powell, were published in such flippant journals as *Life, Puck,* and *Truth,* and convinced me that it would be a waste of time and opportunity to bother further with an education when editors' checks were so astoundingly easy to obtain. My mother, however—my father had died when I was twelve—was dubious of verse-writing as a life's occupation and I consented to try real work and so condescendingly accepted a position as reporter on a Boston evening paper.

"Six months later, having been discharged for cause, I went to Denver, Colorado, and for several years found employment on the paper there. Again out of a job, I yearned for the open spaces and found them in the Grand Valley in western Colorado. I ranched there four years, at odd times pounding out short stories on a decrepit typewriter. Back in Denver, and at work on the *Times,* I collaborated with a brother newspaper man, L. H. Bickford, and produced my part of a first book.

"Subsequently I went to Chicago and read copy on the *Inter-Ocean;* and from there to Philadelphia. In the latter city, at the age of twenty-eight, I finally succeeded in tearing myself away from newspapers, ending a career in which I had variously served as leg-man, court reporter, literary editor, columnist, correspondent, rewrite man, cartoonist, and city editor.

"My release was largely fortuitous, for it happened that a story of mine for boys published in *St. Nicholas Magazine* caught the attention of Ripley Hitchcock, literary adviser for D. Appleton & Company. It was Ripley Hitchcock who had seen possibilities in Edward Noyes Westcott's *David Harum,* after the manuscript had been declined by a dozen others, and it was Ripley Hitchcock who thought he saw possibilities in a doubting and timorous young man named Barbour. The immediate result of our meeting in the old building on Fifth Avenue was *The Half-Back* (published 1899) which, well received then, is now still selling.

"Some one hundred and forty other books have followed that, all but a score or so stories for boys; or boys and girls if you like. It has required fourteen publishers to cope with that production, although the Appleton-Century Company is responsible for the bulk of it. I have, too, contributed at least my share of short stories to the magazines; most of them for the younger generation—since, having accustomed myself to viewing life from the juvenile point, I find it difficult to see it from the grown-ups' angle. I live in Tampa, Florida, and am happily married to a lady who corrects my spelling, reads my proofs, beats me at tennis, and doesn't mind it when I tramp sand into the house after my gardening activities."

February 19, 1944. Died in Pass Christian, Mississippi.

FOR MORE INFORMATION SEE: Stanley J. Kunitz, editor, *Junior Book of Authors,* revised edition, H. W. Wilson, 1951; Obituaries—*New York Times,* February 20, 1944.

(From *Mauis' Summer* by Arnold Edwin Bare. Illustrated by the author.)

ARNOLD EDWIN BARE

BARE, Arnold Edwin   1920-

PERSONAL: Born June 20, 1920, in New York; son of Geoffrey (a teacher) and Lilian (Major) Bare. *Education:* Attended Yale University, New Haven, Conn., two years. *Politics:* Independent Democrat. *Religion:* Protestant. *Home:* 164 East 37th St., New York, N.Y. 10016. *Office:* 1430 Broadway, New York, N.Y. 10018.

CAREER: Exhibitions: Weldon Gallery, 1956. *Awards, honors: Pierre Pidgeon* was a Caldecott Medal runner-up for 1943.

WRITINGS—Self-illustrated: *Mauis' Summer,* Houghton, 1952.

Illustrator: Lee Kingman, *Pierre Pidgeon,* Houghton, 1943; Scott, Foresman, 1965; Lee Kingman, *Ilenka,* Houghton, 1944; Grimm Brothers, *Grimm's Golden Goose,* Houghton, 1947; *Peter Paints the U.S.A.,* Houghton, 1948; *Mikko's Fortune,* Ariel, 1955.

SIDELIGHTS: "*Pierre Pidgeon* was based on drawings made on a trip to French Canada. Travel and illustrating the country you visit can lead to a book. I didn't arrive at a style of painting until I worked at home."

Arnold Edwin Bare's works are included in the Kerlan collection at the University of Minnesota.

FOR MORE INFORMATION SEE: Bertha E. Mahoney and others, compilers, *Illustrators of Children's Books: 1744-1945,* Horn Book, 1947; B. M. Miller and others, compilers, *Illustrators of Children's Books: 1946-1956,* Horn Book, 1958.

BARR, Jene   1900-

PERSONAL: Born July 28, 1900, in Kobrin, Russia; daughter of Joseph and Goldie (Barr) Cohen. *Education:* Graduated from Chicago Normal School of Physical Education, 1920; attended University of Chicago, 1928-29, Chicago Teachers College, 1931, 1933, 1949-50, Art Institute of Chicago, 1932, Northwestern University, 1935-37. *Politics:* Independent. *Religion:* Jewish. *Home:* C/o Bobele, 1085 Tasman Dr. #494, Sunnyvale, Calif. 94086.

CAREER: Board of Education, Chicago, Ill., physical education instructor, 1925-35, classroom teacher, 1935-50, teacher-librarian, 1950-64. Downtown YWCA, Chicago, Ill., teacher of creative writing, 1953-56. Albert Whitman and Co., educational consultant in the Social Studies. *Member:* Society of Midland Authors (chairman, library committee, 1963—), Children's Reading Round Table (program chairman, 1950, president, 1965-66), Illinois Woman's Press Association (chairman, student activities committee,

JENE BARR

How different office work is today. ▪ (From *Busy Office, Busy People* by Jene Barr. Illustrated by Charles Lynch.)

1961—, house chairman, 1961, second vice-president, 1957), Chicago Teacher-Librarian's Club (recording secretary, 1962), Illinois Library Association, National Federation of Press Women. *Awards, honors:* Midwest Award, Children's Reading Round Table, 1959; National Federation of Press Women awards, including first prize for *Texas Pete, Little Cowboy,* 1951, second prize for *Little Circus Dog,* 1950, second prize for *Mr. Mailman,* 1955; Mate Palmer Award of Illinois Woman's Press Association for *Little Circus Dog,* 1950, *Texas Pete, Little Cowboy,* 1951, *Mr. Mailman,* 1955, and *Baseball for Young Champions,* 1959.

WRITINGS: Youth books published by Whitman, except as noted: *Conrad the Clock,* Wilcox & Follett, 1944; *Little Prairie Dog,* 1949; *Little Circus Dog,* 1949; *Surprise for Nancy,* 1950; *Texas Pete, Little Cowboy,* 1950; *Policeman Paul,* 1952; *Fireman Fred,* 1952; *Mike, the Milkman,* 1953; *Baker Bill,* 1953; *Mr. Mailman,* 1954; *Big Wheels! Little Wheels!,* 1955; *Ben's Busy Service Station,* 1956; *Fast Trains! Busy Trains!,* 1956; *Good Morning, Teacher,* 1957; *Dan the Weatherman,* 1958; (with Catherine Bowers) *Here is Chicago* (textbook), University Publishing Co., 1958, revised edition, 1965, 1969, 1973; *This is My Country,* 1959; *Miss Terry at the Library,* 1962; (with others) *How Americans Produce and Obtain Goods and Services* (introductory economics book for young children), Education-Industry Service, 1962; *Mr. Zip and the U.S. Mail,* 1964; *Fire Snorkel Number 7,* 1965; (with Cynthia Chapin) *What Will the Weather Be?,* 1965; *What Can Money Do,* 1967; *Busy Office, Busy People,* 1968.

"Young Champions" Series with Robert J. Antonacci: *Baseball for Young Champions,* 1956, reissued, 1977; *Football for Young Champions,* 1958, reissued, 1976; *Basketball for Young Champions,* 1960, *Physical Fitness for Young Champions,* 1962, reissued, 1975 (all published by McGraw). Contributor to *Illinois Libraries.* Editor of children's column, *Back of the Yards Journal,* Chicago, Ill., 1946-48, women's column, 1947-48, 1952.

SIDELIGHTS: "Because I feel that children are the most important people on earth, and that reading is the most needed basic skill for children, I spent many years writing books for children during my career as a classroom teacher and, later, a teacher-librarian in the Chicago Public Schools.

"The 'Young Champion' series, written with Dr. Robert J. Antonacci, reflects the fact that sports, particularly baseball, represented a turning point in my life. My enjoyment of sports and belief in its values resulted in my becoming first a physical education teacher, which in turn, led to classroom teaching and writing for children.

"I believe that if a child is given an informative and enjoyable book that he can read and understand, he will not only improve in his reading but the feeling of success will encourage him to want to do more reading and in time he will develop a real love for books. Since it is best for this reading process to begin when the child is very young, I began to write 'read-it-yourself' books that I felt were of interest and had meaning for the beginning reader. Further, I have always encouraged young children to use their libraries and get a library card—no age is too young.

"Now retired in California, I am gratified to find that many adults I meet have read my books and now have children of their own who are reading these very same books."

FOR MORE INFORMATION SEE: Chicago Schools Journal, May-June, 1951; *Chicago Daily Tribune,* November 14, 1954; *World Topics Year Book,* 1959.

BAYLOR, Byrd   1924-

PERSONAL: Born in San Antonio, Tex. *Residence:* Arizona and New Mexico.

CAREER: Began as a reporter for an Arizona newspaper; author of children's and adult books. Executive secretary for the Association for Papago Affairs. *Awards, honors: When Clay Sings* illustrated by Tom Bahti, and *The Desert Is Theirs* illustrated by Peter Parnell, were named Caldecott Honor Books in 1973 and 1976, respectively; Catlin Peace Pipe Award, 1974, for *They Put on Masks;* Brooklyn Art Books for Children Citations, 1977, for *The Desert Is Theirs; Hawk, I'm Your Brother* was a Caldecott Honor Book.

WRITINGS—All for children, except as noted; all under name Byrd Baylor, except as noted: (Under name Byrd Baylor Schweitzer) *Amigo* (illustrated by Garth Williams), Macmillan, 1963, reissued, 1973; (under name B. B. Schweitzer) *One Small Blue Bead* (illustrated by Symeon Shimin), Macmillan, 1965; (under name B. B. Schweitzer) *The Chinese Bug* (illustrated by Beatrice Darwin), Houghton, 1968; (under name B. B. Schweitzer) *The Man Who Talked to a Tree* (illustrated by S. Shimin), Dutton, 1968; *Before You Came This Way* (illustrated by Tom Bahti), Dutton, 1969; *Plink, Plink, Plink* (illustrated by James Mar-

**They sat there quietly, as good friends will,
Admiring the view from that rocky hill.**
■ (From *Amigo* by Byrd Baylor Schweitzer. Illustrated by Garth Williams.)

BYRD BAYLOR

shall), Houghton, 1971; *Coyote Cry* (illustrated by S. Shimin), Lothrop, 1972; *When Clay Sings* (ALA Notable Book; illustrated by T. Bahti), Scribner, 1972; *Sometimes I Dance Mountains* (illustrated by Ken Longtemps; photographs by Bill Sears), Scribner, 1973.

Everybody Needs a Rock (ALA Notable Book; illustrated by Peter Parnall), Scribner, 1974; *They Put on Masks* (illustrated by Jerry Ingram), Scribner, 1974; *The Desert Is Theirs* (illustrated by P. Parnall), Scribner, 1975; (editor) *And It Is Still That Way: Legends Told by Arizona Indian Children*, Scribner, 1976; *We Walk in Sandy Places* (photographs by Marilyn Schweitzer), Scribner, 1976; *Hawk, I'm Your Brother* (illustrated by P. Parnall), Scribner, 1976; *Guess Who My Favorite Person Is* (illustrated by Robert Andrew Parker), Scribner, 1977; (for adults) *Yes Is Better Than No*, Scribner, 1977; *The Way to Start a Day* (illustrated by Peter Parnall), Scribner, 1978; *The Other Way to Listen* (illustrated by Peter Parnall), Scribner, 1978.

Also contributor to *Redbook* magazine, *McCall's,* and *Arizona Quarterly.*

SIDELIGHTS: Baylor grew up in the deserts of America's Southwest, and spent many of her childhood summers in Mexico. Her familiarity with the area resulted in a variety of books for children. In *Before You Came This Way,* she described what life in the southwestern canyons might have been like in the prehistoric ages. "It is not only the arts of brush and word that in this book evoke the sense of the past; it is above all the precision with which the authors have understood the unvoiced question with which children approach such novelty.... The explicit inspiration for the work is the American Southwest, but its impact is universal

and intense," wrote a reviewer for *Scientific American.* "The entire book is infused with a sense of wonder and quiet reverence.... Evocative and poetic, a distinguished book," commented Zena Sutherland in an article for *Saturday Review.*

The author's award-winning *The Desert Is Theirs* focused on another characteristic of the land she explored as a young girl. A reviewer for *Horn Book* observed, "[The] author and illustrator [Peter Parnell] have brilliantly integrated myth, folklore, and factual description into a coherent whole.... The unique, multidimensional presentation is eloquent, profound, and totally absorbing."

Guess Who My Favorite Person Is is one of Baylor's more recent books. "You know you're on to something when you sense the exquisite harmony between author and illustrator [Robert Andrew Parker]. Baylor is well-known for her soft, poetic evocation of feelings and she has created a lovely dialogue here.... Parker's paintings are beautiful representations of the scenes and people ...," commented a critic for *Publishers Weekly.* Similarly, a reviewer for the *New York Times* noted, "At its best this dialogue touches lightly and impressionistically; so do the liquid watercolors. ..."

FOR MORE INFORMATION SEE: *Horn Book,* April, 1964, February, 1976, June, 1976; *Saturday Review,* November 8, 1969; *Scientific American,* December, 1969; *Publishers Weekly,* November 7, 1977; *New York Times Book Review,* November 13, 1977.

BELPRÉ, Pura

PERSONAL: Name is pronounced *Poo*-rah *Bell*-pray; born in Cidra, Puerto Rico; came to the United States in the 1920's; married Clarence Cameron White (a musician and composer). *Education:* Educated in Puerto Rico, later attended the New York Public Library School and Columbia University. *Home:* New York City.

CAREER: Author and puppeteer-storyteller. Began telling stories to children as part of the New York Public Library program, later became interested in designing puppets to enhance her stories. *Awards, honors:* Brooklyn Art Books for Children citation, 1973, for *Santiago;* Instituto de Puerto Rico, New York City, citation for introducing the folklore of Puerto Rico in the United States; Bay Area Bilingual Education League and the University of San Francisco, award for distinguished contribution in Spanish literature, 1978.

WRITINGS—Fiction, except as noted: *Perez and Martina: A Puerto Rican Folktale* (illustrated by Carlos Sanchez), Warne, 1932, new edition, 1961, Spanish translation published as *Perez y Martina,* Warne, 1966; *The Tiger and the Rabbit, and Other Tales* (illustrated by Kay Peterson Parker), Houghton, 1946, new edition (illustrated by Tomie de Paola), Lippincott, 1965; *Juan Bobo and the Queen's Necklace: A Puerto Rican Folk Tale* (illustrated by Christine Price), Warne, 1962; *Ote: A Puerto Rican Folk Tale* (illustrated by Paul Galdone), Pantheon, 1969; *Santiago* (illustrated by Symeon Shimin), Warne, 1969, Spanish translation under the same title published by Warne, 1971; (with Mary K. Conwell) *Libros en Espanol: An Annotated List of Children's Books in Spanish* (nonfiction), New York Public Library, 1971; *Dance of the Animals: A Puerto Rican Folk Tale* (illustrated by P. Galdone), Warne, 1972; *Once in Puerto Rico* (illustrated by C. Price), Warne, 1973; *The*

The couples whirled, stamped and bellowed. What tangos and jotas! Waltzes mingled with mazurkas and traditional dances. ■ (From *Dance of the Animals* by Pura Belpré. Illustrated by Paul Galdone.)

PURA BELPRÉ

Rainbow Colored Horse (illustrated by Antonio Martovell), Warne, 1978.

Spanish translator from the English; all published by Harper, except as noted: Munro Leaf, *El Cuento de Ferdinand* ("The Story of Ferdinand"), Viking, 1962; Crosby N. Bonsall, *Caso del Forastero Hambriento* ("Case of the Hungry Stranger"), 1969; Carla Greene, *Camioneros: Que Hacen?* ("Truck Drivers: What Do They Do?"), 1969; Syd Hoff, *Danielito y el Dinosauro* ("Danny and the Dinosaur"), 1969; Leonard Kessler, *Aqui Viene el Ponchado* ("Here Comes the Strikeout"), 1969; Else Holmelund Minarik, *Osito* ("Little Bear"), 1969; Millicent E. Selsam, *Teresita y las Orugas* ("Terry and the Caterpillars"), 1969; Paul Newman, *Ningun Lugar para Jugar* ("No Place to Play"), Grosset, 1971.

ADAPTATIONS—Videotapes: "Profiles in Literature."

SIDELIGHTS: "I grew up in a family of storytellers. My vivid imagination and photographic mind, kept scenes that impressed me as a child very alive. A particular color of a flower and its delicate scent, the sounding of the ripple of water falling from a waterfall, the chirping of birds at early dawn, the rustle of the wind through the trees, the distant chant of the vendors on their way to the market place, and of the sugar cane cart drivers on their way to the sugar cane mill. In my school days I was particularly fond of descriptive passages. I enjoyed them in Spanish which was natural, but also in English which was the second language, and all

through High School, where French became my choice foreign language, which came quite natural, since my father was of French extraction.

"If I hadn't been an assistant in the New York Public Library and assigned to "read" the fairy tale shelves, I would not have become a writer. It was here that I discovered the folklore of the world. I searched avidly for some of the tales I had heard at home, and often told myself, but found not one. To see these folk tales in book form alongside the ones on the shelves became my dream. It began to take form when I went to the library school of the New York Public Library for further library training. In the class of storytelling, the students were asked to write a story to be read at class. I wrote a folk tale, which was my grandmother's favorite, and the one she often told me. It was the romance of a beautiful Spanish cockroach called Martina, and a gallant little Mouse called Perez. It became my first book, and my first dramatization for puppets. It was dramatized by children in the library and throughout the schools. In time it became my first book published in Spanish. It opened the way to the rest of the folk tales that followed.

"My first original story, *Santiago,* is the result of a personal experience. One winter Sunday morning in February, my husband and I were returning from Mass. The snow was high on our way, and just as we reached a garage, a beautiful white hen rushed out and almost tripped me. I was amazed and asked: 'Who do you think will believe me if I tell them that I have seen a beautiful white hen running, running in the streets of New York?' My husband, who had a great sense of humor, replied: 'If she knows what is the best for her, she better keep running or else she will end in a pot of arroz con pollo (chicken rice).' I never forgot that hen. She became the heroine of my story. The story was published in English and Spanish."

Belpre's Spanish ancestry has been incorporated into her puppet shows as well as her books, providing young people of all ages and backgrounds a means for learning more about the Puerto Rican culture. "An enjoyable Puerto Rican folk tale, set down by an accomplished story teller . . . ," wrote a reviewer for *Library Journal* of her book *Orte.* In *Horn Book,* a reviewer said of Belpre's most recent book, *Once in Puerto Rico,* "The stories of heroes and the supernatural . . . will have appeal for story hours or for individual reading. Other tales about specific places . . . and about historical conflicts . . . will hold particular interest for young Puerto Ricans. . . ."

FOR MORE INFORMATION SEE: Lee Bennett Hopkins, *Books Are by People,* Citation, 1969; *Horn Book,* April, 1970, April, 1974; "Children's Literature Conference Begins," *San Francisco Chronicle,* November 17, 1978.

BEWICK, Thomas 1753-1828

PERSONAL: Surname is pronounced *Bu*-ik; born August, 1753, in Cherryburn, near Newcastle, England; died November 8, 1828, in Gateshead, England; son of John (a farmer and tenant collier) and Jane (Wilson) Bewick; married Isabella Elliot, 1786; children: Robert, Jane, Elizabeth. *Home:* Gateshead, England.

CAREER: Wood engraver. Began experimenting and improving wood-engraving techniques while apprenticed to copperplate engraver, Ralph Beilby, 1767-74; started doing illustrations for children's stories around the early 1770's;

Marble bust of Thomas Bewick aged 73, taken from a life mask by E.H. Bailey, 1826.

traveled through England and Scotland, 1776; soon returned to Newcastle to enter into partnership with Beilby, doing metal engravings for a living and wood engravings in his spare time; took complete control of the engraving business by 1800.

WRITINGS: (With Ralph Beilby) *History of British Birds* (self-illustrated), two volumes, Beilby & Bewick, 1797-1804; *A Memoir of Thomas Bewick* (self-illustrated; edited by brother, John Bewick), Longman, Green, 1862, new edition, edited by Iain Bain, Oxford University Press, 1975; *Bewick to Dovaston: Letters 1824-1828,* edited by Gordon Williams, Nattali & Maurice, 1968.

Illustrator: John Gay, *Fables by the Late Mr. Gay,* T. Saint, 1779; Ralph Beilby, *A General History of Quadrupeds,* S. Hodgson, R. Beilby, 1790, reprinted, Scholarly Press, 1976; Oliver Goldsmith, *The Poetical Works of Oliver Goldsmith,* D. Walker, 1794; (with J. Bewick) Joseph Ritson, editor, *Robin Hood: A Collection of All the Ancient Poems,* two volumes, [London], 1795; (with J. Bewick) J. B. Le Grand d'Aussy, *Fabliaux or Tales* (translation from the French by George Lewis Way), W. Bulmer, 1796; Mary Pilkington, *A Mirror for the Female Sex,* [London], 1798; Robert Bloomfield, *Rural Tales, Ballads, and Songs* (engraved from designs by John Thurston), Longman & Rees, 1802; William Somerville, *The Chase: A*

Poem (engraved from design by J. Bewick), [London], 1802; (with J. Bewick) Oliver Goldsmith, *Poems by Goldsmith and Parnell,* W. Bulmer, 1804; Thomas Percy, *The Hermit of Warkworth,* [Alnwick, England], 1805; James Thomson, *The Seasons* (engraved from designs by J. Thurston), J. Wallis, 1805.

John Bunyan, *The Pilgrim's Progress* (engraved from designs by J. Thurston), J. Poole, 1806; (with Luke Clennell) Solomon Hodgson, editor, *The Hive of Ancient and Modern Literature,* third edition, [Newcastle], 1806; John Hodgson, *Poems Written at Lanchester,* [London], 1807; Sydney Melmoth, *Beauties of British Poetry,* third edition, Huddersfield, 1807; Robert Burns, *The Poetical Works of Robert Burns* (engraved from designs by J. Thurston), Catnatch & Davison, 1808; Robert Fergusson, *The Poetical Works of Robert Fergusson,* two volumes, [Alnwick], 1814; Robert J. Thornton, *A Family Herbal,* [London], 1814; Thomas Warton, editor, *The Oxford Sausage; or, Select Poetical Pieces,* [London], 1815; John H. Wynne, *Amusing and Instructive Tales for Youth,* [London], 1815; James Fisher, *A Spring Day,* fifth edition, [Liverpool], 1819; William Markham, *An Introduction to Spelling and Reading English,* [Alnwick], circa 1830; James E. Harting, *Our Summer Migrants,* [London], 1875; (with J. Bewick) Charles Hindley, *A History of the Cries of London,* Reeves & Turner, 1881, reprinted, Singing Tree Press, 1969.

"Natural History" series; published by W. Davison, circa 1814: *A Natural History of Fishes; . . . Foreign Birds; . . . Foreign Quadrupeds; Reptiles, Serpents, and Insects; Water Birds.*

Other illustrations: *A New Lottery of Birds and Beasts,* [Newcastle], 1771; *A New Years Gift for Little Masters and Misses,* [Newcastle], 1777; (with J. Bewick) *Select Fables in Three Parts,* T. Saint, 1784; *Figures of British Land Birds,* S. Hodgson, 1800; (with R. Beilby) *The Holy Bible,* J. Thompson, 1806; *The Holy Bible in Miniature; or, The History of the Old and New Testament,* T. Wilson & Son, 1810; *The Poetical Fabulator; or Beauties in Verse,* T. Wilson & Son, 1810; *Christmas Tales for the Amusement and Instruction of Young Ladies and Gentlemen,* Thomas Wilson, 1811; *The Painter's Budget,* [London], circa 1815; (with Robert Johnson) *The Fables of Aesop and Others* T. Bewick & Son, 1818; *The Youngster's Diary,* [Alnwick], circa 1820; *The Beauties of Aesop and Other Fabulists,* J. Richardson, 1822.

Selections: *A Selection of Engravings on Wood,* Penguin, 1947; *Bewick's Birds,* Hutchinson, 1952; *Wood Engraving of Thomas Bewick,* edited by Reynolds Stone, Dover, 1962; R. Hunter Middleton, *A Portfolio of Thomas Bewick Wood Engravings,* two volumes, Newberry, 1970; James Kirkup, *A Bewick Bestiary,* Mid-Northumberland Arts Group, 1971; *Thomas Bewick: Ten Working Drawing Reproductions,* Cherryburn Press, 1972.

Also designer and engraver of numerous pamphlets, newspapers, shop cards, and other miscellaneous illustrations.

SIDELIGHTS: "In **August, 1753,** I was born, and was mostly entrusted to the care of my aunt Hannah, (my mother's sister) and my grandmother, Agnes Bewick; and the first thing I can remember was, that the latter indulged me in every thing I had a wish for; or, in other words made me a great 'pet.' I was not to be 'snubbed' (as it was called), do what I would; and, in consequence of my being thus suf-

(From *A Treasury of Aesop's Fables.* Illustrated by Thomas Bewick.)

fered to have my own way, I was often scalded and burnt, or put in danger of breaking my bones by falls from heights I had clambered up to.

"The next circumstance, which I well remember, was that of my being put to Mickley school, when very young, and this was not done so much with a view to my learning, as it was to keep me out of '*harm's way.*'—I was sometime at this School without making much progress, in learning my letters & spelling small words—the Master perhaps was instructed not to keep me very close at my book, but in process of time he began to be more & more severe upon me, and I see clearly at this day, that he frequently beat me, when faultless and also for not learning what it was not in my power to comprehend—others suffered in the same way, for he was looked upon as a severe or cross man & did not spare his Rod—his name I do not recollect but he was nicknamed *Shabby Rowans*—he was a tall thin Man, and with a countenance severe & grim he walked about the School Room with the Taws or a switch in his hand, and he no doubt thought he was keeping the Boys to their Lessons. While the gabbering & noise they made was enough to stun any one, and impressed the people passing by, with the Idea that Bedlam was let loose. How long he went on in this way I do not recollect—but like many others, of his profession, who were at that time, appointed to fulfill that most important of all offices, no pains was taken to enquire into the requisite qualifications befitting them for it.—and this Teacher was one of that stamp,—he went on with a senseless System of severity, where ignorance & arrogance were equally conspicuous,—conduct like this sours the minds of some Boys—renders others stupid & serves to make all, more or less disgusted with Learning.

"Upon some occasion or other, he ordered me to be flogged—and this was to be done, by what was called hugging, that is by mounting me upon the back of a stout Boy, who kept hold of my hands over his Shoulders, while the Posteriors was laid bare, & where he supposed he could do the business freely;—in this instance however he was mistaken, for, with a most indignant rage I sprawled, kickt & flung, and as I was told, bit the innocent Boy on the Neck, when he instantly roared out & flung me down, and on my being seized, again by the old man, I rebelled & broke his Shins with my Iron hooped cloggs & ran off—By this time, the Boy's Mother, who was a spirited Woman, & lived close by attracted by the ferment that was raized, flew (I

understood) into the School Room, when a fierce scold ensued between the Master & her.—After this I went no more to his School, but played the Truant every day, and amused myself by making Dams & swimming Boats in a small Bourne which ran through a Place then called 'Colliers-close-Wood,' 'till the Evening, when I returned home with my more fortunate or more obedient School Fellows—How long it was before my abscense from School was discovered I know not, but I got many severe beatings from my father and Mother, in the interval between my utterly leaving the School & the old Masters death—As soon as another School Master (James Burn) was appointed, I was sent to him & he happened to be of a directly opposite character to the late one—with him I was quite happy, and learned as fast as any other of the Boys and with as great pleasure. After the death of this much respected young man, who lived only a very few years after his being appointed schoolmaster, my learning any more at Mickley School was at an End.

"Sometime after this, my Father put me to school under the care of the Rev^d C Gregson of Ovingham & well do I

Bewick's workshop in St. Nicholas' Churchyard, Newcastle.

remember the conversation that passed between them on the occasion—it was little to my credit, for my Father begun by telling him that I was so very unguideable, that he could not do it, & begged of my new master that he would undertake that Task and they both agreed that to 'spare the Rod was to spoil the Child'—and this system was I think too severely acted upon, sometimes upon trivial occasions, & sometimes otherwise.

"After being sometime kept at reading, writing & figures, how long I know not, but I know that as soon as my question was done upon my Slate, I spent as much time as I could find, in filling, with my pencil, all the other spaces of it, with representation of such objects as had struck my fancy, and these were rubbed out (for fear of a beating) before my question was given in. After learning figures as far as Fractions & Decimals &c, I was then put to learn Latin and in this I was for sometime complimented by my Master for the great progress I was making—but as I never knew for what purpose it was that I was put to learn it, & was wearied out with getting off long Tasks, I rather flagged in this department of my Education, and the margins of my Books and every space of spare & blank paper became filled with various kinds of devices or scenes I had met with & these were often accompanied with wretched Rhymes explanatory of them; but as I soon filled all the blank spaces in my Books, I had recourse, at all spare times to the Grave Stones & the Floor of the Church Porch, with a bit of Chalk to give vent to this propensity of mind of figuring whatever I had seen—at that time I had

Thomas Bewick, after a portrait by James Ramsey.

(From *A Treasury of Aesop's Fables.* Illustrated by Thomas Bewick.)

never heard of the word 'drawing' being made use of, nor did I know of any other paintings, besides the Kings Arms in the Church, & the Signs in Ovingham of the Black Bull, the White Horse, the Salmon & the Hounds & Hare—I always thought I could make a far better hunting Scene than the latter, the others were beyond my hand—I remember of my Master's overlooking me while I was very busy with my chalk in the Porch, and of his putting me greatly to the blush, by ridiculing & calling me a conjurer—My Father also found a deal of fault for 'misspending my time in such idle pursuits,' but my propensity to drawing was so routed, that nothing could deter me from persevering in it—and many of my evenings at home, were spent in filling the flags of the Floor & the hearth stone with my chalky designs—

"After I had long scorched my face, in this way, a friend, in compassion, furnished me with a lot of paper, upon which to execute my designs—here I had more scope—pen & Ink and the juice of the Brambleberry made a *grand change*—These were succeeded by a Camel hair pencil & Shells of colours & thus supplied I became completely set up—but of Patterns or drawings I had done—the Beasts & Birds which enlivened the beautiful Scenery of Woods & Wilds, surrounding my native Hamlet, furnished me with an endless supply of Subjects. I now, in the estimation of my rustic Neighbours became an eminent Painter, and the Walls of their Houses were ornamented with an abundance of my rude productions, at a very cheap rate—These chiefly consisted of particular Hunting scenes, in which the portraits of the Hunters, the Horses & of every Dog in the Pack, were in their opinion, as *well as my own,* faithfully delineated.—But while I was proceeding in this to this propensity for drawing—for I early became acquainted, not only with the History & the character of the domestic Animals, but also with those which roamed at large.

"My Mother, who was of a religious turn, had, indeed, all her life endeavoured to make me so too—but as I did not clearly understand her well intended lectures, they made little impression—my father's pithy illustrations, as before hinted at, were much more forcably & clearly made out. I understood them well & their effect operated powerfully upon me—I recollect one instance where I felt the force of this species of education. I might enumerate some others, but this left its *mark upon me*—having fallen in with & joined two untutored lads, in Prudhoe lonning, they jumped over the hedge & filled their pockets with potatoes—The

Cherryburn House, Bewick's birthplace.

Farmer was watching, but they escaped—not having followed their example, I did not offer to fly, but he seized me & threatened what he would do; at this I was extremely distressed & had it not been that I consoled myself with the certainty that my father & mother would believe me on my asserting that I had not stolen any of his potatoes I believe I would have drowned myself.

"I have often reflected since upon the very high importance & of the necessity of instilling this species of education into the minds of youth, for were pains taken to draw forth the pride, naturally implanted in their minds, for the wisest & best purposes, if properly directed, it would exalt human nature, and be of the utmost importance to individuals & to society—it is the want of this & the want of industry that occasions & spreads misery over the land—and how can I doubt it, if my father had been a thief, that I would not have been one also—& if a highwayman & robber, that I might not have been as expert a one as himself—

"In my opinion there are two descriptions of person, who ought to forbear, or to be prevented from marrying—viz those of a base, wicked & dishonest Character, and those who have broken down their constitutions by diseases & debased both mind & body, by their illicit & impure connections & dissipated lives—the latter entails misery upon their innocent tainted ofspring [sic]—and the former by the bad examples they shew to their children which grows upon them with their growth 'till they are perfected in their wickedness & they become a curse to the community in which they live—

"In going along with my narrative, I have noticed some of the first impressions which produced a change, and left a strong effect on my mind. In some of these, the change was quick and decisive; in others of a more tardy nature; and prejudices which were early rooted were not easily removed. Among the worst, was that of a belief in ghosts, boggles, apparitions, &c. These wrought powerfully upon the fears of the great bulk of the people at that time, and, with many, these fears are not rooted out even at this day. The stories so circumstantially told respecting these phantoms and supernatural things, I listened to with the dread they inspired, and it took many an effort, and I suffered much, before it could be removed. What helped me greatly

to conquer fears of that kind was my knowing that my father constantly scouted such idle, or, indeed, such pernicious tales." [*Thomas Bewick: A Memoir Written by Himself*, Oxford University Press, 1975.[1]]

October 1, 1767. Apprenticed to engraver, Ralph Beilby at Newcastle upon Tyne. "Being now nearly fourteen years of age, and a stout boy, it was thought time to set me off to business; and my father and mother had long been planning and consulting, and were greatly at a loss what it would be best to fix upon. Any place where I could see pictures, or where I thought I could have an opportunity of drawing them, was such only as I could think of. A Newcastle bookseller, whose windows were filled with prints, had applied to Mr. Gregson for a boy; and when I was asked if I would like to go to him, I readily expressed my hearty consent; but upon my father making enquiry respecting him, he was given to understand that he bore a very bad character: so that business was at an end. The same year—1767—during the summer, William Beilby and his brother Ralph took a ride to Bywell, to see their intimate acquaintance, Mrs. Simons, who was my godmother, and the widow of the late vicar there. She gave them a most flattering account of me; so much so, that they, along with her and her daughter, set off that same afternoon to Cherryburn to visit us, and to drink tea. When the Newcastle visitors had given an account of their enamellings, drawings, and engravings, with which I felt much pleased, I was asked which of them I should like to be bound to; and liking the look and deportment of Ralph the best, I gave the preference to him. . . . " [Montague Weekley, *Thomas Bewick*, Oxford University Press.[2]]

"I was kept closely employed upon a variety of other jobs, for such was the industry of my master that he refused nothing, coarse or fine—he undertook every thing & did it in the best way he could—he fitted up & tempered his own tools, which he adapted to every purpose & learned me to do the same—this readiness to undertake, brought him in an overflow of work & our work place was filled, with the coarsest kinds of steel stamps—pipe Moulds—Bottle moulds—Brass Clock faces—Book-binders Letters & stamps—Steel, Silver & gold Seals—Mourning Rings—Arms crests & cyphers on silver & every kind of job, from the Silver Smiths—writing engraving of Bills, bank notes,

The Hound and the Huntsman, from "Gay's Fables," 1779.

Bills of parcels, shop bills & cards—these last, with Gent Arms for their Books, he executed as well as most of the first in the Kingdom—& I think upon the whole, he might be called 'an ingeneous self taught Artist'—The higher department of engraving such as Landscape or historical plates, I dare say, was hardly ever thought of by my master, at least not till I was nearly out of my Apprenticeship, when he took it into his head to leave me in charge of the business at home, & of going to London, for the purpose of taking lessons in etching & engraving & practising upon large copperplates—there was however little or no employment in this way in Newcastle, & he had no opportunity of becoming clever at it, so he kept labouring on with such work, as before named, in which I aided him with all my might—I think he was the best master in the World, for learning Boys, for he obliged them to put their hands to every variety of Work—every job, coarse or fine, either in cutting or engraving I did as well as I could, cheerfully . . . but the wearisome business of polishing copper plates & harding & polishing steel seals, was always irksome to me—I had wrought at such as this a long time, & at the coarser kind of engraving, (such as I have noticed before) 'till my hands became as hard & enlarged as those of a blacksmith'—I however in due time, had a greater share of better & nicer work given me to execute.''[1]

1774. Apprenticeship ended. Returned to his childhood house, Cherryburn, for two years. ''The first of October 1774 arrived at last & for the first time in my life I felt myself at liberty—I wrought a few weeks with my old master & then set off to spend the winter at Cherryburn—there I had plenty of work to do, chiefly from my friend Thomas Angus, the printer in Newcastle—I continued there, employed by him & others and when wanted, by my old Mas-

From the little windows at my bed head I noticed all the varying seasons of the year, and when the Spring put in, I felt charmed with the music of Birds, which strained their little throats to proclaim it. ■ (From *Thomas Bewick: A Memoir Written by Himself.* Illustrated by the author.)

ter, 'till the summer of 1776. This was a time of great enjoyment, for the charms of the country was highly relished by me, and after so long an almost abscence from it, gave even that relish a zest, which I have not words to express—I continued to follow wood cutting & other jobs, but often rambled about among old neighbours & became more & more attached to them as well as to my country. In the storms of winter . . . I joined the Nimrods of old,—in spring & summer my favourite sport of angling, was pretty closely followed up—About Christmas, (as I had done before when a boy) I went with my father to a distance to collect the money due to him for his Coals—In these rounds I had the opportunity of *seeing* the kindness & hospitality of the People—the countenances of all, both high & low, beamed with cheerfulness, and this was heightened every where, by the music of old Tunes from the well known exhilerating wild notes of the Northumberland pipes.''[1]

January 4, 1776. Received premium from Society for the Encouragement of Arts for engravings for fable illustrations.

June-August, 1776. Walked to and around Scotland.

October, 1776. Traveled to London to seek work. ''Notwithstanding my being so situated among my friends, & of being so much gratified in seeing such a variety of excellent performances in every Art & science—Painting, statuary, Engraving carving &c were to be seen every day, yet I did not like London—it appeared to me to be a World of itself where every thing in the extreme, might at once be seen—extreme riches—extreme poverty—extreme Grandeur & extreme wretchedness—all of which were such as I had not contemplated upon before. Perhaps I might indeed take too full a view of London on its gloomy side—I could not help it—I tired of it & determined to return home—The Country of my old friends—the manners of the people of that day—the scenery of Tyne side, seemed altogether to form a paradise for me & I longed to see it again—While I was thus turning these matters over in my mind my warm friend & patron Isaac Taylor waited upon me, and upon my telling him I was going to Newcastle, he enquired how long it would be before I returned—never—was my reply, at which he seemed both surprized & displeased—he then warmly remonstrated with me upon this impropriety of my conduct—told me of the prospects before me, and among

Memorial cut to Robert Johnson.

A certain house being much infested with mice, a cat was at length procured, who very diligently hunted after them and killed great numbers every night. ■ (From *The Fables of Aesop.* Illustrated by Thomas Bewick.)

many other matters, that of his having engaged me to draw in the Duke of Richmonds gallery & urged me strenuously to change my mind—I told him that no temptation of gain, of honour, or of any thing else, however great could ever have any weight with me & that I would even enlist for a Soldier—or go & herd sheep at five shillings [a] week as long as I lived. . . .''[1]

June 22, 1777. Formed partnership with Ralph Beilby.

February 20, 1785. Mother died. ''She was possessed of great innate powers of minds, which had been cultivated by a good education, as well as by her own endeavours. For these, and for her benevolent, humane disposition, and good sense, she was greatly respected, and, indeed, revered by the whole neighbourhood.

My eldest sister, who was down from London on a visit to her home at the time of my mother's illness and death, by her over-exertion and anxiety, brought on an illness; and, for the convenience of medical aid, and better nursing, I brought her to my hitherto little happy cot at the Forth, where she died on the 24th June, 1785, aged 30 years. These were gloomy days to me! Some short time before my sister died, upon her requesting me, and my promising her, that I would see her buried at Ovingham, she proposed to sing me a song. I thought this very strange, and felt both sorrow and surprise at it; but she smiled at me, and began

her song of 'All Things have but a Time.' I had heard the old song before, and thought pretty well of it; but her's was a later and a very much better version of it.''[2]

November 15, 1785. Began work on cutting blocks for *A General History of Quadrupeds,* on which day his father died. ''During this time, I observed a great change in the looks and deportment of my father. He had, what is called, 'never held up his head' since the death of my mother; and, upon my anxiously pressing him to tell me what ailed him, he said he had felt as if he were shot through from the breast to the shoulders with a great pain that hindered him from breathing freely. Upon my mentioning medical assistance, he rejected it, and told me, if I sent him any drugs, I might depend upon it he would throw them all behind the fire. He wandered about all summer alone, with a kind of serious look, and took no pleasure in anything, till near the 15th November [1785], which I understand was his birthday, and on which he completed his 70th year, and on that day he died. He was buried beside my mother and sister at Ovingham. After this, I left off my walks to Cherryburn; the main attractions to it were gone, and it became a place the thoughts of which now raked up sorrowful reflections in my mind.

''Some particulars respecting my father, and illustrative of his character, may, perhaps, be thought not uninteresting. I shall give a few such as I recollect them. In his person, he

After a fierce battle between two cocks for the sovereignty of the dunghill, one of them having beaten his antagonist, he that was vanquished slunk away and crept into a corner, where he for some time hid himself; but the conqueror flew up to a high place, and clapped his wings, crowing and proclaiming his victory. An eagle who was watching for his prey, saw him from afar off, and in the midst of his exultation darted down upon him, trussed him up, and bore him away. The vanquished cock perceiving this quitted the place of his retreat, and shaking his feathers and throwing off all remembrance of his late disgrace, returned to the dunghill, and [greeted] the Hens, as if nothing had happened. ■ (From *The Fables of Aesop.* Illustrated by Thomas Bewick.)

was a stout, square-made, strong and active man, and through life was a pattern of health. I was told by some of my aunts, who were older than he, that he was never ill from a disease in his life; and I have heard him say 'he wondered how folks felt when they were ill.' He was of a cheerful temper, and he possessed an uncommon vein of humour and a fund of anecdote. He was much noticed by the gentlemen and others of the neighbourhood for these qualities as well as for his integrity. He had, however, some traits that might be deemed singular, and not in order. He never would prosecute anyone for theft; he hated going to law, but he took it as his own hand, and now and then gave thieves a severe beating, and sometimes otherwise punished them in a singular and whimsical way."[2]

"Having from the time that I was a school Boy, been displeased with most of the cuts in children's books, & particularly with those of the 'Three hundred Animals' the figures of which, even at that time, I thought I could depicture much better than those in that Book; and having afterwards, very often turned the matter over in my mind, of making improvements in that publication—I at last came to the determination of commencing the attempt. The extreme interest I had always felt in the hope of administering to the pleasures & amusement of youth & judging from the feelings I had experienced myself that they would be affected in the same way as I had been, this whetted me up & stimulated me to proceed—in this, my only reward besides, was the great pleasure I felt in imitating nature—That I would ever do any thing to attract the notice of the world, in the manner that has been done, was the farthest thing in my thoughts, & so far as I was concerned myself, at that time, I minded little about any self interested considerations. These intentions, I communicated to my partner, & 'tho he did not doubt of my being able to succeed, from what he had seen of my work, yet being a prudent cautious & thinking man, he wished to be more satisfied, as to the probability of such a publication paying us for our labours—on this occasion, being little acquainted with the nature of such like undertakings, we consulted (our friend) Solomon Hodgson (Bookseller & Editor of the *Newcastle Chronicle*) as to the probability of its success &c when he most warmly encouraged us to proceed—Such Animals as I knew, I drew from memory upon the Wood—others, which

I did not know were copied from Dr. Smellie's abridgement of Buffon & from other naturalists, & also from the Animals which were, from time to time, exhibited in Shows. I made sketches, first from memory, & then corrected & finished the drawings upon the Wood, from a second examination of the different subjects—I begun this business, of cutting the blocks, with the figure of the Dromidary on the 15 of November 1785. . . . I then proceeded in copying such figures (as above named) as I did not hope to see alive—The figures which were done from nature, or from memory so much attracted the notice of our friend, that he most ardently insisted upon our making our work assume a superiour character to that of the 'Shabby Book' we had been only thinking of surpassing—and from the opinion, we had formed of his being better acquainted with business than we were, we offered him a third share free from any expense for the Cuts—a proper agreement was made on the [ ] [sic] of April & he became our partner in the *History of Quadrupeds.*

"While I was busied in drawing & cutting the Figures of the Animals & also in designing & engraving the Vignettes,—Mr Beilby, being of a bookish, or reading turn, proposed, in his evenings at home, to write or compile the descriptions, but not knowing much about natural history, we got Books on that subject to enable him to form a better notion of these matters; with this, I had little more to do, than in furnishing him, in many conversations & written memorandums, of what I knew of Animals, and of blotting out, in his manuscript what was not truth—In this way we proceeded untill the Book was published in 1790.—It is worthy of remark, that while the title page was in hands, Mr. Beilby wished to be made the Author of it and wrote his name as such, 'by R Beilby'—on Mr. Hodgson seeing this, without saying a word he stroked the name out with a pen, while Mr. Beilby was looking on—I knew nothing about this transaction for sometime afterwards, and it might have passed so, for any thing I cared about the Authorship, or whose name was put to it as such.—It was sufficient for me that I had the opportunity of giving vent to my feelings and gratifying my desires in doing my part of the work.

"The greater part of these Wood cuts were drawn & engraved at nights, after the days work of the shop was over. In these Evenings I frequently had the company of my friend & companion the Revd Richard Oliphant who took great pleasure in seeing me work, while, at the same time he read to me, the Sermons he composed for the next Sunday, where he at that time might happen to officiate—I was also often attended, from a similar curiosity, by my friend, the Revd Thomas Hornby, Lecturer of St. John's—he would not, like my friend Oliphant adjourn to a public house & join in a Tankard of Ale but he had it sent for to us at my workplace,—we frequently disagreed in our opinions, as to religious matters—he being, as I thought an intolerant high Churchman—but notwithstanding this, he was a warm well wisher & kind friend to me—and was besides of so charitable a disposition in other respects that his purse was ever open to relieve distress and with an occasional Guinea, he would commission me, anonymously, to dispose of to persons, in want & to sundry other charitable purposes.—

"As soon as the *History of Quadrupeds* appeared in the World, I was surprized to find how rapidly the Book was sold, as well as several successive Editions & this was followed by a glut of praise bestowed upon it—The first time I was obliged to hear personal praises, in this account, was from Dr. David Ure LLD of Glasgow, who called to see me, & not being used to such Compliments I blushed over the Ears & left him talking to Mr. Beilby—These & such like praises, however, excited envy, & was visibly followed by the balance of an opposite feeling, from many people at home, for they raked together & blew up the embers of envy into a transient blaze—but the motives by which I was actuated stood out of the reach of its sparks, & they returned into the heap whence they came & fell into dust—I was much more afraid to meet the praises which was gathering around, than I was of the sneers which they excited, and as soon as the annexed poetry appeared in the paper, I felt obliged on its account, for sometime to shun Swarley's club, of which Geo. Byles was a member, to avoid the warm & sincere compliments that waited me there."[1]

April 20, 1786. Married Isabella Elliot. "I had long made up my mind, not to marry, while my Father & Mother lived, in order that my undivided attention might be bestowed upon them—my Mother, had indeed, sometime before recommended a young Woman in the Neighbourhood to me as a wife—she did not know the young lady intimately,—but she knew she was modest in her deportment, beautiful & handsome in her person & had a good fortune—and in compliance with this recommendation, I soon got acquainted & became intimate with her, but was carefull not to proceed further, and soon discovered that 'tho her character was innocence itself she was mentally one of the weakest of her Sex. The smirking lasses of Tyne side had long thrown out their *jibes* against me as being a Woman hater, but in this they were greatly mistaken—I had indeed been very guarded in my conduct towards them, as I held it extremely wrong & cruel to sport with the feelings of any one of them in making them believe that I was in love with any of them, without really being so, in this (which was one of my resolves) sincerity & truth were my guides—As I ever considered a matrimonial connection as a business of the utmost importance, and which was to last 'till death made the seperation. While, looking about for a partner for life, my utmost attention and anxiety was directed to this important change—I had long considered it to be the duty of every man (in health) on changing his life, to get a healthy woman for his Wife for the sake of his children, and a sensible one, as a companion for his own happiness & comfort—that love is the natural guide in this business, and much misery is attendant upon it, when this is awanting. This being the fixed state of my mind, I permitted no mercinary considerations to interfere. Impressed with these sentiments, I had long . . . looked upon [Isabella] as the most suitable Inmate for me—I had seen her in prosperity and in adversity, and in the latter state she appeared to me to the greatest advantage—in this she soared above her Sex, and my determination was fixed—In due time we were married and from that day to this, no cloud so far as concerned ourselves has passed over us to obscure a life time of uninterrupted happiness."[1]

April 29, 1787. Eldest child, Jane, born.

April 26, 1788. Son, Robert, born.

January 14, 1790. Daughter, Isabella, born.

April 27, 1790. *A General History of Quadrupeds* published.

July 16, 1791. Commenced drawings for *A History of British Birds.* Second edition of *Quadrupeds* published.

Having from the time that I was a school Boy, been displeased with most of the cuts in Children's books, and particularly with those of the "Three hundred Animals" the figures of which, even at that time, I thought I could depicture much better than those in that Book; and having afterwards, very often turned the matter over in my mind, of making improvements in that **publication.** ■ (From *Thomas Bewick: A Memoir Written by Himself.* Illustrated by the author.)

March 7, 1793. Daughter, Elizabeth, born.

April, 1812. Experienced serious illness. Took son, Robert, into partnership.

May 4, 1818. Elected member, Society of Diletlantic of Edinburgh. *Fables of Aesop* published.

November, 1822. Began writing *Memoir.*

February 1, 1826. Wife, Isabella, died. "My dear 'Bell' died, after a long & Painfull illness, on the 1st Feby 1826 Æ 72 (the best of wives & very best of Mothers)."[1]

1827. Completed additional work on *Memoir:* "All Artists (& indeed all Men) ought when necessary to divide their time—by regularly appropriating one portion of it to one

purpose, and another part of it to the varied business that may be set apart for another—in this way a deal of work may be easily got through & the Artist (after leaving off his too intense application) would see, as it were, what he had been doing with *new Eyes*—by which he would be enabled to criticise the almost endless variety of lights, shades & effects &c which awaits his pencil to produce—but the work of the painter may be said to be as endless as the objects which nature continually presents to his view, & it is his judgement that must direct him in the choice of such as may be interesting, or otherwise—in this he will see, what others have done before him & the shoals & quick-sands that have retarded their progress as well as the Rocks they have at last entirely split upon—On his taking a proper survey of all this, he will see the *labour-in-vain,* that has been bestowed upon useless designs, which have & will continue to find their way to a Garret—while those well

Portrait of Thomas Bewick by William Nicholson, c. 1820.

chosen & well executed subjects, will, from their excellence be preserved, with perhaps increasing value for ages to come—In performing all this, great industry will perhaps be required and it ought ever to be kept in mind, that, as in morals nothing is worth listening to but truth—so in arts nothing is worth looking at but such productions as have been faithfully copied from nature but, poetry indeed may launch out [and] take further liberties to charm the intellectual minds of its votaries—It is only such youths as providence has gifted with strong intellectual innate powers, that are perfectly fit to embark in the fine arts—and the power & propensity to do so, is often seen early to bud out & shew itself in the various ways which youth is destined to pursue.

"This is first seen in the young Musician, who without having even learned his ABC breaks out with a random kind of unrestrained freedom to whistle and sing & how often have I been amused at the first assays of the plowboy & how charmed to find him so soon attempt to equal his whistling & singing Master at the plow-stilts, & who with avidity uneasing—never stopped 'till he thought he excelled him—The *future painter* is shewn by his strong propensity to sketch out whatever objects in nature attract his attention, & excites him to imitate them. The Poet indeed has more difficulties to contend with at first, than the others, because he must know language, or be furnished with words wherewith to enable him to express himself even in his first assays, in his dogerel metre & *singsong rhymes*—In all the varied ways, by which Naturalists & Artists are befitted to enlighten, to charm & to embellish civilized society, as they advance through life—if they entertain the true feeling that every production they behold is created not by chance, but by design—[they] will find an encreasing & endless pleasure in the exhaustless stores which *nature has provided,* to attract the attention & promote the happiness of her votaries during the term of their sojourning here.—

"Men so gifted by nature, whether as Artists or in any other way where intellectual powers are to be drawn forth, ought never to despair of rising to eminence, for it is wrong in them to take it into their heads that they can never equal, such men, *of this character,* as have excelled all others in their day—but they ought to keep in mind that the same superintending providence, which gifted these men with talents to excite wonder & to improve Society, from time to time in all Ages—still rules the World & the affairs of Mankind & will continue to do the same for ever—as often as the services of such men are wanted—and this consideration ought to act as a stimulant to their successors, to endeavour to surpass in excellence the brilliant luminaries who have only gone before them to pave the way & enlighten their paths."[1]

November 8, 1828. Died.

His last engraving of a horse was left unfinished. It's title—*Waiting for Death.* The artist made order of his own universe, as he saw it.

From the final pages of his *Memoir:* "In offering these my sentiment & opinions, derived from the observations I have made on my passage thro' life, I have never intended to give offence to good men.—with these sentiments some may be pleased & others displeased—but conscious of the rectitude of my intentions I do not covet the praise of the one, nor fear the censures of the other—it is to another tribunal that I, as well as all other men are to account for their conduct."[1]

FOR MORE INFORMATION SEE: Thomas Bewick, *A Memoir of Thomas Bewick,* edited by J. Bewick, Longman, Green, 1862, new edition by Iain Bain, Oxford University Press, 1975; Hugo Thomas, *Bewick Collector* (bibliography), two volumes, Lovell Reeve, 1866, reprinted, Gale, 1968; Austin Dobson, *Thomas Bewick and His Pupils,* Chatto & Windus, 1884, reprinted, Gale, 1968; Robert Robinson, *Thomas Bewick: His Life and Times,* R. Robinson, 1887, reissued, Graham, 1972; Sydney Roscoe, *Thomas Bewick: A Bibliography,* Oxford University Press, 1953, reissued, Wofsy Fine Arts, 1973; John Jackson, *Thomas Bewick: Wood Engraver,* Signet Press, 1956; T. Bewick, *Bewick to Dovaston: Letters 1824-1828,* Nattali & Maurice, 1968; Jack Armstrong, *Bewick of Cherryburn,* Graham, 1970.

BIEGEL, Paul   1925-

PERSONAL: Born March 25, 1925, in Bussum, Netherlands; son of Herman (a merchant) and Madeleine (Povel) Biegel; married Marijke Straeter (a social worker), September 10, 1960; children: Leonie, Arthur. *Education:* Attended University of Amsterdam. *Home:* Keizersgracht 227, Amsterdam, Netherlands.

CAREER: De Radiobode (radio weekly), Amsterdam, editor, 1948-65; Kövesdi (press agency), Amsterdam, editor, 1965-67; Ploegsma (publishing firm), Amsterdam, editor, 1967-69; Van Holkema en Warendorf (publishing firm), Bussum, writer and advisor, 1969—. *Member:* Dutch Society of Writers (V.V.L.), Dutch Society of Literature. *Awards, honors:* Received best children's book of the year award

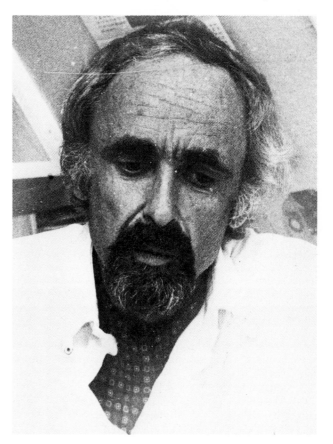

PAUL BIEGEL

Nicky was having a nasty dream. ■ (From *The Seven-times Search,* English version by Gullian Hume and Paul Biegel. Illustrated by Babs Van Wely.)

from Collective Promotion of Dutch Books, 1965, for *Het Sleutelkruid;* award from Children's Jury of Amsterdam, 1970, for *De tuinen van Dorr;* Silver Pencil award from Collective Promotion of Dutch Books, 1972, and prize from Jan Campert Foundation, 1973, for *De twaalf rovers;* Golden Pencil award from Collective Promotion of Dutch Books, 1972, for *De kleine Kapitein;* State Prize for complete works, 1973; Silver Pencil award from Collective Promotion of Dutch Books, 1974, for *Het olifantenfeest.*

WRITINGS: Het Sleutelkruid, Holland, 1964, translation by Hume and Biegel, published as *The King of the Copper Mountains,* Watts, 1969; *Ik wou dat ik anders was,* Holland, 1967, translation by Hume and Biegel, published as *The Seven-Times Search,* Dent, 1971; *De Tuinen van Dorr,* Holland, 1969, translation by Hume and Biegel, published as *The Gardens of Dorr,* Dent, 1975.

De twaalf Rovers, Holland, 1971, translation by Patricia Crampton, published as *The Twelve Robbers,* Dent, 1974,

Puffin, 1977; *De kleine Kapitein,* Holland, 1971, translation by Patricia Crampton, published as *The Little Captain,* Dent, 1971; *Het olifantenfeest,* Holland, 1973, translation by Patricia Crampton, published as *The Elephant Party,* Puffin, 1977; *De kleine kapitein in het land van Waan en Wijs,* Holland, 1973, translation by Patricia Crampton, published as *The Little Captain and the Seven Towers,* Dent, 1973; *Het stenen beeld,* Holland, 1974, translation by Patricia Crampton, published as *Far Beyond and Back Again,* Dent, 1977; *De kleine kapitein en de Schat van Schrik en Vreze,* 1975; *Het Spiegelkasteel,* 1976, translation by Patricia Crampton, published as *The Mirror Castle,* Blackie, 1979; *De Dwergjes van Tuil,* Holland, 1977, translation by Patricia Crampton, published as *The Dwarfs of Nosegay,* Blackie, 1978; *De Rover Hoepsika,* Holland, 1977, translation by Patricia Crampton, published as *The Robber Hopsika,* Dent, 1978.

Other; all published by Holland: *De gouden gitaar* (title means ''The Golden Guitar''), 1962; *Het grote boek* (title means "The Great Book"), 1962; *De Kukelhaan* (title means "Crowcockerel"), 1964; *Het Lapjesbeest* (title means "Patch-Animal"), 1964; *Kinderverhalen* (title means "Children's Stories"), 1966; *De Rattenvanger van Hameln* (title means "The Pied Piper"), 1967; *De zeven fabels uit Ubim* (title means "The Seven Fables from Ubim"), 1970; *Sebastiaan Slorp,* 1971; *Reinaart de Vos* (title means "Reynard the Fox"), 1972; *De Vloek van Woestewolf* (title means "The Curse of Fiercewolf"), 1974; *Twaalf sloeg de klok* (title means "Twelve Chimed the Clock"), 1974; *De Brieven van de Generaal* (title means "Letters from the General"), 1977; *Wie je droomt ben je zelf* (title means "You Are The Ones You Dream Of"), 1977.

Also author of television series, "De Vloek van Woestewolf."

WORK IN PROGRESS: The Stories of Virgil of Nosegay.

SIDELIGHTS: "I was born in an estate-like home with a huge garden, two parents, two brothers, six sisters, a German maid, a gardener, and a dog. I remember a lot, but I am convinced it is the memories without words, of the years before a child has words to its disposition (Adam before he named the things of paradise) that the source of any one's creative urge lies. And the writer, for the rest of his life, tries in vain to find words for it."

Paul Biegel speaks English, French, German, and Dutch.

BLADES, Ann   1947-

PERSONAL: Born November 16, 1947, in Vancouver, British Columbia, Canada; daughter of Arthur Hazelton (an administrator) and Dorothy (a teacher; maiden name, Planche) Sager; divorced. *Education:* University of British Columbia, teaching certificate, 1970; British Columbia Institute of Technology, R.N., 1974. *Home:* 14623 West Beach Ave., White Rock, British Columbia, Canada V4B 2T9.

CAREER: Elementary school teacher in Mile 18, British Columbia, 1967-68, Tache, British Columbia, 1969, and Surrey, British Columbia, 1969-71; part-time registered nurse, Vancouver General Hospital, Vancouver, British Columbia, 1974-75, and at Mt. St. Joseph Hospital, 1975—. *Member:* Writers' Union of Canada, Registered Nurses Association of British Columbia. *Awards, honors:* Book of the year award from Association of Children's Librarians, 1972, and honor list in Austrian and German national book awards, 1977, for *Mary of Mile 18.*

WRITINGS: Mary of Mile 18 (self-illustrated; Child Study Association book list), Tundra Books, 1971; *A Boy of Tache* (self-illustrated; juvenile), Tundra Books, 1973; *The Cottage at Crescent Beach* (self-illustrated; juvenile), Magook Publishers, 1977.

Illustrator: Michael Macklem, *Jacques the Woodcutter,* Oberon, 1977; Betty Waterton, *A Salmon for Simon,* Douglas & McIntyre, 1978.

ANN BLADES

It has stopped snowing, but the path is covered over and the trees seem to grow closer and closer together. If she goes too far from the road, she might not be able to find her way back. ■ (From *Mary of Mile 18* by Ann Blades. Illustrated by the author.)

SIDELIGHTS: Ann Blades' earlier teaching positions were remote—Mile 18 is a small rural community in northern British Columbia, and Tache is an Indian Reservation on Stuart Lake—and she soon found out that the books her students read had no relation to the world they lived in. She began to write her own.

FOR MORE INFORMATION SEE: Chatelaine, February, 1975; *Toronto Globe and Mail,* June 12, 1975.

BOESEN, Victor 1908-
(Jesse Hall, Eric Harald)

PERSONAL: Surname is pronounced *Bo-sun;* born September 7, 1908, in Plainfield, Ind.; son of Jens Eugene and Helene (Petersen) Boesen; married Nancy Hagedorn, October 2, 1940. *Education:* University of Missouri, student, 1928-30. *Politics:* Democrat. *Religion:* "No affiliation." *Home:* 971 Chattanooga Ave., Pacific Palisades, Calif. 90272.

CAREER: Writer. *Wichita Beacon,* Wichita, Kan., reporter, 1930; City News Bureau, Chicago, Ill., reporter and editor, 1931-35; WBBM-CBS Radio, Chicago, Ill., news and commentary writer, 1935-38; KNX-CBS Radio, Los Angeles, Calif., news writer, 1940; *Skyways* (magazine), New York, N.Y., roving correspondent, 1942-44; *Liberty* (magazine), New York, N.Y., Pacific and Far East correspondent, 1945-46, Pacific Palisades Property Owners Association, member of governing board. *Member:* Tokyo Correspondents Club (charter member), Overseas Press Club of America. *Awards, honors:* First Person Award, *Reader's Digest,* 1959.

WRITINGS: (With Joseph Karneke) *Navy Diver,* Putnam, 1962; *They Said It Couldn't Be Done: The Incredible Story of Bill Lear,* Doubleday, 1971; *William P. Lear: From High School Dropout to Space Age Inventor,* Hawthorn, 1974; *Doing Something About The Weather,* Putnam, 1975; *Edward Sheriff Curtis: Visions of a Vanishing Race,* Crowell, 1976; *Edward Sheriff Curtis: Photographer of the North American Indian,* Dodd, Mead, 1977; *Storm: Irving Krick vs. The United States Weather Bureaucracy,* Putnam, 1978. Contributor of articles to approximately 35 national magazines, including *Saturday Evening Post, Collier's, Coronet, Esquire, Nation's Business, Redbook, Family Circle, New Republic, The Reporter, Toronto Star Weekly, Liberty Magazine, Reader's Digest,* and *Look;* and, under pseudonyms Jesse Hall and Eric Harold, to *Skyways* and *West.*

WORK IN PROGRESS: Books on weather control; a book on retirement living.

SIDELIGHTS: "While I've written three children's books, I had little or nothing to do with originating the idea for any of them. I have never thought of myself as a children's writer. Like so much of life, they came about by accident. The first book, *Doing Something About the Weather,* was suggested by the editor of a west coast publishing house one night at a dinner party at the home of one of her writers, a mutual friend. 'You must do something for me!' she exclaimed. We agreed on the subject.

"When I got the outline up—after weeks of research—she said no.

"A year or so later, I acquired a new agent, Jane Browne of Beverly Hills. She asked what I had lying around unsold. I

VICTOR BOESEN

told her about the weather book outline. 'Give it to me,' she said. 'Maybe I can find a place for it.' She did, at Putnam's.

"The juvenile about Bill Lear she thought of because I had done *They Said It Couldn't Be Done* for Doubleday. Hawthorn gave us no arguments.

"The book about Edward Sheriff Curtis came into being after Jane returned from a visit to the publishers in New York, with the word, 'Dodd, Mead is interested in a children's book about Edward Curtis,' naming a man I had never heard of.

"This one, by the way, became the tail to a larger dog: *Visions of a Vanishing Race,* a $30 coffee table affair, published by Crowell. I had the exciting good fortune to turn up original documents on Curtis which not even his family knew about—a thirty year correspondence with his editor at the Smithsonian.

"So you see, it all came about by chance."

BORDIER, Georgette 1924-

PERSONAL: Born July 8, 1924, in Paris, France; daughter of Henri (an engineering consultant of the arts and manufacturing) and Marguerite Bordier; married Vincent Jacques (a commercial artist); children: Claude-Isabelle. *Education:* Studied in the studios of Souverbié, Léger, Lhote, and Courtin. *Home:* 2 bis rue de la Parfumerie, Asnieres 92600, France.

CAREER: Drawing and anatomy teacher at the dance school of the Opera since 1955 and at the masters' program

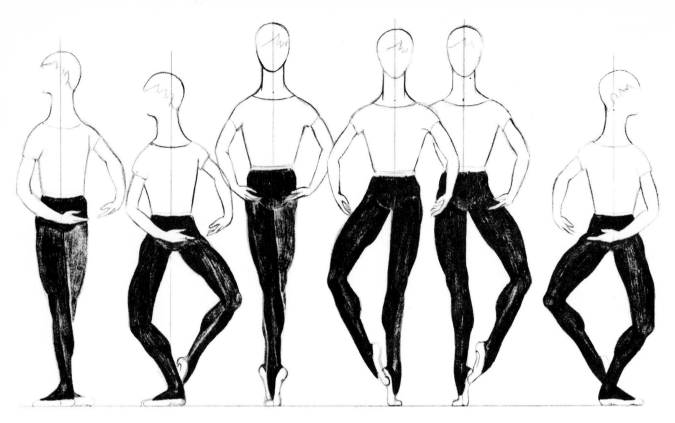

(From *A Young Person's Guide to Ballet* by Noel Streatfeild. Illustrated by Georgette Bordier.)

of the ORTF (the radio and television organization of France). *Awards, honors: A Young Person's Guide to Ballet* was a Children's Book Showcase Title, 1976.

WRITINGS—Self-illustrated: *Anatomiè appliquée á la dance* (title means "Anatomy Applied to Dance"), Amphora, 1975.

Illustrator: G. Guillot and G. Prudhommeau, *Grammaire de la dance classique* (title means "Grammar of Classical Dance"), Hachette, 1969; Noel Streatfeild, *A Young Person's Guide to Ballet*, Warne, 1975.

SIDELIGHTS: "Through the medium of drawing, contact and permanent changes, in as far as the personality and the individual are concerned, are established between the teacher and the child. I envisage creating a book with slides around the three major themes: 'evoking, expressing, creating,' uniting the most beautiful and authentic achievements of the child. This book would be done by children, in spite of them, in their enthusiasm and tenderness, sometimes in their aggressiveness."

BORLAND, Kathryn Kilby 1916-
(Alice Abbott, Jane Land and Ross Land, joint pseudonyms)

PERSONAL: Born August 14, 1916, in Pullman, Mich.; daughter of Paul M. (a diamond broker) and Vinnie (Bensinger) Kilby; married James Borland (a chemist), May 16, 1942; children: James, Susan. *Education:* Butler University, B.S., 1937. *Religion:* Christian Disciple. *Home:* 1050 South Maish Rd., Frankfort, Ind. 46041. *Agent:* Harvey Klinger, 250 W. 57th St., New York, N.Y. 10019.

CAREER: North Side Topics (weekly newspaper), Indianapolis, Ind., editor, 1939-42; free-lance writer. *Member:* Theta Sigma Phi, Kappa Alpha Theta. *Awards, honors:* Co-recipient of Indiana University award for most distinguished children's book by an Indiana author, 1970.

WRITINGS—All with Helen Speicher: *Southern Yankees,* Bobbs-Merrill, 1960; *Allan Pinkerton: Young Detective,* Bobbs-Merrill, 1962; *Eugene Field: Young Poet,* Bobbs-Merrill, 1964; *Phyllis Wheatley: Young Colonial Poet,* Bobbs-Merrill, 1968; *Harry Houdini: Boy Magician,* Bobbs-Merrill, 1969; *Clocks: From Shadow to Atom,* Follett, 1969; *Goodbye to Stony Crick,* McGraw, 1975.

With Speicher, under pseudonym Jane Land and Ross Land, except as indicated: *Miles and the Big Black Hat,* E. C. Seale, 1963; *Everybody Laughed and Laughed,* E. C. Seale, 1964; (with Speicher, under pseudonym Jane Land) *Stranger in the Mirror,* Ballantine, 1974; *To Walk the Night,* Ballantine, 1976; *These Tigers' Hearts,* Doubleday, 1978.

With Speicher, under pseudonym Alice Abbott: *The Third Tower,* Ace Books, 1974; *Goodbye Julie Scott,* Ace Books, 1975.

SIDELIGHTS: Kathryn Borland commented on her association with Helen Speicher: "We are often asked how two people can write together, and it probably does require special circumstances—in our case friendship since childhood, similar viewpoints, and insatiable curiosity about people, events, and places. It is our hope that whatever we write will reinforce the positive values of integrity, love, and responsibility for one another, in addition, of course to the primary purpose of telling a cracking good story.

"It's a bonny day," his father said, "a good day to start school." ■ (From *Allen Pinkerton, Young Detective* by Kathryn Kilby Borland and Helen Ross Speicher. Illustrated by Nathan Goldstein.)

KATHRYN KILBY BORLAND

"We particularly like writing books with a historical background, because we enjoy the research. Quite often some odd fact we turn up triggers an incident in a story, or perhaps an entire new book.

"Our other favorite story-triggerer is travel, in this country or abroad. As a matter of fact, we both love to travel, whether it triggers a story or not.

"As for myself, I have wanted to write ever since I read my first book. I grew up in a family of readers, and am a compulsive reader, ingesting biography, history and mysteries with equally insatiable pleasure. Is there such a thing as a writer who isn't a reader?"

BORTSTEIN, Larry 1942-

PERSONAL: Surname is pronounced Bort-*stine;* born November 25, 1942, in Bronx, N.Y.; son of William and Shirley (Ecker) Bortstein; married Veronica Weber, June 28, 1969; children: Steven. *Education:* City College, New York, N.Y., B.A., 1963. *Religion:* Hebrew. *Home:* 8937 Field St. #57, Broomfield, Colo. 80020. *Office:* Associated Press, 650 15th St., Denver, Colo. 80202.

CAREER: Sports-writer for *New York Mirror,* 1962-63, Associated Press, 1964, National Collegiate Athletic Bureau, 1964-66, Madison Square Garden Basketball Publicity, 1966-67; sports editor for Pyramid Publications, 1967-69; full-time writer on sports topics, 1969-76; *The Pueblo Chieftain,* Pueblo, Colo., staff writer, 1978—; The Associated Press, Denver, Colo., staff writer, 1978—. Ruder & Finn Public Relations Agency, publicity writer on auto racing and tennis. Covered Maccabiah Games in Israel, 1965, Pan-

American Games in Winnipeg, 1967, and Olympic Games in Mexico City, 1968, and Munich, 1972. *Member:* American Society of Journalists and Authors, Football Writers Association of America, U.S. Basketball Writers Association, American Auto Racing Writers and Broadcasters Association, International Motor Press Association, U.S. Tennis Writers Association, Professional Basketball Writers Association, Authors League, Authors Guild, Sigma Delta Chi.

WRITINGS: Football Stars of 1969, Pyramid Publications, 1969; *Super Joe: The Joe Namath Story,* Grosset, 1969; *Len Dawson: Super Bowl Quarterback,* Grosset, 1970; *Football Stars of 1970,* Pyramid Publications, 1970; *Football Stars of 1971,* Pyramid Publications, 1971; (with Henry Berkowitz) *Scuba, Spear and Snorkel,* Cowles, 1971; *Ali: An Intimate Biography,* Tower, 1971; *Who's Who in Auto Racing,* Sports, Inc., 1972; *Who's Who in Golf,* Sports, Inc., 1972; *Who's Who in Pro Hockey,* Sports, Inc., 1972; (with Phil Berger) *The Boys of Indy,* Corwin, 1977; *After Olympic Glory,* Warne, 1978; *David Thompson,* Harvey House, 1979. Editor of magazine, *Auto Racing Sports Stars of 1972;* co-editor of magazine, *Motorcycle Sports Stars of 1972;* contributing editor of *Family Weekly,* 1971-76. Regular contributor of articles on sports to the *Christian Science Monitor,* 1966—.

SIDELIGHTS: "I enjoy the combination of working full time in the news field, as I am now doing with the Denver

LARRY BORTSTEIN

bureau of the Associated Press, and free-lancing for magazines, and writing books in the juvenile area. For nine years I worked full time as a free-lancer, but really found myself unable to muster the necessary discipline to continue free-lancing permanently. I find that many free-lancers who might wish to get into full time employment have a difficult time doing so, more difficult the longer they continue as full time free-lancers. This is, it seems to me, a very unfair and inequitable situation, since many free-lancers are quite skilled and prove themselves over the years to be reliable workers. Yet, often they are perceived as something other than the type of people who are capable of holding down a full time job.

"I enjoy writing for children and young audiences, and also enjoy speaking about books, writers, and writing with young audiences. I take every opportunity I can to address children, since many young people aren't aware that writers are actually living, breathing people. Writing itself often is viewed as something done by old men with beards hovering over a piece of paper. I try to take some of the mystery out of the writing experience for children, while still leaving the impression that writing is a skilled art."

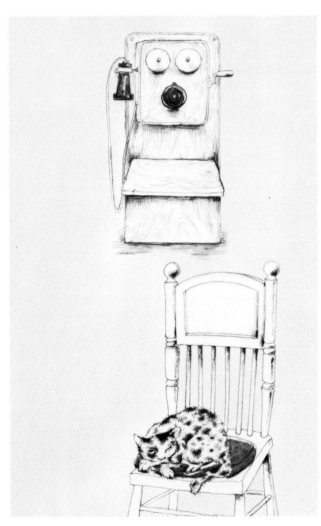

"You win,"
their father gasped at last.
"I'll get us a telephone."
■ (From *Four-Ring Three* by Miriam Anne Bourne. Illustrated by Cyndy Szekeres.)

BOURNE, Miriam Anne 1931-

PERSONAL: Surname rhymes with "torn"; born March 4, 1931, in Buffalo, N.Y.; daughter of Herbert M. (an insurance man) and Caroline (Walker) Young; married Russell Bourne (an editor), August 22, 1953; children: Sarah Perkins, Jonathan, Louise Taber, Andrew Russell. *Education:* Baldwin School, graduate, 1949; Wheelock College, graduate, 1953. *Home:* 6401 81st St., Cabin-John, Md. 20731.

CAREER: Author; owner/proprietor of The Children's Bookshop, a mail-order business at home, 1974—. *Member:* Washington Children's Book Guild.

WRITINGS: Emilio's Summer Day, Harper, 1966; *Raccoons Are for Loving,* Random, 1968; *Tigers in the Woods,* Coward, 1971; *Second Car in Town,* Coward, 1972; *Four-Ring Three* (Junior Literary Guild selection), Coward, 1973; *Nelly Custis' Diary,* Coward, 1974; *Nabby Adams' Diary,* Coward, 1975; *Bright-Lights to See By,* Coward, 1975; *Patsy Jefferson's Diary,* Coward, 1976; *What Is Papa Up to Now?,* Coward, 1977; *The Little Folks at Mount Vernon: A Children's Guide,* Mount Vernon, 1979; *White House Children,* Random House, 1979.

SIDELIGHTS: "Three books (*Second Car in Town, Four-Ring Three, Bright-Lights to See By*) are based on my mother's memories of small-town life in Maine at the beginning of the century. *Tigers in the Woods* came from watching my children's creative play in the fields and woods outside our home in Connecticut. Friends in Bridgeport made me want to write about the city children in *Emilio's Summer Day* and *Raccoons Are for Loving.*

"When we moved from Connecticut to Washington, D.C. (Cabin-John, Maryland is near Washington), I discovered the pleasure of working at the Library of Congress and the Mount Vernon library doing research from which to write books. *Nelly Custis' Diary, Nabby Adams' Diary, Patsy Jefferson's Diary,* and *What Is Papa Up to Now?* grew from the journals and letters of George Washington, John Adams, Thomas Jefferson, and Benjamin Franklin and their families and friends. Visiting the homes of these famous men helped me imagine what it must have been like to be their grand-daughter or daughters."

BOWMAN, John S(tewart) 1931-

PERSONAL: Born May 30, 1931, in Cambridge, Mass.; son of J(ohn) Russell (a teacher) and Ann (a church administrator; maiden name, Stewart) Bowman; married Francesca DiPietro (a social worker), February 11, 1967; children: Michela, Alexander. *Education:* Harvard College, B.A., 1953; attended Trinity College, Cambridge, Mass., 1953-54, University of Munich, 1958-59. *Home:* 53 Massasoit St., Northampton, Mass. 01060.

CAREER: New England Opera Theatre, Boston, Mass., production assistant, 1957; University of Maryland, overseas program, Athens and Crete, Greece, English instructor, 1960; *Natural History,* New York, N.Y., associate editor, 1961-62; Grolier, Inc. (encyclopedia publisher), New York, N.Y., associate editor, 1962-63; free-lance writer, 1963—; University of Massachusetts, Amherst, Mass., visiting lecturer, 1978. *Military service:* U.S. Army, 1954-56. *Member:* Phi Beta Kappa, National Association of Science Writers.

This scene from a 1961 film, "Atlantis, The Lost Continent," is typical of the mixture of periods that people imagine for Atlantis in its prime. There are classic Greek structures, rough hills rising directly behind them and the technologically advanced vessel and harbor light: it is all good fantasy—and harmless fun. ■ (From *The Quest for Atlantis* by John S. Bowman. Jacket illustrated by Howard Berelson.)

WRITINGS: Crete, Secker & Warburg, 1963, revised edition, Jonathan Cape, 1974, Bobbs-Merrill, 1974; *Early Civilizations,* Golden Press, 1966; *The Age of Enlightenment,* Golden Press, 1966; *On Guard,* Doubleday, 1969; *The Quest for Atlantis,* Doubleday, 1971; (editor) *A Book of Islands,* Doubleday, 1972; *Argonaut Guides to Iraklion,* Efstathiadis Brothers, 1974; *Knossos and Santorini,* Efstathiadis Brothers, 1974. Contributor to *New Yorker, Drama Survey, Nature and Science, Interplay, Saturday Review, Harvard Magazine, Parent's Magazine,* and *The Athenian;* also, entry on "Crete" in *Encyclopedia Britannica;* librettos for two produced operas.

WORK IN PROGRESS: Books for young people in various stages of progress; plans for a book on archeology and more opera librettos; an autobiographical memoir about books-in-life; suspense novel.

SIDELIGHTS: John Bowman has lived and traveled extensively in England, France, Germany, Italy, Spain, and Greece; manages "solid French, passable German, and traveler's Italian and Greek."

HOBBIES AND OTHER INTERESTS: Archeology, particularly of the Mediterranean; the theater, particularly the commedia dell'arte; interaction between the sciences and the arts.

BURNINGHAM, John (Mackintosh) 1936-

PERSONAL: Born April 27, 1936, in Farnham, Surrey, England; son of Charles and Jessie (Mackintosh) Burningham; married Helen Gillian Oxenbury (a designer), 1964; children: one son, one daughter. *Education:* Attended Central School of Art, Holborn, London, 1956-59. *Home:* Hampstead, London, England.

CAREER: Author and illustrator. Joined the Friend's Ambulance Unit as an alternative to military service, 1953; spent two years working at farming, slum-clearance, forestry, and school building, traveling through Italy, Yugoslavia, and Israel; designed posters for London Transport and the British Transport Commission; worked for a year on an animated puppet film in the Middle East; turned to writing and illustrating children's books as a means of getting his

JOHN BURNINGHAM

"Well, well!" said Captain McAllister. "A goose on board! She'll have to work her passage if she's coming with us to London." ■ (From *Borka* by John Burningham. Illustrated by the author.)

drawings published, 1963; free-lance designer of murals, exhibitions, three-dimensional models, magazine illustrations and advertisements. His works have been exhibited by the American Institute of Graphic Arts. *Awards, honors:* Kate Greenaway Medal, 1963, for *Borka: The Adventures of a Goose with No Feathers; Mr. Gumpy's Outing* has received numerous awards and honors including, Kate Greenaway Medal, 1970, one of the *New York Times* choice of Best Illustrated Books of the Year, 1971, *Boston Globe-Horn Book* Award (illustration), 1972, and the Children's Book Showcase selection, 1972. *New York Times* Best Illustrated Children's Book Award for *Come Away From The Water, Shirley.*

WRITINGS—All self-illustrated: *Borka: The Adventures of a Goose with No Feathers*, Random House, 1963; *John Burningham's ABC*, J. Cape, 1964, Bobbs-Merrill, 1967; *Trubloff: The Mouse Who Wanted to Play the Balalaika*, J. Cape, 1964, Random House, 1965; *Humbert, Mister Firkin, and the Lord Mayor of London*, J. Cape, 1965, Bobbs-Merrill, 1967; *Cannonball Simp*, J. Cape, 1966, Bobbs-Merrill, 1967; *Harquin: The Fox Who Went down to the Valley*, J. Cape, 1967, Bobbs-Merrill, 1968; *Seasons*, J. Cape, 1969, Bobbs-Merrill, 1971; *Mr. Gumpy's Outing* (Junior Literary Guild selection), Holt, 1970; *Around the World in Eighty Days*, J. Cape, 1972; *Mr. Gumpy's Motor Car*, Macmillan, 1975; *Come Away From The Water, Shirley*, Crowell, 1977.

"Little Book" series: *The Rabbit*, J. Cape, 1974, Crowell, 1975; *The School*, J. Cape, 1974, Crowell, 1975; *The Snow*, J. Cape, 1974, Crowell, 1975; *The Baby*, J. Cape, 1974, Crowell, 1975; *The Blanket*, J. Cape, 1975, Crowell, 1976; *The Cupboard*, J. Cape, 1975, Crowell, 1976; *The Dog*, J. Cape, 1975, Crowell, 1976; *The Friend*, J. Cape, 1975, Crowell, 1976.

Illustrator: Ian Fleming, *Chitty Chitty Bang Bang: The Magical Car*, Random House, 1964; Letta Schatz, editor, *The Extraordinary Tug-of-War*, Follett, 1968.

Also designer of wall-frieze posters, *Birdland*, J. Cape, 1966, Braziller, 1967; *Lionland*, J. Cape, 1966, Braziller, 1967; *Storyland*, J. Cape, 1966, Braziller, 1967.

ADAPTATION—Filmstrip: "Mr. Gumpy's Outing," Weston Woods.

SIDELIGHTS: Burningham uses a wide assortment of materials and techniques in his illustrations, including crayons, charcoal, and india ink. *Borka: The Adventures of a Goose with No Feathers* was not only the author's first attempt at writing and illustrating a children's book, but was also the winner of the Kate Greenaway Medal in 1963. In reviewing Burningham's book, a critic for the *Christian Science Monitor* said, "There is humor, boldness and verve in the story . . . and . . . the well-drawn pictures [are] bright and childlike yet with original and interesting coloring. . . ." Seven years later, Burningham again won the Kate Greenaway Medal. This time the award was for *Mr. Grumpy's Outing*. Of this multi-award winning book a reviewer for the *Library Journal* wrote, "The illustrations, skillfully drawn . . . are outstanding for their very expressive animals and numerous warm, humorous touches. . . . And, the simple, cumulative text and easy, natural attitudes of Gumpy and company are sure to please the picture-book audience."

In addition to his books, Burningham has also created children's wall friezes that measure eight feet long and twelve inches wide.

FOR MORE INFORMATION SEE: Horn Book, June and October, 1971, February and December, 1972, August,

But we could not find the blanket. ■ (From *The Blanket* by John Burningham. Illustrated by the author.)

1976, February, 1978; Doris de Montreville, editor, *Third Book of Junior Authors,* H. W. Wilson, 1972.

BUSONI, Rafaello   1900-1962

PERSONAL: Born February 1, 1900, in Berlin, Germany; came to the United States, 1939; son of a pianist; children: Mario. *Education:* Attended schools in Germany, Switzerland, and the United States. *Home:* New York City.

CAREER: Author and illustrator. Began drawing as a child; quit school to become a painter, 1916; held his first one-man exhibition in Zurich, at the age of seventeen; became interested in children's literature when his son was old enough to enjoy books; worked for Audio-Video Filmstrips, 1948-52; made stage designs for Marionette Films, 1953; served as illustrator on the staff of an encyclopedia; worked on the development of a full-color reproduction method which reduces the costs of line cuts.

WRITINGS—All self-illustrated: *Somi Builds a Church: A Story from Lapland,* Viking, 1943; *Stanley's Africa,* Viking, 1944; *The Man Who Was Don Quixote: The Story of Miguel Cervantes,* Prentice-Hall, 1958.

Illustrator: Bible (Old Testament), *Song of Solomon* (Hebrew), [Berlin], 1922-23; Alison J. (Baigrie) Alessios, *Spear of Ulysses,* Longmans, Green, 1941; Margaret (Culkin) Banning, *Salud! A South American Journal,* Harper, 1941; *Dick Whittington and His Cat,* Grosset, 1941; Howard Melvin Fast, *Lord Baden-Powell of the Boy Scouts,* Messner, 1941; H. M. Fast, *Romance of a People,* Hebrew Publishing, 1941; Harriet F. Bunn, *Johann Sebastian Bach,* Random House, 1942; Josephine Blackstock, *Wings for Nikias,* Putnam, 1942; H. M. Fast, *Goethals and the Panama Canal,* Messner, 1942; Anne (Littlefield) Locklin, *Tidewater Tales,* Viking, 1942; H. M. Fast, *Tall Hunter,* Harper, 1942; Ivan George Heilbut, *Francisco and Elizabeth,* Pantheon, 1942; Katherine (Gantz) Pollock, *Sandalio Goes to Town,* Scribner, 1942; William Saunders Resnick, *Dragonship: A Story of the Vikings in America,* Coward-McCann, 1942;

Helen Dean Fish, *Pegs of History: A Picture Book of World Dates,* Stokes Publishing, 1943; Lorraine and Jerrold Beim, *Sasha and the Samovar,* Harcourt, 1944; Margery (Williams) Bianco, *Forward, Commandos!,* Viking, 1944; J. Blackstock, *Island on the Beam,* Putnam, 1944; Janette Lowrey, *Lavender Cat,* Harper, 1944.

Regina Llewellyn, *Stars Came Down,* Harcourt, 1945; Robin Palmer, *Ship's Dog,* Grosset, 1945; Caroline R. Stone, *Clorinda of Cherry Lane Farm,* Liveright, 1945; Patricia Gordon, *Rommany Luck,* Viking, 1946; Henry William Simon, editor, *Treasury of Grand Opera,* Simon & Schuster, 1946; Elizabeth Townsend, *Johnny and His Wonderful Bed,* Ungar, 1946; Eva (Knox) Witte, *Skookum,* Putnam, 1946; Quail Hawkins, *Mark, Mark, Shut the Door!,* Holiday House, 1947; Fulton John Sheen, *Jesus: Son of*

The day before Christmas was bitterly cold with a few lonely snowflakes flying in the air, and a hard white crust on the ground. ■ (From *Why the Chimes Rang* by Raymond MacDonald Alden. Illustrated by Rafaello Busoni.)

Madame DeFarge knitted with nimble fingers and steady eyebrows, and saw nothing. ■ (From *A Tale of Two Cities* by Charles Dickens. Illustrated by Rafaello Busoni.)

Mary, McMullen, 1947; Charles Dickens, *Tale of Two Cities,* Grosset, 1948; Bernice Sutherland Stark, *Chanco: A Boy and His Pig in Peru,* Messner, 1948; Eugenia Stone, *Robin Hood's Arrow,* Wilcox & Follett, 1948; Honore de Balzac, *Old Man Goriot* (translation from the French by Joan Charles; edited by W. Somerset Maugham), Winston, 1949; Fruma (Kasden) Gottschalk, *Youngest General: A Story of Lafayette,* Knopf, 1949; Rene Prud'hommeaux, *Sunken Forest,* Viking, 1949; E. Stone, *Page Boy for King Arthur,* Wilcox & Follett, 1949.

Dale Collins, *Shipmates Down Under,* Holiday House, 1950; John Faulkner, *Chooky,* W. W. Norton, 1950; Mary Alice Jones, *His Name Was Jesus,* Rand McNally, 1950; Charles George Wilson, *Winds Blow Free: A Story of the American Revolution,* Washburn, 1950; Waldemar Bonsels, *Adventures of Maya the Bee* (translation from the German

by Adele Szold Seltzer), Pellegrini & Cudahy, 1951; Nathaniel Hawthorne, *Pandora's Box,* Limited Editions, 1951; Fritz Muehlenweg, *Big Tiger and Christian,* Pantheon, 1952; R. Prud'hommeaux, *Port of Missing Men,* Viking, 1952; Johann Christoph Friedrich von Schiller, *William Tell,* Heritage Press, 1952; Raymond Macdonald Alden, *Why the Chimes Rang,* Bobbs-Merrill, 1954; Sister Mary Marguerite, *Martin's Mice,* Follett, 1954; H. W. Simon, editor, *Treasury of Christmas Songs and Carols,* Houghton, 1955; R. Prud'hommeaux, *Hidden Lights,* Viking, 1956; Stendhal (pseudonym of Marie Henri Beyle), *Charterhouse of Parma* (translation from the French by Mary Loyd), Heritage Press, 1956; Norman Vincent Peale, *He Was a Child,* Prentice-Hall, 1957; R. M. Alden, *Christmas Tree Forest,* Bobbs-Merrill, 1958; Sister Mary Jean Dorcy, *Mary,* Sheed, 1958; Wilfrid Sheed, *Joseph,* Sheed, 1958; Sidney Rosen, *Doctor Paracelsus,* Little, Brown, 1959.

RAFAELLO BUSONI

Rudyard Kipling, *Captains Courageous,* Hart Publishing, 1960; Louise (Hall) Tharp, *Louis Agassiz: Adventurous Scientist,* Little, Brown, 1961; Carl Lamson Carmer, *The Hudson River,* Holt, 1962; S. Rosen, *The Harmonious World of Johann Kepler,* Little, Brown, 1962; Nicola Ann Sissons, editor, *Myths and Legends of the Greeks,* Hart Publishing, 1962; Stendhal, *The Red and the Black* (translation from the French by C. K. Scott-Moncrieff), Heritage Press, 1964.

"Lands and Peoples" series; all published by Holiday House, except as noted: (And author) *Arabs and the World of Islam,* Cassell, 1939; (and author) *Australia,* Cassell, 1939; (and author) *The Far Far North,* Cassell, 1939; (and author) *Mexico and the Inca Lands,* Cassell, 1939; (and author) *The Negro Lands and East Africa,* Cassell, 1939; (and author) *South Africa and the Congo,* Cassell, 1939; Cateau DeLeeuw, *Dutch East Indies and the Philippines,* 1943; Vernon Ives, *Russia,* 1943; Cornelia Spencer (pseudonym of Grace Yaukey), *China,* 1944; V. Ives, *Turkey,* 1945; Paul V. Falkenberg, *Palestine,* 1946; William Sloane, *British Isles,* 1946; Mary Zwemer Brittain, *Arab Lands,* 1947; Robert Davis, *France,* 1947; Edwin Ben Evans, *Scandinavia,* 1948; C. Spencer, *Japan,* 1948; C. Spencer, *The Low Countries,* 1949; (and author) *Italy,* 1950; Elsa R. Berner, *Germany,* 1951; George Kish, *Yugoslavia,* 1952; Alice Taylor, *Egypt,* 1953; Leonard Stout Kenworthy, *Brazil,* 1954; A. Taylor, *South Africa,* 1954; A. Taylor, *Iran,* 1955; A. Taylor, *India,* 1957.

Also illustrator of trade and text books, including several for the Limited Editions Club and the Heritage Press.

SIDELIGHTS: "Always I wanted to become a painter. I remember struggling with the problem of how to draw a nose 'as it looks' from full face when I was six, and I had my first oil paint set when I was eleven. During the First World War we lived in Switzerland where drawing is considered the very elemental base for any of the fine arts. I tried every technique of the graphic arts: lithography, etching, woodcut, and every means of direct drawing. Although I spent most of my time painting, I cannot remember any period in which I did not make illustrations for my own pleasure. I chose my topics from among plays and operas and wrote the text myself to make the books complete. The text—calligraphy plus original drawings—resulted in manuscript books, and I have made more than twenty such handwritten books. When my son, Mario, was old enough to enjoy books, I got interested in children's books. Quite naturally, out of little talks with my child, evolved my first geographical books which I both wrote and illustrated and which have grown to a list of twenty-one titles." [B. M. Miller and others, compilers, *Illustrators of Children's Books: 1946-1956,* Horn Book, 1958[1]]

FOR MORE INFORMATION SEE: Stanley J. Kunitz, editor, *The Junior Book of Authors,* 2nd edition, revised, H. W. Wilson, 1951; B. M. Miller and others, compilers, *Illustrators of Children's Books, 1946-1956,* Horn Book, 1958.

(Died March, 1962)

CARLSON, Vada F.   1897-
(Florella Rose)

PERSONAL: Born February 27, 1897, in Cody, Neb.; daughter of Fred Lorenzo (employed in building trades) and Hattie F. (Ditson) Rose; married Albert B. Carlson, July 22, 1917 (divorced, 1937); married Jose C. Rodriguez (an artist), January 29, 1972; children: Lois Rose (Mrs. Earl A. Toburen), Wayne B. *Education:* Attended public schools in Cody and Gordon, Neb.; took correspondence courses; attended Mexico City writing school. *Politics:* Republican. *Religion:* Methodist. *Home:* 123 West Fourth St., Winslow, Ariz. 86047.

CAREER: Began working at age sixteen as telephone operator in Cody, Wyo.; writer and woman's page editor on papers in Riverton, Wyo., at various intervals, 1915-32, Concord, Calif., 1932-37, and Pittsburg, Calif., 1938-41; Columbia Steel, Pittsburg, Calif., secretary to foundry superintendent, 1942-45; news editor on paper in Concord, Calif., 1946-48; writer and director of pageant, "Voice of Todos Santos," Chamber of Commerce, Concord, Calif., 1948; publisher of own paper in Oakley, Calif., 1948-49; woman's page editor of *Winslow Mail,* Winslow, Ariz., 1955-56, and *Flagstaff Daily Sun,* Flagstaff, Ariz., 1956-57, 1963-64; *Winslow Mail,* editor, 1965-66; A.R.E. Press, Virginia Beach, Va., editor, 1968-70. *Riverton Ranger,* special writer for golden anniversary edition, 1956, and author of anniversary pageant, *And Still the River.*

MEMBER: National Federation of Press Women (regional director, 1965-67), Arizona Press Women (president, 1957-58), Winslow Arts Association (founder; president, 1962-64), Business and Professional Woman's Club, Order of Eastern Star, Soroptimist Club. *Awards, honors:* Named Woman of Achievement by National Federation of Press Women, Winslow Woman of the Year, by Winslow Chamber of Commerce, Woman of the Year by Arizona Press

(From *High Country Canvas* by Vada F. Carlson. Illustrated by Joel Rodriguez.)

Women, and Business Woman of the Year by Business and Professional Woman's Club, 1965; holder of more than sixty awards for writing.

WRITINGS: We Saw the Sundance, Graphic Press, 1948; *The Desert Speaks* (poetry), Ranger Press, 1956; *This Is Our Valley* (history of Santa Maria Valley), Westernlore, 1959; (with Elizabeth W. White [Indian name, Polingaysi Qoyawayma]), *No Turning Back,* University of New Mexico Press, 1964; (ghost writer for Clara Edge) *Tahirih,* Eerdmans, 1963; *Fluffy and the Flyaway Fly* (juvenile), Whitman Publishing, 1966; (with Gary Witherspoon) *Black Mountain Boy* (juvenile), Navaho Curriculum Center (Rough Rock,

Ariz.), 1968; (editor) *Coyote Legends,* Navaho Curriculum Center, 1968; *The Vision and the Promise* (juvenile), A.R.E. Press, 1969; *The Sacred Summer* (juvenile), A.R.E. Press, 1969.

The Great Migration, A.R.E. Press, 1970; *High Country Canvas,* Northland Press, 1972; *East of the Sun* (anthology), A.R.E. Press, 1972; *Cochise: Chief of the Chiricahuas,* Harvey House, 1973; *John Charles Fremont: Adventurer in the Wilderness* (biography), Harvey House, 1973; *John Wesley Powell: Conquest of the Canyon* (juvenile), Harvey House, 1974. Also author of introduction, *Arizona History,* Western States Historical Publishers, 1975.

Juveniles; under pseudonym Florella Rose; all published by Whitman Publishing: *Peter Picket Pin,* 1953; *Yipee Kiyi,* 1954; *Yipee Kiyi and Whoa Boy,* 1955.

Contributor of articles and poetry to magazines.

WORK IN PROGRESS: The Ancient Pattern-Life of the Hopi with Polingaysi Qoyawayma; *Sunset Crossing,* about early trails in Arizona.

SIDELIGHTS: "I was born near the Rosebud Reservation of the Sioux Indians and have lived near Indians most of my life. My present book concerns the Hopi, as well as early trails through Arizona while it was still a high desert wilderness. As a child I learned to love to read—non-fiction from which I could learn about the world and its fascinating people, and fiction, which thrilled me with its revelation of personalities. I wrote my first story, never published, at the age of fifteen. The title was 'The Tangled Web,' detailing the troubles that came to two girls who attempted to change identities.

"I love to tell stories to small children and for that purpose I invented a tiny boy called Hop-tee-ma-lou who, as one of my granddaughters observed with delight, was always getting into trouble. From which, of course, I eventually extricated him.

"Travel has been a great pleasure and Greece my most loved destination. Mexico has also captivated me. My own country still has its lure and I have visited most of the states. Best of all, I think, is the fact that I have never lost my desire to express myself through the written word. On the way I have garnered my full share of rejections, but eventually the bulk of my writing has found a publisher. I have enough published children's stories for a book, but have not attempted to sell them for this purpose. Perhaps I'll do that—someday. My days are very full. I am interested in history and spend much of my time for the Navajo County Historical Society, taping interviews with old-timers.

"I recommend writing as a profession, especially for girls. One is never too old to write and even in the midst of marriage, homemaking and children, one can write short stories, poetry, news items, and historical bits to fill in until there is time for books."

COLLIER, Christopher 1930-

PERSONAL: Born January 29, 1930, in New York, N.Y.; son of Edmund (a writer) and Katharine (Brown) Collier; married Virginia Wright (a teacher), August 21, 1954; married second wife, Bonnie Bromberger (a librarian), December 6, 1969; children: (first marriage) Edmund Quincy, Sally McQueen, (second marriage) Christopher Zwissler. *Education:* Clark University, Worcester, Mass., B.A., 1951; Columbia University, M.A., 1955, Ph.D., 1964. *Home:* 876 Orange Center Rd., Orange, Conn. 06477. *Office:* Department of History, University of Bridgeport, Bridgeport, Conn. 06602.

CAREER: Teacher in public schools in Greenwich, Conn., 1955-58, and New Canaan, Conn., 1959-61; Columbia University, Teachers College, New York, N.Y., instructor in history, 1958-59; University of Bridgeport, Bridgeport, Conn., instructor, 1961-64, assistant professor, 1964-67, associate professor, 1967-71, professor of history, 1971—, chairman, 1977—. *Military service:* U.S. Army, 1952-54.

Member: American Historical Association, Organization of American Historians, Connecticut Historical Society. *Awards, honors:* Nominated for the National Book Award and received the Newbery Medal for *My Brother Sam is Dead.*

WRITINGS: (Editor) *Public Records of the State of Connecticut 1802-1803,* State Library of Connecticut, 1967; *Roger Sherman's Connecticut: Yankee Politics and the American Revolution,* Wesleyan University Press, 1971; *Connecticut in the Continental Congress,* Pequot, 1973; (with James Lincoln Collier) *My Brother Sam Is Dead* (ALA Notable Book), Four Winds, 1974; *The Bloody Country,* Four Winds, 1976; *Roger Sherman: Puritan Politician,* New Haven Colony Historical Society, 1976; *The Winter Hero,* Four Winds, 1978. Contributor to history journals. Editor, Monographs in British History and Culture, 1967-72; editor of publications, Association for the Study of Connecticut History, 1967-73.

WORK IN PROGRESS: Further research on the history of Connecticut; *Tagliero,* historical novel for teenagers about academic freedom.

SIDELIGHTS: "Most of my writing is done for adults, usually other historians. However, I have been teaching American history to junior and senior high school students, college students, and adults for twenty-five years, and my

(From *My Brother Sam is Dead* by James Lincoln Collier and Christopher Collier.)

CHRISTOPHER COLLIER

books for young people are motivated by a desire to paint the past in colors truer to life than found in most children's literature. In short, I want to correct myths about the American past. Sometimes this calls for rather ugly portraits and gruesome scenes, but just as often history provides dramas of happiness and fulfillment.

"I write with my brother, James Lincoln Collier, because he is a skilled craftsman in the field of children's and young adult literature. He knows how to make characters seem like real-life people, and he knows how to make stories exciting at every turn. Together, I think, we are able to write about the past in a way that is accurate, dramatic, and realistic.

"My books for teen-agers are just as thoroughly researched as are my scholarly works. If we say it snowed three inches on January 4, 1787 in Springfield, Massachusetts, then you can be sure that it really did. We even have dialogue in our historical novels that actually took place—words that I found in letters, diaries, eye-witness accounts, and other sources. Every episode that is found in our books actually happened exactly as we describe it; all we make up are the members of the central family, and all their experiences actually did happen to someone living at their time.

"I began writing because, along with teaching, that is what historians do. But beyond that, I come from a family of writers. My father has written scores of short stories about the West, and biographies of Annie Oakley, Kit Carson, and Buffalo Bill for teen-agers, as well as several other adult and children's books. My uncle, aunt, cousin, brother-in-law,

and several ancestors dating back to the 17th century have been writers, too. My brother has written about thirty books for teen-agers, perhaps a dozen books for adults, and about 700 magazine articles. His son is now writing a book about jazz, and my wife is writing one on figure skating. We all do it because we like to, but we write also as a way of earning a living that makes it possible for us to set our own schedules, take our vacations when we please, and not have to take orders from anyone."

FOR MORE INFORMATION SEE: Horn Book, August, 1975, April, 1976; *Language Arts,* March, 1978.

CUTT, W(illiam) Towrie 1898-

PERSONAL: Born January 26, 1898, in Orkney, Scotland; son of John (a fisherman) and Betsy (Muir) Cutt; married Margaret Nancy Davis (a university lecturer and writer), May, 1948. *Education:* Attended University of Edinburgh; University of Alberta, B.A., 1942, B.Ed., 1947, M.A., 1950. *Politics:* "Neither Right nor Left." *Religion:* Anglican Church of Canada. *Home:* 624 Cornwall St., Victoria, British Columbia, Canada V8V 4L1.

CAREER: Teacher; writer. *Military service:* British Army, 1916-18; served with Gordon Highlanders in France. *Awards, honors: On the Trail of Long Tom* and *Message from Arkmae* were on the Notable Canadian Children's Book list.

...And the fisherman spent some days in the final preparation of creels, boat, and sails for the season's fishing. The creels—lobster traps—used in Orkney were made of wood, wire, and twine. ■ (From *Faraway World* by W. Towrie Cutt. Wood engravings by Joseph Sloan.)

WRITINGS: (Contributor) *The New Orkney Book,* Thomas Nelson, 1966; *On the Trail of Long Tom,* Collins, 1970; *Message From Arkmae,* Collins, 1972; *Seven for the Sea,* Collins, 1972, Follett, 1974; *Carry My Bones Northwest,* Collins, 1973; *Faraway World* (autobiography), Deutsch, 1977; (with wife, Margaret Nancy Cutt) *The Hagboon of Hell and Other Strange Orkney Tales,* Deutsch, 1978.

WORK IN PROGRESS: Research on Orkneymen and Orkney folklore; a fictional story of vanishing islands in the North Atlantic.

SIDELIGHTS: "In my second and third books, I wanted to get children interested in sea mammals, seals and porpoises, as I am against seal slaughter and against experiments with porpoise and dolphin. I also wished to comment upon Indian-white half-breed problems and to outline something of the history here in Canada in my first and fourth books, showing in the first a Metis boy choosing his white heritage and in the fourth a boy choosing to follow his Indian people. In *Faraway World* I wanted to show a boyhood that I myself found happy, and a way of life now lost.

"If there is anything of interest about me, it is probably that my books were published when I was in my seventies. My prescription for the elderly retired: *Make something.* A garden is not subject to the frustrations of a book in progress, which gives joy only when the story pulls instead of being pushed. Publication is hard to attain and when it happens, so slow that it is almost an anticlimax. Yet my relations with my editors—Pamela Royds at Deutsch, Margaret Paull at Collins, and Marci Carifoli at Follett—have brought happiness in my old age."

FOR MORE INFORMATION SEE: *Horn Book,* December, 1974.

DARKE, Marjorie 1929-

PERSONAL: Born January 25, 1929, in Birmingham, England; children: two sons, one daughter. *Education:* Attended Leicester College of Art and Central School of Art, London. *Residence:* Coventry, England.

CAREER: Writer. Worked as textile designer in London, England, 1951-54. *Member:* Society of Authors.

WRITINGS: *Ride the Iron Horse* (illustrated by Michael Jackson), Longman Young Books, 1973; *The Star Trap* (illustrated by Jackson), Longman Young Books, 1974; *Mike's Bike* (illustrated by Jim Russell), Kestrel, 1974; *What Can I Do?* (illustrated by Barry Wilkinson), Kestrel, 1975; *A Question of Courage* (illustrated by Janet Archer), Crowell, 1975; *Kipper's Turn* (illustrated by Mary Dinsdale), Blackie & Son, 1976; *The Big Brass Band* (illustrated by Charles Front), Kestrel, 1976; (contributor) M. R. Hodgkin, editor, *Young Winter's Tales,* Macmillan (London), 1976; (contributor) Dorothy Edwards, editor, *The Read-Me-Another-Story Book,* Methuen, 1976; (contributor) Edwards, editor, *Once Twice Thrice and Then Again,* Lutterworth, 1976; *The First of Midnight* (illustrated by Anthony Morris), Kestrel, 1977; *My Uncle Charlie* (illustrated by Janat Houston), Kestrel, 1977; *A Long Way To Go* (illustrated by Anthony Morris), Kestrel, 1978; *Carnival Day* (illustrated by Nina Sowter), Kestrel, 1979; *Kipper Skips* (illustrated by Mary Dinsdale), Blackie & Son, 1979.

SIDELIGHTS: "As far back as I can remember I have been a kind of dipsomaniac where words are concerned. A solitary child, reading was a major source of pleasure to me, becoming almost an obsession in my teens when I devoured a novel a day. At this point my father objected, book lover though he was, as my school work was suffering. He rationed me severely I thought, allowing me no more than two books a week. Was this a blueprint for authorship? If it was, it did not bear fruit until long after I had left school, been to art college and to work, married and had a family. By the time my children were going to school I felt a real need to swim out of the pleasurable but self-effacing seas of motherhood and do something totally different; something creative and personal. Writing seemed a natural answer and fitted easily into family life.

"A ten year apprenticeship followed when I tried my hand at innumerable forms of writing—thrillers, adult novels, short stories for young and old, television plays. Writing for children evolved out of these years of trial and error, and for the first time I found I was really happy; slotting without difficulty into this particular genre, perhaps because my own childhood and adolescence have remained very clear in my mind. The first novel I felt to be worthy of publication was born—*Ride the Iron Horse,* a story of the coming of an early railway to a remote part of England. It was a success and gave me the much needed encouragement to continue.

"To date my novels for young adults all have historical settings, which may seem strange when one considers the fact that I found school history extremely dull. Acts of Parliament, foreign policies, battle strategy bored me into near sleep. My interest lay in ordinary people, their loves, trials, everyday lives. As a child I often begged my mother and grandmother: 'Tell me about when you were a little girl!'

"Their answers are with me still, so that I feel as strongly linked to the past as I do to the present and future. I love to sink myself into a chosen period, feel it in my bones, try to reproduce it so that the reader too, may know what it was like to be a navvy building an early railway, a Victorian actress, a Suffragette, a slave. . . .

"Ideas for my stories usually originate at unexpected moments—a chance remark in conversation; something I see in the street or on television; a phrase I read in a book, or a newspaper item. Any of these and many others may spark off a train of thought which I like to jot down straight away because they are rare treasures and easily lost. Once an idea takes hold I have a marvellous time letting my mind rove freely, even wildly, as the story begins to take shape, but before it evolves too far I begin research into the particular background. Much of this research is from books, but I find it equally important to visit places and talk to people connected with my current interest. In this way I can begin to experience the period within myself, and in doing so inadvertently have a lot of fun. There was the time I drove a steam traction engine at a rally, and another time when I crawled up and up alarmingly vertical ladders in an old water mill, peering down on the great cogs of wood and iron and the flat milling stones which once had pounded wheat into flour, worked by the mill race I could still hear thundering way beneath my feet. For the sake of *A Question of Courage* I spent a fascinating afternoon with a lady whose sheltered cousin defied her family, went to London and smashed a window because she believed in the Suffragette cause. A deed which put her in prison. Holding the badges Mrs. Pankhurst had presented to her, was for me a very poignant moment. There are, of course, details which defy capture. I never did discover whether Bathbrick was in use as a pan scourer in the late eighteenth century, when researching for *The First of Midnight.* Neither did I find out whether charcoal irons were used by dressmakers in 1912, in the case of *A Question of Courage.* When this happens the only course left open to me is to ruthlessly discard any material where

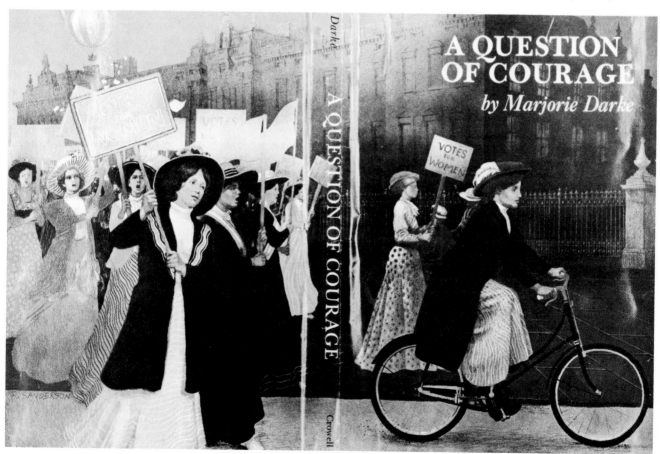

(From *A Question of Courage* by Marjorie Darke. Illustrated by Janet Archer.)

MARJORIE DARKE

there is the smallest element of doubt. It is only fair to the reader.

"Not all my books require this same intensive research. I like to alternate with stories for very young children which can be read aloud. It is a refreshing change playing with the words, building and developing the sounds as well as the storyline. These stories are closely bound to the pictures decorating the book, and I have always been most fortunate in the excellent and sympathetic artists chosen to illustrate them.

"Ultimately there are the sheets of blank paper beside my typewriter, a stack of notes and my head filled with broken jigsaw pieces. I know that the story is hovering there, already independent of me but hidden. Before other people can see it, there is an elusive wall of fog to be pushed away—and that is my job for the next few weeks or months. It is not easy and sometimes it is exasperating, but the moment when my characters begin to direct their own lives and I am merely a recorder of events, then there is an exhilaration, a joy in the writing, which is impossible to define."

FOR MORE INFORMATION SEE: Horn Book, December, 1975.

DAUGHERTY, Charles Michael   1914-

PERSONAL: Born November 17, 1914, in New York City; son of James (the artist and author) and Sonia (a children's author; maiden name Medwedeff) Daugherty. *Education:* Attended Yale University and the Art Students League. *Home:* Westport. Conn.

CAREER: Author and illustrator of books for children. *Military service:* Drafted into the Army, 1941, serving four and a half years.

WRITINGS: So Sailors Say (self-illustrated), Holt, 1941; *Street of Ships* (self-illustrated), Holt, 1942; *Let 'Em Roll* (self-illustrated), Viking, 1950; *Where the Condor Nests* (self-illustrated), Viking, 1955; *Good News* (self-illustrated), Viking, 1956; *The Army: From Civilian to Soldier* (self-illustrated), Viking, 1957; *Wider than the Sky: Aviation as a Career,* Harcourt, 1958; *Mirror with a Memory: The Art of Photography,* Harcourt, 1959; *Wisher* (illustrated by James Daugherty), Viking, 1960; *Searches of the Sea: Pioneers in Oceanography* (illustrated by Don Miller), Viking, 1961; *The Great Archaeologists* (illustrated by Leonard E. Fisher), Crowell, 1962; *City under the Ice: The Story of Camp Century,* Macmillan, 1963; *Robert Goddard: Trail Blazer to the Stars* (illustrated by J. Daugherty), Macmillan, 1964; *Benjamin Franklin: Scientist-Diplomat* (illustrated by John Falter), Macmillan, 1965; *Samuel Clemens* (illustrated by Kurt Werth), Crowell, 1970; (editor) *Six Artists Paint a Portrait: Alfred Chadbourn, George Passantino, Charles Reid, Ariane Beigneux, Robert Baxter, Ann Toulmin-Rothe,* North Light, 1974.

Illustrator: Katherine B. Shippen, *Bright Design,* Viking, 1949; Eric P. Swenson, *South Sea Shilling,* Viking, 1952.

SIDELIGHTS: Charles Michael Daugherty's first book was *So Sailors Say,* of which the *New York Times* commented, "This is a first book that promises well. The author's style is pleasant and easy and he combines an interesting, swiftly moving tale with enough practical information about boat building and sailing to encourage any boy who lives near a pond to follow Davey's example and build a boat of his own." *Secret of Ships,* his second effort, was reviewed by a *Books* critic, who wrote, "The straightforwardness of the story is convincing; the events are so striking that a lurid style would have spoiled them. . . . As for South Street itself, the special charm of that waterfront pervades the story, and inspires most of its line drawings of the period." The *New York Times* added, "Mr. Daugherty has the knack of telling a lively tale that sustains the interest; he knows ships and writes of them with contagious enthusiasm. . . ."

Speaking of *Let 'Em Roll,* the *New York Herald Tribune* wrote, "The style is brisk, and the sketches are excellent and helpfully factual at the right places. Any boy of about twelve who is interested in movies from any angle will be absorbed. This is no very special piece of good writing, and the adventure is, of course, a fantastic bit of luck. But it is good to suggest that boys take an attitude toward the movies which is both critical and creative." The *New York Times* added, "In a pleasing style, mature but never heavy, the author succeeds, though his central character sometimes seems secondary to the information. . . ."

The *Chicago Tribune* review of *Where the Condor Nests* included, "Charles Daugherty, the author, and Peter Winkler, the young man in his book, both joined archaeological expeditions as photographers. As a result the reader gets the benefit of imagination and reality blended very neatly, with adventure coming out on top." *Kirkus* commented, "A fanciful story set in Peru combines photography, archaeology,

Strong and courageous, an expert skier and sailor, Dr. Nansen was also a scientist trained in zoology and biology. In his student days he had made his first voyage to northern waters aboard a sailing vessel. From that time on, his thoughts and aspirations were directed toward the polar regions. ■ (From *Searchers of the Sea* by Charles Michael Daugherty. Illustrated by Don Miller.)

and illegal treasure hunting for the stuff of its adventure, but the result is over-dressed melodrama rather than real excitement."

Mirror with a Memory was reviewed by a *New York Times* critic who called it, "A broad and stimulating introduction for the young to the whole of photography. . . . The emphasis throughout is on developing individual ability to see and to feel more than the obvious and to produce photographs that have significance and beauty."

The *Christian Science Monitor* called *The Great Archaeologists,* "A lively history of the development of modern archaeology told in terms of the men who contributed to its early days. Each chapter has its suspense and climax, each its appeal to spirited young adventurers. . . ." *Horn Book* commented, "This inviting-looking book traces the steps in the development of archaeology by briefly discussing the men whose work has advanced the science, from Johann

Joachim Winckelmann, whose writings in the middle eighteenth century set a precedent for a systematic method of collecting and evaluating antiquities, to Henri Breuil, the greatest twentieth-century authority on prehistoric cave art. . . . The book shows the progression of archaeology in which new areas and new phases (underwater exploration and the development of the carbon-14 dating technique, for example) are continually opening. . . ."

The *Christian Science Monitor* described *Robert Goddard: Trail Blazer to the Stars:* "The life story of America's greatest rocket pioneer, Robert Goddard, written by Charles Daugherty and illustrated by his father, James, reads like a joint labor of love. Youngsters 9 and up will find it warm, humorous, and often moving, yet compact and succinct. . . ."

HOBBIES AND OTHER INTERESTS: Traveling.

FOR MORE INFORMATION SEE: Bertha Mahony Miller and others, compilers, *Illustrators of Children's Books, 1946-1956,* Horn Book, 1958.

DAVIS, Paxton 1925-

PERSONAL: Born May 7, 1925, in Winston-Salem, N.C.; son of James Paxton (a tobacco executive) and Emily (McDowell) Davis; married Wylma Elizabeth Pooser, June 6, 1951 (divorced, 1971); married Peggy Camper, July 21, 1973; children: Elizabeth Keith, Anne Beckley, James Paxton III.

PAXTON DAVIS

Education: Virginia Military Institute, cadet, 1942-43; Johns Hopkins University, B.A., 1949. *Politics:* Democrat. *Religion:* Presbyterian. *Home:* Fincastle, Va. 24090. *Agent:* Curtis Brown Ltd., 575 Madison Ave., New York, N.Y. 10021.

CAREER: Reporter for *Winston-Salem Journal,* Winston-Salem, N.C., 1949-51, *Richmond Times Dispatch,* Richmond, Va., 1951-52, *Twin City Sentinel,* Winston-Salem, N.C., 1952-53; Washington and Lee University, Lexington, Va., assistant professor, 1953-58, associate professor, 1958-

63, professor of journalism, 1963-76. *Military service:* U.S. Army, 1943-46, served two years in China-Burma-India Theater; became sergeant; received two battle stars for Burma campaigns of 1944-45. *Awards, honors:* First place in interpretive reporting, Virginia Press Association, 1951; fellow, Bread Loaf Writers' Conference, 1956; Shenandoah Award for distinguished writing, 1956.

WRITINGS: Two Soldiers: Two Short Novels, Simon and Schuster, 1956; *The Battle of New Market: A Story of VMI,* Little, 1963; *One of the Dark Places,* Morrow, 1965; *The*

Ah, but a man's reach... ■ (From *A Flag at the Pole* by Paxton Davis. Illustrated by Harold Little.)

Seasons of Heroes, Morrow, 1967; *A Flag at the Pole*, Atheneum, 1976; *Ned*, Atheneum, 1978. Contributor of short stories to *Playboy, Hopkins Review, Bluebook*, and *Shenandoah*, poems to *Shenandoah* and *Lyric*. Book editor, *Roanoke Times*, Roanoke, Va., 1961—. Contributing editorial columnist to *Roanoke Times* and *World News*, 1976—.

FOR MORE INFORMATION SEE: Horn Book, April, 1977.

de la MARE, Walter   1873-1956
(Walter Ramal)

PERSONAL: Born April 25, 1873, in Charlton, Kent, England; died June 22, 1956, in Twickenham, Middlesex, England; buried at St. Paul's Cathedral in London; son of James Edward (a church warden) and Lucy Sophia (Browning; a distant relative of Robert Browning) de la Mare; married Constance Ingpen, 1899 (died, 1943); children: two daughters, two sons. *Education:* Attended St. Paul's Cathedral Choir School, London. *Home:* Twickenham, England.

CAREER: Poet and novelist. Worked for the Anglo-American Oil Company as a clerk and as writer and editor of its house organ, 1890-1908. Granted a Civil List pension, 1908, which enabled him to devote all of his time to writing. *Member:* Athenaeum Club. *Awards, honors:* James Tait Black Memorial Prize, 1922, for *Memoirs of a Midget;* Carnegie Medal, 1947, for *Collected Stories for Children;* Champion of Honour, 1948; Order of Merit, 1953; honorary degrees from several universities, including Oxford, Cambridge, St. Andrews, Bristol, and London.

WRITINGS—For children: (Under pseudonym Walter Ramal) *Songs of Childhood*, Longmans, Green, 1902, reprinted, Dover, 1968 [other editions illustrated by Estella Canziani, Longmans, Green, 1923; Marion Rivers-Moore, Faber, 1956]; *The Three Mulla-Mulgars*, Duckworth, 1910, reissued as *The Three Royal Monkeys* (illustrated by Mildred E. Eldridge), Faber, 1969 [other editions published under the original title illustrated by Dorothy P. Lathrop, Knopf, 1919; J. A. Shepherd, Selwyn & Blount, 1924]; *A Child's Day: A Book of Rhymes* (illustrated by Carine Cadby and Will Cadby), Constable, 1912 [another edition illustrated by Winifred Bromhall, Holt, 1923]; *Peacock Pie: A Book of Rhymes*, Constable, 1913, revised edition, Faber, 1969 [other editions illustrated by W. Heath Robinson, Constable, 1916; Jocelyn Crowe, Holt, 1936; Edward Ardizzone, Faber, 1946; Barbara Cooney, Knopf, 1961]; *Down-Adown-Derry: A Book of Fairy Poems* (illustrated by D. P. Lathrop), Holt, 1922; *Miss Jemima* (illustrated by Alec Buckels), B. Blackwell, 1925, reissued as *The Story of Miss Jemima* (illustrated by Nellie H. Farnam), Grosset & Dunlap, 1940; (with others) *Number Three Joy Street: A Medley of Prose and Verse for Boys and Girls*, Appleton, 1925; (with others) *Number Four Joy Street*, Appleton, 1926; (with others) *Number Five Joy Street*, Appleton, 1927; (editor with Thomas Quayle) *Readings* (illustrated by C. T. Nightingale), Knopf, 1927; *Old Joe* (illustrated by C. T. Nightingale), B. Blackwell, 1927; *Lucy* (illustrated by Hilda T. Miller), B. Blackwell, 1927; *Told Again: Old Tales Told Again* (illustrated by A. H. Watson), Knopf, 1927, reissued as *Tales Told Again* (illustrated by Alan Howard), Faber, 1959; (with others) *Number Six Joy Street*, Appleton, 1928; *Poems for Children*, Holt, 1930; (editor) *Tom Tiddler's Ground* (illustrations from Thomas Bewick), Collins, 1931 [another edition illustrated by Margery Gill, Knopf, 1962]; (with Harold Jones) *This Year: Next Year*, Holt, 1937; *The*

WALTER de la MARE

Old Lion, and Other Stories (illustrated by Irene Hawkins), Faber, 1942; *Mr. Bumps and His Monkey* (illustrated by D. P. Lathrop), J. C. Winston, 1942.

Poems: *Poems*, J. Murray, 1906; *The Listeners, and Other Poems*, Constable, 1912, Holt, 1916; *The Sunken Garden, and Other Poems*, Beaumont Press, 1917; *Motley, and Other Poems*, Holt, 1918; *The Veil, and Other Poems*, Constable, 1921, Holt, 1922; *Thus Her Tale* (illustrated by William Ogilvie), Porpoise Press, 1923; *Alone*, Faber & Gwyer, 1927; *Stuff and Nonsense*, Holt, 1927 [another edition illustrated by Margaret Wolpe, Faber, 1957]; *The Captive, and Other Poems*, Bowling Green Press, 1928; *Snowdrop* (illustrated by C. Guercio), Faber, 1929; *News* (illustrated by B. Freedman), Faber, 1930; *The Fleeting, and Other Poems*, Knopf, 1933; *Memory, and Other Poems*, Holt, 1938; *Bells and Grass: A Book of Rhymes* (illustrated by F. Rowland Emett), Faber, 1941, reissued, Viking, 1964 [another edition illustrated by D. P. Lathrop, Viking, 1942]; *Time Passes, and Other Poems*, Faber, 1942; *The Burning-Glass, and Other Poems*, Viking, 1945 [another edition illustrated by John Piper, Faber, 1946]; *Inward Companion*, Faber, 1951; *Winged Chariot*, Faber, 1951; *Winged Chariot, and Other Poems* (issued in England as two separate titles, *Inward Companion* and *Winged Chariot*), Viking, 1951; *O Lovely England, and Other Poems*, Faber, 1953, Viking, 1956; *The Winnowing Dream* (illustrated by Robin Jacques), Faber, 1954.

Novels: *Henry Brocken: His Travels and Adventures in the Rich, Strange, Scarce-Imaginable Regions of Romance*, J. Murray, 1904; *The Return*, Putnam, 1911; *Memoirs of a Midget*, Collins, 1921, Knopf, 1922; *At First Sight*, C. Gaige, 1928.

Short stories: *The Riddle, and Other Tales*, Knopf, 1923; *Broomsticks, and Other Tales*, Knopf, 1925; *The Connois-*

And he waited in the tree-top like a Starling,
 Till the Moon was gotten low;
When all the windows in the walls were darkened,
 He softly in did go.
■ (From *Peacock Pie* by Walter de la Mare. Illustrated by Barbara Cooney.)

C. Armstrong Gibbs), Beaumont Press, 1921 [other editions illustrated by D. P. Lathrop, Knopf, 1923; Gwendolen Raverat, Faber, 1942]; *Ding Dong Bell*, Knopf, 1924; (editor) *Eighteen-Eighties: Essays*, Macmillan, 1930, reprinted, Scholarly Press, 1971; *Desert Islands and Robinson Crusoe*, Farrar & Rinehart, 1930; *Lewis Carroll*, Faber, 1932, reprinted, Folcroft, 1973; *Early One Morning in the Spring*, Macmillan, 1935; *Poetry in Prose*, H. Milford, 1935, Oxford University Press, 1937, reprinted, Folcroft, 1969; *Pleasures and Speculations*, Faber, 1940, reprinted, Books for Libraries, 1969; *Chardin, 1699-1799*, Faber, 1948, Pitman, 1950; *Private View* (essays on literature), Faber, 1953.

Collections and selections: *Collected Poems, 1901-1918*, two volumes, Holt, 1920; *Selected Poems*, Holt, 1927; *Seven Short Stories* (illustrated by John Nash), Faber, 1931; *Poems, 1919 to 1934*, Constable, 1935, Holt, 1936; *Stories, Essays, and Poems*, Dent, 1941; *Best Stories of Walter de la Mare*, Faber, 1942; *Collected Rhymes and Verse* (illustrated by Berthold Wolpe), Faber, 1944 [another edition illustrated by Errol le Cain, Faber, 1970]; *Collected Stories for Children* (illustrated by I. Hawkins), Faber, 1947 [another edition illustrated by Robin Jacques, Faber, 1967]; *Rhymes and Verses: Collected Poems for Children* (illustrated by Elinore Blaisdell), Holt, 1947, reissued, 1967; *Collected Tales* (edited by Edward Wagenknecht), Knopf, 1950; *Selected Poems* (edited by R. N. Green-Armytage), Faber, 1954, reissued, 1973; *Walter de la Mare: A Selection from His Writings* (edited by Kenneth Hopkins), Faber, 1956; *Best Stories*, Faber, 1957; *The Story of Joseph* (illustrated by E. Ardizzone), Faber, 1958; *The Story of Moses* (illustrated by E. Ardizzone), Faber, 1959; *A Penny a Day* (illustrated by P. Kennedy), Knopf, 1960; *The Story of Samuel and Saul* (illustrated by E. Ardizzone), Faber, 1960; *Poems* (edited by Eleanor Graham; illustrated by M. Gill), Penguin, 1962; *A Choice of de la Mare's Verse* (edited, and with an introduction, by W. H. Auden), Faber, 1963; *The Complete Poems of Walter de la Mare*, Faber, 1969, Knopf, 1970; *Secret Laughter* (illustrated by M. Gill), Penguin, 1969; *Eight Tales*, Arkham House, 1971.

seur, and Other Stories, Knopf, 1926; *On the Edge: Short Stories*, Faber, 1930, Knopf, 1931; *The Lord Fish* (illustrated by Rex Whistler), Faber, 1933; *A Froward Child*, Faber, 1934; *Nap, and Other Stories*, Nelson, 1936; *The Wind Blows Over*, Macmillan, 1936, reprinted, Books for Libraries, 1970; *The Picnic, and Other Stories*, Faber, 1941; *The Magic Jacket, and Other Stories* (illustrated by Irene Hawkins), Faber, 1943 [another edition illustrated by Paul Kennedy, Knopf, 1962]; *The Scarecrow, and Other Stories* (illustrated by I. Hawkins), Faber, 1945; *The Dutch Cheese* (illustrated by D. P. Lathrop), Knopf, 1931 [another edition illustrated by I. Hawkins, Faber, 1946]; *A Beginning, and Other Stories*, Faber, 1955; *Ghost Stories*, Folio Society, 1956.

Editor: *Come Hither: A Collection of Rhymes and Poems for the Young of All Ages*, Knopf, 1923, revised edition, 1969; *Stories from the Bible* (illustrated by Theodore Nadejen), Cosmopolitan Book, 1929 [other editions illustrated by I. Hawkins, Faber, 1947; E. Ardizzone, Knopf, 1961]; *Animal Stories*, Faber, 1939, Scribner, 1940; *Behold this Dreamer: Of Reverie, Night, Sleep, Lovedreams, Nightmare, Death, the Unconscious, the Imagination, Divination, the Artist, and Kindred Subjects*, Knopf, 1939, reprinted, Greenwood Press, 1969; *Love*, Faber, 1943, W. Morrow, 1946.

Other: *Rupert Brooke and the Intellectual Imagination: A Lecture*, Sidgwick & Jackson, 1919, Harcourt, 1920, reprinted, Haskell House, 1972; *Crossings: A Fairy Play* (music by

ADAPTATIONS—Movies: "Reading Out Loud: Archibald MacLeish" (readings of Walter de la Mare's poems; 28 minutes; black & white), Westinghouse Broadcasting, 1960.

SIDELIGHTS: **April 25, 1873.** Born at Charlton, a village in the county of Kent, England. His father, James Edward, descendent from an old Huguenot family, was a church warden. Through his mother, Lucy Sophia Browning, he was related to the poet Robert Browning. "What a bundle of skills and ideas one inherits. Is there any scientist who denies that we inherit ideas? ... Aren't children sometimes old, just as old people may be young? Aren't we born with all the talents we shall ever have: isn't the bucket as full as it ever will be? If we are born with a capacity for courage, we shall be courageous, if the occasion arises; if not, not. You can't acquire courage or any other virtue if you haven't got it: you can only improve it with practice." [Russell Brain, *Tea With Walter de la Mare,* Faber, 1957.[1]]

"I was carried off to my christening, a few days after my earthly footlights went up, transferred puking and puling into my godmother's arms, and thence into my Uncle Abraham's. Whether or not this swaddled-up infant which he poised over the font emitted the customary challenge, whether or not, that is, I cried, I cannot recall. Nor her, nor him, alas! After that ceremony, the play really began. How much of comedy, how much of tragedy, of farce and melodrama was to go to its unfolding? Of this, at that not wholly passive moment perhaps, I hadn't presumably the faintest inkling. Time alone could show, as indeed it has." [Walter de la Mare, introduction to *When I Was a Child,* edited by Edward Wagenknecht, Dutton, 1946.[2]]

1877. Father died and the family moved to London. De la Mare was four. Although he was raised by his mother, in later years he became increasingly fond of his father whom he had hardly known. "How near to you are people in your imagination, for example, someone who has died? Do they exist in space at all? Can you go back in memory to your childhood and if so, how big are you then? Can you remember putting your fingers on the edge of the table when your eyes were just level with it?"[1]

1878. De la Mare was educated at the Choir school of St. Paul's Cathedral. "I can remember myself at the age of five sitting before the fire, with two nice old ladies watching me eat calves' feet jelly, which was quite tasteless because I was so homesick, and I can still feel the relief I felt when the maid came and said: 'You're called for.' "[1]

"Even at the age of five—or less—we seem to have been able to summarise the kind, the characters, the personalities, and even the more or less concealed relations between a complete bevy of grown-ups. How?—with so little (and yet how much) of earthly life in our new knapsacks? We neither argue, analyse, nor explain; we know. Not that early memo-

(From *The Lord Fish* by Walter de la Mare. Illustrated by Rex Whistler.)

ries are necessarily of greater value than those we now derive from our daily routine when awake or asleep, in dream. But they are apt to be more intense and salient, sharper, more emotional and vivifying, less alloyed with prejudice and reflection.

"Nor, assuredly, is a young child unable to reflect, or to criticise, or to test the dictates of his elders. Little Edmund Gosse once prayed to a chair. And I myself, when I was very young used to pray (not to) but for the Devil.

"'Early memories,' all of them. But *how* early is the earliest likely to be? How far back at most into one's primal existence can one carry the flickering lamp of Memory—and without delusion? How deep into the ooze of the else-forgotten can the plummet sound? Is, after all, the acutely conscious mind of a child here for the first time? Not so, declares Wordsworth, in his famous Ode. Our birth is but a sleep and a *forgetting*. And isn't it Plato who declares that, rather than learning the things of our world, we recollect them? Moreover, the ideas, or divinations, of Henry Vaughan, of Traherne and William Blake, concerning the innate simplicity, innocence and enraptured acceptance of Nature's splendour and loveliness, are not necessarily opposed to this view:

> Happy those early days when I
> Shined in my angel infancy,
> Before I understood this place
> Appointed for my second race"[2]

1889-1890. Founded and edited *The Choristers' Journal* for St. Paul's Cathedral Choir School. Reportedly, he was a good student. "It was an Archbishop of Canterbury who gave me the first money I earned. When I was a chorister at St. Paul's, they had a service in connexion with a pan-Anglican congress, and the Archbishop came, and I had to hold, or uphold, or generally keep from harm his train. He gave me half-a-crown, which he had to borrow from his chaplain. I remember the Bishop of the Niger was there: he was as black as your hat, but I suppose that is what you would expect."[1]

Spring, 1890. Left school at the age of seventeen and became a bookkeeper in the city offices of the Anglo-American Oil Company. He remained with the company for eighteen years, but in his spare time he wrote short stories and poems. "We are said to grow up. In physique we do; in knowledge and experience we grow wider; we may wither at the root. Do we intrinsically much change? 'I can't help thinking,' says Mr. Forest Reid, a faithful friend indeed of the young, 'that I was in those early days very much what I am now.' That too is my own impression. We grow in many directions, better or worse, but not, intrinsically, very different. If this is true of mankind in general, then we may all happily look forward to sharing familiar company when we are very old—on the verge of our second childhood, in fact. Then we shall more easily be able perhaps 'to make both ends meet!' "[2]

1893. "I remember when I was about twenty, meeting a girl at a dance. She wasn't very forthcoming, and to tease her I said: 'You will always remember to-night.' She said: 'Shall I? Why?' and I said: 'You'll remember these curtains'—and one or two things. Now I remember them all, and I expect she has long ago forgotten. By telling other people they will remember things, you remember them yourself."[1]

1895. "Kismet" a short story appeared in *The Sketch* and represented his first break into print.

1899. Married Constance Ingpen. Became the father of four children: two daughters, two sons. "I approve of marriage—I think that's the way to put it—but that is no reason why one should disapprove of unmarriage. It seems to me more a question of convention than of ethics or morals."[1]

1902. First book of poems, *Songs of Childhood,* published under the anagrammatic pseudonym, Walter Ramal. "... Owing to the kindness of Andrew Lang [then reader for Longmans, who published this collection] and of Charles Longman, my first book of rhymes had appeared, *Songs of Childhood.* First snowdrop of the year, first primrose, first cuckoo-call and returning swallows, first memories, first love—all such firsts may carry with them a thrill or delight or edge or sweetness, and perhaps even a magic, of their own. So, however faulty it may be, however far short it may have fallen of hope or wish or intention—so may a first book. There is a peculiar joy in seeing what has been all but a secret source of interest and pleasure out in the open, so to speak. Some of the rhymes in that collection had been written during the last years of Queen Victoria, and had then been shared solely with my mother. Moreover I hid myself behind a pen-name. Charming—with its pale-blue cloth, parchment spine, gilded Longman *Ship,* and Dickie Doyle frontispiece—charming though the little volume was in outward appearance, its welcome hardly resembled that bestowed on hot cakes. But there it actually was, in print." [Walter de la Mare, introduction to *Bells and Grass,* Viking, 1942.[3]]

1904. First novel, *Henry Brocken,* published. "The creative artist does not make up a character bit by bit; he finds him whole.

"Suppose I were to say: 'Her footsteps were so light that she passed along the passage without the housemaid's perceiving her.' Already you have a description of two people, and the housemaid who did not 'perceive her' is a different person from one who did not notice her. This selection of the precise word is something that Henry James was good at, but Chekhov even better.

"Which seems more real, a character in fiction, someone you have imagined, someone you have dreamed about, or someone you know but who is absent? Most people say a character in fiction, but how odd! Why should a character in fiction seem more real than an actual person?"[1]

1906. *Poems* published. "Why must a poem have a meaning? We don't ask what is the meaning of a piece of music—why of a poem?"[1]

1908. At the age of thirty-five, left the oil company. De la Mare was granted a civil list pension which enabled him to devote full time to writing.

1910. Second novel, *The Return,* published. That same year, *The Three Mulla-Mulgars,* a story written for and read aloud to the author's four children, was published.

1913. *Peacock Pie* published. This book of rhymes established de la Mare as a writer. "In 1913, another collection of rhymes, called *Peacock Pie,* was published. Needless to say, this title for it was not in the least intended to suggest a delicacy. Indeed, I had never so much as tasted a peacock pie, although I had frequently feasted my eyes on one in the

(From *This Year: Next Year* by Walter de la Mare and Harold Jones.)

I twist and turn
I creep, I prowl,
Likewise does he,
The Crafty soul...
■ (From *Bells and Grass* by Walter de la Mare.
Illustrated by Dorothy P. Lathrop.)

windows of Mr. Pimm's restaurant in Cheapside—the bird itself, or rather its lovely but vacant plumage, seated in splendour upon the pastry's moulded upper-crust. No. The book contained a piece called 'The Mad Prince'; and that begins:

'Who said, "Peacock Pie?"'

Hence the spectacular title."[3]

1921. Only play, "Crossings," published. The first performance of this play was given on June 21, 1919 by the boys of Wick School, Hove. That same year, *Memoirs of a Midget,* illustrated by Florence Thompson, de la Mare's daughter, was published.

1923. *Come Hither,* the first of many anthologies de la Mare was to compile, was published.

1924. *Ding Dong Bell* published. The book consisted entirely of imaginary epitaphs. "What does all this preoccupation with graves mean? Isn't it perhaps one up for the grave? It can't be such a bad place. Have you noticed that we always attribute consciousness to the dead—imagine them lying there, six feet deep, and aware of their loneliness? Can a corpse feel, when it's been dead a week?"[1]

1929. Edited *Stories from the Bible.* "The stories contained in this volume are versions of but a few of the narratives related in the first nine books of the Old Testament of the Bible, 'that inestimable treasure which excelleth all the riches of the earth.'

"The Bible, it is said, is not being read nowadays so much as it used to be: while there *was* a time when, it is recorded, a load of hay would be paid gladly for the loan of a manuscript Testament for an hour a day. Wholly apart from the profound truth that 'simple men of wit may be edified much to heavenly living by reading and knowing of the Old Testament,' this statement, if true, implies a loss beyond measure

to mind and heart, and particularly to the young—its wisdom and divination, truth and candour, simplicity and directness. All that man is or feels or (in what concerns him closely) thinks; all that he loves or fears or delights in, grieves for, desires and aspires to is to be found in it, either expressed or implied. As for beauty, though this was not its aim, and the word is not often used in it—it is 'excellent in beauty'; and poetry dwells in it as light dwells upon a mountain and on the moss in the crevices of its rocks. In what other book—by mere mention of them—are even natural objects made in the imagination so whole and fair; its stars, its well-springs, its war-horse, its almond tree?

"That there are difficulties for those unfamiliar with its pages no one with any knowledge of the subject would deny. The very simplicity and austerity of the Old Testament stories, their conciseness, the slight changes that have occurred in the meaning or bearing of English words, occasional obscurities and repetitions in the text, are among them. My small endeavour has been to lighten some of these difficulties, while yet keeping as close to the spirit of the text as I am capable of. In many passages I have kept even to the letter. Apart from that, remembrance of what the matchless originals as in the Bible itself meant to me when I was a child is still fresh and vivid in mind, and these renderings are little more than an attempt to put that remembrance as completely as I can into words." [Introduction to *Stories from the Bible,* edited by Walter de la Mare, Knopf, 1961.[4]]

1931. *Tom Tiddler's Ground,* an anthology for children was published. The anthology was such a success that a second edition was called for in 1932. In his own introduction, de la Mare instructed the reader on the subject of poetry. "There are many kinds of rhymes in this book—mere jingles, game-rhymes, nursery rhymes and poems. Some are old, some are new. Some are rather roughly made, they jog and stumble when they ought to dance: others are among the most lovely and perfect things that have ever been made out of English words. But every one has its own kind of goodness, and gives its own kind of pleasure, and many of them I have loved since I was a child.

"None the less, this is only a little book. It gives only a glimpse of the great feast of English poetry. But that is much. There was once an Irishman who made a henhouse for his chickens. When it was finished, he cut a large hole in the door for his full-sized hens to go in at and to come out of—and a little hole for the chicks! Still, whichever one they used, they *all came out.*

"They all came out into the same great farmyard—with its ricks and its barns and its moss-grown stones, and its grass and its pigs and its geese and its ducks and its wild birds, and its fields and meadows over the wall. And the woods beyond *them,* and the hills beyond them, and the blue sky with its clouds and skylarks beyond and above them too. And so into the full light of the morning. In the same way, from the rhymes and poems in this book, you can go out into the wonderful riches of mind and heart revealed in our great English poetry.

"Not all the poems in it are merry, lively and sparkling, not all are so plain and simple that they almost sing themselves. There are enough of these, however, to prove that poetry is not dry or dull or something you have to wait to enjoy until you are grown up. Why, even babies of three can chirrup and dance to 'Mary, Mary!' and to 'Old King Cole.' Some of the poems are serious, some are tragic; many are easy to understand, a few will be difficult. But I do not know of any true poem, however sorrowful it may be, that is not a comfort to read and to remember and a good deal else beside. Nor do I know of any true poem, however difficult it may seem at the first reading of it, that has not become much clearer as soon as I have begun to *try* to understand it. Some poems may always remain difficult; and there are many other things in life and in books that only the wisest can understand. Still, one can at least try to understand, and as a wise friend who loves both poetry and children once said to me, it is often what seem to be the simplest things that most need explaining.

"We can, too, and particularly when we are young, delight in the sound of the words of a poem, immensely enjoy them—the music and rhythm and lilt, feel its enchantment and treasure it in memory, without realising its *full* meaning—just as we can listen to a wren or blackbird singing without knowing what that singing means.

"It is best, therefore, to try to find your way in a poem for yourself. It is next best to find someone to help you who not only cares for it but has also had to find his or her way, and may in turn have been helped in doing so. In this book I have tried, where it seemed wanted, and very often when I wanted it myself, to give this help.

"Apart from meaning, many questions may be asked about poems, the answers to which will be full of interest and yet not necessary to the enjoyment of the poems. Why, for example, Old King Cole called for three fiddlers and not for seven; who—*if* he was ever anybody else—Jack Horner really was; why such and such a line of a poem is good grammar though it may not seem so; when any particular poem was written, and what kind of man the writer was; and last, why one *ought* to like it. All such knowledge may be interesting and valuable, but it is not necessary to one's delight; and there are very few 'oughts' in regard to the love of poetry. Let your eyes, mind, heart and spirit feed on it, and see what happens.

"Nevertheless, it is always good, so far as it is possible, to *understand* what one reads. A deep and vivid understanding only adds to the joy it gives, and a few words may clear away a difficulty.... Where, however, in the pages that follow, there seems to be no difficulty and there is yet an explanation, the explanation can easily be left unread. Besides, I may not always have given the right explanation! In any case always go back to the poem again after reading anything that may have been said about it.

"To learn to love books and reading is one of the very best things that can happen to anybody. So, too, with pictures and with music. Poetry in particular *wears* well. The longer you care for it in itself the better it gets. You can see the spring's first tuft of primroses, or watch a tom-tit with a nut, or the evening star, or the kitchen fire, or a pond in the moonlight, or a butterfly on a wild rose, or your mother's face, or even a cat washing her own—you can do all these things ninety-nine times and still find them as new and lively and odd and mysterious and interesting at the hundredth. And so it is with old rhymes and all the old tales and poems one cares for most. Love them once, you love them always.

"Read slowly; *say* the words over either aloud or to yourself as you read; listen carefully to the sound of them as well as to the sense; try to see and hear in your mind all that the poem tells of; think while you read; and don't give any poem up merely because you fail to like it immediately. You never can tell; sooner or later there may come a moment when you

They laid him lifeless on a bier,
They lapped him up in ermine;
They lit a candle, inches thick,
His Uncle preached the sermon.
■ (From *Bells and Grass* by Walter de la Mare. Illustrated by Dorothy P. Lathrop.)

will hear 'in the silence of morning the song of the bird.'" [Introduction to *Tom Tiddler's Ground,* edited by Walter de la Mare, Knopf, 1961.[5]]

1932. *Lewis Carroll* published. De la Mare had the opportunity to meet the original Alice on one occasion, "... when she was an old woman, rather peevish, and there was nothing of Alice left in her at all....

"I once wrote a book about [Lewis Carroll], and I said something which I still think is true—that he did something which had never been done before. There is nothing like the world of Alice, and the poems and parodies are wonderful. Isn't it curious that Lewis Carroll became attached to little girls, and pushed them out when they became—what was it?—twelve? I suppose Freud would have had a name for it, but I would much rather not know what it is."[1]

1942. *Bells and Grass,* a book of rhymes, was published when the author was nearly seventy. The introduction, written by de la Mare, began on rather a sad note. "As this small volume will be the last collection of its kind that I shall make, I should like to explain in a few words how it came into being—notwithstanding the days in which we are now living.

"About a year ago I was looking through a jackdaw jumble of old papers and old letters—the contents of a packing case, a Tate sugar-box, which had been left undisturbed since 1924. A bonfire merrily blazing away under the blue skies of early May soon disposed of most of this hoard. But among a

In a few days the ship put off from the quay and out of
the Port of London gliding over the sparkling Thames
(for in those days its waters were clear as crystal and
full of fish), and so out to sea. ■ (From *Tales Told
Again* by Walter de la Mare. Illustrated by Alan
Howard.)

few old manuscripts in the box I came across a commonplace book, bound in black leather. It had been completely
forgotten; yet at a glimpse it at once came welling up into
memory again. About twenty pages of it had been crammed,
top to bottom, with pencil scribblings, many of them dated
1905, the remainder of a date not later, I think, than 1906.
Some of these were marked 'Copied.' A few are still incom-
pletely readable even by the writer of them!

"The rhymes, then, in this forgotten old commonplace book
were 'made-up' more than thirty-five years ago. It is rather
odd experience to read again anything written in the distant
past which has long ago passed out of recollection—even if it
be only an old letter to butcher, baker, or candle-stickmaker.
It is like chancing on a half-forgotten photograph—as I also
did that morning: the photograph of a moon-faced boy in a
surplice. It may be a happy experience; it may be a sadden-
ing one; it may be a mingling of both.

"A last word may be said about the rhymes themselves. As
with those in the earlier books, some of them tell of actual
and personal memories. Most of them, whether fanciful or
not, are concerned with the imagined and the imaginary. The
'I' in a rhyme is not necessarily 'me.' A small boy, for example, who is not even a nephew-much-removed tells how he
lost his 'magic' stone called *Kiph*. Imaginary children of
differing sorts and ages (though all of the same parentage)
are speaking in 'Nicoletta,' in 'The Voice,' in 'The Feather,'

in 'The Shadow,' in 'Somewhere.' It is a small girl who in
'Poor Bird' discovers that a fish hasn't any toes. An imaginary grown-up, looking back into the past, is rhyming in 'No
Bed,' another in 'The Small Phantom.' Another and a
woman this time—is watching her Charles in '*Hark!*' sea-
gulls are squawking in 'The Storm,' and nobody in particular
is relating the tale that is all end and little beginning called
'Pigs.' And so with the rest.

"There was perhaps little need to make this explanation.
What otherwise, the contents of this book are in themselves,
it is certainly not for me to say. To write anything solely to
please someone else is rather dangerous; and particularly if it
happens to be in rhyme. To write for one's own delight and
out of sheer impulse and desire to do so is less dangerous,
though one may of course keep such things to oneself! To
hope to please others with what has been so written is a wil-
dish aspiration, but an aspiration which it should not be too
difficult even to condone. It may not be *too* difficult, perhaps, even when the writer is distinctly 'old' in birthdays,
and when those 'others'—whatever *their* age in birthdays
may be—were not only born young, but young will always
remain.''[3]

1943. Wife, Constance, died. "To be in love is to recognise
the divine in the loved one, and to be divine yourself.''[1]

1947. *Collected Stories for Children* awarded the Carnegie
Medal of the Library Association. The writer of *Chosen for
Children* (published by the Library Association) said, "Walter de la Mare's *Collected Stories for Children* was a new
book of 1947 in a bibliographical, not a literary, sense. Each
of the seventeen tales had been printed before, one as long
ago as 1900. The publication of the *Collected Stories* offered, however, the last opportunity for the Library Association to recognise the unique contribution which Walter de la
Mare had made to children's literature. For nearly half a
century he had devoted to children the same qualities which
had made him so distinctive and memorable a writer of prose
and verse for adults. No other writer had given so gener-
ously of his best to children, so that it was impossible to say
that *Peacock Pie* was inferior to *Motley* or *The Three Mulla-
Mulgars* to *The Return*. It was therefore a cause for rejoicing that the Library Association had interpreted in so liberal
a spirit its regulations by honouring a book which so richly
summed up a life devoted to the delight and the understanding of children.... *Collected Stories for Children* is representative of the creative work of forty years. It has, nevertheless, a remarkable unity in mood and style, however
diverse the subject-matter and the treatment.... Walter de
la Mare is in all these stories a fine craftsman and a sensitive
observer. He never condescends to his readers, and he
never forgets that, of all the wonders in the world which he
explores so profoundly and so sadly, the greatest wonder is
the child's fresh and penetrating vision.'' [Leonard Clark,
The Bodley Head Monographs: Walter de la Mare, Bodley
Head, 1960.[6]]

1948. Named Companion of Honour by King George VI.
De la Mare was awarded honorary degrees from several
universities, including Oxford, Cambridge, St. Andrews,
Bristol, and London. Russell Brain, a friend of the elderly de
la Mare, recalled the poet reminiscing on one of these receptions of an honorary degree from London University when
that institution honored another famous Englishman as well
as de la Mare. "He recalled receiving an honorary degree
from London University at the same time as Churchill. They
sat side by side on the platform, and in the course of the
Chancellor's speech Churchill turned to W. J. [de la Mare]

By the kindness of the captain of *The Old Lion*, it had been arranged that Jasper should come aboard—it was his wish—and return to Africa. ■ (From *Mr. Bumps and His Monkey* by Walter de la Mare. Illustrated by Dorothy Lathrop.)

WALTER de la MARE

and said: 'What a lovely scene!' Some minutes later he said the same thing again. Churchill had to reply on behalf of the honorary graduates, and recalled his schooldays, and declined 'mensa.' He said that he hadn't paid much attention to learning when he was at school, and now he was sorry. However, there was one compensation: it enabled him to stay under one good English master. W. J. said that it tickled him to sit with Churchill, both wearing robes: it reminded him of two of his old aunts.''[1]

1953. Awarded the Order of Merit. The poet was eighty. ''It is odd, when you are preparing for something all your life, to be surprised when it happens; as though you were dribbling across a field and surprised when you scored a goal.''[1]

June, 1954. Fell on the back of his head and slightly injured his brain. The accident had an extraordinary effect on him. Thereafter, de la Mare had difficulty writing and visualising his surroundings. Because of his symptoms he became increasingly interested in experiencing in his own person the relationship between the brain and the mind. Two months after his injury he wrote a friend: ''I was absolutely delighted at your kindly smile over my suggestion that the brain might be compared, not very strictly, to a lump of three-dimensional mosaic (which of course can be 'cracked' by a fall).... My symptoms haven't yet ceased. They make life rather odd at times and I wonder when 'they' will notice it....''[1]

1955. De la Mare was comfortably established at his home at Twickenham. ''I have hardly been outside this room for two years, and I ought not to get the credit for being philosophical about it, for I hardly feel it as a deprivation. It is the inward life that matters. This is true of love. You may love someone who is unworthy, and whom you know to be unworthy. And is not interest a form of love? Admiration certainly is.''[1]

April, 1956. At age eighty-three de la Mare wrote: ''How old, then, are the young? And how young is it possible for the old in years to remain—without, that is, being merely immature, undergrown, or silly? Is this in fact a question of age, of mere time? I doubt if it is. Even one's body seems in certain respects to be independent of the mechanical hands of a clock, and of an earth spinning on in space, as we are told, through its four strange and lovely seasons, in its annual revolution round the sun. We know very little what we mean by Time. I have seen a baby apparently of only twenty-four hours' experience in this world that yet was not only the minute image of, but also looked even older than its grandmother. I have seen grandmothers with eyes as guileless and youthful as a frank and happy seven-year-old's; and, clearly, with hearts to match. The body ages: that is certain. No old ewe, whatever its inclinations may be, can gambol, leap, and pirouette like a lamb. Every seven years, it is said, as with an umbrella that has been repaired—new ferrule, new stick, new handle, new ribs, new silk or alpaca—the body itself is renewed. Yet it continues to age and at last wears out.

''None the less, handle to ferrule, we ourselves remain much the same umbrella. The self within is still the self within, however much knowledge and experience, and whatever treasures of memory it may have acquired. It is still the silkworm in its cocoon, whatever the quality of the silk may be. As the years go by, we put away childish things. We have to. And yet what we love and delight in when we are young we may continue to love and delight in when we are old; and not much less ardently, perhaps. So with all that is meant by heart, feelings, mind, the fancy, and the imagination.''[3]

May, 1956. Two years after his brain injury, de la Mare was still pondering the concept of consciousness. ''Our whole perception depends on our body, so when we die we lose not only our bodies but our whole apparatus of thought: we leave two vacua. So everyone should try to write something, so that some of his thought may be left. . . . It was Berkeley who said we don't perceive a tree, but only our idea of it. But if that is true it seems odd that no one ever noticed it before. What do we perceive when we perceive a tree? It is not the specialist's tree, nor the tree's tree. There can be nothing but a lot of different people's ideas. Do you think a tree is conscious? A friend of mine is writing a history of consciousness. If you had to write a history of consciousness where would you begin?''[1]

June 21, 1956. Became ill during the night. It was clear that he was dying. He remarked to a friend who visited his death bed, ''All these onlookers! There are so many of them. I wonder where they come from.''[1]

June 22, 1956. Died at Twickenham, Middlesex, England at the age of eighty-three. De la Mare was buried in the crypt of St. Paul's Cathedral. ''How much less afflicting at times would my present have been if I had had the fore sight to remind myself how beguiling it would appear as the past.'' [John Atkins, *Walter de la Mare: An Explanation,* C. J. Temple, 1947.[7]]

FOR MORE INFORMATION SEE: Edward B. Shanks, "Poetry of Mr. Walter de la Mare," in his *First Essays on Literature,* Collins, 1923; John Freeman, "Walter de la Mare," in his *English Portraits and Essays,* Hodder & Stoughton, 1924; Rodolphe L. Megroz, *Walter de la Mare: A Biography and Critical Study,* Hodder & Stoughton, 1924, reprinted, R. West, 1973; Coulson Kernahan, "Walter de la Mare," in his *Five More Famous Living Poets,* Butterworth, 1928; Edward L. Davison, "Walter de la Mare," in his *Some Modern Poets,* Harper, 1928; Forrest Reid, *Walter de la Mare,* Faber, 1929, reprinted, R. West, 1973; Rica Brenner, "Walter de la Mare," in her *Ten Modern Poets,* Harcourt, 1930; Thomas J. Hardy, "Faerie Way of Writing," in his *Books on the Shelf,* P. Allan, 1934; John A. Atkins, *Walter de la Mare: An Exploration,* Temple, 1947, reprinted, Haskell House, 1975; Edward Wagenknecht (editor), *When I Was a Child,* Dutton, 1946; John Atkins, *Walter de la Mare: An Explanation,* C. J. Temple, 1947; Harold H. Child, "Mr. de la Mare's World," in his *Essays and Reflections,* Cambridge University Press, 1948; *Tribute to Walter de la Mare on His Seventy-Fifth Birthday,* Faber, 1948; Henry C. Duffin, *Walter de la Mare: A Study of His Poetry,* Sidgwick & Jackson, 1949, reprinted, Folcroft, 1973.

Graham Greene, "Walter de la Mare's Short Stories," in his *Lost Childhood, and Other Essays,* Viking, 1952; Kenneth Hopkins, *Walter de la Mare,* Longmans, Green, 1953, reissued, 1969; David Cecil, *Walter de la Mare: A Checklist,* Cambridge University Press, 1956; Russell Brain, *Tea with Walter de la Mare,* Faber, 1957; Paula Bianco, "Walter de la Mare," *Horn Book,* June, 1957; E. Farjeon, "Walter de la Mare," *Horn Book,* June, 1957; H. Read, "Walter de la Mare," *Horn Book,* June, 1957; D. Cecil, "Prose Tales of Walter de la Mare," in his *Fine Art of Teaching,* Bobbs-Merrill, 1957; Frank Magill, editor, *Cyclopedia of World Authors,* Harper, 1958; Louis Untermeyer, *Lives of the Poets,* Simon & Schuster, 1959; Leonard Clark, *The Bodley Head Monograph: Walter de la Mare,* Bodley Head, 1960; Doris R. McCrosson, *Walter de la Mare,* Twayne, 1966; Brian Doyle, editor, *Who's Who of Children's Literature,* Schocken Books, 1968; Forrest Reid, *Walter de la Mare: A Critical Study,* Scholarly Press, 1970.

For children: Stanley J. Kunitz and Howard Haycraft, editors, *Junior Book of Authors,* second edition revised, H. W. Wilson, 1951; Leonard Clark, *Walter de la Mare,* Walck, 1961; Laura Benét, *Famous Poets for Young People,* Dodd, Mead, 1964.

Obituaries: *New York Times,* June 23, 1956; *Illustrated London News,* June 30, 1956; *Newsweek,* July 2, 1956; *Publishers Weekly,* July 2, 1956; *Time,* July 2, 1956; *Commonweal,* July 6, 1956; *Wilson Library Bulletin,* September, 1956; *Americana Annual, 1957; Britannica Book of the Year, 1957.*

DENSLOW, W(illiam) W(allace) 1856-1915

PERSONAL: Born May 5, 1856, in Philadelphia, Pennsylvania; died March 29, 1915; son of William Wallace, Sr. (a botanist) and Jane Eva Denslow; married Annie McCartney, 1882 (divorced); married Ann Waters Holden, 1896 (divorced); married Frances Golsen Doolittle, December 24, 1903. *Education:* Studied at the Cooper Union Institute, 1870-71, and the National Academy of Design, 1872-73, both in New York City.

W.W. Denslow, ca. 1859.

CAREER: Illustrator of books and magazines and designer of costumes and scenery. Early jobs included office boy for the Orange Judd Company, painting advertisements on barns, illustrating atlases, drawing local landmarks, and lecturing on art history, and working as a cowboy; did newspaper work for the *Chicago Herald* and the *Rocky Mountain News* (Denver), and also worked on periodicals in San Francisco.

WRITINGS—All illustrated by the author: *Denslow's Picture Books,* series of 18 booklets, G. W. Dillingham, 1903; (with Paul West) *Pearl and the Pumpkin,* G. W. Dillingham, 1904; (with Dudley A. Bragdon) *Billy Bounce,* G. W. Dillingham, 1906; *When I Grow Up,* Century, 1909.

Illustrator: L. Frank Baum, *Father Goose: His Book,* G. M. Hill, 1899; Baum, *The Wonderful Wizard of Oz,* G. M. Hill, 1900, reissued as *The Wizard of Oz,* Rand McNally, 1971; Baum, *Dot and Tot of Merryland,* G. M. Hill, 1901; (editor) *Mother Goose,* P. McClure, 1901; Clement C. Moore, *Night before Christmas,* G. W. Dillingham, 1902; Isabel M. Johnston, *Jeweled Toad,* Bobbs-Merrill, 1907.

Also author of a series of newspaper stories entitled *Scarecrow and the Tin Man.*

SIDELIGHTS: **May 5, 1856.** Born in Philadelphia, the son of a botanist, the family relocated quite often during his childhood. He had particularly fond memories of family life along New York's Hudson River. "In the summer I rowed a skiff and in winter sailed an ice boat. I not only had as good a

(From *The Wonderful Wizard of Oz* by L. Frank Baum. Illustrated by W.W. Denslow.)

time as ever fell the lot of a boy, but I also unconsciously laid the foundation for a love of nature. I am quite sure that I would not now appreciate the beauties of landscape quite as keenly as I do had it not been for a constant association with scenery such as the Hudson alone affords." [Douglas Greene and Michael P. Hearn, *W. W. Denslow,* Clarke Historical Library, 1976.[1]]

In his drawings, Denslow displayed an exuberant sense of humor, sketching caricatures of his teachers who were not amused by the young artist. "There was precious little printed then for a boy to laugh at, and I made up my mind that someday I'd furnish . . . [children] the laugh material."[1]

1870. Attended Cooper Institute. Took drawing course and joined the "Salmagundi Club," a group of bohemian artists who delighted in drawing self-parodies.

1872. Entered the National Academy of Design. Continued his studies with particular emphasis on drawing the human body.

June 1, 1872. Denslow's first published picture appeared in *Hearth and Home.* It was a picture puzzle woodcut.

1874. Worked on *Daily Graphic,* the first American daily pictorial newspaper.

1876. Between jobs, Denslow accepted commission to draw advertisements for chewing tobacco. "I turned out what I considered a fair job and forgot all about it. Shortly after, however, I made a trip through the New England states, and wherever I went I was confronted with that tobacco sign. At

first I was rather pleased at seeing my handiwork so profusely displayed, but soon I began to see the defects in my work—and I acknowledge now they were many and glaring. I grew to detest this particular showcard, and the more I saw of it the more repugnant it became. But I could not escape it. At the hotel, the barbershop, the grocery—even on the fences—this horrid example of crude art stared me in the face. It became my *bete noir.* I shivered with apprehension wherever I went, I dreamed of it at night, I trembled lest anyone should discover that my hand drew the horrible object."[1]

1882. After some years of wandering, settled in Philadelphia. Opened an artist's firm and married Annie McCartney.

1883. Denslow and wife separated. He began drinking heavily. A son was born, whom Denslow later refused to acknowledge.

1885. Moved to New York. Denslow drew theatrical posters and humorous caricatures of famous personalities.

1888. Became newspaper artist for *Chicago Herald.* He also became an alcoholic and took the cure.

1890. Went West to work for the *Denver Rocky Mountain News.* "In a hut high up in the Rockies a miner had posted my tobacco card. A cow puncher on a Colorado ranch had the horror stuck up in the back of his shed. Absolutely I could not escape. For years the card continued to haunt me. Even yet I fear to look at a billboard lest I be confronted by that reminder of youthful indiscretion."[1]

Pushed further west and actually became a cowboy in an attempt to live in the myth of the West, re-experiencing horse

(From *Jack and the Beanstalk,* adapted and illustrated by W.W. Denslow.)

riding for the first time since his youth. "Before I had time to even think, the animal humped its back into the form of a rainbow and at the same instant leaped into the air as if shot from a mortar. It then seemed to me that I continued up for a delightfully indefinite period after the broncho had returned to earth. But at last I reached a turning point in my career and began to descend with equal velocity. My recollection is decidedly hazy as to the exact circumstances of my contact with the ground. How I could have piled myself up in a manner to escape instant death is a matter which has always been a standing marvel to me."[1]

1891. Moved to San Francisco. Denslow covered news events—including an execution at San Quentin. "Cloudy and threatening sky, the ideal day for a hanging. The sunrise is a blood red streak over the low distant hills with dark gray masses of cloud above and the angry black waters of the bay beneath. Angry but beautiful. . . . I did not feel at all badly during the execution except when the officials . . . were strapping down the man's arms, etc. And then only for a moment. I suppose I was too busy. The execution was more like making away with a vicious dog than anything else I know of."[1]

1893. Returned to Chicago, drew illustrations of the World's Fair, known as the Columbian Exposition. "It is literally stunning, the immensity of the thing. Miles of ground covered with tremendous and artistic buildings. My first

L·FRANK BAUM

(From *Father Goose: His Book* by L. Frank Baum. Illustrated by W.W. Denslow.)

thoughts were, knowing that they are only intended for short use of six months, . . . what a magnificent ruin they must make when all is finished."[1]

One of the many spectacles of the fair was the first Ferris Wheel: "When we got under the wheel and looked aloft, my courage oozed out the holes in my socks. I flatly refused to climb so they made a sling or a bowline, as they called it, and proceeded to hoist us by steam power. . . . I have been on Pike's and other Peaks but never so high as it appeared to me on that bloomin' wheel."[1]

1894. Discouraged with career as illustrator, Denslow contemplated his position and the alternatives: "I float, as it were, with the stream, enjoying life as I float. I *do* have a good time and no mistake, besides that I work very hard, being at it night and day. . . . When one gets to be a newspaperman it is much like a disease, hard to get out of. Of course, I should like to do something better, but a big salary and solid comfort make one hesitate to lean to something else; besides I am well thought of where I am. . . .

"Nearly all Chicago publishing, engraving, and printing firms monopolize everything. The businessman is the great man; he is the whole thing; and he shows it clearly and distinctly. The artist or writer, what is he? He is my hired man, my money buys him, to me belongs the credit."[1]

February 20, 1896. Married Ann Holden, daughter of a Chicago newspaperwoman friend. "An easy chair, a long cool pipe, well seasoned, the Arcadia Mixture, and good rare old books; say what more do you want?"[1]

(From *Dot and Tot of Merryland* by L. Frank Baum. Illustrated by W.W. Denslow.)

Drawing "A Spectre of Christmas Eve" from *Carter's Monthly*, March, 1898. ■ (Courtesy of the Library of Congress.)

1898. Association with Roycrofters productions began. Denslow designed book covers, cartoons, posters and even buildings.

March 16, 1899. First work with L. Frank Baum, *Father Goose: His Book,* was published and received critical acclaim for its inventive use of color illustrations.

September, 1900. The Baum and Denslow collaboration, *The Wonderful Wizard of Oz,* published. A particularly difficult challenge was making the Scarecrow and the Tin Woodman believable. "I made twenty-five sketches of those two monkeys before I was satisfied with them. You may well believe that there was a great deal of evolution before I got that golf ball in the Scarecrow's ear or the funnel on the Tin Man's head. I experimented and tried out all sorts of straw waist-coats and sheet-iron cravats before I was satisfied."[1]

1901. Denslow suffered a breakdown and was sent to a Michigan sanitarium.

April, 1901. A rift developed between Baum and Denslow.

May, 1901. Returned to work and received a commission to prepare a new edition of *Mother Goose.* "I don't always adhere to the text of the familiar nursery rhymes. I believe in pure fun for the children, and I believe it can be given them without any incidental gruesomeness. In my *Mother Goose* I did not hesitate to change the text where the change would give a gentler and clearer tone to the verse. The comic element isn't lost in this way. . . . So when I illustrate and edit childhood classics I don't hesitate to expurgate. I'd rather please the kids than any other audience in the world."[1]

1902. A final split developed as Baum and Denslow feuded during the production of the theatrical version of *The Wonderful Wizard of Oz.*

September 17, 1903. Divorced wife, Ann.

December 24, 1903. Married Frances Doolittle. They honeymooned on a Bermuda Island, which Denslow later bought. "I have bought an island . . . containing about 10 acres of rocks, soil and cedar trees. On this island I am now building a mansion, a cottage and a dock. This keeps me busy in the afternoon while the books for babes take up my time in the forenoon. As this is where I work to the best advantage I wish to make it as comfortable as possible.

"By order of King Denslow I. Monarch of Denslow Island and Protector of the Coral Reefs. On Friday, January 15, in the Year of Our Lord 1904, and of the reign of our Glorious Majesty the First, the faithful subjects of the King will assemble at the foot of Christopher Street to send their Monarch on his way, whence he will take his triumphant march to the newly-acquired lands in the country of perpetual summer, the same being Denslow Island among the Bermudas. There he will open the palace of the King with due ceremony, christening its portals with a whole bottle of drawing ink, and inscribing on the sill the magic emblem of his dynasty, the seahorse.

"Of course, in going ahead with the formation of my kingdom I have had to use the greatest diplomacy. If the government at Washington had got wind of it in the early stages, I have no doubt that they would have sent a fleet to Denslow Island to blow it out of the water. England, too, would have

(From *The Wizard of Oz* by L. Frank Baum. Illustrated by W.W. Denslow.)

Self-caricature. ■ (From *The Inland Printer,* December, 1900.)

W.W. Denslow, 1899.

stepped in with a transport of troops, and the whole affair would have been off."[1]

1904. Appearance of series of picture books featuring Denslow's specialty—animals drawn in human situations, displaying human emotions.

1908. Reeling from an assortment of theatrical failures, Denslow received the last major commission of his life—from *St. Nicholas* Magazine.

August, 1909. Severe financial hardships and a renewed bout with alcoholism forced Denslow to mortgage his Bermuda Island and return to advertising, a career he detested.

March 29, 1915. Denslow contracted pneumonia and died at the age of fifty-eight.

FOR MORE INFORMATION SEE: Michael P. Hearn, "W. W. Denslow: The Forgotten Illustrator," *American Artist,* May, 1973; Douglas G. Greene and M. P. Hearn, *W. W. Denslow,* Central Michigan University Press, 1976; Doris de Montreville and Elizabeth D. Crawford, editors, *Fourth Book of Junior Authors and Illustrators,* H. W. Wilson, 1978.

EGYPT, Ophelia Settle 1903-

PERSONAL: Born February 20, 1903, in Clarksville, Tex.; daughter of Green Wilson (a teacher) and Sarah (a teacher; maiden name, Garth) Settle; married Ivory Lester Egypt (a waiter), June, 1940 (died, November, 1953); children: Ivory

Lester, Jr. *Education:* Howard University, B.A., 1925; University of Pennsylvania, M.A., 1926, M.S., 1944, further graduate study, 1949-50; attended Columbia University. *Home:* 1933 Alabama Ave. S.E., Washington, D.C. 20020.

CAREER: Orange County Training School, Chapel Hill, N.C., teacher, 1925-26; Fisk University, Nashville, Tenn., researcher and instructor in social sciences, 1928-33; St. Louis Provident, St. Louis, Mo., assistant consultant, 1933-35; Flint Goodridge Hospital, New Orleans, La., director of social service department, 1939—; Howard University, Washington, D.C., assistant professor and field work supervisor in medical school, 1939-51; Juvenile Court, Washington, D.C., probation officer, 1950-52; Iona R. Whipper Home, executive director, 1952-54; case worker for unmarried mothers in Washington, D.C., 1954-56; Parkslands Neighborhood Clinic, Planned Parenthood of Metropolitan Washington, D.C., founder and director, 1956-68; writer, 1968—. Consultant to governmental agencies and social service organizations. *Member:* Garfield Douglas Civic Association, Anacostia Historical Society. *Awards, honors:* Named Iota Phi Lambda Sorority's woman of the year, 1963; International Womens Year Award, Club Twenty, 1975.

WRITINGS: James Weldon Johnson (biography for children), Crowell, 1974. Conducted interviews with ex-slaves published as *Unwritten History of Slavery,* Fisk University, Micro Card Editions, 1968. Contributor of articles to periodicals.

WORK IN PROGRESS: A story for children; preparing a group of ex-slave interviews for publication.

SIDELIGHTS: "I've been scribbling little jingles since elementary school days but it was in high school that I wrote my first poem. I didn't like what my history book said about Dred Scott, the slave who took his case to the Supreme Court to prove that he should be free since he had lived outside slave territory. My poem said that the Court was wrong when it decided that he was *not* free and that he had no right to freedom since a slave could not be a citizen. It wasn't a very good poem but it made my point. I read it proudly in class and my teacher and classmates liked it.

"Most of my writing began like the poem about Dred Scott. Some incident in my life or in my family or work starts ideas moving around in my head and the first thing I know, I'm dreaming about that subject and thinking about it more and more. That's the way I started writing the story about my early childhood. One day, at work, after I had become a professional social worker, I was helping a young mother who wanted to give up her baby for adoption. She loved him very much but she knew she could not take care of him or give him the kind of life she wanted him to have. But she had a hard time making up her mind. After many discussions, she decided to give him up. After he left the office with his new parents, his mother wept as she talked with me about her feeling of loss and aloneness and her firm conviction that she had done the right thing.

"Somehow, that mother's experience started me thinking about my own mother who had died before my fifth birthday. I began wondering how she had felt about me and my younger brothers as she became aware of the nearness of her death. My own feeling of loss overwhelmed me and before the day ended, I sat down to the typewriter and tried to put my feeling on paper. Often that is the way I begin, but I do

The words from the stories always seemed to spin James away from his small bed. ■ (From
James Weldon Johnson by Ophelia Settle Egypt. Illustrated by Moneta Barnett.)

OPHELIA SETTLE EGYPT

have to sit at my typewriter and struggle for hours day after day. Incidently, that story is still unpublished.

"I had to work even harder on *James Weldon Johnson*. It was almost three years from the time I selected his name from a list of biographies the publisher wanted done. I had known him and his wife personally and had loved listening to him talk about his experiences and read from his writings. Doing a biography about him was much harder than I thought because so many things had to be left out and so much research had to be done. Hardest of all, I had to learn to write short sentences and use words that had meaning for young children.

"Fortunately, other members of the Black Writers Workshop of Washington, D.C. were experiencing similar problems and we had the expert leadership of two beautiful writers, Sharon Bell Mathis and Eloise Greenfield who gave me invaluable assistance and encouragement. My editor also provided skilled, understanding guidance. Earlier influences include my English teachers, friends and family and such writers as Charles S. Johnson under whom I worked at Fisk University when I interviewed more than 100 former slaves and Langston Hughes who was always willing to read my material and encourage me to keep writing. More recently, another poet and writer, Sterling Brown, has helped me in countless ways with my ex-slave manuscript.

"My favorite work, based on interviews with men and women who had been slaves is still unpublished but I hope that it will be available in a few years. Those aged men and women reminded me of my own grandparents who had been slaves. I remember how we used to sit around the fireplace spellbound listening to their stories of life in slavery. So talking to men and women who had been children during slavery, was like having my grandparents come alive again. Now I am trying to make these old people's stories come alive for children. I hope I can help youngsters feel the pride and excitement I experienced as I listened to my own grandparents.

"To the children who want to become writers, I'd like to say begin now. Write about your own experiences and feelings, the people you see every day, and all the world around you. There is beauty there as well as ugliness, joy as well as sorrow and pain. I also want my writing to say to children, especially Black children, life can be hard and discouraging, but never as bad as slavery. If slave parents could find a way to survive and make good lives for themselves and their children, surely you can do it. Work and stick together. Love and help each other. No matter how poor or how rich or successful you become, always reach out to those around you. Lend a helping hand, even to those who seem hopeless, remembering always that 'There but by the grace of God, go I.'"

EWING, Juliana (Horatia Gatty) 1841-1885 (Juliana Horatia Gatty)

PERSONAL: Born August 3, 1841, in Ecclesfield, Yorkshire, England; died May 13, 1885, in Bath, England; buried at Trull, Somerset, England; daughter of Alfred (a clergyman) and Margaret (an author and editor of children's stories; maiden name Scott) Gatty; married Alexander Ewing (an Army officer and hymn writer), June 1, 1867. *Education:* Tutored by her mother in music, art, languages, philosophy, and theology.

CAREER: Writer of books for children. Her stories first appeared in Charlotte Yonge's *The Monthly Packet*, in 1861. Most of Ewing's subsequent works appeared in *Aunt*

JULIANA HORATIA EWING

Judy's Magazine (founded and edited by her mother) before publication in book form.

WRITINGS: Melchior's Dream, and Other Tales, Bell, 1862 (includes *A Bit of Green, The Blackbird's Nest*); (contributor) Margaret Gatty, *Aunt Judy's Letters* (illustrated by C. S. Lane), [London], 1862; *Mrs. Overtheway's Remembrances* (illustrated by J. A. Pasquier and Joseph Wolf), Bell, 1869 [other editions illustrated by M. V. Wheelhouse, Bell, 1908; C. E. Brock, in *The Children's Bookcase,* volume seven, edited by Edith Nesbit, Frowde & Hodder, 1911; T. B. Hickling, S. W. Partridge, 1911]; *The Brownies, and Other Tales* (illustrated by George Cruikshank), Bell, 1870 (includes *The Land of the Lost Toys, Amelia and the Dwarfs,* and others) [other editions illustrated by Alice B. Woodward, Bell, 1910; E. H. Shepard, Dutton, 1954]; *A Flat-Iron for a Farthing; or, Some Passages in the Life of an Only Son,* Bell, 1873, reprinted, Faith Press, 1959 [other editions illustrated by Helen Allingham, Bell, 1884, reissued, Watergate Classics, 1948; M. V. Wheelhouse, Bell, 1908].

Lob Lie-by-the-Fire; or, The Luck of Lingborough, and Other Tales (illustrated by G. Cruikshank), Bell, 1873 (includes *Timothy's Shoes, The Peace Egg, Old Father Christmas,* and others) [other editions illustrated by Randolph Caldecott, E. & J. B. Young, 1885; A. B. Woodward, Bell, 1908; Florence Wyman Ivins, Oxford University Press, 1937], later reissued in *Lob Lie-by-the-Fire [and] The Story of a Short Life* (with illustrations from H. M. Brock and R. Caldecott), Dutton, 1964; *Six to Sixteen: A Story for Girls* (illustrated by Allingham), Bell, 1875 [another edition illustrated by M. V. Wheelhouse, Bell, 1908]; *Jan of the Windmill* (first published in *Aunt Judy's Magazine,* 1872-73, as "The Miller's Thumb"; illustrated by Allingham), Bell, 1876, reissued, H. Z. Walck, 1960 [another edition illustrated by M. V. Wheelhouse, Bell, 1908]; *A Great Emergency, and Other Tales,* Bell, 1877 [another edition illustrated by M. V. Wheelhouse, Bell, 1908], reissued in *A Great Emergency [and] A Very Ill-Tempered Family,* Gollancz, 1967, reprinted, Schocken Books, 1969.

We and the World: A Book for Boys, [London], 1880 [other editions illustrated by M. V. Wheelhouse, Bell, 1910; W. L. Jones, Little, Brown, 1912]; *Old Fashioned Fairy Tales,* Society for Promoting Christian Knowledge (S.P.C.K.), 1882 [another edition illustrated by Graham Robertson, Bell, 1920, reprinted, 1953]; *Brothers of Pity, and Other Tales,* S.P.C.K., 1882; *A Week Spent in a Glass Pond* (illustrated by R. André), Wells, Gardner, 1883; *Master Fritz* (illustrated by André), S.P.C.K., 1883; *A Sweet Little Dear* (illustrated by André), S.P.C.K., 1883; *Three Little Nest Birds* (illustrated by André), S.P.C.K., 1883; *Touch Him If You Dare* (illustrated by André), S.P.C.K., 1884; *Little Boys and Wooden Houses* (illustrated by André), S.P.C.K., 1884; *Tongues in Trees* (illustrated by André), S.P.C.K., 1884; *Jackanapes* (illustrated by R. Caldecott), E. & J. B. Young, 1884 [other editions illustrated by Frederick C. Gordon, Dutton, 1893; Josephine E. Bruce, D. C. Heath, 1900; Tasha Tudor, Oxford University Press, 1948]; *Daddy Darwin's Dovecot* (illustrated by R. Caldecott), S.P.C.K., 1884 [another edition illustrated by Etheldred B. Barry, D. Estes, 1898]; combined edition of *Jackanapes, together with Daddy Darwin's Dovecot [and] Lob Lie-by-the-Fire* (illustrated by R. Caldecott), S.P.C.K., 1884, reprinted, University Microfilms, 1966.

Poems of Child Life and Country Life, six volumes (illustrated by R. André), S.P.C.K., 1885; *The Story of a Short*

Now, it is certainly true that a curve may be either concave or convex; but I had heard of the bridge of a nose, and knew well enough which way the curve should go; and I had a shrewd suspicion that if so very short a nose as mine, with so much and so round a tip, could be said to be curved at all, the curve went the wrong way. ■ (From *Mrs. Overtheway's Remembrances* by Juliana Horatia Ewing. Illustrated by J.A. Pasquier and J. Wolf.)

Life (illustrated by Gordon Browne), S.P.C.K., 1885 [other editions illustrated by A. F. Schmitt, D. C. Heath, 1900; Ruth M. Hallock, Rand, McNally, 1903], later reissued in *Lob Lie-by-the-Fire [and] The Story of a Short Life* (with illustrations from H. M. Brock and R. Caldecott), Dutton, 1964; *Mary's Meadow [and] Letters from a Little Garden* (illustrated by G. Browne), E. & J. B. Young, 1866 [another edition illustrated by M. V. Wheelhouse, S.P.C.K., 1915]; *Dandelion Clocks, and Other Tales* (illustrated by G. Browne and others), S.P.C.K., 1887; *The Peace Egg: A Christmas Mumming Play* (illustrated by G. Browne), E. & J. B. Young, 1887; *Mother's Birthday Review* (illustrated by R. André), S.P.C.K., 1888; *Snapdragon and Old Father Christmas* (illustrated by G. Browne), E. & J. B. Young, 1888; *Leaves from Juliana Horatia Ewing's "Canada Home"* (edited and illustrated by E. S. Tucker), Roberts Brothers, 1896.

Rhymes; all illustrated by R. André and published by S.P.C.K.: *A Soldier's Children,* 1883; *Blue Red; or, The Discontented Lobster,* 1883; *Our Garden,* 1883; *The Blue*

Bells on the Lea, 1884; *Doll's Housekeeping,* 1884; *The Doll's Wash,* 1884; *Papa Poodle and Other Pets,* 1884.

Collections: *Complete Works,* 18 volumes, S.P.C.K., 1894-96; *Juliana Horatia Ewing's Works,* 11 volumes, Little, Brown, 1908.

ADAPTATIONS—Plays: Mary Salome, *Amelia and the Dwarfs,* Burns & Oates, 1906; M. E. Smith, *The Fairy Shoes* (adaptation of *Timothy's Shoes*), J. Curwen, 1916; J. A. Townsend, *Amelia's Dream* (adaptation of *Amelia and the Dwarfs*), Sheldon Press, 1924; Jane Colquhoun, *The Story of the Brownies* (adaptation of *The Brownies*), County of Kent Girl Guides, 1956; Esmee Mascall, *Brownies and Boggarts* (adaptation of *The Brownies*), McDougall's Educational Co., 1957.

SIDELIGHTS: **August 3, 1841.** Born in Ecclesfield, Yorkshire, the second of seven children of Alfred Gatty, a curate, and Margaret Scott. Margaret Gatty, Juliana's mother, was a writer, also. Her writing was spawned by financial hardship and the expenses of educating her sons. Her daughters were tutored at home. In 1866 she became the editor of a new children's magazine called *Aunt Judy's Magazine,* which was Juliana's nickname and the title of a book of "Tales" by her mother.

1844. Ewing precociously recited her catechism in Sunday School and was rewarded with a prayer book. Her deep religious sentiments were embodied in all her writings and buoyed her up in times of suffering.

Juliana Ewing wrote a short story in 1873, which her family attests to as a complete self-portrait. The name of it was "Madam Liberality." "It was not her real name; it was given to her by her brothers and sisters. People with very marked qualities of character do sometimes get such distinctive titles to rectify the indefiniteness of those they inherit and those they receive in baptism. The ruling peculiarity of a character is apt to show itself early in life, and it showed itself in Madam Liberality when she was a little child.

"Plum-cakes were not plentiful in her home when Madam Liberality was young, and, such as there were, were of the 'wholesome' kind—plenty of breadstuff, and the currants and raisins at a respectful distance from each other. But, few as the plums were, she seldom ate them. She picked them out very carefully, and put them into a box, which was hidden under her pinafore.

"When we grown-up people were children, and plum-cake and plum-pudding tasted very much nicer than they do now, we also picked out the plums. Some of us ate them at once, and had then to toil slowly through the cake or pudding, and some valiantly dispatched the plainer portion of the feast at the beginning, and kept the plums to sweeten the end. Sooner or later we ate them ourselves, but Madam Liberality kept her plums for other people.

"When the vulgar meal was over—that commonplace refreshment ordained and superintended by the elders of the

Ecclesfield Hall. ■ (From *Juliana Horatia Ewing and Her Books* by Horatia K.F. Eden. Drawing by Juliana Horatia Ewing.)

"See to the crows, the pretty black crows!" ■ (From *Jan of the Windmill* by Juliana Horatia Ewing. Illustrated by Helen Paterson.)

household—Madam Liberality would withdraw into a corner, from which she issued notes of invitation to all the dolls. They were 'fancy written' on curl-papers, and folded into cocked hats.

"Then began the real feast. The dolls came and the children with them. Madam Liberality had no toy tea-sets or dinner-sets, but there were acorn-cups filled to the brim, and the water tasted deliciously, though it came out of the ewer in the night-nursery, and had not even been filtered. And before every doll was a flat oyster-shell covered with a round oyster-shell, a complete set of complete pairs which had been collected by degrees, like old family plate. And, when the upper shell was raised, on every dish lay a plum. It was then that Madam Liberality got her sweetness out of the cake. She was in her glory at the head of the inverted tea-chest, and if the raisins would not go round the empty oyster-shell was hers, and nothing offended her more than to have this noticed. That was her spirit, then and always. She could 'do without' anything, if the wherewithal to be hospitable was left to her.

"When one's brain is no stronger than mine is, one gets very much confused in disentangling motives and nice points of character. I have doubted whether Madam Liberality's besetting virtue were a virtue at all. Was it unselfishness or love of approbation, benevolence or fussiness, the gift of sympathy or the lust of power, or was it something else? She was a very sickly child, with much pain to bear, and many pleasures to forego. Was it, as the doctors say, 'an effort of nature' to make her live outside herself, and be happy in the happiness of others?

"Madam Liberality was accustomed to disappointment.

"From her earliest years it had been a family joke, that poor Madam Liberality was always in ill-luck's way.

"It is true that she was constantly planning; and, if one builds castles, one must expect a few loose stones about one's ears now and then. But, besides this, her little hopes were constantly being frustrated by Fate.

"If the pigs or the hens got into the garden, Madam Liberality's bed was sure to be laid waste before any one came to the rescue. When a picnic or a tea-party was in store, if Madam Liberality did not catch cold, so as to hinder her from going, she was pretty sure to have a quinsy from fatigue or wet feet afterwards. When she had a treat, she paid for the pleasurable excitement by a head-ache just as when she ate sweet things they gave her tooth-ache." [Horatia K. F. Eden, *Juliana Horatia Ewing and Her Books,* S.P.C.K., 1885.[1]]

Ewing was ill most of her life, having a weak constitution throughout childhood. "But, if her luck was less than other people's, her courage and good spirits were more than common. She could think with pleasure about the treat when she had forgotten the head-ache.

"One side of her face would look fairly cheerful when the other was obliterated by a flannel bag of hot camomile flowers, and the whole was redolent of every possible domestic remedy for toothache, from oil of cloves and creosote to a baked onion in the ear. No sufferings abated her energy for fresh exploits, or quenched the hope that cold, and damp, and fatigue would not hurt her 'this time.'

"In the intervals of wringing out hot flannels for her quinsy she would amuse herself by devising a desert island expedition, on a larger and possibly a damper scale than hitherto, against the time when she should be out again.

"It is a very old simile, but Madam Liberality really was like a cork rising on the top of the very wave of ill-luck that had swallowed up her hopes.

"Her little white face and undaunted spirit bobbed up after each mischance or malady as ready and hopeful as ever."[1]

1859. Emerged from the nest and began taking an interest in the outside world. Due to her efforts, a village library was established in this year which flourished beyond her short life (forty-four years). She also began teaching a Sunday school class on the liturgy. Her first stories were published during this "parochial" phase of her home/village life.

"Madam Liberality grew up into much the same sort of person that she was when a child. She always had been what is termed old-fashioned, and the older she grew the better her old-fashionedness became her, so that at last her friends would say to her, 'Ah, if we all wore as well as you do, my dear! You've hardly changed at all since we remember you in short petticoats.' So far as she did change, the change was for the better. (It is to be hoped we do improve a little as we get older.) She was still liberal and economical. She still planned and hoped indefatigably. She was still tender-hearted in the sense in which Gray speaks—

'To each his sufferings: all are men
    Condemned alike to groan,
The tender for another's pain,
    The unfeeling for his own.'

"She still had a good deal of ill-health and ill-luck, and a good deal of pleasure in spite of both. She was happy in the happiness of others, and pleased by their praise. But she was less head-strong and opinionated in her plans, and less fretful when they failed. It is possible, after one has cut one's wisdom-teeth, to cure oneself even of a good deal of vanity, and to learn to play the second fiddle very gracefully; and Madam Liberality did not resist the lessons of life.

"GOD teaches us wisdom in divers ways. Why He suffers some people to have so many troubles, and so little of what we call pleasure in this world, we cannot in this world know. The heaviest blows often fall on the weakest shoulders and how these endure and bear up under them is another of the things which God knows better than we."[1]

1862. *Melchior's Dream* published. Just as she had saved her childhood treats for others, Ewing took the proceeds from her first edition of this book and bought hangings for the local church and treated two of her sisters to vacations.

Ewing and her mother were extremely close as their correspondence underscores. Margaret Gatty recognized early that her daughter's gift surpassed her own and she encouraged her to continue.

April 13, 1863. "MY DEAREST MOTHER,—I could knock my head off when I think that *I* am to blame for not being able to send you word yesterday of the happy conclu-

sion of this affair!! * * I cannot apologize enough, but assure you I punished myself by two days' suspense (a letter had been misdirected to the surgeon which delayed his visit). I did intend to have asked if I might have spent a trifle with the flower-man who comes to the door here, and bring home a little adornment to my flower-box as a sugar-plum after my operation * * now I feel I do not deserve it, but perhaps you will be merciful!

"It was a tiresome operation—so choking! He (Mr. Smith, the surgeon) was about an hour at it. He was more kind and considerate than can be expressed; when he went I said to him, 'I am very much obliged to you, first for telling me the truth, and secondly for waiting for me.' For when I got 'down in the mouth,' he waited, and chatted till I screwed up my courage again. He said, 'When people are reasonable it is barbarous to hurry them, and I said you were that when I first saw you.'"[1]

1864. Advised her friend Eleanora Lloyd on the methods of teaching catechism from her experience:

"Ecclesfield. August 19, 1864.

"MY DEAREST ELEANOR,

It is with the greatest pleasure that I 'sit down' and square my elbows to answer one question of your letter. The one about the Liturgical Lessons. . . . My dear old Eleanor—I am such a bad hand myself—that I feel it perfectly ludicrous to attempt to help you—but here are a few results of my limited experience which are probably all wrong—but the best I have to offer!

"Don't teach all the school.

"Make up a 'Liturgical Class' (make a favour of it if possible) of mixed boys and girls.

"Have none that cannot read.

"Tell them to bring their Prayer-books with them on the 'Liturgy Day.'

"If any of them say they have none—let nothing induce you to supply them.

"Say 'Well, you must look over your neighbour, but you ought to have one for yourself—I can let you have one for 2*d.*, so when you go home, "ask Papa," and bring me the 2*d.* next time.'

"Never give the Prayer-book 'in advance'—! (I never *pressed* the Prayer-books on them, or insisted on their having them. But gradually they all wanted to have them, and I used to take them with me, and they brought up their 2*d.*'s if they wanted any. The class is chiefly composed of Dissenters, but they never have raised any objection, and buy Prayer-books for children who never come to Church. The first prize last time was very deservedly won by the daughter of the Methodist Minister.)

"If you know any that cannot afford them, give them in private.

"One's chief temptation is to attempt too much. The great art is to make a good *skeleton* lesson of the leading points, and fill in afterwards.

(From *Jackanapes* by Juliana Horatia Ewing. Illustrated by Jessie Wilcox Smith.)

"*Wait* a long time for your answers.

"Repeat the question as simply as possible, and keep saying—Now *think—think*. One generally gets it in time.

"Lead up to your answer: thus—

"*Eleanor*. 'S. Augustine was a missionary Priest from—now answer all together?'

"*The whole Class*. Rome.

"*Eleanor*. 'Now who was S. Augustine?—All together.'

"The result probably will be that one or perhaps two will give the whole answer—and then you can say—

"'That's right. But I want you all to say it. Now together. Who was S. Augustine?'

"Then you will get it from all. . . .

"Excuse all this ramble. I have no doubt I have bored you with a great deal of chaff—but I hardly know quite what you want to know. As to the subject—it is a Hobby with me—so excuse rhapsodies!"[1]

1865. Writing profits accrued during this time, enabled her to take her eldest brother to Antwerp and Holland. She wrote to her sister:

*"Hotel de Vieux, Doellen,
The Hague,
September 27, 1865.*

"DEAREST D—,

This morning we had a great treat! We took an open carriage and drove from the Hague to Scheveningen on the coast. All the way you go through an avenue of elms, which is lovely. It is called 'the Wood,' and to the left in Sorgoliet, where the Queen mother lives, . . . Scheveningen is a bare-looking shore, all sand, and bordered with sandbanks, or Dunes. It was *fiercely* hot, scorching, and not an atom of shade to be had; but in spite of sun, slipping sandbank-seat, sand-fleas, and a hornet circling round, I did make a sketch, which I hope to finish at home.

"Both Regie and I bathed, and it was *delicious*—an utterly calm sea, and I enjoyed it thoroughly. The bathing machines seem to be a Government affair. They and the towels are marked with a *stork,* and you take a ticket and get your gown and towels from a man at a 'bureau' on the sands. I must tell you, this morning when we came down, we found breakfasting in the *salle-á-manger* our Dutch friend, the bulb merchant. We had our breakfast put at his table, and had a jolly chat. It was so pleasant! Like meeting an old friend. He has gone, I am sorry to say, but I have made great friends with Stephanie's father; he cannot speak a word of English, so we can only talk in such French as I can muster; but he is very pleasant, and his children are so nice! eight—four boys and four girls. The wife is Dutch, and I do not think can speak French, so I do not talk to her.

"After dinner the *maître d'hôtel* asked us if we would not go to 'the Wood' (on the road to Scheveningen), and hear the military band—so we went. I can't describe it. It was like nothing but scenes in a theatre. Pitch dark in all the avenues, except for little lamps like tiny tumblers fixed on to the trees, and so on to the Pavilion, which was lighted up by chains of similar lamps like an illumination—and round which—seated round little green tables—were gathered, I suppose, about two thousand people. Their politeness to each other—the perfect good-behaviour, the quiet and silence during the music, and the buzz and movement when it was over, were wonderful. The music was very good. R. and I had each a tiny cup of coffee, and a little brandy and water, for it was very cold!! Now I have come in, and he has gone back, I think. Stephanie was there, and lots of children. As I lay awake last night I heard the old watchman go round. He beats two pieces of wood together and calls the hours of the night. I saw a funeral too, this morning, and the coachman wears a hat like this—[*Sketch*]. In the streets we have met men in black with cocked hats. They are 'Ansprekers,' who go to announce a man's death to his friends.

"*Friday night. Michaelmas Day.* Hotel Pay Bas, Rotterdam.—Back again! and to-morrow at 8:15 a.m. we go back to dear old Antwerp. For the solemn fact has made itself apparent, that the money will not hold out till to-morrow week, as we intended. So we must give up our dear Captain, and come home in the *Tiger*!! We shall be with you D. V. on Saturday week, starting on Wednesday from Antwerp. We have been to the Poste Restante, and got dear Mother's letter, to my infinite delight. I am so glad Miss Yonge likes 'the Brownies.'

"Your ever loving, JUDY"[1]

1866. Margaret Gatty began editing *Aunt Judy's Magazine* with the help of her four daughters. Nearly all the rest of Ewing's writing appeared in her mother's publication.

About this time she met and fell in love with Alexander Ewing. They wanted to marry, but her family opposed it. Although they admired many of his qualities, they objected to the uncertainty of his future in the military life and were probably also unwilling to give up her help (writing) at home. Ewing took no part in the argument, but wrote a friend of her future husband's suitability: "He is very clever. A beautiful musician—good linguist—well read, etc.—a dab at meteorology, photography, awfully fond of dogs, good rider, finally a high free mason (a knight Templar) and . . . a mesmerist! Don't laugh at me! I am awfully happy." [Gillian Avery, *Mrs. Ewing,* Henry Z. Walck, 1964.[2]]

June 1, 1867. Married Alexander Ewing and a week later left for Fredericton, New Brunswick, Canada, where he was stationed.

Margaret Gatty missed her terribly, and wrote: "I dare not begin to think of how I feel at Julie thus going across the water. But one thing is certain. She could not have been happy *without* him. And her happiness is the only really important point. Children must go *forward* and *outward,* the old folks must be contented that is so."[2]

June 10, 1867. A letter to her mother from the "S. S. China" during her honeymoon. "I staggered up yesterday morning to have my first sight of an iceberg. . . . The sea was dark-blue, a low line of land (Cape Race) was visible, and the iceberg stood in the distance dead white, like a lump of sugar. . . . I think the first sight of Halifax was one of the prettiest sights I ever saw. When I first came up there was no horizon, we were in a sea of mist. Gradually the horizon line appeared—then a line of low coast—muddy-looking at first—it soon became marked with lines of dark wood—then the shore dotted with grey huts—then the sun came out—the breeze got milder—and the air became strongly redolent of pine-woods. Nearer, the coast became more defined, though still low, rather bare, and dotted with brushwood, and grey stones low down, and crowned always with 'murmuring pines.' As we came to habitations, which are dotted, and sparkle along the shore, the effect was what we noticed in Belgium, as if a box of very bright new toys had been put out to play with, red roofs—even red houses—cardboard-looking churches—little bright wooden houses—and stiffish trees mixed everywhere. It looks more like a quaint watering-place than a city, though there are some fine buildings. . . . We took a great fancy to the place, which was like a new child's picture book, and I was rather disappointed to learn it is not to be our home. But Fredericton, where we are going, has superior advantages in some respects, and will very likely be quite as pretty.''[1]

Began the eighteen years of her wandering married life with more than the expected discomforts of army life due to her delicate physical and home-loving nature. Her writing output in the next six years more than doubled that of the previous six.

Despite her moving from place to place, her life was still easier than those of her sisters at home, since her parents required inordinate assistance.

Characteristically, Ewing made the best out of any inconveniences of military life, studying carefully the ''flora and fauna'' of her new locales.

1867. Her first stories from her new home were published, *An Idyl of the Wood* and *The Three Christmas Trees*.

June 19, 1867. Wrote her mother from Halifax. ''Rex and I went down to the fish-market that I might see it. Coming back we met an old North American Indian woman. Such a picturesque figure. We talked to her, and Rex gave her something. I do not think it half so degraded-looking a type

as they say. A very broad, queer, but I think acute and pleasant-looking face. Since I came in I have made two rather successful sketches of her. She wore an old common striped shawl, but curiously thrown round her so that it looked like a chief's blanket, a black cap embroidered with beads, black trousers stuffed into moccasins, a short black petticoat, and a large gold-coloured cross on her breast, and a short jacket trimmed with scarlet, a stick and basket for broken victuals. She said she was going to catch the train! It sounded like hearing Plato engaged for a polka! . . . ''[1]

August 23, 1867. A letter to her dear friend Eleanora Lloyd, from her new home in New Brunswick.

''MY DEAREST OLD ELEANORA,

''I have been a wretch for not having written to you sooner. It seems strange there should remain any pressure of business or hurry of life in this place, where workmen look out of the windows of the house (our house and a fact!); they are repairing nine at a time, and boys swing their buckets and dawdle to the well for water, as if Time couldn't be lounged and coaxed off one's hands!! And yet busy I have been, and every nail has been a scramble. Getting into our house was no joke, attending sales and shops, buying furni-

We sat so long together on one big footstool by the fire, with our arms around each other, and the book resting on our knees, that Kitty called down blessings on my godmother's head for having sent a volume that kept us both so long out of mischief. ■ (From *Old Father Christmas* by Juliana Horatia Ewing. Illustrated by Gordon Browne and other artists.)

(From *Lob Lie-by-the-Fire* by Juliana Horatia Ewing. Illustrated by Randolph Caldecott.)

ture—ditto, ditto—as to paying and receiving calls on lovely days with splendid sketching lights—they have been thorns in the flesh—and, worst of all, regular colonial experiences of servants—one went off at a day's notice—and for two or three days we had *nobody* but Rex's *orderly,* such a handy, imperturbable soldier, who made beds, cooked the dinner, hung pictures, and blew the organ with equal urbanity. He didn't know much—and in the imperfect state of our cuisine had few appliances—but he affected to be *au fail* at everything—and what he had not got, he 'annexed' from somewhere else. One of our maids uniformly set tumblers and wine-glasses with the tea set, and I found 'William' the Never-at-fault cleaning the plate with knife-powder, and brushing his own clothes with the shoe brush. However, we have got a very fair maid now, and are comfortable enough.

"Our house is awfully jolly, though the workmen are yet about. The drawing-room really is not bad. It is a good-sized room with a bay window—green carpet and sofa in the recess—window plant shelf—on one long side of the wall—a writing-table between two book-shelves—and oh! my dear, I cannot sufficiently say the pleasure as well as *use* and *comfort* all my wedding presents have been to me. You can hardly estimate the comforting effect of these dear bits of civilization out here, especially at first when we were less comfortable. But the *refinements* of comfort, you know, are not to be got here for love or money as we get them at home. Your dear book and inkstand and weights (uncommonly useful at this juncture of new postage), etc.,

look so well on my writing-table—on which are also the Longleys' Despatch Box—Frank Smith's blotting book— my Japanese bronzes, Indian box, Chinese ditto, Japanese candlestick and Chinese shoes, etc. of Rex's—our standing photos, table bookstand, etc., etc. You can't imagine how precious any knick-knacks have become. My mother's coloured photo that Brownie gave me is propped in the centre—and we have bought a mahogany bracket for my old Joan of Arc!! We have hired a good harmonium. Altogether the room really looks pretty with a fawn-coloured paper and the few water colours up—round table, etc., etc. Our bedroom has a blue and white paper, is a bright, airy, two-windowed room, with a *lovely* eastward view over the river—the willows—and the pine woods. Our abundant space mocks one's longing to invite a good many dear old friends to visit one!

"People are wonderfully kind here. They really keep us in vegetables, and I have a lovely nosegay on my table at this moment. There is a very pleasant Regiment (22nd) here, with a lovely band. On my birthday Rex gave me Asa Gray's *Botany,* a book on botany generally, and on North American plants in particular. Some of the wild-flowers are lovely. One (Pigeon Berry) [*sketch*] has a white flower amid largish leaves—thus. It grows about as large as wild anemone, in similar places and quantities. When the flower falls the stamens develop into a thick *bunch* of *berries,* the size and colour of holly berries, only *brighter* brilliant scarlet, and patches of pine wood are covered with them.

"My dear, you *would* like this place! . . .

"Your ever loving,
"J. H. EWING."[1]

Her love of animals, as reflected in her "tales" appears in many of her letters:

"To H. K. F. G.

September 29, 1867.

". . . I have fallen head over ears in love with another dog. Oh! bless his nose! . . . His name is Hector. He is a *white* pure bull-dog. His face is more broad and round—and delicious and ferociously good-natured—and affectionately ogreish—than you can imagine. The moment I saw him I hugged him and kissed his benevolence bump, and he didn't even *gowly powl.* . . .

"TO MRS. GATTY.

[*Fredericton,* 1867?]

". . . Talking of stories, if I only can get the full facts of his history, I think I shall send A. J. M. a short paper on a Fredericton Dog. Did I ever tell you of him? He has the loveliest face I ever saw, I think, *in any Christian.* He knows us quite well when we go up the High Street where he lives. When he gets two cents (1*d.*) given him, he takes it in his mouth to the nearest store and buys himself buscuits [sic]. I have seen him do it. If you only give him *one* cent he is dissatisfied, and tries to get the second. The Bishop told me he used to come to Church with his master at one time; he would come and behave very well—TILL the offertory. Then he rose and *walked after the alms-collectors,* wagging his tail as the money chinked in, because he wanted his penny for his biscuits!!! He is a large dog—part St. Bernard, and has magnificent eyes. But (my *poor*!) they shaved him this summer like a poodle! There is a bear in the officers' quarters here—he belongs to the regiment. I have patted him, but he catches at one's clothes. To see him *patting* at my skirts with his paw was delicious—but I don't like his *head,* he looks very sly!"[1]

When confronted with the various new flowers in New Brunswick, she began a notebook of sketches of them. She named them their scientific names, and her husband (Major Ewing) added as many popular names as he could learn from Peter, a friendly Melicete Indian. She introduced several New World (North American) flowers into her stories such as the Tabby-Striped Arum named the Jack-in-the-Pulpit by poet Whittier. She also wrote a whole story about a species of Trillium called "The Blind Hermit and the Trinity Flower."

In several letters to her mother she writes of other flowers:

"April 17, 1868.

"We are beginning now to talk of 'Mayflower expeditions.' I think I shall give one to a few select friends. I had thought of a child's one, but a nice old school-mistress here gives one for children, and I think one raid of the united juvenile population on the poor lovely flowers is enough. The Mayflower is a lovely wax-like ground creeper with an exquisite perfume. It is the first flower, and is to be found before the snow has left the woods. . . .

"May 12, 1868.

May 18, 1868.

". . . I am awfully busy with my garden, and people are very kind in giving me things. To-morrow we go to the Rowans, and I am to ransack *his* garden! I do think the exchange of herbaceous perennials is one of the joys of life. You can hardly think how delicious it feels to *garden* after six months of frost and snow. Imagine my feelings when Mrs. Medley found a bed of seedling bee larkspurs in her garden, and gave me at least two dozen!!! I have got a whole row of them along a border, next to which I *think* I shall have mignonette and scarlet geraniums alternately. It is rather odd after writing Reka Dom, that I should fall heir to a garden in which almost the only 'fixture' is a south border of lilies of the valley! . . ."[1]

1869. Despite her love of her new home and husband, she expressed her recurring homesickness in letters to her mother.

"TO MRS. GATTY.

Fredericton, N.B.
Easter Monday, 1869.

"You are very dear and good about our ups and downs, and it makes me doubly regret that I cannot reward you by conveying a perfectly truthful *impression* of our life, etc. here to your mind. I trace in your very dearness and goodness about it, in your worrying more about discomfort for me in our moves than about your own hopes of our meeting at Home, how little able one is to do so by mere letters. I wish it did not lead you to the unwarrantable conclusion that it is because you are 'weak and old' that you do not appreciate the uncertainties of our military housekeeping, and can only 'admire' the coolness with which I look for-

(From *The Story of a Short Life* by Juliana Horatia Ewing.)

ward to breaking up our cosy little establishment, just when we were fairly settled down. You can hardly believe how well I understand your feelings for me, *because I have so fully gone through them for myself.*

"I never had D.'s 'spirit' for a wandering life, and it is out of the fulness of my experience that I *know,* and wish unspeakably that I could convey to you, how very much of one's shrinking dread has all the *unreality* of fear of an *unknown* evil. When I look back to all I looked forward to with fear and trembling in reference to all the strangenesses of my new life, I understand your feelings better than you think. I am too much your daughter not to be strongly tempted to 'beat my future brow,' much more so than to be over-hopeful. Rex is given that way too in his own line; and we often are brought to say together how inexcusable it is when everything turns out so much better than we expected, and when 'God' not only 'chains the dog till night,' but often never lets him loose at all! Still the natural terrors of an untravelled and not herculean woman about the ups and downs of a wandering, homeless sort of life like ours are not so comprehensible by him, he having travelled so much, never felt a qualm of sea-sickness, and less than the average of home-sickness, from circumstances. It is one among my many reasons for wishing to come Home soon, that one chat would put you in possession of more idea of our passing home, the nest we have built for a season, and

...Little Miss Jane Johnson, and her "particular friend" Clarinda, sat under the big oak-tree on the Green, and Jane pinched Clarinda's little finger till she found that she could keep a secret and then she told her in confidence that she had heard from Nurse and Jemima that Miss Jessamine's niece had been a very naughty girl, and that that horrid, wicked officer had come for her on his black horse and carried her right away. ■ (From *Jackanapes* by Juliana Horatia Ewing. Illustrated by Amy Sacker.)

the wood it is built in, and the birds (of many feathers) amongst whom we live, than any *letters* can do. . . .

"You can imagine the state of (far from blissful) ignorance of military life, tropical heat, Canadian inns, etc., etc., in which I landed at Halifax after such a sudden wrench from the old Home, and such a very far from cheerful voyage, and all the anecdotes of the summer heat, the winter cold, the spring floods, the houses and the want of houses, the servants and the want of servants, the impossibility of getting anything, and the ruinous expense of it when got! which people pour into the ears of a new-comer just because it is a more sensational and entertaining (and *quite* as stereotyped) a subject of conversation as the weather and the crops. The points may be (isolately) true; but the whole impression one receives is alarmingly false! And I can only say that my experience is so totally different from my fears, and from the cook-stories of the 'profession,' that I don't mean to request Rex to leave Our Department at present! . . ."[1]

1869. The Ewings visited England in the autumn bringing their new dog Trouvé with them. They received a tremendous welcome from both the village and the Gatty family.

They were next stationed in Aldershot, where they stayed until 1877. She loved the climate, pine trees, theatricals, concerts and regimental balls. Their small military bungalow she considered a test of her homemaking abilities and these years were her most productive by far.

The disadvantages of this life she conceded in "The Story of a Short Life" (*Aunt Judy's,* 1882) where she described how: ". . . only the publicity and squalor of the back-premises of the 'Lines'—their drying clothes and crumbling mud walls, their coal-boxes and slop-pails—could exceed the depressing effects of the gardens in front, where such plants as were not uprooted by the winds perished of frost and drought, and where, if some gallant creeper had stood fast and covered the nakedness of your wooden hovel, the Royal Engineers would arrive one morning . . . and tear down the growth of years before you had finished shaving, for the purpose of repainting your outer walls."[2]

She expressed her interest in the ordinary soldiers in two other accounts—*Lob Lie-by-the-Fire* (1874) and *Jackanapes* (1879).

October, 1873. Her much loved mother died. She wrote a short memoir in the November issue of *Aunt Judy's,* which she and her sister Horatia took over for the next two years. A letter to her husband about Margaret Gatty:

"TO A. E.

> *Ecclesfield Vicarage, Sheffield.*
> Sunday, Oct. 5, 1873.

". . . It is all over. She *is* with your Father and Mother, and the dear Bishop, and my two brothers, and many an old friend who has 'gone before.' Had she been merely a friend she is one of those whose loss cannot but be felt more as years and experience make one realize the value of certain noble qualities, and their rarity; but if GOD has laid a heavy cross upon us in this blow,—which seems such a blow in spite of long preparing!—He has given us every comfort, every concession to the weaknesses of our love in the accidents of her death. . . . It was an ideal end. GOD Who had permitted her to suffer so sorely in body, and to be often visited in old times—by dread of death and of 'death-agonies,' parted the waves of the last Jordan, and she 'went through dryshod!' . . . The sense of her higher state is so overwhelming, one *cannot* indulge a *common* sorrow. For myself I can only say that I feel as if I were a child again in respect of her. She is as much with *me* now, as with any of her children, even if I am in Jamaica or Ceylon. *Now* she knows and sees my life, and I have a feeling as if she were an ever-present *conscience* to me (as a mother's *presence* makes a child alive to what is right and what is wrong), which I hope by GOD's grace may never leave me and may make me more worthy of having had such a Mother. . . ."[1]

1877. The happy years at Aldershot ended and the wandering began. Her husband was posted to Manchester and she stayed behind to pack, something she'd do much of in the next few years. They lived in Bowdon, outside of Manchester for the year.

September, 1878. Major Ewing was stationed at York and the couple moved to Fulford, near York. She decorated their new home only to have to move once again.

March, 1879. Her husband was dispatched to Malta.

October, 1879. Wrote the piece on the military entitled *Jackanapes.* In June of that year she'd met Randolph Caldecott whose illustrations she'd greatly admired. She and Horatia asked him for a colored illustration for *Jackanapes* before it was even written. Since colors took long to print, she suggested a "scene" to him because he wouldn't be able to read it in time.

At the end of October, she started for Malta to join her husband, but she became so ill travelling through France that her youngest sister and her friend Mrs. R. H. Jelf went to Paris and took her back to England as soon as she could be moved. Her grief at only passing through Paris was expressed to her husband: "You must show your wife Paris! I sobbed myself nearly to bits in the cab as we came away through those lovely streets, and thought of you, and how you love it. . . . When we drove past the Louvre and it was open, I was wild to go in and just see Raphael's St. Margaret, but on the whole we daren't risk it, and I collapsed almost directly afterwards."[2]

She was advised by her doctor not to travel again for several months. Her husband came home for Christmas, but she was still unfit to travel. Before she could join him in Malta, he was sent on to Ceylon, in which climate she could never live healthily.

She was very unhappy about not being with her husband in his new surroundings and about not having her own home in which to entertain her many friends. She was plagued financially also, as money wasn't always forthcoming from her husband or her publishers. She never got enough for her work. Hence long correspondences with her publishers of whom she wrote: "The moment we come to *deal*, the firm's only notion of business is to depreciate and beat me down."[2]

Randolph Caldecott wrote to her regarding the cost of illustrating her *Jackanapes,* affirming his belief that all publishers should be treated like tradesmen: "I should have no scruple in touching the very bottom of a publisher's coffer. I am sorry to say that I know them a little too well."[2]

Only two years before her death she wrote that she'd only received twenty pounds in royalties on ten books that year: "I've been nearly twenty years at it, and never got beyond our old groove with nine volumes. Some doing well up to a few thousands, others (like *Lob Lie-by-the-Fire*) having brought me in about seven pounds ten shillings in six or seven years!"[2]

1880. Her back ailment was diagnosed as spinal neuralgia, but to modern ears the symptoms resembled cancer. Her niece specifically mentioned cancer in a biography. She described some of her symptoms in a letter to her husband: "Head and spine very shaky this morning so that I could not get warm; but I wrapped in my fur cloak, and went out into the sunshine, up and down, up and down the churchyard flags. A sunny old kirkyard is a nice place, I always think, for aged folk and invalids to creep up and down in."[2]

Her illness she bore with great patience and good spirits, making the best of a bad situation. She wrote to her husband often and he responded with brilliantly written letters, which cheered her.

January 31, 1880. To Major Ewing in Ceylon.

"*Greno House,* Tuesday.

"Harry Howard drove me up yesterday. It was *just* as much as I could bear; but I lay on the sofa till dinner, and went to bed at eight, and though my head kept me awake at

Up went her arms to shield his ears from a wellmerited cuffing; but fate was kinder to him than he deserved. It was only an old man (prematurely aged with drink and consequent poverty) whose faded eyes seemed to rekindle as he also gazed after the pigeons, and spoke as one who knows. ■ (From *The Brownies and Other Stories* by Juliana Horatia Ewing. Illustrated by E.H. Shepard.)

first, I did well on the whole. Breakfast in bed, a bigger one than I have eaten for three weeks, and since then I have had an hour's drive. The roughness of the roads is unlucky, but the air *divine*! Such sweet sunshine, and Greno Wood, with yellow remains of bush and bracken, and heavy mosses on the sandstone walls, and tiny streams trickling through boggy bits of the wood, and coming out over the wall to overflow those picturesque stone troughs which are so oddly numerous, and which I had in my head when I wrote the first part of 'Mrs. Overtheway.'"[1]

She described Yorkshire: "Very dear to me are all your 'tender and true' regards for the old home—the grey-green nest (more grey than green!) a good deal changed and weatherbeaten, but not quite deserted—which is bound up with so much of our lives! . . . Another chord of sympathy was very strongly pulled by your writing of the 'grey-green fields,' and sending your love to them. No one I ever met has, I think, *quite* your sympathy with exactly what the external world out-of-doors is to me and has been ever since I can remember. From days when the batch of us went-out-walking with the Nurses, and the round mossedge holes in the roots of gnarled trees in the hedges, and the red leaves of Herb Robert in autumn, and all the inexhaustible wealth of hedges and ditches and fields, and the Shroggs, and the brooks, were happiness of the keenest kind—to now when it is as fresh and strong as ever; it has been a pleasure which has balanced an immense lot of physical pain."[2]

July 23, 1880.

> "*Ecclesfield, Sheffield.* July 23, 1880.

"MY DEAR MR. CALDECOTT,

"I am sending you a number of *Jackanapes* in case you have lost your other.

"I have made marks against places from some of which I think you could select easy scenes; I mean easy in the sense of being on the lines where your genius has so often worked.

"I will put some notes about each at the end of my letter. What I now want to ask you is whether you *could* do me a few illustrations of the vignette kind for *Jackanapes,* so that it might come out at Christmas. Christmas *ought* to mean October, so it would of course be very delightful if you could have completed them in September—and as soon as might be. But do not WORRY your brain about dates. I would rather give it up than let you feel the fetters of Time, which, when they drag one at one's work, makes the labour double. But if you will begin them, and *see* if they come pretty readily to your fingers, I shall only too well understand it if after all you can't finish in time for this season!"[1]

October, 1880. She met John Ruskin and he encouraged her to publish her own work, "and to mention me in the next *Fors Clavigera* as having joined him in defying the publishing brotherhood. It was an overwhelming temptation to go hand in hand with *him* in anything! But one's safe way in doubt is—to do what is most *right,* and my intercourse with Bell [her publisher] has not been such as to justify me in subscribing to an attack on his honesty."[2]

1882. Her health improved somewhat, but she was still in a weakened condition. A letter to her husband.

"TO A. E.

> January 4, 1883.

"Caldecott says his difficulty over my writing is that 'the force and finish' of it frightens him. It is painted already and does not need illustration; and he has lingered over *Jackanapes* from the conviction that he could 'never satisfy me!!' This difficulty is, I hope, now vanquished. He is hard at work on a full and complete edition of *Jackanapes,* of which he has now begged to take the entire control, will 'submit' paper and type, etc. to me, and hopes to please. 'But you are so particular!'

"I need hardly say I have written to place everything in his hands. I am 'not such a fool as' to think I can teach *him*! (though I am insisting upon certain arrangements of types, etc., etc., to give a *literary*—not Toy Book—aspect to the volume).

"André I *know* I help. But then only a man of real talent and mind would accept the help and be willing to be taught. The last batch of *A Soldier's Children* that came had three pages that grated on me.

"For 1, I sent him a sketch! said the lady must wear a bonnet in church, and her boys must take off their hats!

That she must kneel *forwards,* be dressed in a deep sealskin with heavy fox edge, and have her eyes *down,* and the children must kneel *imitating her,* and I should like an old *brass* on the wall above them with one of those queer old kneeling families in cuff.

"For 2, I said I could not introduce child readers to the cells, and I begged for an old Chelsea Pensioner showing his good conduct medal to a little boy.

"3. I suggested the tomb of a Knight Crusader, above which should fall a torn banner with the words, 'In Coelo Quies.'

"Now if he had kicked at having three pictures to do utterly over again, one could hardly have wondered, pressed as he is. But, back they came! 'I am indeed much indebted to you,' the worst he had to say! The lady in No. 1 now *is* a lady; and as to the other two, they will be two of the best pages of the book. Old Pensioner first-rate, and Crusader under torn banner just leaving 'Coelo Quies,' a tomb behind 'of S. Ambrose of Milan' with a little dog—and a snowy-moustached old General, with bending shoulders and holding a little girl by the hand, paying *devoir* at the Departed Warrior's tomb in a ray of rosy sunlight!!

"This is the sort of way we are fighting through the Ewing-André books."[1]

1883. Her husband returned in May and was stationed at Taunton. She was uplifted by his presence and the comfort of having her own home and garden again. They named it Villa Ponente.

November, 1884. Her last writing was again about flowers. She began a series of "Letters From a Little Garden" in *Aunt Judy's Magazine.*

The last three months of her life were filled with pain and suffering, which she bore with the greatest patience and courage. Her last letters were dictated from what was to be her deathbed. These were to her good friend Marny Jelf:

> [Written with a typewriter.]

"TO MRS. JELF.

> *Taunton.* December 23, 1884.

"DEAREST MARNY,

"My right arm is disabled with neuralgia, and Rex is working one of his most delightful toys for me. He says I brought my afflictions on myself by writing too prolix letters several hours a day. I've got very much behindhand, or you'd have heard from me before. I must try and be highly condensed. Gordon Browne has done some wonderful drawings for *Laetus.* Rex was wild over a *Death or Glory* Lancer, and I think he (the Lancer) and a Highlander would touch even Aunty's heart. They will rank among her largest exceptions. I can't do *any* Xmas cards this year; I can neither go out nor write. I hoped to have sent you a little Xmas box, of a pair of old brass candlesticks such as your soul desireth. D. and I made an expedition to the very broker's ten days ago, but when I saw the dingy shop choke-full of newly-arrived dirty furniture, and remembered that these streets are reeking with small-pox—as it refuses to 'leave us at present'—I thought I should be foolish to go

Then he could creep into the cowhouse and lie in the straw against the white cow's back. ■ (From *Lob Lie-by-the-Fire* in *Lob Lie-by-the-Fire* [*and*] *The Story of a Short Life* by Juliana Ewing. Illustrated by Randolph Caldecott.)

in. D. knows of a pair in Ecclesfield, and I have commissioned her to annex them if possible; but they can't quite arrive in time. . . .

"Your loving, J. H. E.

"TO MRS. JELF.

January 22, 1885.

"DEAREST M.,

"I am *so* pleased you like the brazen candlesticks.

"I have long wanted to tell you how *lovely* I thought all your Xmas cards. Auntie's snow scene was exquisite—and your Angels have adorned my sick-room for nearly a month! Most beautiful.

"I know you'll be glad I had my first 'decent' night last night—since December 18!—No very lengthy vigils and no pain to *speak* of. No pain to growl about to-day. A great advance.

"Indeed, dear—I should not only be glad but *grateful* to go to you by and by for a short *fillip*. Dr. L— would have sent me away now if weather, etc. were fit—or I could move.

"After desperate struggles—made very hard by illness—I hope to see *Laetus* in May at *one shilling*. Gordon Browne doing well. Do you object to the ending of *Laetus*—to Lady Jane having another son, etc.?

"*Taunton.* February 16, 1885.

"MY DEAREST MARNY,

Rex is 'typing' for me, but my own mouth must thank you for your goodness, for being so ready to take me in. By and by I shall indeed be grateful to go to you. But this is not likely to be for some weeks to come. You can't imagine what a Greenwich pensioner I am. I told my doctor this morning that he'd better send me up a wood square with four wheels, like those beggars in London who have no limbs; for both my legs and my right arm were *hors de combat,* and to-day he has found an inflamed vein in my left, so *that* has gone into fomentations too.

"But in spite of all this I feel better, and do hope I shall soon be up and about. But he says the risk of these veins would be likely to come if I over-exerted myself, so—anxious as I am to get to purer air, I don't think it would do to move until my legs are more fit. May I write again and tell you when I am fit for Aldershot? Dr. L—

MRS. EWING

highly approves of the air of it, but at present he thinks lying in bed the only safe course. Do thank dear Aunty next time you write to her for her goodness, and tell her that in my present state I should make her seem quite spry and active. A thousand thanks for the *Pall Mall*. I do *not* neglect one word of what you say; but I need hardly say that I can't work at present. . . .

> "Your loving,
> J. H. E."[1]

In February she was operated on twice for the removal of a growth from her spine. These she endured courageously, thankful for her ability to tolerate chloroform well. Her early understanding of pain is evident again in her heavily autobiographical story "Madam Liberality". . . . She described a session with a dentist which she experienced as a child: "Madam Liberality staggered home, very giddy, but very happy. Moralists say a great deal about pain treading so closely on the heels of pleasure in this life, but they are not always wise or grateful enough to speak of the pleasure which springs out of pain. And yet there is a bliss which comes just when pain has ceased, whose rapture rivals even the high happiness of unbroken health; and there is a keen pleasure about small pleasures hardly earned, in which the full measure of those who can afford anything they want is sometimes lacking. Relief is certainly one of the most delicious sensations which poor humanity can enjoy!"[1]

Her description of religious tracts applied to her literary and life philosophy: "Young writers of talent break almost invariably. No class of literature is a more striking example of the blunder of throwing away powder and shot than tracts—and I sometimes wonder if any recognized form of literature has more in its power. It is almost next to drama for what it has to work upon, the highest hopes, the deepest sufferings of humanity . . . and a real artist needs strong warrants of Conscience when he dips into those primary colours. In a fit of enthusiasm Ruskin wanted to lay a tax on all colours but Black, Prussian blue, Vandyke brown, and Chinese white. I suspect it would be greatly to the advantage of *our* Art if to depict some of the deeper emotions and experiences of Humanity were forbidden . . . till years of discretion. 'Make your *white* precious' is a quaint saying of Ruskin's which I often recall when I write."[2]

May 13, 1885. She died quietly and painlessly, having made all of her "white precious."

FOR MORE INFORMATION SEE: Horatia K. F. (Gatty) Eden, *Juliana Horatia Ewing and Her Books* (illustrated from sketches by Juliana Horatia Ewing), S.P.C.K., 1885, reprinted, Gale, 1969; Emma Marshall, *Women Novelists of Queen Victoria's Reign,* Hurst & Blackett, 1897; E. V. Lucas, "Old and the Young Adam," in *All of a Piece,* Lippincott, 1937; W.K.L. Clarke, "Mrs. Ewing and Her Books," in *Eighteenth Century Piety,* Macmillan, 1944; Christabel Maxwell, *Mrs. Gatty and Mrs. Ewing,* Constable, 1949; Marghanita Laski, *Mrs. Ewing, Mrs. Molesworth, and Mrs. Hodgson Burnett,* A. Barker, 1950; Marcia Dalphin, "Mrs. Gatty and Mrs. Ewing," *Horn Book,* May, 1950; Roger Lancelyn Green, *Tellers of Tales,* Ward, 1953, revised edition, F. Watts, 1965; Gillian Elise Avery, *Mrs. Ewing,* Bodley Head, 1961, reissued, Walck, 1964; M. A. Downie, "Mrs. Ewing in Canada," *Horn Book,* December, 1967; Brian Doyle, editor, *Who's Who of Children's Literature,* Schocken Books, 1968; Laura Benét, *Famous Storytellers for Young People,* Dodd, 1968.

FEELINGS, Muriel (Grey)   1938-

PERSONAL: Born July 31, 1938, in Philadelphia, Pennsylvania; married Thomas Feelings (an author and illustrator), February 18, 1969 (divorced, 1974); children: Zamani, Kamili. *Education:* Attended Philadelphia Museum School of Art, 1957-60; Los Angeles State College, B.A., 1963.

CAREER: Author. Teacher, 1964-70, in New York and Uganda, East Africa. *Member:* Columbian Design Society (New York). *Awards, honors: Moja Means One: Swahili*

MURIEL FEELINGS

8 **nane**
(nah·nay)

Busy market stalls are stocked with fruits, vegetables, meats, fish, clothes, jewelry, pottery, and carvings.

(From *Moja Means One* by Muriel Feelings. Illustrated by Tom Feelings.)

Counting Book (illustrated by Tom Feelings) was a runner-up for the Caldecott Medal, 1972, and was cited by the Brooklyn Art Books for Children, 1973.

WRITINGS: Zamani Goes to Market (illustrated by husband, Tom Feelings), Seabury Press, 1970; *Moja Means One: Swahili Counting Book* (ALA Notable Book; illustrated by T. Feelings), Dial Press, 1971; *Jambo Means Hello: Swahili Alphabet Book* (ALA Notable Book; illustrated by T. Feelings), Dial Press, 1974.

SIDELIGHTS: **July 31, 1938.** Born in Philadelphia, Pennsylvania, and grew up there. Feelings studied at the Philadelphia Museum School of Art and completed her formal education at California State College in Los Angeles (1963), where she majored in art and minored in education and Spanish.

1964-70. Taught Spanish and art in the secondary and elementary schools of Philadelphia and New York and in Uganda, East Africa. In Uganda she taught art in a boys' senior secondary school in Kampala, the capital. "I have found a great satisfaction in my teaching years with Black children of various age levels—seeing their development and their pride in learning about their heritage. My most rewarding experience was the two years in Africa; both the life and work. I was met with much warmth by the students and people as a whole. I found the rural African life probably the most congenial, as people there have an intact culture; and hospitality and warmth are a built-in part of the culture. I traveled to Kenya, Tanzania, to various parts of Uganda, and to Central Africa."

February 18, 1964. Married Thomas Feelings, a fellow author and illustrator.

1970. *Zamani Goes to Market,* illustrated by her husband, was published. The hero in the book was named after their son, Zamani. "*Zamani Goes to Market* was inspired by collective impressions of my visits to various parts of East Africa, but many features were inspired by experiences during a two-week stay with a family in a Kenya village."

1971. *Moja Means One: Swahili Counting Book* published. A *Horn Book* review said, "On the plus side, illustrations in shades of brown and smoke evoke the beauty of rural Africa. On the minus side, the counting device is confusing.... [This book] could be used in a story hour for all young children as a way of introducing the sights and sounds of eastern Africa." According to *Saturday Review,* "A small child will need an adult's help with this counting book, as the word or words that identify the numbered objects are used in a sentence.... The book is addressed 'To all Black children living in the Western Hemisphere, hoping you will one day speak the language—in Africa.'"

Of *Jambo Means Hello: Swahili Alphabet Book, Horn Book* wrote, "The words of this Swahili alphabet book speak of respect and friendship, mothers and fathers and children, worship and celebration, succulent food, majestic animals, and of greetings to companions and strangers. But the beautiful vision of African life in the text merely hints of the community breathtakingly captured in the illustrations, which draw on the ambience of the words but move into the realm of the sublime."

FOR MORE INFORMATION SEE: Horn Book, February and March, 1972, August and December, 1974.

FIELD, Eugene   1850-1895

PERSONAL: Born September 3, 1850, in St. Louis, Missouri; died November 4, 1895, in Chicago, Illinois; son of Roswell Martin (a lawyer) and Frances (Reed) Field; married Julia Sutherland Comstock, October 16, 1873; children: five sons, three daughters. *Education:* Attended Williams College, Williamstown, Massachusetts; Knox College, Galesburg, Illinois; and the University of Missouri. *Home:* "Sabine Farm," Buena Park, Illinois.

CAREER: Journalist and poet. Worked on the editorial staff of several newspapers, including the *St. Joseph Gazette,* 1875-76; *St. Louis Journal* and *St. Louis Times-Journal,* 1876-80; *Kansas City Times,* 1880-81; *Denver Tribune,*

1881-83. Wrote column entitled "Sharps and Flats" for the *Chicago Morning News* (called the *Chicago Record* after 1890), 1883-95. His writings are mainly collections of newspaper contributions.

WRITINGS—Poems: *A Little Book of Western Verse,* [Chicago], 1889, Scribner, 1890; *Second Book of Verse,* M. E. Stone, 1892; *With Trumpet and Drum,* Scribner, 1892, reprinted, Books for Libraries, 1970; *Love-Songs of Childhood,* Scribner, 1894, reprinted, 1969; *Lullaby-Land* (illustrated by Charles Robinson), Scribner, 1894; *Songs, and Other Verse,* Scribner, 1896; *The Eugene Field Book: Verses, Stories, and Letters for School Reading,* Scribner, 1898, reprinted, Books for Libraries, 1969; *A Little Book of Tribune Verse,* Tandy, Wheeler, 1901; *Little Willie,* privately printed, 1901, also published as *The Immortal Little Willie,* J. H. Nash, 1929; *Poems of Childhood* (illustrated by Maxfield Parrish), Scribner, 1904, reissued, 1974; *Hoosier Lyrics,* M. A. Donohue, 1905; *The Clink of Ice, and Other Poems Worth Reading,* M. A. Donohue, 1905; *John Smith, U.S.A.,* M. A. Donohue, 1905; *Sister's Cake, and Other Poems,* Hurst, 1908; *Cradle Lullabies,* Canterbury, 1909; *The Poems of Eugene Field,* Scribner, 1910; *Christmas Tales and Christmas Verse* (illustrated by Florence Storer), Scribner, 1912; *Penn-Yan Bill's Wooing Poem,* Torch Press, 1914; *The Mouse and the Moonbeam,* W. E. Rudge, 1919.

The Symbol and the Saint, W. E. Rudge, 1924; *Wynken, Blynken, and Nod, and Other Child Verses,* C. E. Graham, 1925 [other editions illustrated by Fern B. Peat, Saafield Publishing, 1930; Helen Page, Follett, 1956; Clare McKinley, Rand McNally, 1956; Susan Perl, Dell, 1964; Barbara Cooney, Hastings House, 1970; Holly Johnson, F. Warne, 1973]; *Child Verses* (illustrated by Helene Nyce), Saafield Publishing, 1927; *Fiddle-Dee-Dee, and Other Verses* (illustrated by H. Nyce and Shawn O'Rosson), Saafield Publishing, 1929; *The Sugar-Plum Tree, and Other Verses* (illustrated by F. B. Peat), Saafield Publishing, 1930.

Other: *The Tribune Primer,* [Denver], 1882; *Culture's Garland, Being Memoranda of the Gradual Rise of Literature, Art, Music, and Society in Chicago, and Other Western Ganglia,* Ticknor, 1887; *A Little Book of Profitable Tales,* J. Wilson, 1889, reprinted, Books for Libraries, 1969; (with brother, Roswell M. Field) *Echoes from the Sabine Farm: Adaptations from Horace,* Scribner, 1892; *The Holy Cross, and Other Tales,* Stone & Kimball, 1893, reprinted, Books for Libraries, 1969; *The House: An Episode in the Lives of Reuben Baker, Astronaut, and of His Wife, Alice,* Scribner, 1893; *Eugene Field: An Auto-Analysis,* R. R. Donnelley, 1896; *The Love Affairs of a Bibliomaniac,* Scribner, 1896, reprinted, R. West, 1973; *Second Book of Tales,* Scribner, 1896; *Florence Bardsley's Story: The Life and Death of a Remarkable Woman,* W. I. Way, 1897; *The Temptation of Friar Gonsol,* Woodward & Lothrop, 1900; *Sharps and Flats,* Scribner, 1900; *Nonsense for Old and Young* (illustrated by John C. Frohn), H. A. Dickerman, 1901; *The Stars: A Slumber Story,* New Amsterdam Book Co., 1901; *The Complete Tribune Primer* (illustrated by Frederick Opper), Mutual Book Co., 1901, reprinted, Dillon Press, 1967; *In Wink-A-Way Land,* M. A. Donohue, 1905; *The Gingham Dog and the Calico Cat* (illustrated by H. Page), Follett, 1956; *A Comic Primer* (illustrated by Wendy Watson), Peter Pauper Press, 1966.

Collections and selections: *The Writings in Prose and Verse of Eugene Field,* 12 volumes, Scribner, 1898-1901; *Some Poems of Childhood* (illustrated by Gertrude A. Kay; edited by Bertha E. Mahony), Scribner, 1931; *Favorite Poems by*

Eugene Field (illustrated by Malthe Hasselriis), Grosset & Dunlap, 1940; *The Lullaby Book of Poems,* Schori Press, 1963; *The Works of Eugene Field,* eight volumes, Scholarly Press, 1976.

ADAPTATIONS—Movies and filmstrips: "Little Boy Blue" (motion picture), Metro-Goldwyn-Mayer, 1936; "Gingham Dog and Calico Cat" (filmstrip; color, for kindergarten and primary grades), Stillfilm, 1949; "Winkin, Blinkin, and Nod" (filmstrip; color, for kindergarten and primary grades), Stillfilm, 1949; "The Owl and the Pussy-Cat [and] Wynken, Blynken, and Nod" (filmstrip; color, with a phonodisc and text booklet), Weston Woods, 1967.

Plays: Anne (Coulter) Martens, *The Mouse Who Didn't Believe in Santa,* adaptation of *The Mouse and the Moonbeam,* Dramatic Publishing, 1963; A. Martens, *The Lonesome Little Shoe* (one-act), Dramatic Publishing, 1964.

Other: Reginald De Koven and others, composers of music, *Songs of Childhood,* Scribner, 1896.

SIDELIGHTS: **September 3, 1850.** Born in St. Louis, Missouri. The exact date of Field's birthdate is uncertain. He gave both September 2nd and September 3rd, preferring the latter. Family tradition inclines to September 2nd. It was Field's feeling that if any of his friends forgot September 2nd, their consciences would prick them to make amends on September 3rd. "I am a scion of an illustrious family. . . . Sir John Field was an astronomer; he loved to 'rear his head among the stars,' and it was with them that he passed a lifetime, and to them that he devoted his genius and talents.

"John Field his son was a preacher, a godly man who gave his life, not to the stars, but to the creator of stars.

"Zachariah Field was a farmer, devoted to pastoral life; contented with his farm and his flocks he dared not lift his eyes to the stars, but under their mystic light paid worship to them and his maker.

"Joseph Field was a physician. He went about doing good, and a generation of undertakers rose up and called him blessed.

"Seth Field was a lawyer; he shone in the legal firmament, a worthy satellite of Kent and Blackstone, and his son, Martin Field, trod the same path of glory, leaving behind a record as pure and bright as the first rays of the evening star.

"Roswell M. Field was a lawyer, too, and now we find Eugene Field, the son of R. M. Field, the great-great-great-great grandson of Sir John Field, the astronomer, a pure, bright light in the world of literature, a star rising from the horizon and destined ere long to occupy a blazing position in the zenith." [Slason Thompson, *Life of Eugene Field,* D. Appleton, 1927.[1]]

1856. His mother died.

"TO MY MOTHER

"How fair you are, my mother!
Ah, though 'tis many a year
Since you were here,
Still do I see your beauteous face,
And with the glow
Of Your dark eyes cometh a glow
Of long ago.

So gentle, too, my mother!
  Just as of old, upon my brow,
  Like benedictions now,
Falleth your dear hands' touch;
  And still, as then,
A voice that glads me over-much
  Cometh again,
  My fair and gentle mother!"[1]

Field's father, Roswell Martin Field, received fame for his courtroom defense of Dred Scott, but had little time for his sons. Field and brother, Roswell, were cared for by their cousin, Mary Field French (a spinster of about thirty years) in Amherst, Mass.

"To Mary Field French
"A dying mother gave to you
  Her child a many years ago;
How in your gracious love he grew,
  You know, dear, patient heart, you know.

"The mother's child you fostered then
  Salutes you now and bids you take
These little children of his pen
  And love them for the author's sake."

[Robert Conrow, *Field Days: The Life, Times and Reputation of Eugene Field,* Scribner, 1974.[2]]

"... I find myself thinking of my boyhood, and of the hills and valleys and trees and flowers and birds I knew when the morning of my life was fresh and full of exuberance. Those years were spent among the Pelham hills, very, very far from here; but memory o'erleaps the mountain ranges, the leagues upon leagues of prairie, the mighty rivers, the forest, the farming lands, o'erleaps them all; and today, by that same sweet magic that instantaneously undoes the years and space, I seem to be among the Pelham hills again. The yonder glimpse of the Pacific becomes the silver thread of the Connecticut, seen, not over miles of orange groves, but over broad acres of Indian corn; instead of the pepper and eucalyptus, the lemon and the palm, I see (or I seem to see) the maple once more and the elm and the chestnut trees, the shagbark walnut, the hickory, and the birch. In those days, these rugged mountains of this southland were unknown to me; and the Pelham hills were full of marvel and delight, with their tangled pathways and hidden stores of wintergreen and wild strawberries. Furtive brooks led the little boy hither and thither in his quest for trout and dace, while to the gentler minded the modest flowers of the wildwood appealed with singular directness. A partridge rose now and then from the thicket and whirred away, and with startled eyes the brown thrush peered out from the bushes."[1]

The Field brothers made frequent visits to their grandmother in Newfane, Vermont. "... My lovely old grandmother was one of the very elect. How many times have I carried her footstove for her and filled it in the vestry room. I have frozen in the old pew while grandma kept nice and warm and nibbled lozenges and cassia cakes during the meeting. I remember the old sounding board. There was no melodeon in that meetinghouse, and the leader of the choir pitched the tune with a turning fork. As a boy I used to play hi-spy in the horse shed. But I am not so old—no, a man is still a boy at forty, isn't he?"[1]

"Yes, grandma was Puritanical—not to the extent of persecution, but a Puritan in the severity of her faith and in the exacting nicety of her interpretation of her duties to God and

EUGENE FIELD

mankind. Grandma's Sunday began at six o'clock Saturday evening; by that hour her house was swept and garnished, and her lamps trimmed, every preparation made for a quiet, reverential observance of the Sabbath Day."[2]

"The old homestead was to the south of the common; it was a long two-story frame house with narrow windows and a green front door, upon which there was a curious little brass knocker and a brass door plate bearing the name 'General Martin Field.' Above the door was an archaic window or transom in the shape of a fan. Three acres of land were around the house, a large front yard and a side yard and an orchard; there were numerous outbuildings, a museum (for my grandfather was an amateur naturalist), a woodshed, a barn, an ice-house and a carriage house. In the carriage house was a monster chaise, and I used to wonder whether there ever was a horse big enough and strong enough to haul it. There was a long gravel walk leading from the front gate to the front door, and on each side of this walk there was a flower-bed, in which, at the proper season, prim daffodils bloomed. On the picket fence which divided the front and side yards there was a sun dial, and just to the north of this dial stood a sassafras tree. . . ."[1]

The longest visit "lasted seven months and the dear old lady got all the grandsons she wanted. She did not invite us to repeat the visit."[1]

The Field boys had the benefit of their grandmother's gracious presence and exemplary life until they were well into their teens. It was during these visits that Field developed his extraordinary love for pets. According to Roswell: "Unlike other boys, he seemed to carry his pets into a higher sphere and to give them personality. For each pet, whether dog, cat, bird, goat or squirrel—he had the family mistrust of a horse—he not only had a name, but it was delight to fancy that each possessed a peculiar dialect of human speech, and each he addressed in the humorous manner conceived.

When in childhood he was conducting a poultry annex to the homestead, each chicken was properly instructed to respond to a peculiar call, and Finniken, Minniken, Winniken, Dump, Poog, Boog seemed to recognize immediately the queer intonations of their master with an intelligence that is not usually accorded to chickens.''[1]

Field once said, ''[If] I could be grateful to New England for nothing else, I should bless her forevermore for pounding me with the Bible and the Spelling Book.''[1]

As a child, Field was encouraged by his devout Congregationalist grandmother to write sermons. Said to have been written at age nine and taking for his text the fifteenth verse of the thirteenth chapter of Proverbs:

> *Good understanding giveth favor:*
> *But the way of the transgressor is hard.*

Field proceeded: ''The life of a Christian is often compared to a race that is hard and to a battle in which a man must fight hard to win; these comparisons have prevented many from becoming Christians.

''But the Bible does not compare the Christian's faith as one of hard labor. But Solomon says wisdom's ways are ways of pleasantness and her paths are peace. Under the word transgressor are included all those that disobey their maker, or in shorter words, the ungodly. Every person looking around him will see many who are transgressors and whose lot is very hard.

''I remark, secondly, that conscience makes the way of the transgressors hard; for every act of pleasure, every act of guilt his conscience smites him. The last of his stay on earth will appear horrible to the beholder. Some time, however, he will be stayed in his guilt. A death in the family of some favorite object, or be attacked by some disease himself is brought to the portals of the grave. Then for a little time, perhaps, he is stayed in his wickedness, but before long he returns to his worldly lusts. Oh, it is indeed hard for a sinner to go down into perhaps perdition over all the obstacles which God has placed in his path. But many, I am afraid, do go down into perdition, for wide is the gate and broad the way that leadeth to destruction, and many there be that go in after it.

''Suppose now there was a fearful precipice and to allure you there your enemies should scatter flowers on its dreadful edge, would you if you knew that while you were strolling about on that awful rock that night would settle down on you and that you would fall from that giddy, giddy height, would you, I say, go near that dreadful rock? Just so with the transgressor, he falls from that height just because he wishes to appear good in the sight of the world. But what will a man gain if he gain the whole world and lose his own soul,''[1]

Fall, 1865. Entered a private school of the Rev. James Tufts, Monson, Mass. Here he took his greatest lessons from the birds, insects, and smaller animals that abounded in the Monson meadows.

In his recollections of those early school days, Tufts remembered that ''in his studies [Field] was about fitted for an ordinary high school, except in arithmetic. He had read a little Latin, enough to commence Caesar. I found him an average boy in his lessons, not dull, but not a quick and ready scholar like his father, who graduated from Middlebury College at the age of fifteen, strong and athletic.

''He did not seem to care much for his books, or his lessons anyway, but was inclined to get along as easily as he could, partly on account of his delicate health, which made close study irksome, and partly because his mind was very juvenile and undeveloped. His health improved gradually, while his interest in his studies increased slowly but steadily. Judge Forbes, of Westboro, for a time his roommate and a remarkable scholar, remarked on reading his journal that his chum occasionally took up his book for study when his teacher came around, though he was not always particular which side up the book was. And so it was through life.

''Eugene gave little if any indication of becoming a poet, or even a superior writer, in his youth. He was always, however, bright and lively in conversation, abounding in wit, self-possessed, and never laughing at his own jokes, showing, too, some of that exhaustless fountain of humor in which he afterward excelled. But he did not like close application, nor did he have patience to correct and improve what he wrote, as he afterward did when his taste was more cultivated. In declamation Eugene always excelled, reciting with marked effect 'Spartacus,' 'The Soldier of the Legion' and 'The Dream of Clarence' from Shakespeare. He inherited from his father a rich, strong, musical and sympathetic voice, which made him a pleasant speaker and afterward a successful public reader.''[1]

1869. Barely able to pass the entrance examination, Field entered Williams College. A fellow student, Solomon B. Griffin, gave his view of the Field who flitted across the campus. ''. . . I struck up an acquaintance with him at Smith's college book store and the post office. Field was raw and not a bit deferential to established customs, and so the secret society men were not attracted to him. The 'trotting' or preliminary attentions to freshmen constitute a great and revered feature of college life. When I saw Field 'trotting' a lank and gawky freshman, for the 'Mills Theological Society,' the humor of it appealed to one soaked in the traditions of a college town, and we 'became acquainted.' Field left the class about as I came in.''[1]

April 27, 1869. Field returned to Monson. According to Tuft, ''He was too smart for the professors at Williams; because they did not understand him, they could not pardon his eccentricities. Eugene was not much of a student, but very much of an irrepressible boy. There was no malice in his pranks, only the inherited disposition to tease somebody and everybody.''[1]

July 5, 1869. Summoned to St. Louis by the serious illness of his father, who died a week later.

Autumn, 1869. Entered the sophomore class at Knox College, Galesbury, Illinois. Here he tried his prentice hand at reporting college affairs for a local newspaper.

Fall, 1870. Junior class at the University of Missouri, Columbia, Missouri. The historian of the University left the following impression of Field at his third Alma Mater. ''Eugene was an inattentive, indifferent student, making poor progress in the studies of the course—a genial, sportive, song-singing fun-making companion. Nevertheless he was bright, sparkling, entertaining and a leader among 'the boys.' In truth he was in intellect above his fellows and a genius along his favorite lines. He was prolific of harmless pranks and his school life was a big joke.''[1]

Failed his math class and was almost expelled from the University after conducting a raid on the president's wine cellar.

...That give great joy to me
While the Dinkey-Bird goes singing
In the amfallela tree.
■ (From *Poems of Childhood* by Eugene Field. Illustrated by Maxfield Parrish.)

The occasion prompted what has been labeled as "Field's first printed poem"—the final lines of which he wrote in mock Latin.

> "The frightened pueri all crowd,
> Around the Doctor, who aloud,
> Proclaims ut he will have to see,
> Then ranged before the Faculty.
> Sed gloria to that Faculty.
> Doctor cavet, pueri, free."[2]

1871. Field never completed college. His share of his father's estate was under the guardianship of his father's executor, Melvin L. Gray, and the watchful care of Mrs. Gray. "My acquaintance with Mrs. Gray began in 1871. I was at that time just coming of age, and there were many reasons why I was attracted to the home over which this admirable lady presided. In the first place, Mrs. Gray's household was a counterpart of the household to which my boyhood life in New England has attached me. Again, both Mr. and Mrs. Gray were old friends of my parents; and upon Mr. Gray's accepting the executorship of my father's estate, Mrs. Gray felt, I am pleased to believe, somewhat more than a friendly interest in the two boys, who, coming from rural New England life into the great, strange, fascinating city, stood in need of disinterested friendship and prudent advice. I speak for my brother and myself when I say that for the period of twenty years we found in Mrs. Gray a friend as indulgent, as forbearing, as sympathetic, as kindly suggestive and as disinterested as a mother, and in her home a refuge from temptation, care and vexation."[1]

1872. Accompanied by a college chum and future brother-in-law, Edgar V. Comstock, "I visited Europe, spending six months and my patrimony in France, Italy, Ireland, and England."[1]

"The English . . . appear to set themselves up as the lords of Creation, as if the little isle of England were in any way better than other little isles. Not so with the American. He is all smiles to everyone, free with his money, into everything, friendly with even the garcons and porters. I can't say that I approve of this miscellaneous friendliness but it is perfectly characteristic of the American abroad."[2]

"We have been two months in Nice, and a month or so traveling in Italy. Two weeks we passed in Naples, and a most delightful place we found it. . . . I climbed Vesuvius and peered cautiously into the crater. It was a glorious sight. Nothing else like it in the world! Such a glorious smell of Brimstone! Such enlivening whiffs of hot steam and sulphuric fumes! Then, too, the grand veil of impenetrable white smoke that hung over the yawning abyss! No wonder people rave about this crater, and no wonder Pliny lost his life in coming too near the fascinating monster. The ascent of Vesuvius is no mean undertaking and I advise all American parents to train their children especially for it, by drilling them daily upon their back-yard ash-heaps. I was an hour climbing up the cone, which cannot be more than fifteen hundred feet. . . . Coming down the mountain is rare fun. The sand and ashes are so deep that the descent may be made upon a dead run. Clad in old garments and with my pedal extremities encased in my 'monitor gaiters,' I astonished the natives by my celerity and recklessness. I was much disappointed in Pompeii."[1]

The only letters to reach America during his European sojourn were to ask Mr. Gray for additional funds for the expedition. When the two tourists reached Naples, they were promptly met with a "No funds available" cable notice. Returned to St. Louis.

May, 1873. Reporter for St. Louis *Evening Journal*.

Selected as the journalist to accompany Carl Schurz, a candidate for reelection to the United States Senate, on a political campaign through Missouri.

October 16, 1873. After a two year engagement and considerable parental hesitation, "I married Miss Julia Sutherland Comstock of St. Joseph, Missouri, at that time a girl of sixteen. We have had eight children—three daughters and five sons.

> "*What though these years of ours be fleeting,*
> *What though the years of youth be flown?*
> *I'll mock Old Tempus with repeating:*
> *'I love my love and her alone.'*
>
> "*And when I fall before his reaping,*
> *And when my stuttering speech is dumb,*
> *Think not my love is dead or sleeping,*
> *But that it waits for you to come.*"[1]

On the occasion of their eighth wedding anniversary, in 1881, Field wrote his wife, "You have had a hard time, Julia. You loved and married a boy. You were the mother of a boy's children. You are the mother of a big, foolish and yet affectionate boy's children today."[2]

1875. City editor of the St. Joseph Gazette.

> "*Oh, many a peck of apples and of peaches did I get*
> *When I helped 'em run the local on the St. Jo*
> *Gazette.*"[1]

Spring, 1876. Returned to St. Louis. Editorial writer on the St. Louis *Journal* and the *Times-Journal*.

Field employed several methods of obtaining "needful" money from Gray. Once he threatened to go on the stage under the assumed name of Melvin L. Gray. "Very well, if you cannot make such a paltry advance out of my estate, I shall be compelled to go on the variety stage. But as I cannot keep my own name I will take yours and shall have lithographs struck off at once reading, 'To-night, M. L. Gray, Banjo and Speciality Artist.'"[1] Gray advanced the needed funds.

Field repudiated the charge that he disrespected Gray from whom he received every evidence of affection. "A copy of last Saturday's St. Louis *Spectator* has just arrived and I am equally surprised, pained and indignant to find in it a personal article about myself which represents me in the untruthful light of having been disrespectful and impudent to you. I believe you will bear me out when I say that my conduct towards you has upon all occasions been respectful and gentlemanly. I may not have been able to repay you the many obligations you have placed me under, but I have always regarded you with feelings of affectionate gratitude and I am deeply distressed lest the article referred to may create a widely different impression. Of course it makes no difference to you, but as gratitude is about all I have in the world to bestow on those who are good and kind to me, it is not right that I should be advertised—even in a joking way—as an ingrate."[1]

The little stars were the herring fish
   That lived in that beautiful sea—
"Now cast your nets wherever you wish—
   Never afeard are we";
     So cried the stars to the fishermen three:
       Wynken,
       Blynken,
       And Nod.

The little stars were the herring fish
    That lived in that beautiful sea—
"Now cast your nets wherever you wish—
    Never afeard are we";
So cried the stars to the fishermen three:
    Wynken
    Blynken
    And Nod.

■ (From *Wynken, Blynken and Nod* by Eugene Field. Illustrated by Barbara Cooney.)

1879. "I wrote and published my first bit of verse in 1879. It was entitled 'Christmas Treasures.' Just ten years later I began to write verse very frequently."[1]

1880. Moved to Kansas City. Managing editor of the *Times.*

1881-1883. Moved to Denver. Managing editorship of the *Tribune.* Given the assignment to make the *Tribune* "hum." Started a column headed "Odds and Ends," to which he was the chief contributor, and "The Tribune Primer," of which the following are examples:

"THE WASP

"See the Wasp. He has pretty yellow Stripes around his Body, and a Darning Needle in his Tail. If you will Pat the Wasp upon the Tail, we will Give you a Nice Picture Book.

"THE NASTY TOBACCO

"What is that Nasty-looking object? It is a Chew of To-bacco. Oh, how naughty it is to use the Filthy weed. It makes the teeth black and spoils the Parlor Carpet. Go Quick and Throw the Horrid Stuff Away. Put it in the Ice Cream Freezer or in the Coffee Pot, where Nobody can see it. Little Girls, you should never chew Tobacco.

"THE MUCILAGE

"The Bottle is full of Mucilage. Take it and Pour some Mu-cilage into Papa's Slippers. Then when Papa comes Home it will be a Question whether there will be more Stick in the Slippers than on your Pants."[1]

April 26, 1883. Melville E. Stone of the *Chicago Morning Press* urged Field to join the staff. Stone received the following acceptance letter:

"DEAR MR. STONE:

"Had I supposed you were going to be in Denver a day longer I should have tried to have another talk with you and I believe we could have settled the question of my coming to Chicago. I repeat that I was much pleased by the way you talked relative to my casting my lot with the *News,* and I want to assure you once more that when I go to you it will be with the intention of staying. As I intimated to you while you were here, I cannot leave the *Tribune* people in the lurch. I have a contract with them till August 2, and, while I could get out of that contract I would prefer abiding strictly by it. Would it suit you as well, providing we agree to other details, that I delay my coming to you till September 1? I will contract with you for two or three years, to do the work you specify, for $50 per week the first year, $50.50 per week the second year. If you choose to contract for three years, I shall want $55 the third year. The reason I tack on the 50 cents for the second year is to gratify a desire I have to be able to say I am earning a little more money each year. This is a notion I have happily been able to gratify ever since I began reporting at $10 a week.

"Will you people allow me $100 for the expense of breaking up housekeeping here and removing to Chicago? I am a deucedly poor man or I would not suggest such a thing. An attempt at honesty in the profession has kept me gloriously hard up, with a constantly increasing family. However, as you are not running a charity enterprise, I beg you will not consider this last suggestion if it seems an improper one. I trust to hear from you at your earliest convenience.

"Yours very truly,

EUGENE FIELD"[1]

August, 1883. Moved his family and belongings to Chicago. An ever increasing family made a salary which seemed sufficient in Denver seem restrictive in Chicago. This situation gave point to an incident when his daughter asked her father to give her an appropriate text to recite to her Sunday school teacher; Field schooled her to rise and declaim with dramatic conviction: "The Lord will provide; my father can't."[1]

August 31, 1883. Started a column, "Sharps and Flats," which contained serious prose and verse as well as whimsical humor.

"I am neither a poet nor an author. I am simply a newspaper man, seeking to do somewhat towards improving newspaper literature. I am a thistle, standing in a bleak but fertile prairie; if the high winds scatter my seed hither and thither, I shall be content, for then other thistles will issue therefrom and make the prairie beautiful after a fashion. But, presently advancing culture will root up the thistles and then more beautiful flowers will bloom in our stead; that conviction pleases me most.

"If I have an honest purpose it is to give lie to the absurd heresy that a newspaper writer cannot write literature for his newspaper.

"It is with this ambition in view that I have put aside all pecuniary considerations and given my work freely and cheerfully to the newspaper. So little do I regret this alleged folly and so much in earnest am I in it that I shall probably continue in this way of doing to the end of my life."[2]

Slason Thompson offered the following description of him: "He was ... in his thirty-third year. If Eugene Field had ever stood up to his full height he would have measured slightly over six feet. But he never did and was content to shamble through life, appearing two inches shorter than he really was. Shamble is perhaps hardly the word to use. But neither glide nor shuffle fits his gait any more accurately. It was simply a walk with the least possible waste of energy. It fitted Dr. Holmes' definition of walking as forward motion to prevent falling. And yet Field never gave you the impression

that he was about to topple over. His legs always acted as if they were weary and would like to lean their master up against something. As to what that something might be, he would probably have answered 'Pie.'

"Field's arms were long, ending in well-shaped hands, which were remarkably deft and would have been attractive had he not at some time spoiled his fingers by the nail biting habit. His shoulders were broad and square, and not nearly as much rounded as might have been expected from his position while writing. It was not the stoop of his shoulders that detracted from his height, but a certain settling together, if I may so say, of the couplings of his backbone. He was large boned throughout, but without the muscles that should have gone with such a frame. He would probably have described himself as tall, big, gangling. He had no personal taste or pride in clothing, and never to my knowledge came across a tailor who took enough interest in his clothes to give him the benefit of a good fit or to persuade him to choose a becoming color. For this reason he looked best dressed in a dress suit, which he never wore when there was any possibility of avoiding it. His favorite coat was a sack, cut straight, and made from some cloth in which the various shades of yellow, green and brown struggled for mastery.

"But it was of little consequence how Field's body was clothed. He wore a 7⅜ hat and there was a head and face under it that compelled a second glance and repaid scrutiny in any company. The photographs of Field are numerous and preserve a fair impression of his remarkable physiognomy. None of the paintings of him that I have seen do him justice, and the etchings are not much of an improvement on the paintings. The best photographs only fail because they cannot retain the peculiar death-like pallor of the skin and the clear, innocent china-blue of the large eyes. These eyes were deep set under two arching brows, and yet were so large that their deep setting was not at first apparent. Field's nose was a good size and well shaped, with an unusual curve of the nostrils strangely complementary to the curve of the arch above the eyes. There was a mole on one cheek, which Field always insisted on turning to the camera and which the photographer very generally insisted on retouching out in the finishing. Field was wont to say that no photograph of him was genuine unless that mole 'was blown in on the negative.' The photographs all give him a good chin, in which there was merely the suggestion of that cleft which he held marred the strength of George William Curtis's lower jaw.

"The feature of his face, if such it can be called, where all portraits failed, was the hair. It was so fine that there would not have been much of it if it had been thick, and as it was quite thin there was only a shadow between it and baldness. Even its color was illusive—a cross between brown and dove color. Only those who knew Field before he came to Chicago have any impression as to the color of the thatch upon that head which never during our acquaintance stooped to a slouch hat. The formal black or brown derby for winter and the seasonable straw hat for summer seemed necessary to tone down the frivolity of his neckties, which were chosen with a cowboy's gaudy taste. To the day of his death Field delighted to present neckties, generally of the made-up variety, to his friends, which, it is needless to say, they never failed to accept and seldom wore. Often in the afternoon as it neared two o'clock he would stick his head above the partition between our rooms and say:

"'Come along, Nompy'—his familiar address for the writer—'come along and I'll buy you a new necktie.'

"'The dickens take your neckties,' would be my reply.

"Whereupon with the philosophy of which he never wearied, Field would rejoin:

"'Very well, if you won't let me buy you a necktie, you must buy me a lunch.'

"And off we would march to Henrici's coffee-house around the corner on Madison street, generally gathering Ballantyne and 'Snip' in our train as we passed the kennel of the managing editor of what was to be the newspaper with the largest morning circulation in Chicago."[1]

As an avid baseball "fan," Field devoted more than a score of paragraphs to the national game. Next to baseball, fishing was the sport out of which he got the most enjoyment. "So reclining on cushions, protected from the ardor of Sol, with the attention divided between a delightful book and a red bob—what enjoyment would be keener or greater than that of the angler?"[1]

With a miscellaneous collection of books numbering 3,500, Field turned book-collecting into his favorite hobby. He advised: "I hope that you will keep right along collecting, but do not buy too many French, German, Latin, and Italian books; that is not particularly profitable. You ought to be able to get together a splendid lot of American first editions, and if I were you I would certainly do that. In time Americans will be immensely valuable. Keep on piling up autograph letters, and don't forget to keep the letters you get from contemporaneous people; these may in time become of great interest and value. The fad of extra-illustrating has never possessed me, and I am hoping that it will not, for the reason that I could never make it profitable, since I never dispose of what I secure. I have absolutely no sense of barter—no, I am simply a royal and unmitigated sucker.

"You know that when Diogenes returned from his cruise about Athens, under the auspices of a lantern, his friend Socrates asked him what his racket had been. 'I have been hunting for an honest man,' replied he of the tub. 'Indeed!' queried Soc. 'and did you find any?' 'No, that I did not,' quoth Diog.; 'but I ran across a heap of—fools.' 'So?' saith Soc., 'and now, by Pallas! tell me the names of them.' 'That were a tedious job,' answered Diogenes; 'but I don't mind telling you that the chiefest and veriest—fool of 'em all was a gangling, cadaverous, lantern-jawed, lop-eared, flat-footed Missourian named Field!' 'By the dog, you speak truly!' cried Soc. 'When it comes to the quintessence of damphoolery, Eugene does indeed take the cake!'

"The amount of reading I am doing appals me. I fear its variety demoralizes me. With biographies of Landor, Peter Parley, Coleridge, Wordsworth, Leslie (the painter), Burns, Congreve, and Lamb, I am mixing up Baker's *Wild Beasts and their Ways,* divers works on dyspepsia and nervous diseases, Miller's *Songs of the Sierras,* Jeaffreson's *Doctors,* and a multitude of other books treating of all subjects from fairy mythology down to scatologic rites. I am wondering whether from this curious mass I shall expiscate anything of use to me in my work. My Muse has had a month's rest. I am beginning to think of giving the old girl another whirl. I am inclined to try my hand at a series of Russian lyrics, having become much interested in Ralston's *Folk-Songs.*" [Francis Wilson, *The Eugene Field I Knew,* Scribner, 1898[3]]

"All books are not for everybody; in literature there is a distinct aristocracy of intelligence. There are many people who should be prevented by law from reading the songs of Solomon. Literature is not so likely to be unfit for readers as readers are likely to be unfit for literature."[2]

"I have been a great theatre-goer."[1] When Modjeska came to town, he was a constant one.

The "Sharps and Flats" contained a review on Emma Abbott (a singer) whose artistic talents hovered above the requirements of a church sociable. Field's critique followed:

"Ten Years a Songbird: Memoirs of a Busy Life

"Miss Abbott is a lady for whom we have had for a number of years—ever since her debut as a public singer—the highest esteem. She is one of the most conscientious of women in her private walk, conscientious in every relationship and duty and practice that go to make the sum of her daily life. This conscientiousness, involving patience, humility, perseverance, and integrity, has been, we think, the real secret of her success."[1]

On the operatic stage Madam Marcella Sembrich was his favorite prima donna. "It is not all surprising that Madame Sembrich caught on so grandly night before last. She is the most comfortable-looking prima donna that has ever visited Chicago. She is one of your square-built, stout-rigged little ladies with a bright honest face and bouncing manners. . . . Her audience was a coldly critical one, of course, and it sat like a bump on a log until Sembrich made her appearance in the mad scene where Lucheer gives her vocal circus in the presence of twenty-five Scotch ladies in red, white and green dresses, and twenty-five supposititious Scotch gentlemen in costumes of the court of Louis XIV. Instead of sending for a doctor to assist Lucheer in her trouble, these fantastically attired ladies and gentlemen stand around and look dreary while Lucheer does grand and lofty tumbling, and executes pirouettes and trapeze performances in the vocal art. Then the audience began to wake up. . . . When she finally struck up high F sharp in the descending fourth of D in alt, one gentleman from the South Side, who had hired a dress coat for the occasion, broke forth in a hearty 'Brava!' This encouraged a resident of the North Side to shout 'Bravissimo!' and then several dudes from the Blue Island district raised the cry of 'Bong,' 'Tray beang' and 'Brava!' The vast audience seemed crazed with delight and enthusiasm. Even the pork merchants and grain dealers in the family circle vied with each other in hoarsely wafting Italian words of cheer at the triumphant Sembrich. One man was put out by the ushers because he so far forgot himself and the eclat of the occasion as to shout in vehement German: 'Mein Gott in Himmel das ist ver tampt goot!'

"It was an ovation, but it was no more than Sembrich deserved—bless her fat little buttons."[1]

October, 1889. Field seldom varied his routine of work or took a vacation. However, "ill health compelled me to visit Europe; there I remained fourteen months, that time being divided between England, Germany, Holland and Belgium.

"The attack of indigestion with which I am suffering began last June, resulting from irregularity in hours of eating and sleeping and from too severe application to work. The contemplated voyage will do me good, I think, and I hope to gather much valuable material while I am abroad. I shall seek to acquaint myself with such local legends as may seem to be capable of treatment in verse. Most of my time will be spent in London, in Paris and in Holland. I expect to find among the Dutch much to inspire me. I carry numerous letters of introduction—all kinds of letters except letters of credit. I regret that the potent name of Rothschild will not figure in the list of my trans-Atlantic acquaintances."[1]

From London he wrote: "Talk about weather, this is the most abominable climate I ever experimented with. Elsewhere I should have been well long ago; but I am so nervous that I dread travel and the excitement incident thereto. My inclination is to stay in the house, keep warm, read and write, and digest my simple food.

"What exceeding folly was it that tempted me to cross the sea in search of what I do not seem able to find here—a righteous stomach? I have been wallowing in the slough of despond for a week, and my digestive apparatus has gone wrong again. I have suffered tortures that would have done credit to the inventive genius of a Dante; and the natural consequences is, that I am as blue as a whetstone."[3]

November 13, 1889. "I am now, so to speak, in God's hands. Getting the four children fitted out for school and paying a quarter's tuition in advance has reduced me to a condition of financial weakness which fills me with the gloomiest apprehension. You of fertile resource must tell me what I am to do. I will not steal; to beg I am ashamed. My bank account shows £15. Verily, I am in hell's hole."[1]

Having placed four children in school at Hanover, Field wrote: "I am now feeling quite as I felt when I was in my original condition—perhaps I should say my normal condition of original sin."[1]

1891. Eldest son, Melvin, died. "On Thursday, the 28th ultimo, we laid Melvin's remains to rest finally in Graceland Cemetery. The lot I selected and bought is in a pretty, accessible spot, sheltered by two oak trees, just such a spot as the boy himself, with his love for nature, would have chosen. The interment was very private, none being present but the family. Others were in the cemetery making preparations for the observance of Decoration Day. Of this number were many Germans and these, attracted by the appearance of the pretentious German casket in which our boy's body lay, gathered around wonderingly. They were curious to know the story of the casket, for they had not seen one like it for many years. But the ceremony, however painful, was beautiful—beautiful in the caressing glory of the sunlight that was all around, in the fragrant velvety verdure that composed the bed to which we consigned the ashes of the beloved one, in the gentle music of the birds that nested hard by and knew no fear and in the love which we bore him and always shall."[1]

Fall, 1893. Suffered an attack of pneumonia. On doctor's advice visited California.

Winter, 1894. Wrote and had printed *An Auto-Analysis*. This document according to his biographer, Slason Thompson, is an ingenious mingling of fact and fiction. Within it's content Fields gave an account of all his likes and dislikes. ". . . I am fond of the quaint and curious in every line. I am very fond of dogs, birds and all small pets—a passion not approved of by my wife.

"My favorite flower is the carnation, and I adore dolls.

"My favorite hymn is 'Bounding Billows.'

"My favorites in fiction are Hawthorne's *Scarlet Letter*, *Don Quixote* and *Pilgrim's Progess*.

"I greatly love Hans Christian Andersen's Tales, and I am deeply interested in folk-lore and fairy tales. I believe in ghosts, in witches, and in fairies.

"I should like to own a big astronomical telescope and a twenty-four-tune music box.

"My favorite actor is Henry Irving; actress, Mme. Modjeska.

"I dislike 'Politics,' so called.

"I should like to have the privilege of voting extended to women.

"I am unalterably opposed to capital punishment.

"I favor a system of pensions for noble services in literature, art, science, etc. I approve of compulsory education.

"If I had my way, I should make the abuse of horses, dogs and cattle a penal offense; I should abolish all dog laws and dog-catchers, and I would punish severely everybody who caught and caged birds.

"I dislike all exercise and play all games very indifferently.

"I love to read in bed.

"I believe in churches and schools: I hate wars, armies, soldiers, guns and fireworks.

"I like music (limited).

"I have been a great theatre-goer.

"I enjoy the society of doctors and clergymen.

"My favorite color is red.

"I do not care particularly for sculpture or for paintings; I try not to become interested in them, for the reason that if I were to cultivate a taste for them I should presently become hopelessly bankrupt.

"I am extravagantly fond of perfumes.

"I am a poor diner, and I drink no wine, or spirits of any kind: I do not smoke tobacco.

"I dislike crowds and I abominate functions.

"I am six feet in height, am of spare build, weigh 160 pounds and have shocking taste in dress.

"But I like to have well-dressed people about me.

"My eyes are blue, my complexion pale, my face is shaven, and I incline to baldness.

"It is only when I look and see how young and fair and sweet my wife is that I have a good opinion of myself.

"I am fond of companionship of women, and I have no unconquerable prejudice against feminine beauty. I recall with pride that in twenty-two years of active journalism I have always written in reverential praise of womankind.

"I favor early marriage.

"I do not love all children.

"I have tried to analyze my feelings toward children, and I think I discover that I love them, in so far as I can make pets of them.

"I believe that, if I live, I shall do my best literary work when I am a grandfather."[1]

July, 1895. Bought Sabine Farm. It was "provided with all the modern conveniences, including an ample porch and a genial mortgage."[1]

August, 1895. Field gave expression to the home he dearly loved.

"MY SABINE FARM

"At last I have a Sabine farm
Abloom with shrubs and flowers;
And garlands gay I weave by day
Amid those fragrant flowers;
And yet, O fortune hideous,
I have no blooming Lydias;
And what, ah, what's a Sabine farm to us
     Without its Lydias?

"Within my cottage is a room
Where I would fain be merry;
Come one and all unto that hall,
     Where you'll be welcome, very!
I've a butler who's Hibernian—
But no, I've no Falernian!
And what, ah, what's a Sabine farm to you
     Without Falernian?

"Upon this cosey Sabine farm
     What breeds my melancholy?
Why is my Muse down with the blues
     Instead of up and jolly?
A secret this between us:
I'm shy of a Maecenas!
And what, oh, what's a Sabine farm to
     Me without Maecenas!"[1]

November 4, 1895. Died of heart failure at the Sabine Farm in Chicago, Illinois. ". . . Just a dropping to sleep here and an awakening yonder.

"How good it is to live in this beautiful world of ours; how varied and countless are the blessings bestowed upon us, how sweet is the beneficence of Nature; how dear is the companionship of humanity!"[1]

FOR MORE INFORMATION SEE: Slason Thompson, *Eugene Field: A Study in Heredity and Contradictions,* Scribner, 1901, reprinted, Beekman, 1973; Charles H. Dennis, *Eugene Field's Creative Years,* Doubleday, 1924, reprinted, Scholarly Press, 1971; R. A. Day, "Birth and Death of a Satirist: Eugene Field and Chicago's Growing Pains," *American Literature,* January, 1951; Robert Conrow, *Field Days: The Life, Times, and Reputation of Eugene Field,* Scribner, 1974.

For children: Laura Benét, *Famous American Poets,* Dodd, 1950; Mae (Trovillion) Smith, *Famous Pets of Famous People,* Dodd, 1950; L. Benét, *Famous American Humorists,* Dodd, 1959; L. Benét, *Famous Poets for Young People,*

The stock was of pine and the barrel of tin,
The "bang" it came out where the bullet went in.
■ (From *The Sugar Plum Tree and Other Verses* by Eugene Field. Illustrated by Fern B. Peat.)

Dodd, 1964; Kathryn Kilby Borland and Helen Ross Speicher, *Eugene Field: Young Poet,* Bobbs-Merrill, 1964; L. Edmond Leipold, *Famous American Poets,* Denison, 1969; L. E. Leipold, *Great American Poets,* Denison, 1973.

FREEDMAN, Russell (Bruce) 1929-

PERSONAL: Born October 11, 1929, in San Francisco, Calif.; son of Louis N. (a publishers' representative) and Irene (Gordon) Freedman. *Education:* Attended San Jose State College (now University), 1947-49; University of California, Berkeley, B.A., 1951. *Home and office:* 280 Riverside Dr., New York, N.Y. 10025.

CAREER: Associated Press, San Francisco, Calif., newsman, 1953-56; J. Walter Thompson Co. (advertising agency), New York, N.Y., television publicity writer, 1956-60; Columbia University Press, New York, N.Y., associate staff member, *Columbia Encyclopedia,* 1961-63; Crowell-Collier Educational Corp., New York, N.Y., editor, 1964-65; New School for Social Research, New York, N.Y., instructor of writing workshops, 1969—; free-lance writer, particularly for young people. *Military service:* U.S. Army, Counter Intelligence Corps, 1951-53. *Member:* Authors League of America, American Civil Liberties Union.

WRITINGS—Books for young people; all published by Holiday House, except as noted: *Teenagers Who Made History,* 1961; *2000 Years of Space Travel,* 1963; *Jules Verne: Portrait of a Prophet,* 1965; *Thomas Alva Edison,* Study-Master, 1966; *Scouting With Baden-Powell,* 1967; (with James E. Morriss) *How Animals Learn,* 1969; (with

His mother held him in her arms and pressed him close to the warmth of her belly. ▪ (From *The First Days of Life* by Russell Freedman. Illustrated by Joseph Cellini.)

RUSSELL FREEDMAN

Morriss) *Animal Instincts,* 1970; *Animal Architects,* 1971; (with Morriss) *The Brains of Animals and Man,* 1972; *The First Days of Life,* 1974; *Growing Up Wild: How Young Animals Survive,* 1975; *Animal Fathers,* 1976; *Animal Games,* 1976; *Hanging On: How Animals Carry Their Young,* 1977; *How Birds Fly,* 1977; *Getting Born,* 1978; *How Animals Defend Their Young,* Dutton, 1978. Contributor to *Columbia Encyclopedia,* 3rd edition, Scholastic Magazines, and to *Cricket.*

FOR MORE INFORMATION SEE: Horn Book, December, 1963.

GARDNER, Martin   1914-

PERSONAL: Born October 21, 1914, in Tulsa, Okla.; son of James Henry and Willie (Spiers) Gardner; married Charlotte Greenwald, October 17, 1952; chidren: James Emmett, Thomas Owen. *Education:* University of Chicago, B.A., 1936. *Home:* Hastings-on-Hudson, New York.

CAREER: Author and editor. Editor, University of Chicago literary magazine, *Comment;* reporter, Tulsa *Tribune;* contributing editor, *Humpty Dumpty's Magazine;* writer in the mathematical games department of *Scientific American,* 1957—. *Military service:* United States Naval Reserve, 1942-46.

WRITINGS: In the Name of Science, Putnam, 1952, revised edition published as *Fads and Fallacies in the Name of Science,* Dover, 1957; *Mathematics, Magic and Mystery,* Dover, 1956; *Logic, Machines and Diagrams,* McGraw, 1958, reprinted as *Logic, Machines, Diagrams and Boolean Algebra,* Dover, 1968; *The Arrow Book of Brain Teasers* (juvenile; illustrated by William Hogarth), Scholastic, 1959; *The Scientific American Book of Mathematical Puzzles and*

Diversions, Simon & Schuster, 1959, 6th edition, Scribner, 1975; *Science Puzzlers,* (juvenile; illustrated by Anthony Ravielli), Viking, 1960; *Mathematical Puzzles* (juvenile; illustrated by Anthony Ravielli), Crowell, 1961; *The Second Scientific American Book of Mathematical Puzzles and Diversions,* Simon & Schuster, 1961; *Relativity for the Million* (illustrated by Anthony Ravielli), Macmillan, 1962, revised edition published as *The Relativity Explosion,* Random House, 1976; *The Ambidextrous Universe* (illustrated by John Mackey), Basic Books, 1964, revised edition, Scribner, 1979.

Archimedes, Mathematician and Inventor (juvenile; illustrated by Leonard E. Fisher), Macmillan, 1965; *New Mathematical Diversions from Scientific American,* Simon & Schuster, 1966; *The Numerology of Dr. Matrix,* Simon & Schuster, 1967; *The Unexpected Hanging, and Other Mathematical Diversions,* Simon & Schuster, 1969; *Never Make Fun of a Turtle, My Son* (juvenile; illustrated by John Alcorn), Simon & Schuster, 1969; *Perplexing Puzzles and Tantalizing Teasers* (juvenile; illustrated by Laszlo Kubinyi), Simon & Schuster, 1969; *Space Puzzles* (juvenile; illustrated by Ted Schroeder), Simon & Schuster, 1971; *Sixth Book of Mathematical Games from Scientific American,* W. H. Freeman, 1971; *Codes, Ciphers, and Secret Writing* (juvenile), Simon & Schuster, 1972; *The Flight of Peter Fromm,* W. Kaufmann, 1973; *The Snark Puzzle Book* (illustrations from Henry Holiday and John Tenniel), Simon & Schuster, 1973; *Mathematical Carnival,* Knopf, 1975; *The Incredible Dr. Matrix,* Scribner, 1976; *Mathematical Magic Show,* Knopf, 1977; *More Perplexing Puzzles and Tantalizing Teasers* (juvenile; illustrated by Laszlo Kubinyi), Simon & Schuster, 1977.

Editor: *The Wizard of Oz and Who He Was,* Michigan State University Press, 1957; *Great Essays in Science,* Pocket

MARTIN GARDNER

Find the Best Words

The bull in this picture has just swallowed a time bomb that is set to go off in five minutes. Which of the four words below do you think best describes the situation?

Awful
Abominable
Dreadful
Shocking

(From *Perplexing Puzzles and Tantalizing Teasers* by Martin Gardner. Illustrated by Laszlo Kubinyi.)

Books, 1957, reissued, Washington Square Press, 1963; Sam Loyd, *Best Mathematical Puzzles of Sam Loyd,* Dover, 1957; Lewis Carroll, *The Annotated Alice: Alice's Adventures in Wonderland [and] Through the Looking Glass,* C. N. Potter, 1960, revised edition, Penguin Books, 1971; Charles C. Bombaugh, *Oddities and Curiosities of Words and Literature,* Dover, 1961; Lewis Carroll, *The Annotated Snark,* Simon & Schuster, 1962; Samuel Taylor Coleridge, *The Annotated Ancient Mariner,* Bramhall House, 1965; Lewis Carroll, *The Nursery "Alice,"* McGraw, 1966; Rudolf Carnap, *Philosophical Foundations of Physics,* Basic Books, 1966, reissued as *An Introduction to the Philosophy of Science,* Basic Books, 1974; E. L. Thayer, *The Annotated Casey at the Bat,* C. N. Potter, 1967; Henry E. Dudeney, *Five Hundred Thirty-Six Puzzles and Curious Problems,* Scribner, 1967; Boris Kordemski, *The Moscow Puzzles,* Scribner, 1972; Lewis Carroll, *The Wasp in a Wig,* C. N. Potter, 1977; Kobon Fujimura, *The Tokyo Puzzles,* Scribner, 1978; *Aha! Insight, Scientific American,* W. H. Freeman, 1978.

SIDELIGHTS: "As a small child my greatest reading experiences were the books of L. Frank Baum. I have tried to repay him by writing about him in books and magazines, and doing the introductions for a continuing series of Dover paperback reprints that now includes Baum's first two Oz books and five of his early non-Oz fantasies. There is no question that Baum was our country's greatest writer of juvenile fantasy, and it is one of the scandals of American letters that only in recent decades has this been recognized by critics and librarians. I am proud to have played a role in hastening this inevitable recognition.

"During the eight years that I was on the staff of *Humpty Dumpty's Magazine* I wrote each month a short story (about the adventures of Humpty Junior), a poem of moral advice, and did all the activity features that involved damaging a page. Twenty of my doggerel poems were revised (the little egg was replaced by a boy named Tom or by his sister Rose) and published as *Never Make Fun of a Turtle, My Son.* The eighty or more short stories (I also wrote stories for a short-lived Parents Institute periodical called *Piggity,* which for a time I edited) have not been reprinted in book form except for a few that found their way into anthologies.

"My earliest hobby was magic and I have retained an interest in it ever since. Although I have written no general trade books on conjuring, I have written a number of small books that are sold only in magic shops, and I continue to contribute original tricks to magic periodicals. My second major hobby as a child was chess, but I stopped playing after my college days for the simple reason that had I not done so, I would have had little time for anything else. The sport I most enjoyed watching as a boy was baseball, and most enjoyed playing was tennis. A hobby I acquired late in life is playing the musical saw."

GESSNER, Lynne 1919-
(Merle Clark)

PERSONAL: Given name originally Merlyn; born June 10, 1919, in Preston, Cuba; daughter of American parents, Emery Thomas (an accountant for Cuba Division, United Fruit Co.) and Minnie (an artist; maiden name, Richards) Clark; married Malcom J. Gessner (an architectural draftsman), April 2, 1944; children: Dianne Lynne (Mrs. John B. Doyle), Deborah Dee (Mrs. Dean L. McMann). *Education:* Attended Portland State College (now University), 1962,

LYNNE GESSNER

1963, and Phoenix College, 1964. *Politics:* Republican. *Religion:* Christian Scientist. *Home:* 6507 East Holly St., Scottsdale, Ariz. 85257.

CAREER: Former medical secretary and office manager; full-time writer, 1973—. *Awards, honors:* Nominee Newbery Award for *Navajo Slave,* 1977.

WRITINGS: Trading Post Girl (juvenile), Fell, 1968; *Lightning Slinger* (juvenile), Funk, 1968; (under name Merle Clark) *Ramrod* (adult western), Tower, 1969; *Bonnie's Guatemala Adventure,* Putnam, 1970; *Navajo Slave* (juvenile), Harvey House, 1976; (contributor) *Baleful Beasts and Eerie Creatures* (anthology), Rand McNally, 1976; *Malcolm Yucca Seed,* Harvey House, 1977; *To See a Witch,* Nelson, 1978; *Danny,* Harvey House, 1978. Contributor of six stories to *Encyclopaedia Britannica* Reading Training program, and short stories and articles to juvenile, adult, senior citizen, and religious magazines, and to Sunday newspaper supplements; a story published in *Jack & Jill* is included in a Canadian school reader.

WORK IN PROGRESS: Nobody's Boy, a study of suicide; *Stories of Dolphins from Ancient Times until Today; Hell's Highway,* a historical book of World War II, scheduled for a 1979 publication; *The Mystery Of The Great Horned Owl.*

SIDELIGHTS: "My early childhood was spent in the West Indies, primarily in Cuba and in Nicaragua. I also lived at an Indian trading post in the 1930's, and have traveled extensively, going to Europe several times, to Hawaii, Alaska, Canada and Mexico.

"My American born grandfather, being an adventurer, had an interesting life, most of it spent in Central and South

He raced past the children and stood shyly before his parents, looking down at his dusty shoes.
■ (From *Malcolm Yucca Seed* by Lynne Gessner. Illustrated by William Sauts Bock.)

HAGGARD, H(enry) Rider   1856-1925

PERSONAL: Born June 22, 1856, in Bradenham, Norfolk, England; died May 14, 1925, in London, England; son of William Meybohm Rider (a barrister) and Ella (Doveton) Haggard; married Louisa Margitson, 1880; children: three daughters. *Education:* Educated at Garsington and Ipswich Grammar School. *Home:* Ditchingham, Norfolk, England.

CAREER: Author. Private secretary to Sir Henry Bulwer, Governor of Natal, South Africa, 1875; Registrar and Master of the High Court in the Transvaal, 1877-79; resigned to take up ostrich farming, 1879; called to the Bar, 1884; abandoned law, 1885, to devote his time to writing. Haggard was an expert in agricultural matters and in international affairs; he traveled around the world, 1912-17, as a member of the Dominions Royal Commission. *Member:* Athenaeum Club, National Club, Cecil Club. *Awards, honors:* Created Knight, 1912; Knight Commander of the Order of the British Empire, 1919.

WRITINGS—Novels: *Dawn,* Hurst & Blackett, 1884, J. W. Lovell, 1887; *The Witch's Head,* G. Munro, 1885; *King Solomon's Mines,* Cassell, 1885, reprinted, Hart, 1976 [other editions illustrated by Paul Hogarth, Penguin, 1958; Will Nickless, Collins, 1959; Charles Keeping, Blackie, 1961; Frank Kramer, Hart, 1960; Alan E. Cober, Collier Books, 1962; Hookway Cowles, Macdonald, 1965; David Gentleman, Imprint Society, 1970]; *She,* Harper, 1886, reprinted, Hart, 1976 [other editions illustrated by Maurice Greiffenhagen and Charles H. M. Kerr, Longmans, Green, 1915; W. Nickless, Collins, 1957; H. Cowles, Macdonald, 1963]; *A Tale of Three Lions,* J. W. Lovell, 1887, a later edition published as *Allan the Hunter,* Lothrop, 1898; *Jess,* Harper, 1887, reissued, Hutchinson, 1972; *Allan Quatermain,* Harper, 1887 [other editions illustrated by C.H.M. Kerr, Longmans, Green, 1914; H. Cowles, Macdonald, 1963]; *My Fellow Laborer* [and] *The Wreck of the Copeland,* G. Munro, 1888; *Mr. Meeson's Will,* J. W. Lowell, 1888, reprinted, Arno, 1976; *Colonel Quaritch, V. C.,* J. W. Lovell, 1888; *Maiwa's Revenge,* Harper, 1888 [another edition illustrated by H. Cowles, Macdonald, 1965]; *Cleopatra, being an Account of the Fall and Vengeance of Harmachis, the Royal Egyptian, as Set Forth by His Own Hand* (illustrated by R. C. Woodville and M. Greiffenhagen), Longmans, Green, 1889 [another edition illustrated by H. Cowles, Macdonald, 1958]; *Allan's Wife,* G. Munro, 1889, reissued, Macdonald, 1963.

(With Andrew Lang) *The World's Desire,* Harper, 1890, reissued, Ballantine, 1972 [another edition illustrated by Geoffrey Whittam, Macdonald, 1963]; *Beatrice,* Harper, 1890; *Eric Brighteyes* (illustrated by Lancelot Speed), United States Book Co., 1891, reissued Newcastle, 1974; *Nada the Lily,* Longmans, Green, 1892, reissued, Macdonald, 1963 [another edition illustrated by H. Cowles, Collins, 1957]; *Montezuma's Daughter,* Longmans, Green, 1893, reprinted, American Reprints-Rivercity Press, 1976 [other editions illustrated by M. Greiffenhagen, Longmans, Green, 1920; H. Cowles, Macdonald, 1965]; *The People of the Mist,* P. F. Collier, 1894 [another edition illustrated by Jack Matthew, Macdonald, 1958]; *Joan Haste,* Longmans, Green, 1895; *Heart of the World,* Longmans, Green, 1895, reissued, Newcastle, 1976 [another edition illustrated by H. Cowles, Macdonald, 1965]; *The Wizard,* Longmans, Green, 1896; *Doctor Therne,* Longmans, Green, 1898; *Swallow,* Longmans, Green, 1898.

H. Rider Haggard, age 41.

Black Heart and White Heart, and Other Stories, Longmans, Green, 1900; *Lysbeth: A Tale of the Dutch,* Longmans, Green, 1901 [another edition illustrated by G. P. Jacomb Hood, Longmans, Green, 1918]; *Pearl-Maiden: A Tale of the Fall of Jerusalem,* Longmans, Green, 1903, reissued, T. Stacey, 1972; *Stella Fregelius: A Tale of Three Destinies,* Longmans, Green, 1903; *The Brethren,* McClure, Phillips, 1904 [another edition illustrated by H. Cowles, Macdonald, 1963]; *Ayesha, the Return of She,* Doubleday, Page, 1905, reprinted, American Reprints-Rivercity Press, 1976 [other editions illustrated by W. Nickless, Collins, 1957; H. Cowles, Macdonald, 1965]; *Benita: An African Romance* (illustrated by Gordon Browne), Cassell, 1906 [another edition illustrated by H. Cowles, Macdonald, 1965]; *The Way of the Spirit,* Hutchinson, 1906; *The Spirit of the Bambatse,* Longmans, Green, 1906; *Margaret,* Longmans, Green, 1907; *The Lady of the Heavens,* Authors and Newspapers Association, 1908, also published as *The Ghost Kings* (illustrated by Arthur C. Michael), Cassell, 1908; *The Yellow God,* Cupples & Leon, 1908; *The Lady of Blossholme,* B. Tauchnitz, 1909.

Queen Sheba's Ring (illustrated by Sigurd Schou), Doubleday, Page, 1910 [another edition illustrated by Geoffrey Whittam, Macdonald, 1965]; *Morning Star* (illustrated by A. C. Michael), Longmans, Green, 1910, reissued, T. Stacey, 1972; *The Mahatma and the Hare* (illustrated by W. T. Horton and H. M. Brock), Holt, 1911; *Red Eve* (illustrated by A. C. Michael), Doubleday, Page, 1911; *Marie* (illustrated by A. C. Michael), Cassell, 1912 [another edition illustrated by H. Cowles, Macdonald, 1959]; *The Wanderer's Necklace* (illustrated by A. C. Michael), Longmans, Green, 1914; *Allan and the Holy Flower* (illustrated by M. Greiffenhagen), Longmans, Green, 1915 [another edition illustrated by H. Cowles, Macdonald, 1963]; *Finished,* Paget Literary Agency, 1916 [another edition illustrated by H. Cowles, Macdonald, 1962]; *The Ivory Child* (illustrated by A. C.

Michael), Longmans, Green, 1916 [another edition illustrated by H. Cowles, Macdonald, 1958]; *Elissa; or, The Doom of Zimbabwe*, Hodder & Stoughton, 1917; *Moon of Isreal*, Longmans, Green, 1918; *Love Eternal*, Longmans, Green, 1918; *When the World Shook, being an Account of the Great Adventure of Bastin, Bickley, and Arbuthnot*, Longmans, Green, 1919, reprinted, Arno, 1975.

The Ancient Allan, Longmans, Green, 1920; *She and Allan*, Longmans, Green, 1920, reissued, Newcastle, 1975 [another edition illustrated by H. Cowles, Macdonald, 1960]; *Smith and the Pharoahs, and Other Tales*, Longmans, Green, 1921; *The Virgin of the Sun*, Doubleday, Page, 1922; *Wisdom's Daughter: The Life and Love Story of She-Who-Must-Be-Obeyed*, Doubleday, Page, 1923; *Heu-Heu; or, The Monster*, Doubleday, Page, 1924, reissued, Hutchinson, 1972; *Queen of the Dawn: A Love Tale of Old Egypt*, Doubleday, Page, 1925; *Treasure of the Lake*, Doubleday, Page, 1926, reissued, Hutchinson, 1971; *Allan and the Ice-Gods: A Tale of Beginnings*, Doubleday, Page, 1927, reissued, Hutchinson, 1971; *Marion Isle*, Doubleday, Doran, 1929 (published in England as *Mary of Marion Isle*, Hutchinson, 1929); *Belshazzar*, Doubleday, Doran, 1930.

Other: *Cetywayo and His White Neighbors; or, Remarks on Recent Events in Zululand, Natal, and the Transvaal*, Truebner, 1882; *A History of the Transvaal*, New Amsterdam Book Co., 1899; *A Farmer's Year* (illustrated by G. Leon Little), Longmans, Green, 1899; *The Last Boer War*, Kegan Paul, 1900, reprinted, Books for Libraries, 1973; *The New South Africa*, Pearson, 1900; *A Winter Pilgrimage, being an Account of Travels through Palestine, Italy, and the Island of Cyprus*, Longmans, Green, 1901; *Rural England, being an Account of Agricultural and Social Researches Carried Out in the Years 1901 and 1902*, Longmans, Green, 1902; *The Poor and the Land, being a Report on the Salvation Army Colonies in the United States and at Hadleigh, England*, Longmans, Green, 1905; *A Gardener's Year*, Longmans, Green, 1905; *Regeneration, being an Account of the Social Work of the Salvation Army in Great Britain*, Longmans, Green, 1910; *Rural Denmark and Its Lessons*, Longmans, Green, 1911; *The Days of My Life: An Autobiography* (edited by C. J. Longman), Longmans, Green, 1926.

Collections and selections: *The Favorite Novels of H. Rider Haggard*, Blue Ribbon Books, 1928; *The Works of H. Rider Haggard*, W. J. Black, 1928; *Three Adventure Novels: She, King Solomon's Mines [and] Allan Quatermain*, Dover, 1951; *Five Adventure Novels*, Dover, 1951; *Lost Civilizations: Three Adventure Novels*, Dover, 1953.

ADAPTATIONS—Movies: "She," Lucoque, Ltd., 1916, William Fox, 1917, RKO Radio Pictures, 1935, Metro-Goldwyn-Mayer, starring Ursula Andress, 1965; "The Grasp of Greed," adaptation of *Mr. Meeson's Will*, Bluebird Photoplays, 1916; "Heart and Soul," adaptation of *Jess*, William Fox, 1917; "Moon of Isreal," R-C Pictures, 1927; "King Solomon's Mines," Gaumont British Picture Corp. of America, 1937, Loew's, starring Stewart Granger and Deborah Kerr, 1950; "Watusi," adaptation of *King Solomon's Mines*, Metro-Goldwyn-Mayer, 1959; "The Vengeance of She," Hammer Film Productions, 1967.

SIDELIGHTS: **June 22, 1856.** Born in Bradenham, Norfolk, England. Son of William Meybohm Rider (a barrister) and Ella Doveton Haggard. "I am the eighth child of the family of ten—seven sons and three daughters—who were born to my father and mother. As it chanced I first saw the light . . . not at Bradenham Hall, which at the time was let, but at the Wood Farm on that property whither, on her return from travelling in France, my mother retired to be confined. A few years ago I visited the room in which the interesting event took place. It is a typical farmhouse upper chamber, very pleasant in its way, and to the fact of my appearance there I have always been inclined, rather fancifully perhaps, to attribute the strong agricultural tastes which I believe I alone of my family possess.

"My father was a typical squire of the old sort, a kind of Sir Roger de Coverley. He reigned at Bradenham like a king, blowing everybody up and making rows innumerable. Yet I do not think there was a more popular man in the county of Norfolk. Even the servants, whom he rated in a fashion that no servant would put up with nowadays, were fond of him. He could send back the soup with a request to the cook to drink it all herself, or some other infuriating message. He could pull at the bells until feet of connecting wire hung limply down the wall, and announce when whoever it was he wanted appeared that Thorpe Idiot Asylum was her proper home, and so forth. Nobody seemed to mind in the least. It was 'only the Squire's way,' they said.

"My father was regular in attendance at church. We always sat in the chancel on oak benches originally designed for the choir. If he happened to be in time himself and other parishioners, such as the farmers' daughters, happened to be late, his habit was, when he saw them enter, to step into the middle of the nave, produce a very large old watch which I now possess . . . and hold it aloft that the sinners as they walked up the church might become aware of the enormity of their offence.

"He always read the Lessons and read them very well. There were certain chapters, however, those which are full of names both in the Old and New Testaments, which were apt to cause difficulty. It was not that he was unable to pronounce these names, for having been a fair scholar in his youth he did this better than most. Yet when he had finished the list it would occur to him that they might have been rendered more satisfactorily. So he would go back to the beginning and read them all through again.

"My mother was married when she was twenty-five years of age, and children came in what ladies nowadays would consider super-abundance. The eldest, my sister Ella, was born in Rome in March 1845, while they were still upon a marriage tour, and subsequently, in quick succession, the others followed. The last of us, my brother Arthur, appeared in November 1860—well do I remember my father in a flowered dressing-gown telling us to be quiet because we had a little brother. This allows nearly sixteen years between the eldest and the youngest, including one who came into the world still-born. Although she had ten children living, my mother never ceased to regret this boy, and I remember her crying when she pointed out to me where he was buried in Bradenham churchyard.

"My mother never was a beauty in the ordinary sense of the word, but in youth, to judge by the pictures which I have seen of her (photographs were not then known), she must have been very refined and charming in appearance, and indeed remained so all her life. Her abilities were great; taking her all in all she was perhaps the ablest woman whom I have known, though she had no iron background to her character; for that she was too gentle. Her bent no doubt was literary, and had circumstances permitted I am sure she would

(From the movie "She," starring Helen Mack and Randolph Scott. Copyright 1935 by RKO Pictures.)

have made a name in that branch of art to which in the intervals of her crowded life she gravitated by nature. Also she was a good musician, and drew well. Of her mental abilities I have however spoken in a brief memoir which I published as a preface to a new edition of my mother's poem, 'Life and its Author.'

"I think that the greatest of her gifts, however, was that of conversation. No more charming companion could be imagined. Also she had the art of drawing the best out of anyone with whom she might be talking, as the sympathetic sometimes can do. In a minute or two she would find which was his or her strongest point and to this turn the conversation. Notwithstanding the tumultuous nature of her life, her illnesses and other distractions, she contrived to read a great deal, and to keep herself *au courant* with all thought movements and the political affairs of the day. Further she did her very best to teach her numerous children the truths of religion, and to lead them into the ways of righteousness and peace. I fear, however, that at times we got beyond her. It is not easy for any woman to follow and direct all the physical and mental developments of a huge and vigorous family who are continually coming and going, first from schools and elsewhere, and later from every quarter of the world.

"She never complained, but I cannot think that the life she was called upon to lead was very congenial to her. When young in India, where at that time English ladies were rare, as was natural in the case of one of her charm who was known also to be a considerable heiress, she was much sought after and fêted. Then she returned to England and married, and for her the responsibilities of life began with a vengeance, to cease no more until she died. These indeed were complicated by the fact that a time came when she had to think a good deal about ways and means, especially after my father, who had the passion of his generation for land, insisted upon investing most of her fortune in that security just at the commencement of its great fall in value. Her various duties, including that of housekeeping, of which she was a perfect mistress, left her scarcely an hour to follow her own literary and artistic tastes. All she could do was to give a little attention to gardening, to which she was devoted.

"It seems that I was a whimsical child. At least Hocking, my mother's maid, a handsome, vigorous, black-eyed, raw-boned Cornishwoman who spent most of her active life in the service of the family, informed me in after years that nothing would induce me to go to sleep unless a clean napkin folded in a certain way was placed under my head, which napkin I called 'an ear.' To this day I have dim recollections of crying bitterly until this 'ear' was brought to me. Also I was stupid. Indeed, although she always indignantly denied the story in after years, I remember when I was about seven my dear mother declaring that I was as heavy as lead in body and mind.

"I fear that I was more or less of a dunderhead at lessons. Even my letters presented difficulties to me, and I well recollect a few years later being put through an examination by my future brother-in-law, the Rev. Charles Maddison Green, with the object of ascertaining what amount of knowledge I had acquired at a day school in London, where we then were living at 24 Leinster Square.

"The results of this examination were so appalling that when he was apprised of them my indignant father burst into the room where I sat resigned to fate, and, in a voice like to that of an angry bull, roared out at me that I was 'only fit to be a greengrocer.' Even then I wondered mildly why this affront should be put upon a useful trade. After the row was over I went for a walk with my brother Andrew who was two years older than myself and who, it appeared, had assisted at my discomfiture from behind a door. Just where Leinster Square opens into a main street, I think it is Westbourne Grove—at any rate in those days Whiteley had a single little shop not far off at which my mother used to deal—there is, or was, a fruit and vegetable store with no glass in the window. My brother stood contemplating it for a long while. At last he said:

"'I say, old fellow, when you become a greengrocer, I hope you'll let me have oranges cheap!'

"To this day I have never quite forgiven Andrew for that most heartless remark.

"After all it was not perhaps strange that I did not learn much at these London day schools—for I went to two of them. The first I left suddenly. It was managed by the head master and an usher whose names I have long forgotten. The usher was a lanky, red-haired, pale-faced man whom we all hated because of his violent temper and injustice. On one occasion when his back was turned to the class to which I belonged, that I presume was the lowest, I amused myself and my companions by shaking my little fists at him, whereon they laughed. The usher wheeled round and asked why we were laughing, when some mean boy piped out:

"'Please, sir, because Haggard is shaking his fists at you.'

"He called me to him and I perceived that he was trembling with rage.

"'You young brute!' he said, 'I'll see you in your grave before you shake your fists at me again.'

"Then he doubled his own and, striking me first on one side of the head and then on the other, knocked me all the way down the long room and finally over a chair into a heap of slates in a corner, where I lay a while almost senseless. I recovered and went home. Here my eldest sister Ella, noticing my bruised and dazed condition, cross-examined me till I told her the truth. An interview followed between my father and the master of the school, which resulted in the dismissal of the usher and my departure. Afterwards I met that usher in the Park somewhere near the Row, and so great was my fear of him that I never stopped running till I reached the Marble Arch.

"After this my father sent me to a second day school where the pupils were supposed to receive a sound business education.

"Then came the examination that I have mentioned at the hands of my brother-in-law. As a result I was despatched to the Rev. Mr. Graham, who took in two or three small boys (at that time I must have been nine or ten years of age) at Garsington Rectory near Oxford.

"The Rectory, long ago pulled down, was a low grey house that once had served as a place of refuge in time of plague for the Fellows of one of the Oxford colleges.

"After my time at Mr. Graham's, of whom I have spoken, came to an end, how or when I do not know, the question arose as to where I should be sent to school. All my five elder brothers, except Jack the sailor, had the advantage of a public school education. ∴ . . When it came to my turn, however, funds were running short, which is scarcely to be wondered at, as my father has told me that about this time the family bills for education came to £1200 a year. Also, as I was supposed to be not very bright, I dare say it was thought that to send me to a public school would be to waste money. So it was decreed that I should go to the Grammar School at Ipswich, which had the advantages of being cheap and near at hand.

"Never shall I forget my arrival at that educational establishment, to which my father conducted me. We travelled *via* Norwich, where he bought me a hat. For some reason best known to himself, the head-gear which he selected was such as is generally worn by a curate, being of the ordinary clerical black felt and shape. In this weird head-dress I was duly delivered at Ipswich Grammar School. As soon as my father had tumultuously departed to catch his train, I was sent into the playground, where I stood a forlorn and lanky figure. Presently a boy came up and hit me in the face, saying:

"'Phillips' (I think that was his name) 'sends this to the new fellow in a parson's hat.'

"This was too much for me, for underneath my placid exterior I had a certain amount of spirit.

"'Show me Phillips,' I said, and a very big boy was pointed out to me.

"I went up to him, made some appropriate repartee to his sarcasm about my hat, and hit him in the face. Then followed a fight, of which, as he was so much larger and stronger, of course I got the worst. However, I gained the respect of my schoolfellows, and thenceforth my clergyman's hat was tolerated until I managed to procure another.

"I spent two or three years at Ipswich. At that time it was a rough place, and there was much bullying of which the masters were not aware. . . .

"I took my part in the school games and was elected captain of the second football team, but did not stay long enough at Ipswich to get into the first. Not much more returns to me about this period of my life that is worthy of record. Although I believe that I was popular among my schoolmates, who showed their affection by naming me 'Nosey' in allusion to the prominence of that organ on my undeveloped face, I did not care for school, and found it monotonous, with the result that my memories concerning it are somewhat of a blur.

"Such was the circle in which I grew up. I think that on the whole I was rather a quiet youth, at any rate by comparison. Certainly I was very imaginative, although I kept my

(From the movie "King Solomon's Mines," starring Stewart Granger. Released by Metro-Goldwyn-Mayer. Copyright 1950 by Loew's Inc.)

thoughts to myself, which I dare say had a good deal to do with my reputation for stupidity. I believe I was considered the dull boy of the family. Without doubt I was slow at my lessons, chiefly because I was always thinking of something else. Also to this day there are subjects at which I am extremely stupid. Thus, although I rarely forgot the substance of anything worth remembering, never could or can I learn anything by heart, and for this reason I have been obliged to abandon the active pursuit of Masonry. Moreover all mathematics are absolutely abhorrent to me, while as for Euclid it bored me so intensely that I do not think I ever mastered the meaning of the stuff." [*The Days of My Life: An Autobiography,* Volume I, edited by C. J. Longman, Longmans, Green, London, 1926.[1]]

1875. As a result of his father's intervention, Haggard was appointed to the staff of Sir Henry Bulwer, Lieutenant-Governor of Natal, South Africa. Haggard was nineteen. "Now before we go on to Natal where the real business of my life began, I will stop for a moment to take stock of myself as I was in those days at the age of nineteen.

"I was a tall young fellow, quite six feet, and slight; blue-eyed, brown-haired, fresh-complexioned, and not at all bad-looking. The Zulus gave me the name of 'Indanda,' which meant, I believe, one who is tall and pleasant-natured. Men-

tally I was impressionable, quick to observe and learn whatever interested me, and could already hold my own in conversation. Also, if necessary, I could make a public speech. I was, however, subject to fits of depression and liable to take views of things too serious and gloomy for my age—failings, I may add, that I have never been able to shake off. Even then I had the habit of looking beneath the surface of characters and events, and of trying to get at their springs and causes. I liked to understand any country or society in which I found myself. I despised those who merely floated on the stream of life and never tried to dive into its depths. Yet in some ways I think I was rather indolent, that is if the task in hand bored me. I was ambitious and conscious of certain powers, but wanted to climb the tree of success too quickly—a proceeding that generally results in slips."[1]

August, 1875. Arrived in Africa. "Of the year or so that I spent in Natal I have not much to say that is worthy of record. The country impressed me enormously. Indeed, on the whole I think it the most beautiful of any that I have seen in the world, parts of Mexico alone excepted.

"Then there were the Zulu Kaffirs living in their kraals filled with round beehive-like huts, bronze-coloured, noble-looking men and women clad only in their *moochas,* whose herds of cattle wandered hither and thither in charge of a little lad. From the beginning I was attracted to these Zulus, and soon began to study their character and their history."[1]

December, 1876. Appointed to the staff of Sir Shepstone, which was sent to the Transvaal to annex the territory for England. "At the end of 1876 Sir Theophilus Shepstone was appointed Special Commissioner to the Transvaal. His commission was a wide one, for, although this was not known at the time, it gave him powers, if he thought fit, to annex the country, 'in order to secure the peace and safety of our said colonies and our subjects elsewhere.' When the vastness of the territories and the questions concerned are considered, this was a great authority to leave to the discretion of a single man. But thus was the British Empire made before the days of cables, when everything depended upon the judgment of the officers on the spot.

"I think that we trekked from Maritzburg on December 20, 1876, and took thirty-five days to traverse the four hundred odd miles between it and Pretoria in our ox-waggon. It was my first real introduction to African travel, and I greatly enjoyed the journey, hot as it was at that time of year.

"Well do I remember our leisurely progress over the plains, the mountains, and the vast, rolling high veld of the Transvaal territory. Still I can see the fearful sweeping thunderstorms that overtook us, to be followed by moonlit nights of surpassing brilliancy which we watched from beside the fires of our camp. Those camps were very pleasant, and in them, as we smoked and drank our 'square-face' after the day's trek, I heard many a story of savage Africa from Sir Theophilus himself, from Osborn and from Fynney, who next to him, perhaps, knew as much of the Zulus and their history as any living in Natal.

"There were never any quarrels among us of Shepstone's staff during that long journey or afterwards. Indeed we were a band of brothers—as brothers ought to be. Personally I formed friendships then, especially with Osborn and Clarke, that endured till their deaths and I trust may be renewed elsewhere."[1]

Summer, 1877. Appointed temporary Registrar and Master of the High Court in the Transvaal. "Not very long after the Annexation the Master and Registrar of the High Court died, and after some reflection the Government appointed me to act in his place. It is not strange that they should have hesitated, seeing that I was barely twenty-one years of age and had received no legal training. Moreover in those days the office was one of great importance."[1]

Spring, 1878. Appointed Registrar and Master of the High Court, a position he retained until 1879. In a letter to his father, Haggard demonstrated his self-satisfaction at having secured his position. "I have won the day with reference to my appointment as Master and Registrar.... I believe I am by far the youngest head of Department in South Africa. I have also the satisfaction of knowing that my promotion has not been due to any favouritism. My connection with the Chief has been against me rather than otherwise, because people in his position are very slow about doing anything that can be construed into favouritism. He was good enough, I believe, to speak very kindly about me when he settled the matter of my appointment this morning, saying that 'he thought very highly of me and was sure that I should rise.' This turn of affairs to a great extent settles the question of my going anywhere else. I am very glad to have got the better of those lawyers who petitioned against me, and also to

have held the office so much to the satisfaction of the Government as to justify them in appointing so young a man. When I began to act eight months since I had not the slightest knowledge of my work, a good deal of which is of course technical, and what is more there were no records, no books, indeed nothing from which I could form an idea of it, nor had I anyone to teach me. In addition I had to deal with a lot of gentlemen whose paths were the paths of self-seeking, who did their utmost to throw obstacles in my way. These difficulties I have, I am glad to say, to a great extent overcome, and I intend now to make myself thoroughly master of my position. Of course the very fact of my rapid rise will make me additional enemies, especially the five or six disappointed candidates, but I don't mind that...."[1]

Summer, 1878. With his friend, Arthur Cochrane, built a home in the Transvaal. "We named it 'The Palatial,' and it has since become well known as 'Jess's Cottage.' It was a funny little place consisting of two rooms, a kitchen, etc., and having a tin roof. I remember how tiny it looked when the foundations were dug out. I believe that it still stands in Pretoria."[1]

1879. Resigned his position to take up ostrich farming with his friend, Cochrane. "Cochrane and I took it into our heads that we would shake off the dust of Government service and farm ostriches. As a beginning we purchased some three thousand acres of land at Newcastle in Natal from Mr. Osborn, together with the house that he had built when he was Resident Magistrate there. We had never seen the land and did not think it worth while to undertake the journey necessary to that purpose, as it lay two hundred miles away. In this matter our confidence was perfectly justified, since my dear friend Osborn had scrupulously undervalued the whole estate, which was a most excellent one of its sort.

"I forget what we paid him for it, but it was a very modest sum. Or rather we did not pay him at the time, as we wished to keep our working capital in hand, nor do I think that he demanded any security in the shape of mortgages or promissory notes. He knew that we should not fail him in this matter, nor did we do so.

"On my part it was a mad thing to do, seeing that I had a high office and was well thought of; yet, as it chanced, the wisest that I could have done. Had I stopped on at Pretoria, within two years I should have been thrown out of my employment without compensation, as happened to all the other British officials when Mr. Gladstone surrendered the Transvaal to the Boers after our defeat at Majuba, or at any rate to those of them who would not take service under the Dutch Republic, as I for one could never have consented to do.

"So my life at Pretoria came to an end. Cochrane and I rode away one morning to a Boer stead somewhere in the neighbourhood of where Johannesburg now stands, and bought and paid for our ostriches. I think that Cochrane must have driven them down to Hilldrop, our new home near Newcastle in Natal, for I have no recollection of assisting in the business. Nor do I remember ever visiting Hilldrop until I came thither eighteen months or more later with my wife."[1]

August, 1879. Returned to England. "When I reached home everyone was very glad to see me, especially my mother, but my father did not welcome my reappearance with wholehearted enthusiasm. He remarked with great candour that I should probably become 'a waif and a stray,' or possibly—my taste for writing being already known—'a miserable

(From the movie "Watusi," starring George Montgomery and Taina Elg. Copyright 1959 by Metro-Goldwyn-Mayer.)

penny-a-liner.' I am sure I do not wonder at his irritation, which, were I in his place to-day, I should certainly share. He saw that I had thrown up my billet and he had no faith in the possibilities of African farming.

"However, things righted themselves by degrees, as somehow they generally do when one is young and not afraid to take chances."[1]

Fall, 1879. Met Louisa Margitson and became engaged at the end of a week. "... Not long after my arrival in England I did the wisest and best deed of my life and engaged myself to be married.

"My dear wife was a schoolfellow of my sister Mary, and was staying with her at Bradenham when we met. After a short acquaintance we became engaged, and at first all went well enough; subsequently, however, her guardians—for she was not yet of age—after consenting to her engagement, reconsidered the matter and wished her to break it off. I do not altogether blame them, since at the moment my prospects were not particularly brilliant. As it chanced, however, my wife, perhaps the most upright and straightforward woman whom I ever knew, was not one of a nature to play fast and loose in such matters. She declined, whereupon one of her

guardians, who was a lawyer, made her a ward in Chancery. Well do I remember appearing before Vice-Chancellor Malins, a kindly old gentleman and man of the world, upon whose gouty toe I inadvertently trod when shaking hands with him. He soon sifted the matter out and approved of the engagement, making certain directions as to settlements, etc. The net result of the whole business was that, including the cost of the settlements, a very moderate estate was mulcted in law expenses of a sum of nearly £3000!

"In after days I and my wife's relations, with most of whom, by the way, I never had any difference at all, as they were no parties to these proceedings, became and remained the best of friends. So I wish to say no more of the matter except that I regret those moneys which went in quite useless law costs."[1]

August 11, 1880. Married. "The end of the business was that after about a year of these excursions and alarums we were duly married.... I being twenty-four and my wife within a few months of twenty-one, and departed from this house to Norwich in a carriage drawn by four grey horses with postilions. This is interesting, as I believe it must have been one of the last occasions upon which postilions were used for such a purpose in England, except of course in the case of royal personages. At any rate I have never seen or heard of them since in this connection, and how we came to have them I do not quite know. I can see them now in their gay dress and velvet caps touching up the grey steeds with their short whips. We made quite a sensation on our thirteen-mile journey to and through Norwich; but oh! were we not glad when it was all over.''[1]

November, 1880. With his bride, sailed for South Africa. ''My wife and I with two servants, a Norfolk groom of the name of Stephen—I forget his surname—who, a little touched up, appears as Job in my book *She,* and a middle-aged woman named Gibbs who had been my wife's maid before marriage, three dogs, two parrots, and a 'spider' carriage, which was built to my special order in Norwich, left England somewhere towards the end of 1880. I think that we reached Natal before Christmas, and were greeted with the news of the Bronker's Spruit massacre, for I can call it by no other name. In short, we found that the Transvaal was in open rebellion.

''It was indeed a pleasant situation. Newcastle, whither we desired to proceed, lies very near the Transvaal border, and the question was, Did I dare to take my wife thither? For some weeks we remained in Maritzburg, staying part of the time with Sir Theophilus and Lady Shepstone, and the rest in an hotel. Literally I was at my wits' end to know what to do. . . .

''At length my wife, who, I think, take her altogether, is the most courageous woman I ever met, announced that she would have no more of it: her house was at Newcastle two hundred miles away, and, Boers or no Boers, thither she would go.

''So I bought two good horses—which afterwards died of the sickness—harnessed them to the 'spider,' and we started.

''I must add a few words about our farming life. Our estate, Rooipoint, covered something over three thousand acres. At any rate it was a large property lying between the Newcastle town lands and the Ingagaan River, in the centre of which rose a great flat-topped hill, the Rooi or Red Point, that gave it its name. From the very crest of this hill flowed, and doubtless still flows a strong and beautiful spring of water, though why water should appear at the top of a mountain instead of the bottom is more than I can say. At the foot of this mount we erected the steam-driven grinding mill which I had bought in England, our idea being that we should make our fortunes or at any rate do very well as millers. Whether this anticipation would or would not have been realised is more than I can tell, as we did not keep the farm long enough to learn.

''Still our efforts were by no means confined to this mill. Thus we started the making of bricks, for which there was a good market in Newcastle. I used to labour at this business, and very hard work it was.

''Besides our milling and brick-making we were the first to farm ostriches in that part of Natal. In my experience the ostrich is an extremely troublesome bird. To begin with he hunts you and knocks you down. When attacked by an ostrich the only thing to do is to lie down quite flat. In this position it cannot strike you with its bludgeon-like foot, nor is its beak adapted to pecking, though it can and does dance and roll upon you and sit upon your head as though it were an egg which it wished to hatch.

''Such is a rough outline of our various agricultural and other operations on the Rooipoint farm. Personally they form my pleasantest recollections of the place, though, were I to start again, I would not have so many irons in the fire. On the whole we made a good deal of money, though our outgoings and losses were also heavy. To farm successfully in Natal requires, or required, much capital and, owing to the poor quality of the Kaffir labour, incessant personal supervision. These Kaffirs, however, who were most of them our tenants, were in many ways our best friends; moreover they afforded us constant amusement when they were not engaged in driving us mad by their carelessness.''[1]

May 23, 1881. First son, Arthur John ''Jock,'' born. ''The child is a very perfect and fine boy, he weighed nine pounds just after birth, and is a very well nourished child. He has dark blue eyes and is a fair child with a good forehead. As regards his dear mother I cannot tell you how thankful I am that the business is so far over.'' [Lilias Rider Haggard, *The Cloak That I Left,* Hodder and Stoughton, London, 1951.[2]]

August, 1881. Left South Africa. ''So at last we bade farewell to Hilldrop, which neither of us ever has, nor I suppose ever will, see again except in dreams. I remember feeling quite sad as we drove down the dusty track to Newcastle, and the familiar house, surrounded by its orange trees, grew dim and vanished from our sight.

''There my son had been born; there I had undergone many emotions of a kind that help to make a man; there I had suffered the highest sort of shame, shame for my country; there, as I felt, one chapter in my eventful life had opened and had closed.''[1]

Autumn, 1881. ''On our return to England in the autumn of 1881 we went to stay at Bradenham for a while and rested after our African adventures.

''Before Christmas we moved to a furnished house at Norwood. Here, having all my way still to make in the world, I set to work in earnest. First of all I entered myself at Lincoln's Inn, but found to my disgust that before I could do so I was expected to pass an examination in Latin, English History and, I think, Arithmetic. My Latin I had practically forgotten, and my English History dates were somewhat to seek. I represented to the Benchers that, after having filled the office of Master of the High Court of the Transvaal, this entrance examination was perhaps superfluous, but they were obdurate on the matter. So I set to work and, with the assistance of a crammer, in a month learned more Latin than I had done all the time I was at school; indeed, at the end of a few weeks I could read Caesar fluently and Virgil not so ill. The end of it was that I passed the examination at the head of the batch who went up with me, or so I was given to understand.

''Another thing that I did was to write my first book, *Cetewayo and His White Neighbours, or Remarks on Recent Events in Zululand, Natal and the Transvaal.* It contained about two hundred and fifty closely printed pages in the first of its editions, and represented a great amount of labour. I was determined that it should be accurate, and to ensure this I purchased all the Blue-books dealing with the period of which I was treating, and made précis of them, some of which I still possess.

''But it is one thing for an unknown person to write a book of this character, and quite another for him to persuade anyone to publish it.''[1]

Christmas, 1882. Moved to Ditchingham, his wife's home which she had inherited.

January 6, 1883. Eldest daughter, Angela, born.

Fall, 1883. First novel, *Dawn,* completed. "I worked at that book morning, noon, and night, with the result that at length my eyesight gave out, and I was obliged to finish the writing of it in a darkened room."[2]

March, 1884. Third child born. "She was named Dorothy, after the heroine of *The Witch's Head,* or in full, Sybil Dorothy Rider. My recollection of this period is that it was rather lonely, at any rate for me, since my friends were African, and Africa was far away. However, I worked very hard, as indeed I have done without intermission since I was a rather idle boy at school, both at writing and the study of the Law. Between the intervals of work I took walks with a dear old bulldog I had, named Caesar, who appears in *Dawn,* and a tall Kaffir stick made of the black and white *umzimbeetwood,* which I still have, that reminded me of Africa. At times, too, I got a day's shooting on our own land or elsewhere.

"However, I had so many resources in my own mind, and so much more to do than I could possibly compass, that all these matters troubled me not at all. I was determined to make a success in the world in one way or another, and that of a sort which would cause my name to be remembered for long after I had departed therefrom, and my difficulty was to discover in which way this could best be done—in short, to search out the line of least resistance. So I possessed my soul in patience and worked and worked and worked. Often I wonder what estimate those who lived about me, and whom I met from time to time, formed of the studious young man who was understood to have been somewhere in Africa. I imagine that it was not complimentary, for if I understood them they did not understand me."[1]

1885. Called to the bar. Moved to London. "Now with a wife and three children I was practically beginning life again in a small furnished house in West Kensington at the age of twenty-eight or thereabouts.

"After my arrival in London I began to attend the Probate and Divorce Court. Soon I found, however, that if I was to obtain a footing in that rather close borough, I must do so through a regular gate, and I entered into an arrangement with Bargrave (now Sir Henry Bargrave) Deane to work in his chambers."[1]

Wrote the romance, *King Solomon's Mines,* which was an instant success. "Whether I wrote *King Solomon's Mines* before or after I entered Bargrave Deane's chambers I cannot now remember, but I think it must have been before. At any rate I recollect that we brought up from Ditchingham a certain pedestal writing-desk, which had always been in the house and has returned thither, for it now stands in my wife's bedroom, and added it to the somewhat exiguous furniture of our hired abode. It stood in the dining-room, and on it in the evenings—for my days were spent in the Temple—I wrote *King Solomon's Mines.* I think the task occupied me about six weeks. When the tale was finished I hawked it round to sundry publishers, Hurst and Blackett among them, none of whom if I remember rightly, thought it worth bringing out.

"At length, I know not how, the manuscript, which to-day presents a somewhat battered appearance, reached the late

...**I introduce the world to Ayesha and the Caves of Kôr.** ■ (From *She: A History of Adventure* by H. Rider Haggard. Illustrated by Maurice Greiffenhagen.)

W. E. Henley, who appears to have brought it to the notice of Mr. Andrew Lang. How I first came into contact with my friend Andrew Lang—that is, where and when I met him—I cannot recall. *King Solomon's Mines,* which was produced as a five-shilling book, proved an instant success.

"Truly in those days my industry was great. While on my summer holiday in 1885 I wrote *Allan Quatermain,* the sequel to *King Solomon's Mines,* from the first word to the last, although it did not appear until about a couple of years later, after it had run through *Longman's Magazine.*"[1]

December, 1886. *She* published. "I remember that when I sat down to the task my ideas as to its development were of the vaguest. The only clear notion that I had in my head was that of an immortal woman inspired by an immortal love. All the rest shaped itself round this figure. And it came—it came faster than my poor aching hand could set it down.

"Well do I recall taking the completed manuscript to the office of my literary agent, Mr. A. P. Watt, and throwing it on the table with the remark: 'There is what I shall be remembered by.'

"It would seem, therefore, that between January 1885 and March 18, 1886, with my own hand, and unassisted by any secretary, I wrote *King Solomon's Mines, Allan Quatermain, Jess* and *She.* Also I followed my profession, spending many hours of each day studying in chambers, or in Court, where I had some devilling practice, carried on my usual correspondence, and attended to the affairs of a man with a young family and a certain landed estate."[1]

January, 1887. Traveled to Egypt. "From a boy ancient Egypt had fascinated me, and I had read everything concerning it on which I could lay hands. Now I was possessed by a great desire to see it for myself, and to write a romance on the subject of 'Cleopatra,' a sufficiently ambitious project.

"On my arrival in England what between success and attacks I found myself quite a celebrity, one whose name was in everybody's mouth. I made money; for instance I sold *Cleopatra* for a large sum in cash, and also *Colonel Quaritch, V.C.,* a tale of English country life which Longman liked—it was dedicated to him—and Lang hated it so much that I think he called it the worst book that ever was written. Or perhaps it was someone else who favoured it with that description. Some of this money I lost, for really I had not time to look after it, and the investments suggested by kind friends connected with the City were apt to prove disappointing. Some of it I spent in paying off back debts and mortgages on our property, and in doing up this house which it sadly needed, as well as countless farm buildings, and a proportion was absorbed by our personal expenditure. For instance we moved into a larger house in Radcliffe Square and there entertained a little, though not to any great extent, for we never were extravagant. Also I became what is called famous, which in practice means that people are glad to ask you out to dinner, and when you enter a room everyone turns to look at you. Also it means that bores of the most appalling description write to you from all over the earth, and expect answers."[1]

June, 1888. Trip to Iceland.

August, 1888. Began the novel, *Eric Brighteyes,* based on his Icelandic trip. "*Eric* came out in due course, and did well enough. Indeed as a book it found, and still continues to find, a considerable body of readers. My recollection is, however, that it was reviewed simply as a rather spirited and sanguinary tale. Lang was quite right. The gentlemen who dispense praise and blame to us poor authors have not, for the most part, made a study of the sagas or investigated the lands where these were enacted. I wonder if it has ever occurred to the average reader how much the writer of a book which he looks at for an hour or two and throws aside must sometimes need to know, and what long months or years of preparation that knowledge has cost him? Probably not. My extended experience of the average reader is to the effect that he thinks the author produces these little things in his leisure moments, say when he, the reader, would be smoking his cigarettes, and this without the slightest effort." [*The Days of My Life: An Autobiography,* Volume II, edited by C. J. Longman, Longmans, Green, London, 1926.[3]]

December 9, 1889. His mother died at Bradenham.

June, 1889. Began *Nada the Lily,* which was finished in January. "It is true that in such a book as *Nada the Lily* there is much slaughter. But all this is a matter of history. A tale of the days of Chaka which left out his slayings and battles would be false to the facts and merely ludicrous. Omelets cannot be made without the breaking of eggs. Would such critics then argue that this tale and others like it should be left untold? If so, I hold that they are wrong, since these give

a picture which, from the circumstances of my youth, perhaps I alone in the world can paint, not only of some very remarkable men, but of a state of savage society which has now passed away and may never recur.

"Personally I hate war, and all killing, down to the destruction of the lower animals for the sake of sport, has become abominable to me. But while the battle-clouds bank up I do not think that any can be harmed by reading of heroic deeds or of frays in which brave men lose their lives."[3]

January, 1890. With his wife, Haggard accepted an invitation to Mexico.

February, 1890. Beloved son, Jock, died unexpectedly at the age of nine after an attack of measles and an unsuspected complication of a gastric ulcer. Haggard and his wife received the news in Mexico. "It is strange, but when I went to Mexico I knew, almost without doubt, that in this world he and I would never see each other more. Only I thought *it was I who was doomed to die.* Otherwise it is plain that I should never have started on that journey. With this surety in my heart—it was with me for weeks before we sailed—the parting was bitter indeed. The boy was to stay with friends, the Gosses. I bade him good-bye and tore myself away. I returned after some hours. A chance, I forget what, had prevented the servant, a tall dark woman whose name is lost to me, from starting with him to Delamere Crescent till later than was expected. He was still in my study—about to go. Once more I went through that agony of a separation which I knew to be the last. With a cheerful face I kissed him—I remember how he flung his arms about my neck—in a cheerful voice I blessed him and bade him farewell, promising to write. Then he went through the door and it was finished. I think I wept.

"I said nothing of this secret foreknowledge of mine, nor did I attempt to turn from the road that I had chosen because I was aware of what awaited me thereon. Only I made every possible preparation for my death—even to sealing up all important papers in a despatch-box and depositing them in Messrs. Gosling's Bank, where I knew they would be at once available.

"But alas! my spirit saw imperfectly. Or perhaps *knowing* only that Death stood between us, I jumped to the conclusion that it was on me of an older generation that his hand would fall, on me who was about to undertake a journey which I guessed to be dangerous, including as it did a visit to the ruins of Palenque, whither at the time few travellers ventured. It never occurred to me that he was waiting for my son.

"About six weeks later—for I may as well tell the story out and be done with it—that hand fell. My presentiments had returned to me with terrible strength and persistence. One Sunday morning in the Jebbs' house in Mexico City, as we were preparing to go to church, they were fulfilled. Mrs. Jebb called us to their bedroom. She had a paper in her hand. 'Something is wrong with one of your children,' she said brokenly. 'Which?' I asked, aware that this meant death, no less, and waited. 'Jock,' was the reply, and the dreadful telegram, our first intimation of his illness, was read. It said that he had 'passed away peacefully' some few hours before. There were no details or explanations.

"Then in truth I descended into hell. Of the sufferings of the poor mother I will not speak. They belong to her alone.

"I can see the room now. Jebb weeping by the unmade bed, the used basins—all, all. And in the midst of it myself—with a broken heart! Were I a living man when these words are read—why, it would be wrong that I should rend the veil, I who never speak of this matter, who never even let that dear name pass my lips. But they will not be read till I, too, am gone and have learned whatever there is to know. Perhaps also the tale has its lessons. At any rate it is a page in my history that cannot be omitted, though it be torn from the living heart and, some may think, too sad to dwell on."[3]

The tragedy changed Haggard. Thereafter he became apprehensive. For a time, he lost his health, friends, and state of mind. "As for myself, I was crushed; my nerves broke down entirely, and the rest of the Mexican visit, with its rough journeyings, is to me a kind of nightmare. Not for many years did I shake off the effects of the shock; indeed I have never done so altogether. It has left me with a heritage of apprehensions, not for myself personally—I am content to take what comes—but for others. My health gave out. I left London, which I could no longer bear, and hid myself away here in the country. The other day I found a letter of this period, sent to me as an enclosure on some matter, in which the writer speaks of me as being 'quite unapproachable since the death of his only son.' So, indeed, I think I was. Moreover, at this time the influenza attacked me again and again, and left me very weak.

"We did not come home at once—what was the good of returning to the desolated home? Our boy had died in a strange house and been brought to Ditchingham for burial. What was the good of returning home? So there, far away, in due course letters reached us with these dreadful details and heart-piercing messages of farewell.

"And now I have done with this terrible episode and will get me to my tale again. The wound has been seared by time—few, perhaps none, would guess that it existed; but it will never heal. I think I may say that from then till now no day has passed, and often no hour, when the thought of my lost boy has not been present with me. I can only bow my head and murmur, 'God's will be done!'"[3]

1891. Returned to England. "When I returned from Mexico in 1891 I fell into very poor health. Everything, especially my digestion, went wrong, so wrong that I began to think that my bones would never grow old. Amongst other inconveniences I found that I could no longer endure the continual stooping over a desk which is involved in the writing of books. . . . From that time forward I have done a great deal of my work by means of dictation, which has greatly relieved its labour. Some people can dictate, and others cannot. Personally I have always found the method easy, provided that the dictatee, if I may coin a word, is patient and does not go too fast.

"Of the next few years of my life there is not much to tell. I lived here at Ditchingham in a very quiet and retired fashion, rarely visiting London, wrote a few novels, and for recreation occupied myself with farming and gardening, for which occupations I have always had an instinctive taste. The work that I did was a good deal attacked: it was the fashion to attack me in those days. Possibly owing to my ill-health some of it may not have been quite up to the mark; I do not know. What I do know is that I grew heartily tired of the writing of stories."[3]

December 9, 1892. Youngest daughter, Lilias, born. "After the birth of my youngest child, Lilias, which to my great joy

There at the end of the long stone table, holding in his skeleton fingers a great white spear, sat *Death* himself, shaped in the form of a colossal human skeleton, fifteen feet or more in height. ■ (From *King Solomon's Mines* by Henry Rider Haggard. Illustrated by Will Nickless.)

happened at the end of the year 1892, my health and spirits began to mend and my energy to return, largely owing, I think, to the treatment of my friend Dr. Lyne Stivens. I was still a youngish man, but had reached that time of life when I felt that if I was to make any change of occupation it must be done at once. And I longed to make a change, for this humdrum existence in a country parish, staring at crops and cultivating flowers, was, I felt, more suitable to some aged man whose life's work was done than to myself. Also at this time the unrealities of fiction-writing greatly wearied me, oddly enough much more than they do at present, when they have become a kind of amusement and set-off to the more serious things and thoughts with which my life is occupied."[3]

April 22, 1893. Father died. "In 1893 my dear father died as the result of a chill which he caught in waiting about for the poll to be declared at an election in cold weather. It was sad to see a man of his great strength and energy fading away and becoming so subdued and gentle, qualities which were not natural to him. After one extraordinary recovery from the jaundice, or whatever it was that had attacked him, believing himself to be strong again, he began to travel and pay visits in winter, and thus brought on a return of his ailment. I was not actually present at his death-bed, as I could only reach Bradenham on the following day. He left me one of his executors and, as he was dying, told our old servant Hocking to give me his watch and chain, which I think had been his father's before him. I have it now, still marking the hour at which it ran down under his pillow on that night. His last words, spoken almost as he expired, were:

"'God is everywhere! He is in this room, is He not?'

"He looked fine and peaceful in death; as I think I have said, he was very handsome, and in many ways a remarkable man. I never knew anyone who resembled him in the least or who was the possessor of half his energy. God rest him!"[3]

1895. Entered politics. Defeated for the seat of East Norfolk. "... I almost carried one of the most difficult seats in England. But almost is not quite, and the awful expense attendant upon contesting a seat in Parliament (in a county division it costs, or used to cost, over £2000) showed me clearly that, unless they happen to be Labour members, such a career is only open to rich men. Also I came to understand that it would be practically impossible for me both to earn a living by the writing of books and to plunge eagerly into Parliamentary work, as I know well that I should have done. Even if I could have found the time by writing in the mornings—which, where imaginative effort is concerned, has always been distasteful to me—my health would never have borne the double strain.

"So that dream had to be abandoned, for which I am sorry. Indeed, a legislative career is about the only one of which the doors are not shut to the writer of fiction, as is proved by many instances, notably that of Disraeli."[3]

In the same year, elected to the Athenaeum Club.

1900. Traveled to Cypress and the Holy Land. "The Holy Land impressed me enormously, although it is the fashion of many travellers to say that there they find nothing but disappointment...."[3]

1901 and **1902.** Published *Rural England,* an account of agricultural and social researches carried out during that year. "Of *Rural England,* the heaviest labour of all my laborious life, there is really not very much to say. There it is. I shall never forget the remark of my daughter Dolly, a young lady with a turn for humour, when these two great volumes—they contain as many words as would more than fill five novels—arrived from Messrs. Longmans and, portly, blue and beautiful, stood before us on the table. 'My word, Dad!' she said, 'if *I* had written a book like that, *I* should spend the rest of my life sitting to stare at it!'[3]

Winter, 1904. Returned to Egypt with his eldest daughter. *The Way of the Spirit* and *Morning Star* are based on this trip. "Early in 1904 I took my daughter Angela on a trip to Egypt, returning by way of Italy and Spain.... I enjoyed that trip in Egypt very much. The place has a strange fascination for me, and if I could afford it I would go there every year."[3]

1905. Sent to the United States as Commissioner to report on the Labour Colonies established by the Salvation Army. Established a lifetime friendship and correspondence with Theodore Roosevelt, who was then President. "I wonder if we shall ever meet again? No I do not wonder, for I am sure we shall *somewhere* for we have too much in common not to do.... A great man indeed but oh! how misunderstood by millions. It was well worth coming to America just for those few hours of comradeship."[2]

That same year Haggard saw another book published while he was a patient in a nursing home. "In the intervals of all this Commission business I retired for a month or five weeks into a nursing home to undergo an operation which the effects of my long journey made necessary.

"Never shall I forget that place!—the lodging-house-like little drawing-room where patients were received, and where I had to wait in my dressing-gown while my room was made ready for the operation; the dreadful noise caused by the carriages of theatre-goers returning home at night or by the rattle of the mail-carts over the stone-paved road; the continual operations; the occasional rush of the nurses when it was announced that a patient was passing away; and so forth.

"I had never taken a major anaesthetic before, and I must say I did not find the process pleasant. I can still see the face of my friend Dr. Lyne Stivens, and the jovial, rubicund countenance of the late Professor Rose, bending over me as through a mist, both grown so strangely solemn, and feel the grip of my hand tightening upon that of the nurse which afterwards it proved almost impossible to free.

"Then came the whirling pit and the blackness. I suppose that it was like death, only I hope that death is not quite so dark!

"From this blackness I awoke in a state of utter intoxication to find the nurses of the establishment gathered round me with sheets of paper and the familiar, hateful autograph books in which, even in that place and hour, they insisted I should write. Heaven knows what I set down therein: I imagine they must have been foolish words, which mayhap one day will be brought up against me.

"Another question: Why cannot the public authorities establish really suitable nursing homes for paying patients? This would be a great boon to thousands, and, I should imagine, self-supporting.

"However, of one of these nurses at any rate, a widow, I have grateful recollections. I amused myself, and, I trust her, by reading *Ayesha* aloud to her during my long wakeful hours—for she was a night nurse.

"This book *Ayesha,* which was published while I was in the nursing home, is a sequel to *She,* which, in obedience to my original plan, I had deliberately waited for twenty years to write. As is almost always the case, it suffered somewhat from this fact, at any rate at the hands of those critics with whom it is an article of faith to declare that no sequel can be good. Still, I have met and heard from many people who like *Ayesha* better than they do *She.*"[3]

1906. Made a member of the Royal Commission on Coast Erosion, a position he held for five years. "I worked hard on that Royal Commission. During the five years of its life, indeed, I only missed one day's sitting, and that was because the steamer from Denmark could not get me there in time. Shortly after the commencement of its labours I was nominated the Chairman of the Unemployed Labour and Reclamation Committee, which involved a good deal of extra, but important and interesting, business. Also I was the Chairman of two of the tours that were made by committees of the Commission to inspect the coasts of Great Britain and Ireland, during which tours I am glad to say there were no differences of opinion or other troubles, such as have been known to arise on similar occasions."[3]

1911. His work on the Royal Commission ended. "I missed that Commission very much; since its sittings took me to London from time to time, and gave me a change of mental occupation and interests. Indeed I do not remember ever being more consistently depressed than I was during the first part of the following winter. Here, as I no longer shoot, I had nothing to do, except the daily grind of romance-writing, relieved only by Bench business, my farm affairs, and an afternoon walk through the mud with the two spaniels, Bustle and Jeekie, and a chat after church on Sunday upon the affairs of the nation with my fellow-churchwarden, friend and neighbour, Mr. Carr, the squire of this place. Also bronchitis, which had threatened me for some years, troubled me much. I thought that I had shaken it off, but caught it again during a cold snap, staying at a Cambridge college, whither I went to address a large meeting upon the possibility of establishing agricultural training institutions upon the Danish model. So I returned here, enjoyed the bronchitis, and began to write this autobiography, for really it seemed as though everything had come to an end.

"Then of a sudden things changed, as they have a way of doing in life. Thus one morning about Christmas-time I found amongst my correspondence a communication from the Prime Minister informing me that the King had been pleased to confer a knighthood upon me. I had often thought and said that I did not think I should care to be knighted. Indeed when a year or two before it was suggested to me through a semi-official channel on behalf of a very powerful Minister, that if I wished for a baronetcy it might perhaps be arranged, I said at once, and firmly, that I did not. Baronetcies are for rich men who have male heirs, not for persons like myself.

"However, I took the knighthood when it was definitely offered, on the ground that it is a mistake to refuse anything in this world; also that a title is useful in the public service, and especially so abroad. Moreover, it was Recognition, for which I felt grateful; for who is there that does not appreciate recognition particularly after long years of, I hope, disinterested toil?"[3]

January, 1912. Knighted in the New Year Honours List. On the 11th of that same month, Haggard was appointed to the Dominions Royal Commission. "I need scarcely say that to my mind this was recognition—with a vengeance. Charles Longman remarked when I told him the news, at which he was delighted, 'I would rather have heard this than that they had given you a peerage. Anyone can be a peer, but to be one of the six men chosen to represent the United Kingdom on a great Empire inquiry of this sort is a real honour.'

"I agree with him, especially as I have no wish to be a peer. Also to me the compliment seemed the more marked for the reason that it was paid to an individual who first became known to the public as a writer of romantic literature, an occupation that does not dispose the British nation to take those who follow it seriously. Now I saw that all my long years of toil in investigating and attempting to solve the grave problems which lie at the root of the welfare of our country had not been without effect upon the minds of its rulers, and I felt proportionately grateful and honoured.

"Of course the acceptance of this Royal Commissionership involves serious sacrifices in my case, exclusive of that of

...Just as I was sinking exhausted, a hand shot down into the water and caught me by the ears.... ■ (From *The Mahatma and the Hare* by H. Rider Haggard. Illustrated by H.M. Brock.)

long separation from my family. Thus it will necessitate the partial shutting down of my home here; and how I am to carry on my literary work in the intervals of so much public labour, really I do not know! I felt, as did my wife, and still feel that such considerations should not be allowed to interfere with the execution of what I look upon as a high and honourable duty."[3]

February, 1914. After more than thirty years, returned to his beloved South Africa. In July, he returned home. "So ends my visit to South Africa—on the whole it has been successful, if sad in some ways. I am truly and deeply grateful for the extreme kindness with which I have been welcomed everywhere, in fact I have experienced quite a little triumph. Affectionate as was my greeting I think really it was more to do with the fact I am sort of curiosity, a survival from a past generation, than to my own individuality. Also my subsequent career has interested those among whom I spent the first years of my manhood, when I was concerned with great men and great events.

"So to South Africa, farewell, which is the dominant word in my life. It is a fair land of which the charm still holds my heart and whose problems interest me more than ever. How

H. Rider Haggard, drawing by S. van Abbé.

will they work out their fate I wonder? When I have gone to sleep or may be to dream on elsewhere. My name will perhaps always be connected with Africa if it remains a white man's 'house' and even if it does not—perhaps. It is impossible for me to avoid contrasting the feelings with which I leave it now that I have grown old, with those with which I bade good-bye to its shores in 1881 when I was young. Then life was before me, I had hopes and ambitions. Now life is practically behind me, with its many failures and its few successes."[3]

January-August, 1916. Sent to South Africa, Australia, and Canada by the government to investigate the prospects of ex-servicemen settling in the Dominions of England. Haggard spent exhausting months travelling, speaking, interviewing and attending official lunches, dinners and receptions. In Canada he was informed that it was proposed and agreed by the Geographical Board of Canada to name a mountain on the line of the Grand Trunk Pacific Railway, Mount Sir Rider and the glacier which flowed down it Haggard Glacier. "Here they give my name to a towering Alp—in Norfolk they would not bestow it upon the smallest 'pightle' [a small, odd corner of land]. Truly no man is a prophet in his own country!"[2]

September, 1917. Presented his entire collection of manuscripts to the Castle Museum of Norfolk. "Since Norfolk has been the home of my family for several generations and I am Norfolk born, I have given them to the Castle Collection—the gift of a Norfolk man to Norfolk. All the same it made me rather sad to part with them. . . ."[2]

In the same month he sold his Norfolk farm of thirty years. "I have made nothing if return on capital is taken into account, but I have gained a vast amount of experience—and perhaps I am well out of the business."[2]

May, 1918. Returned to his family home at Bradenham. "It is odd at the end of life coming back to houses at which one has spent its beginnings, for then such become one vast and

living memory. Every bit of furniture, every picture on the walls, every stone and tree bring forgotten scenes before the eye, or find tongues and talk. Scenes in which dead actors played, voices that can stir the air no more. Where are they all? Where do they hide from the searchlight of our love? Well, ere long the play of our generation will be finished and we too shall learn. Bradenham . . . where I first saw the light, you are a sad spot for me, the echoes from your old walls are many and dear."[2]

November, 1918. World War I ended. Haggard wrote a chilling prophesy in his diary: "So it comes about that our nation emerges from the struggle more potent, more splendid than ever she has shone before, laughing at all disloyalties, with mighty opportunities open to her grasp. How she will use them in the years to come, I shall never see. The Germans will neither forgive nor forget; neither money nor comfort will tell with them henceforth. They have been beaten by England and they will live and die to smash England—she will never have a more deadly enemy than the new Germany. My dread is that in future years the easy-going, self-centred English will forget that just across the sea there is a mighty, cold-hearted and remorseless people waiting to strike her through the heart. For strike they will one day, or so I believe."[2]

January, 1924. Returned to Egypt with his daughter, Lilias.

November, 1924. After a luncheon in his honor, Haggard was taken ill with an attack which the doctors put down to violent digestive upset, chill and exertion. He never fully recovered.

December, 1924. At home in Ditchingham he fought a losing battle with pain, weakness and depression.

Spring, 1925. His doctors decided that he must be operated on in London.

May 14, 1925. Died at a nursing home in London, England. "After all what is it, this death? As I grow older I seem to understand the hope and beauty of it, and though doubtless I shall recoil afraid, to rejoice that life should close so soon. Better to die than to see those we love die. For to most of us existence here at the best is unhappy. Goodness and the desire to better the state of others are the only happy things in it, and the first in our half-brutal nature is hard to attain. But I think it can be attained if opportunity and space endure, and then, our many past sins, errors and foulness of thought and deed notwithstanding, why should we fear to die? Surely those men are made who in their little day reject the offerings of religion, for through faith the communion of the creature with his Maker is real and possible to him who seeks it, whatever the fashion of his seeking, and without that communion light is not. Love also is real and immortal, not lust, but the love of children and friends and fellow-beings—*that* light shall always shine. For myself I hope to live long enough to win sufficient success and money to do some little good to others. If I fail in the attempt . . . may the earnest endeavour be accepted! At least we should try, since all we have, intelligence, attributes, means, is but lent to us. I wonder if you will set me down as a simple religious enthusiast or as a little mad with my notions of the efficacy of faith and prayer. Perhaps I am the latter—sorrow breeds it—but at least my madness is a star to follow. . . ."[3]

Haggard's wife and children laid his ashes beneath the slab of black marble in the chancel of Ditchingham Church. On the stone was cut the short sentence he himself had written:

HALE, Edward Everett 1822-1909
(Colonel Frederic Ingham)

PERSONAL: Born April 3, 1822, in Boston, Massachusetts; died June 10, 1909, in Boston, Massachusetts; son of Nathan Hale (owner and editor of the Boston *Daily Advertiser;* nephew of the Revolutionary War hero of the same name) and Sarah Preston (Everett) Hale (sister of the orator and author, Edward Everett); brother of the author, Lucretia Peabody Hale, and of the painter, Susan Hale; married Emily Baldwin Perkins, 1852; children: Ellen, Arthur, Charles, Philip, Herbert, Harry, Roberta, Edward Everett, Jr. *Education:* Attended private schools until the age of thirteen; graduated from Harvard University, 1839, S. T. D., 1879.

CAREER: Clergyman, author, poet, and social reformer. As a college student, worked for the Boston *Daily Advertiser;* taught school for two years; ordained Unitarian clergyman, 1846, following an independent study of theology; served as minister of the Church of Unity, Worcester, 1846-56, and of the South Congregational Church of Boston, 1856-99; elected Chaplain of the United States Senate, 1903-09. Promoter of the Chautauqua Circles and Lend-a-Hand Clubs, and various philanthropic organizations; chairman, Massachusetts Commission for International Justice. *Awards, honors:* LL.D., Dartmouth College, 1901, Williams College, 1904.

WRITINGS—Fiction: *The Man without a Country* (first published in the *Atlantic Monthly,* 1863), Ticknor & Fields, 1865, later published in *The Man without a Country, and Other Tales,* 1868, reprinted, Books for Libraries Press, 1971 [other editions include those illustrated by Nella F. Binckley, Platt & Peck, 1910; L. J. Bridgman, Page, 1917; Milo Winter, Whitman, 1927; Edward A. Wilson, Limited Edition Club, 1936, reissued, Heritage Press, 1961; Everett Shinn, Random House, 1940; Leonard Everett Fisher, F. Watts, 1960]; (under pseudonym Colonel Frederic Ingham) *Ten Times One Is Ten: The Possible Reformation,* Roberts Brothers, 1871.

Ups and Downs: An Every-day Novel, Roberts Brothers, 1873; *Our New Crusade: A Temperance Story,* Roberts Brothers, 1875; *G.T.T.; or, The Wonderful Adventures of a Pullman,* Roberts Brothers, 1877; *Philip Nolan's Friends: A Story of the Change of Western Empire,* Scribner, Armstrong, 1877, reprinted, Literature House, 1970; *Back to Back: A Story of Today,* Harper, 1878; *Mrs. Merriam's Scholars: A Story of the "Original Ten,"* Roberts Brothers, 1878; *In His Name* (first published in the monthly, *Old and New,* 1873), Fairbanks, Palmer, 1882 [a later edition illustrated by G. F. Jacomb-Hood, Roberts Brothers, 1888]; *Our Christmas in a Palace: A Traveller's Story,* Funk & Wagnalls, 1883; *Daily Bread: A Story of the Snow Blockade,* J. S. Smith, 1883; *The Fortunes of Rachel,* Funk & Wagnalls, 1884.

Red and White: A Christmas Story, J. S. Smith, 1887; *My Friend the Boss: A Story of Today,* J. S. Smith, 1888; *Mr. Tangier's Vacations: A Novel,* Roberts Brothers, 1888; *Four and Five: A Story of a Lend-a-Hand Club,* Roberts Brothers, 1891; (with sister, Lucretia P. Hale) *The New Harry and Lucy: A Story of Boston in the Summer of 1891,* Roberts Brothers, 1892; *East and West: A Story of New-Born Ohio,* Cassell, 1892 (published in England as *The New Ohio: A Story of East and West,* Cassell, 1892); *Sybil Knox; or, Home Again: A Story of Today,* Cassell, 1892; *One Good Turn,* J. S. Smith, 1893; *For Fifty Years: Verses Writ-*

EDWARD EVERETT HALE

ten on Occasion, in the Course of the Nineteenth Century, Roberts Brothers, 1893; *My Double and How He Undid Me,* Lamson, Wolffe, 1895; (with his children and others) *New England History in Ballads* (poems and songs; illustrated by Ellen D. Hale, Philip L. Hale, and Lilian Hale), Little, Brown, 1906.

Short stories: *If, Yes, and Perhaps,* Ticknor & Fields, 1868, reprinted, Garrett Press, 1969; *The Ingham Papers: Some Memorials of the Life of Captain Frederic Ingham,* Fields, Osgood, 1869; *His Level Best, and Other Stories,* Roberts Brothers, 1872, reprinted Garrett Press, 1969; *Christmas Eve and Christmas Day: Ten Christmas Stories* (illustrated by F.O.C. Darley), Roberts Brothers, 1873, reprinted, Books for Libraries, 1969; *Crusoe in New York, and Other Tales,* Roberts Brothers, 1880, reprinted, Garrett Press, 1968; *Christmas in Narragansett,* Funk & Wagnalls, 1884; *The Brick Moon, and Other Stories,* Little, Brown, 1899, reprinted, Books for Libraries, 1970; *Sunday Afternoon Stories for Home and School,* Office of Lend-a-Hand Record (Boston), 1901.

For children: *Boys' Heroes,* Lothrop, 1865; *How to Do It,* J. R. Osgood, 1871; *The Life of George Washington Studied Anew,* Putnam, 1888; *Afloat and Ashore,* Searle & Gorton, 1891; *Hands Off,* J. S. Smith, 1895; *A Safe Deposit,* J. S. Smith, 1895; *Susan's Escort, and Others* (illustrated by W. T. Smedley), Harper, 1897 (includes, among other stories, *Aunt Caroline's Present, Colonel Clipsham's Calendar, Susan's Escort,* all published separately by J. S. Smith, 1895); *How to Live,* Little, Brown, 1902.

Nonfiction: *Letters on Irish Emigration,* Phillips, Sampson, 1852, reprinted, Books for Libraries, 1972; *Kansas and Nebraska,* Phillips, Sampson, 1854, reprinted, Books for Libraries, 1972; *Sybaris and Other Homes,* Fields, Osgood,

1869, reprinted, Arno, 1971; *Workingmen's Homes*, J. R. Osgood, 1874; *One Hundred Years Ago: How the War Began*, Lockwood, Brooks, 1875; *Sketches of the Brothers Everett*, Little, Brown, 1878; *What Career? Ten Papers on the Choice of a Vocation and the Use of Time*, Roberts Brothers, 1878; *The Kingdom of God and Twenty Other Sermons*, Roberts Brothers, 1880; *The Life in Common and Twenty Other Sermons*, Roberts Brothers, 1880; (with sister, Susan Hale) *The Story of Spain*, Putnam, 1887; (with son, Edward E. Hale, Jr.) *Franklin in France*, Roberts Brothers, 1887-88, reprinted, B. Franklin, 1969; *How They Lived in Hampton*, J. S. Smith, 1888, reprinted, Arno, 1971.

The Story of Massachusetts, Lothrop, 1891; *The Life of Christopher Columbus*, G. L. Howe, 1891, reissued as *The Story of Columbus as He Told It Himself*, J. S. Smith, 1893; *A New England Boyhood* (autobiographical), Cassell, 1893, new edition (with foreword by Edwin D. Mead), Little, Brown, 1927, reprinted, Scholarly Press, 1970; *If Jesus Came to Boston*, Lamson, Wolffe, 1895; *Studies in American Colonial Life*, Chautauqua Century Press, 1895; *Ralph Waldo Emerson, Together with Two Early Essays of Emerson*, Brown, 1899, reprinted, Folcroft, 1973; *A Permanent Tribunal: The Emperor of Russia and His Circular regarding Permanent Peace*, G. H. Ellis, 1899; *Addresses and Essays on Subjects of History, Education, and Government*, Little, Brown, 1900; *Memories of a Hundred Years*, Macmillan, 1902, revised and enlarged edition, 1904; *"We the People": A Series of Papers on Topics of Today*, Dodd, 1903; *The Foundations of the Republic*, J. Pott, 1906.

Travel books: *Ninety Days' Worth of Europe*, Walker, Wise, 1861; *Seven Spanish Cities, and the Way to Them*, Roberts Brothers, 1883; *Historic Boston and Its Neighborhood*, Appleton, 1898; *Young Americans in the Orient*, Lothrop, 1900; *Tarry at Home Travels*, Macmillan, 1906; series written with Susan Hale and published by Lothrop—*A Family Flight through France, Germany, Norway and Switzerland*, 1881; *A Family Flight over Egypt and Syria*, 1882; *A Family Flight around Home*, 1884; *A Family Flight through Mexico*, 1886; *Young Americans Abroad: Being a Family Flight of Four Young People and Their Parents through France and Germany*, 1898.

Editor: *The Rosary of Illustrations of the Bible* (prose and poetry), Phillips & Sampson, 1849; *The President's Words: A Selection of Passages from the Speeches, Addresses, and Letters of Abraham Lincoln*, [Boston], 1866; (and contributor) *Six of One by Half a Dozen of the Other: An Everyday Novel*, Roberts Brothers, 1872; *Silhouettes and Songs Illustrative of the Months*, Lockwood, Brooks, 1876; *Lights of Two Centuries: Artists, Sculptors, Prose Writers, Composers, Poets, and Inventors* (biography), A. S. Barnes, 1887; (and contributor) *Sunday-School Stories on the Golden Texts of the International Lessons of 1889*, Roberts Brothers, 1889.

Stories of War Told by Soldiers, Roberts Brothers, 1879; *Stories of the Sea Told by Sailors*, Roberts Brothers, 1880; *Stories of Adventure Told by Adventurers*, Roberts Brothers, 1881; *Stories of Discovery Told by Discoverers*, Roberts Brothers, 1882; *Stories of Invention Told by Inventors and Their Friends*, Roberts Brothers, 1885.

Collections: *The Works of Edward Everett Hale*, ten volumes, Little, Brown, 1898-1901.

Founder and editor of the monthly magazine, *Old and New* (1870-75), which was later absorbed by *Scribner's Magazine*.

ADAPTATIONS—Movies and filmstrips: "The Man without a Country" (motion pictures), Jewel Productions, 1917, Fox Film, 1925, Vitaphone, 1938, Young American Films, 1953; "As No Man Has Loved" (motion picture), adaptation of *The Man without a Country*, Fox Film, 1925; "The Man without a Country" (filmstrip), Encyclopaedia Britannica Films, 1956.

Opera: Arthur Guiterman, librettist, *The Man without a Country* (music by Walter Damrosch), produced in New York at the Metropolitan Opera, 1937.

SIDELIGHTS: **April 3, 1822.** Born in Boston. Fourth of eight children. "I was born in a house which stood where Parker's larger lunch-room now fronts the Tremont House. We moved from this house to that on the corner of School Street, lately purchased by Mr. Parker to enlarge his hotel, and in 1828 we moved again to the new house, which was, and is, No. 1 Tremont Place. It is now two or three stories higher than it was then; but some parts of the interior are not changed. Behind it was a little yard, with a wood-house, called a 'shed,' on top of which the clothes were dried. This arrangement was important for our New England childhood.

"I was the youngest of four children who made the older half of a large family. By a gap between me and my brother Alexander,—who afterwards was lost in the government service in Pensacola,—'we four' were separated from the 'three little ones.' It is necessary to explain this in advance, in a history which is rather a history of young life in Boston than of mine alone.

"My father . . . was an experienced teacher in young life, and he never lost his interest in the business of education. My mother had a genius for education, and it is a pity that, at an epoch in her life when she wanted to open a girls' school, she was not permitted to do so. They had read enough of the standard books on education to know how much sense there was in them, and how much nonsense. Such books were about in the house, more or less commented on by us young critics as we grew big enough to dip into them.

"At the moment I had no idea that any science or skill was expended on our training. I supposed I was left to the great American proverb . . . 'Go as you please.' But I have seen since that the hands were strong which directed this gay team of youngsters, though there was no stimulus we knew of, and though the touch was velvet. An illustration of this was in that wisdom of my father in sending me for four years to school to a simpleton.

"The genius of the whole, shown by both my father and mother, came out in the skill which made home the happiest place of all, so that we simply hated any engagement which took us elsewhere, unless we were in the open air. I have said that I disliked school, and that I did not want to go down on the wharves, even with that doubtful bribe of the molasses casks. At home we had an infinite variety of amusements. At home we might have all the other boys, if we wished. At home, in our two stories, we were supreme. The scorn of toys which is reflected in the Edgeworth books had, to a certain extent, its effect on the household. But we had almost everything we wanted for purposes of manufacture or invention. Whalebone, spiral springs, pulleys, and catgut, for perpetual motion or locomotive carriages; rollers and

And, what with collecting the milk from the hill-farms, on the one hand, and then carrying it for delivery at the three o'clock morning milk-train, on the other hand, any hours which you, dear reader, might consider systematic, or of course in country life, were certainly always set aside.
■ (From *Christmas Eve and Christmas Day* by Edward E. Hale. Illustrated by F.O.C. Darley.)

planks for floats—. . . and were obtainable. In the yard we had parallel bars and a high cross-pole for climbing. When we became chemists we might have sulphuric acid, nitric acid, litmus paper, or whatever we desired, so our allowance would stand it.

"I was not more than seven years old when I burned off my eyebrows by igniting gunpowder with my burning-glass. My hair was then so light that nobody missed a little, more or less, above the eyelids. I thought it was wisest not to tell my mother, because it might shock her nerves, and I was a man, thirty years old, before she heard of it. Such playthings as these, with very careful restrictions on the amount of powder, with good blocks for building, quite an assortment of carpenter's tools, a work-bench good enough, printing materials *ad libitum* from my father's printing-office, furnished endless occupation." [Edward Everett Hale, *A New England Boyhood,* Little, Brown, 1928.[1]]

Life in New England was a constant joy.

Spring. "As the snow melted, and the elms blossomed, and the grass came, the Common opened itself to every sort of game. We played marbles in holes in the malls. We flew kites everywhere, not troubled, as boys would be now, by trees on the cross-paths, for there were no such trees. The old elm and a large willow by the Frog Pond, were the only trees within the pentagon made by the malls and the burial-ground. Kite-flying was, as it is, a science; and on a fine summer day, with south-west winds, a line of boys would be camped in groups, watching or tending their favorite kites as they hung in the air over Park Street. Occasionally a string would break. It was a matter of honor to save your twine. I remember following my falling kite, with no clue but the direction in which I saw it last, till I found that the twine was lying across a narrow court which opened where the Albion Hotel is now. There were two rows of three-story houses which made the court, and my twine festooned it, supported by the ridge-poles of the roofs on either side. I rang a door-bell, stated my case, and ran up, almost without permission, into the attic. Here I climbed out of the attic window, ran up the roof as *Teddy the Tyler* might have done, and drew in the coveted twine. For the pecuniary value of the twine we cared little; but it would have been, in a fashion, a disgrace to lose it."[1]

Summer. "Joy, joy, joy! Of a hot summer day in June, when I was nine years old, I was asked how I would like to learn to swim. Little doubt in the mind of any boy who reads this what my answer was. I and my elder brother, who was twelve, were to be permitted to go to the swimming school. This was joy enough to have that year marked with red in our history.

"... Dr. Francis Lieber, who had been exiled from Germany a few years before, had come to Boston, and had established first his gymnasium and then his swimming school. Swimming schools were and are thoroughly established on the continent of Europe, and the Germans have a special reputation for skill in swimming. With the gymnasium I had little or nothing to do but what I have told. I was, indeed, quite too small to be put through its exercises.

"The swimming school was in water which flowed where Brimmer Street and the houses behind it are now built. It was just such a building as the floating baths are now which the city maintains, but that it enclosed a much larger space. Of this space a part had a floor so that the water flowed through; the depth was about five feet. To little boys like me it made little difference that there was this floor, for we could be as easily drowned in five feet of water as if there were fifteen.

"With great delight I carried down my little bathing drawers, which were marked with my own number so that they might always hang upon my peg. With the drawers and my towels I proceeded to a little cell, just such as the bathers at South Boston have now, with the great advantage, however, that its door was made of sail-cloth. You selected a cell on the northern side, so that when you went into the water you could draw your sail-cloth into the sun, and the sun would heat it well through; then, after your bath, you stood wrapped up in this warm linen shroud, and the luxury was considered exquisite.

"So soon as you were undressed and ready—and this meant in about one minute—you took your turn to be taught. A belt was put around you under your arms; to this belt a rope was attached, and you were told to jump in. You jumped in and went down as far as gravity chose to take you, and were then pulled up by the rope. The rope was then attached to the end of a long belt, and you were swung out upon the surface of the water. Then began the instruction.

"'O-n-e;—two, three:' the last two words spoken with great rapidity—'one' spoken very slowly. This meant that the knees and feet were to be drawn up very slowly, but were to be dashed out very quickly, and then the heels brought together as quickly.

"Boys who were well built for it and who were quick learned to swim in two or three lessons. Slender boys and little boys who had not much muscular force—and such was I—were a whole summer before they could be trusted without the rope. But the training was excellent, and from the end of that year till now I have been entirely at home in the water. I think now that scientific and systematic training in swimming is a very important part of public instruction, and I wish we could see it introduced everywhere where there is responsible oversight of boys or girls at school.''[1]

Entered school at age two. "At my own imprudent request, not to say urgency, I was sent to school with two sisters and a brother, older than I, when I was reckoned as about two years old. The school was in an old-fashioned wooden house which fronted on a little yard entered from Summer Street. We went up one flight of narrow stairs, and here the northern room of the two bedrooms of the house was occupied by Miss Susan Whitney for her school, and the southern room, which had windows on Summer Street, by Miss Ayres, of whom Miss Whitney had formerly been an assistant. Miss Whitney afterwards educated more than one generation of the children of Boston families. I supposed her to be one of the most aged, and certainly the most learned, women of her time. I believe she was a kind-hearted, intelligent girl of seventeen, when I first knew her. I also supposed the room to be a large hall, though I knew it was not nearly so large as our own parlors at home.

"It may have been eighteen feet square. The floor was sanded with clean sand every Thursday and Saturday afternoon. This was a matter of practical importance to us, because with the sand, using our feet as tools, we made sand pies. You gather the sand with the inside edge of either shoes from a greater or less distance, as the size of the pie requires. As you gain skill, the heap which you make is more and more round. When it is well rounded you flatten it by a careful pressure of one foot from above. Hence it will be seen that full success depends on your keeping the sole of the shoe exactly parallel with the plane of the floor. If you find you have succeeded when you withdraw the shoe, you prick the pie with a pin or a broom splint provided for the purpose, pricking it in whatever pattern you like. The skill of a good pie-maker is measured largely by these patterns. It will readily be seen that the pie is better if the sand is a little moist. But beggars cannot be choosers, and while we preferred the sand on Mondays and Fridays, when it was fresh, we took it as it came.

"I dwell on this detail at length because it is one instance as good as a hundred of the way in which we adapted ourselves to the conditions of our times. Children now have carpets on their kindergarten floors, where sand is unknown; so we have to provide clay for them to model with, and put a heap of sand in the back yard. Miss Whitney provided for the same needs by a simpler device, which I dare say is as old as King Alfred.

"I cannot tell how we were taught to read, for I cannot remember the time when I could not read as well as I can now. There was a little spelling-book called *The New York Spelling-Book,* printed by Mahlon Day. When, afterwards, I came to read about Mahlon in the book of Ruth, my notion of his was of a man who had the same name as the man who published the spelling-book. My grandfather had made a spelling-book which we had at home. Privately, I knew that, because he made it, it must be better than the book at school, but I was far too proud to explain this to Miss Whitney. I accepted her spelling-book in the same spirit in which I have often acted since, falling in with what I saw was the general drift, because the matter was of no great consequence. For reading-books we had Mrs. Barbauld's *First Lessons, Come, Hither, Charles, Come to Mamma;* and we had *Popular Lessons,* by Miss Robbins, which would be a good book to revive now, but I have not seen it for sixty years.

"The school must have been a very much 'go-as-you-please' sort of place. So far it conformed to the highest ideals of the best modern systems. But it had rewards and punishments. I have now a life of William Tell which was given me as a prize when I was five years old. By way of showing what was then thought fit reading for boys of that age I copy the first sentence: 'Friends of liberty, magnanimous hearts, sons of sensibility, ye who know how to die for your independence and live only for your brethren, lend an ear to my accents. Come! hear how one single man, born in an uncivilized clime, in the midst of a people curbed beneath the rods of an oppressor, by his individual courage, raised this people so abashed, and gave it a new being'—and so, and so on. My brother Nathan had *Rasselas* for a prize, and my sister Sarah had a silver medal, 'To the most amiable,' which I am

THE MAN WITHOUT A COUNTRY

The text of *The Man Without a Country* was transcribed into a textbook for stenographers by Gregg Publishing. Illustrated by Frank T. Merrill.

"Home!! Mr. Nolan!!! I thought you were the man who never wanted to hear of home again!" ■ (From *The Man Without a Country* by Edward Everett Hale. Illustrated by Everett Shinn.)

sure she deserved, though the competition extended to the whole world."[1]

1828. Moved to No. 1 Tremont. "Just before I was six years old I was transferred from Miss Whitney's school to another school which was in the immediate neighborhood, being in the basement of the First Church, which was then in Chauncy Street. It stood, I think, just where Coleman & Mead's great store stands. There were three or four large rooms under the church, which were rented as school-rooms; and it being thought that I was large enough to go to a man's school, I was sent there, to my great delight, with my friend Edward Webster [son of Daniel Webster]. We were very intimate from days earlier than this . . . and it was a great pleasure to us that we could go to school together. He had been at Miss Ayres's, so that only an entry parted us. There was no thought of sending me to a public school.

"My father and mother had both very decided, and, I have a right to say, very advanced, views on matters of education; and advanced education was then a matter everywhere in the air. The Boston Latin School had been made a first-rate school for preparing boys for college, under the eye and care of Benjamin Apthorp Gould, some ten years before. But there was no public school of any lower grade, to which my father would have sent me, any more than he would have sent me to jail. Since that time I have heard my contemporaries talk of the common school training of the day, and I do not wonder at my father's decision. The masters, so far as I know, were all inferior men; there was constant talk of 'hiding' and 'cow-hides' and 'ferules' and 'thrashing,' and I should say, indeed, that the only recollections of my contemp-

oraries about those school-days are of one constant low conflict with men of a very low type. So soon as a boy was sent to the Latin School—and he was sent there at nine years of age—all this was changed into the life of a civilized place. Why the Boston people tolerated such brutality as went on in their other public schools I do not know, and never have known; but no change came for some years after.

"For the next three years the only object, so far as I was concerned, was to have me live along and get ready for the Latin School. I have always been glad that I was sent where I was—to a school without any plan or machinery, like Miss Whitney's, very much on the go-as-you-please principle, and where there was no strain put upon the pupil. I disliked it, as I disliked all schools; but here, again, I regarded the whole arrangement as one of those necessary nuisances which society imposes on the individual, and which the individual would be foolish if he quarrelled with, when he did not have it in his power to abolish it. I had no such power, and therefore went and came as I was bidden, only eager every day to exchange the monotonies of school life for the more varied and larger enterprises of the play-room or of the Common.

"I have said that advanced education was in the air. It will be hard to make boys and girls of the present day understand how much was then expected from reforms in education. Dr. Channing was at his best then, and all that he had to say about culture and self-culture impressed people intensely—more intensely, I think, than was good for them. There was rumors from Europe of Fellenberg's school at Hofwyl. At Northampton the Round Hill School was started in 1823 on somewhat similar plans. In England Lord Brougham and the set of people around him were discussing the 'march of intellect,' and had established a Society for the Promotion of Useful Knowledge, whose name has lived after it. I may say here, in a parenthesis, that the first time I ever heard of the 'march of intellect' was when I saw a very funny play, in which a clever boy named Burke was the hero in the 'march of intellect.' He appeared in half a dozen characters, to teach half a dozen subjects; and it was a capital satire on the idea that everything could be taught by professors.

"Mr. Webster, Mr. Edward Everett, my father, and other gentlemen in their position established the 'Useful Knowledge Society' of Boston. The reign of Lyceums and Mechanics' Institutes had begun. Briefly, there was the real impression that the kingdom of heaven was to be brought in by teaching people what were the relations of acids to alkalies, and what was the derivation of the word 'cordwainer.' If we only knew enough, it was thought, we should be wise enough to keep out of the fire, and we should not be burned.

"So it was that any novelty, when it was presented at a school-room door, was even more apt to be accepted than it is now; and, as every reader of these lines knows, such things are accepted pretty willingly now. So I remember that I was taught 'geometry' when I was six years old—or that I thought I was—from a little book called *The Elements of Geometry*. I could rattle off about isosceles triangles when I was six, as well as I can now. And I had other queer smattering bits of knowledge, useful or useless, which were picked up in the same way.

"At school there was a school library, from which we borrowed books, because we liked the mechanism of it. We had much better books at home; but of course it was good fun to have your name entered on a book, and to return them once a week, and so on.

"My father was one of the best teachers I ever knew. When he had a moment, therefore, from other affairs to give to our education, it was always well used; and we doubtless owed a great deal to him which we afterwards did not know how to account for. Among other such benefactions, I owe it that for these three or four years, when really I had nothing to do but to grow physically, I was placed with a simple, foolish man for a teacher, and not with one of the drivers, who had plans and would want to make much of us. Among other notions of my father, right or wrong as the case may be, was this: that a boy could pick up the rudiments of language quite early in life. So the master was told that Edward Webster and I, and perhaps some other boys, were to be taught the paradigms of the Latin grammar at once. We also had given to us little Latin books, which we spelled away upon. One was a translation of Campe's German version of *Robinson Crusoe* into Latin. It was thought that the interest of the book would induce us to learn the meaning of the words. But the truth was, we were familiar with Defoe's *Robinson Crusoe*, and regarded this as a low and foolish imitation, of which we made a great deal of fun. All the same, the agony with which some boys remember their first studies of '*amo, amas, amat*,' is wholly unknown to me. I drifted into those things simply, and by the time I was sent to the Latin School the point had been gained, and I knew my '*penna, pennae, pennae*,' and my '*amo, amas, amat*,' as well as if I had been born to them."[1]

With his sister, Lucretia (Peabody Hale), he published a magazine. "Perhaps two of us put together our paper, folded it and pinned it in the fold, and then made a magazine. Of magazines there were two,—*The New England Herald*, composed and edited by the two elders of the group, and *The Public Informer*, by my sister Lucretia and me. I am afraid that the name 'Public Informer' was suggested wickedly to us little ones, when we did not know that those words carry a disagreeable meaning. But when we learned this, afterwards, we did not care. I think some of the Everetts, my uncles, had had a boy newspaper with the same name. When things ran with perfect regularity, *The New England Herald* was read at the breakfast table one Monday morning, and *The Public Informer*, the next Monday morning. But this was just as it might happen. They were published when the editors pleased, as all journals should be, and months might go by without a number. And there was but one copy of each issue. It would be better if this could be said of some other journals." [Jean Holloway, *Edward Everett Hale: A Biography*, University of Texas Press, 1956.[2]]

1835. Entered college at age thirteen. "But when the business of actually going to college began I had none of this light-hearted feeling. It was all very pleasant to go around . . . to furniture stores, with money enough to buy the chairs, and carpet, and washbowl, and other apparatus with which one was to begin independent life. It was interesting to go out . . . to 22 Stoughton, and assist in putting the carpet down, in hanging the curtains, and in determining where my desk should be, and where my brother's should be, and so in beginning upon housekeeping. But when all this was over, when I had been to morning prayers for the first time, and had gone through the routine of morning recitations, and the first recitation of the afternoon—recitations which were all child's play to boys who had been as well trained as we—when I sat in the broad window seat, and looked out on the setting sun, behind Mount Auburn, as it happened, then the bitterness of the situation revealed itself to me. I was thoroughly and completely homesick.

(From *The Man Without a Country* by Edward Everett Hale. Illustrated by Edward A. Wilson.)

"I said to myself, perhaps I said aloud, 'This is one day of three hundred and sixty-five, and that will make one year. At the end of that year I shall have gone through one of four such years.' And I wondered how I ever could survive the deadly monotony of such a service. It was not till the next year that I read, in Miss Martineau's *Travels*, that happy anecdote of the Jersey apprentice boy, who, when nine years old, was forever wishing for the Fourth of July. Someone asked him why he was so eager to have the Fourth of July come, and he said: 'When that has come I shall have only eleven more years to serve.' I repeat this tale of homesickness because, although it was an exaggerated feeling, it expresses well enough my dislike for the routine of college, a dislike which accompanied me to its very close. Other fellows took the thing more simply and philosophically. Newton, of my own class, a fine fellow who died young, said to me once that he attended every chapel exercise, morning and evening through the whole time he was in Cambridge. 'Why should I not?' he said. 'I had not the attractions which you had in Boston; Cambridge was my home. The rule was to be in chapel twice a day; I might as well be there as anywhere else.' He was undoubtedly the happier and, I think, the better man, because he could accept the routine of life with such good nature.

"As for the business which took us to college, more than half of us soon found out that we had been too well prepared. As Hayward used to say, 'We had overrun the game.' That is the great merit of the elective system, if it holds in the freshman year of a college—that a boy or young man can take hold where he is prepared to go forward. For us, however, we were set on reading Livy and Xenophon. These authors are easier after you have 'the hang of it' than the Latin and Greek which we had been reading for some time before at school. We could almost read them at sight. Our teachers in these two languages regarded the whole thing as a bore; they were preparing for other fields in life, and they had taken their tutorships by the way, without any idea that they were to interest us in language or that there was much interest in it; at least that is the impression which they left upon our minds. It was simply a dull school exercise. It may be said in passing that one of the great difficulties of our present college system comes from the fact that in general boys, for the last year they are in the preparatory school, have been under the care of a gentleman of spirit, and intelligence, and eagerness in education, who makes them his companions, who gives them such enthusiasm as he has in the studies which they are pursuing. For then they pass into the hand of some instructor who has just graduated, who does not know much, and very likely does not know how to teach what he knows. Thus, from a superior, picked man, one of the best educators in the country, perhaps, a boy passes under the direction of a frightened novice, with whom the college is trying an experiment whether he will or will not succeed. Of course, in theory, the best educators ought to have the charge of those pupils who need education most. But in practice, I fancy, it is very hard, in the charge of colleges, to make the professors of most ability take those elementary duties upon themselves. Certainly in very few colleges do they take any such duty.

"In my senior year a dramatic event crossed the dreadly monotony of college life, which sent a knot of us into the laboratory for the whole of one Sunday. At morning chapel President Quincy, with a good deal of emotion, told us that breakfast at commons must be delayed a little while on account of an accident which had happened in the kitchen. It proved that two of the waiters had gone to sleep, in one of the rooms in the basement which was assigned for their bedroom, with a pan of charcoal burning. They had only been discovered just before the chapel service, and both of them were unconscious. At that moment the doctors were with them, hoping to re-arouse the vitality which was almost gone. When we came to breakfast a message came upstairs from this sick room, to know who there was at breakfast who could make oxygen. I ran down at once, and Dr. Wyman and Dr. Webster explained to me that they wanted to try the experiment of feeding the exhausted lungs with pure oxygen. When I found that it was not for immediate use only, but that the treatment was to be continued through the day, I told Dr. Webster that we should have to start the furnace in the Davy Club laboratory, and he bade me do so. With two or three others of the men most interested in chemistry I went up to that laboratory, and till ten o'clock in the evening we were sending down rubber bags of oxygen for these poor fellows to breathe. Whether it did them any good or not I do not know; eventually one of them recovered and the other died."[1]

1839. Class day. "This will be as good a place as any to tell the varying fortunes of class day itself, of which I happen to remember one of the most important crises. Class day seems to have originated as early as the beginning of the century. The class itself chose a favorite speaker as orator, and someone who could write a poem, and had its own exercises of farewell. There grew up side by side with those farewell exercises the custom by which the class treated the rest of the college, and eventually treated every loafer in Cambridge. As I remember the first class days which I ever saw, they were the occasions of the worst drunkenness I have ever known. The night before class day some of the seniors—I do not know but what all—went out to the lower part of the yard, where there was still a grove of trees, and 'consecrated the grove,' as the phrase was, which meant drank all the rum and other spirits that they liked. Then, on the afternoon of class day, around the old elm tree, sometimes called Rebellion Tree and sometimes Liberty Tree, which stood and stands behind Hollis, all the college assembled, and every other male loafer who chose to come where there was a free treat. Pails of punch made from every spirit known to the Cambridge innkeepers, were there for everybody to drink. It was a horrid orgy from end to end, varied, perhaps, by dancing round the tree.

"With such memories of class day President Quincy, in 1838, sent for my brother and one or two others of the class of that year in whom he had confidence, to ask what could be done to break up such orgies. He knew he could rely on the class for an improvement in the customs. They told him that if he would give them for the day the use of the Brigade Band, which was then the best band we had in Boston, and which they had engaged for the morning, they felt sure that they could change the *fête*. The conditions, observe, were a lovely July day, the presence in the morning at the chapel, to hear the addresses, of the nicest and prettiest girls of Boston and neighborhood with their mammas, and the chances of keeping them there through the afternoon. Mr. Quincy gladly promised the band, and when the day came, it became the birthday of the modern 'class day,' the most charming of *fêtes*. Word was given to the girls that they must come to spend the day. In the chapel Coolidge delivered a farewell oration. Lowell, alas! was at Concord, not permitted to come to Cambridge to recite his poem; it had to be printed instead. When the ode had been sung the assembly moved up to that shaded corner between Stoughton and Holworthy. The band people stationed themselves in the entry of Stoughton, between 21 and 24, with the window open, and the 'dancing on the green' of which there are still traditions, began. The wind instrument men said afterward that they never played for dancing before, and that their throats were bone dry, and I suppose there was no girl there who had ever before danced to the music of a trombone. When our class came along, in 1839, we had the honor of introducing fiddles. I shall send this paper to the charming lady—the belle of her time—with whom I danced in the silk gown in which I had been clad when I delivered the class poem of my year. Does she remember it as well as I do?

"Commencement was a function far more important than the exhibitions or than class day, which, to speak profanely, were side shows. No audience can ever be persuaded to sit six hours or more to hear perhaps thirty addresses. So now, while a certain theory is maintained that certain of the best scholars in the large graduating class prepare addresses, by far the larger number of them are excused, and only five or six speakers, representing four or five branches of the university, actually address the audience. No one has to be in the theatre more than two hours."[1]

September 9, 1839. Became schoolmaster of the Latin School he had attended.

April 3, 1841. Two years out of college, Hale taught in the Boston Latin School and read theology. "I am nineteen years old and all day I have been thinking more of the future than I often do—not because it is my birthday but because half a dozen odd circumstances have called it up to me, and obliged me to remember that I shall not always be a boy, nineteen years old—living in my own home, and drawing my quarter's salary from the city. Another year I shall have left the Latin School, shall have begun to devote myself exclusively to my profession, a profession the proper preparation for which I think no one understands—I am sure I do not myself. I shall be obliged to take the responsibility of preparing myself for its solemn duties very much in my own way. I shall have the responsibility too of not wasting time, when I have no master but myself.

"While thinking of all this I am glad—very glad—that I am only nineteen. To be sure only nineteen involves more than a quarter of the longest lease of life, but if I had entered college three or four years older than I did, and there are theorists enough who will tell me that I should have done so—I should not now feel quite so easy as I do. I should not have quite so much time at my disposal before forcing myself on the active duties of life.

"After all, I have lately persuaded myself that we are apt to trouble ourselves a great deal too much about these active duties. God made me, I believe, to be happy, and placed me here that my powers might be developed and improved and so fitted for a superior state of existence; if then by my labor in the community I support myself and do my duty to those of my fellow beings who are more unfortunate than I, I conceive that nothing more is or need be required of me. As for ambition I have less and less of the schoolboy stamp of it every day that I live. My air castles now are to live a life of literary quiet and repose, to spend my time in such manner as may be most pleasant to myself without infringing on the rights or pleasures of my neighbors, or fretting myself about the improving my study or other labor in the highest degree, of the advantages put into my hands. My time is best im-

proved when it is passed most happily. I know of nothing to make me suppose that man was meant to be a utilitarian machine." [Edward E. Hale, Jr., *The Life and Letters of Edward Everett Hale,* Volume I, Little, Brown, 1917.[3]]

1841. Resigned as schoolmaster of the Latin School. Secured post of junior assistant in geological survey of New Hampshire. "My connexion with the Latin School is at an end—I resigned at the end of the second year having obtained all the good I could from it, (and, I believe, a great deal too) and as much as I cared to of the worst effects. So that I am not so mechanically restricted by set hours as I have been, though I manage to keep pretty busy."[3]

Fall, 1842. Began religious career as preacher. ". . . At some times I feel greatly discouraged about it, looking at the divided and I believe the quarrelsome feeling among all parties on religious points,—and at my own inability to come up to what I wish to do. At the same time I am more and more satisfied as to the immense effect which may be produced by the clergy, if they act in the proper way. I am also, however, every day more and more satisfied that I embarked on the profession too young, and regret more and more that I persuaded myself to enter in its practice when I did:—for I feel younger and younger, less and less experienced every day that I preach. I suppose I may live through all this. There would be something almost ridiculous in a man's entering at any time with much confidence on a profession for which nobody was ever fully prepared. I am at present supplying the pulpit at Watertown for a few Sundays:—the Church which Dr. Francis has left the College, but for the future my plans are not at all definite. A scheme . . . of an excursion to some of our young societies in the west, quite fell through.

"I observe, with profound regret, the religious struggles which come into many biographies, as if almost essential to

The Negroes were, most of them, out of the hold, and swarming all around the dirty deck, with a central throng surrounding Vaughan and addressing him in every dialect and patois of a dialect, from the Zulu click up to the Parisian of Beledjereed. ■ (From *The Man Without a Country* by Edward Everett Hale. Illustrated by Leonard Everett Fisher.)

Hale, the young minister, from a daguerreotype, 1855.

the formation of the hero. I ought to speak of these, to say that any man has an advantage, not to be estimated, who is born, as I was, into a family where the religion is simple and rational; who is trained in the theory of such a religion, so that he never knows, for an hour, what these religious or ir-religious struggles are. I always knew God loved me, and I was always grateful to him for the world he placed me in. I always like to tell him so, and was always glad to receive his suggestions to me. . . . I can remember perfectly that when I was coming to manhood, the half-philosophical novels of the time had a deal to say about the young men and maidens who were facing the 'problem of life.' I had no idea whatever what the problem of life was. To live with all my might seemed to me easy; to learn where there was so much to learn seemed pleasant and almost of course; to lend a hand, if one had a chance, natural; and if one did this, why, he en-joyed life because he could not help it, and without proving to himself that he ought to enjoy it.''[2]

Winter, 1844. Preached in Washington. He declined an invi-tation to settle there, feeling that he was too inexperienced. ''Here in Washington are ambition, fashion, a civic self con-ceit, ignorance, want of intellectual action among all classes, degradation and ignorance of the free blacks, very little comparative influence of religion, and slavery.

''Wake them up in twenty or thirty years?

''Tears!!!!!''[3]

1845. Preached in Worcester, where he remained for six months and finally accepted a call.

April 29, 1846. Ordained a minister of the Church of the Uni-ty, Worcester, Massachusetts, Hale believed the Church to be one of the active social factors in American life, working toward the upbuilding of the community in which it existed. ''The only value of such an assemblage of men of heart and spirit, at work in the walks of moral and religious effort is, that they assure themselves whether they are doing their share in the great positive work of the world's redemption. In that work all men of conscience and life—in whatever calling—are engaged. All of them, however, engaged, are seeking to lift up the civilization of the world. We meet here,—in these philanthropic assemblies to see whether we,—in our several lines of action, are doing our share—and keeping up with the immense well trained work of other la-borers. It is the work of the world's salvation which is given us to urge along—with such powers as God endows us with.''[3]

1851. His sister, Sarah, died.

October 15, 1852. Married Emily Perkins. Honeymooned in Berkshires.

February 11, 1854. Ellen Day ''Nelly'' born.

1856. Ended his service as minister of the Church of the Unity. ''It is strange enough how much ten years has put us through. After I had finished my two sermons yesterday in the midst of a tremendous randan I had a soothed feeling of rest and satisfaction come over me such as I have never seen described. . . . It was the finishing of a ten year's job, some-thing as McClure may have felt when he got his men paid off and everything done—only more so. . . . I never experienced anything like it, except in the afternoon before I was mar-ried—and in the rest of the night after I was engaged. God grant that it last through these next months but I have no hope it will.

''It has been infinitely strange, almost as solemn, as novelty as Niagara, to have nothing to do this last week, to feel a ten year's job is over (not to use the word *job* in a poor sense). I can feel the blood vessels of my brain dropping back to a normal condition after the effort and excitement of the last two months, as your foot expands for hours after you have had a tight boot on; till the 18th of October it is play time. That day is the installation.''[2]

October 18, 1856. Installed as minister of South Congrega-tional Church in Boston. ''We are getting entirely ensconced in our new quarters & duties. . . . I had not had so much time to myself in ten years. I knew that that was a mere lull, and so of course it proves. But I do have my time at command thus far as I have scarce ever had in Worcester:—and I think I can make this continue. There is also the luxury of preach-ing, con amore, old sermons; about which there is this to be said, that to a congregation which has heard them before it is just as odious to preach an old sermon, as it is to finish a story at a dinner party—when by the manner of the guests you observe that they have heard it before. But to preach an old sermon to a congregation which has not heard it, is just as agreeable as to find a brand new audience for one of your old stories. You tell it, if possible, with all the more gusto because you have told it before. Be it remarked in passing that of Whitfield's preaching and all itinerant preaching, (very likely therefore, even of Paul's and Luke's and Barna-bas's), this repetition of old sermons has been a great ele-ment of power.''[2]

Before the *Nautilus* got round from New Orleans to the Northern Atlantic coast with the prisoner on board, the sentence had been approved, and he was a man without a country.
■ (From *The Man Without a Country* by Edward Everett Hale. Illustrated by Leonard Everett Fisher.)

1859. Traveled through Europe. The trip resulted in the book, *Ninety Days Worth of Europe,* published in 1861. "You cannot conceive of the *randan* and confusion of the first week at home. . . .

"I found everybody well; my own family here and at Brookline. . . .

"Our establishment here at Worcester Street . . . has taken up its line of march again quite steadily. Emily has been at Hartford almost all the time I was in Europe. She came back with the children on Wednesday, I the next Tuesday morning for we had a villainous voyage. My boy [first son, Arthur] is a new element which quite varies as you may suppose, many lines of our proceeding, he makes Nelly feel a great deal older and more confident. She had profited by my absence to learn to read; an accomplishment for which I have so little respect that as long as I was here I had not permitted her to aspire to. In revenge for which that her feet may keep pace with her head I have sent her to a little folks' dancing school kept at Brookline by Sarah Phillips. . . ."[3]

1861. The Civil War brought Hale into a national sphere. Until the war, he had been content to minister solely to his Boston congregation. At the close of the war he believed that the Church had a social obligation which reached far beyond the boundaries of the pulpit. To this end he worked thereafter. "War has begun. I am exquisitely sorry, now that it is here. I did not know that I could be so sorry about anything out of the family. . . .

"Until 1861 I was only known in Boston as an energetic minister of an active church. I didn't want anything else. I believe now, as then, that if anything is going to be done it is to be done through that agency. Then the war came along. I was in the Massachusetts Rifle Corps. Then I was in the

Sanitary Commission. To save the country—that brought one into public life, and I have never got back into simple parish life again."[3]

1863. *The Man Without a Country,* possibly Hale's most famous story, was published. "This story was written in the summer of 1863, as a contribution, however humble, towards the formation of a just and true national sentiment, a sentiment of love to the nation. It was at the time that Mr. Vallandingham had been seen across the border. It was my wish, indeed, that the story might be printed before the autumn elections of that year as my 'testimony' regarding the principles involved in them, but circumstances delayed its publication till the December number of the *Atlantic* appeared."[3]

April, 1865. The Civil War ended. "We are wild with victory. The sense of it comes again and again and again and yet we do not feel it. . . . Grant had said from day to day he thought they would surrender, but except that, the news announced itself without other omen than steady victory every time. Sheridan struck their retreat. Fayetteville, —where Lee's headquarters were at our last date, is the head of batteau navigation on the Appomattox two miles S. W. from Richmond, the largest village in Prince Edward's county. Our telegraphs must have been laid to that neighborhood in the seven days between the fall of Richmond and the surrender.

"I got the news in the paper yesterday morning. They had been firing salutes since 5 o'clock in Chester Square, but none of us had waked up. All day long we did nothing that we ever did before. The enthusiasm of the time was splendid. . . . We had a very good impromptu service at church,—which seemed the natural thing to do."[3]

September, 1865. The Civil War had marked a turning point in Hale's ministerial career. Having worked endlessly for peace during the war, Hale was no longer content to minister solely to his Boston congregation. At the end of the war, Hale was very much a public man, eager to bring peace and social justice to all the American people. "Simply then I have a right to call this summer and autumn halcyon days;—storm breeders, if you please, but for that God may care and will. What I know is that I am well, successful and happy; that my wife and children are well and happy, that I am as near out of debt as a man of my temperament is likely to be, and am on the way to be farther out. That so far as I know or care, good men think well of me, and that so far as I know or care, I have no enemies.

"Going then into the radii of the outside circles, to speak first of my profession. I entered my profession with little ambition for success in it. I soon abandoned that, I mean that I was soon satisfied that the New England minister who thought that theology was his province because he must be a theologian, was as much mistaken as the soldier would be who thought mathematics was his province because every soldier must be a mathematician. I soon satisfied myself that the profession in our time could not subsist on or by or in its old standards. For myself, I understood that my work of the ministry should be carried out with certain different methods, in search of certain results·not aimed at in the ministry of the generation before me.

"Or without saying that I started upon any definite plan, I soon saw that the man who meant to move the community by moral agencies for its good, needed a wider base for his operations than any deference given to the pulpit, even in its best successes, would give him. My theory is that the pulpit gives a man the influence which he must use in other walks and spheres than the pulpit alone. All which I say only by the way in this memoir, which is not a memoir of my plan of life. I say it only that I may say that this theory of the profession, has so far as I am concerned succeeded. I do not know that it would find any imitators. I even doubt whether it would. . . . And thus while no one would call me what I never aspired to be, the most distinguished preacher in our communion, I suppose I would be popularly called our most successful minister. Whether called so, or not, in an attached congregation eager to forestall my wishes I have the evidence of that sort of success, so far as I can ask for it, of the deeper evidences of the more true professional success I do not care to speak here.

"Now to go outside what is personal to me, on which I have lingered unwilling enough because these are confessions of gratitude. Perfectly satisfied myself that this country is to be made a civilized nation by the practical application of the Christian religion, I was of course dissatisfied that this Unitarian body of which I am conscientiously a member and minister, should sulk on one side and leave to accident or providence the propagation of such views, and their practical introduction in politics, in education, and the other functions of society. So soon then as I found I had any influence in the more general councils of this body, I exerted myself to see an effort made that we might assert ourselves as a communion as the advance body in Christian civilization not satisfied with any position in the rear. This theory of our position is certainly getting itself recognized in our churches and throughout the country. The apologetic vein of speech on our side, and the condescending tone on other sides have wholly disappeared. We understand ourselves and other people understand us as being a leading power for good or for evil in the working out of the fortunes of the land. It is a

great thing, it is a great source of personal comfort and happiness to see such an advance in the self respect of the Ecclesiastical body to which in conscience one belongs.

"In that body just now circumstances make me a leader. Such sort of leadership is lost as it is won, without any effort or any fault of one's own, and I know that this will fly away as idly and foolishly as it came. While it lasts it is a satisfaction to have it, not to grumble because 'they' do not do this or that, but to have quite as much right and opportunity as any one to say whether 'they' shall or shall not do this or that. While I certainly expect to yield this with a good grace, I will not fail to insert among these satisfactions the present hold on it.

"I must ascribe to the same accidental hold of that influence the position which I have in the councils of the Freedman's Aid, the Emigrant Aid, the Soldier's Memorial, and which I have had in the Sanitary. The reconstruction of the country is, in my point of view, much more in the hands of these agencies, if they be bravely and broadly administered than it is in the hands of the Government itself. I am certainly glad, therefore, to be of counsel in the administration of their affairs.

"For any influence on the community which their affairs may demand, I have as good an influence with the press, or as warm an entrée as one can ask for. Accident rather than desert has made me a contributor and a favored contributor to the *Daily,* the *Examiner,* the *Atlantic Monthly,* and the *Register.* These journals are glad to have me write for them as often as I will, and excepting the *Register* compensate me for writing, the *Daily* and the *Atlantic Monthly* handsomely. Godkin who edits the *Nation* and Norton who edits the *North American* have urged me most cordially to write for them. If I do not do so, it is because I like my other organs better, and do not need those vehicles to the public ear.

"And I will not close this memoir, written as a detailed expression of gratitude and, God knows, without a thought of boasting, without saying one thing more. All such real satisfactions as these may be embittered after all by a tight shoe, or a bad corn, or by those moral or mental annoyances for which these are the metaphorical names. A man may be harassed by his neighbours, by his parish, by this party, by his rivals. I am not conscious of any such harassment. First of all, I am eager to say that the body of men with whom I have most to do, viz. my own parish and its officers; are eager to find out how I can be most at ease. In the way of money, in the command of my time, in leaving me free from surveillance, in satisfying themselves to let me do my own work in my own way, and in persuading themselves that I am doing it when they do not see that I am, they give me all the freedom so far as I can see that a man has who has an 'independent fortune so called.' In giving virtually to my direction the expenditure of more than $10,000 a year in charitable or benevolent undertakings, they give me most of the satisfaction which a man of fortune would have in expending that amount on his charities; they take away the only annoyances which can connect with life on a salary paid by other men."[3]

1866. Mother died. Hale was deeply devoted to his family and considered himself the mainstay. "I felt a hundred years older after my mother died. Till then there was some one who thought of me as a boy, and measured me by a boy's standard, not to say with a mother's infinite tolerance and love. Since then I have had to wobble on as one of the present generation, wholly conscious myself that I am as much a boy as I ever was." [Edward E. Hale, Jr., *The Life and Let-*

(From the television production of "Man Without a Country," starring Cliff Robertson.)

ters of Edward Everett Hale, Volume II, Little, Brown, 1917.[4]]

March 17, 1868. Hale's second son, Charles Alexander, died in childhood. "The little fellow died at seven this morning. The doctors forewarned us of it when they went last night, but till the last minute I believed he was steadily gaining, and he was spared all pain. A noble boy and precious memory."[4]

September, 1869. Youngest son, Robert Beverley, was born. The family consisted of one daughter and six sons.

November, 1869. Moved to 39 Highland Street, Boston, which remained Hale's home until his death. "We are just pulling through the last miseries of our move from Milton. This house is not yet in order,—but is very convenient and comfortable. . . ."[4]

December, 1869. Established a monthly magazine, *Old and New.* "I am in the thick of the arrangement for the new review. But for the worries of my house, I believe I could have issued the first number Dec. 14, which means Jan. 1st. But I have almost determined not to begin till March 1. . . . Hurd and Houghton are to be the publishers, the Unitarian Association furnishing half the capital. I hope to give Nathan [my brother] regular work in its editing. I relieve myself from a good deal of other denominational duty by taking this in hand, which is, I suppose as much in my line, as anything I

can put my hand to. I enjoyed very much what I did in editing the *Examiner.*

"**June 12, 1870.** We have taken *Old and New* from Hurd and Houghton, and are publishing for ourselves, under Roberts Brothers imprint. I suppose we may count the journal as just established, not firmly but hopefully. To the public we take a very imperious tone, and in New England, our sales are so large that all New England supposes that we have really gained the top of magazinedom. Our sales at the West and on the Pacific also are large, but in the Middle States we cannot keep the hold we thought we had. The magazine would fully pay for itself with a regular sale of 9,000 copies. We have often made that sale, but on weak numbers, I mean numbers which sell badly, we have fallen as low as 7500."[4]

1873. Second trip abroad with his wife. "We have had the shortest passage out ever made by this boat, so there must have been some good angel or other on board. Till this morning we have had almost all sail set, which is very unusual, and means, of course, that the wind has been nearly fair all the time. Four days bring you past the banks of Newfoundland. Three days may be fairly called the English part of the passage,—there we see Fastnet Light tonight, if all is well, and do not reach Liverpool until Saturday morning. You will observe that three more days are left in the middle of the Atlantic itself. To this portion of the globe the sailors give the happy title of the Devil's Hole, and I am sure it is very

Hale, the patriarch, 1902.

well named. At least we found very rough weather there, and were all pretty sick till it got through, having started on our first four days with the idea that we were to be let off very easily."[4]

July, 1873. Returned from Europe to his new summer home at Matanuck. "Here I am in the new home. You cannot think how charming it is. I have come in from the piazza with its view as wide as . . . in Switzerland, and with the serene infinity of the stars in half-heaven, with new wonder at the world's beauty. I had just been up stairs, and had heard the Lord's Prayer in the four versions, as to language and expression, of the four older boys. They have been good boys all day, and give in their loyal manly work in the morning good promise for our holiday.

"As for the house itself you cannot think how nice it is. In the first place it is pretty. . . . It is completely finished, to the last iota, and finished more thoroughly than any country house I ever saw. . . . The furniture is ample, and particularly pretty, new ingrain carpets of charming colors all over the house, pretty wicker furniture in the parlor, and in short everything you could wish and much more than you expect. The furniture alone must have cost two thousand dollars. It has been very dry, so that they have been sadly disappointed about their grass. But you know this hillside made no great pretences that way ever, and the prospect for next month seems better. I hear the surf of the sea as I write, and the moonlight and stars are delightful.

"It is lovely here. I look out, as I write, on the pretty pond close behind the house. From the piazza, at a distance, is the eternal sea, not so far but we hear its unrhythmed laughter at night, and see the white lines of the breakers. Just at the left Pt. Judith light flashes—as we sit at night on our piazza, and I believe Block Island light has been seen on the right.

"I have been young and now am old. I am ashamed to say what a relief I find it that I have no *visitor's duties* to discharge. The oversight of the children and the presiding at dinner are as nothing in the comparison. As for the oversight of the children, the freedom and the open-air of the place are all in all to them, and in such solace nineteen-twentieths of the ordinary care vanishes. As for eating and the provision for it, we are yet living on the feudal homage of our new neighbors, and I cannot yet tell how hard it is to be. I know this, that Wednesday in Boston I lugged out two boxes of blackberries literally five miles on a tired arm to treat my children with, having paid 95 cents for them, and that the next night here I found many more and much finer on my table which they had picked themselves on the hill-side."[4]

1875. *Old and New* sold.

1876. Trip to Texas to do documentary research. "This place [San Antonio] is wonderfully satisfactory. In the first place it is completely foreign. The hotel I am in, a very good one, is much such a hotel as I was in Linz and at Pesth, built round an open square in which the people have tables and their meals in summer. The town is built on both sides of a lovely, narrow river, full of rapid water, and overhung everywhere by willows and mesquit, and acacia which looks like a willow. Over this river go no end of bridges, some broad, some only footpaths. The streets are not wide, but let you now and then, just where you least expect it, into great Spanish plazas. The Americans do their best to introduce their own style of building two and three stories high. But the Spanish is so much more sensible that even in the new buildings it holds its own, while the old ones were so solid that they are still occupied, and are indeed, in many cases, hard to pull down. The whole aspect of the town, therefore, is like Buda, if you crossed to go there, and I guess rather like what you found in the cities lower down on the Danube. The notice to people to cross the bridge on a walk is in English, German, and Spanish.

"The Alamo, the scene of the horrible Famine massacre, is still standing close by this hotel. The Cathedral, like that in New Orleans, has been modernized and in part rebuilt. But in many many instances you see stone gargoyles projecting to let water off roofs, without the least suspicion on anybody's part that they are picturesque or old-fashioned.

"As for costume, no two people by any accident are dressed alike. There is a large enough number of Mexicans to make an evident Spanish look in costume, and some of their customs prevail over the Yankees. Thus they have a peculiar felt hat, with something like a serpent coiled round it, and we saw yesterday that herdsmen and drovers who are not at all Mexicans wore these, got up in a very showy way, I have no doubt at some New York factory. Think by the way of meeting a herd of 1800 cattle slowly walking towards Brighton and death across the prairies, driven by two or three men, who simply walk their horses (or gallop them) back and forth at right angles behind the line of march to hurry up stragglers. The rest, if they think, like many a poor devil, suppose that because they go to destruction slowly they do not go at all."[4]

March 2, 1882. His beloved brother, Charles, died. "Our poor dear Charley died last night. I was with him almost all day,—but he knew nothing and nobody, and died without any struggle. It is the last of the series of paralytic attacks, of which the first came in July, 1876."[4]

February, 1891. Always very interested in travel, Hale went to California to deliver a series of lectures. "Every inch of the journey is interesting. You have all the satisfaction of Europe, in that it is all new, and a curious feeling of home-ishness; that you are in your own country. I have but just made out, that I am more in the midst of Americans than I have been for forty years. In these three or four days at San Diego, I have seen one Chinaman, one negro, and one Irishman; all the rest apparently, of pure Yankee blood and manners. The charm is inexpressible. You have all the pleasure of foreign traveling, and you are all the time at home; as if some one brought you in your parlour stereoscopes from Europe.

"The flora is absolutely new. Even when I thought I saw peach trees they were apricots. I had never seen orchards of English walnuts. We saw one enormous ranch which was in Indian corn last year, and but one. That is hardly an exception, in novelty, the stalks are so high. Olives, oranges, lemons, limes, guavas, apricots. Walnuts, eucalyptus, cypress, agave occasionally, not in bloom but in fruit, thirty feet high; palms of four or five varieties, Norfolk Island pines,—take that for a rapid catalogue."[4]

April 3, 1892. At seventy, Hale was still active in the church and still maintained a sense of social obligation that his ministry brought him. "I have written twenty-five books but I'm not an author; I'm a parish minister. I don't care a snap for the difference between Balzac and Daudet. That isn't important in life. I do care about the difference between the classes of men who migrate to this country."[4]

October 8, 1895. Youngest son, Robert Beverly, died. "I am waiting for the hour of our dear Rob's funeral. His mother is upstairs, where she has lain for four weeks and so weak that they dare not tell her of his death.

"He is the purest, noblest and most faultless human being in the shape of a man whom I have ever seen. As my sister Sarah seemed to me in the shape of a woman. . . .

"His fight with fever at the last was so terrible that I was not going to look upon his face again, so sad was the expression, almost of agony, when he was dying. But Phil [my son] told me I should see nothing of this, and it was true. As Phil said, it was just the look of interest in a new problem before him, and there was the dear smile on his face which belonged to his determination to solve that problem. I changed my order for the church,—I had said the coffin should not be opened there,—and told Frank Smith to leave it open for any one to see his face who wanted.

"Dear Phil said 'You knew I confided everything to him, and I would take his advice about very little things. Whatever I asked about, however trifling, he would not answer without this little pause in which he should make a decision, and with just this expression which he has now of a new experience before him.'

"Several of the boys were here last night, who are the pall-bearers of today. They have but one thing to say, and that is of his force of character and of his intense love for everybody."[4]

Statue of Hale by B.V. Pratt, Boston, Massachusetts.

May 15, 1899. Resigned as minister of the South Congregational Church of Boston where he had served for forty-three years. "It is forty-three years since I accepted this charge. I feel sure of the regard of every one in the congregation, now that I leave the pulpit, I am still as truly as ever a member of the dear old South Congregational.

"But I have known,—oh, for a long time, that the church needs a minister as well as a preacher. And nothing but the kindness of every member of the congregation has justified me in remaining so long in a charge where I have left so many of a minister's duties unfulfilled. My conscience has been relieved by . . . the . . . members of the committee, of all the members of the church, of the South Friendly, of the Alliance, and all our workers of every name. But all the same, the church ought to have a young and active minister.

"I am not young and I am not active. . . .

"The years which have passed in . . . service have been happy years to me. I have seen the children of those who called me, and their children's children, grow up to manhood and womanhood. And in all the relations between me and those whom I love to call my people there has never been an unkind word or jar.

"Do not encourage any suggestion that I may recall this resignation. We *ought* to place this duty in other hands. And of course *ought* is final."[4]

December, 1903. Elected Chaplain of the Senate. "For I also am an office of the United States now, I am *Chaplain of the Senate*. This calls me to Washington every winter. And Washington is no longer the Virginia mud-hold. . . . It is really a beautiful city, with many of the conveniences and luxuries of civilised life."[4]

January 4, 1904. The beginning of Hale's last large public service as Chaplain of the Senate which he retained until his death. "First day of service. Mr. Lodge introduced me to Mr. Frye in the Vice-President's room. I entered the Senate with the Secretary, and took the Vice-President's seat. Mr. Frye who is acting President of the Senate came a minute after. He tapped with the gavel. I rose and the Senate rose. I read 'Wherefore we say Abba, Father,' and then repeated the Lord's Prayer."[4]

Spring, 1909. Returned to 39 Highland Street in Boston in the early Spring and spent the last months of his life quietly. He constantly thought he might be able to preach but was not able to do so.

June 8, 1909. "They are curiously like each other, these days, and I do not even go around the Island. But we sometimes have a visit from the Doctor, and sometimes we do not. . . . It was a lovely day and I spent all the time on the deck, from half past ten till five. Had a very good night."[4]

June 10, 1909. Died in Boston at the age of eighty-seven. "Live with all your might, and you will have more life with which to live."[4]

FOR MORE INFORMATION SEE: Edward Everett Hale, *A New England Boyhood*, Cassell, 1893, new edition (with foreword by Edwin D. Mead), Little, Brown, 1927, reprinted, Scholarly Press, 1970; Hale, *Memories of a Hundred Years*, Macmillan, 1902; Edward E. Hale, Jr., *The Life and Letters of Edward Everett Hale*, Little, Brown, 1917; Edwin Wildman, *Famous Leaders of Character in America, from the Latter Half of Nineteenth Century*, Page, 1922; June Barrows Mussey, editor, *Yankee Life by Those Who Lived It*, Knopf, 1947; (for children) Elizabeth Rider Montgomery, *Story behind Great Stories*, McBride, 1947; E. Coleman, *Edward Everett Hale: Preacher and Publisher*, Bibliographic Society of America, 1952; Jean Holloway, *Edward Everett Hale: A Biography*, University of Texas Press, 1956, reprinted, 1965; Sam Moskowitz, *Explorers of the Infinite*, World, 1963; Robert L. Straker, *Horace Mann and Others*, Antioch Press, 1963.

HITTE, Kathryn   1919-

PERSONAL: Surname is pronounced Hit; born November 23, 1919, in Pana, Ill.; daughter of Dudley Clement (a musician) and Zeta (Kelligar) Hitte; married William D. Hayes (an author of children's books and illustrator), April 2, 1960. *Education:* Illinois College, A.B. (cum laude), 1942; University of Illinois, B:S. in Library Science, 1944. *Home:* New York City. *Office:* Room 2525, 500 Fifth Ave., New York, N.Y. 10036.

CAREER: Children's librarian in Whiting, Ind., 1944-45; New York (N.Y.) Public Library, children's librarian, 1945-50; editorial consultant and writer for children, 1950—. Storyteller, actress, and playwright for children and adults, 1970—. *Member:* Authors League of America, Authors Guild.

WRITINGS: A Letter for Cathy, Abingdon, 1950; *Lost and Found*, Abingdon, 1951; *Surprise for Susan*, Abingdon, 1953; *The Shoe Book*, Golden Press, 1959; *The Button Book*, Golden Press, 1959; *Hurricanes, Tornadoes, and Blizzards*, Random, 1960; *I'm an Indian Today*, Golden Press, 1961; *The Other Side of the Fence*, American Book Co., 1963; *Richie and the Junk*, American Book Co., 1963; *The Brave and the Free*, American Book Co., 1964; *Where Will We Go?*, American Book Co., 1965; *New in the City*, American Book Co., 1965; (with husband, William D. Hayes) *Let's Fly*, American Book Co., 1965; *When Noodlehead Went to the Fair*, Parents Magazine Press, 1968; *Boy, Was I Mad!*, Parents Magazine Press, 1969; (with William D. Hayes) *Mexicali Soup*, Parents Magazine Press, 1970; *What Can You Do Without a Place to Play?*, Parents Magazine Press, 1971.

Plays—For children and young people: "Queexing Along," "They All Had Fun," "Uptown, Downtown, Cross-Town Bus," "Silver Gunsight," (with William D. Hayes) "To Catch a Prince."

Plays—Adult: "Chinese Nightingale," (with William D. Hayes) "Spotlight."

ADAPTATIONS: Beauty and the Beast, Cinderella, Pinocchio, The Emperor's New Clothes, The Birthday of the Infanta, Trial and Error (from a story by William D. Hayes). Many of the above have been produced in professional and children's theatres in New York City, San Diego and elsewhere.

KATHRYN HITTE

And some get kind of nervous when they're doing the wash. ■ (From *What Can You Do Without a Place to Play?* by Kathryn Hitte. Illustrated by Cyndy Szekeres.)

Contributor of fiction, non-fiction, poetry and plays to reading textbooks and anthologies published in the United States, Canada and Europe. Author of teaching materials for basic reading and language arts programs and of audio-visual materials, including "Pathways to Phonic Skills" (three recordings). Contributor of poetry and fiction to *Jack and Jill, Humpty Dumpty, Scholastic* Magazine and other periodicals.

WORK IN PROGRESS: Two books of fiction and a full-length play; completion of some unfinished fiction of the late William D. Hayes.

SIDELIGHTS: "I cannot remember when I did not want to be a writer. Even when I was excited about other things—mostly acting—I wanted to write, *too*. As a child, I wrote a lot of poems and stories and plays. They weren't just for me; I always wanted other people to read them or to listen to them. I read a lot, too; books were just about the most wonderful thing in the world. I was very fortunate in having a mother to whom books and reading were vital, too. My mother was always ready to listen to a poem or a story, or to help with ideas, encouragement, and enthusiastic interest. From the time I was quite young, she took me to the library with her nearly every day. I was so happy there, always, that when I grew up I decided to combine writing with being a librarian—a children's librarian. I did so for some years; it was as a children's librarian that I began to write for children. And I'm still very happy whenever I'm in a library!

"I've been fortunate, too, in having a writer-illustrator-husband to share ideas with, to share school and library visits with, sometimes to write stories with—and to agree with about the joys (and importance) of children's books.

"When young readers ask about writing, I tell them yes, of course it's fun to write, and when a story is going well it becomes truly exciting; but that writing is also hard work, very hard work, and it's lonely work. I like people very much; I like to be with them; so after a spell of writing, I need to get 'out in the world' and do things with people, or where I can see other people and mingle with them. This, of course, helps feed the imagination—for people make stories—and so my writing fires are rekindled and I can sit down again to the lonely sessions.

"A question often asked is 'where do your ideas come from?' Mine may come from happenings I observe or hear of or read about. They may come from children themselves—from watching children or from visiting them. But mostly I cannot tell where an idea has come from. It floats, perhaps, in the back of my imagination until I am ready for it—or until it is ready for me. A wonderful thing is that the more I write, the more ideas I get. I think this is true of any of the creative arts, and it is probably true for workers in other realms as well: that is, that *using* the creative imagination keeps it going and helps to develop it.

"Occasionally I write a draft of a story very quickly, and then revise. But usually I write slowly, polishing the pages—the paragraphs, the sentences—as I go, working from notes and simplified plot outlines. I'm very conscious of *sound*—not just the sounds of the particular words I choose to use, but the rhythm of the sentences. Along with many another writer, I want the 'unconscious' sound—the unheard sounds and rhythms that a reader may not even be aware of—to help express what I'm saying. So I read my work aloud constantly as it progresses. I'm even inclined to act it out.

"Sometimes I write at my typewriter in an office; sometimes with pen or pencil in a library. I like to work outdoors when I can, too; nature seems to help me think and write the way I want to. And what's the way I most want to? Why, in a way that will make the reader—*some* reader—care about the story as much as I cared about my favorite books when I was a child."

HOBBIES AND OTHER INTERESTS: Reading, travel, theater, music, and certain facets of nature study.

FOR MORE INFORMATION SEE: Horn Book, April, 1969.

HOOKS, William H(arris) 1921-

PERSONAL: Born November 14, 1921, in Whiteville, N.C.; son of Ulysses G. (a farmer) and Thetis (Rushing) Hooks. *Education:* University of North Carolina, B.A., 1948, M.A., 1950; also attended American Theatre Wing, New School for Social Research, and Bank Street College. *Home:* 387 Bleecker St., New York, N.Y. 10014. *Office:* Publications Division, Bank Street College, 610 West 112th St., New York, N.Y. 10025.

The three of us were the first ones to hit the cafeteria. ■ (From *The 17 Gerbils of Class 4A* by William H. Hooks. Illustrated by Joel Schick.)

CAREER: High school teacher of history and social studies in Chapel Hill, N.C., 1949; Hampton Institute, Hampton, Va., instructor of history and dance, 1950; Brooklyn College of the City University of New York, Brooklyn, N.Y., choreographer at Opera Workshop, 1960-64; owner of dance studio in New York, N.Y., 1965-70; Bank Street College, New York City, member of staff in Publications Division, 1970-72, chairman of division, 1972—. Vice-president of Ballet Concepts, Inc.; choreographer for New Jersey Opera Guild, Paramount Pictures, outdoor dramas, and off-Broadway productions; also choreographer for his own dance company. Managing editor of Bank Street College's "Bank Street Readers," revised edition, "Discoveries: An Individualized Approach to Reading," "Tempo Series," and "Education Before Five." *Military service:* U.S. Army, Medical Corps, 1942-46; became technical sergeant. *Member:* Phi Beta Kappa.

WRITINGS: The Seventeen Gerbils of Class 4A (juvenile), Coward, 1976; *Maria's Cave* (juvenile), Coward, 1977; *Doug Meets the Nutcracker* (juvenile), Warne, 1977; (with Ellen Galinsky) *The New Extended Family: Day Care That Works,* Houghton, 1977; *Crossing The Line* (young adult novel), Knopf, 1978. Reviewer for *Dance Digest.* Associate editor of "U.S.R.D. Readers," "Bank Street Unit Readers," and "Captain Kangaroo" television scripts.

SIDELIGHTS: Hooks has acted as educational consultant to CBS, NBC weekend specials, the Peabody Award-winning ABC "Afterschool Specials," and all of the ABC Saturday morning children's programs. A producer and choreographer, he has been involved in a wide variety of productions, including thirteen historical outdoor dramas, such as "Unto These Hills" on the Cherokee Indian Reservation.

William Hooks, with co-author Ellen Galinsky.

HOYT, Olga (Gruhzit) 1922-

PERSONAL: Born November 16, 1922, in Columbus, Ga.; daughter of Oswald Martin (a research pathologist) and Elfriede (Nerica) Gruhzit; married Edwin P. Hoyt (an author), May 24, 1947; children: Diana Palmer, Helga Martin (Mrs. Benjamin Berliner), Christopher Martin. *Education:* University of Michigan, B.A., 1943. *Home and office:* 1010 Koloa St., Honolulu, Hawaii 96816.

CAREER: Chrysler Corp., Detroit, Mich., instructor and inspector in airplane wing factory, 1943; U.S. Office of War Information, with news division, New York, N.Y., 1944-45, assistant news editor in Beirut, Lebanon, 1945; *Time,* New York, N.Y., researcher, 1945-47, stringer in Colorado Springs, Colo., 1951-54; North American Newspaper Alliance, free-lance correspondent in Europe, 1947-48, London, 1975; *Denver Post,* Denver, Colo., columnist and book reviewer, 1949-50; *Colorado Springs Free Press,* Colorado Springs, Colo., book editor and columnist, 1951-55; *New York Times,* New York, N.Y., children's book reviewer, 1957-64; Gemini News Service, London, England, correspondent, 1977—; researcher for her author-husband. *Member:* Alpha Phi.

WRITINGS: If You Want a Horse (juvenile), Coward, 1965; *Witches* (juvenile), Abelard, 1969; *The Bedouins* (juvenile), Lothrop, 1969; *Aborigines of Australia* (juvenile), Lothrop, 1969; (with husband, Edwin P. Hoyt) *Censorship in America,* Seabury, 1970; *American Indians Today* (juvenile), Abelard, 1972; (with Edwin P. Hoyt) *Freedom of the News Media* (juvenile), Seabury, 1973; *Demons, Devils,*

and Djinn (juvenile), Abelard, 1974; *Exorcism* (juvenile), Watts, 1978. Contributor to *Saturday Review, Baltimore Sun, Guardian* (London) and other Gemini News Service newspapers. First woman editor, *Gargoyle* (University of Michigan monthly magazine), 1942.

SIDELIGHTS: "I have always been interested in editorial work, since my college days, and was lucky enough after I went to New York, in 1943, to be able to secure editorial jobs. The most exciting of which was my stint in Beirut, Lebanon, as assistant news editor for the Office of War Information. There I found myself doing various jobs, from putting out news releases, to writing fashion articles for the Arab and French newspapers. Research for *Time* Magazine in New York gave me my first love for researching, and a good thing, for I have been researching for my writer-husband for over twenty years.

"I started my own writing when we lived on a farm in Connecticut, and we owned three horses, for our young daughters. Unfortunately they went to school, and I was left tending the horses, whom I feared greatly. But, by taking care of them, I learned to love them, and realized how much my girls did *not* know about taking care of horses, and what a responsibility they were. Thus, I wrote my first book, *If You Want a Horse,* to try to present to young girls (and boys) the needs of horses, and how they should be housed, fed, and so on. From then on, my researches led me to write later books. In recent years I became intrigued with the interest in the occult and mysticism from the beginnings of recorded history. It was interesting to discover how different peoples

OLGA HOYT

in different ages believed in magic and mysticism and, thus, I wanted to record this information for young readers.

"I research and edit for my husband, and he edits for me. It is a fine relationship, and we help each other to present what we hope are good books. I receive much guidance from him since he has had vast experience, and has had over 125 books for young adults, and adults, published, ranging from war exploits to biograpy, to novels.

"Hawaii is a delightful and fascinating (because of the mixture of the races) place to live, and I hope to write an adult novel about life here in the near future."

HOBBIES AND OTHER INTERESTS: Bird raising (cockatiels), gardening (orchids), painting.

HUGHES, Shirley 1929-

PERSONAL: Born July 16, 1929, in Hoylake, near Liverpool, Eng.; married to an architect; children: two sons, one daughter. *Education:* Attended Liverpool Art School and Ruskin School of Drawing and Fine Art, Oxford University. *Address:* 63 Lansdowne Road, London W11, Eng.

CAREER: Author and illustrator of books for children. *Awards, honors:* Other Award, 1976, from the Children's Rights Workshop, for *Helpers.*

WRITINGS—All self-illustrated: *Lucy and Tom's Day,* W. R. Scott, 1960; *The Trouble with Jack,* Bodley Head, 1970; *Lucy and Tom Go to School,* Gollancz, 1973; *Sally's Secret,* Bodley Head, 1973; *Helpers,* Bodley Head, 1973, published in America as *George the Babysitter,* Prentice-Hall, 1977; *Lucy and Tom at the Seaside,* Gollancz, 1976; *Dogger,* Bod-

ley Head, 1977; *It's Too Frightening for Me!,* Hodder & Stoughton, 1977; *Moving Molly,* Bodley Head, 1978.

Illustrator: Doris Rust, *Story a Day,* Faber, 1954; Rust, *All Sorts of Days,* Faber, 1955; Diana Ross, pseudonym of Diana Denney, *William and the Lorry,* Faber, 1956; Edward H. Lang, *Curious Adventures of Tabby,* Faber, 1956; D. Rust, *Animals at Number Eleven,* Faber, 1956; Allan C. McLean, *Storm over Skye,* Harcourt, 1957; Rust, *Animals at Rose Cottage,* Faber, 1957; Rust, *Mixed-Muddly Island,* Faber, 1958; Louisa May Alcott, *Little Women,* Blackie, 1960; Dorothy Clewes, *The Singing Strings,* Collins, 1961; Hans Christian Andersen, *Fairy Tales,* Blackie, 1961; Margaret McPherson, *The Shinty Boys,* Harcourt, 1963; Ruth Sawyer, *Roller Skates,* Bodley Head, 1964; Mabel E. Allan, *Mystery on the Fourteenth Floor,* Abelard-Schuman, 1965; Helen Morgan, *A Dream of Dragons, and Other Tales,* Faber, 1965; Margaret Storey, *Kate and the Family Tree,* Faber, 1965; Storey, *The Smallest Doll,* Faber, 1966; Donald Bisset, *Little Bear's Pony,* Benn, 1966; Angela Bull, *Wayland's Keep,* Collins, 1966; Barbara Ireson, editor, *The Faber Book of Nursery Stories,* Faber, 1966; Margaret J. Baker, *Porterhouse Major,* Prentice-Hall, 1967; M. MacPherson, *The New Tenants,* Harcourt, 1968; John Randle, *Grandpa's Balloon,* Benn, 1968; Helen Cresswell, *A Day on Big O,* Follett, 1968; Ursula M. Williams, *A Crown for a Queen,* Meredith Press, 1968; Leonard Clark, compiler, *Flutes and Cymbals,* Crowell, 1969; Ann Thwaite, *The Holiday Map,* Follett, 1969; U. M. Williams, *The Toymaker's Daughter,* Meredith Press, 1969; Sara Corrin, editor, *Stories for Seven-Year-Olds, and Other Young Readers,* F. Watts, 1969.

Ruth Ainsworth, *The Ruth Ainsworth Book,* F. Watts, 1970; Helen Morgan, *Satchkin Patchkin,* M. Smith, 1970; Helen Griffiths, *Moshie Cat,* Holiday House, 1970; M. E. Allan, *The Wood Street Secret,* Abelard-Schuman, 1970; Jo Rice, *Robbie's Mob,* World's Work, 1971; H. Cresswell, *Rainbow Pavement,* Benn, 1971; H. Griffiths, *Federico,* Hutchinson Junior Books, 1971; Dorothy Edwards, *More Naughty Little Sister Stories,* Methuen, 1971; U. M. Williams, *The Three Toymakers,* T. Nelson, 1971; S. Corrin, editor, *Stories for Eight-Year-Olds, and Other Young Readers,* Faber, 1971; H. Morgan, *Mother Farthing's Luck,* Faber, 1971; Charles Perrault, *Cinderella; or, The Little Glass Slipper,* Walck, 1971; Barbara Sleigh, *The Smell of Privet,* Hutchinson, 1971; Nina Bawden, *Squib,* Gollancz, 1971; Elizabeth Goudge, *The Lost Angel: Stories,* Hodder & Stoughton, 1971; Julia Cunningham, *Burnish Me Bright,* Heinemann, 1971; Robina B. Willson, *Dancing Day,* Benn, 1971; Mary Stewart, *The Little Broomstick,* Brockhampton, 1971, Morrow, 1972; Frances M. Fox, *The Little Cat That Could Not Sleep,* Faber, 1971, Scroll Press, 1972; H. Morgan, *Mary Kate,* T. Nelson, 1972; U. M. Williams, *Malkin's Mountain,* T. Nelson, 1972.

Margaret Kornitzer, *The Hollywell Family,* Bodley Head, 1973; M. Storey, *The Family Tree,* T. Nelson, 1973; D. Edwards, *When My Naughty Little Sister Was Good,* Penguin, 1973; M. Mahy, *The Second Margaret Mahy Story Book,* Dent, 1973; Ruth Ainsworth, *Another Lucky Dip,* Penguin, 1973; S. Corrin, editor, *Stories for Five-Year-Olds, and Other Young Readers,* Faber, 1973; R. Ainsworth, *The Phantom Fisherboy: Tales of Mystery and Magic,* Deutsch, 1974; D. Edwards, *My Naughty Little Sister and Bad Harry,* Methuen, 1974; Jean Sutcliffe, *Jacko, and Other Stories,* Puffin Books, 1974; Jenny Overton, *The Thirteen Days of Christmas,* T. Nelson, 1974; S. Corrin, editor, *Stories for Under Fives,* Faber, 1974; Alison Farthing, *The Gauntlet*

Fair, Chatto, 1974; Joan Drake, *Miss Hendy's House,* Brockhampton Press, 1974; D. Bisset, *Hazy Mountain,* Penguin, 1975; Marjorie Lloyd, *Fell Farm Campers,* Puffin Books, 1975; M. Mahy, *The Third Margaret Mahy Story Book,* Dent, 1975; M. E. Allan, *The Sign of the Unicorn: A Thriller for Young People,* White Lion, 1975.

H. Morgan, *Mrs. Pinny and the Blowing Day,* Puffin Books, 1976; Noel Streatfeild, *New Town: A Story about the Bell Family,* White Lion, 1976; Streatfeild, *The Painted Garden: A Story of a Holiday in Hollywood,* Puffin Books, 1976; D. Edwards, *My Naughty Little Sister Goes Fishing,* Methuen, 1976; M. E. Allan, *The Wood Street Rivals,* Methuen, 1976;

On the way home Dave walked beside the pushchair giving Joe licks off his ice-cream. Joe kicked his feet about and shouted for more in-between licks. ■ (From *Dogger* by Shirley Hughes. Illustrated by the author.)

SHIRLEY HUGHES

Ruth Tomalin, *The Snake Crook,* Faber, 1976; M. Mahy, *The First Margaret Mahy Story Book: Stories and Poems,* Dent, 1976; Sara and Stephen Corrin, editors, *Stories for Six-Year-Olds, and Other Young Readers,* Penguin, 1976; M. E. Allan, *The Wood Street Helpers,* Methuen, 1976; Allan, *The Wood Street Group,* Methuen, 1976; Allan, *Away from Wood Street,* Methuen, 1976; Allan, *Fiona on the Fourteenth Floor,* Dent, 1976; Winifred Finlay, *Tattercoats, and Other Folk Tales,* Kaye & Ward, 1976, Harvey, 1977; Alison M. Abel, editor, *Make Hay While the Sun Shines,* Faber, 1977; Helen Cresswell, *Donkey Days,* Benn, 1977; Ruth Ainsworth, *The Phantom Roundabout and Other Ghostly Tales,* Deutsch, 1977; Helen Young, *A Throne for Sesame,* Deutsch, 1977; Dorothy Edwards, *My Naughty Little Sister and Bad Harry's Rabbit,* Methuen, 1977; Oliver T. Selfridge, *The Trouble Was Dragons,* Addison-Wesley, 1977; Alison Utley, *From Spring to Spring,* Faber, 1977; Sarah and Stephen Corrin (editors), *More Stories for Seven-Year-Olds,* Faber, 1978; Brenda Sivers, *The Snailman,* Little, Brown, 1978; Ursula Moray-Williams, *Bogwoppit,* Hamish Hamilton, 1978; Nancy Northcote, *Pottle Pig,* Kaye and Ward, 1978.

SIDELIGHTS: "Like most illustrators, I think in pictures. The words come later, as captions for a silent movie which has already unfolded inside my head. I worked as an illustrator for many years before I got round to writing my own stories. That didn't happen until I had young children of my own. Illustrating, like acting, instrumental playing, or any of the other interpretive arts, is largely concerned with trying to use your imaginative powers to get inside another person's skin, to identify with the story and work out from there, using your technique—black and white line, full colour, or whatever is specified by the publisher—to illuminate the drama of the narrative, give a visual form and style to the characters and their background, and to enhance the look of the printed page in a way which will delight and entertain the reader. All this springs from a passion to communicate with an audience whom you may never see.

"I don't know of any pleasure in the world to compare with sitting down, pencil in hand, in front of a lovely piece of blank white drawing paper, with a lot of ideas buzzing about in your head, clamouring to get down onto the drawing-board. Once work is underway, of course, you are at grips with the usual hair-raising problems. Using inks and brushes, putting down washes of colour, trying to translate the vitality of rough sketches into finished art work, can go wrong at any stage no matter how experienced you are. It's a more tactile, sensuous activity than sitting in front of a typewriter. But there are certain tranquil times when it's more like working on a piece of embroidery, and you can happily be listening to music or even a radio talk at the same time—something unthinkable for a writer. When you're working on a story by another person you're in a supportive role, which is in some ways easier because you always have that other imagination to draw upon. But making up a story of your own and doing the pictures too is something very close to the heart, and, in the end, the greatest pleasure of all.

"I grew up during the war, in a large suburban house with a garden. The grown-ups were all frantically involved with food-rationing, blackouts, placing evacuees (we had five under seven-year-olds billeted on us at one point) and getting up parcels of comforts for the forces. Although I can remember seeing the night sky over towards Liverpool raked by searchlights and tracer shells and vivid with fires from the incendiary bombs, I look back on it as a quiet uneventful life on the whole. Convinced as one is at that age of one's own immortality, the social and academic pressures being practically non-existent, there was an unlimited amount of time in which to mooch about. The main problem was that drawing paper was in short supply, but we did very well with the backs of old envelopes. We wrote plays and acted them to whatever audience could be press-ganged into watching, and we wrote stories and drew the pictures to go with them. We had plenty of books, many of them old ones left over from a time which, as luck would have it, was a kind of golden age of illustration. The worlds of Dulac, Rackham and Ernest Shephard were especially seductive in the midst of drab wartime austerity.

"Later I studied costume design with the idea of designing for the theatre, but after a spell as general dogsbody in a repertory, painting scenery flats, mending tights, and sticking green hair onto the heads of trolls, I thought better of it, no doubt, to the great relief of the management. After a long spell of academic fine-art training, which included a daily confrontation with a life-model—a testing and sometimes daunting discipline at the time, but one which I've never regretted—I returned to an old abiding passion to illustrate and write stories, and I have been immersed in it ever since.

"Bringing up my own family, experiencing the usual domestic dramas, and knowing what it's like to have to read the same story aloud every night for weeks on end, made me turn to trying to produce books with which young children can strongly and warmly identify, with pictures which they can turn back to and explore for themselves, and a text which wouldn't bore the adult or older child who is sharing it with them. Observing people, and trying to draw them out of my head, is a challenge which holds an endless fascination for me. Depicting human situations, dramatic or domestic, farcical, fantastic, realistic or romantic, is what I like best."

FOR MORE INFORMATION SEE: Lee Kingman and others, compilers, *Illustrators of Children's Books, 1957-1966,* Horn Book, 1968.

HÜLSMANN, Eva   1928-

PERSONAL: Born September 2, 1928; in Metz, France; daughter of Franz (a colonel) and Berta (Hinsberg) Hülsmann; married Aldo Andina (a factory director; deceased), March 20, 1969. *Education:* Attended art school in Cologne and Berlin, Germany. *Home:* Via Ciceri Visconti, 18 Milano, Italy 20137.

CAREER: Illustrator; painter. *Exhibitions:* Galleria Barbaroux, Milano, 1958; several collectives as Mostra degli Illustratori, Bologna, 1966-75; Famiglia Meneghina, Milano, 1977; Cricket Travelling Art Exhibit, United States, 1977, 1978. *Member:* Famiglia Artistica, Famiglia Meneghina.

WRITINGS—Self-illustrated: *Arte Decorative,* Edizioni di Scienze ed Arti (Milano), 1954.

Illustrator: Cesare Conci, *Coleotteri* (title means "Beatles"), Aldo Martello (Milano), 1959; Cesare Conci and M. Torchio, *Pesci* (title means "Fish"), Aldo Martello, 1961; Enzo De Michele, *Pietre Preziose* (title means "Precious Stones"), Aldo Martello, 1965; Otto von Frisch, *Europäische Vögel* (title means "European Birds"), Verlag J. F. Schreiber (Esslingen), 1967; Alberto Manzi (co-illustrator), *Gli Animali intorno a noi,* (title means "Animals About Us"), Bompiani (Milano), 1968; Alberto Manzi (co-illustrator), *Gli Animali e il loro ambiente* (title means "Animals in Their World"), Bompiani, 1968; Veronika de Osa, *Das Tier als Symbol* (title means "The Animal as a Symbol"), Rosgarten Verlag (Konstanz), 1968; Jean Chapman, *Die Wunschkatze* (title means "The Wishcat), Verlag Friedr. Oetinger (Hamburg), 1969.

Helmut E. Adler, *Bird Life,* Sterling, 1970; Otto von Frisch, *Das Wasser und Seine Tiere* (title means "The Water and it's Animals"), Atlantis Verlag (Zurich), 1970; Giulio Mortari, *Fiori Per Lei* (title means "Flowers for Her"), Capitol (Bologna), 1971; G. V. Wahlert, *Das Schädelkabinett* (title means "Skulls"), Basilius Press (Basel), 1972; Gisela Dannholz, *Die Bären* (title means "The Bears"), Verlag Friedr. Oetinger, 1972; H. Melles, *Der Kleine Igel* (title means "The Little Hedgehog"), Siebert Verlag (Bad Aibling), 1972; H. Melles, *Wo die Tiere wohnen* (title means "Animals Homes"), Siebert Verlag, 1972; H. Melles, *Was macht . . .* (title means "What Does . . . "), Siebert Verlag, 1972; H. Melles, *Warum?* (title means "Why?"), Siebert Verlag, 1972; Otto von Frisch, *Der Hamster und die Eidechse* (title means "The Hamster and the Lizard"), Atlantis Verlag, 1972; O. Del Rio, *300 Milioni di anni fa* (title means "Paleontology"), Capitol, 1974; Christine Adrian, *Tiere pflegen und verstehen* (title means "How to Nurse and to Understand Animals"), Kosmos Franckh (Stuttgart), 1976; Gerald Summers, *Owned by an Eagle,* Collins (London), 1976; Margaret Rau, *The Giant Panda At Home,* Knopf, 1977; Margaret Rau, *The Great Eastern Kangaroo at Home,* Knopf, 1978. Work has appeared in *Cricket* since 1973.

SIDELIGHTS: "I always liked animals very much and I wouldn't be sorry if I had been born an animal. The more you study animal behavior, the more you become aware of how polite and kind they are to each other—if human beings were civilized like that, it would be a better world. Did you

EVA HÜLSMANN

ever hear about a war between lion nations? Even a tiger, when it is not hungry, lies peacefully in the grass.

"I also like them for their beauty, some are so graceful, so perfect, so aristocratic they take your breath away. And how clumsy our body is confronted with their swiftness, how they can hump, fly, run.

"As I like them so much, I became an *animal painter* and as you can see, I did a lot of books about them. I like to draw them exactly as they are, because I think that it is impossible to do better than nature did: my task is only to express the feeling which nature gives to me and to transmit it, if I can. Certain feelings are better expressed when the animals are depicted in a surrealistic atmosphere.

"I have grown up in Germany. There are several artists between my ancestors and, notwithstanding, I first thought to study natural history, later on I decided for sculpture. I studied sculpture in Germany and I was very happy with that. But later on, as I needed money, I became aware that sculpture is awfully expensive, but rarely remunerative. To earn money I had to learn painting and as studying time was over, I had to learn it by myself. For this I may have a technique of my own, mixing pastel and water colours. First I did drawings for printed clothes (the book, *Arte decorative,* was the conclusion of this period). Then I began to introduce myself to the publishers and now I am doing what I consider as my inclination.

"In the meantime I went to Italy. I married an Italian who was the best husband of the world, but unfortunately he died and left me alone. My main company actually are my tropical birds. I don't keep birds which live better in freedom, but tropical birds, once they have arrived here, I can save them only by buying them and let them fly around in my flat. I own

(From *The Giant Panda at Home* by Margaret Rau. Illustrated by Eva Hülsmann.)

a nice terrace and I covered it with a wire-net, so the little ones can fly on the terrace and in the flat as they like. I have sixteen birds and I hope that they are quite happy.

"My languages are German, Italian, French and English. With my husband I made several journeys in Europe and after his death I came to America. I liked it very much—I hope to come back soon."

HUMPHREY, Henry (III) 1930-

PERSONAL: Born April 26, 1930, in Mineola, N.Y.; son of Henry, Jr. (an editor) and Cathleen (Murphy) Humphrey; married Deirdre O'Meara (a writer), July 20, 1957; children: Nora Alexandra, Maud Gonne, Daphne O'Meara, Eloise Arnold, Deirdre Mary. *Education:* Attended New York University, 1949-51. *Home:* 166 Newtown Turnpike, Weston, Conn. 06883. *Agent:* Anita Diamant, Writer's Workshop, Inc., 51 East 42nd St., New York, N.Y. 10017; and Betty Marks, 51 East 42nd St., New York, N.Y. 10017.

CAREER: Channel 5-Television, New York City, film director, 1952-57; Cunningham & Walsh (advertising agency), New York City, account executive, 1957-62; Doherty, Clifford, Shenfield & Steers (advertising agency), New York City, account executive, 1962-63; Sullivan, Stauffer, Colwall & Bayles (advertising agency), New York City, account executive, 1963-65; free-lance photographer and writer for children, 1965—.

WRITINGS—For children: all with own photographs: *What Is It For?*, Simon & Schuster, 1969; *What's Inside*, Simon & Schuster, 1972; *Sights and Sounds of Flying*, Little, Brown, 1972; *Farm*, Doubleday, 1978.

WORK IN PROGRESS: A book on ocean sailing for young adults, publication by McKay expected in 1979-80; a children's book, *When Is Now?*, with wife Deidre Humphrey, publication by Doubleday expected in 1980; a book on photography for young people, publication by Simon & Schuster expected in 1980.

SIDELIGHTS: "I don't know if it's ever inevitable that someone becomes an author, but I suppose my hide would have to have been even thicker than it is for me to have avoided it. My father is an editor; my sister is a poet and professor of creative writing; my wife is an author, and so is her father. My friends include Nils Bodecker and Richard and Patsy Scarry who, as everybody knows, are enormously successful in writing and illustrating books for children.

"But, strangely enough, I didn't consciously try to become an author. I'm a photographer specializing in a photojournalistic approach to pictures for corporate brochures and an-

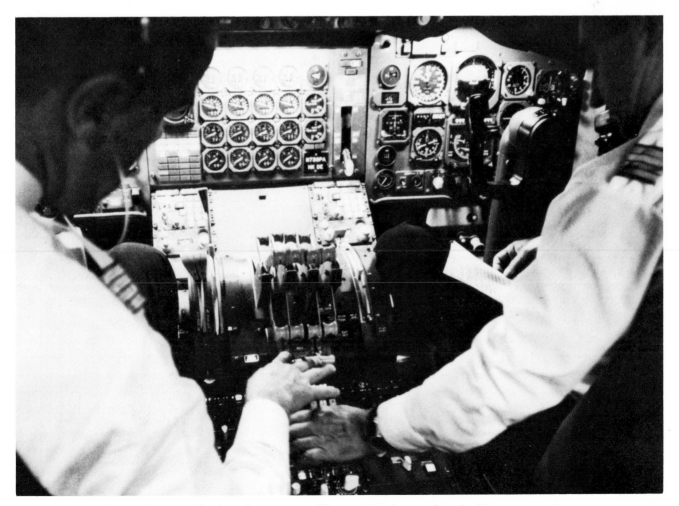

By punching keys like those found on an adding machine, the two of you feed the computers the exact position (in degrees of latitude and longitude) of the airport you are leaving. ■ (From *The Sights and Sounds of Flying*, text and photographs by Henry Humphrey.)

nual reports. I got an idea for a photographic children's book *What Is It For?* which would show children the end use of some very familiar objects found in cities and towns everywhere (manhole cover, not-for-deposit mailbox, standpipe connector, etc.). I thought it would be fine if a couple of thousand were published, then I could put one under my arm and show corporate prospects what a clever photographer I am. It was picked by the *New York Times* as one of the ten best illustrated children's books of the year, and Simon & Schuster went back on press with the book almost immediately. 'Well, this is fun!' I thought to myself, and I've been hopelessly hooked on children's books ever since.

"I can't imagine a more important audience to reach than young people. They can be so enthusiastic, but so easily turned off by boredom. One of the best parts of doing books is receiving an occasional letter from a reader to whom the book meant something.

"Where do ideas come from? I'm trained to see things. Some of them I don't understand and my curiosity is piqued. What I want more than anything is that my books will excite curiosity in my readers."

JEFFERIES, (John) Richard   1848-1887

PERSONAL: Born November 6, 1848, near Swindon, Wiltshire, England; died August 14, 1887, at Goring, Sussex, England; son of James Luckett (a farmer) and Elizabeth (Gyde) Jefferies; married Jessie Baden, 1874; children: two. *Education:* Attended schools in Wiltshire, England.

CAREER: Novelist and naturalist. Reporter and reviewer for the *North Wilts Herald,* 1866; started writing novels, 1870; wrote articles for the *Pall Mall Gazette,* in London, beginning 1877; continued writing until his death, in spite of a painful illness that began about 1882.

WRITINGS—Fiction: *The Scarlet Shawl: A Novel,* [London], 1874; *Restless Human Hearts: A Novel,* three volumes, [London], 1875; *World's End,* three volumes, [London], 1877; *Greene Ferne Farm,* Smith, Elder, 1880, reissued, W. Foster, 1947; *Wood Magic: A Fable,* two volumes, Cassell, 1881, reissued, Third Press, 1974; *Bevis: The Story of a Boy,* three volumes, Sampson, Low, 1882, new edition, edited by Brian Jackson and illustrated by Ernest Howard Shepard, Puffin, 1974 [another edition illustrated by Harry Rountree, Duckworth, 1913]; *The Dewy Morn: A Novel,* Bentley, 1884; *After London; or, Wild England,* Cassell, 1885, reissued, Arno, 1975; *Amaryllis at the Fair: A Novel,* Harper, 1887, reissued, Westaway Books, 1948.

Nonfiction: *Jack Brass: Emperor of England* (political pamphlet), [London], 1873; *Reporting, Editing, and Authorship,* [London], 1873; *A Memoir of the Goddards of North Wilts,* [Swindon], 1873; *Suez-cide!! or, How Miss Britannia Bought a Dirty Puddle and Lost Her Sugar-Plums,* [London], 1876; *The Gamekeeper at Home: Sketches of Natural History and Rural Life,* [London], 1878; *Wild Life in a Southern County,* Smith, Elder, 1879, new edition, illustrated by Charles Frederick Tunnicliffe, Lutterworth, 1949 [another edition published as *An English Village* (illustrated by Clifton Johnson), Little, Brown, 1903]; *The Amateur Poacher,* Roberts Brothers, 1879.

Hodge and His Masters, two volumes, Smith, Elder, 1880, reissued, MacGibbon & Kee, 1966 [another edition published as *A Classic of English Farming: Hodge and His*

Masters, edited by Henry Williamson, Faber, 1946]; *Round about a Great Estate,* Roberts Brothers, 1880; *Nature near London,* Chatto & Windus, 1883; *The Story of My Heart* (autobiographical), Longmans, Green, 1883, reissued, Macmillan, 1968; *The Red Deer,* Longmans, Green, 1884; *The Life of the Fields* (papers originally published in *Time, Graphic,* and other periodicals), Chatto & Windus, 1884 (excerpt published as *The Pageant of Summer,* T. B. Mosher, 1905).

The Open Air (papers originally published in *Standard, English Illustrated,* and other periodicals), Chatto & Windus, 1885, Harper, 1886; *Field and Hedgerow: Being the Last Essays of Richard Jefferies,* edited by his wife, Jessie Jefferies, Longmans, Green, 1889, reissued, Lutterworth, 1948; *The Toilers of the Field,* Longmans, Green, 1892; *The Hills and the Vale,* Duckworth, 1909; *The Wood from the Trees,* Pilot Press, 1945.

Selections: *Beauty Is Immortal,* edited by Samuel J. Looker, Aldridge, 1948; *Chronicles of the Hedges, and Other Essays* (illustrated by the author and his uncle, John Luckett Jefferies), edited by S. J. Looker, Phoenix House, 1948; *The Jefferies Companion,* edited by S. J. Looker, Phoenix House, 1948; *The Old House at Coate,* edited by S. J. Looker, Harvard University Press, 1948, reissued, Books for Libraries, 1970; *Field and Farm* (illustrated by the author and J. L. Jefferies), edited by S. J. Looker, Phoenix House, 1957.

Collections: *Jefferies' England: Nature Essays* (photographs by Will F. Taylor), edited by S. J. Looker, Constable, 1937, Harper, 1938; *The Nature Diaries and Note-Books of Richard Jefferies,* edited by S. J. Looker, Grey Wall Press, 1941; *The Works of Richard Jefferies,* edited by C. Henry Warren, Eyre & Spottiswoode, 1948.

SIDELIGHTS: **November 6, 1848.** Born John Richard Jefferies on "Coate Farm," near Swindon, in North Wiltshire. The second of five children. Father, James Luckett Jefferies, a farmer, excelled in architecture, music and painting. He was a man with a great love for books. Jefferies received little formal education, but read constantly, borrowing books from neighbors. "Almost the first thing I did with pen and ink as a boy was to draw a map of the hamlet with the roads and lanes and paths, and I think some of the ponds, and with each of the houses marked and the occupier's name. Of course it was very roughly done, and not to any scale, yet it was perfectly accurate and full of detail. . . ." [Richard Jefferies, "My Old Village," *Field and Hedgerow,* Longmans, Green and Co., 1889.[1]]

He roamed the countryside studying wildlife: "There have been few things I have read of or studied, which in some manner or other I have not seen illustrated in this county while out in the fields.

". . . An epitome of the natural world, and . . . if anyone has come really into contact with its productions, and is familiar with them, and what they mean and represent, then he has a knowledge of all that exists on earth.

"All the grasses of the meadow were my pets, I loved them all; and perhaps that was why I never had a 'pet,' never cultivated a flower, never kept a caged bird, or any creature. Why keep pets when every wild, free hawk that passed overhead in the air was mine? I joyed in his swift, careless flight, in the throw of his pinions, in his rush over the elms and miles of woodland; it was happiness to see his unchecked life. What more beautiful than the sweep and curve of his going through the azure sky?'' [Richard Jefferies, ''Hours of Spring,'' *Field and Hedgerow,* Longmans, Green and Co., 1889.[2]]

1856. ''[I have been] out shooting with papa. We shot several Rabbits. I have rowed the Boat from one end of the water to the other with Mama and two others. I have caught some fishes, but they are dead.'' [Edward Thomas, *Richard Jefferies: His Life and Work,* Kennikat Press, reissued, 1972.[3]]

1863. At age fifteen he ran away with a boy cousin to France intending to walk to Moscow. The venture failed and he returned to the farm.

March, 1866. Joined the staff of the *North Wilts Herald* as a writer, reporter and reviewer. ''The first object of the reporter should . . . be to acquire an insight into the real state of things, to get behind the scenes, so as to thoroughly comprehend the outward show placed before the public.

''The reporter, while going about the country studying as he goes its topography, antiquities, traditions, and general characteristics, will have ample opportunities of amassing materials for original sketches in the paper. . . . He can then write a local history, or, taking an old tradition, or a noted spot, for the centre-piece, weave a short story out of his imagination around it.'' [Richard Jefferies, *Reporting, Editing, and Authorship* (pamphlet), John Snow (London), 1873.[4]]

Began his courtship of Jessie Baden of Day House Farm.

While on the staff of the newspaper he wrote the *History of Malmesbury* and the *History of Swindon,* later reprinted as *Jefferies Land.* Of this period he later wrote: ''I was not more than eighteen when an inner and esoteric meaning began to come to me from all the visible universe, and indefinable aspirations filled me. I found them in the grass fields, under the trees, on the hill-tops, at sunrise, and in the night. There was a deeper meaning everywhere. . . .

''I was sensitive to all things, to the earth under, and the star-hollow round about; to the least blade of grass, to the largest oak. They seemed like exterior nerves and veins for the conveyance of feeling to me. Sometimes a very ecstasy of exquisite enjoyment of the entire visible universe filled me. I was aware that in reality the feeling and the thought were in me, and not in the earth or sun; yet I was more conscious of it when in company with these.'' [Richard Jefferies, *The Story of My Heart: My Autobiography,* Longmans (London), 1883.[5]]

August 28, 1868. After a disease they could find no cause for: ''Thank God I am getting better now, and can sit up in bed; but I am so miserably weak, and my legs are as thin as a grasshopper's. . . . But when I come to think it over calmly, I can almost thank God that I have been ill, for it has made me pause and think, and I can now see what a wrong and even wicked course I have been secretly pursuing for a long time, and I hope I shall take warning. God has been very merciful to me this time. I never found my Bible a consolation before, but I have during the last two or three days, for its promises are full of mercy, and I have found it true, for I have prayed earnestly and God has answered me. . . .

RICHARD JEFFERIES

''Above all, I am in the country, and can see the green grass out of my window, and it is quiet. . . .

''I have such a longing to see the sea.''[2]

September, 1870. After a long holiday at Dover, Ostend and Hastings, he wrote to a neighbor of Coate Farm:

''Dear Sir,

''I once told you that if ever I found myself in a difficulty I should come to you for help, and you were kind enough to say you would give it if it lay in your power. The truth is, I know no other to whom I can turn, for you are the only man I am acquainted with who has a generous sentiment. I have plenty of friends and relatives who have plenty of money, and who, so long as they believe me to be in a good position, will be ready enough to do anything for me, but let them once understand that I have got into a difficulty, they will shrug up their shoulders—as the old song says: 'they will give unto those who don't want it.' My pride, I think a proper pride, prevents me from asking these people. I could remain here with my kind aunt as long as I liked, but the truth would come out, and although she would not alter, yet the rest would look down upon me with contempt, and my presence would expose her to unpleasant remarks which I could not bear. I cannot return home for something of the same kind of reason—in one word, I have no other resource but you, and if you do not or cannot help I must turn navvy or starve. The fact is, I have had to learn the same bitter lesson that you have learnt, only upon a smaller scale—namely, that good nature is another name for foolery. I gave away so much that I left myself insufficient to live upon while my plans were growing up to bear fruit, and the consequence was I have had to abandon them at the very moment when a little more time would have given me success and made me independent.

"All is not lost, but while the grass grows the steed starves. What I have to ask is—will you allow me to live a little time with you, until I can work myself up again? May I come to your house and remain with you until I shall be able to get a position again? I do not ask you to give this to me, but to lend it, for I have little doubt but that in time I shall be able to repay you every farthing of the cost, which I will do the very uttermost. I am to all intents and purposes penniless. The only securities I can give you for repayment are these: I have a small silver watch which cost £4, a small Albert gold chain which cost £3, and a massive gold chain which cost 8 guineas, a diamond scarf-pin which cost 10 guineas, a double-barrelled gun which cost £7 (I have the warranty), and a gig which I don't know the value of. Besides these, I have about 200 books, all standard and expensive works. They cost me full £60, and are in good condition. These are all my effects: besides, I am young and strong, and I should not object to bear a hand upon the farm when required; in fact, I should like to. I know something about it, having often done so for amusement at home. In actual coin I have only £1 left, and one or two franc-pieces. I forget, I have a small collection of coins in my cabinet at home, among them a gold 7s. 6d. piece, which you can have too. There are also 2 model steam-engines, a locomotive and a stationary. The locomotive cost £3 or £4.

"I cannot go home. I would sooner starve. I can only go home when I am independent.

"I could sell these little things, but that money would soon go; besides, it would be very wretched to lose them, for some I value dearly. . . .

"What I want is a bed and to live with you. I can write anywhere. . . .

"If you would send a telegram, I should be obliged.

"You remember, perhaps, my once asking you to become a subscriber to a novel I wished to publish. You agreed, but said that you thought people would much sooner subscribe or buy a copy of my *History of Swindon,* if it was made larger and published as a book. I said nothing, but at once dropped the idea of a novel, and went to work collecting material. I got a whole box full of papers and old deeds, and wrote out a book in manuscript. I had it estimated, and even had 500 circulars printed to advertise. This is the only manuscript I have by me, but I feel little doubt I shall soon be able to work my way up again."[2] The neighbor took him into his home.

February, 1871. After returning to Coate Farm, continued his writing. "Very few were rejected, but none brought any return."[2]

July, 1871. Writing and earning money from the *North Wilts* and the *Swindon Advertiser.* His father threatened to turn him out of doors. Home was unhappy. "[His mother was] very unwell . . . nervous and liable to make herself miserable over the merest trifle . . . we live so unsociably in this house."[2]

1872. Wrote a letter to the *London Times* on "The Wiltshire Laborer." It was used as the basis of a leading editorial. His earnings from magazines and newspapers continued to be meagre.

1873. "The Future of Farming" published in *Fraser's Magazine.* "The farm was no longer self-supporting. It was necessary to keep account-books, a thing never done before. The words 'profit and loss' were introduced and began to be thoroughly understood. To make a 'profit' the farm must become a business; a business required a certain amount of speculation; speculation means capital. These men had not got capital. . . .

"Though tenants quit and farms are to let, the face of the country is not apparently altered. The arable lands are ploughed and sown, and harrowed and rolled; corn is ripening, herds are grazing in the meadows. Farmyards present the same appearance; there are still ricks and labourers moving about, carthorses harnessed, and the very barndoor fowls picking among the chaff. It is hard to believe that everything is in such decay.

"The changes which have been crowded into the last half-century have been so numerous and so important that it would be almost reasonable to suppose the limit had been reached for the present, and that the next few generations would be sufficiently occupied in assimilating themselves to the new conditions of existence.

"But so far from this being the case, all the facts of the hour point irresistibly to the conclusion that the era of development has but just commenced." [Richard Jefferies, "The Future of Farming," *Fraser's Magazine,* 1873.[6]]

Other articles followed on this subject, the history of agriculture and agricultural criticism.

1874. First novel published, *The Scarlet Shawl.* Contributed to cost of publication.

July, 1874. Married Jessie Baden.

1875. Moved to Victoria Street, Swindon. There his first child was born. *Restless Human Hearts* published.

1877. Moved to a London suburb, Surbiton. "From my home near London I made a pilgrimage almost daily to an aspen by a brook. . . .

"I am very fond of what I may call a thickness of the people such as exists in London; I dream in London quite as much as in the woodlands; I like the solitude of the hills and the hum of the most crowded city; I dislike little towns and villages. . . .

"[In London] is the presence of man in his myriads, it is a curious thing that your next-door neighbour may be a stranger, but there are no strangers in a vast crowd. They all seem to have some relationship, or rather, perhaps, they do not rouse the sense of reserve which a single unknown person might. Still, the impulse is not to be analyzed; these are mere notes acknowledging its power. [The neighbourhood of the city induced] a mental, a nerve-restlessness [out in the Surrey fields]; the hills and vales, and meads and woods, are like the ocean upon which Sinbad sailed; but coming too near the loadstone of London, the ship wends thither, whether or no—at least, it is so with me; and I often go to London without any object whatever, but just

Coate Farm. The gable window above the pear tree was in Jeffries' study.

because I must, and, arriving there, wander whithersoever the hurrying throng carries me. . . .

"Let the meads be never so sweet, the mountain-top never so exalted, still to Fleet Street the mind will return."[2]

1878. *The Gamekeeper at Home* published. Excerpted from this book are his thoughts and feelings of the "outside" life: "It's indoors, sir, as kills half the people; being indoors three parts of the day, and next to that taking too much drink and vittals [sic]. Eating's as bad as drinking; and there ain't nothing like fresh air and the smell of the woods. You should come out here in the spring, when the oak timber is throwed (because, you see, the sap be rising, and the bark strips then), and just sit down on a stick fresh peeled—I means a trunk, you know—and sniff up the scent of that there oak-bark. It goes right down your throat, and preserves your lungs as the tan do leather. And I've heard say as folk who work in the tan-yards never have no illness. There's always a smell from the trees, dead or living. I could tell what wood a log was in the dark by my nose; and the air is better where the woods be. The ladies up in the great house sometimes goes out into the fir plantations—the turpentine scents strong, you see—and they say it's good for the chest; but, bless you, you must live in it. People go abroad, I'm told, to live in the pine forests to cure 'em: I say these here oaks have got every bit as much good in that way.

"I never eat but two meals a day—breakfast and supper; what you would call dinner—and maybe in the middle of the day a hunch of dry bread and an apple. I take a deal for breakfast, and I'm rather lear [hungry] at supper; but you may lay our oath that's why I'm what I am in the way of health. People stuffs theirselves, and by consequence it breaks out, you see. It's the same with cattle; they're overfed, tied up in stalls, stuffed, and never no exercise, and mostly oily food, too. It stands to reason they must get bad; and that's the real cause of these here rinderpests, and pleuro-pneumonia, and what-nots. At least, that's my notion. I'm in the woods all day and never comes home till supper—'cept, of course, in breeding time, to fetch the meal and stuff for the birds—so I gets the fresh air, you see; and the fresh air is the life, sir. There's the smell of the earth, too—'specially just as the plough turns it up—which is a fine thing; and the hedges and the grass are as sweet as sugar after a shower. Anything with a green leaf is the thing, depend upon it, if you want to live healthly.

"I never signed no pledge; and if a man asks me to take a glass of ale, I never says him no. But I ain't got no barrel at home; and all the time I've been in this here place I've never been to a public. Gentlemen give me tips—of course they does; and much obliged I be; but I takes it to my missus. Many's the time they've asked me to have a glass of champagne or brandy when we've had lunch under the hedge; but I says no, and would like a glass of beer best, which I gets, of course. No; when I drink, I drinks ale: but most in general I drinks no strong liquor. Great coat!—cold weather! I never put no great coat on this thirty year. These here woods be as good as a topcoat in cold weather. Come off the open fields with the east wind cutting into you, and get inside they firs and you'll feel warm in a minute. If you goes into the ash-wood you must go in farther, because the wind comes more between the poles."[2]

1879. *The Amateur Poacher* published. "Every now and then [his] shot when he fired high cut the twigs out of the ash by me. Then came the distant noise of the beaters' sticks, and the pheasants, at last thoroughly disturbed, flew out in twos and threes at a time. Now the firing grew fierce, and the roll of the volleys ceaseless. It was impossible to jam the cartridges fast enough in the breech.

"A subtle flavour of sulphur filled the mouth, and the lips became dry. Sunshine and gleaming leaves and sky and grass seemed to all disappear in the fever of the moment. The gun burned the hands, all blackened by the powder; the metal got hotter and hotter; the sward was poached and trampled and dotted with cases; shots hissed through the air and pattered in showers on the opposite plantation; the eyes, bleared and bloodshot with the smoke, could scarce see to point the tube. Pheasants fell, and no one heeded; pheasants escaped, and none noticed it; pheasants were but just winged and ran wounded into the distant hedges; pheasants were blown out of all living shape and could hardly be gathered up. Not a word spoken; a breathless haste to load and blaze; a storm of shot and smoke and slaughter." [Richard Jefferies, *The Amateur Poacher*, Roberts Brothers, 1879.[7]]

1880. "Round About a Great Estate" published in *Pall Mall Gazette*. "Reclining on the sweet short sward under the hawthorn on the Down I looked over the Idover plain, and thought of the olden times. As I gazed I presently observed, far away beside some ricks, the short black funnel of an engine, and made it out to be a steam-plough waiting till the corn should be garnered to tear up the stubble. How much meaning there lay in the presence of that black funnel! There were the same broad open fields, the same beautiful crops of golden wheat, the same green hills, and the same sun ripening the grain. But how strangely changed [were] all human affairs. . . ." [Richard Jefferies, "Round About a Great Estate," *Pall Mall Gazette,* 1880.[8]]

1881. *Wood Magic* published. The beginning of a chain of diseases.

1882. *Bevis* published, his most famous novel.

1883. *The Story of My Heart: My Autobiography* published. Considered greatest achievement. "I began to make efforts to express these thoughts in writing, but could not succeed to my liking. Time went on, and harder experiences, and the pressure of labour came, but in no degree abated the fire of first thought. Again and again I made resolutions that I would write it, in some way or other, and as often failed. I could express any other idea with ease, but not this.

"Burning on, the great sun stood in the sky, heating the parapet, glowing steadfastly upon me as when I rested in the narrow valley grooved out in prehistoric times. Burning on steadfast, and ever present as my thought. Lighting the broad river, the broad walls; lighting the least speck of dust; lighting the great heaven; gleaming on my finger-nail. The fixed point of day—the sun. I was intensely conscious of it; I felt it; I felt the presence of the immense powers of the universe; I felt out into the depths of the ether. So intensely conscious of the sun, the sky, the limitless space, I felt in the midst of eternity then, in the midst of the supernatural, among the immortal, and the greatness of the material realised the spirit. By these I saw my soul; by these I knew the supernatural to be more intensely real than the sun. I touched the supernatural, the immortal, there that moment.

Jefferies, as a young man.

". . . I grasp death firmly in conception as I can grasp this bleached bone."[5]

March 27, 1884. "To me it seems as if I wrote nothing, more especially since my illness, for this is the third year I have been so weakened. To me it seems as if I wrote nothing, for my mind teems with ideas, and my difficulty is to know what to do with them. I not only sketch out the general plan of a book almost instantaneously, but I can see every little detail of it from the first page to the last. The mere writing—the handwriting—is the only trouble; it is very wearying. At this moment I have several volumes complete in my mind. Scarce a day goes by that I do not put down a fresh thought. I have twelve notebooks crammed full of ideas, plots, sketches for papers, and so on."[2]

Jefferies wrote in the essay "Nature in the Louvre" turned down by *Longman's Magazine* about this time: "Here is the difference between genius and talent. Talent has lined the walls with a hundred clever things, and could line miles of surface; genius gives but one example, and the clever things are silenced. Here is the difference between that which expresses a noble idea, and that which is dexterously conventional. The one single idea dominates the whole. Here is the difference, again, between the secret of the heart, the aspiration of the soul, and that which is only the workmanship of a studio ancient or modern." [Richard Jefferies, "Nature in the Louvre," *Field and Hedgerow,* Longmans, Green and Co., 1889.[9]]

September, 1885. Illness struck him down once again. "I cannot do anything. Whatever I wish to do, it seems as if a voice said, 'No, you must not do it.' Feebleness forbids. I think I would like a good walk. 'No.' I think I would like to write. 'No.' I think I would like to rest. 'No.' Always 'No' to everything. Even writing this . . . has made the spine ache almost past endurance. I cannot convey . . . how miserable it is to be impotent—to feel yourself full of ideas and work and to be unable to effect it. It is absolutely maddening. Still, the autumn comes on, and there is no staying it.''[2]

"Our bodies are full of unsuspected flaws, handed down it may be for thousands of years, and it is of these that we die, and not of natural decay. . . . The truth is, we die through our ancestors; we are murdered by our ancestors. Their dead hands stretch forth from the tomb and drag us down to their mouldering bones.'' [Henry S. Salt, *Richard Jefferies: His Life and Ideals,* Kennikat Press, 1905, 1970.[10]]

August 14, 1887. Tuberculosis set in. At 38, Jefferies died in poverty. ''I begin to think that my senses have deceived me. It is as they say. No one else seems to have seen the sparkle on the brook, or heard the music at the hatch, or to have felt back through the centuries; and when I try to describe these things to them they look at me with stolid incredulity. No one seems to understand how I got food from the clouds, nor what there was in the night, nor why it is not so good to look at it out of window. They turn their faces away from me, so that perhaps after all I was mistaken, and there never was any such place or any such meadows, and I was never there.

'' And perhaps in course of time I shall find out also, when I pass away physically, that as a matter of fact there never was any earth.''[1]

> ''Touched by his hand, the wayside weed
> Becomes a flower: the lowliest reed
> Beside the stream
> Is clothed with beauty; gorse and grass
> And heather where his footsteps pass
> The brighter seem.''

[*Sir Bevis,* edited by Eliza Josephine Kelley, Atheneum, 1899.[11]]

FOR MORE INFORMATION SEE: Richard Jefferies, *The Story of My Heart,* Longmans, Green, 1883, reissued, Macmillan, 1968; Henry S. Salt, *Richard Jefferies: His Life and His Ideals,* Sonnenschein, 1894, reprinted, Kennikat, 1970, Folcroft, 1973; Edward Thomas, *Richard Jefferies: His Life and His Work,* Little, Brown, 1909, reprinted, Kennikat, 1972, Folcroft, 1973; Samuel J. Looker and Crichton Porteous, *Richard Jefferies: Man of the Fields,* Verry, 1964; William J. Keith, *Richard Jefferies: A Critical Study,* University of Toronto Press, 1965.

KALASHNIKOFF, Nicholas   1888-1961

PERSONAL: Born May 17, 1888, in Minusinsk, Siberia, Russia; emigrated to the United States in 1924, naturalized in 1930; son of a farmer; married Elizabeth Lawrence (an editor). *Education:* Studied at schools in Irkutsk; later attended Moscow University for two years.

CAREER: Author of books for children. At age 16, participated in the 1905 rebellion of the Russian masses and was exiled by the government to northern Siberia for four years. Joined the Russian Army during World War I with the rank

"There, there, lad," Turgen soothed him with tender strokes and pats. "What are you afraid of? I will soon make you well and take you back to your family. Who am I but an old man? There is no harm in me. Besides, who would dare to lift a hand against such a splendid fellow? Lie still. Trust me." ■ (From *The Defender* by Nicholas Kalashnikoff. Illustrated by Claire and George Lauden, Jr.)

of captain; commanded the People's Army of Siberia as a general during the Russian Civil War, defeating Ataman Semenoff at Irkutsk, 1919. Forced to flee to China upon Bolshevik victory. *Awards, honors:* Runner-up for the Newbery Medal, 1952, for *The Defender;* received a MacDowell Fellowship for *They That Take the Sword.*

WRITINGS: They That Take the Sword, Harper, 1939; *Jumper: The Life of a Siberian Horse* (illustrated by Edward Shenton), Scribner, 1944, reissued, Oxford University Press, 1963; *Toyon: A Dog of the North and His People* (illustrated by Arthur Marokvia), Harper, 1950, reissued, The World's Work, 1960; *The Defender* (Ala Notable Book; illustrated by Claire and George Louden, Jr.), Scribner, 1951, reissued, 1967; *My Friend Yakub* (illustrated by Feodor Rojankovsky), Scribner, 1953, reissued, Oxford University Press, 1961.

SIDELIGHTS: At age sixteen, Kalashnikoff joined the revolutionary process in Russia and participated in the ensuing rebellion of 1905. This revolutionary activity cost the young student his education, a year in solitary confinement

NICHOLAS KALASHNIKOFF

followed by confinement to the arctic. His experiences in the polar region provided the materials for his writings.

FOR MORE INFORMATION SEE: Muriel Fuller, editor, *More Junior Authors,* H. W. Wilson, 1963.

(Died August 17, 1961)

KARP, Naomi J. 1926-

PERSONAL: Born October 17, 1926, in New York, N.Y.; daughter of Nathan I. (an attorney) and Jennie (a teacher; maiden name, Friedman) Kaplan; married Martin E. Karp (a business executive), March 14, 1948; children: Betsy (Mrs. Jeffrey J. Davis), Leslie (Mrs. David Goldenberg), Jonathan. *Education:* Attended University of Wisconsin, Madison, 1946; Queens College (now of the City University of New York), B.A., 1948. *Politics:* Democrat. *Religion:* Jewish. *Home:* 12 Ave. Bel Air, 1180 Brussels, Belgium.

CAREER: Westport News, Westport, Conn., political reporter, 1964-69; Capitol Correspondent, Hartford, Conn., owner of syndicate, 1969-71; Chatham Press, Riverside, Conn., public relations director, 1971-73; free-lance writer, 1973—. Member of board of trustees of Norwalk Public Library, 1972-77. *Member:* Authors League of America.

WRITINGS: Nothing Rhymes with April (juvenile), Harcourt, 1974; *The Turning Point* (juvenile; selection of Junior Literary Guild and Jewish Book Club), Harcourt, 1976; *The Bystander* (adult novel), 1978.

SIDELIGHTS: "When my parents moved to Laurelton in the southeastern corner of the borough, it was, in the minds of our Bronx and Manhattan relatives, still Indian territory. My mother was a schoolteacher who during the Depression,

when my father's law practice was reduced to guiding his clients safely through the bankruptcy courts, supported the family by holding three consecutive daily jobs, working each day from eight a.m. to ten p.m. Why she was so irritable was beyond me as I sat, head buried in a book, while she ironed, vacuumed, and prepared the following day's meals until well past midnight.

"My earliest desire was to become a detective, but I later realized the impracticality of this ambition and decided instead on a career as a French chanteuse. The fact that I found my greatest pleasure and facility in scibbling poems, short stories, and essays was, strangely, unconnected to future aspirations. With the exception of arithmetic and home arts, I was an outstanding student at P.S. 132, called to the stage twice during graduation ceremonies to receive the history and English medals. With each trip I clutched my mandatorily self-made dress as the bodice slowly separated from the skirt.

"Obviously, growing up in the 1930's had a profound effect on me, for these years are the source of material for my two children's books. Although neither is autobiographical,

She sat down at the desk, curled her legs around the front legs of the chair so that her toes pointed in opposite directions, and began. ■ (From *Nothing Rhymes with April* by Naomi J. Karp. Illustrated by Pamela Johnson.)

NAOMI J. KARP

much of the background and characters are related to events about which I was concerned, more deeply than I knew at the time. What I have written about is the effects of outside forces on this most sensitive period of childhood."

The Turning Point deals with a young Jewish girl who moves from the Bronx, in 1938, to an anti-Semitic suburb.

KHERDIAN, David   1931-

PERSONAL: Born December 17, 1931, in Racine, Wis.; son of Melkon (a chef) and Veron (Dumehjian) Kherdian; married Kato Rozeboom, January 21, 1967 (divorced, 1970); married Nonny Hogrogian (an artist and illustrator), March 17, 1971. *Education:* University of Wisconsin, B.S. (philosophy), 1960. *Politics:* None. *Religion:* Armenian Orthodox. *Home address:* P.O. Box 626, Aurora, Ore. 97002.

CAREER: Was a door-to-door magazine salesman and became, at nineteen, the company's youngest field manager; worked as shoe salesman, bartender, day laborer, factory worker; The Sign of the Tiger (used book store), Racine, Wis., owner, 1961-62; The Book House (used book store), Fresno, Calif., manager, 1962-63; Northwestern University, Evanston, Ill., literary consultant, 1965; Giligia Press, East Chatham, N.Y., founder and editor, 1966-73. Instructor in poetry, Fresno State College (now California State University, Fresno), 1969-70; poet-in-the-schools, State of New Hampshire, 1971-72. Writer and designer of theatre program, Santa Fe Theatre Co., 1968. Poetry judge, Vincent Price awards in creative writing, Institute of American Indian Arts, Santa Fe, 1968. *Military service:* U.S. Army, 1952-54. *Member:* P.E.N.

WRITINGS: David Meltzer: A Sketch from Memory and Descriptive Checklist, Oyez, 1965; *A Biographical Sketch*

and Descriptive Checklist of Gary Snyder, Oyez, 1965; *A Bibliography of William Saroyan, 1934-1964,* Roger Beacham, 1965; (compiler) *William Saroyan Collection* (catalog), Fresno County Free Library, 1966; *Six Poets of the San Francisco Renaissance: Portraits and Checklists,* introduction by William Saroyan, Giligia, 1967; (with Gerald Hausman) *Eight Poems,* Giligia, 1968; (author of introduction) Hausman, compiler, *The Shivurrus Plant of Mopant, and Other Children's Poems,* Giligia, 1968; *Six San Francisco Poets,* Giligia, 1969.

On the Death of My Father and Other Poems, introduction by Saroyan, Giligia, 1970; (editor with James Baloian) *Down at the Santa Fe Depot: Twenty Fresno Poets,* Giligia, 1970; *Homage to Adana,* limited edition, Perishable Press, 1970, Giligia, 1971; *Looking over Hills,* illustrations by wife, Nonny Hogrogian, Giligia, 1972; (editor) *Visions of America: By the Poets of Our Time,* illustrations by N. Hogrogian, 1973; *A David Kherdian Sampler,* COF Press, 1974; *The Nonny Poems,* Macmillan, 1974; (editor) *Settling America: The Ethnic Expression of Fourteen Contemporary Poets,* Macmillan, 1974; *Any Day of Your Life,* Overlook Press, 1975; (contributor) *Father Me Home, Winds,* edited by Art Cuelho and Dean Phelps, Seven Buffaloes Press, 1975; (editor) *Poems Here and Now,* illustrations by N. Hogrogian, Morrow, 1976; (editor) *The Dog Writes on the Window with His Nose and Other Poems,* illustrated by N. Hogrogian, Four Winds Press, 1976; (editor) *Traveling America With Today's Poets,* Macmillan, 1977; (editor) *If Dragon Flies Made Honey,* illustrated by Jose Aruego and Ariane Dewey, Morrow, 1977; *Country Cat, City Cat,* illustrated by Nonny Hogrogian, Four Winds, 1978; *I Remember Root*

DAVID KHERDIAN

Cat
Missak on his
rocktop moss
covered throne
(in our fern and
flower garden)
sits and catches
flies and keeps
his belly warm.
■ (From *Country Cat, City Cat* by David Kherdian.
Woodcuts by Nonny Hogrogian.)

River, Overlook Press, 1978; (editor) *I Sing The Song Of Myself,* Morrow, 1978; *The Road from Home: The Story of an Armenian Girl,* Morrow, 1979.

Broadsides: *Letter to Virginia in Florence from Larkspur, California,* Giligia, 1966; *Mother's Day,* Gary Chafe and Sanford M. Dorbin, 1967; *Kato's Poem,* Giligia, 1967; *My Mother Takes My Wife's Side,* illustrations by Judi Russell, Giligia, 1969; *O Kentucky,* Giligia, 1969; *Outside the Library,* privately printed, 1969; *Root River,* illustrations by Bob Totten, Perishable Press, 1970; *Bird in Suet,* illustrations by N. Hogrogian, Giligia, 1971; *Hey Nonny,* illustrations by N. Hogrogian, privately printed, 1972; *Poem for Nonny,* illustrations by N. Hogrogian, Phineas Press, 1973; *Onions from New Hampshire,* illustrations by N. Hogrogian, privately printed, 1973; *In the Tradition,* illustrations by N. Hogrogian, University of Connecticut, 1974; *16:IV:73,* illustrations by N. Hogrogian, Arts Action Press, 1975; *Anniversary Song,* Bellevue Press, 1975; *Remembering Mihran,* The University of Massachussetts, 1975; *Melkon,* Isat Pragbhara Press, 1976; *Dafje Vartan* (Salal Series VI), Prescott Street Press, 1978.

Work represented in many anthologies, including: Edward Field, *A Geography of Poets,* Bantam Books, 1969; Jack Antreassian, editor, *Ararat: A Decade of Armenian-American Writing,* Armenian General Benevolent Union of America, Inc., 1969; Gerald Hausman and David Silverstein, editors, *The Berkshire Anthology,* Bookstore Press, 1972; Ward Abbott, editor, *Desert Review Anthology,* Desert Review Press, 1974; Michael McMahon, *Flowering After Frost: The Anthology of Contemporary New England Poetry,* Branden Press, 1975; Gerald Haslam and James D. Houston, *California Heartland: Writing from the Great Central Valley,* Capra Press, 1978. Contributor to magazines. Editor, *Ararat,* 1970-71.

WORK IN PROGRESS: Working on a juvenile novel, tentative title *Me and Joe's Story.*

SIDELIGHTS: "I was an only child for nearly twelve years, and I was headstrong and willful and a loner. I had a real *Huckleberry Finn* childhood in many ways. Best of all, there wasn't any art around—there was the really raw stuff (by the Americans) of movies, circus, vaudeville, parades, etc.; and there was the church music and the recitation of poems (by the Armenians), and the folklore, which consisted mainly of the tales of the incomparable Nassredin Hodja. So there was little to stand between oneself and one's own naked reality and experience of life. I kept flunking in grade school because I would not accept that books could represent life. I insisted on verifying everything for myself, and I found everything wanting. So that's what saved me. The only art I remember from childhood were these rock gardens that certain Americans in my hometown like to build—probably the Germans. These I loved. . . . Then, when I was nineteen, I read Theodore Dreiser's *The Stoic,* and *that* did it. For years and years I did nothing but read. Everything that remotely stank of literature, I read. So that when I began writing poetry at the age of 35, I had all the experience and reading I would need for my purposes." [From an article entitled, ''An Interview with David Kherdian,'' by Ara Baliozian, *The Armenian Post,* January 12, 1978.]

"I was in on the Poet-In-The-Schools program about the time it began. This was in New England (New Hampshire) and the year was 1971, I believe.

"Poetry had been spoiled for me in the grades, and when I began entering the classrooms and talking to the teachers I had the eerie sensation that I was being taken back in time: the same stupidity and insolence on the part of the teachers and principals, the same prison atmosphere, the same tubercular smell; and, of course, the same unhappy students. And the teachers in the grades didn't seem to know any more about poetry now then they did when I was in school back in the 30's and 40's. There weren't any good books, and that was a big part of the problem. The contemporary anthologies were puerile, and the ancient tomes (virtually the same books I was taught from) were full of the most incredible sing-song, ding-dong poetry imaginable.

"It was this that caused me to become an anthologist. I wanted to give the children something good to read.

"The anthologies I have compiled so far run the gamut: *The Dog Writes on the Window with His Nose and Other Poems* (ages five—eight); *If Dragon Flies Made Honey* (ages six—nine); *Poems Here and Now* (roughly fifth grade through junior high); and the trilogy for Macmillan: *Visions of America by the Poets of Our Time; Settling America: The Ethnic Expression of Fourteen Contemporary Poets,* and *Traveling America with Today's Poets* as well as *I Sing the Song of Myself.* These are for all ages, and have been used in college as well as high school courses.

"Above all, what I wanted to do was make my anthologies from the poems of living American poets. A collection of my own poems for children, *Country Cat, City Cat,* may be the culmination of my work in this field—that is, living poetry by living poets for living children. I hope the reputation of poetry has been helped, and the poor, beleaguered American poem has been served."

HOBBIES AND OTHER INTERESTS: Trout fishing.

FOR MORE INFORMATION SEE: Fresno Bee, September 2, 1962, July, 26, 1964, April 16, 1966; *Booklover's Answer,* September-October, 1963; *Racine Journal Times,* May 19, 1967, July 14, 1971; *The New Mexican,* March 5, 1968, July 28, 1968; *Hoosharar,* December 1, 1970; *The Armenian-Mirror Spectator,* February 6, 1971, July 24, 1971; *Boston Herald Traveler,* March 1, 1972; Moses Yanes, *The Visit,* COF Press, 1974; Carolyn Riley, editor, *Contemporary Literary Criticism,* Volume VI, Gale, 1976; *Poet and Critic,* Volume 9, Number 1, 1975; *The Armenian Post,* January 12, 1978.

LAND, Barbara (Neblett) 1923-

PERSONAL: Born July 11, 1923, in Hopkinsville, Ky.; daughter of Robert Trawick and Jacqueline (Barbour) Neblett; married Myrick Ebben Land (a writer, editor, and teacher), February 26, 1949; children: Robert Arthur, Jacquelyn Myrick (Mrs. Pierre LaRamee). *Education:* University of Miami, B.A., 1944; Columbia University, M.S., 1946, further study, 1959. *Politics:* Democrat. *Religion:* Episcopalian. *Home:* 100 North Arlington Ave., Reno, Nev. 89501. *Agent:* Sterling Lord Agency, 660 Madison Ave., New York, N.Y. 10021.

CAREER: Miami Herald, Miami, Fla., reporter, 1940-47; *Life* magazine, New York City, reporter, 1948-49; *New York Times,* New York City, reporter, 1955-57; Columbia University, Graduate School of Journalism, instructor in journalism, 1962-63, lecturer, 1963-65; Book-of-the-Month Club, New York City, reader and editor, 1969-72; University of Queensland, Brisbane, Australia, tutor in journalism, 1973-75; full-time writer, 1975—. Conducted a series of in-

BARBARA LAND

terviews with scientists for Columbia University Oral History collection, 1960-65. Gave broadcasts for Australian Broadcasting Corp., Armed Forces Network (Germany), and Municipal Broadcasting. *Member:* Authors Guild. *Awards, honors:* Pulitzer travel scholarship, 1946; Sloan-Rockefeller fellowship for advanced science writing program at Columbia University, 1959.

WRITINGS—Juvenile: (With husband, Myrick Land) *Jungle Oil,* Coward, 1957; (with M. Land) *The Changing South,* Coward, 1958; (with M. Land) *The Quest of Isaac Newton,* Doubleday, 1960; *The Quest of Johannes Kepler,* Doubleday, 1963; (with M. Land and Robert Oswald) *Lee: A Portrait of Lee Harvey Oswald,* Coward, 1967; *The Telescope Makers,* Crowell, 1968; *Evolution of a Scientist,* Crowell, 1973.

WORK IN PROGRESS: Women of the Antarctic.

SIDELIGHTS: "My father always told me, when I was a child, 'You can do anything you really want to do. Just make up your mind and *do* it.'

"Not quite believing it could be that easy for a girl, I used to test him with questions about unlikely activities.

    'Could I be a doctor?'
    'Of course.'
    'A fireman?'
    'If you want to.'

'Could I go to the moon?'
'If anybody can.'
'Well, how about being . . . a football player?'

"I never really wanted to be a football player, but I did want to go to the South Pole with Admiral Richard E. Byrd. He had taken a Boy Scout with him in 1928. By 1933, when I was old enough to read about Byrd's adventures in the Antarctic, it seemed to me only fair that a girl should be included next time around. It didn't work out that way, but nearly thirty years later I interviewed Byrd's Boy Scout for *Science World* magazine. He had grown up to be Dr. Paul Siple, leader of the team of scientists who manned the first permanent research station at the very bottom of the world. As he described to me the all-male world of Antarctic science, I felt again my childhood fascination with ice and snow—anything polar. Still, it seemed unlikely that I—or any other woman of my generation—would be allowed to work at the South Pole. I was wrong. All over the world there were women, in various fields of science, determined to show that they could survive the hostile Antarctic climate and make valuable contributions. Some of these women are working in Antarctica right now—but only since 1969. I am currently talking with them and writing about their experiences. I remember my father's encouraging words, now repeated by my husband and children, and am still trying to visit Antarctica myself."

LANG, Andrew 1844-1912
(A. Hugh Longway)

PERSONAL: Born March 31, 1844, in Selkirk, Scotland; died July 20, 1912, in Banchory, Aberdeenshire, Scotland; son of John (a county sheriff-clerk) and Jane Plenderleath (Sellar) Lang; married Lenora Blanche Alleyne, 1875. *Education:* Attended St. Andrews University and University of Glasgow, 1861-63; graduated from Balliol College, Oxford (first in classics), 1868. *Home:* Kensington, London, England.

CAREER: Journalist, historian, and poet. Oxford University, Merton College, fellow, 1868-75; began journalism career, 1875. *Member:* Royal British Academy (fellow), Society for Psychical Research (founder; president, 1911), Athenaeum Club. *Awards, honors:* LL.D., St. Andrews University, 1888, Oxford University, 1904.

WRITINGS—Fiction: *The Princess Nobody: A Tale of Fairy Land* (illustrated by Richard Doyle), Longmans, Green, 1884; (under pseudonym A. Hugh Longway) *Much Darker Days,* Longmans, Green, 1884; (with May Kendall) *That Very Mab,* Longmans, Green, 1885; *In the Wrong Paradise, and Other Stories,* K. Paul, Trench, 1886; *The Mark of Cain,* J. W. Arrowsmith, 1886, reissued, Folcroft, 1973; *The Gold of Fairnilee* (illustrated by E. A. Lemann), J. W. Arrowsmith, 1888, reissued as the title story of a collection of tales, Gollancz, 1967; *Prince Prigio* (illustrated by Gordon F. Browne), J. W. Arrowsmith, 1889, reissued with *Prince Ricardo,* Dutton, 1961 [another edition illustrated by Robert Lawson, Little, Brown, 1942]; *Old Friends: Essays in Epistolary Parody,* Longmans, Green, 1890, reprinted, AMS Press, 1970; (with Henry Rider Haggard) *The World's Desire,* Longmans, Green, 1890, reissued, Ballantine, 1972; *Prince Ricardo of Pantouflia* (illustrated by G. F. Browne), Longmans, Green, 1893, reissued with *Prince Prigio,* Dutton, 1961; *My Own Fairy Book* (illustrated by G. F. Browne, T. Scott, and E. A. Lemann), Longmans, Green, 1895; *A Monk of Fife: A Romance of*

ANDREW LANG

the Days of Jeanne d'Arc, Longmans, Green, 1895, reprinted, AMS Press, 1968; (with Alfred Edward Woodley Mason) *Parson Kelly,* Longmans, Green, 1900; *The Disentanglers,* Longmans, Green, 1901, reprinted, AMS Press, 1970. Supposed author, with others, of *Bess, He, It,* and *King Solomon's Wives* (parodies on H. R. Haggard's novels), all published by N. L. Munro, 1887.

Poems: *Ballads and Lyrics of Old France, with Other Poems,* Longmans, Green, 1872; *XXII Ballades in Blue China,* Kegan Paul, 1880; *XXII and X: XXXII Ballades in Blue China,* Kegan Paul, 1881; *Helen of Troy,* G. Bell, 1882; *Ballades and Verses Vain,* Scribner, 1884; *Rhymes a la Mode,* Kegan Paul, 1885; *Grass of Parnassus: Rhymes Old and New,* Longmans, Green, 1888; *Ban and Arriere Ban: A Rally of Fugitive Rhymes,* Longmans, Green, 1894; *New Collected Rhymes,* Longmans, Green, 1905.

Anthropology, mythology, and occult: *Custom and Myth,* Longmans, Green, 1884, revised, 1885, reprinted, EP Publishing, 1974; *Myth, Ritual, and Religion,* two volumes, Longmans, Green, 1887, reissued, AMS Press, 1968; *Cock Lane and Common-Sense,* Longmans, Green, 1894, reprinted, AMS Press, 1970; *Modern Mythology,* Longmans, Green, 1897, reissued, AMS Press, 1968; *The Book of Dreams and Ghosts,* Longmans, Green, 1897, reprinted, Causeway, 1974; *The Making of Religion,* Longmans, Green, 1898, reprinted, AMS Press, 1968; *Magic and Religion,* Longmans, Green, 1901, reprinted, AMS Press, 1971; *Social Origins,* Longmans, Green, 1903; *The Secret of the Totem,* Longmans, Green, 1905, reprinted, AMS Press, 1970; *The Clyde Mystery: A Study in Forgeries and Folklore,* J. MacLehose, 1905.

Biographies: *Life, Letters, and Diaries of Sir Stafford Northcote,* W. Blackwood, 1890; *The Life and Letters of John Gibson Lockhart,* Scribner, 1897, reprinted, AMS Press, 1970; *Prince Charles Edward,* Goupil, 1900, reissued, AMS Press, 1967; *Alfred Tennyson,* Dodd, 1901, reprinted, Richard West, 1973; *John Knox and the Reformation,* Longmans, Green, 1905, reprinted, Kennikat, 1967; *Sir Walter Scott,* Scribner, 1906, reprinted, Richard West, 1973; (for children) *The Story of Joan of Arc,* Dutton, 1906; *The Maid of France, being the Story of the Life and Death of Jeanne d'Arc,* Longmans, Green, 1908; *Sir George Mackenzie: King's Advocate of Rosehaugh,* Longmans, Green, 1909.

History and travel: *Oxford: Brief Historical and Descriptive Notes,* Seeley Service, 1882; *St. Andrews* (illustrated by T. Hodge), Longmans, Green, 1893; *Pickle the Spy; or, The Incognito of Prince Charles,* Longmans, Green, 1897, reprinted, AMS Press, 1970; *The Companions of Pickle,* Longmans, Green, 1898; *A History of Scotland from the Roman Occupation,* four volumes, W. Blackwood, 1900-07, reprinted, AMS Press, 1970; *The Mystery of Mary Stuart,* Longmans, Green, 1901, reprinted, AMS Press, 1970; *James VI and the Gowrie Mystery,* Longmans, Green, 1902; *The Valet's Tragedy and Other Studies,* Longmans, Green, 1903, reprinted, AMS Press, 1970; *Historical Mysteries,* Smith, Elder, 1904; *Portraits and Jewels of Mary Stuart,* J. MacLehose, 1906; *A Short History of Scotland,* W. Blackwood, 1911; (with John Lang) *Highways and Byways in the Border* (illustrated by Hugh Thomson), Macmillan, 1912.

Literature and criticism: *The Library,* [London], 1876, reissued, Folcroft, 1973; *Letters to Dead Authors,* Scribner, 1886, reprinted, Richard West, 1973; *Books and Bookmen,* G. J. Coombes, 1886, reprinted, AMS Press, 1970; *Letters on Literature,* Longmans, Green, 1880, reissued, Folcroft, 1973; *Lost Leaders,* Longmans, Green, 1889; *How to Fail*

Once upon a time there lived a King and Queen who loved each other so much they were never happy unless they were together. ■ (From *Red Fairy Book,* edited by Andrew Lang. Illustrated by Marc Simont.)

Now in the next kingdom everything was as different as it could possibly be. The King was sulky and savage, and never enjoyed himself at all. ■ (From *Red Fairy Book,* edited by Andrew Lang. Illustrated by Marc Simont.)

in Literature, Field & Tuer, 1890, reprinted, AMS Press, 1970; *Essays in Little,* Henry & Co., 1891, reprinted, AMS Press, 1968; *Homer and the Epic,* Longmans, Green, 1893, reprinted, AMS Press, 1970; *Adventures among Books,* Longmans, Green, 1905, reprinted, Books for Libraries, 1970; *The Puzzle of Dickens' Last Plot,* Chapman & Hall, 1905, reprinted, Richard West, 1973; *Homer and His Age,* Longmans, Green, 1906; *La Jeanne d'Arc de M. Anatole France* (a criticism of France's *La Vie de Jeanne d'Arc*), [Paris], 1909; *The World of Homer,* Longmans, Green, 1910, reissued, Folcroft, 1973; *Sir Walter Scott and the Border Minstrelsy,* Longmans, Green, 1910, reprinted, AMS Press, 1968; *History of English Literature from "Beowulf" to Swinburne,* Longmans, Green, 1912, reprinted, AMS Press, 1969; *Shakespeare, Bacon, and the Great Unknown,* Longmans, Green, 1912, reprinted, AMS Press, 1968.

Other: (With William Ernst Henley) *Pictures at Play; or, Dialogues of the Galleries* (illustrated by Harry Furniss), Longmans, Green, 1888, reprinted, AMS Press, 1970; *Angling Sketches* (illustrated by William G. Burn-Murdoch), Longmans, Green, 1891.

Contributor: R. Barclay, editor, *A Batch of Golfing Papers,* Simpkin, Marshall, 1892; Allan G. Steel, *Cricket,* Longmans, Green, 1890; Hedley Peck, *The Poetry of Sports,* Longmans, Green, 1896; Horace G. Hutchinson, *Famous Golf Links,* Longmans, Green, 1891; Peter H. Brown, *The Union of 1707: A Survey of Events,* G. Outram, 1907.

Editor: *English Worthies,* nine volumes, Longmans, Green, 1885-87; *Ballads of Books,* Longmans, Green, 1888, reissued, Folcroft, 1973; Charles Perrault, *Perrault's Popular Tales,* Clarendon Press, 1888; *The Blue Fairy Book* (illustrated by Henry Justice Ford and George Percy Jacomb-Hood), Longmans, Green, 1889, reissued, McGraw, 1966 [other editions illustrated by Manning De Villeneuve Lee, Macrae Smith, 1926; Frederick Richardson, John C. Win-

With such eagerness she danced! ■ (From *The Twelve Dancing Princesses* by Andrew Lang. Illustrated by Adrienne Adams.)

ston, 1930; Ben Kutcher, Longmans, Green, 1948; Reisie Lonette, Looking Glass Library, 1959]; *The Red Fairy Book* (illustrated by H. J. Ford and Lancelot Speed), Longmans, Green, 1890, reissued, McGraw, 1967 [other editions illustrated by Gustaf Tenggren, McKay, 1924; M. De V. Lee, Macrae Smith, 1927; F. Richardson, John C. Winston, 1930; Marc Simont, Longmans, Green, 1948; R. Lonette, Looking Glass Library, 1960].

The Blue Poetry Book (illustrated by H. J. Ford and L. Speed), Longmans, Green, 1891, reissued, Folcroft, 1973; *The Green Fairy Book* (illustrated by H. J. Ford), Longmans, Green, 1892, reissued, Dover, 1965 [another edition illustrated by R. Lonette, Looking Glass Library, 1960]; *The True Story Book* (illustrated by L. Bogle, Lucien Davis, and others), Longmans, Green, 1893; *The Yellow Fairy Book* (illustrated by H. J. Ford), Longmans, Green, 1894, reissued, McGraw, 1967 [another edition illustrated by Janice Holland, Longmans, Green, 1948]; *The Red True Story Book* (illustrated by H. J. Ford), Longmans, Green, 1895; Sir Walter Scott, *Poetical Works*, A. & C. Black, 1895; *The Animal Story Book* (illustrated by H. J. Ford), Longmans, Green, 1896; *The Blue True Story Book* (illustrated by H. J. Ford, L. Davis, and others), Longmans, Green, 1896; Robert Burns, *The Poems and Songs of Robert Burns*, Methuen, 1896; Izaak Walton, *The Compleat Angler*, Dent, 1896; *A Collection of Ballads*, Chapman & Hall, 1897; *The Pink Fairy Book* (illustrated by H. J. Ford), Longmans, Green, 1897, reissued, Dover, 1967; *The Nursery Rhyme Book* (illustrated by L. Leslie Brooke), Warne, 1897, reissued, Dover, 1972; *The Arabian Nights Entertainments*, Longmans, Green, 1898, reissued, Books for Libraries, 1969; *The Red Book of Animal Stories*, Longmans, Green, 1899, reissued, Tuttle, 1972.

The Grey Fairy Book (illustrated by H. J. Ford), Longmans, Green, 1900, reissued, Dover, 1967; *The Violet Fairy Book* (illustrated by H. J. Ford), Longmans, Green, 1901, reissued, McGraw, 1967; *The Book of Romance* (illustrated by H. J. Ford), Longmans, Green, 1902; *The Crimson Fairy Book* (illustrated by H. J. Ford), Longmans, Green, 1903, reissued, Dover, 1967 [another edition illustrated by B. Kutcher, Longmans, Green, 1947]; *The Brown Fairy Book* (illustrated by H. J. Ford), Longmans, Green, 1904, reissued, McGraw, 1966; *The Red Romance Book* (illustrated by H. J. Ford), Longmans, Green, 1905; *The*

Orange Fairy Book (illustrated by H. J. Ford), Longmans, Green, 1906, reissued, Dover, 1968 [another edition illustrated by Christine Price, Longmans, Green, 1949]; *The Olive Fairy Book* (illustrated by H. J. Ford), Longmans, Green, 1907, reissued, Dover, 1968; *Poets Country* (illustrated by Francis S. Walker), T. C. & E. C. Jack, 1907; *Tales of a Fairy Court* (illustrated by Arthur A. Dixon), Collins, 1907; *Tales of Troy and Greece* (illustrated by H. J. Ford), Longmans, Green, 1907, new edition illustrated by Edward Bawden, Faber, 1968; Jean Ingelow, *Poems*, Longmans, Green, 1908; Lenora B. Lang (his wife), *The Book of Princes and Princesses*, Longmans, Green, 1908; L. B. Lang, *The Red Book of Heroes*, Longmans, Green, 1909.

The Lilac Fairy Book (illustrated by H. J. Ford), Longmans, Green, 1910, reissued, Dover, 1968; L. B. Lang, *All Sorts of Stories*, Longmans, Green, 1911; L. B. Lang, *The Book of Saints and Heroes* (illustrated by H. J. Ford), Longmans, Green, 1912; James Annesley, *The Annesley Case*, W. Hodge, 1913; L. B. Lang, *The Strange Story Book*, Longmans, Green, 1913; J. B. Poquelin de Moliere, *Moliere's Les Precieuses Ridicules*, second edition, Clarendon Press, 1926.

Selected tales from books edited by A. Lang: *Rose Fairy Book* (illustrated by Vera Bock), Longmans, Green, 1951; *The Adventures of Odysseus* (illustrated by Joan Kiddell-Monroe), Dutton, 1962; *Fifty Favourite Fairy Tales* (edited by Kathleen Lines; illustrated by Margery Gill), Nonesuch Press, 1963, published in America as *Fifty Favorite Fairy Tales*, F. Watts, 1964; *The Twelve Dancing Princesses* (illustrated by Adrienne Adams), Holt, 1966; *Little Red Riding Hood* (illustrated by Jean Winslow), Golden Press, 1967; *More Favorite Fairy Tales* (edited by K. Lines; illustrated by M. Gill), F. Watts, 1967; *Read Me Another Fairy Tale* (illustrated by Wallace Tripp), Grosset, 1967; *The Story of Robin Hood, and Other Tales of Adventure and Battle* (illustrated by H. J. Ford), Schocken Books, 1968; *King Arthur: Tales of the Round Table* (illustrated by Charles Mozley), large type edition, F. Watts, 1968; *To Your Good Health: A Russian Folk Tale* (illustrated by Mehli Gobhai), Holiday House, 1973.

Translator: (With Samuel Henry Butcher) Homer, *The Odyssey*, Macmillan, 1879, reissued, 1966; Theocritus, *Theocritus, Bion, and Moschus*, Macmillan, 1880; (with Walter Leaf and Ernest Myers) Homer, *The Iliad of Homer*, Macmillan, 1883, reissued, Modern Library, 1968; *Aucassin and Nicolette*, David Nutt, 1887, new edition published as *The Song-Story of Aucassin and Nicolette* (illustrated by Fritz Kredel), Gravesend Press, 1957; Charles Deulin, *Johnny Nut and the Golden Geese*, Longmans, Green, 1887; (with Paul Sylvester) *The Dead Leman and Other Tales from the French*, second edition, Swan, Sonnenschein, 1889; *The Miracles of Madame Saint Katherine of Fierbois*, Way & Williams, 1897; Homer, *The Homeric Hymns*, G. Allen, 1899, reprinted, Books for Libraries, 1972.

ADAPTATIONS—Plays: Paul T. Nolan, *A Groom for the Loveliest Mouse* (one-act), Edgemoor, 1971.

Recordings: "Snow-White and Rose-Red," read by Glynis Johns, music by Dick Hyman, Caedmon Records, 1973; "Princess Rosette" (tape cassette), Spoken Arts, 1974; "Little Wildrose and Other Andrew Lang Fairy Tales," read by Cathleen Nesbitt, Caedmon Records, 1974.

The Lion and the unicorn
Were fighting for the crown;
The lion beat the unicorn
All around the town.

■ (From *The Nursery Rhyme Book*, edited by Andrew Lang. Illustrated by L. Leslie Brooke.)

SIDELIGHTS: **March 31, 1844.** Born at Selkirk, a Scottish border country. "It was worth while to be a boy then in the south of Scotland and to fish the waters haunted by old legends, musical with old songs. . . . Memory brings vividly back the golden summer evenings by Tweedside, when the trout began to plash in the stillness—brings back the long, lounging solitary days beneath the woods of Ashiesteil—days so lonely that they sometimes, in the end, begat a superstititous eeriness. One seemed forsaken in an enchanted world; one might see the two white fairy deer flit by, bringing to us, as to Thomas the Rhymer, the tidings that we must back to Fairyland.

"A boy of five is more at home in Fairyland than in his own country.

"The majority of dwellers on the Border are born to be fishers. Like the rest of us in that country, I was born an angler, though under an evil star, for, indeed, my labours have not been blessed, and are devoted to fishing rather than to the catching of fish. . . . My first recollection of the sport must date from about the age of four—the sunlight on a shining bend of a highland stream, and my father, standing in the shallow water, showing me a huge yellow fish.

". . . I see myself, with a crowd of other little children, sent to fish with crooked pins, for minnows . . . the parr disdained our baits, and for months I dreamed of what it would have been to capture him, and often thought of him in church. In a moment of profane confidence my younger brother once asked me: 'What do *you* do in sermon time? I 'said he in a whisper—' mind you don't tell—*I* tell stories to myself about catching trout.' To which I added a similar confession, for even so I drove the sermon by.

"Beyond a strong opinion that I should be a 'goat' at the Last Day, I can remember no religious speculations of my own. The idea of the Deity made little impression; the Shorter Catechism, which had to be learnt by heart, seemed meaningless, and did not even excite curiosity. . . .

Taffy was a Welshman, Taffy was a thief; Taffy came to my house and stole a piece of beef.
■ (From *The Nursery Rhyme Book,* edited by Andrew Lang. Illustrated by L. Leslie Brooke.)

I do remember thinking that the Angels who made love to the daughters of men, were the gods—Apollo and Zeus and Hermes—under another name. One's infant reason was mythological, not theological in bias.

"... I read every fairy tale I could lay my hands on. ... my first memories of romance. One story of a White Serpent, with a wood-cut of that mysterious reptile, I neglected to secure, probably for want of a penny, and I have regretted it ever since." [Roger Lancelyn Green, *Andrew Lang,* Bodley Head (London), 1962.[1]]

Apart from reading, Lang engaged in another border sport favorite, cricket. "The first time I ever saw ball and bat must have been about 1850. The gardener's boy and his friends were playing with home-made bats, made out of firwood with the bark on, and with a gutta-percha ball. The game instantly fascinated me."[1] This skill soon failed him, owing to ill-health and defective eyesight.

Day-boy at Selkirk Grammar School.

1854. Edinburgh Academy, living for his first two years "a rather lonely small boy in the house of an aged relation."[1] Spent most of his time living "like a young hermit" in the world of books, reading Scott, Dickens, Lever, Dumas, Ariosto, Byron, Pope, and Longfellow and then: "I tried Tennyson, and instantly a new light of poetry dawned, a

Deedle, deedle, dumpling, my son John
Went to bed with his trousers on;
One shoe off, the other shoe on,
Deedle, deedle, dumpling, my son John.
▪ (From *The Nursery Rhyme Book,* edited by Andrew Lang. Illustrated by L. Leslie Brooke.)

new music was audible, a new god came into my medley of a Pantheon, a god never to be dethroned."[1]

1856. Moved into the house of schoolmaster D'Arcy Wentworth Thompson. "One can never say how much one owes to a schoolmaster who was a friend of literature, who kept a house full of books, and was himself a graceful scholar and an author.

"As a humble student of savage life, I have found it necessary to make researches into the manners and customs of boys. If you meet them in the holidays, you find them affable and full of kindness and good qualities. . . . But boys at school and among themselves, left to the wild justice and traditional laws which many generations of boys have evolved, are entirely different beings. [For example:] Tall stools were piled up in a pyramid, and the victim was seated on top, near the roof of the room. The other savages brought him down from this bad eminence by hurling other stools at those which supported him."[1]

Detesting the classical subjects at first, he wrote: "I hated Greek with a deadly and sickening hatred; I hated it like a bully and a thief of time. . . ."[1]

Homer awakened Lang's intellectual energies and aspirations toward an academic career. "From the very first words, in which the Muse is asked to sing the wrath of Achilles, Peleus' son, my mind was altered, and I was the devoted friend of Greek. Here was something worth reading about; here one knew where one was; here was the music of words, here were poetry, pleasure and life. . . . The very sound of the hexameter, that long, inimitable roll of the most various music, was enough to win the heart, even if the words were not understood, full as they are of all nobility, all tenderness, all courage, courtesy and romance. The *Morte d'Arthur* itself, which about this time fell into our hands, was not so dear as the *Odyssey*."[1]

November, 1861. Entered the University of St. Andrews into the residence at St. Leonard's Hall. "With St. Andrews it was a case of love at first sight, as soon as I found myself under the grey sky, and beheld the white flame of the breakers chasing over the brown wet barrier of the pier. [It was] the happiest time of my life, ever dear and sacred in memory."[1]

With friend, Allan Menzies, founded *The St. Leonard's Magazine.* "I was the editor and usually wrote two-thirds or more of the *Magazine* on Friday night by the glimmer of stolen candle-ends."[1] In 1863, the University produced a properly printed magazine to which Lang contributed.

1864. Elected to a Snell Exhibition (the most coveted of classical scholarships to Oxford) at the University of Glasgow. ". . . Was nearly dead after a winter at Glasgow University, the Head [H. H. Almond] very kindly allowed me to come to Loretto for the summer term to read Greek with Mr. Beilby, fresh from Cambridge."[1]

January, 1865. Entered Oxford. "How fair Oxford seemed after the black quadrangle and heavy air of Glasgow . . . in one of October's crystal days with the elms not yet stripped of their gold, and with the crimson pall of red leaves swathing the tower of Magdalen, Oxford looks almost as beautiful as in the pomp of spring.

"What is learned of literature, at Oxford, is learned from reading the best literature, that of Greece and Rome, and

from reading for human pleasure, there *is* no other way. Schools of literature, examinations and all, ought to be abolished."[1]

In a light-hearted letter to his little cousin, Adele Sellar, Lang wrote: "[I'm writing] because I had no novels or books, and Latin and Greek History and Philosophy, Logic and Metaphysics, Politics and other extras, give me a headache—so you can't expect me to have anything to say."[1] Ending the letter with an account of how to understand Hegel. "You begin by thinking of *nothing* for a long time, till you're quite sure you grasp the situation, and then you think of *something*, only it must not be anything in particular, and gradually you see that something and nothing are both the same, and there you are!"[1]

1869. Won the Open Fellowship to Merton College.

September, 1869. His parents died within two days of one another.

Autumn, 1872. Health broke down alarmingly. Fled to Mentone on the Riviera suffering from acute lung trouble.

1874. Friendship with Robert Louis Stevenson, also "ordered south" for health reasons.

Decided to leave Oxford upon the termination of his Fellowship. "Unfortunately, life at Oxford is not all beauty and pleasure. Things go wrong somehow. Life drops her happy mask.

"Oxford, that once seemed a pleasant porch and entrance into life, may become a dingy ante-room, where we kick our heels with other weary, waiting people. At last, if men linger there too late, Oxford grows a prison. . . . It is well to leave the enchantress betimes, and to carry away few but kind recollections.

> "Because within a fair forsaken place
> The life that might have been is lost to thee."[1]

April 17, 1875. Married Leonora Blanche Alleyne. Set up housekeeping in Kensington which remained their home for the rest of Lang's life, though part of his later winters were spent at St. Andrews on account of his health.

For almost forty years Lang was to pursue a journalistic career. He contributed leaders to the *Daily News,* literary articles to the *Morning Post,* and other papers, reviewed for *The Academy,* and wrote monthly topical paragraphs for *Longman's Magazine* under the title, "At the Sign of the Ship."

Wrote on a variety of subjects for the ninth edition of the *Encyclopedia Britannica,* the articles ranging from ghosts to crystal-gazing.

January, 1879. Completed the prose translation of the *Odyssey* in collaboration with S. H. Butcher.

1883. *Iliad* appeared in collaboration with Walter Leaf and Ernest Myers.

As an accomplished critic, he wrote: "Writing about contemporary books is the merest journalism. It is pleasant to praise what one thinks good, and to our deeply fallen nature it is not always unpleasant to blame what one thinks bad;

THE FAITHFUL SERVANT & THE THREE EAGLES

(From *The Crimson Fairy Book*, edited by Andrew Lang. Illustrated by H.J. Ford.)

The Princess Gets Her Letter

(From *The Olive Fairy Book,* edited by Andrew Lang. Illustrated by H.J. Ford.)

but to be literature, writing about books ought to deal with classics—Homer, Moliere, Shakespeare, Fielding, and so on.''[1]

1889. *The Blue Fairy Book* published. In reading and arranging the contents, he experienced, ''perhaps, as much pleasure as the child who reads them or hears them for the first time . . . I still tremble for Puss in Boots when the Ogre turns into a lion; and still one's heart goes with the girl who seeks her lost and enchanted lover, and wins him again in the third night of watching and of tears.

''This collection, made for the pleasure of children and without scientific purpose, includes nursery tales which have a purely literary origin.''[1]

In the introduction to *The Blue Fairy Book,* he wrote: ''When the Princess awakens, after her betrothal to the Yellow Dwarf, and hopes it was a dream, and finds on her finger the fatal ring of one red hair, we have a brave touch of horror and of truth. All of us have wakened and struggled with a dim evil memory, and trusted it was a dream, and found, in one form or other, a proof, a shape of that ring of red hair.''[1]

Reviewing refined attempts at ''modern'' fairy tales, he wrote: ''In the old stories, despite the impossibility of the

incidents, the interest is always real and human. The princes and princesses fall in love and marry—nothing could be more human than that. Their lives and loves are crossed by human sorrows. In many the lover and his lady are separated by a magic oblivion: someone has kissed the prince, and he instantly forgets his old love, and can only be recovered by her devotion. This is nearly the central situation of the Volsunga Saga, though there it ends tragically, whereas all ends well in a fairy tale. The hero and heroine are persecuted or separated by cruel stepmothers or enchanters; they have wanderings and sorrows to suffer; they have adventures to achieve and difficulties to overcome. They must display courage, loyalty and address, courtesy, gentleness and gratitude. Thus they are living in a real human world, though it wears a mythical face, though there are giants and lions in the way. The old fairy tales which a silly sort of people disparage as too wicked and ferocious for the nursery, are really 'full of matter,' and unobtrusively teach the true lessons of our way-faring in a world of perplexities and obstructions.''[1]

1890. *The Red Fairy Book* published. ''The best of all were naturally selected for the earlier volume . . . in a second gleaning of the fields of Fairy Land we cannot expect to find a second Perrault. But there are good stories enough left and it is hoped that some in the *Red Fairy Book* may have the attraction of being less familiar than many of the old friends.''[1]

1892. *The Green Fairy Book* appeared. ''First there was the *Blue Fairy Book;* then, children, you asked for more, and we made up the *Red Fairy Book;* and when you wanted more still, the *Green Fairy Book* was put together. . . . If we have a book for you next year, it shall not be a fairy book.''[1]

Old King Cole
Was a merry old soul,
And a merry old soul was he;
He called for his pipe,
And he called for his bowl,
And he called for his fiddlers three.

■ (From *The Nursery Rhyme Book,* edited by Andrew Lang. Illustrated by L. Leslie Brooke.)

The True Story Book appeared the following year.

Of his Fairy Book collections, Lang confesses that: "My part has been that of Adam, according to Mark Twain, in the Garden of Eden. Eve worked, Adam superintended. . . . I find out where the stories are, and advise, and, in short, superintend. *I do not write the stories out of my own head*. The reputation of having written all the fairy books (a European reputation in nurseries and the United States of America) is 'the burden of an honour unto which I was not born.' Nobody can write a *new* fairy tale; you can only mix up and dress up the old, old stories, and put the characters into new dresses."[1]

After 1900 Lang showed less and less interest in contemporary literature. His journalism became tired and faded, yet, unfortunately he still needed to write his weekly articles in *The Morning Post* and *The Illustrated London News* for financial reasons. "If Nora died tomorrow, and I were unemployed, my finances would be, after all these thirty-five years, where they were when I was twenty-four. I have not made friends of the Mammons of any sort, and am of little use to other anti-Mammonites."[1]

A History of English Literature published two days after his death, he described as "that intolerable and grievous labour, undertaken only for money—I'd have written as much for nothing about Homer."[1]

Out of his last years one clear picture of Lang has been preserved by his friend Alice King Stewart with whom he used to stay on his way to or from St. Andrews. "Andrew Lang was tall but inclined to stoop, with a rather slight figure. He was very active for his years. In my mind's eye I see him slouching easily along with his hands in his pockets, but I think that this attitude was to get a better view of things as he walked along. He was supposed not to have the use of one eye, and in the other he wore an unmounted monocle, which always seemed to be popping in and out and was only restrained from loss by a black elastic cord. Certainly with his one good eye he saw more than most people with two. His eyes were dark brown, matching his moustache. He had a fine intellectual head, sometimes held rather to one side when looking at objects, partly because of the blind eye. His hair never looked as if it had recently seen a barber, and the brindled locks, which Robert Louis Stevenson described, were white when I knew him. . . .

"His voice was high-pitched, rather thin in quality, and he had a slight burr in pronouncing the letter 'R.' He had a habit of cutting short his sentences and moving on to an entirely different topic and, as he was also apt to murmur his words into his moustache, one had to be alert in following his talk. . . .

"Every year he and Mrs. Lang used to stay with me, and I always found him a most charming guest, easily entertained and interested in such a wonderful variety of subjects. With strangers he was not always easy to amalgamate, especially as so many were either afraid of him or wondered what were suitable subjects of conversation. . . . This was largely caused, not from rudeness, but from the fact that he was naturally a shy man and highly strung, moreover he did not suffer fools gladly. He was really tender-hearted to the last degree, even to the fish dangling on his hook when fishing."[1]

July 20, 1912. Died of angina pectoris at Banchory, Aberdeenshire. "My mind is gay, but my soul is melancholy.

ANDREW LANG

"One gift the fairies gave me: (three
They commonly bestowed of yore)
The love of books, the golden key
That opens the enchanted door."[1]

Greatly averse to all publicity, Lang refused to have any authorized biography published or for his letters to appear after his death. His widow obeyed this request, saying: "My wrists ached for weeks after tearing up Andrew's papers."[1]

FOR MORE INFORMATION SEE: Roger Lancelyn Green, *Andrew Lang: A Critical Biography,* Edmund Ward, 1946; (for children) Elizabeth Rider Montgomery, *Story behind Great Stories,* McBride, 1947; *Concerning Andrew Lang; Being the Andrew Lang Lectures Delivered before the University of St. Andrews, 1927-1937,* Oxford University Press, 1949; James Bell Salmond, *Andrew Lang and Journalism,* Thomas Nelson, 1950; R. L. Green, *Tellers of Tales,* revised edition, F. Watts, 1965; (for children) Laura Benét, *Famous English and American Essayists,* Dodd, 1966; Brian Doyle, editor, *Who's Who of Children's Literature,* Schocken Books, 1968; J. Weintraub, "Andrew Lang: Critic of Romance," *English Literature in Transition,* Number 1, 1975.

LATHAM, Barbara 1896-

PERSONAL: Born June 6, 1896, in Walpole, Mass.; daughter of Allen (a teacher) and Caroline (Walker; a teacher) Latham; married Howard Cook (an artist), May 26, 1927. *Education:* Attended Norwich Art School, Pratt Institute, Art Students League and Andrew Dasburg's Class (Woodstock, N.Y.). *Politics:* Independent. *Religion:* Protestant. *Home:* 250 East Alameda, Apartment 137, Santa Fe, N.M. 87501.

BARBARA LATHAM

CAREER: Artist; illustrator. Norwich Art School, Norwich, Conn., teacher, 1920; Mrs. Josef Hoffmans School for Girls, Aiken, S.C., teacher, 1922; Norcross Publishing Co., New York, N.Y., designer of Christmas cards. *Exhibitions*—One man shows: Weyhe Gallery, New York, N.Y.; Dallas Museum, Dallas, Texas; Witte Memorial Museum, San Antonio, Texas; Sweet Briar College, Virginia; Converse Art Gallery, Norwich, Conn., Amarillo Tri-State Fair, Amarillo, Texas; Santa Fe Museum, Santa Fe, N.M.; Highlands University, Las Vegas, N.M.; Roswell Museum, Roswell, N.M.

Group Shows: Whitney Museum, New York, N.Y.; National Academy of Design, New York, N.Y.; National Arts Club, New York, N.Y.; Association of American Artists; Brooklyn Museum International, Brooklyn, N.Y.; Chicago Museum International, Chicago, Ill.; West of Mississippi Show, Colorado Springs, Colo.; Cedar State Utah State University, Cedar, Utah; Pennsylvania Academy of Fine Arts Water Color Annual; Philadelphia Print Club, Philadelphia, Pa.; Philadelphia Art Alliance, Philadelphia, Pa.; Library of Congress, Washington, D.C.; Carnegie Institute; Los Angeles County Museum, Los Angeles, Calif.; Corcoran Gallery; Pennell; Denver Museum, Denver, Colo.; Mortimer Levitt Gallery, New York, N.Y.; Kennedy Galleries, New York, N.Y.; Rochester Memorial Art Gallery Print Club; American Institute of Graphic Arts, Metropolitan Museum, New York, N.Y.; University of Tulsa, Tulsa,

Okla.; Brooklyn Museum Annual Print Show, Brooklyn, N.Y.

Permanent Collections: Metropolitan Museum, Print Collections, New York, N.Y.; Newark Museum, Newark, N.J.; Philadelphia Museum, Philadelphia, Pa.; Slater Hall Museum, Norwich, Conn.; Library of Congress, Washington, D.C.; Santa Fe Museum, Santa Fe, N.M.; University of Minnesota, St. Paul, Minn.; Tulsa University, Tulsa, Okla.; Roswell Museum, Roswell, N.M.; Archives of American Art, Smithsonian Institute, Washington, D.C.

WRITINGS—Self-illustrated: *Perrito's Pup,* Knopf, 1946.

Illustrator: Lily Duplaix, *Pedro, Nina and Perrito,* Harper, 1939; Janette Lowrey, *The Silver Dollar,* Harper, 1940; Leah Gale, *Hurdy-Gurdy Holiday,* Harper, 1942; Marion Lansing, *Calling South America,* Ginn, 1945; Irma S. Black, *Maggie A Mischievous Magpie,* Holiday House, 1949; *Dusty,* Holiday House, 1950; Mary Adrian, *Honey Bee,* Holiday House, 1952; Jean Fiedler, *The Green Thumb Story,* Holiday House, 1952; Paul M. Sears, *Downy Woodpecker,* Holiday House, 1953; Marion Marcher, *Monarch Butterfly,* Holiday House, 1954; Paul M. Sears, *Tree Frog,* Holiday House, 1954; Stella Sanders, *Flying Horse Shoe Ranch,* Viking, 1955; J. Frank Dobie, *Tales of Old Time Texas,* Little, Brown, 1955; Gladys Conklin, *I Like Caterpillars,* Holiday House, 1958; Gladys Conklin, *I Like Butterflies,* Holiday House, 1960; Jean Lee Latham, *The Frightened Hero,* Chilton, 1965. Has illustrated several textbooks for Ginn. Illustrations have also appeared in *Art Digest, Forum, McCall's, Horn Book,* and many newspapers.

SIDELIGHTS: "The illustrations for *Hurdy-Gurdy Holiday* were the most fun to do. I was sent up to the Bronx Zoo to find a suitable monkey. The keeper brought me Jimmy and shut us both up in a small supply room. Jimmy was

(From *Hurdy-Gurdy Holiday* by Leah Gale. Illustrated by Barbara Latham.)

locked in a cage which he promptly unlocked. Then he climbed onto my shoulder, unwrapped my turban-like hat and began to pull down my hair. I managed to get the door open a crack and called the keeper who came in with bananas for Jimmy and locked him up more securely. But he reached through the wire cage and grabbed my pencil which apparently tasted better than the bananas. I started with another pencil but as soon as he realized that I was drawing him, he rested his folded arms on his knees and hid his head only peeking out with one eye. I tried to distract him by putting my foot against the cage, then he reached out and chewed a piece of the rubber sole of my shoe. So I got the keeper again to bring some very special goodies which interested Jimmy.

"I took several trips to the zoo and finally got enough sketches. By this time Jimmy and I were friendly and he sang to me like a little bird when he saw me coming. I knit him a little red suit and cap, but the keeper and I together could never get it on him. Long after when I visited the zoo a little monkey rushed out from all the others and sang his little bird song of welcome.

"The Hurdy-Gurdy Man was also an adventure. I met him on the street but he didn't speak English so I wrote a note with my address asking him to pose for me the next day. His friends explained the note to him and the next day we heard a great deal of noise down the street and then lots of clumping up our eight flights of stairs and very loud singing. He had indulged in a bit of encouragement. But he would never come again so I hunted up his living quarters—actually a bar on Canal Street. I walked in and he invited me to breakfast, a glass of whiskey. After that he kept a friend on watch to warn him when I approached so that he could slip out the back door.

"About the caterpillar and butterfly books, I raised the caterpillars in my studio from eggs either sent by the author or found by me. Each kind of caterpillar lived on a bunch of leaves which they especially liked. They didn't wander off until all the leaves were eaten. The tiger swallowtail wouldn't put out his red horns because he was used to me, but one day I accidentally dropped a pencil on him and out popped the horns with a smell which filled my whole studio. Neither the caterpillars nor the butterflies minded my watching them.

"The magpie in *Maggie a Mischievous Magpie* was our pet for two years. When the puppies were born she was fascinated and wanted to play with them.

"When we had callers, Maggie would watch them and then hop up onto someone's lap and suddenly snatch the cigarette out of their mouth, then hop to the floor and carefully hide it under a corner of the rug or she would carefully lift an ice cube out of a drink and repeat this until she had a little pile of them.

"I am very fond of animals and when in the country am seldom without a small baby animal in one of my pockets. As to the techniques—having been a commercial artist in New York, I am familiar with some processes of reproduction. My books were mostly done in the direct positive process and I did the color separation. This is a lot of work for which an artist gets no extra pay but I found it fascinating and got some excellent results. However, it is a very meticulous process and too much for aging eyes so I gave it up and now paint entirely in oil.

Latham, self-portrait.

FOR MORE INFORMATION SEE: Bertha E. Mahoney and others, compilers *Illustrators of Children's Books: 1744-1945,* Horn Book, 1947; B. M. Miller and others, compilers, *Illustrators of Children's Books: 1946-1956,* Horn Book, 1958.

LEIPOLD, L. Edmond 1902-

PERSONAL: Born August 5, 1902, in Minnesota; son of George August (a businessman) and Emma (Thieling) Leipold; married Gladys Huffman, July 27, 1923; children: Jean (Mrs. Dwayne Mahlberg), L. Edmond, Jr., Darel, Lance. *Education:* St. Cloud State College, student, 1923-24; University of Minnesota, Ph.D., 1942; Harvard University, postdoctoral study, 1943. *Home:* 777 Excelsior Blvd., Excelsior, Minn. 55331.

CAREER: Superintendent of schools in Montgomery, Minn., 1928-36; Nokomis Jr. High School, Minneapolis, Minn., principal, 1942-63; writer, 1963—. Professor at University of Colorado, Greeley, 1947-59, and New Mexico State University, 1961-65. *Member:* Minnesota Association of Secondary Principals (executive secretary, 1965-66), Minneapolis Retired Teachers (president, 1976-77), Retired Gentlemen's Club (Minnetonka, 1973), Excelsior Senior Citizens (president, 1976-77), Scholia Fraternity, Excelsior Club (honorary rotarian, 1978). *Awards, honors:* Distinguished Award Medal, St. Cloud University, 1968; Distinguished Service Award, City of Minneapolis, 1977; Good Neighbor Award, WCCO T.V., 1977.

WRITINGS—All published by Denison—juveniles: *When Our Country Was Very Young,* 1967; *Our Country Grows Up,* 1968; *America Becomes Free,* 1968; *Come Along to*

East Germany, 1968; *Makers of a Better America*, 1969; *Americans Born Abroad*, 1970; *Great American Poets*, 1970; *Folk Tales of England*, 1970; *Folk Tales of Russia*, 1970; *Folk Tales of France*, 1970; *Folk Tales of Italy*, 1970; *Folk Tales of Arabia*, 1970; *Folk Tales of Germany*, 1970; *Folk Tales of Greece*, 1970; *They Gave Their Lives*, 1971; *Great American Artists*, 1971; *Heroes of Today*, 1972; *The Astronauts*, 1972; *Come Along to Luxembourg*, 1972; *Heroes of a Different Kind*, 1973; *Come Along to Saudi Arabia*, 1974.

Adult: *Famous American Musicians*, 1967; *Famous American Women*, 1967; *Famous American Indians*, 1967; *Famous American Founders of Our Cities*, 1967; *William P. Lear: Designer and Inventor*, 1967; *Famous American Heroes in Time of War*, 1967; *Gordon A. Yock: Merchandising Expert*, 1967; *Famous American Engineers*, 1968; *Famous American Negroes*, 1968; *Famous American Fiction Writers*, 1968; *Ronald Reagan: Governor and Statesman*, 1968; *Jeno F. Paulucci: Merchant Philanthropist*, 1968; *Lawrence M. Weitzel: Mechanical Specialist*, 1968; *Famous American Labor Leaders*, 1969; *Famous American Athletes*, 1969; *Famous American Poets*, 1969; *Famous American Artists*, 1969; *Famous American Crusaders for a Cause*, 1969; *Richard M. Nixon: President*, 1969; *Win Stephens: Business and Civic Leader*, 1969; *Cecil E. Newman: Newspaper Publisher*, 1969.

Famous American Founders of Fortunes, Volume I, 1970; *Famous American Founders of Fortunes*, Volume II, 1970; *A Pictorial Biography of the Harold Greenwoods*, 1970; *Harold W. Greenwood: Financier*, 1970; *Famous American Doctors*, 1971; *Famous American Citizens Born Abroad*, 1971; *Famous American Explorers of Our Land*, 1971; *Christiaan Barnard: The Man with the Golden Hands*, 1971; *Eddie Shipstad: Ice Follies Star*, 1971; *Famous American Architects*, 1972; *Famous American Teachers*, 1972; *Famous American Scientists and Astronauts*, 1972; *Charles Lindbergh: Aviation Pioneer*, 1972; *Alton S. Newell: Recycling Expert*, 1973; *Walter M. Ringer: Keeping at It*, 1977; Contributor of about eighty-five articles to education journals.

WORK IN PROGRESS: Personal writings at present.

SIDELIGHTS: "My school experiences, from kindergarten to Harvard University, have always been, to me, thrilling and excitable. My journeys abroad have been fascinating. Every one has been the 'best of all.' When I consider the tremendous changes that have gone on in this world during

During the reign of Caliph Haroun Al-Raschid, most honored of rulers, there lived in Bagdad a poor porter by the name of Sindbad. ■ (From *Folk Tales of Arabia* by L.E. Leipold. Illustrated by Howard E. Lindberg.)

L. EDMOND LEIPOLD

my life time, I can hardly believe it. To have lived through them has been a rewarding experience. Had I shuffled off this mortal coil at an early age, one could hear today moans of regret coming from my tomb. It has been a privilege to write about them. . . .''

LORRAINE, Walter (Henry) 1929-

PERSONAL: Born February 3, 1929, in Worcester, Mass.; married wife, Anita; children: Marc, Tamsin (daughter). *Education:* Graduated from the Rhode Island School of Design. *Home:* Newton, Mass.

CAREER: Houghton, Mifflin, Boston, Mass., book designer and production manager of juvenile books; illustrator of books for young people. Has also taught at the Museum of Fine Arts School and Boston University. *Military service:* Served for two years in the Navy. *Awards, honors: I Will Tell You of a Town* and *Dear Rat* were included among the Ten Best Illustrated Children's Books of the *New York Times* in 1956 and 1961, respectively.

ILLUSTRATOR: Daphne Rooke, *Twins in South Africa,* Houghton, 1955; Alistair Reid, *I Will Tell You of a Town,* Houghton, 1956; Reid, *Fairwater,* Houghton, 1957; Katherine Love, compiler, *A Little Laughter,* Crowell, 1957; A. Reid, *Allth,* Houghton, 1958; Emilie W. McLeod, *One Snail and Me,* Little, Brown, 1961; Julia Cunningham, *Dear Rat,* Houghton, 1961; Ogden Nash, *The Adventures of Isabel,* Little, Brown, 1963; Margaret Holt, *David McCheever's 29 Dogs,* Houghton, 1963; Cora Annett, *The Dog Who Thought He Was a Boy,* Houghton, 1965; Sidney B. Simon, *The Armadillo Who Had No Shell,* Norton, 1966; Constance B. Hieatt, reteller, *Sir Gawain and the Green Knight,* Crowell, 1967; Sandol S. Warburg, *From Ambledee to*

Zumbledee: An ABC of Rather Special Bugs, Houghton, 1968; Judy Hawes, *My Daddy Longlegs,* Crowell, 1972; Albert S. Fleischman, *McBroom Tells a Lie,* Little, Brown, 1976.

SIDELIGHTS: Born in Worcester, Massachusetts on February 3, 1929, Walter Lorraine received his art training from the Rhode Island School of Design. Later he served two years in the United States Navy.

Lorraine has taught at the Museum of Fine Arts School and Boston University. As the manager of trade children's books for Houghton Mifflin in Boston, Lorraine has been involved with many illustrators in his publishing career and is a distinguished illustrator of many children's books himself. ''I was told one time that the average life of an illustrator is ten years. A frightening thought for those interested in the field. . . .

''Good illustrators have something to say. Whatever their techniques or styles, they always make a particular individual statement. Whether to convey fact or fiction, they are essentially story tellers—no less than writers—who use pictures instead of words. Their artistic talent, and they must always have artistic talent, is but a tool to achieve that end. Their primary interest is in the story rather than only in the color or the design. They will sacrifice the visual if necessary to get across that verbal idea. There is a saying that there is art in architecture but that architecture is not art. Whatever the beauty of the building, it still has to function properly for the people who live in it. The same can be said for illustration. Most assuredly good book illustration should be artistic, but its first and foremost function is to communicate clearly the idea of the book.

''A picture book, to be most effective, must have such an integration of words and pictures that neither will function well without the other. A good book is a Gestalt, where the whole is truly greater than the sum of its parts. The function of words and pictures is the same: to communicate an idea. To divide the two for judgment defeats the purpose.

''Each piece of writing has a beat, a rhythm that is uniquely of that writing's particular world. The most effective illustrators can sense that beat and pick it up and then can play it back, jazz fashion, with exciting variations of expression brought from their own experience that will enhance and extend the message. . . .

''To best make this play, illustrators themselves must have considerable experience with life and be sensitive to it. But most essential, they must be able to read. Interpretation is the thing, a creative joining with the world of the text. Far too many aspiring illustrators do not choose to read and therefore never understand the basic concept of illustration.

''I mean this in a symbolic sense. Of course they read the text and possibly do get the facts straight but they come to that text more to impose their will upon it rather than to interact openly with it—a jazz player with a totally foreign beat to the music at hand.

''A good illustrator's work though it may have the flavor of its time will always be fresh in its content and storytelling quality. Anyone who loves good books can find examples, Tenniel, Rackham, Caldecott, A. B. Frost, Wyeth, Ernest Shepard—all knew well the true world of the illustrator; I think of Juliet Kepes' *Five Little Monkeys* (Houghton) that is as fresh today as the day it was published back in 1952.

"Genuine hair restorer, gents!" he was calling out. "Step up for Heck Jones's Secret Double-Strength Bald-Headed Elixer! Guaranteed to grow hair on a hen's egg." ■ (From *McBroom and the Beanstalk* by Sid Fleishman. Illustrated by Walter Lorraine.)

Maurice Sendak has this ability ot communicate ideas and feelings. It is the content of the work that matters. His art technique has varied over the years yet his simple line drawings for *A Hole is to Dig* (Harper) speak as eloquently for that subject as do his far more intricate and elegant mood illustrations for Randall Jarrell's *The Animal Family* (Pantheon).

"The function of words and pictures is the same, to tell a story or communicate an idea. To separate the two for analysis in books like H. A. Rey's *Curious George* (Houghton) would be folly.

"When selecting an illustrator for a particular book the above concepts should be paramount. People differ in their experience and individual interpretation of situations. It is the person, the illustrator and his or her ability to interpret a text that is the prime concern. Illustrators who through their art can clearly show emotion and character with a strong story line that is easily readable, who can say this is the way I think, yet also who can say this is what the author had in mind—such illustrators are the ones for the job. Illustrators must have convictions about their work and not want to compromise it but be imaginative and free thinking enough to be able to join that special world and play a proper accompaniment to the best of that particular text.

"The problem of interpretation is critical. How to illustrate the simple text line, 'The young boy ran to the store to buy a loaf of bread.' Possibly no two illustrators would react the same. Should the message be 'young boy,' 'the store,' 'the bread' or perhaps the running is the thing. As a simple example one would not use an illustrator whose natural interests were serious and sober to illustrate a humorous story. The combination could work but this would be very unlikely. As a more subtle example, writing can be sharp and staccato in feeling. An illustration style that utilizes a sharp jagged line, all other things being equal, will capture the beat of that writing. A soft and flowing line would never do.

"So the illustrating process is a complex one and the selection of illustrators has far more facets than most people realize. I believe that every good picture book should be a solid coordinated unit of text and illustration—a complete format. I believe that good illustration is to be read, not merely looked at...." [From an article entitled, "On Illustrators—My View," by Walter Lorraine, *The Calendar*, March-August, 1975.[1]]

FOR MORE INFORMATION SEE: Bertha M. Miller and others, compilers, *Illustrators of Children's Books, 1946-1956*, Horn Book, 1958; *Horn Book*, December, 1963; Lee Kingman and others, compilers, *Illustrators of Children's Books, 1957-1966*, Horn Book, 1968.; *The Calendar*, March-August, 1975.

MASSIE, Diane Redfield

PERSONAL: Born in Los Angeles, Calif.; daughter of James Gilbert (an insurance agent) and Marion (a teacher; maiden name, Haskell) Redfield; married David M. Massie (a professor); children: Caitlin, Tom. *Education:* Attended Los Angeles City College, Occidental College, and Los Angeles County Art Institute. *Residence:* Hunterdon County, N.J. *Agent:* Janet A. Loranger, P.O. Box 113, West Redding, Conn. 06896.

DIANE REDFIELD MASSIE

CAREER: Author and illustrator of books for children. Professional oboist with Honolulu Symphony for five seasons. *Awards, honors:* Honor Book Award from Book Week Children's Spring Book Festival, 1965, for *A Turtle and a Loon;* design award from Chicago's Book Clinic, 1966, for *A Birthday for Bird; MacGregor Was a Dog* and *The Baby Bee Bee Bird* were selected and read by Captain Kangaroo on television.

WRITINGS—All juvenile; all self-illustrated: *The Baby Bee Bee Bird*, Harper, 1963, 1978; *Tiny Pin*, Harper, 1964; *A Turtle and a Loon*, Atheneum, 1965; *MacGregor Was a Dog*, Parents' Magazine Press, 1965; *A Birthday For Bird*, Parents' Magazine Press, 1966; *Cockle Stew*, Atheneum, 1967; *King Henry the Mouse*, Atheneum, 1968; *Dazzle*, Parents' Magazine Press, 1969; *Walter Was a Frog*, Simon & Schuster, 1970; *The Monstrous Glisson Glop*, Parents' Magazine Press, 1970; *Zigger Beans*, Parents' Magazine Press, 1971; *Good Neighbors*, (Weekly Reader Children's Book Club), 1972, McGraw, 1972; *Briar Rose and the Golden Eggs*, Parents' Magazine Press, 1973; *Turtle's Flying Lesson*, (Weekly Reader Children's Book Club), 1973, Grosset, 1973; *The Lion's Bed* (Weekly Reader Children's Book Club), 1974; *The Komodo Dragon's Jewels*, Macmillan, 1975; *The Thief in the Botanical Gardens* (Weekly Reader Children's Book Club), 1975; *Sloth's Birthday Party* (Weekly Reader Children's Book Club), 1976; *Brave Brush-Tail Possum* (Weekly Reader Children's Book Club), 1979; *Chameleon Was a Spy*, Crowell, 1979. Also author of several one-act plays. Contributor of poems to *Humpty Dumpty*.

WORK IN PROGRESS: Muskrat's Hotel; A Blue Narwhal to Borneo, a book of rhymes.

SIDELIGHTS: "I entered the field of children's books by the back door, as it were. I had been trained as a musician and spent five seasons playing first oboe in the Honolulu Symphony. I met my husband there, who was in the Navy, and after he was discharged, we came East. It was not easy to find work in New York, though I joined Local 802 (musician's union). (In the music business, one needs to know contractors and other musicians. I didn't in New York, hence, no work.) After my daughter, Caitlin, was born and had reached the age for stories, I began to think in terms of children's books.

"As a child, I had loved to make up stories. I used to put on plays and puppet shows for my family and neighbors. The theater fascinated me. Years later, while in Honolulu working as a musician, I wrote, directed and acted in several comedies, using my musician friends as actors.

"So story telling to my daughter began this interest anew. Sometimes with an especially liked story, I would go down-

stairs later and write it down. The next day, I would simplify the language, etc.

"Often I would make a 'dummy' with pictures accompanying the text. These first dummies are the ones I showed to publishers when I decided to try to sell my stories. Harper and Row published my first book, *The Baby Bee Bee Bird,* and I have been involved with children's books ever since.

"My son, Tom, has passed the 'picture book' and 'easy reader' age I write for, but he still acts as critic as does my husband, David. I value their opinions.

"I think my favorite occupation is writing rhymes. Several of my books are in rhyme and two are collections of rhymes. A rhyme offers fascinating possibilities with a strict form. I find it like working a puzzle.

**"Your chair is next to the Captain,"
said the waiter, carrying the bread.**
■ (From *The Komodo Dragon's Jewels* by Diane Redfield Massie. Illustrated by the author.)

"My other great love, of course, will always be the theater. I still write plays (adult) and I make elaborate animal costumes. (These have been for my children for Halloween.) Now, I make dramatic bird costumes for myself when I'm invited to costume parties. I have a blue heron suit, a lamengier vulture costume, and a scarlet ibis costume. These are made with felt, ribbons, silver or gold metallic fringe, sequins, etc. The heads are 'feathered' with felt and ribbons, have long beaks of felt, and beautiful glass eyes surrounded by glittering sequins, etc. The bodies have wings, tail, etc., using the same materials. I suppose this can be called a 'hobby.' I also like to paint (I am studying oil painting) and I like very much to cook.

"We live in the country and look out over fields and woods. These circumstances, I think, color the stories I write, which are about animals (however anthropomorphic) in their natural surroundings."

FOR MORE INFORMATION SEE: Horn Book, June, 1965, August, 1975.

MAYER, Mercer   1943-

PERSONAL: Born in Little Rock, Ark.; married wife, Marianna (an author), now divorced.

CAREER: Has been an art director in an advertising agency, but is presently a full-time author and illustrator of children's books. *Awards, honors: Everyone Knows What a Dragon Looks Like* was selected as one of the *New York Times* Choice of Best Illustrated Books of the Year, and was part of the American Institute of Graphic Arts Book Show, both in 1976; it also won the Irma Simonton Black Award in 1977; *While the Horses Galloped to London* was selected as part of the Children's Book Showcase, 1974; *Frog Goes to Dinner* received the Brooklyn Art Books for Children Citation, 1977.

WRITINGS—All self-illustrated: *A Boy, a Dog, and a Frog,* Dial, 1967; *There's a Nightmare in My Closet,* Dial, 1968; *Terrible Troll,* Dial, 1968; *If I Had . . . ,* Dial, 1968; *I Am a Hunter,* Dial, 1969; *Frog, Where Are You?,* Dial, 1969; *A Special Trick,* Dial, 1970; (with Marianna Mayer) *Mine,* Simon & Schuster, 1970; *The Queen Always Wanted to Dance,* Simon & Schuster, 1971; (with M. Mayer) *A Boy, a Dog, a Frog, and a Friend,* Dial, 1971; (with M. Mayer) *Me and My Flying Machine,* Parents' Magazine Press, 1971; *A Silly Story,* Parents' Magazine Press, 1972; *Frog on His Own,* Dial, 1973; *Bubble, Bubble,* Parents' Magazine Press, 1973; *Mrs. Beggs and the Wizard,* Parents' Magazine Press, 1973; *What Do You Do with a Kangaroo?,* Four Winds, 1974; *One Monster after Another,* Golden Press, 1974; *Two Moral Tales,* Four Winds, 1974; *Two More Moral Tales,* Four Winds, 1974; *Walk, Robot, Walk,* Ginn, 1974; *You're the Scaredy-Cat,* Parents' Magazine Press, 1974; *Frog Goes to Dinner,* Dial, 1974.

Just for You, Golden Press, 1975; (with M. Mayer) *One Frog Too Many,* Dial, 1975; *The Great Cat Chase: A Wordless Book,* Four Winds, 1975; *Professor Wormbog in Search for the Zipperump-a-Zoo,* Golden Press, 1976; *Liza Lou and the Yeller Belly Swamp,* Parents' Magazine Press, 1976; *Ah-*

(From *Frog Goes to Dinner* by Mercer Mayer. Illustrated by the author.)

Choo, Dial, 1976; *Four Frogs in a Box*, Dial, 1976; *Hiccup*, Dial, 1976; *There's a Nightmare in My Cupboard*, Dent, 1976; *Just Me and My Dad*, Western, 1977; *Little Monster's Word Book*, Western, 1977; *Oops*, Dial, 1977; *Professor Wormbog's Gloomy Kerploppus: A Book of Great Smells*, Western, 1977; (editor) *The Poison Tree, and Other Poems*, Scribner, 1977.

Illustrator: John D. Fitzgerald, *The Great Brain*, Dial, 1967; Liesel M. Skorpen, *Outside My Window*, Harper, 1968; George Mendoza, *The Gillygoofang*, Dial, 1968; Sidney Offit, *The Boy Who Made a Million*, St. Martin's, 1968; G. Mendoza, *The Crack in the Wall, and Other Terribly Weird Tales*, Dial, 1968; Sheila LaFarge, *Golden Butter*, Dial, 1969; J. D. Fitzgerald, *More Adventures of the Great Brain*, Dial, 1969; Kathryn Hitte, *Boy, Was I Mad!*, Parents' Magazine Press, 1969; Warren Fine, *The Mousechildren and the Famous Collector*, Harper, 1970; Jean R. Larson, *Jack Tar*, M. Smith, 1970; Barbara Wersba, *Let Me Fall before I Fly*, Atheneum, 1971; Jane H. Yolen, *The Bird of Time*, Crowell, 1971; Jan Wahl, *Margaret's Birthday*, Four Winds, 1971; J. D. Fitzgerald, *Me and My Little Brain*, Dial, 1971.

Candida Palmer, *Kim Ann and the Yellow Machine*, Ginn, 1972; Mildred Kantrowitz, *Good-Bye Kitchen*, Parents' Magazine Press, 1972; J. Wahl, *Grandmother Told Me*, Little, Brown, 1972; J. D. Fitzgerald, *The Great Brain at the Academy*, Dial, 1972; Mabel Watts, *While the Horses Galloped to London*, Parents' Magazine Press, 1973; J. D. Fitzgerald, *The Great Brain Reforms*, Dial, 1973; B. Wersba, *Amanda Dreaming*, Atheneum, 1973; J. D. Fitzgerald, *The Return of the Great Brain*, Dial, 1974; Fitzgerald, *The Great Brain Does It Again*, Dial, 1975; John Bellairs, *The Figure in the Shadows*, Dial, 1975; Jay Williams, *Everyone Knows What a Dragon Looks Like*, Four Winds, 1976; *Mercer's Monsters*, Western, 1977; J. Williams, *The Reward Worth Having*, Four Winds, 1977.

SIDELIGHTS: **1943.** Born in Little Rock, Arkansas. Attended elementary school in Camden, Arkansas. Traveled widely with his family throughout the United States before settling in Hawaii. Mayer graduated from Theodore Roosevelt High School in Honolulu and attended the Honolulu Academy of Arts. He and his mother were commissioned to decorate the Kahala Hilton Hotel with collage wall panels. He was also a political cartoonist for the International

(From *Ah-Choo* by Mercer Mayer. Illustrated by the author.)

Brotherhood of Teamsters in Honolulu. Mayer received additional art training at the Art Students League in New York City. "My one philosophy as an artist is to learn how to draw the human figure, which is the most complicated and delicately balanced form in nature. Once that is mastered, an artist can compete and succeed in any area of the arts he or she wishes. Without this mastery, the artist will limit himself tremendously. I have drawn all my life. One of my earliest memories is of looking at a book illustrated by N. C. Wyeth."

"My main desire in writing and illustrating is to expand the childhood fantasy world which adults forget all about but which is something that I have never lost touch with."

1971. *The Queen Always Wanted to Dance,* his own book, was a Junior Literary Guild selection. The Mayers lived in Sea Cliff, Long Island, New York with Marianna Mayer's fifteen-year-old sister, an art student.

1973. Bought a fifteen acre farm near Roxbury, Connecticut where they raised horses. With three horses and two dogs the couple could also observe many frogs, muskrats and turtles in the river running next to their property. "But our main special interest is trying to keep this mammoth old Colonial house from caving in."

1974. *Frog Goes to Dinner,* the fifth book in Mayer's "Frog" series was published. The author-illustrator does not see himself as their creator. "They have not so much been created by me, but rather given to me. One day I will sit down and wonder, 'will I ever think of another frog book?' 'Oh, probably not,' comes the answer, and then a few days later, there it is. One, two, three, I have the theme and the plot. The time then goes into polishing the rough dummy. But try as I might I cannot deliberately think up one of those silly books. I've now come to the conclusion that I am Frog's creation, which is just fine with me. After all, the responsibility of thinking up new things to make books about is overwhelming."

1975. The sixth "Frog" book, *One Frog Too Many* was published. "I had been trying for about a year to come up with a sixth 'Frog' book, making false starts and getting nowhere. Then Marianna heard Phyllis [Fogelman; his editor] talking about 'Frog in a Box,' said 'That's it!' and just reeled off the whole plot. I reached for pencil and paper and started working on the dummy right there."

1976. *Ah-Choo* and *Hiccup,* two almost wordless picture books for children, were published. *Ah-Choo* was created at a workshop for elementary school teachers in New Orleans when Mayer was asked how he goes about creating a new book. The subject exploded from the sketches he drew for his audience. "The first picture I drew was an elephant, for no other reason than I thought elephants would show up best to a large crowd. I truly had no intention of actually creating a new book.

"Next I drew a picture of my elephant coming upon a small mouse selling flowers. 'What could possibly happen next?' I asked my audience, and before anyone could answer I had an idea: of course, the elephant sneezes. Well, before I knew it, my demonstration turned into the actual creation of a new book, which delighted everyone, myself included. On the airplane coming home I sketched in the rest of the dummy, this time on Eastern Airlines stationery."

On that same airplane trip *Hiccup* was created. "Sitting there a few thousand feet above the ground I thought, what about a hippopotamus with the hiccups, and a new project was born. This all may seem easy, and it is when it finally comes, but before I arrive at a publishable story there are stacks of dead ends."

1976. Illustrated *Everyone Knows What a Dragon Looks Like,* which was written by Jay Williams. The book was selected as one of the *New York Times* Choice of Best Illustrated Books of the Year for 1976 and won the Irma Simonton Black Award in 1977. "Being an author-illustrator has its problems because editors have a tendency not to ask if I would like to illustrate someone's else's work. Usually I am very busy, but on rare occasions I would love to, and Jay Williams' manuscript was one of those rare occasions.

"I knew form the start I didn't want to draw a historical document. I wanted this book to come directly from me as if I lived in China. But I made no bones about being a Westerner. The China I drew is a China of the heart. I surrounded myself with Chinese art and books. I pored over everything Chinese I could find. I China-fied myself. Then I tried to forget it all and began to sketch. It was wonderful fun, a very rich experience."

Many of Mercer Mayer's books do not contain words, but tell a story through pictures. Most critics agree that in books such as *Frog, Where Are You?* and *A Boy, a Dog, a Frog and a Friend* words are not needed and that it is easy for children to follow the action through the pictures.

Mayer's drawings for *A Poison Tree and Other Poems* were critiqued in *Horn Book* by a reviewer who described the book as, "A new anthology for young people in which the illustration is fully as significant as the poetry but does not supersede it. For each poem a full-page drawing complements an emotion expressed by the poet, often from the point of view of a child. . . . With alternating misty grays and sepia—a strikingly different style for the artist—the full-page illuminations subtly project inspiration and ecstasy and other emotions. Some of the illustrations are executed brilliantly in chiaroscuro: a dark face with light in the eyes; a spider web in the moonlight; a crouching giant under a sickle moon and stars."

FOR MORE INFORMATION SEE: Horn Book, December, 1969, June, 1971, October, 1973, December, 1974, February and April, 1975.

McCRADY, Lady 1951-

PERSONAL: Born October 13, 1951, in Indianapolis, Ind.; daughter of Harry E. (a musician; engineer) and Louise (Benson; The Shirret Lady) McCrady. *Education:* Sir John Cass School, London, England; Syracuse University, B.F.A. (cum laude), 1973.

CAREER: Free-lance illustrator, 1973—. *Exhibitions:* Numerous one-person and group shows in New York and Connecticut. Paintings and original book illustrations owned by The Hartford Collection, Hartford, Conn., and in various private collections in New England and New York. *Member:* Illustrators Guild, Kappa Kappa Gamma fraternity.

WRITINGS: (Self-illustrated) *Miss Kiss and the Nasty Beast,* Holiday House, 1979.

Illustrator: Parent's Nursey School, *Kids Are Natural Cooks*, Houghton, 1971, 1974; Charles Keller, *Glory, Glory How Peculiar*, Prentice, 1976; Tobi Tobias, *An Umbrella Named Umbrella*, Knopf, 1976; Inez Maury (author), Norah Alemany (translator), *My Mother the Mail Carrier*, Feminist Press, 1976; Mary Calhoun, *The Witch's Pig*, Morrow, 1977; Rose Lagerkrantz, *Tulla's Summer*, Harcourt, 1977; Steven Kroll, *If I Could Be My Grandmother*, Pantheon, 1977; Mary Calhoun, *Jack the Wise and the Cor-* *nish Cuckoos*, Morrow, 1978; Bonnie Carey, *Grasshopper to the Rescue*, 1979; Jan van Pelt, *The Day the Zoo Caught the Flu*, Harvey House, 1979; Jane Feder, *The Night Light*, Dial, 1979.

SIDELIGHTS: "I work primarily in pencils. I am strongly influenced by the eccentric world around me, the mysticism of the universe, the wonderment of nature."

"That's my umbrella," Anne said.
"Prove it," Lucy Paladino said.
■ (From *An Umbrella Named Umbrella* by Tobi Tobias. Illustrated by Lady McCrady.)

LADY McCRADY

McDERMOTT, Gerald   1941-

PERSONAL: Born in 1941, in Detroit, Mich,; married Beverly Brodsky (an artist), 1969. *Education:* Graduated from the Pratt Institute of Design. *Residence:* Hudson River Valley, New York.

CAREER: Began taking art lessons at the age of four; as an adolescent became a regular member of the "Storyland" radio program, Detroit, Mich.; took a year off from his studies at Pratt to visit animation studios in Eastern and Western Europe; hired as a graphic designer for New York City's public television station; filmmaker; illustrator and reteller of folk tales. *Awards, honors: Anansi the Spider* was named a Caldecott Honor Book in 1973, and received the Lewis Carroll Shelf Award in 1975; *Arrow to the Sun* was selected for the American Institute of Graphic Arts Children's Book Show, 1973-74, awarded the Caldecott Medal in 1975, and the Brooklyn Art Books for Children Citation in 1977. McDermott's film version of his book, *Anansi the Spider,* was awarded the Blue Ribbon at the American Film Festival, 1970.

WRITINGS—Reteller of folk tales; all self-illustrated: *Anansi the Spider: A Tale from the Ashanti,* Holt, 1972; *The Magic Tree: A Tale from the Congo,* Holt, 1973; *Arrow to the Sun: A Pueblo Indian Tale,* Viking, 1974; *The Stonecutter: A Japanese Folk Tale,* Viking, 1975.

ADAPTATION—Filmstrips: "Anansi the Spider," "Arrow to the Sun," "Moments Spent," "The Magic Tree," "The Stonecutter," all Weston Woods.

SIDELIGHTS: **1941.** Born in Detroit, Michigan, Gerald McDermott's art career began at the age of four when his parents enrolled him at the Detroit Institute of Arts. "I've been on a journey past paper mountains, flying men, foolish spiders, talking trees, and the flaming arrows of the solar fire. It has been a journey of discovery through the bizarre and exotic forms of world mythology. The Rainbow Trail has become a path for my work as an artist. . . .

"The purpose of my journey has been to explore and share the evocative qualities of these ancient tales with those still open to the message of myth.

"Animated films and illustrated books have carried me along this path of exploration. The choice of these media grew out of early experience with several forms of artistic expression. Encouraged and supported by my parents, I attended special classes at the Detroit Institute of Arts from the age of four. Every Saturday, from early childhood through early adolescence, was spent in those halls. I virtually lived in the museum, drawing and painting and coming to know the works of that great collection. I've kept a brush in my hand ever since." [From an article entitled, "On the Rainbow Trail," by Gerald McDermott, *Horn Book,* April, 1975.[1]]

1950-1952. "A brief but glorious career as a child radio-actor had its influence. From the age of nine until eleven (that is, until my voice suddenly changed), I was heard regularly in a show that specialized in dramatizing folk tales and legends. Working with professional actors and learning how music and sound effects are integrated in a dramatic context were indispensable experiences for a future filmmaker."[1]

As a teenager, McDermott was influenced by the Bauhaus principles incorporated in the special curriculum at his high

GERALD McDERMOTT

school. "... I was directly influenced by motion pictures, especially those animated epics that evoked a dream world. My view of these changed, however, under the discipline of Bauhaus-based design training at Cass Technical High School. As my ideas and tastes formed, I began to feel sure that the medium of animation could offer more than giggling, white-gloved mice."[1]

McDermott's art training continued at the Pratt Institute of Design in New York after graduation from high school. During his final year there, the young artist made his first animated film, "The Stonecutter." "... During my college years ... I began to experiment with animated films. My principal goal was to design films that were highly stylized in color and form. I also hoped to touch upon themes not dealt with in conventional cartoons. Instinctively, I turned to folklore as a source for thematic material.

"'The Stonecutter,' a Japanese folk tale taken from a childhood storybook, was my first animated film. It is an ancient fable of a man's foolish longing for power—a tale of wishes and dreams that can be understood on many levels. Its attraction was its elegant simplicity and magical quality. In its structure and symbolism, 'The Stonecutter' prefigures my later films: The story contains in microcosm the basic theme of self-transformation that was consciously developed in my later work.

"While my approach to the graphic design of 'The Stonecutter' was unconventional, traditional animation techniques were used to set the designs in motion. I've continued to utilize these methods because they offer the greatest possible degree of control over the final film. The basic device is the storyboard, a series of about one hundred quick sketches outlining the high points of the action. This serves as a visual script and is referred to continually throughout the many months of production."[1]

McDermott's works were based on folk tales. Early in his career he met Dr. Joseph Campbell, an authority on the relationship between mythology and psychology and a great influence on McDermott's later works. "Soon after finishing my first film, I had the immense good fortune to meet Joseph Campbell. Dr. Campbell has written extensively and eloquently of the relationships between mythology and modern psychology. In his four-volume study, *The Masks of God,* he has traced the evolution of myth and its function in world culture. Campbell has shown that the prime function of mythology is to supply the symbols that carry the human spirit forward, 'to waken and give guidance to the energies of life.' These ideas, illuminated in Campbell's *The Hero with a Thousand Faces,* became the basis for all my subsequent work.

"During the production of *Flight of Icarus, Anansi the Spider,* and *The Magic Tree,* I consulted with Campbell on the meanings of the tales that I had chosen to animate. He pointed out that all these mythical stories, even though from cultures as disparate as Japan, ancient Crete, and Africa, share a common theme. Rather than being simple fables that attempt to explain natural phenomena or justify social systems, they deal with the universal idea of the hero quest. Its classic form is delineated by Campbell: *'A hero ventures forth from the world of common day into a region of supernatural wonder: fabulous forces are there encountered and a decisive victory is won: the hero comes back from this mysterious adventure with the power to bestow boons on his fellow man.'*

"One can visualize this quest as a circular journey where certain symbols, clothed in the garments of the culture that created the myth, are encountered again and again. Tasaku, the lowly stonecutter, seeks to rise in power through the transforming magic of a mountain spirit; Daedalus and Icarus seek release with magic wings; Mavungu seeks happiness with a magic princess. All journey forth and undergo a series of supernatural events.

"Even that lovable rogue, Anansi, goes on a journey. He is a trickster, a comic shadow of the mythic hero. No mystical experience beckons Anansi; he simply 'gets lost and falls into trouble.' His descent into the abyss consists of being swallowed by a large fish. He has no inner resources with which to save himself; instead, these are divided among six spider sons. His sons do manage to rescue him, but because of this division, the celestial reward of the moon eludes them all.

"In each of these films, I was concerned with the circular journey of the individual who sets forth on a quest of self-fulfillment. In psychological terms, he must make a break with the past, overcome obstacles to change, and grow. Ideally, the seeker can then return, his full potential realized, and take his place in society with the 'wisdom and power to serve others.'"[1]

Late 1960's. Moved with his wife, Beverly Brodsky (a fellow artist) to Southern France for a few years. Before leaving, however, the young filmmaker became acquainted with George Nicholson who is now the editorial director of Viking Junior Books. This acquaintance led to a new career for McDermott as a book illustrator and reteller of folk tales. The transition from film to printed page was not an easy one. "This jarring shift from a medium of time to a medium of space posed some special problems. When George Nicholson, ... put forth the idea of book adaptations of my African folklore films, it seemed an easy task. After all, four thousand discarded animated drawings were stacked up in my studio. Why not simply shuffle through them, choose forty, and send them off to the printer? Because the result would be a souvenir program of the film—a totally unacceptable solution.

"We returned to the orginal film storyboard, and I tried to reconceive the visual material in a series of doublepage spreads. It was an unsettling experience because the control I enjoyed as a film director was lost. There was no longer a captive audience in a darkened room, its gaze fixed upon hypnotic flickering shadows. Gone were the music and sound effects and the ability to guide the viewer through a flow of images with a carefully planned progression. Now the reader was in control. The reader could begin at the end of the book or linger for ten minutes over a page or perhaps merely glance at half a dozen others. As an artist, I was challenged to resolve these problems."[1]

1973. Returned to the United States. His book, (based on the African myth) *Anansi the Spider,* was named a Caldecott Honor Book.

1974. *Arrow to the Sun: A Pueblo Indian Tale* was published by Viking. The book was selected for the American Institute of Graphic Arts Children's Book Show. "When I began my work on *Arrow to the Sun* ... I knew from the outset that the book and the film would be conceived concurrently. With the sensitive and patient collaboration of my editor at Viking, Linda Zuckerman, and my art director, Suzanne Hal-

Anansi. He is "spider" to the Ashanti people. ■ (From *Anansi the Spider,* adapted and illustrated by Gerald McDermott.)

dane, I sought to solve the problems of continuity and design present in the earlier books. The introduction of large areas of quiet space, filled with solid, rich color, improves the pacing. The use of the Rainbow Trail motif, a multicolored band, helps to guide the reader's eye across the page. The elimination of text from many spreads allows the images to speak. These are some of the techniques that eased my passage as an artist. Though story line and character design were shared, the book in form, texture, and color took on a life of its own.

"In outline and impact, this ancient, pre-Conquest Pueblo Indian tale is a perfect example of the classic motif of the hero quest. The hero of this myth, which is the creation of a solar-oriented culture, is a young boy who must seek his true father. The object of his search, the Lord of the Sun, embodies the constancy and power of life-sustaining solar fire—a symbol that is central to Pueblo ritual. The sun, in Carl Jung's phrase, is 'the classic symbol of the unity and divinity of self.'

"Corn, the staff of life for the people of the pueblos, is an important companion symbol to the sun. The constant, life-sustaining warmth of the sun nurtures the golden ears of corn. In searching for a graphic motif that would unite these two concepts, I slowly turned an ear of corn in my hands, studying the color, texture, and form. Then I broke the ear in half. At that moment, the symbol hidden beneath the surface was revealed—a moment re-created in my film. The cross section of the ear of corn, with its concentric rings and radiating rays of kernels, forms a perfect image of the sun.

"If one looks at the tip of an ear of corn—an important ritual article in Pueblo culture—one sees that four kernels come together to form a quadrilateral sign. I took this flowered cross, with its four kernel rays, and bound it by a solar circle. This became the unifying visual element in my retelling of *Arrow to the Sun.* It first appears as the spark of life, then as the hero's amulet. It identifies him as he proceeds on his journey through a landscape permeated with the golden hues of sun and corn.

"The Boy is a child of the divine world and the world of men. He is the offspring of Sky Father and Earth Mother—a lineage he shares with other great heroes of world mythology. '[T]he hero destined to perform miracles . . . can have no earthly father. . . . his seed has to be planted by heavenly powers. His mother, however, is earthly, and so he is born both god and man. Always the chosen one unites within himself in this way the two spheres.'

"His questing path is the Rainbow Trail—a multihued border motif that appears in the sand paintings, pottery designs, and weaving of the Southwest. It runs through the pages of my book as well; down through the sky to the pueblo, across the earth, blazing up to the sun, framing the drama of the kivas, and bursting forth at the moment of the hero's assimilation to the sun.

"The Arrowmaker is encountered on the Rainbow Trail. He is a *shaman*—a man of magical powers. Only he has an open eye and the inner vision required to perceive the Boy's true heritage. He provides the supernatural aid that enables the Boy to continue his journey. The magical arrow that he fashions releases the Boy from his earthbound state, just as one of wisdom opens the closed mind of another. He sends the Boy on the self-revealing way of the father seeking hero.

"Upon passing through the fiery sun door, the Boy confronts the mighty Lord of the Sun. This is hardly the completion of the journey, however, but the beginning of the true challenge. Despite its colorful surface and happy conclusion, like similar myths, 'its content proper refers to a terrifyingly serious reality: initiation, that is, passing, by way of a symbolic death and resurrection, from ignorance and immaturity to the spiritual age of the adult.'

"The Boy must descend into the abyss of the ceremonial chambers—the four kivas—to prove his heritage. He must face these tests and emerge reborn from the dark womb of the kiva. A true hero, he accepts the challenge, 'Father, . . . I will endure these trials.' Lions, serpents, and bees await the Boy. In the ensuing confrontations, though threatened by these creatures, he is not destroyed. Significantly, neither does he destroy the animals, for they represent the dark forces of our own unconscious. They are the shadow beings of the dream state, the internal demons that torment us and block our growth. We cannot destroy them, but we can calm them and integrate them with our functions. We can assume their positive qualities and put them at our service.

"This interpretation is quite different from the one we might apply to the mythology of the West which is most familiar to us. It represents a kinship and reverence for the natural world that is opposed to Greek and Hebrew tradition. Heracles destroys the titanic snake, the Hydra. He kills the lion, strips it, and wears its skin as a symbol of his dominance. Absolute domination is the message of these myths. But for our Indian hero, the human world and the animal world are reconciled. The Boy assumes the strengths of the lions, even as they become purring kittens at his feet. He overcomes the squirming chaos of the serpents and creates a circle, a symbol of wholeness and unity as is the corn-sustaining sun. (The serpents inhabit the maizefield and devour the corn-destroying rodents.) The bees, which can sting with killing power, instead give the miracle gift of sun-colored honey to the Boy.

"The deepest point of the descent into the abyss occurs in the Kiva of Lightning. Here flashes the polar opposite of the constant warmth of the sun. Unpredictable and violent, it

shatters the immature form of the Boy. When he emerges from this final crisis, he is reborn and 'filled with the power of the sun'—filled with a spiritual awareness born of his trials. If this solar symbolism seems remote, perhaps we should listen to the response of a nine-year-old to *Arrow to the Sun:* 'I think that the Lord of the Sun knew all along who the Boy really was, but he made the Boy go through the tests anyway, so that the Boy would know who he was.'

"The journey on the Rainbow Trail is near its end. The Boy, radiant in his new garments, returns to earth bearing the message of his father. He began as an individual searching for his true identity, isolated from his community. He completes the journey as a self-aware messenger of life-sustaining powers, ready to take his place in the community. As Joseph Campbell has observed, 'The ultimate aim of the quest, if one is to return, must be . . . the wisdom and power to serve others.' Surrounded by the people of his village, joined with the Corn Maiden, watched over by Sky Father and Earth Mother, enclosed within the arc of the Rainbow Trail, the hero steps onto the World Center and joins in the Dance of Life.''[1]

1975. *Arrow to the Sun* awarded the Caldecott Medal.

1977. *Arrow to the Sun* awarded the Brooklyn Art Books for Children citation. McDermott lives with his wife in the Hudson River Valley, New York. "The Rainbow Trail of the artist has come full circle. It is not an end, but a continuation, an ever-repeated cycle. The challenge is eternal: to descend again and again into the 'image-producing abyss' to discover visual evocations of the compelling myths of mankind.''[1]

FOR MORE INFORMATION SEE: Horn Book, December 1972, August, 1974, April, June, and August, 1975; *New York Times Book Review,* May 5, 1974; *Bulletin of the Center for Children's Books,* November, 1974; *Publishers Weekly,* May 19, 1975; Priscilla Moulton, "Gerald McDermott," *Horn Book,* August, 1975; Lee Kingman, editor, *Newbery and Caldecott Medal Books: 1966-1975,* Horn Book, 1975; James Auer, "Gerald McDermott: Myths Inspire Winner of Caldecott Award," *Authors in the News,* Volume 2, Gale, 1976.

McPHERSON, James M. 1936-

PERSONAL: Born October 11, 1936, in Valley City, N.D.; son of James Munro (a high school teacher) and Miriam (Osborn) McPherson; married Patricia A. Rasche, December 28, 1957; children: Joanna Erika. *Education:* Gustavus Adolphus College, B.A., 1958; Johns Hopkins University, Ph.D., 1963. *Politics:* Democratic. *Religion:* Presbyterian. *Home:* 15 Randall Rd., Princeton, N.J. 08540. *Office:* Department of History, Princeton University, Princeton, N.J. 08540.

CAREER: Princeton University, Princeton, N.J., instructor, 1962-65, assistant professor, 1965-66, associate professor of history, 1966—. *Member:* American Historical Association, Association for the Study of Negro Life and History, Organization of American Historians, Southern Historical Association, Phi Beta Kappa. *Awards, honors:* Proctor and Gamble faculty fellowship; Anisfield-Wolff Award in Race Relations, 1965, for *The Struggle for Equality: Abolitionists and the Negro in the Civil War and Reconstruction;* Guggenheim fellowship; National Endowment for the Humanities fellowship.

JAMES McPHERSON

WRITINGS: The Struggle for Equality: Abolitionists and the Negro in the Civil War and Reconstruction, Princeton University Press, 1964; (editor) *The Negro's Civil War: How American Negroes Felt and Acted in the War for the Union,* Pantheon, 1965; (contributor) Martin B. Duberman, editor, *The Anti-Slavery Vanguard: New Essays on Abolitionism,* Princeton University Press, 1965; (editor) *Marching Toward Freedom: The Negro in the Civil War, 1861-1865,* Knopf, 1968; (contributor) Barton J. Bernstein, editor, *Towards a New Past: Dissenting Essays in American History,* Pantheon, 1968; (with others) *Blacks in America: Bibliographical Essays,* Doubleday, 1971; *The Abolitionist Legacy: From Reconstruction to the NAACP,* Princeton University Press, 1975. Contributor of articles to *American Historical Review, Journal of American History, Journal of Negro History, Caribbean Studies, Phylon, Mid-America,* and other publications.

SIDELIGHTS: "I grew up in small towns in North Dakota and Minnesota, where my father was a teacher and later a school superintendent. He still teaches high school in Minnesota, and my mother teaches elementary school. Thus, I acquired my interest in teaching as a career from living in a family of teachers. One of my brothers is a college teacher and both of my sisters have taught elementary school. I became fascinated with American history while in college, and it was natural that I should combine my interest in teaching and history to become a teacher of history and a writer of books about American history that I hope have been useful in teaching and learning.

"Having grown up in the far northern part of the United States, I conceived an interest, a romanticized one, no doubt, in the most exotic and distant part of the country, the South, and I took up serious study of the South in graduate school. Living in Baltimore during my years of graduate

study, and also during the early years of the civil rights movement (1958-1962), I became fascinated by the history of race relations in the South. Being a northerner, I became further interested in the role that northerners had played in trying to change southern race relations in the past. Thus, I studied the 19th-century abolitionists and wrote two books about their role during and after the Civil War in trying to obtain equal rights, equal justice, and education for the freed slaves. This naturally led me into an interest in black history, and I also wrote two books about the history of blacks in the Civil War. Most of my books were written for a college-level audience or higher, but when a publisher suggested in 1967 that I adapt my book, *The Negro's Civil War,* to be used in high schools, I readily agreed because of my longstanding interest in public school education. I enjoyed the experience of writing *Marching Toward Freedom.* My two youngest brothers were then in junior high and high school, and I tried out the book on them as I was writing it in order to see whether it would appeal to a high-school age audience. They liked it, and I hope that other students who have read it have also liked it."

FOR MORE INFORMATION SEE: Book World, May 5, 1968; *Commonweal,* May 24, 1968; *National Observer,* November 4, 1968.

MERCER, Charles (Edward) 1917-

PERSONAL: Born July 12, 1917, in Stouffville, Ontario; son of Alfred Tennyson and Alma (Hoover) Mercer; married Alma Sutton, 1940. *Education:* Brown University, A.B. (cum laude), 1939. *Home and office:* 1137 East 36th St., New York, N.Y. 10016. *Agent:* Mitch Douglas, International Creative Management, 40 West 57th St., New York, N.Y. 10016.

CAREER: Washington Post, Washington, D.C., reporter, 1939-42; Associated Press, New York, N.Y., 1946-49, variously reporter, editor, feature writer, then television columnist, 1957-59; free-lance writer, 1959-66; G. P. Putnam's Sons, New York, N.Y., senior editor, 1966-1975, vice-president and co-director of books for young readers, 1975—. *Military service:* U.S. Army, Military Intelligence, 1942-46, became first lieutenant; recalled to active duty, 1950-52. *Member:* Phi Beta Kappa, Pi Delta Epsilon, Alpha Delta Phi.

WRITINGS: The Narrow Ledge, Morrow, 1951; *There Comes A Time,* Putnam, 1955; *Rachel Cade* (Literary Guild selection), Putnam, 1956; *The Drummond Tradition,* Putnam, 1957; *Enough Good Men,* Putnam, 1960 (Literary Guild selection); *Pilgrim Strangers,* Putnam, 1961; *The Reckoning,* Putnam, 1962; *Gift of Life,* Putnam, 1963; *Alexander the Great* (nonfiction), Horizon, 1963; *Alexander the Great* (nonfiction), Horizon, 1963; *Legion of Strangers* (nonfiction), Holt, Rinehart & Winston, 1964; *The Trespassers,* Putnam, 1964; *Beyond Bojador,* Holt, Rinehart & Winston, 1965; *Promise Morning,* Putnam, 1966; *Let's Go to Africa* (juvenile), Putnam, 1967; *Let's Go to Europe* (juvenile), Putnam, 1968; *The Minister* (Readers Digest Condensed Book selection), Putnam, 1970; *Roberto Clemente* (juvenile), Putnam, 1974; *Gerald Ford* (juvenile), Putnam, 1975; *The Castle on the River,* Popular Library, 1975; *Witch Tide,* Popular Library, 1976; *Jimmy Carter* (juvenile), Putnam, 1977; *Miracle at Midway* (juvenile; Junior Literary Guild selection), Putnam, 1977; *Monsters in the Earth: The Story of Earthquakes* (juvenile), Putnam, 1978. Short stories and novelettes have appeared in *McCall's, Saturday Eve-*

Every place you stop, you eat good meals. No wonder the French tell you they are the best cooks in the world. ■ (From *Let's Go to Europe* by Charles Mercer. Illustrated by Charles Dougherty.)

ning Post, Good Housekeeping, Collier's, Redbook and *Cosmopolitan.*

SIDELIGHTS: "I have always enjoyed telling stories, whether true ones or made up. My most successful book commercially was a novel, *Rachel Cade,* published in 1956, which sold many hundreds of thousands of copies, was made into a movie and translated into nine languages. For a while I was weary with being known as the author of that book, as if I were not writing other, perhaps better books. But time takes care of such things. Today *Rachel Cade* is out of print and younger readers have never heard of it.

"I think it is my interest in telling a good story that has drawn more of my creative attention in recent years to younger readers, both as a writer myself and as an editor trying to help other writers. There are more good true stories to tell than ever can be published. I think it very important to interest the very young in reading as soon as possible. It can be done, among other ways, by telling them what young life was like to interesting people as various as Roberto Clemente and Jimmy Carter. At an older so-called young adult reading level I know that I have interested the young in history by telling the fabulous true story of the Battle of Midway in World War II. And anyone who thinks science is dull need only read the facts about earthquakes to see that study of cause and effect in the natural world is like a fascinating mystery story."

MOLARSKY, Osmond   1909-

PERSONAL: Born November 17, 1909, in Boston, Mass.; son of Abram and Sarah Ann (Shreve) Molarsky; married Aileen Olsen (an author), December 23, 1951; married second wife, Margaret Gibbons, 1970. *Education:* Swarthmore College, B.A., 1934. *Residence:* Ross, Calif. *Agent:* Curtis Brown Ltd., 60 East 56th St., New York, N.Y. 10022.

CAREER: Producer of marionette shows, 1929-36, traveling with a chautauqua troupe; writer of scripts for documentaries for U.S. Office of Education, 1938-39; J. Walter Thompson Agency, New York, N.Y., advertising copywriter, 1953-57; KVIE-TV (educational television), Sacramento, Calif., writer-producer, 1966; KNEW (radio), Oakland, Calif., commentator and host of a telephone talk program, 1968—. *Military service:* U.S. Naval Reserve, 1943-46; became lieutenant senior grade. *Awards, honors:* His play, "No! Not the Russians!" was the winner in *Stage* Magazine one-act play contest, 1937; *Reader's Digest* Foundation Award for best educational television program for "Gold Was Where You Found It," 1966, and for "Secrets of the Brook," 1967.

WRITINGS—All juvenile except as indicated: (contributor) *Best Plays from Stage* (anthology), Dodd, 1938; *Piper, the Sailboat That Came Back,* New York Graphic Society, 1965; (with Virginia Brown, Billie Phillips, and Jo Paul) *Out*

The day Arnold McWilliams got out of the hospital his three best friends were sitting on his front stoop, waiting for him to come home. ■ (From *Where the Good Luck Was* by Osmond Molarsky. Illustrated by Ingrid Fetz.)

Jumped Abraham, McGraw, 1967; *Song of the Empty Bottles*, Walck, 1968; *Right Thumb, Left Thumb*, Addison-Wesley, 1969; *Where the Good Luck Was*, Walck, 1970; *The Bigger They Come*, Walck, 1971; *Take It or Leave It*, Walck, 1971; *Song of the Smoggy Stars*, Walck, 1972; *The Good Guys and the Bad Guys*, Walck, 1973; *Montalvo Bay*, Walck, 1976; *The Fearless Leroy*, Walck, 1977; *Robbery in Right Field*, Walck, 1978; *A Different Ball Game*, Coward, 1979. Writer of documentary film scripts for industry, government, and labor unions. Writer with Hardie Gramatky of a monthly juvenile feature, "Letters from Ellsworth Elephant," in *Family Circle*, 1960-63.

SIDELIGHTS: "My strongest career influence was my post impressionist artist parents, who felt that none but the creative life was worth while and that people who did life's mundane chores such as managing corporations or performing brain surgery were little better than peasants. We were possibly the poorest family in Nutley, New Jersey between the World Wars but without doubt the greatest snobs. My father's unworldliness was expressed typically the year the New Jersey car license plates came out in green and orange. Offended by this color scheme, he repainted them, from his palette, in a combination of pastel greys and blues.

"Ironically, both my brother and I were discouraged from being painters, as too uncertain a way of making a living and, more or less, by default, fell into other forms of creative activity. My brother is an author and composer and I have been writing, these many years. But I often think that I have a greater untapped inherited talent for painting than for writing.

"Midway through high school, my brother and I began to experiment with marionettes and the summer of my freshman year at Swarthmore College, I signed a contract to travel with the Swarthmore Chautauqua, presenting a marionette show in the afternoon, acting in a comedy at night and driving a truck most of the night to reach the next tent in time for the following afternoon's performance. My brother was too young for the trip and I trained my roommate, James A. Michener (*Hawaii*, etc.) to puppeteer and be my assistant. This experience is reported in his autobiographical novel, *Fires of Spring*.

"The marionettes were an expression of my interest in the theater and a play I wrote and produced in college and which later won a national playwriting contest, led to the writing of the DuPont 'Cavalcade of America,' historical radio drama series, and other dramatized documentaries. This and many other types of writing, including advertising, was essentially commercial and not what my parents would have understood as art. They would have approved of my juvenile books, which I began to write in 1966.

"As a writer of juveniles, most of my ideas and inspiration come from recollections of my own childhood, transposed to a new time and setting, usually the inner city. My first book was written at the suggestion of an elementary school teacher in a ghetto school in Washington, D.C., who deplored the absence of books with which her students could identify. Most of my stories are designed for children whose interests are more advanced than their ability to read. Now, however, as a San Francisco suburbanite, I find myself writing about suburban type children and situations. I have had no children of my own, but for certain background details I now have a ready reference source in a ten-year-old step granddaughter. If the age of my leading characters seems to advance, as future books are published, no doubt this will be because Kathy is growing up.

"Although I have never been an athlete, I always have felt the need for violent exercise and now, in my later sixties,

OSMOND MOLARSKY

play on the town soccer team, belong to a fencing club and cruise the coast of California in a large sailboat, assisted only by my wife, Peggy, who is my age.''

FOR MORE INFORMATION SEE: Children's Book World, November 3, 1968; *Horn Book,* April, 1969; *Young Readers' Review,* October, 1969.

MONJO, F(erdinand) N. 1924-1978

PERSONAL: Born in 1924, in Stamford, Conn.; married a teacher and author; children: three sons, one daughter. *Education:* Graduated from Columbia University. *Residence:* New York City.

CAREER: American author and editor. *Awards, honors:* National Book Award, 1974, for *Poor Richard in France.*

WRITINGS: Indian Summer (illustrated by Anita Lobel), Harper, 1968; *The Drinking Gourd* (AlA Notable Book; illustrated by Fred Brenner), Harper, 1970; *The One Bad Thing about Father* (illustrated by Rocco Negri), Harper, 1970; *Pirates in Panama* (illustrated by Wallace Tripp), Simon & Schuster, 1970; (translator with Nina Ignatowicz) Reiner Zimnik, *The Crane,* Harper, 1970; *The Jezebel Wolf* (illustrated by John Schoenherr), Simon & Schuster, 1971; *The Vicksburg Veteran* (illustrated by Douglas Gorsline), Simon & Schuster, 1971; *Rudi and the Distelfink* (illustrated by George Kraus), Windmill Books, 1972; *The Secret of the Sachem's Tree* (illustrated by Margot Tomes), Coward, 1972; *Slater's Mill* (illustrated by Laszlo Kubinyi), Simon & Schuster, 1972; (editor) Patricia Lauber, *Clarence and the Burglar* (illustrated by Paul Galdone), Coward, 1973; *Me and Willie and Pa: The Story of Abraham Lincoln and His Son Tad* (illustrated by D. Gorsline), Simon & Schuster, 1973; *Poor Richard in France* (illustrated by Brinton Turkle), Holt, 1973.

Grand Papa and Ellen Aroon: Being an Account of Some of the Happy Times Spent Together by Thomas Jefferson and His Favorite Granddaughter (illustrated by Richard Cuffari), Holt, 1974; *King George's Head Was Made of Lead* (illustrated by M. Tomes), Coward, 1974; *The Sea Beggar's Son* (illustrated by C. Walter Hodges), Coward, 1974; *Letters to Horseface: Being the Story of Wolfgang Amadeus Mozart's Journey to Italy, 1769-1770* (illustrated by Don Bolognese and Elaine Raphael), Viking, 1975; *Gettyburg: Tad Lincoln's Story* (illustrated by D. Gorsline), Dutton, 1976; *The Porcelain Pagoda* (illustrated by Richard Egielski), Viking, 1976; *Willie Jasper's Golden Eagle* (illustrated by D. Gorsline), Doubleday, 1976; *Zenas and the Shaving Mill* (illustrated by R. Cuffari), Coward, 1976.

SIDELIGHTS: Ferdinand N. Monjo was born in Stamford, Connecticut in 1924. He acquired his sense of history during his Stamford childhood. His father's family were fur merchants who sent ships to the Arctic to trade with the Eskimos for sealskins. They had emigrated from Spain to this country in 1850. His mother's family were Mississippi natives and he had often heard stories about his great-grand-mother during the Civil War when, as a young woman, she had managed to run a half-deserted plantation. "Listening to stories like these brought history alive so vividly for me that I was never able to read it, later, as if it were a mere collection of facts and dates. Hearing my two families discuss the past—often with considerable heat and color—made it clear to me that people like Grant and Lincoln certainly had been flesh and blood creatures. And if this were true, why then, I could begin to imagine that perhaps even such remote creatures as Elizabeth of England or Caesar (or even Sir Edmund Andros) might once have been alive."

As a child one of his greatest loves was playing the piano. "Forty years ago, when I was a little boy growing up in Stamford, Connecticut, I actually *liked* to practice the piano. I know that's hard to believe, but it's true. (Not the scales and the hard parts, to tell the truth. But the melodies.) And of all the music I ever learned to play, I loved Mozart's best.

"Now I have a long and unusual first name; it is Ferdinand. This meant that I really *had* to have a nickname; it was Buster. And, of course, I had to have a piano teacher; and her name was Lony Warinka Lyman. She was part Russian and part French, and she had studied music at the Brussels Conservatoire. She could play Mozart's sonatas four hundred times better than I could. Sometimes, when she played something especially wonderful of Mozart's for me—to show me how it ought to sound—I'd say, 'Oh, Madame Lyman, how *beautiful* that is!'

"Then she would laugh, as if she had done nothing at all remarkable, and answer in her pretty French accent, 'Oh, vell, Buster! Vhat do you suppose? Zat's *music!*' So it was. And always so perfectly lovely, that there was nothing more to say about it.'' [From an article entitled, "Meet Your Author—F.N. Monjo," Ferdinand N. Monjo, *Cricket Magazine,* September, 1975.[1]]

Another youthful love of his was Indian stories—this love later manifested itself in his first book for children, *Indian Summer.* "As a child, I was fascinated by—no, addicted to—stories of Indian attacks, Indian raids, Indian captives. I was not the eager young racist, gloating over the Indian's stupidity and eager to watch his downfall, mind you. I was quite the young romantic. And Indian stories (the bloodier and more exciting the better) represented the apogee of reading, pleasure. I will never forget the breathless excitement

Everyone else in the village was wondering about them, too. ■ (From *The Secrets of the Sachem's Tree* by F.N. Monjo. Illustrated by Margot Tomes.)

...Those wild winds were seeking to pile us up on the coast of Chile. ■ (From *The Porcelain Pagoda* by F.N. Monjo. Drawings by Richard Egielski.)

with which I read (in the second grade) of what happened to Daniel Boone's daughter, Jemimah Boone, when, as a little girl, she was captured by Indians (and weeks later rescued). As I remember it, the Indians in the story were pretty damned virile. They scared the hell out of me, and I would have given anything if I could have become one of them, and could have been initiated into their tribe that very day. I didn't think they were stupid or 'negative' either. And I knew—even back then, in 1930—that they had abundant cause for the hostility they felt for the frontiersmen." [From an article entitled, "Monjo's Manifest Destiny," by F. N. Monjo, *Library Journal,* May 15, 1974.[2]]

Monjo was graduated from Columbia University in New York. In the 1950's he became an editor for children's books, a profession which he retained for more than twenty years. At one time he was editor-in-chief of the Junior Library at American Heritage and editor-in-chief of Golden Press.

The first of many historical fiction books for children which he was to write, *Indian Summer,* was published in 1969. "... I do not want to write or to publish any stories, ever, that are in any way harmful to children. I think children are the most important national resource that any country can

possess. Too valuable to be lied to, or to be gratuitously insulted."[2]

In 1969 Monjo became vice-president and editorial director of books for children at Coward, McCann and Geoghegan. Prior to this position he had been editor-in-chief of children's books at Harper & Row. He and his wife lived in New York City with their four children. He continued to write historical fiction books throughout the 1970's. "... As an editor, I began to realize that most of the fun of history lay in the details that most children's books seemed to omit. So I resolved to try writing some books for young children, limited to incidents or mere glimpses from history, but allowing enough leisure and space to be able to include the details that help so much to bring a scene to life."

Many of Monjo's historical-fiction books were written from a child's point of view in an effort to humanize our forefathers. "We can—if we insist upon it—overwhelm our six and eight-year-olds with vast, monolithic, unsmiling profiles. I remember, as a child, seeing newsreels of Gutzon Borglum chopping those giant, grim faces of Washington, Lincoln, and Teddy Roosevelt into the Dakota cliffs.

In a way I'm glad they're there. But, as a child, I couldn't imagine that they represented anyone who had ever been a little boy, or that any one of those men had ever cracked a joke or made a pass or fallen on his face. No. They rose up seven stories tall, just as formidable and as poised and as eternal and as unbelievable as the statues of the Egyptian Pharaohs on the Nile.

"I suppose that back in the 1930's, when I was a child, all of us were still more or less in the grip of something I have come to think of as the D.A.R. syndrome. This is a disease in which all great Americans are assumed to have been desperately single-minded, antiseptic, humorless, and perfect. Patients afflicted with this malady believed that their symptoms could be eased by acts of prostration at the feet of heroic statues of the great. Children were urged to participate in these austere rites. But, unfortunately, this joyless hero worship did not lead us to the results we might have hoped for. Instead, it led my generation to boredom and, eventually, to Watergate.

"As a result, I decided that I would try to offer some flawed, partial, impressionistic, and irreverent portraits of great Americans to children today. I wanted these shirt-sleeve miniatures to contain only those details that a young child might be likely to admire and understand. I wanted to be sure to include any jokes and mistakes the great men themselves might have made. I wanted to show their foibles and to present the hero not as a huge, remote icon—but, instead, as an intimate, palpable, fallible surprise." [From an article entitled, "Great Men, Melodies, Experiments, Plots, Predictability, and Surprises," by F. N. Monjo, *Horn Book,* October, 1975.[3]]

Monjo presented sketches of his personalities in his books, rather than an entire biography—his purpose being to invite the young reader to read more about a famous American. "I am frequently asked, 'How can you present a whole life in all its complexity for the understanding of children?' The most fruitful effort—in terms of breaking ground for me as an author—was a little book I wrote ... [in 1970] about Theodore Roosevelt called *The One Bad Thing About Father.* I decided after some reading on the subject that the chief thing I wanted to convey was a sense of T. R.'s surprising dyna-

Grandfather and I are playing chess in his cabin. There's nothing Grandfather loves better than playing chess. ■ (From *Poor Richard in France* by F.N. Monjo. Illustrated by Brinton Turkle.)

mism. But how was I to do that? He had had a long, complicated career. He had lost a wife when he was a young man and had married another. He had been under-Secretary of the Navy, and he had had to resign that post when he wanted to go off to war in Cuba and lead the Rough Riders in the Spanish-American War. How in the world was I ever going to be able to get across to eight-year-olds facts and situations such as these? What could I say to them that would be meaningful about resigning from a cabinet post or losing a wife and finding another? I read all the juvenile books currently available about T. R. and found that all of them dodged the question and simply related the facts in chronological order. As a result, it seemed to me, all of them were dull. And since they had to be brief, all of them read like encyclopedia articles. This was exactly what I did not want to duplicate.

"So I decided, instead, to present Teddy Roosevelt quite differently—telling no more about him than his seven or eight-year-old son Quentin might have done. This meant, simply, that when I came upon facts and situations which I felt an eight-year-old boy would not have understood, I left them out. It also meant that I produced nothing resembling a definitive biography of T. R. I was able to produce only a glimpse of a great man, and yet just such a glimpse as his own little boy might have had. A very sketchy result but, I hope, a lively one.

"This is what I feel I can do: give a child his first authentic taste of a great figure from the past. I can't possibly give the full outline of the great man or the full impact of his doctrines or the full summary of his life's accomplishment. But if that first taste is not bitter and if it leaves the reader perhaps eager to read more on the subject, so much the better. I shall certainly not have satisfied a child's interest in T. R. or Lincoln or Jefferson, but I may have got it started."[3]

In 1974 his book *Poor Richard in France,* which incorporated his idea of a child's point of view of history, won the National Book Award. "Benjamin Franklin, when he went to France to try to persuade the French to help us with the Revolution in 1776, took with him his staid, conservative, sober seventeen-year-old grandson, Temple Franklin, as well as his lively seven-year-old grandson, Benjamin Franklin Bache. Perhaps I've let Benny Bache speak with more irreverence then he ever possessed, though I know that he later grew up to be a highly critical and sarcastic journalist who opposed the Establishment—the Federalist regimes of Washington and Adams."[3]

Monjo was the author of more than twenty books for children which primarily dealt with biographical or historical fiction. He tried to base his stories on as much historical fact as was possible. His research involved many hours and much of this research was done at the New York Society Library. "I have been asked where I draw the line between biography and fictionalized biography and what is the moral obligation of the author to distinguish between fact and fiction in juvenile biographies. . . .

"Now, there is no question that I do invent some scenes and some dialogue, so I should not be listed, as I sometimes am, as a writer of nonfiction. I write, and keep confessing that I write, historical fiction. I take some pains to declare this in the notes I put at the back of all my books, even though the material presented is, I suppose, about ninety-eight percent fact. But when I wrote *Me and Willie and Pa*—about Abraham Lincoln and his son Tad—I allowed Tad, quite unhistorically for all I know, to ask his father what emancipation was all about. And I allowed Lincoln, quite without sanction in any document, to explain it to Tad, as Petroleum V. Nasby might have done. Petroleum V. Nasby was the nom de plume of a popular humorist of the day, David Ross Locke. And it is certifiably true that Lincoln relished and chuckled over Nasby's books. But I have no document nor any authority I can point to proving that Lincoln ever quoted Nasby to Tad. Lincoln could have done so, but I have no reason to suppose he did. So, I call the book historical fiction. Most of it is based on fact, but it contains some minor incidents and exchanges which may never have occurred."[3]

Those in the publishing world who knew Monjo stressed that it was fun to work with him. His friends considered him witty, enthusiastic and with a talent for mimicry. Monjo died at the age of fifty-four in New York City on October 9, 1978.

A memorial fund was established in Monjo's name at the New York Society Library. "We need to inspire our gifted young people to make an attempt at greatness. We need to make them want to reach out after that splendid, elusive, brass ring known as achievement and make it theirs. Our age is more tawdry than we wish it to be, and we yearn for some heroes and heroines for ourselves and for the future. I have not yet utterly abandoned the Western world. It has produced many men and women who still make my skin prickle. I have not yet abandoned the American experiment, for it has produced large numbers of people whom I wish I might have emulated. That is why I would like my books to arouse young people. To make them understand that all great human beings were once uncertain children, unaware of their powers. I want my books to incite children to dare to do something marvelous. For, if they dare, perhaps they will succeed."[3]

FOR MORE INFORMATION SEE: New York Times Book Review, November 3, 1968, November 16, 1975; *School Library Journal,* November, 1968; *Publishers Weekly,* October 8, 1973, November 17, 1975; Mary Gloyne Byler, *American Indian Authors for Young Readers,* Association on American Indian Affairs, 1973; *Bulletin of the Center for Children's Books,* March, 1974, October, 1975, April, June, September, October, November, 1976; F. N. Monjo, "Monjo's Manifest Destiny," *Library Journal,* May 15, 1974; *Horn Book,* August, 1970, August and October, 1971, April, 1973, February and December, 1974, April and October, 1975, February, June, August, October, 1976; *Cricket Magazine,* September, 1975; *Children's Literature Review,* Volume 2, Gale, 1976.

(Died October 9, 1978)

NIELSEN, Kay (Rasmus) 1886-1957

PERSONAL: Given name pronounced "Kigh": born March 12, 1886, in Copenhagen, Denmark; died in 1957; son of Martinius Nielsen (an actor); married Ulla Pless-Schmidt, 1926. *Education:* Studied art in Paris, 1904-11, at the Academie Julien, the Academie Collarossi, and with Lucien Simon. *Home:* Los Angeles, California.

CAREER: Author and illustrator. First exhibition of art work, London, England, 1912; first American exhibition, New York City, 1917; Royal Theater, Copenhagen, Denmark, set designer, 1918-1922; also painted several murals for school libraries, Los Angeles.

WRITINGS: Tag med til Island, A. Frost-Hansen (Copenhagen), 1945; *Danske, Norske og Svenske Keramiske Maerker,* Andreassens (Copenhagen), 1948; *Du Lille: En Lille Bog for Alle Moedre* (illustrated by Ruth Rossen), A. Frost-Hansen, 1949; *Postkort fra den Iberiske Halvoe,* Nytaar (Copenhagen), 1952; *Fager er Lien, om Brennu Njal og Hans Soenner,* A. Frost-Hansen, 1956; *Postkort fra Greekenland,* P. Malling (Copenhagen), 1959; *Pasquinate eller Romerske Novemberelegier,* Privattryk (Copenhagen), 1960 *Lidt om Balloner ude og Hjemme,* G. W. Ventilation (Copenhagen), 1962; *Danske Antikviteter,* C. A. Reitzel (Copenhagen), 1963; *Fire Byer,* Thaning & Appel (Copenhagen), 1963; *Danmark Set fra Luften* (photographs by Torkild Balslev), Lademann (Copenhagen), 1968, translation by Georg Rona published as *Denmark As Seen from Above,* Lademann, 1968; (with Per Eilstrup and Holger Rasmussen) *Vore Gamle Herregaarde* (photographs by T. Balslev and Joergen Groenlund), Lademann, 1968; *Antikfund* (photographs by Aage Jespersen), Lademann, 1969; *Noget om Whisky,* Erichsen (Copenhagen), 1970; *Antikvitets ABC: Haandbog for Samlere,* Lademann, 1972.

Editor; all published Thaning & Appel: (With Gunnar Buchwald) *Antikvitetsaarbogen,* 1963; *Gode Ord om Helbred,* 1967; *Gode Ord om Mad,* 1967; *Gode Ord om Musik,* 1967; *Gode Ord om Rejser,* 1967; *Gode Ord om Vin,* 1967; *En Glaedelig Begivenhed,* 1968; *Sagt om Hunde,* 1968; *Sagt om Heste,* 1969; *Sagt om Oel og Braendevin,* 1969; *Sagt om Tobak,* 1969; *Til Dig fra Mig,* 1969; *Danske Ordsprog,* 1970; *Ord om Venskab,* 1970; *Ord om Lykken,* 1970; *Sagt om Vejret,* 1970.

Illustrator: Arthur Thomas Quiller-Couch, editor, *In Powder and Crinoline,* Hodder & Stoughton, 1913; Peter Christen Asbjörnsen and Jörgen Engebretsen Moe, *East of the Sun and West of the Moon: Old Tales from the North,* Hod-

"Don't drink!" cried out his little Princess, springing to her feet, "I would rather marry a gardener!" ■ (From *Twelve Dancing Princesses and Other Fairy Tales* by A.T. Quiller-Couch. Illustrated by Kay Nielsen.)

Just as they bent down to take the rose a big dense snowdrift came and carried them away.
■ (From *East of the Sun, West of the Moon: Old Tales from the North* by Peter Christen Asbjörnsen and Jörgen Engebretsen. Illustrated by Kay Nielsen.)

Then he coaxed her down and took her home. ■ (From *East of the Sun, West of the Moon: Old Tales from the North* by Peter Christen Asbjörnsen and Jörgen Engebretsen. Illustrated by Kay Nielsen.)

der & Stoughton, 1914, Doran, 1922; A. T. Quiller-Couch, *Twelve Dancing Princesses and Other Fairy Tales,* Doran, 1923; Hans Christian Andersen, *Fairy Tales,* Doran, 1924; Jacob Ludwig Karl and Wilhelm Karl Grimm, *Hansel and Gretel and Other Stories,* Hodder & Stoughton, 1925; R. Wilson, editor, *Red Magic: A Collection of the World's Best Fairy Tales from All Countries,* J. Cape, 1936; *Old Tales from the North,* Seattle Book, 1975.

SIDELIGHTS: **March 12, 1886.** Born in Copenhagen, Denmark. "Both my father and mother were artists. My father, Professor Martinius Nielsen ... was in his youth an actor in the classical repertoire. He became the leading and managing director of the Dagmartheater in Copenhagen, which under his directorate became the modern literary stage.

"My mother, Oda Nielsen, [was an] actress to the court of the royal theater in Copenhagen. . . . In her youth she lived in Paris and brought home the great French repertoire from the eighties. Later she joined the Dagmartheater and the repertoire thereon. Her love for the French she kept in her songs [repertoire Yvette Gilbert] and she also became and still is the interpretess of the songs of the Old Danish folklore.

"In this tense atmosphere of art, I was brought up. I remember men as Ibsen, Bjornsen, Lie, Grieg, Sinding, Brandes and many others probably unknown to the American public. Since early boyhood I have been drawing. When the Sagas were read to me I drew down the people therein. Anything I heard about I tried to put in situations on paper. I heard much and saw much concerning art, but I never really intended to be an artist myself.

"When I was twelve years of age I was taken out of school and given my own teachers. I had a vague idea of being a medical man, but when I was seventeen, I suddenly broke off from books and went to Paris to study art.

"I lived in Paris at Montparnasse for seven years and I frequented several schools of art. First the 'Academie Julien' and under Jean Paul Laurence, thereafter 'Collarossi' under Kristian Krog, and several others; the last was Lucien Simon. I worked and lived in the usual routine of French school life, always working from nature, but in my hours off the school I did drawings out of my imagination. . . . Or, inspired from reading, I did drawings to Heine, Verlaine, Hans Andersen. These drawings, most of them done in black and white, became numerous and in 1920 they were seen by London people and an exhibition was offered by Dowdeswel and Dowdeswel.

"I was brought up in a classical view concerning art, but I remember I loved the Chinese drawings and carvings in my mother's room brought home from China by her father. And this love for the works of art from the East has followed me. My artistic wandering started with the early Italians over Persia, India, to China." [*Contemporary Illustrators of Children's Books,* Horn Book, 1930.[1]]

1911. Left Paris for London.

1912. "I had my first show held by Dowdeswel and Dowdeswel, consisting of the drawings done in my Paris days. After this I worked for England entirely."[1]

The Book of Death, a series of black and white drawings were the principal illustrations selected for the exhibition.

These illustrations were unfortunately never issued in book form. The originals are therefore in private collections or have been lost.

1913. Exhibition at Leicester Galleries featuring the book, *In Powder and Crinoline.* Nielsen submitted his original water colors and entered the second phase of his career by utilizing the Chinese colorists for inspiration.

1915. *East of the Sun, West of the Moon,* water color exhibition at Leicester Galleries. These twenty-five illustrations proved to be Nielsen's best.

1917. First show in America with Scott & Fowles, New York.

1919. Nielsen and collaborator Johannes Poulsen mounted a production of *Aladdin* at the Danish State Theater. Nielsen designed both sets and costumes.

1922. Nielsen and Poulsen mounted a production of *Scaramouche* for which Nielsen made drawings for the published score of the music by Sibelius.

February, 1924. His edition of *Hans Andersen* was exhibited at the Leicester Galleries.

1925. *Hansel and Gretel: Stories from the Brothers Grimm* published. Nielsen offered twelve colored plates.

1926. Married twenty-two-year-old Ulla Pless-Schmidt.

1930. Last exhibition at Leicester Square where the *Red Magic* drawings (his last publication) and the illustrations for *The Brothers Grimm* were on sale.

1936. Traveled to Hollywood with Poulsen to mount a production of "Jedermann" by Hugo von Hofmannsthal, and to design the aetherial "Bald Mountain" sequence for "Fantasia" for Walt Disney.

1939. Second World War broke out in Europe. Nielsen sent for Ulla who had remained in Denmark. During this period, the Disney connection ended in a suspension when plans for "The Little Mermaid" on which Nielsen was working were given up. It was rumored that he was not pleased to see his designs altered during the process of animation. Nielsen began to face financial reverses, a difficult prospect for one who had been accustomed to an easier life style.

Hildegarde Flanner, a California neighbor to the Nielsens, offered the following insight into Nielsens' life in their native Denmark. "In Denmark they had lived in an aura of two generations of theater, art and the lights of family prominence. Now they lived chiefly with memories, the illumination of the past. Domestically it had been a correct and pleasant existence. 'In winter it was night most of the day,' Ulla told us, 'and the house-boy—he was from Java—toward evening would come into the drawing room and turn on more lights and bring us our drinks. Then he would prepare the dinner.' At this point she sighed, remembering that the dishes from breakfast and luncheon lay unwashed in her sink. 'And in summer when we gave an evening party we would make it beautiful for the company. We borrowed the night blooming Cereus from the botanical garden. Ah, it was all excellent, and with music.' But how well she could pretend that everything was 'oughkeigh.' (I told her that was the way it was spelled.) To dine there was an occasion, never merely a meal. Fabulous ries taffel, lace ta-

The Cottage was built of bread and cake. ■ (From *Hansel and Gretel and Other Stories* by Jacob Ludwig Karl and Wilhelm Karl Grimm. Illustrated by Kay Nielsen.)

blecloth, candles, and the silver that did not sink in the North Sea.... As a lady who had never worked for her living she would once in a while break down and work to clean her own house, but just as often, as a lady, she ignored the dirt as an element of life beneath her notice, and when guests were coming to dinner I have heard her say haughtily, 'When I see the whites of their eyes I start to get ready.''' [Hildegarde Flanner Monhoff, "An Elegy" from *The Unknown Paintings of Kay Nielsen,* edited by David Larkin, Bantam Books, 1977.[2]]

The Nielsens decided to raise chickens to ease their financial worries. Flanner wrote: "Their friend, the Danish pianist and entertainer Victor Borge, had a profitable business in rearing and selling Cornish game chickens. Along with creatures in general, the Nielsens had a true heart for chickens. They understood, even liked the silly ways of chickens, knew how to talk to them, and had a sentimental memory of the many chickens they had kept at their country home in Denmark. Soon, going into their house one might hear the soft sleepy cheeping of baby chicks in the small kitchen, cosy in their baskets or in incubators made by Kay. It was a pleasant greeting but an unsettling one to catch these barnyard voices only a few feet away while one stood uncertainly in the proprieties of the drawing room. And finally and somehow, and in spite of many preparations and much work, the enterprise Cornish Game Hen came to nothing.

"It was not easy to see why an artist of Kay's reputation should find his abilities asking for employment. Yet it was easy to see that his disadvantage lay in the narrowness of his range in a day that was suspicious of fantasy—unless neurotic or Joycean—that 'the Golden Age of Illustration' in which his name had been notable along with those of Morris, Beardsley, Boecklin, Pyle, Rackham, Dulac and their brotherhood had closed, and however vital his skill in decoration he had no ease in self-promotion.... Apprehension about money became chronic, and also there was the crucial matter of ill-health. In spite of his tall appearance of well-being, Kay was not strong and Ulla, since no one dares be sick without plenty of cash, did not mention the fact that she was threatened with diabetes."[2]

1942. Miss Jasmine Britton, supervising librarian of the Los Angeles school system, secured from the Pollia Foundation a commission for Nielsen to paint a mural in the library of the Central Junior High School (a modest, multi-racial, and low-income community). Miss Britton recalled: "We built a moving platform for Kay to reach the top. It took him much longer than we expected. He was not well and he smoked continually. I had a problem in war times to find a carton of cigarettes a week.... We paid Kay every two weeks $200."[2] The mural required three years of measuring, climbing, painting, smoking and coughing to finish.

Arthur Millier, art critic of the *Los Angeles Times,* reviewed the presentation of the mural as "one of the most beautiful wall paintings in America. The mural has so impressed Los Angeles educators, that the artist is already at work on sketches for a mural project in another high school here."[2]

1946. The Board of Education of the Central Junior High School, Los Angeles, announced that the school building which contained the Nielsen mural was needed for administration headquarters. Nielsen's mural was stripped from the wall and replaced with charts of urban school districts for decor.

Britton outraged by this act, threatened to expose it to the *Los Angeles Times.* The mural was a gift to the City of Los Angeles and painted by an artist with a reputation on two continents and in England. Shaken politicians offered to move the mural to the newly built Sutter Junior High in the San Fernando Valley, Los Angeles. Unfortunately much of the mural had been totally destroyed by faulty removal and storage. Flanner recalled: "Too shocked to contemplate the ruin, Kay at first refused to work on it. Eventually he was persuaded to do so, however. Characteristically he drove himself mercilessly, often working ten hours and more a day, starting high up on the scaffolding in the cool of the morning and gradually descending to work at lower levels as the heat built up near the ceiling. Ulla and a decorator, Einar Petersen, worked with him. The entire restoration took two years and unquestionably was a drain on Kay's health. The sickening blow to Kay's pride and sensibilities was a matter his shocked friends avoided probing."[2]

Painted a second mural, "The Canticle of the Sun," for the library of the Emerson Junior High School, Los Angeles.

1947. Nielsen completed for the Wong Chapel in the First Congregational Church of Los Angeles an altar painting based on the Twenty-Third Psalm. With the completion of the Wong Chapel painting, Nielsen was again out of work. According to Flanner: "The blank wall they had stared at before was once more coldly staring back at them. They groaned, and their groans were gallant. No one had to pity them. Their friends brought them unnecessary luxuries—exotic hors d'oeuvres and caviar—gifts that would not vulgarly suggest they needed sensible food."[2]

It was to be six years before Nielsen received another commission.

1949. Flanner wrote: "At length anxiety and hope together took them home to Denmark. It was not a simple departure ...just before sailing their cabin was so crowded with things brought along for Kay's comfort that he had no room to lie down."[2]

1952. Returned to the States, but America again failed them and they returned to Denmark once more. Nielsen described the final sojourn in Denmark. "I sat all day in blankets inside a cloud of my freezing breath."[2]

1953. Helen Britton Holland, sister of Jasmine, sent Nielsen fifteen hundred dollars as first payment on a third wall painting, commissioned for Whitman College in Walla Walla, Washington.

June 1957. Died in obscurity. Flanner offered a final sketch of the illustrator. "Ordinarily he wore a tweed jacket, the pockets full of cigarettes for which he was always groping. In other repects he seemed to resemble that Lohan of the Buddhistic discipleship who was represented in the company of a tame crane and an adoring deer. He has been likened to St. Francis, but I prefer the Lohan, of whom I have an old painting which by a strange chance looks enough like Kay Nielsen to have been his Asiatic brother. Kay all his life had an affinity for the Oriental. He was a very talented man yet he was so free of opinions that he left none behind for any portrait by quotation. His work must speak instead. Intellectually he did not have strong identifications but in his feelings he had empathy for many aspects of man and nature. Asked today what they recall most about him people invariably answer, 'He never said an unkind word about anybody.'''[2]

I see the star. ■ (From *Red Magic: A Collection of the World's Best Fairy Tales*, edited by R. Wilson. Illustrated by Kay Nielsen.)

FOR MORE INFORMATION SEE: Bertha E. Mahony, editor, _Illustrators of Children's Books: 1744-1945,_ Horn Book, 1947; Kay Nielsen, _Kay Nielsen,_ Coronet, 1975; Welleran Poltarnes, _Kay Nielsen: An Appreciation,_ Green Tiger, 1976; _The Unknown Paintings of Kay Nielsen,_ edited by David Larkin, Bantam, 1977.

NORTH, Joan 1920-

PERSONAL: Born February 15, 1920, in Hendon, London, England; daughter of Frank Wevil Gordon (a metallurgist) and Gladys May (Paybody) North; married C. A. Rogers (now Astor Professor of Mathematics at University College, University of London), February 24, 1952; children: Jane Petronelle Rogers, Petra Nell Rogers. _Education:_ Attended schools in England prior to 1932, in China, 1932-35, Lowther College, Wales, 1935-36, King's College, University of London, 1938-39. _Home:_ 8 Grey Close, London NW, 11, England.

CAREER: Variously employed for brief periods in social work, nursing, with British Broadcasting Corp., and in publications department of Tate Gallery, London, England; now free-lance writer. _Military service:_ British Woman's Auxiliary Air Force, 1940-45; became leading aircraftswoman. _Member:_ Society of Authors, Buddhist Society, College of Psychic Studies.

WRITINGS: Emperor of the Moon, Bles, 1956; _The Cloud Forest,_ Hart-Davis, 1965, Farrar, 1966; _The Whirling Shapes,_ Farrar; 1967; _The Light Maze,_ Farrar, 1971.

SIDELIGHTS: "When I was a child, my father worked in North China and we travelled a good deal, often coming home on leave to England. Consequently, I have never felt rooted in any particular place. I do remember, with affection, the Blue Funnell boats we used (the journey took about five weeks). They all had ancient Greek Homeric names. It was at the age of eight on the _Sarpedon_ that I read a translation of the _Illiad_ and wept over the fall of Troy. The other book offered me was _Black Beauty,_ so altogether it was a tearful voyage.

"At home I devoured what books were available (and I suppose this is what led me to writing later). I believe it is one of Evelyn Waugh's characters who reads _Alice in Wonderland_ and Havelock Ellis's _Psychology of Sex_ at the same period. This certainly happened to me for the simple reason that both books were there—and we only had a small bookshelf.

"My early creative efforts were directed to putting on plays (apart from the private imaginary stories I pursued alone and with certain friends). I lived a good deal in my imagination. Writing things down was harder work—at once more satisfying and less so. More in that there was something visible actually achieved; less in the loss of freedom and narrowing of focus. Words were so much clumsier a medium.

"I never plan a book ahead. Perhaps writing would be easier if I did. I start with an incident that catches my imagination and make myself plod on until, in desperation, a story unravels itself. It's like taking a torch into a dark place; by its light one dimly discerns the shape ahead and often, when one gets close to it, it surprises one, which is fun. I do not write my books especially for children—more for myself—the child I was and still am."

NUSSBAUMER, Paul (Edmund) 1934-

PERSONAL: Born May 2, 1934, in Luzern, Switzerland; son of Paul (a technician) and Rösli (Dreher) Nussbaumer; married Mares (Jans; a marionette puppeteer), February 2, 1962; children: Nicolas Emanuel, Melchio Peter. _Education:_ Primar und Realschulen (primary and secondary schools), Meiringen, Switzerland; Kunstgewerbeschule (art school), Luzern, Switzerland; Grafisches Atelier, Olten, Switzerland. _Religion:_ Catholic. _Home:_ Sonnhalden, CH—6024 Hildisrieden, Luzern, Switzerland.

CAREER: Painter; illustrator. _Awards, honors:_ Grant of the Federal Department of the Interior, 1956, 1966, 1967; Kiefer-Hablitzel Grant, 1967; _William Tell and His Son_ received Biennale der Illustrationen Bratislava Silbermedaille, 1967, and Jugenbuchpreis der Schweiz, 1974.

WRITINGS—Self-illustrated: (With Palmer Brown) _Anna Lavinias wunderbare Reise_ (title means "The Wonderful Journey of Anna Lavinia"), Benziger (Zurich), 1958; (with Ulrich Gisiger) _Arrah der Zigeuner_ (title means "Arrah the Gypsy"), Benteli (Bern), 1964; (with wife, Mares) _Ihr Kinderlein kommet_ (juvenile), Atlantis (Zurich), 1964, published in the U.S. under the title _Away in a Manger,_ Harcourt, 1965; (with Bettina Hürlimann) _Der Knabe des Tell_ (juvenile), Atlantis, 1965, published in America under the title _William Tell and His Son,_ Harcourt, 1966; (with Alfred Eidenbenz) _Onkel Toms wundersame Reise_ (title means "Uncle Toms' Wonderful Journey"), Schweizerspiegel (Zurich), 1965; (with Ursule Williams) _Der schwarze Max_ (title means "Black Max"), Benziger, 1966; (with Bettina Hürlimann) _Barry_ (juvenile), Atlantis, 1967, published in America under the title _Barry: The Story of a Brave St. Bernard,_ Harcourt, 1968; (with Johan Fabricius) _Hentjes ganz besonderer Winter_ (title means "Hentjes' Very Special Winter"), Sauerländer (Aarau), 1969; (with Rudolf Reichlin) _Der Bauernhof_ (juvenile; title means "The Farm"), Atlantis, 1969; (with Ludwig Bechstein) _Hans im Glück_ (juvenile; title means "Lucky John"), Harlekin-Verlag (Luzern), 1970; (with Gottfried Burgin) _Pony-Ranch_ (juvenile), Atlantis, 1972; (with Retus de Selva) _Die rote Katzenfamilie_ (juvenile; title means "The Red Cat-Family"), Werner Classen Verlag (Zurich), 1974.

Illustrator: _Im Wunderland_ (Volumes I and II; textbook; title means "In Wonderland"), Kant. Lehrmittelverlag, (Luzern), 1966; _Daheim_ (textbook; title means "At Home"), Kant. Lehrmittelverlag, 1966; Alexander Pushkin, _Eugen Onegin Dramen_ (title means "Eugen Onegin Dramas"), Edito-Service (Geneva), 1967; Guy de Maupassant, _Mademoiselle Fifi: Une Vie_ (title means "A Life"), Maurice Goron Editeur d'art (Paris), 1968; Sagenmappen, _Wallis_ (title means "Traditions"), Wallis, Mengis and Sticher (Luzern), 1968; Sagenmappen, _Innerschweiz_ (title means "Traditions of Inner Switzerland"), Mengis and Sticher, 1969.

Sagenmappen, _Luzern,_ Mengis and Sticher, 1970; Grimm Brothers, _Hansel and Gretel_ (juvenile), Harlekin-Verlag, 1971; Johanna Spyri, _Heidi,_ Volume 1 (juvenile), Benziger, 1971; Alain Fournier, _Le Grand Maulnes_ (title means "The Big Maulnes"), Edito-Service, 1971; Hans Bender, _Wunschkost,_ Edito-Service, 1971; C. F. Meyer, _Jürg Jenatsch,_ Edito-Service, 1971; _Als die Eisenbahn noch Konig war_ (juvenile; title means "The Time the Train was Still King"), Harlekin-Verlag, 1972; Sagenmappen, _Berner Oberland_ (title means "Traditions of Berner Oberland"), Mengis and Sticher, 1972; Sagenmappen, _Bünder_ (title means "Tradi-

Tell grew pale. To shoot an apple from the head of his son? What if he missed? Should he refuse to shoot?

"If you do not shoot, you must die anyhow, and the boy, too," said Gessler. ■ (From *William Tell and His Son* by Bettina Hürlimann. Illustrated by Paul Nussbaumer.)

tions of Graubünden"), Mengis and Sticher, 1973; Sagen-mappen, *Ostschweizer* (title means "East-Switzerland"), Mengis and Sticher, 1974; Silvia Sempert, *Na meh Guet Nacht-Geschichtli* (juvenile; title means "Some More Good-Night Stories"), Ex-Libris (Zurich), 1974; *Solothurner Sagen* (title means "Traditions of Kanton"), Solothurn, Mengis and Sticher (Luzern), 1975; Hans Manz, *Der schwarze Wasserbutz* also titled as *Die schönsten Sagen der Schweiz* (juvenile; title means "The Most Beautiful Traditions of Switzerland"), Huber Fraunfeld, 1976; Gilbert Cesbron, *La Tradition Fontquernie* (title means "Tradition of Fontquernie"), Edito-Service (Geneva), 1976; Johanna Spyri, *Heidi,* Volume I and II, (juvenile), Benziger (Zurich), 1976; Adolf Heizmann, *Der Kaiser bracht Soldaten* (juvenile; title means "The Emperor Needs Soldiers"), Schweizer Jugendschriftenwork (Zurich), 1977; Grimm Brothers, *Die zertanzten Schuhe* (juvenile; title means "The Shoes used by Dancing"), Aktion Blindenhörbücherei (Zurich), 1978.

SIDELIGHTS: "I was born in Lucerne on May 2, 1934. I have little recollection of the city since I was only two years old when my parents moved from there to Meiringen which was to become my home. My father worked as a depot chief

for the train station—the trains which took me to and from our cramped little town. My father's specialty was the 'steam engines.' They also became my interest, but not in a technical sense, for they were 'steam horses' to me. I drew these huge, black, steam-spitting machines in all dimensions and techniques. At the age of five, I sold one of these sketches for one frank and since that day desired to become nothing other than an artist. Two, perhaps three years later came the period of 'The Romans.' I painted enormous slaughter scenes—my [Karl May] phantasies reached all the way to the 'Indian' slaughters.

"These developments were rapidly interrupted with my entrance examination into secondary school. My instructor forbade my many drawings and insisted on a concentration of arithmetic, reading, and writing. I studied these basics, but barely passed the examinations. Then came the years of decision making regarding a profession. My father quite naturally wanted to know nothing about my becoming an artist—I was to become a technician. Father's dream did not bear much fruit.

"At the age of sixteen I entered an art school in Lucerne where I studied for five glorious years. My mentor, Swiss

PAUL NUSSBAUMER

surrealist, Max von Moos, awakened in me the great joy for illustration and painting. Again came a period of [painting] the Romans, the Indians, the Cowboys, the Wild West . . . it was heavenly!

"At twenty-one with schooling behind me, I wanted to become an artist, and set out for Rome with little money in my pocket. After six months my dream was shattered. I was penniless and had to take a position as designer of a window showcase for a large clothing store. Every year came Christmastime and with it the three kings, the winter scenes, the entire magic of winter. And here was the start of my first book. The Christmas story, *Away in a Manger*, was born. Much was held together with the first book—my marriage, a move to Tessin, the collaboration with Bettina Hürlimann. The story of the first book was actually written by my wife, Mares. This is how my books came about and the time came as well when I was able to make a living as painter and illustrator.

"We moved back to the south of Switzerland and have for the last fourteen years lived in the wide-open spaces of the country not far from Lucerne. I've concentrated more on my illustrations these last few years. I painted murals in schools, orphanages, kindergartens, hospitals, and restaurants. It is here that I give [children] my own 'child world'."

FOR MORE INFORMATION SEE: Bettina Hürlimann, *Die Welt im Bilderbuch,* Atlantis, 1965; *Graphis,* number 131, 1967; *Bookbird,* February, 1970; Bettina Hürlimann, *Sieben Häuser,* Artemis, 1976.

PARNALL, Peter 1936-

PERSONAL: Born in 1936, in Syracuse, N.Y.; married; children: one son, one daughter. *Education:* Attended Cornell University and Pratt Institute School of Art. *Home:* Waldoboro, Me.

CAREER: Left Cornell University shortly after entering and drifted through the southwestern United States, holding a variety of jobs; returned to New York and attended Pratt Institute for two years before taking the job as art director for a travel magazine; worked for five years as an art director for an advertising agency; free-lance designer; author and illustrator of books for children. *Awards, honors:* The *New York Times* named *A Dog's Book of Bugs* by Elizabeth Griffen and *Knee-Deep in Thunder* by Sheila Moon as the best illustrated children's books of the year in 1967 and *Malachi Mudge* by Edward Cecil for the same honor in 1968; Christopher Award for Children's Book Category, 1971, for *Annie and the Old One* by Miska Miles; the American Institute of Graphic Arts Children's Book Show selected *When the Porcupines Moved In* by Cora Annett for the 1971-72 exhibition and *Year on Muskrat Marsh* by Berniece Freschet for the 1973-1974 exhibition; *Annie and the Old One* by M. Miles and *The Desert Is Theirs* by Byrd Baylor received the Brooklyn Art Books for Children Citation in 1973 and 1977 respectively; *The Desert Is Theirs* by B. Baylor and *Hawk, I'm Your Brother* by B. Baylor were named Caldecott Medal Honor Books in 1976 and 1977 respectively.

WRITINGS—All self-illustrated: *The Mountain,* Doubleday, 1971; *The Great Fish,* Doubleday, 1973; *Alfalfa Hill,* Doubleday, 1975; *A Dog's Book of Birds,* Scribner, 1977.

Illustrator: Wayne Short, *The Cheechakoes,* Random House, 1964; Mary Francis Shura, *A Tale of Middle Length,* Atheneum, 1966; Elizabeth Griffen, *A Dog's Book of Bugs,* Atheneum, 1967; Sheila Moon, *Knee-Deep in Thunder,* Atheneum, 1967; Edward Cecil (pseudonym of Cecil Maiden), *Malachi Mudge,* McGraw, 1968; Frank Lee DuMond, *Tall Tales of the Catskills,* Atheneum, 1968; Jean Craighead George, *The Moon of the Wild Pigs,* Crowell, 1968; Murray Goodwin, *Underground Hideaway,* Harper, 1968; Walt Morey, *Kavik the Wolf Dog,* Dutton, 1968; Patricia Coffin, *The Gruesome Green Witch,* Walker & Co., 1969; Miska Miles, *Apricot ABC,* Little, Brown, 1969; Peggy Parish, *A Beastly Circus,* Simon & Schuster, 1969.

Aileen Lucia Fisher, *But Ostriches,* Crowell, 1970; George Mendoza, *The Inspector,* Doubleday, 1970; Jan Wahl, *Doctor Rabbit,* Delacorte, 1970; Cora Annett, *When the Porcupine Moved In,* F. Watts, 1971; Angus Cameron, *The Nightwatchers,* Four Winds Press, 1971; G. Mendoza, *Big Frog, Little Pond,* McCall, 1971; G. Mendoza, *Moonfish and Owl Scratchings,* Grosset, 1971; M. Miles, *Annie and the Old One,* Little, Brown, 1971; J. Wahl, *The Six Voyages of Pleasant Fieldmouse,* Delacorte, 1971; Margaret Hodges, *The Fire Bringer,* Little, Brown, 1972; Jane Yolen and Barbara Green, *The Fireside Song Book of Birds and Beasts,* Simon and Schuster, 1972; Mary Anderson, *Emma's Search for Something,* Atheneum, 1973; Mary Ann Hoberman, *A Little Book of Little Beasts,* Simon & Schuster, 1973; Laurence P. Pringel, *Twist, Wiggle, and Squirm: A Book about Earthworms,* Crowell, 1973; Miriam Schlein, *The Rabbit's World,* Four Winds Press, 1973; Byrd Baylor, *Everybody Needs a Rock* (ALA Notable Book), Scribner, 1974; Berniece Freschet, *Year on Muskrat Marsh,* Scribner, 1974; Keith Robertson, *Tales of Myrtle the Turtle,* Viking, 1974.

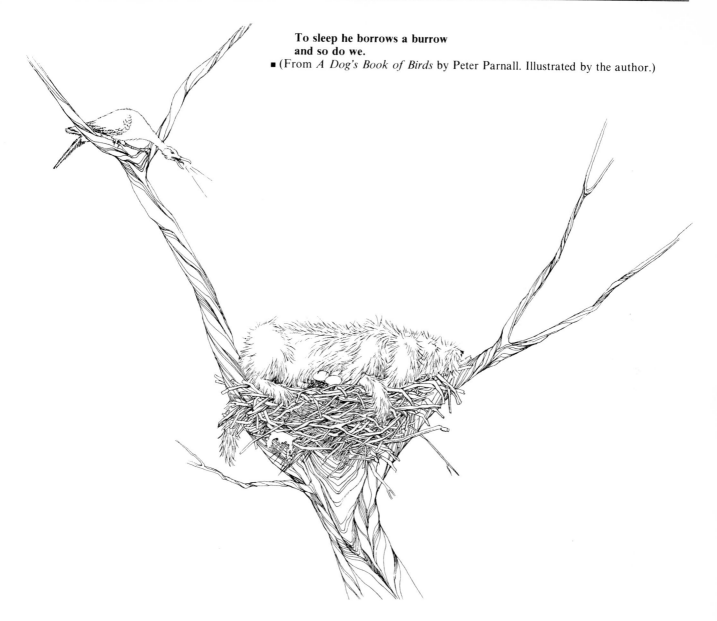

**To sleep he borrows a burrow
and so do we.**
■ (From *A Dog's Book of Birds* by Peter Parnall. Illustrated by the author.)

B. Baylor, *The Desert Is Theirs,* Scribner, 1975; Sally Carrighar, *The Twilight Seas,* Weybright & Talley, 1975; Millard Lampell, *The Pig with One Nostril,* Doubleday, 1975; Alice Schick, *The Peregrine Falcons,* Dial Press, 1975; B. Baylor, *Hawk, I'm Your Brother,* Scribner, 1976. B. Baylor, *The Way To Start a Day,* Scribner, 1977; B. Baylor, *The Other Way to Listen,* Scribner, 1978.

SIDELIGHTS: Peter Parnall spent his childhood in the country where he developed a fondness for animals. His interest in wildlife inspired him to become a veterinarian. Parnall enrolled in Cornell University to qualify for a position in the science of animal care, but he soon realized his preference for drawing animals was stronger than his desire to study them.

Parnall left college and wandered from job to job throughout the southwestern United States. The wayfaring young man eventually returned to New York to study advertising at Pratt Institute. It wasn't long, however, before Parnall dropped out of the academic environment to pursue a career as an art director. After working several years in the advertising industry, Parnall developed his own illustrative style,

but at the same time became disillusioned with the field and the people in it.

By the 1960's Parnall turned to illustrating books for children. The illustrator is still deeply interested in animals, and often finds inspiration for many of his works by taking long walks to watch deer and other wild creatures.

In *The Mountain* Parnall gave a pictorial account of how man could destroy nature. "[*The Mountain*] is a pleasure to look at. Judging from this picture biography of a mountain, it is no surprise that the author has won prizes in graphic arts . . . ," noted a reviewer for the *New York Times*. In an article for *Saturday Review,* Zena Sutherland wrote, "*The Mountain* is one of the best [books on ecology and conservation] for young children: simply written, beautifully illustrated, with no preaching from the author."

Parnall's *Alfalfa Hill* described the effect of winter on a hill in New Jersey. "Parnall's prose poem describes [the seasonal] changes, and his piercing line drawings effectively record the changing habitat . . . ," commented a reviewer for *Booklist*. In reviewing the same book, a critic for the *Bulletin of*

PETER PARNALL

the Center for Children's Books observed, "The illustrations are superb, black and white lines with all of this artist's usual spare elegance, his distinctive veining of trees, and a soft realism in depicting animals. . . ."

Parnall now lives on a farm in Maine, raising sheep, logging, and illustrating two to three books per year. He sells limited edition prints of his works.

FOR MORE INFORMATION SEE: Lee Kingman and others, compilers, *Illustrators of Children's Books, 1957-1966*, Horn Book, 1968; *Saturday Review*, September 18, 1971; Doris de Montreville and Donna Hill (editors), *Third Book of Junior Authors*, H. W. Wilson, 1972; *New York Times Book Review*, January 2, 1972; *Horn Book*, October 1975; *Booklist*, November 15, 1975; *Bulletin of the Center for Children's Books*, February, 1976.

PIATTI, Celestino   1922-

PERSONAL: Born January 5, 1922, near Zurich, Switzerland; married Marianne Piatti-Stricker (an artist). *Education:* Attended the School for Applied Arts in Zurich, Switzerland, 1937. *Residence:* Basel, Switzerland.

CAREER: Apprentice in graphic arts, 1938-42; commercial artist in studio of Fritz Buehler, Zurich, Switzerland, 1944-48; opened his own studio, 1948; Deutscher Taschenbuch Verlag, Munich, Germany, designer of paperback book covers, 1961-63; author, illustrator, and designer. *Awards, honors:* Several of Piatti's posters have been given annual awards by the Swiss Federal Department of the Interior.

WRITINGS: (With wife, Marianne Piatti, and Hansbeat Stricker) *Reisen mit Pinsel, Stift, und Feder: Skizzenblaetter und Aufzeichnungen*, Werner & Bischoff, 1962; *The Happy Owls* (ALA Notable Book; self-illustrated), Atheneum, 1963; *Eulenglueck*, Artemis Verlag, 1963; (with Hans Schumacher) *ABC der Tiere* (self-illustrated), Artemis Verlag, 1965, translation by Jon Reid published as *Celestino Piatti's Animal ABC*, Atheneum, 1966; (with Ursula Huber) *Zirkus Nock* (self-illustrated), Artemis Verlag, 1967, translation by Barbara Kowal Gollob published as *The Nock Family Circus*, Atheneum, 1968; (with Ursula Piatti) *Der Kleine Krebs*, Artemis Verlag, 1973, translation published as *The Little Crayfish*, Bodley Head, 1974.

Illustrator: Edzard Hellmuth Schaper, *Die Legende vom Vierten Koenig*, J. Hegner, 1961, reissued, 1972; William Saroyan, *Zirkusluft*, Artemis Verlag, 1968; Aurel von Juechen, *Die Heilige Nacht*, Artemis Verlag, 1968, translation by Cornelia Schaeffer published as *The Holy Night: The Story of the First Christmas* (ALA Notable Book), Atheneum, 1968; Max Bolliger, *Der Goldene Apfel*, Artemis Verlag, 1970, translation by Roseanna Hoover published as *The Golden Apple: A Story*, Atheneum, 1970.

ADAPTATIONS—Film: "The Happy Owls," produced by Weston Woods.

SIDELIGHTS: Celestino Piatti was born at Wangen near Zurich, Switzerland on January 5, 1922. He studied at the Kunstgewerbeschule (School for Applied Arts) in Zurich in 1937 and served a four year apprenticeship in graphic design until 1942. After working as a commercial artist for Fritz Bühler in Basil, Switzerland, he opened his own studio with his wife in 1948.

CELESTINO PIATTI

O
Who's this who hangs
Yet takes no chances?
Orangutan!
He hides in branches

(From *Celestino Piatti's Animal ABC,* text by Jon Reid.)

In 1961 he began to design paperback book covers. Piatti read every book for which he supplied the cover because he felt that he needed to know his subject thoroughly before he designed its book cover.

After designing book covers, he began to illustrate children's books, including his successful book, *The Happy Owls,* written in 1963.

Piatti lives in Basil, Switzerland with his wife, Marianne. He is widely known as an advertising and poster artist as well as an illustrator for children's books.

As a commercial artist, Celestino Piatti entered exhibits all over the world, winning the poster competition at the Foire Internationale de Lyon in 1959, and at the Kieler Woche in Germany in 1961.

Commenting on *The Happy Owls,* Virginia Haviland wrote in *Horn Book,* "Unlike the usual traditional fable with its acceptable moral, this has an inconclusive lesson, for two contented owls fail to convince an assemblage of bickering barnyard fowls that there is reason for rejoicing in the delights of the season. Sharply clear to the picture-book child is the impressionistic art: the huge piercing-eyed owls, spirited geese, peacock, hens, and ducks, the surrealistic flower, and the variety of trees. A fresh visual experience." Alice Dalgliesh, writing in *Saturday Review,* commented, "[This] book demands attention because of the posterlike quality of its pictures, the artist's use of color, and the excellent color reproduction. . . . Children may find this either an amusing or a sad ending according to the way that it strikes their fancy. . . ."

Book Week's comments on *Celestino Piatti's Animal ABC* included, "For visual pleasure, this humorous and handsome ABC is my favorite of the books I've seen this spring. Great sweeping black lines nearly a quarter of an inch thick outline the main forms of Celestino Piatti's big, boldly colored and patterned animals on each page. . . . They are unmistakably modern, clever, and decorative, showing the inspiration of Douanier Rousseau crossed with that of Chagall, and are only surpassed by Andre Francois' wonderfully original creatures. The text is pitifully obvious and flat, perhaps because there was an attempt to keep too close to the original.''

FOR MORE INFORMATION SEE: *Graphis,* number 66, 1956, and number 115, 1964; *Saturday Review,* June 27, 1964; *Horn Book,* August, 1964, June, 1966; *Book Week,* May 15, 1966; Lee Kingman and others, compilers, *Illustrators of Children's Books, 1957-1966,* Horn Book, 1968; Doris de Montreville and Donna Hill, editors, *Third Book of Junior Authors,* H. W. Wilson, 1972.

PYLE, Howard   1853-1911

PERSONAL: Born March 5, 1853, in Wilmington, Delaware; died November 9, 1911, in Florence, Italy; son of William (owner of a leather business) and Margaret Churchman (Painter) Pyle; married Anne Poole (a singer), April 12, 1881. *Education:* Attended private schools, art school in Philadelphia for three years, and Art Student's League in New York. *Religion:* Quaker. *Home:* Wilmington, Delaware.

CAREER: Author, artist, painter, teacher of illustration, and writer of children's stories: employed as an illustrator for *Scribner's Monthly;* taught illustration at Drexell Institute of Arts and Sciences in Philadelphia, 1894-1900, later establishing his own art school in Wilmington. *Member:* National Institute of Arts and Letters, Associate National Academy, 1905, National Academy, 1907, Century Club of New York, and Franklin Inn Club of Philadelphia.

WRITINGS—All self-illustrated, except as noted: *The Merry Adventures of Robin Hood of Great Renown, in Nottinghamshire,* Scribner, 1883, reissued, Dover, 1968 [other editions illustrated by Lawrence Beall Smith, Grosset & Dunlap, 1952; Paul Busch, Whitman, 1955; Benvenuti, Golden Press, 1962; Jo Polseno, Grosset & Dunlap, 1965; Don Irwin, Childrens Press, 1968]; *Otto of the Silver Hand,* Scribner, 1883, reissued, F. Watts, 1971; *Pepper and Salt; or, Seasoning for Young Folk,* Harper, 1886, reissued, Dover, 1967; *The Wonder Clock; or, Four and Twenty Marvellous Tales, Being One for Each Hour of the Day* (with verses by sister, Katherine Pyle), Harper, 1888, reissued, Dover, 1965; *The Rose of Paradise,* Harper, 1888; *Men of Iron,* Harper, 1891, reissued, Scholastic Book Services, 1968 [another edition illustrated by Clark B. Fitzgerald, Webster, 1949]; *Book of Pirates,* Harper, 1891, later published as *Howard Pyle's Book of Pirates,* edited by Merle Johnson, Harper, 1921, reprinted, Harper, 1965; *A Modern Aladdin; or, The Wonderful Adventures of Oliver Munier,* Harper, 1892; *The Story of Jack Ballister's Fortunes,* Century, 1895; *Twilight Land,* Harper, 1895, reprinted, Dover, 1968; *The Garden behind the Moon: A Real Story of the Moon Angel,* Scribner, 1895; *The Price of Blood: An Extravaganza of New York Life in 1807,* R. G. Badger, 1899.

The Story of King Arthur and His Knights, Scribner, 1903, reissued as *The Book of King Arthur,* Childrens Press, 1969 [another edition illustrated by Sergio Leone, Grosset & Dunlap, 1965]; *The Story of the Champions of the Round Table,* Scribner, 1905, reprinted, Scribner, 1968; *Stolen Treasure* (stories), Harper, 1907; (with Winthrop Packard, Molly Elliot Seawell, and others) *Strange Stories of the Revolution,* Harper, 1907; *The Story of Sir Launcelot and His Companions,* Scribner, 1907; (with J. H. Upshur, Paul Hull, Reginald Gourlay, and others) *Adventures of Pirates and Sea-Rovers,* Harper, 1908; *The Ruby of*

HOWARD PYLE

Kishmoor, Harper, 1908, reprinted, C. F. Braun, 1965; *The Story of the Grail and the Passing of Arthur,* Scribner, 1910.

Other Writings: *Within the Capes,* Scribner, 1885; (with others) *School and Playground* (stories), D. Lothrop, 1891; (editor) Alexandre Olivier Exquemelin, *The Buccaneers and Marooners of America,* Macmillan, 1891, reprinted, Gryphon Books, 1971; *The Divinity of Labor* (address), J. Rogers, 1898; *Rejected of Men: A Story of Today,* Harper, 1903; (contributor) William Dean Howells, editor, *Shapes That Haunt the Dusk,* Harper, 1907; (contributor) Katherine N. Birdsall and George Haven Putnam, editors, *The Book of Laughter,* Knickerbocker Press, 1911; *King Stork* (illustrated by Trina Schart Hyman), Little, Brown, 1973.

Illustrator: *Yankee Doodle: An Old Friend in a New Dress,* Dodd, 1881; Alfred Lord Tennyson, *Lady of Shalott,* Dodd, 1881; Charles Carleton Coffin, *Old Times in the Colonies,* Harper, 1881; Rossiter Johnson, *Phaeton Rogers,* Scribner, 1881; William Makepeace Thackery, *The Chronicle of the Drum,* Scribner, 1882; Helen Campbell, *Under Green Apple Boughs,* Fords, Howard, 1882; Will Carlton, *Farm Ballads,* Harper, 1882; James Baldwin, *Story of Siegfried,* 1882; C. C. Coffin, *Building the Nation: Events in the History of the United States from the Revolution to the Beginning of the War between the States,* Harper, 1883; Horace E. Scudder, *A History of the United States of America Preceded by a Narrative of the Discovery and Settlement of North America and of the Events Which Led to the Independence of the Thirteen English Colonies for the Use of Schools and Academies,* Sheldon, 1884; Oliver Wendell Holmes, *Illustrated Poems,* Houghton, 1885; Francis S. Drake, *Indian History for Young*

Folks, Harper, 1885; Driedrich Knickerbocker (pseudonym of Washington Irving), *A History of New York,* two volumes, Grolier Club, 1886; Thomas Wentworth Higginson, *A Larger History of the United States of America,* Harper, 1886; Will Carlton, *City Ballads,* Harper, 1886; James Baldwin, *Story of the Golden Age,* Scribner, 1887, illustrations reprinted in *Odysseus, the Hero of Ithaca* by Mary E. Burt, Scribner, 1898; Thomas Buchanan Read, *The Closing Scene,* Lippincott, 1887; Elbridge S. Brooks, *Storied Holidays: A Cycle of Historic Red-Letter Days,* D. Lothrop, 1887; Edmund Clarence Stedman, *The Star Bearer,* D. Lothrop, 1888; Wallace Bruce, *Old Homestead Poems,* Harper, 1888.

Lafcadio Hearn, *Youma: The Story of a West Indian Slave,* Harper, 1890; Harold Frederic, *In the Valley,* Scribner, 1890; John Greenleaf Whittier, *The Captain's Well,* New York Ledger, 1890; James Lane Allen, *Flute and Violin, and Other Kentucky Tales and Romances,* Harper, 1891; Oliver Wendell Holmes, *One Hoss Shay, with its Companion Poems,* Houghton, 1892; Holmes, *Poetical Works of Oliver Wendell Holmes,* two volumes, Houghton, 1892; Holmes, *Dorothy Q., Together with A Ballad of the Boston Tea Party and Grandmother's Story of the Bunker Hill Battle,* Houghton, 1893; Holmes, *Autocrat of the Breakfast Table,* two volumes, Houghton, 1893; John Flavel Mines, *A Tour around New York* [and] *My Summer Acre,* Harper, 1893; C. C. Coffin, *Abraham Lincoln,* Harper, 1893; Mary E. Wilkens, *Giles Corey,* Harper, 1893; Thomas A. Janvier, *In Old New York,* Harper, 1894.

W. D. Howells, *Stops of Various Quills,* Harper, 1895; E. S. Brooks, *Great Men's Shoes,* Putnam, 1895; E. S. Brooks, *The True Story of George Washington,* D. Lothrop, 1895; A. Conan Doyle, *The Parasite: A Story,* Harper, 1895; Robert Louis Stevenson, *The Novels and Tales of Robert Louis Stevenson,* three volumes, Scribner, 1895; Harriet Beecher Stowe, *Writings of Harriet Beecher Stowe,* two volumes, Riverside Press, 1896; Silas Weir Mitchell, *Hugh Wynne, Free Quaker,* Century, 1896; T. N. Page, *In Ole Virginia,* Scribner, 1896; Henry Van Dyke, *First Christmas Tree,* Scribner, 1897; Woodrow Wilson, *George Washington,* Harper, 1897; Francis Parkman, *Works of Francis Parkman,* three volumes, Little, Brown, 1897-98; Henry Cabot Lodge, *Story of the Revolution,* Scribner, 1898; Ernest Ingersoll, *The Book of Oceans,* Century, 1898; Mary E. Wilkens, *Silence, and Other Stories,* Harper, 1898; Margaret Deland, *Old Chester Tales,* Harper, 1899; Paul Leicester Ford, *Janice Meredith, A Story of the American Revolution,* two volumes, Dodd, 1899.

Poster advertisement by Pyle for *To Have and To Hold.* ■ (Courtesy of the Delaware Art Museum.)

The Great Red Fox goeth to the store-house and helps himself to the good things. ❦

(From *The Wonder Clock* by Howard Pyle. Illustrated by the author.)

(From *The Merry Adventures of Robin Hood* by Howard Pyle. Illustrated by the author.)

(From *Pepper and Salt: or, Seasoning for Young Folk* by Howard Pyle. Illustrated by the author.)

Mary Johnston, *To Have and to Hold,* Houghton, 1900; Edwin Markham, *The Man with the Hoe, and Other Poems,* Doubleday, 1900, illustrations reprinted in *Modern Pen Drawings European and American,* edited by Charles Holmes, The Studio, 1901; John Lothrop Motley, *Works of John Lothrop Motley,* Harper, 1900; Nathaniel Hawthorne, *Complete Writings of Nathaniel Hawthorne,* Houghton, 1900; Maud Wilder Goodwin, *Sir Christopher: A Romance of a Maryland Manor in 1644,* Little, Brown, 1901; Robert Neilson, *Captain Renshaw; or, The Maid of Cheapside: A Romance of Elizabethan London,* L. C. Page, 1901, illustrations reprinted in *A History of American Art,* by Sadakichi Hartman, L. C. Page, 1901; Woodrow Wilson, *A History of the American People,* five volumes, Harper, 1902, reprinted with additional illustrations, Harper, 1918; *Har-*

per's Encyclopedia of United States History, ten volumes, Harper, 1902; James Russell Lowell, *The Poetical Works of James Russell Lowell,* five volumes, Riverside Press, 1904; Wilbur F. Gordy, *A History of the United States,* Scribner, 1904.

Justus Miles Forman, *The Island of Enchantment,* Harper, 1905; J. B. Cabell, *The Line of Love,* Harper, 1905; John Greenleaf Whittier, *Snow Bound: A Winter Idyl,* Houghton, 1906; J. B. Cabell, *Gallantry: An Eighteenth Century Dizain,* Harper, 1907; Henry Peterson, *Dulcibel: A Tale of Old Salem,* Winston, 1907; J. B. Cabell, *Chivalry,* Harper, 1909; L. E. Chittenden, *Lincoln and the Sleeping Sentinel,* Harper, 1909; Margaret Sutton Briscoe, John Kendrick Bangs, and others, *Harper's Book of Little Plays,* Harper, 1910; William Makepeace Thackery, *The Works of William Makepeace Thackery,* edited by Lady Ritchie, Harper, 1910; William Gilmore Beymer, *On Hazardous Service: Scouts and Spies of the North and South,* Harper, 1912; Don Seitz, *The Buccaneers,* Harper, 1912; Fanny E. Coe, *Founders of Our Country,* American Book Co., 1912; J. B. Cabell, *The Soul of Melicent,* F. Stokes, 1913; W.H.W. Bicknell, *Etchings,* Bibliophile Society, 1913; Margaret Deland, *Around Old Chester,* Harper, 1915; W. F. Gordy, *Stories of Later American History,* Scribner, 1915; Mark Twain (pseudonym of Samuel Longhorne Clemens), *Saint Joan Of Arc,* Harper, 1919; Francis J. Dowd, editor, *Book of the American Spirit,* Harper, 1923; Henry Gilbert, *Robin Hood,* Parents' Magazine Press, 1964.

Contributor of illustrations and writings to various periodicals and newspapers, including Chicago *Tribune, Collier's Weekly, Cosmopolitan, Harper's Monthly, Harper's Young People, Ladies' Home Journal, St. Nicholas,* and *Scribner's.*

ADAPTATIONS—Movies: "The Black Shield of Falworth," adaptation of *Men of Iron,* starring Tony Curtis and Janet Leigh, Universal Pictures, 1954.

Plays: Sophie L. Goldsmith, *Wonder Clock Plays,* Harper, 1925; Mary T. Pyle, *Robin Hood Plays Matchmaker* (one-act), Dramatists Play Service, 1939; M. T. Pyle, *The Apple of Contentment* (one-act), Dramatists Play Service, 1939; M. T. Pyle, *Three Strangers Come to Sherwood* (one-act), Dramatists Play Service, 1942.

Recordings: "Tales of King Arthur and his Knights," read by Ian Richardson, Caedmon, 1975.

SIDELIGHTS: **March 5, 1853.** Born in Wilmington, Delaware. "Everything must have a beginning, and I often think that my beginning must have begun in a very bright and happy childhood. First of all there was my mother—the best mother, I believe, that any boy ever had, unless it is the mother of my own boys. My mother loved good books and such pictures as were thought to be good in those days. Not only did she like such things herself, but she took care that I should like them, too.

"We children . . . did not have so many books as children have nowadays; but many that we had were very good. Long before I could read myself, I had heard the story of *Robinson Crusoe,* and *Gulliver Among the Pygmies and Giants.* I knew the *Tangleweed Tales* and *Wonder Book* very well, and *A Midsummer Night's Dream* and *Ivanhoe* had been read aloud to me. I was acquainted with *Pilgrim's Progress,* and knew the best of Grimm's *German Fairy Tales* almost by heart. *Slovenly Peter* I loved, and likewise

Pyle on the front porch of his new studio, built in 1900.

the *Original Poems* and the *Arabian Nights*. All these things we had when I was a little boy, and, after all, there is not much better literature to be found even nowadays than these and others I could name; such my mind was fed upon in those early days.

"As I have said, my mother was very fond of pictures; but especially was she fond of pictures in books. A number of prints hung on the walls of our house: there were engravings of Landseer and Holman Hunt's pictures, and there was a colored engraving of Murillo's Madonna standing balanced on the crescent moon, and there was pretty smiling Beatrice Cenci, and several others that were thought to be good pictures in those days. But we—my mother and I—liked the pictures in books the best of all. I may say to you in confidence that even to this very day I still like the pictures you find in books better than wall pictures.

"As for our picture-books: not only did we have the old illustrated Thackeray and Dickens novels, and Bewick's Fables, and Darley's outline drawings to Washington Irving's stories, and others of that sort, but the *London Punch* (and there were very great artists who drew pictures for the *London Punch* in those days) and the *Illustrated London News* came into our house every week. I can remember many and many an hour in which I lay stretched out before the fire upon the rug in the snug warm little library, whilst the hickory logs snapped and crackled in the fireplace, and

the firelight twinkled on the andirons, and the snow, maybe, was softly falling outside, covering all the far-away fields with a blanket of white,—many and many an hour do I remember lying thus, turning over leaf after leaf of those English papers, or of that dear old volume of the *The Newcomes* (the one with the fables on the title-page), or of *The Old Curiosity Shop* where you may see the picture of Master Humphrey with the dream people flying about his head. So looking at the pictures, my mother, busy with the work in her lap, would tell me the story that belonged to each.

"Thus it was that my mother taught me to like books and pictures, and I cannot remember the time when I did not like them; so that time, perhaps, was the beginning of that taste that led me to do the work I am now doing.

"Then the house I lived in in those early days was the quaintest, dearest old place you can imagine. It was built of stone, and there were really three houses joined together. There was an old part built about 1740, I think. Standing against that was another part built about 1780, and then my father built an addition that stood against the 1780 part of the house, so when you went from one of these parts to another, you had to go up one step and down another.

"In front of the house was a grassy lawn with a terraced bank (I used to roll over and over down that bank in the soft warm grass on a summer's day), and there was a little

(From *The Story of Jack Ballister's Fortunes* by Howard Pyle. Illustrated by the author.)

(From *Howard Pyle's Book of Pirates* by Howard Pyle. Illustrated by the author.)

Queen Morgana loses Excalibur his sheath. ■ (From *The Story of King Arthur and His Knights.* Illustrated by Howard Pyle.)

grove, or park of trees, to one side, and beyond you could see the turnpike road. I remember that every now and then there would be a train of Conestoga wagons that would pass along the highroad in a great cloud of dust, carrying lime from Lancaster County in Pennsylvania to the neighboring town for export. These big wagons were always very wonderful to me. They looked like great, clumsy ships that had come from afar, and sometimes the leading team of eight mules, bedecked with gay harness trimmed with crimson leather and brass, were adorned with silver bells that rang a merry tune as they passed in the bright sunshine along the highway.

"On the other side of the house to a little distance was a garden of old, old-fashioned roses and sweet shrubs that filled the air with fragrance when they were abloom. And there were beds of tulips and daffodillies, and there were graveled walks edged with box, and a greenhouse of shining glass at the lower end of the garden. And there was a wooden summer-house at the end of one of the graveled walks, and altogether it was such a garden as you would hardly find anywhere outside of a storybook. It seems to me that when I think of that garden I cannot remember anything but bloom and beauty, air filled with the odor of growing things, and birds singing in the shady trees in such a fashion as they do not sing nowadays.

"When you take into consideration such a mother as I had, and such a home as I lived in in those early years of my

childhood life, you may easily imagine that my mind was always very full of the thought of making pictures and of writing books.

"I cannot remember the time when I was not trying to draw pictures.

"At the time of the beginning of the Civil War we were all very loyal in our family. For many years I had an original picture, drawn by myself and tinted with water-color (I was eight years old when I made it), representing a bandy-legged zouave waving a flag and brandishing a sword as he threatened a wretched Confederate with annihilation. There was lots of smoke and bombshells in the picture, and a blazing cannon and an array of muskets and bayonets passing behind a hill, so that you would not have to draw all the soldiers who carried them. Accompanying this picture was a legend telling how the cannon-thunder roars, how the sword flashes in the air and falls upon the enemy of the nation. The text, I remember; concluded with the words, 'Ded! Ded! Ded! is the cesioner!' (Secessionist! I was never a good hand at spelling.)

"And as for writing—I must tell you a story about myself. There was a great rock by the garden wall where there were ferns and ivy. I remember one time—I think it was spring-time, and I know that the afternoon sun was very bright and warm—I was inspired to write a poem. My mother gave me some gilt-edged paper and a lead pencil, and I went out to this rock where I might be alone with my inspiration and purpose. It was not until I had wet my pencil point in my mouth, and was ready to begin my composition, that I realized that I was not able to read or write. I shall never forget how helpless and impotent I felt.

"I must have been a very, very, little boy at that time, for in those days a boy was sent to school almost as soon as he was old enough to wear trousers.

"Such was my early childhood.

"Maybe that was the beginning of such success as has since come to me, now that I am more than fifty years old. I cannot fix my sight on any other beginning.

"After those few bright early years there came a sad time when we had to quit our beautiful home, never to return to it again. Then there succeeded other life pictures: there was the house in town: there was another house in the country; there were long years of school, where I was not very good with my studies, but where I filled my slate and my Caesar full of pictures; there was another weary time when my parents tried, I believe, to prepare me for college, and when they finally had to surrender to my disinclination to study and send me to an art school.

"After that there follows the memory of a struggle in New York, in New York where the rushing and turbulent life was like a strong and powerful torrent and one had, like a young swimmer, to struggle with might and main to make head against the sweeping current, all full of other swimmers." [*Women's Home Companion,* Volume 39, April, 1912.[1]]

"I had been in New York for a year and a half, perhaps, when I painted my first important picture. It was made in black and white and called *The Wreck in the Offing.* A crew of a life-saving station were in a room playing cards by the light of a lantern. The door burst open and a man in oilskins, streaming with spray and rain, told the news of the disaster. I spent weeks on that picture. When it was finished five cents was the total sum of my remaining cash resources. I knew the idea was worth $15, even if the picture were rejected. But I neglected to consider that the art editor might be absent. It was a shock, therefore, when I found that he had gone home for the day. However, I left the picture.

"Walking back to my studio, miles away, I stopped to see Frederick Church, who was always kind to young artists, but I could not bring myself to the point of letting him know that I was penniless. I told the young man who shared my studio that I was ill and had lost my appetite. But when they had gone to the restaurant I searched my old clothing and found half a dollar; it paid for my dinner that night, my breakfast next morning, and my car fare back to *Harper's.*

"My nerves were on edge when at last I faced the art editor. My picture, big as a house, was standing on his desk. I felt sure, the minute I saw it, that it had been declined. 'Mr. Harper,' the art editor said, 'has looked at your picture and likes it. Indeed, he intends to give it a double page in the *Weekly*.'

"Since that eventful morning, my ways have been in pleasant places. I was paid $75 for *The Wreck in the Offing,* and the first thing I did was to take a friend to Delmonico's for luncheon. I want to add that I thought I foresaw the time when illustrating would be a very important part of art life in this country. I never lost confidence in my early judgment, and I am glad I have lived to see American illustrating a dignified and major factor in our national art evolution." [*Harper's Weekly,* Volume 53, June 12, 1909.[2]]

Left New York and returned to Wilmington. "I found the diversions in New York too many and attractive for sustained and serious effort. When I made up my mind to move I didn't linger, but packed my effects and bought a ticket.

"I come to my studio in the morning and stay until six o'clock in the summer, and so long as I can see in the winter. When I shut the doors of this building I shut my mind to paints, pencils, and pictures. I don't think of art except when I am here. I don't talk it. I stand up while I work and that is all the physical exercise I ever get. My recreation is found in the social life of the fine old city of Wilmington, and it is equal to the best in the United States."[2]

1883. First book, *The Merry Adventures of Robin Hood,* published.

1886. *Pepper & Salt* published.

1888. *The Wonder Clock* and *Otto of the Silver Hand* were published.

1894. Began teaching illustration at the Drexel Institute of Arts and Science in Philadelphia.

1900. Set up his own art school in Wilmington. His students included Maxfield Parrish, N. C. Wyeth, Frank Schoonover, Jessie Wilcox Smith and Thornton Oakley.

1903. Wrote to Scribner's suggesting he re-tell the adventures of King Arthur and his knights of the Round Table.

Pyle at his easel, 1898.

Told to go ahead, over the next seven years produced four volumes.

1910. "All these images pass before my memory, but nowhere do I find a single place (except it be in those early childhood days) whereupon I may set my finger, and say, 'Here my fortunes began.' Those fortunes, they grew as I grew, and came I know not how—like gray hairs, as I said, and gathering years. So if there really was a beginning of such success as has come to me, it must have been in those bygone days of forty-five years ago, and more."[1]

November 9, 1911. Died in Florence, Italy. "But though success comes thus, one knows not whence nor how, yet you must not think that it ever comes to him who sits with his hands in his lap, waiting for its arrival in the course of time. It only comes to him who strives from day to day to do the best he can with the work that lies immediately before him to accomplish.

"Yet in that striving, he who would succeed must arm himself with three vital and most necessary weapons. First, he must have ceaseless industry; second, he must have

"Uff!" said she. "Here is a smell of Christian blood in the house." ■ (From *King Stork* by
Howard Pyle. Illustrated by Trina Schart Hyman.)

The Spy, painting by Howard Pyle. ■ (From *Harper's New Monthly* Magazine, February, 1905.)

limitless ambition of purpose; third, he must possess unquenchable enthusiasm, coupled with a determination to succeed. Given these three, and something else besides—the gift of imagination—and it matters not, I believe, whether the life of a man begins in a cobbler's shop or a grocery store, or whether it begins in such an illuminating joyfulness in beautiful things as that which brightened my early childhood. With any beginning, success will, of a surety, be his who makes himself truly deserving of it.''[1]

FOR MORE INFORMATION SEE: F. Hopkinson Smith, *American Illustrators,* Scribner, 1892; Willard S. Morse and Gertrude Brinckle, compilers, *Howard Pyle: A Record of His Illustrations and Writings,* Wilmington Society of the Fine Arts, 1921, reprinted, Singing Tree Press, 1969; Charles D. Abbott, *Howard Pyle: A Chronicle,* Harper, 1925; Grace Irwin, "Howard Pyle and Some Others," in *Trail-Blazers of American Art,* Harper, 1930; Charles D. Abbott, "Writing Illustrator," in *Careers in the Making,* edited by I. M. R. Logie, Harper, 1942; Robert Lawson, "Howard Pyle and His Times," in *Illustrators of Children's Books,* compiled by B. E. Mahony and others, Horn Book, 1947.

Henry C. Pitz, "Howard Pyle, Father of American Illustration," in *American Artist,* December, 1951; Loring Holmes Dodd, *Generation of Illustrators and Etchers,* Chapman & Grimes, 1960; Elizabeth Nesbitt, *Howard Pyle,* Walck, 1966; Brian Doyle, editor, *Who's Who of Children's Literature,* Schocken Books, 1968; H. C. Pitz, *Brandywine Tradition,* Houghton, 1969; Richard McClanathan, editor, *Brandywine Heritage: Howard Pyle, N. C. Wyeth, Andrew Wyeth, James Wyeth,* New York Graphic Society, 1971; *Howard Pyle* (paintings; introduction by Rowland Elzea), Scribner, 1975; H. C. Pitz, *Howard Pyle: Writer, Illustrator, Founder of the Brandywine School,* Potter, 1975.

For children: Elizabeth Rider Montgomery, *Story behind Great Books* (illustrated by Friedebald Dzubas), McBride, 1946; Montgomery, *Story behind Great Stories,* McBride, 1947; Carolyn Sherwin Bailey, *Candle for Your Cake,* Lippincott, 1952; Laura Benét, *Famous Storytellers for Young People,* Dodd, 1968.

RUMSEY, Marian (Barritt) 1928-

PERSONAL: Born May 18, 1928, in Nebraska City, Neb.; daughter of John L. (a medical doctor) and Sara (Thomas) Barritt; married William J. Rumsey, August 31, 1948; children: William, Thomas. *Education:* San Diego State College, student, 1945-46. *Home:* Box 77044, Station C, Atlanta, Ga. 30357.

WRITINGS: Seal of Frog Island, Morrow, 1960; *Devil's Doorstep,* Morrow, 1966; *Shipwreck Bay,* Morrow, 1966; *High Country Adventure,* Morrow, 1967; *The Beaver of Weeping Water,* Morrow, 1969; *Danger on Shadow Mountain,* Morrow, 1970; *Lost in the Desert,* Morrow, 1971; *Lion on the Run,* Morrow, 1973; *Carolina Hurricane,* Morrow, 1977.

SIDELIGHTS: "Until I was a teen, I lived in the small, gold mining town of Oatman, Arizona where my father was the doctor for the mines and the surrounding towns. It was here I began my writing, and it started because often I could not find the exact sort of reading material I wanted. It seemed logical to write my own stories, and these invariably

"I didn't mean to hit you," he cried miserably, the tears rolling down his face. ■ (From *The Beaver of Weeping Water* by Marian Rumsey. Illustrated by Lydia Rosier.)

reflected my own experiences and especially the wilderness that I loved.

"After the mines closed, my family moved to La Jolla, California, and it was here that I finished my education. When I married, I began a new type of life style that I found delightful. My home became a small, traveling sailboat, and my two sons, William and Thomas, were raised abroad and educated by correspondence school until they attended college. It was not long before we added a camper coach to our possessions, and when not traveling by sea, we were on the move over land. This outdoor life definitely added vast new localities and subject matter that I included in my writings. It was also an adventurous and sometimes dangerous life, and I became acquainted with a new world of self-sufficiency for survival. I discovered, too, that this also applied to children, for if unexpectedly facing dangerous situations alone, these children showed a determination and a natural instinct to face the problem with considerable adultness. I was so impressed by this, that I began to write my books for young people.

"My books have their beginnings with my own experiences, and since my greatest enjoyment is time spent away, alone, and enjoying nature, these always play an important part of each story. But most of all, I love to write about young people and that lightly hidden gift that nature has given them, self-sufficiency."

SACKSON, Sid 1920-

PERSONAL: Born February 4, 1920, in Chicago, Ill.; son of Aaron J. (an engineer) and Esther (Rosen) Sackson; married Bernice P. Berdick, September 7, 1941; children: Dana R., Dale (Mrs. Dale E. Friedman). *Education:* City College (now of the City University of New York), B.S., 1943. *Religion:* "No organized religion." *Home and office:* 1287 Arnow Ave., Bronx, N.Y. 10469.

CAREER: Licensed civil engineer; U.S. Department of the Navy, Brooklyn, N.Y., civilian chief engineering draftsman, 1940-46; Corbett-Tinghir Co., New York City, engineering designer, 1946-48; City of New York, Traffic Dept., traffic engineer, 1948-51; The Dorr Co., Stanford, Conn., engineering designer, 1951-55; Shapiro Associates, New York City, engineer and programmer, 1955-70; writer and inventor of games, 1962—. *Member:* New York Game Associates (was president; the New York Game Associates is now defunct).

WRITINGS: A Gamut of Games (adult), Random House, 1969; *Beyond Tic Tac Toe: Challenging and Exciting New*

SID SACKSON

Games to Be Played with Colored Pens Or Pencils (juvenile), Pantheon, 1975; *Beyond Solitaire: Challenging New Games for One to Play with Colored Pens and Pencils* (juvenile), Pantheon, 1976; *Beyond Words* (juvenile), Pantheon, 1976; *Beyond Competition: Six Dynamic New Games for Two or More Players to Win Together* (juvenile), Pantheon, 1977. Author of game review column "Sackson on Games," later changed to "Briefings" in *Strategy and Tactics,* 1969—. Contributor to *Washington Post;* contributing editor to *Games* magazine, 1977.

WORK IN PROGRESS: Another book for Pantheon; several new games for publication in the U.S. and in Europe; research on old and new games.

SIDELIGHTS: "When I was in first grade, the high point of the day would occur when the teacher distributed pages from a magazine and instructed us to circle the words we knew. The positioning of the circles and their relationship to each other interested me much more than the words themselves. I evolved rules for joining the circles, set objectives for the growing chains, and thereby created my first game. . . .

"Now, many years after my initial discovery of games in the first grade, I am just as intrigued by what makes a game tick as I was then. I have created several hundred games of my own, but I am just as fascinated by one created by a friend, one I buy in a store, or one I rediscover in a library or museum. With this as a spur—and helped by travels through the United States, Canada, and Europe—my collection of games and books on games (in eight languages) has grown to be what is, to the best of my knowledge, the largest privately owned collection." His games include "Acquire," "Sleuth," "Bazaar," "Executive Decision," "Venture," "Monad," "Focus," "Major Battles and Campaigns of General George S. Patton," "Major Campaigns of General Douglas MacArthur," "Totally," "The Winning Ticket," "The Harry Lorayne Memory Game," and "Charlie and the Chocolate Factory Game."

SANCHEZ-SILVA, Jose Maria 1911-

PERSONAL: Born November 11, 1911, in Madrid, Spain; son of Lorenzo (a journalist) and Adoracion (Garcia-Morales) Sanchez-Silva; married Maria del Carmen Delgado, 1933; children: six. *Education:* Attended schools in Madrid; later studied at El Dabate (a journalism school), Madrid.

CAREER: Began working as an errand boy, kitchen worker, and at other odd jobs as an adolescent; worked for several newspapers before joining the staff of *Arriba,* Madrid, as reporter, 1939, later becoming editor-in-chief, and finally assistant director, 1944; *Revista de las Artes y los Oficios* (Review of Arts and Crafts), editor, beginning 1946; temporarily retired from the newspaper business to devote his time to traveling and writing books in the 1950's. *Member:* General Society of Spanish Authors (appointed to council, 1963). *Awards, honors:* Francisco de Sales prize, 1942; National Prize for Literature (Spain), 1944, 1957; National Prize for Journalism (Spain), 1945; Mariano de Cavia prize, 1947; Rodriguez Santamaria prize, 1948; received an audience with Pope Pius XII, 1957; Grand Cross of the Order of Cisneros (Spain), 1959; Virgen del Carmen prize, 1960; award for special services from the Government of Peru, 1962; Grand Cross of Merit (Spain), 1964; Grand Cross of the Order of Alfonso X (Spain), 1968; tied for Hans Christian Andersen Award, 1968.

Marcelino comia con los frailes, justamente enfrente del padre Superior. ■ (From *Marcelino Pan y Vino* by José Maria Sànchez-Silva. Edited by Edward R. Mulvihill and Roberto G. Sanchez.)

WRITINGS: Un Paleto en Londres: La Vuelta al Mundo y Otros Viajes, Editora Nacional (Madrid), 1952; *Adelaida y Otros Asuntos Personales* (illustrated by Lorenzo Goni), Editora Nacional, 1953; *Marcelino Pan y Vino: Cuento de Padres a Hijos* (illustrated by L. Goni), [Madrid], 1953, translation by Angela Britton published as *Marcelino: A Story from Parents to Children,* Newman Press, 1955 [another edition translated by John Paul Debicki published as *The Miracle of Marcelino,* Scepter, 1963]; *Historias de Mi Calle,* [Madrid], 1954; *Quince o Veinte Sombras,* Ediciones CID (Madrid), 1955; *El Hereje: Cuento para Mayores* (illustrated by Alvaro Delgado), A. Aguado (Madrid), 1956; *Fabula de la Burrita Non* ("Little Donkey Odd"; illustrated by L. Goni), Ediciones CID, 1956; *Tres Novelas y Pico,* A. Aguado, 1958.

Cuentos de Navidad ("Christmas stories"; illustrated by Jose Francisco Aguirre), Editorial Magisterio Espanol (Madrid), 1960; *Adios, Josefina!* (illustrated by L. Goni), Alameda (Madrid), 1962, translation by Michael Heron published as *The Boy and the Whale* (illustrated by Margery Gill), McGraw, 1964; *San Martin de Porres,* Secretariado Martin de Porres (Palencia), 1962; *Colasin, Colason,* Editora Nacional, 1963; *Pesinoe y Gente de Tierra,* [Madrid], 1964; *Cartas a un Nino Sobre Francisco Franco,* [Madrid], 1966; *Tres Animales Son,* Doncel (Madrid), 1966; *Adan y el Senor Dios* ("Adam and the Lord"; illustrated by L. Goni), Tall. Graf. Escelicer (Madrid), 1967; *Un Gran Pequeno* (il-

lustrated by Jose Luis Macias S.), Editorial Marfil (Alcoy), 1967, translation by M. Heron published as *Ladis and the Ant* (illustrated by David Knight), Bodley Head, 1968, McGraw, 1969; *El Segundo Verano de Ladis* (illustrated by J. L. Macias S.), Editorial Marfil, 1968, translation by Isabel Quigly published as *Second Summer with Ladis* (illustrated by D. Knight), Bodley Head, 1969; (with Luis de Diego) *Luiso* (illustrated by L. Goni), Doncel, 1969.

Also author of *El Hombre y la Bufanda* ("The Man and the Neckcloth"), 1934; *Aventura en Cielo* ("Adventures in Heaven"); *El Espejo Habitado* ("The Lived-In Mirror"); and *Historias Menores* ("Little Stories"). Scriptwriter for the motion picture, "Ronda Espanola," 1952.

SIDELIGHTS: As a journalist, Jose Sanchez-Silva has traveled throughout the world covering various news stories ranging from an assignment for *Arriba* in Italy to the 1948 winter Olympic games in England. In addition to his busy life as a reporter, the author managed to write a book about every two years. His works have been translated into twenty-six languages and some have been used as textbooks by students learning Spanish in Europe and the United States.

One of Sanchez-Silva's later books, *Ladis and the Ant,* told the story of a small boy named Ladis and his encounter with an extraordinary ant. A reviewer for the *New York Times* noted, "The scientific information he [Ladis] learns on his explorations is memorable, because the insects concerned have been affectionately endowed with personalities."

FOR MORE INFORMATION SEE: Doris de Montreville, editor, *Third Book of Junior Authors,* H. W. Wilson, 1972.

JOSE MARIA SANCHEZ-SILVA

MIROSLAV SASEK

SASEK, Miroslav   1916-

PERSONAL: Born November 18, 1916, in Prague, Czechoslovakia; children: Dusan Pedro. *Education:* Educated in Prague, and at l'Ecole des Beaux Arts, in Paris. *Residence:* Munich, Germany.

CAREER: Worked for Radio Free Europe, Munich, Germany, 1951-57; author and illustrator. *Awards, honors: New York Times* Choice of Best Illustrated Children's Books of the Year, 1959, for *This Is London,* and 1960, for *This Is New York;* Boys' Clubs of America Junior Book Award, 1961, for *This Is New York.*

WRITINGS—"This Is" series, all illustrated by the author and published by Macmillan: *This Is Paris* (ALA Notable Book), 1959; . . . *London,* 1959, revised edition, 1970; . . . *New York,* 1960; . . . *Rome,* 1960; . . . *Venice,* 1961; . . . *Edinburgh,* 1961; . . . *Munich,* 1961; . . . *San Francisco,* 1962; . . . *Israel,* 1962; . . . *Cape Kennedy,* 1964; . . . *Ireland,* 1964; . . . *Hong Kong,* 1965; . . . *Greece,* 1966; . . . *Texas,* 1967; . . . *the United Nations,* 1968; . . . *Washington, D.C.,* 1969; : . .*Australia,* 1970; . . . *Historic Britain,* 1974.

Other: *Stone Is Not Cold,* Citadel Press, 1961.

ADAPTATION—Filmstrip: "This Is New York" produced by Weston Woods.

SIDELIGHTS: "Children need 'Baedekers,' too!" This conclusion led Miroslav Sasek to begin illustrating and writing travel books for children about the world's greatest cities.

Sasek was born and educated in Czechoslovakia. In 1946 when the Communists gained power in his homeland, Sasek

Edinburgh's highest monument commemorates Sir Walter Scott, her greatest son. ▪ (From *This is Edinburgh* by Miroslav Sasek. Illustrated by the author.)

...And a fishing fleet in the Lagoon. ▪ (From *This is San Francisco* by Miroslav Sasek. Illustrated by the author.)

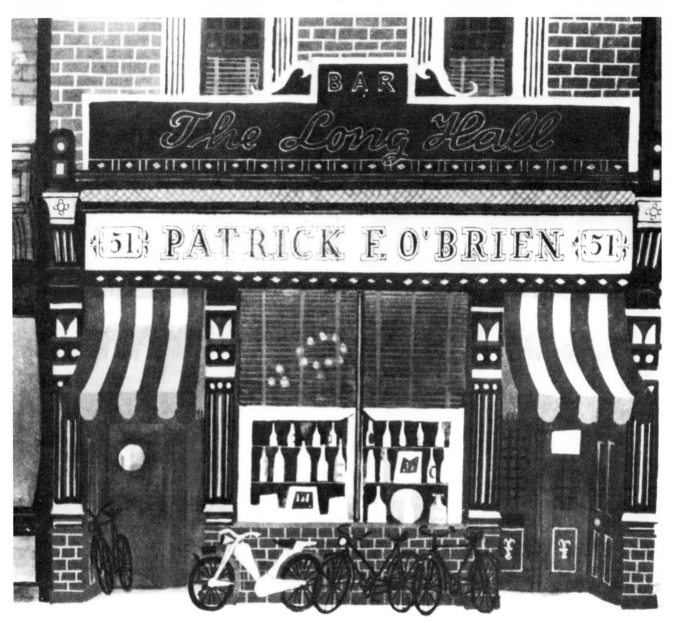

**But for the 500,000 freshmen who wear
the "Pioneer's Pin" of a teetotaller,
there are only soft drinks in any pub.**
■ (From *This is Ireland* by Miroslav Sasek. Illustrated by the author.)

went to Paris where he studied at l'Ecole des Beaux Arts. Eventually, he settled in Munich, Germany.

A three-week vacation in Paris gave Sasek the idea for writing travel books for children, and *This Is Paris* appeared in 1959. The London *Times Literary Supplement* review included, "A beautifully produced picture book destined to delight young and old alike.... Use of colour is enchantingly fresh and vivid. The text consists of brief and very simple comments on the sketches with factual explanations which add to our knowledge of Paris and gently remind us of much we had forgotten. Each picture is a pleasing design with imaginative use of detail." The *New York Times* added, "With a minimum of words and a maximum of illustrations, *This Is Paris* captures the magic of mankind's capital city."

"There are not many words in Miroslav Sasek's *This Is London,*" observed a reviewer in the London *Times Literary Supplement,* "but those few are most memorable.... The colour is magnificent and uninhibited, the draughtsmanship brilliant but unobtrusive (one gradually realizes that these bold, stylized drawings are minutely accurate as well as true in general impression). The humour is characteristic and pervasive but always subordinate. The jokes are all pointed." The *San Francisco Chronicle* added, "The second largest city in the world, seen through an artist's eye, emerges in a brilliant galaxy of pictures accompanied by clear, concise information about each."

Sasek had originally intended to write only three books of this nature—about Paris, London, and Rome. However, the success of the first three encouraged him to do more, and in dig the grave of Robert Kennedy. Sasek described these experiences as a "continuing nightmare," and *This Is Washington, D.C.* reflects this, according to some critics. Comments in the *Bulletin of the Center for Children's Books* included, "Like other Sasek books, this is distinguished by the impressive exactness of the architectural details in pictures of sites and buildings, and by the rakish drawing of people; it includes general information about the city and minor details of exhibits, as well as the text about and painting of points of major interest that constitute the bulk of the book. The whole is an attractive and fairly comprehensive guide to the city; it lacks only the flavor and the feeling of a metropolitan personality that gave the earlier Sasek books about great cities such verve."

This Is Historic Britain is Miroslav Sasek's latest book. "Another in the series of oversize books filled with beautifully detailed pictures of sights and sites of a city or a country," wrote a critic in the *Bulletin of the Center for Children's Books.* "Sasek's text is, as always, packed with facts that would be interesting to a sightseer, and the book can serve as an adjunct to a historical unit of the curriculum, but the primary appeal is visual: carefully detailed and accurate paintings in restrained color of the period architecture found in castles, cathedrals, and historic buildings throughout England, Scotland, and Wales."

FOR MORE INFORMATION SEE: New York Times, May 10, 1959; *Times Literary Supplement,* May 29, 1959, and December 4, 1959; *San Francisco Chronicle,* February 28, 1960; Lee Kingman and others, compilers, *Illustrators of Children's Books, 1957-1966,* Horn Book, 1968; Lee Bennett Hopkins, *Books Are by People,* Citation Press, 1969; *Times Literary Supplement,* June 26, 1969; Doris de Montreville and Donna Hill, *Third Book of Junior Authors,* H. W. Wilson, 1972; *Bulletin of the Center for Children's Books,* October, 1969, and February, 1975.

SEWARD, Prudence   1926-

EDUCATION: Studied at Northwood College, Harrow Art School, and the Royal College of Art.

CAREER: Illustrator. *Member:* Royal Watercolor Society, Society of Painter-Etchers and Engravers. *Awards, honors:* Rome Scholarship in Engraving, 1949-51.

ILLUSTRATOR: Richard Parker, *The House that Guilda Drew,* Brockhampton Press, 1963; Douglas Wilkinson, *Sons of the Arctic,* Clarke, Irwin, 1965; Eileen H. Colwell (editor), *A Second Storyteller's Choice,* Walck, 1965; Paul Berna, *The Clue Of The Black Cat,* Pantheon, 1965; Betty Roland, *Jamie's Summer Visitor,* McGraw, 1967; Paul Berna, *A Truckload of Rice,* Pantheon, 1968; Emily Dickinson, *A Letter to the World,* Bodley Head, 1968, Macmillan, 1969; Elfrida Vipont Foulds, *The Pavilion,* Oxford University Press, 1969; Joan G. Robinson, *Charley* (ALA Notable Book), Coward-McCann, 1969.

Eileen Bell, *Tales from the End Cottage,* Penguin, 1970; Eileen Bell, *More Tales from End Cottage,* 1972; Alison Farthing, *Skip Saturday,* Chatto, 1972; Elizabeth Roberts, *All about Simon and His Grandmother,* Methuen, 1973, Penguin, 1975, published in America as *Jumping Jackdaws! Here Comes Simon,* Rand McNally, 1975; John Cunliffe, *The Farmer, the Rooks and the Cherry Tree,* Deutsch, 1974; Rumer Godden, *Candy Floss and Impurity Jane,*

This pub, the Cheshire Cheese, is one of the oldest.
■ (From *This is London* by Miroslav Sasek. Illustrated by the author.)

the 1960's, there appeared several Sasek books on European and American cities. He also expanded his scope to include entire countries, as well as points of interest, such as Cape Kennedy and the United Nations.

In 1968, Sasek came to Washington, D.C. to complete the research for a book on that city. He was in the city at the time of the riots which followed the assassination of Martin Luther King, Jr. He was still there when Robert Kennedy was assassinated, and was sketching the gravesite of John F. Kennedy when guards asked him to leave so that they could

Whatever their age, children would follow for preference a clue which the police would consider outside the range of their investigations. ■ (From *A Truckload of Rice* by Paul Berna. Translated by John Buchanon-Brown. Illustrated by Prudence Seward.)

Penguin, 1975; Joyce Donoghue, *Playtime Stories,* Penguin, 1975; Marie Hynds, *The Golden Apple,* Blackie & Son, 1976. Illustrated *First Book of Nursery Rhymes* for Watts. Work has also appeared in *Cricket* Magazine.

SIDELIGHTS: "I was born in London in 1926. My father was a wine merchant and I was educated at private schools. After two years in Rome, at the end of my art training, I returned to London and became a free-lance illustrator until 1976 when I went to work in the prints and drawings department of the British Museum. After nearly two years there, I was accepted at Camberwell School of Art in the prints and drawings conservation course. I have one daughter, a student of law. I live in an old cottage on the Norfolk-Suffolk border and a 'pied-a-terre' in Islington, London.

"I lived and worked as a free-lance illustrator in Toronto, Canada for three years in the 60's. I illustrated some books for the main publishing houses there."

SHECTER, Ben 1935-

PERSONAL: Born April 28, 1935, in New York, N.Y. *Education:* Attended City College of New York and Yale School of Drama. *Residence:* New York, N.Y.

CAREER: Started working in the field of window display; became a costume and scenic designer for opera, ballet, theater, and television, beginning 1962; author and illustrator of books for children. His works have been exhibited by the American Institute of Graphic Arts. *Military service:* U.S. Army, 1958-60. *Awards, honors: The Hating Book* by Charlotte Zolotow was named by *House Beautiful* as one of the ten best children's books for 1969.

WRITINGS: Emily, Girl Witch of New York (self-illustrated), Dial, 1963; *Jonathan and the Bank Robbers* (self-illus-

trated), Dial, 1964; *Partouche Plants a Seed,* Harper, 1966; *Conrad's Castle* (self-illustrated), Harper, 1967; *Inspector Rose* (self-illustrated), Harper, 1969; *If I Had a Ship* (self-illustrated), Doubleday, 1970; *Someplace Else* (self-illustrated), Harper, 1971; *Across the Meadow* (self-illustrated), Doubleday, 1972; *Game for Demons,* Harper, 1972; *Stone House Stories* (self-illustrated), Harper, 1973; *The Whistling Whirligig* (self-illustrated), Harper, 1974; *Molly Patch and Her Animal Friends,* Harper, 1975; *The Toughest and Meanest Kid on the Block,* Putnam, 1975; *The Stocking Child,* Harper, 1976; *Hester the Jester,* Harper, 1977; *The Hiding Game* (self-illustrated), Parents' Magazine, 1977; *A Summer Secret,* Harper, 1977.

Illustrator: Joan M. Lexau, *Millicent's Ghost,* Dial, 1962; Miriam Anne Bourne, *Emilio's Summer Day,* Harper, 1966; Nancy Brelis, *The Mummy Market,* Harper, 1966; Charlotte Zolotow, *If It Weren't for You,* Harper, 1966; Barbara Borack, *Grandpa,* Harper, 1967; Janet Chenery, *The Toad Hunt,* Harper, 1967; J. M. Lexau, *Every Day a Dragon,* Harper, 1967; Nathaniel Benchley, *A Ghost Named Fred,* Harper, 1968; Mary Church, *John Patrick's Amazing Morning,* Doubleday, 1968; C. Zolotow, *My Friend John,* Harper, 1968; Aileen Lucia Fisher, *Clean as a Whistle,* Crowell, 1969; C. Zolotow, *The Hating Book,* Harper, 1969; Sandra Hochman, *The Magic Convention,* Doubleday, 1971; Marjorie Weinman Sharmat, *Getting Something on Maggie Marmelstein,* Harper, 1971; C. Zolotow, *A Father Like That,* Harper, 1971; Millicent Selsam, *More Potatoes,* Harper, 1972; Robert Wahl, *What Will You Do Today, Little Russell?,* Putnam, 1972; Felice Holman, *The Escape of the Giant Hogstalk,* Scribner, 1974; C. Zolotow, *The Summer Night,* Harper, 1974; Nancy Jewell, *Cheer Up, Pig!,* Harper, 1975; M. W. Sharmat, *Maggie Marmelstein for President,* Harper, 1975; Charlotte Herman, *The Difference of Ari Stein,* Harper, 1976; M. W. Sharmat, *Mooch the Messy,* Harper, 1976.

SIDELIGHTS: Raised in Brooklyn, N.Y., Ben Shecter had easy access to museums, libraries, and numerous cultural events. This, plus the advantage of having an encouraging and understanding father, filled young Shecter with dreams of becoming a set designer for stage productions.

A chance meeting with Franco Zeffirelli at a party led to an introduction to Gian Carlo Menotti. As a result of that introduction, Shecter went to Italy in the summer of 1962 to attend the Spoleto Festival of Two Worlds and began his career as a scenic designer. At around the same time, Shecter did a series of drawings about a little girl in a haunted house which served as the basis for Joan Lexau's book *Millicent's Ghost* and introduced Shecter to the world of book illustration.

Shecter eventually began to write as well as illustrate books for children. In *Someplace Else,* the author-illustrator told the story of an eleven-year-old boy adjusting to a move to a new neighborhood. "The author writes with rare humor and affection, etching incidents so clearly one feels that the story must stem from his own experience. And one feels fortunate in being able to share them," noted a critic for *Book World.* A *Horn Book* reviewer commented, "The author writes with telling economy, using the right details; and if his story is nostalgic in a manner that pleases the adult, it is nevertheless lively and direct in its revelation of childish behavior and feelings."

FOR MORE INFORMATION SEE: Lee Kingman and others, compilers, *Illustrators of Children's Books, 1957-*

BEN SHECTER

I say, "Ollie cat,
what do you know about the pond?"
He answers, "Meow, I want some milk."
"No answer, no milk," I say.
■ (From *A Summer Secret* by Ben Shecter. Illustrated by the author.)

1966, Horn Book, 1968; *Book World,* November 7, 1971; *Horn Book,* February 1972, December, 1974; Doris de Montreville and Donna Hill, editors, *Third Book of Junior Authors,* H. W. Wilson, 1972.

SHEKERJIAN, Regina Tor (Regina Tor)

PERSONAL: Married Haig Shekerjian. *Education:* Graduated from Skidmore College, Saratoga Springs, N.Y.; studied art at the Art Students League and at the University of Mexico; attended the New School for Social Research.

CAREER: Author and illustrator. *Exhibition:* Artwords and Bookworks, Los Angeles Institute of Contemporary Art, 1978. *Member:* Author's League. *Awards, honors:* Discovering Israel received the National Jewish Book Award for the best juvenile of the year, 1960; certificates of merit from the Society of Illustrators.

WRITINGS—Under name Regina Tor: *Getting to Know Korea,* Coward, 1953; (self-illustrated) *Getting to Know Germany,* Coward, 1954; (self-illustrated) *Getting to Know Puerto Rico,* Coward, 1955; (self-illustrated) *Getting to Know Canada,* Coward, 1956; *Getting to Know the Philippines* (illustrated by Haris Petie), Coward, 1958; *Getting to Know Greece* (illustrated by Don Lambo), Coward, 1959; (with Eleanor Roosevelt) *Growing Toward Peace,* Random House, 1960; (self-illustrated) *Discovering Israel,* Random House, 1960.

Illustrator—under name Regina Shekerjian: (And editor with husband, Haig Shekerjian) *A Book of Christmas Car-*

Three of them are going down the road. Peter the Rat, Peter the Butterfly, and the boy called Peter. ■ (From *The Boy, the Rat, and the Butterfly* by Beatrice de Regniers. Illustrated by Haig and Regina Shekerjian.)

ols, Harper, 1964, revised, 1977; (and editor with H. Shekerjian) *A Book of Ballads, Songs, and Snatches,* Harper, 1966; (with H. Shekerjian) *Children of the Kingdom,* Book 4, Allyn & Bacon, 1966, confraternity edition, 1967; (with H. Shekerjian) Jay Williams, *Life in the Middle Ages,* Random House, 1966; Charlotte Zolotow, *River Winding,* Abelard-Schuman, 1970; (with H. Shekerjian) Beatrice De Regniers, *The Boy, the Rat, and the Butterfly,* Atheneum, 1971; Pearl Buck, *The Chinese Story Teller,* John Day, 1971; Nancy Willard, *19 Masks for the Naked Poet,* Kyack Books, 1971; (with H. Shekerjian) *The Adventures of Tom Thumb,* Scholastic, 1972; (with H. Shekerjian) *King Midas and the Golden Touch,* Scholastic, 1973; Marianna Prieto (compiler), *Play It in Spanish: Spanish Games and Folk Songs for Children,* John Day, 1973; (with H. Shekerjian) Nancy Willard, *The Merry History of a Christmas Pie,* Putnam, 1974; Julie Dannenbaum, *Menus for All Occasions,* Saturday Review Press, 1974; (with H. Shekerjian) Nancy Willard, *All On a May Morning,* Putnam, 1975; (with H. Shekerjian) Nancy Willard, *The Well-Mannered Balloon,* Harcourt, 1976. Short stories, poetry and articles have appeared in *Experiment, Story, Opinion, Decade, Glass Hill, American Heritage, Junior Natural History* and others. Along with H. Shekerjian has done several "papertexts" published by Simon & Schuster and numerous collections of literature-texts for schools.

SIDELIGHTS: Horn Book commented on Regina Tor's *Getting to Know Puerto Rico:* "Puerto Rico, U.S.A.—her historic past (briefly) and her present problems. Directly and concisely this unbroken narration of facts covers the island's economy, social life, and traditions. Emphasis rests on 'Op-

eration Bootstrap' and the efforts of the U.S.A. to improve life for her crowded, underprivileged Puerto Rican citizens. Young readers should find it pleasant and easy as well as informative reading." *Kirkus* added, "Contemporary Puerto Rico, with its good elements coming more and more into focus, is briskly shown with due attention given to the small details of nature and social life which add color. The clean, well designed pictures are in soft grey and orange."

Kirkus said of *Getting to Know Greece:* "A country of contrasts, both its most primitive and sophisticated aspects are drawn here in a language which suggests that the author both knows and appreciates her subject." *Library Journal* commented, "One of the greatest advantages of the 'Getting to Know' series is the fine choice of countries for study.... These, including this newest on Greece, are most welcome. Readers will acquire a variety of information about the country to help them understand its significance today." The comments of the *New York Times* included, "It has a smooth if uninspired text. The drawings are slight but pleasant. The book as a whole gives a very sketchy idea of the country's past. It does better with its present, though the treatment seems overly romantic and sunny. From reading *Getting to Know Greece,* one would hardly guess that a life-and-death Communist uprising was suppressed barely ten years ago."

Growing toward Peace, written with Eleanor Roosevelt, tells "The story of man's long search for peace culminating in the United Nations," according to *Horn Book.* "The

REGINA SHEKERJIAN

tasks of the United Nations," commented the *Christian Science Monitor,* "are thoroughly, simply, and inspiringly described and well illustrated with photographs, prints, and drawings." The *New York Times* added, "Mrs. Roosevelt, with Helen Ferris, told some of this a decade ago in *Partners: United Nations and Youth.* This new book is much briefer, very concise, but no less moving in its statements of the UN's function and the world's need."

SNOW, Donald Clifford   1917-
(Thomas Fall)

PERSONAL: Born in 1917. *Home:* New York, N.Y.

CAREER: Author of books for young adults. *Awards, honors:* Runner-up for the Nancy Bloch Award, 1967, for *Canalboat to Freedom.*

WRITINGS—All under pseudonym Thomas Fall: *Prettiest Girl in Town,* Harper, 1950; *The Justicer,* Rinehart, 1959; *Eddie No-Name* (illustrated by Ray Prohaska), Pantheon, 1963; *Edge of Manhood* (illustrated by Henry C. Pitz), Dial, 1964; *My Bird Is Romeo* (illustrated by Louise Gordon), Dial, 1964; *Wild Boy* (illustrated by H. C. Pitz), Dial, 1965; *The Profit and the Loss,* D. McKay, 1965; *Canalboat to Freedom* (ALA Notable Book; illustrated by Joseph Cellini), Dial, 1966; *Dandy's Mountain* (illustrated by Juan Carlos Barberis), Dial, 1967; *Dandy's Summer,* Dial, 1967; *Goat Boy of Brooklyn* (illustrated by Fermin Rocker), Dial, 1968; *Jim Thorpe* (illustrated by John Gretzer), Crowell, 1970; *The Ordeal of Running Standing,* McCall, 1970; *Emily and the Killer Hawk,* Scholastic Book Service, 1976.

SIDELIGHTS: "I was born in a house my grandfather built in the Ozark Mountains and grew up in Oklahoma among many families of the Caddo, Cheyenne, Comanche, Wichita and other American Indians. I have Cherokee ancestory on one side of my own family. Indian children whose parents did not speak English, were my playmates, although I was not personally raised in an Indian home.

DONALD CLIFFORD SNOW

"After I finished college and worked for a while in the oil business in Oklahoma and Texas, I decided to try to become a full time writer. It was natural for Indian subjects to be in the front of my mind. Many of my books for both adult and juvenile markets have, therefore, involved the tragic confrontation between Indians, the native Americans, and the whites who pioneered into the Indian country. My own mother was brought by her father, a farmer-minister, from Tennessee into Indian Territory in 1905.

"I have had no greater satisfaction in my life than receiving letters from young readers throughout the United States as my books have been used in their school and public libraries.

"My private interests, outside the writing and publishing worlds, are centered around the world of nature (I live in the mountains of upstate New York) and of music. I am not a musician, but I am a devoted fan of both country and jazz music. Very privately, I play the piano, banjo, guitar, mandolin and fiddle—but only enough to enjoy some amateur sessions with neighbors and friends who play stringed instruments.

"My ambition is to continue writing books for young readers; they are, after all, the only readers who really matter."

Donald Snow's Cherokee heritage is reflected in many of his writings. Barbara Wersba, writing in the *New York Times Book Review* had the following comments about *Edge of Manhood:* "Needless to say, inherent in this story is a document of the white man's profound injustice to the Indian. [The author] has let the facts speak for themselves, and by leaving them unstressed, has made a deeper statement than any treatise on the subject. Misguided by images of television 'redskins,' our children know all too little of the American Indians' culture, suffering, or decline. This book will make an important contribution."

The Ordeal of Running Standing was described by a *Horn Book* critic as "an authentic, compelling story of [an Indian] man and woman tragically trapped in a moment of history." Observed the *New York Times Book Review:* "If there is any truth in Shaw's celebrated quip that America went directly from savagery to decadence, it can be found in the crisis of the Indian . . . [His] super-Western dramatizes a bitter chapter of this larcenous history and enlivens it with frontier humor. . . .' "

One critic has described Snow as having "a rare talent for writing about adolescence." His book, *Dandy's Mountain* is an example. According to *Book World,* "In the hands of a less skillful writer, the preoccupation with the dictionary could have become an exercise in cleverness, but [the author] has made Dandy a believable girl. . . . [He has depicted her] mother and father as real people with a relationship between themselves as well as with their children. . . . [He] sees adults as an important part of young people's lives, primarily giving them help when they need it, but otherwise lending quiet strength to young people who must learn to accept responsibility for their own actions. . . ."

FOR MORE INFORMATION SEE: New York Times Book Review, November 1, 1964, November 29, 1970; *Book World,* September 24, 1967; *Horn Book,* December, 1970.

"Once he hopped a freight train only to learn that it was going in the wrong direction." ■ (From *Jim Thorpe* by Thomas Fall. Illustrated by John Gretzer.)

VICTORIA CAROLYN STOREY

STOREY, Victoria Carolyn 1945-
(Vicky Martin)

PERSONAL: Born May 22, 1945, in Windsor, Berkshire, England; daughter of Lancelot Arthur (a banker) and Jean (Slocock) Martin; married Thomas Michael Storey (a chartered accountant), July 28, 1969; children: Eleanor, Susannah, Harriet. *Education:* Winkfield Place, cordon bleu, 1962; attended Byam Shaw School of Art, 1962-65. *Politics:* Conservative. *Religion:* Church of England. *Home:* Newell Farm House, Lower Beeding, Horsham, Sussex, England. *Agent:* John Farquharson Ltd., Bell House, Bell Yard, London, WC2A 2UU, England.

CAREER: Has worked as a cook, 1965-66, a receptionist, 1966-67, and a dealer in antiques, 1967-68; writer, 1968—.

WRITINGS: (Under name Vicky Martin) *September Song,* Macmillan, 1969, Nelson, 1971; *The Windmill Years,* Macdonald & Janes, 1978. Author of nearly sixty short stories and about seven serials.

SIDELIGHTS: "As a child I was an obsessive reader of everything I could lay my hands on. Although I kept note books from my early teens, recording the best and worst moments of my life, I never thought of being a professional writer until my last year at art school. I had always loved drawing and painting and intended to make a career as a commercial artist. After three years at art school I realised I would never be good enough.

"I turned to writing and was surprised to find that I could express myself far more easily in this way. I began to sell short stories and then serials. I left art school and embarked on a variety of jobs and wrote at the same time. I always wanted to write a novel and I did write a teen-aged book, but this was followed by several years of serials and short stories. However, I have now completed *The Windmill Years* and am halfway through another book, so at last I am settled with the type of writing I really want to do.

"My childhood was happy and secure. Nevertheless, I was an anxious child, a worrier. My teens were rather unhappy as I was large and shy and late to mature. Only since my marriage have I found the security to relax and develop. My eight married years have been packed with events—the birth of three daughters, my husband's changing occupations—but we have just bought a farm and hope to settle here permanently.

"My family is very important to me. I grew up in a large, affectionate circle of people and they are a very necessary background to my life. I still long to write 'the great novel,' but I am more realistic about myself now, in my early 30's, and I doubt if I have the depth. I shall be happy to produce well-written and readable stories about reasonably believable people."

HOBBIES AND OTHER INTERESTS: Fashion, cooking, house decoration, antiques, travel.

SULLIVAN, Thomas Joseph, Jr. 1947-
(Tom Sullivan)

PERSONAL: Born March 27, 1947, in Boston, Mass.; son of Thomas Joseph and Marie (Kelly) Sullivan; married Patricia Steffen, May 17, 1969; children: Blythe Patrice, Thomas Joseph III. *Education:* Attended Providence College, 1965-67; attended Harvard University, 1969. *Politics:* Republican. *Religion:* Roman Catholic. *Home address:* P.O. Box 7000-17, Redondo Beach, Calif. 90277.

CAREER: Singer and songwriter. Gives public lectures. Member of board of directors of Los Angeles Braille Institute and Up with People (Tucson). Delegate to Republican National Convention, 1976; member of President Ford's committee on job opportunities for the handicapped.

WRITINGS—Under name Tom Sullivan: (With Derek Gill) *If You Could See What I Hear* (autobiography), Harper, 1975; *Adventures in Darkness* (autobiography; young adults), McKay, 1976. Has written for (and performed on) "M.A.S.H.," CBS-TV; "Airport 77," "Dark Ride," for television.

WORK IN PROGRESS: A series of books on the senses, for small children.

SIDELIGHTS: "My foremost interest in life is to live each day to its fullest, using every gift given to me to its potential. Because of an inconvenience (blindness) it seems I have spent a good deal of my life struggling against the labels that society puts on any minority group, thereby placing limits on that group. I have, as my books point out, done a lot of crazy things, just to prove I could do them. Then, in my middle

Tom Sullivan on horseback. ■ (From *If You Could See What I Hear* by Tom Sullivan and Derek Gill.)

twenties an incident happened which gave me the incentive to write my own story.

"I have a vital interest in the well-being of our country, and am becoming more and more active in politics, handicapped education, and giving motivational lectures to many organizations around the world. In short, where there is a need before me I try to do my part.

"If I were to sum up my own personal philosophy, it would be that yesterday is only a memory, tomorrow is a dream, but we must live well for this moment—focus our attention on the now, the present, what is happening today."

Sullivan is also a composer and arranger—music being the main thrust of his life. He also enjoys athletic talents. After winning the high school nationals in wrestling, Sullivan went on to the Olympic trials in 1968. He runs six miles a day and is a fanatic golfer shooting in the low 90's and has played in many celebrity tournaments around the country.

FOR MORE INFORMATION SEE: Los Angeles Times, November, 1975.

TARRY, Ellen   1906-

PERSONAL: Born September 26, 1906, in Birmingham, Ala.; children: Elizabeth, Tarry Patton. *Education:* Attended Alabama State University, Fordham University and Bank Street Writers' Laboratory, New York City. *Home:* 65 West 96th St., New York, N.Y.

CAREER: Began professional career as teacher, later worked for a time as a newspaperwoman, and social worker; author of books for children; served at one time as deputy assistant to the Regional Administrator for Equal Opportunity, Department of Housing and Urban Development.

WRITINGS: Janie Belle (illustrated by Myrtle Sheldon), Garden City Publishing, 1940; *Hezekiah Horton* (illustrated by Oliver Harrington), Viking, 1942; (with Marie Hall Ets) *My Dog Rinty* (illustrated by Alexander and Alexandra Alland), Viking, 1946, new edition, 1964; *The Runaway Elephant* (illustrated by O. Harrington), Viking, 1950; *The Third Door: The Autobiography of an American Negro Woman,* McKay, 1955, reissued, Negro Universities Press, 1971; *Katharine Drexel: Friend of the Neglected* (illustrated by Donald Bolognese), Farrar, Straus, 1958; *Martin de Porres: Saint of the New World* (illustrated by James Fox), Vision Books, 1963; *Young Jim: The Early Years of James Weldon Johnson,* Dodd, 1967.

WORK IN PROGRESS: A book on Pierre Toussaint, the post-Revolutionary Black citizen of New York.

SIDELIGHTS: **September 26, 1906.** Born in Birmingham, Alabama. "If my family had lived in New York, Boston, or Philadelphia, a casual observer might have considered us an average American family. But Birmingham, Alabama, was our home, so we were not considered average—or American. Anthropologists would probably have said that my father was a mulatto and my mother an octoroon. I do not know what scientific name they might have used to describe my two sisters and me. I do know a lot of unscientific names that were used, but I was a young lady before I really understood them. Mama once laughingly said we were a 'duke's mixture'; to me, that seemed closer to the truth than anything else.

"Papa, who was a barber by trade, was born in Athens, Alabama, about 1868. He settled in Birmingham when the Magic City was still a tiny village close to the coal mines and steel mills that were pouring riches into the pockets of Northern industrialists. Mama migrated from the country, in this case, a small Gone-with-the-Wind community a few miles on the Alabama side of the Georgia-Alabama line.

"Papa's customers were all white. Most of them were wealthy, too. And though Mama sewed for the wives of some of the men Papa shaved, they might never have met if a strong March wind had not blown her hat off one day when she was crossing a street in the Negro business district.

"Mama and Papa were married in one of the biggest weddings that had ever taken place at Reverend Buckner's church. I must have heard a great deal about it, because I once told a new neighbor all about the wedding. I even described Mama's dress and the dresses her bridesmaids wore. When the curious woman asked how I knew all this, I told her I had to know, because I was sitting on the front seat all during the ceremony.

"Mama was furious when she heard what I had said. Papa laughed.

"'Maybe Ellen was on the front seat,' he said, 'because she was born nine months and five days later.'" [Ellen Tarry, *The Third Door: The Autobiography of an American Negro,* McKay, 1955.[1]]

1911. "Ida Mae was born when I was five. I was not happy over having a sister. I did not want to share the joy of being 'Bob Tarry's little girl.'

"I used to hear old women, who had nothing to do except sit on the front porch and talk, say Papa had a right to be so crazy about me because I 'looked like he spit me out.' Although I thought he was the most wonderful man in the world, every night when I said my prayers I asked God to let me wake up looking like my pretty blue-eyed mother with her red-gold hair. So it did not help for Ida Mae to be born looking so much like Mama, even though the fuzz on her head was not red but the color of corn silk.

"[In time] I soon learned to take care of the baby, to wash diapers in an emergency, and to iron the rough-dried clothes."[1]

1913. "When I was seven years old I went to school. . . . The children in my class had been repeating a chant about 'yaller is roguish, but black is honest,' and calling me 'cat-eyes' for about a week before I understood that they did not like the way I looked. In Mama's Mirror my reddish hair, gray eyes, and fair complexion showed me as I had always been and I wondered why the children had started calling me names. The same children teased me because I was so tall for my age and said I would 'never see seven again' until I was 'a hundred and seven.' I decided that getting to know boys and girls who teased and said mean things about you was all a part of going to school. It never occurred to me to fight back, because Mama said only 'common people' fought. Whenever the children started pulling my long thick braids some of the older girls who went to our church always showed up in time to rescue me.

"This was also the year I told my first story, planted my first tree, and saw my first snowstorm.

"The summer before I was eight I spent with relatives on a farm. It was the Sunday before school was to start when I came home. There on the front porch was Papa—with a new mustache. A nurse in a white uniform was sweeping leaves off the steps, leaves that had fallen from my tree. Inside I found a new baby—another sister—named Elizabeth after Aunt Lizzie next door. I did not want *her* either. But she was little and blue and did not look at all like Mama. Instead of feeling angry at her for being born, I felt sorry for her. . . .

"'Little Sister' was really the sweetest baby. Ida Mae treated her like another toy. Yet the baby seldom cried at Ida Mae's roughness."[1]

September, 1918. "I started my last semester at Slater [Elementary] School and my new teacher inspired me to reach for the moon. We had only been in school a few days when she told us to write a composition on the most interesting experience we had during the summer. I could not write about raiding watermelon patches; blackberry hunting was tame. Until the night before the composition was to be turned in, I could not think of a subject. I just sat with my pencil and pad in my hands and looked out the window. Suddenly I noticed a calendar on the wall. On the calendar was a picture of an Indian camp scene. A wigwam stood among a cluster of russet-leaved trees with a thick forest in the background and a lake in front. Before the wigwam smoldered the embers of a campfire. A full moon shone on the lake and an Indian brave drifted downstream in a canoe—his oar raised. I thought about a camping trip we had planned, one that got rained out. I closed my eyes and rushed the Indian on about his business. Then I grouped my family about the fire and we told stories and sang songs until it was time to wrap up in our blankets.

"The next day I turned in a descriptive composition on a camping trip outside Eutaw, Alabama. After the papers were corrected, the teacher picked my composition out and asked me to come to the front and read it to the class. I did and the other children were as quiet as could be. I could not understand why nobody said anything after I finished and I looked around at the teacher. Her plain, irregular-featured ebony face was beautiful with a glow that was new to me. Years later, I saw the same look on the face of a nurse who held a newborn baby in her hands. She left her desk and put one arm around my shoulders. For a moment I wondered if I had been caught in another 'story.'

"'Someday,' she said, ending my suspense, 'someday Ellen is going to be a writer!'"[1]

Summer, 1921. Her father died suddenly. "As painful as was the longing in our hearts, it was the physical act of waiting for Papa each night, then remembering that he would not come, that was hardest."[1]

Sent to a Catholic boarding school, St. Francis de Sales Institute in Rock Castle, Virginia, instead of the local high school. Ellen Tarry was not raised a Catholic, but her parents believed that she would only receive a sound college preparation from a private school. At that time the Birmingham Board of Education placed a strong emphasis on industrial education in their Negro high schools. "One month after Papa's death I went to Rock Castle. . . . Bit by bit I built up a wall of resistance to the Catholic practices that were a vital part of the daily routine at St. Francis de Sales. I made no secret of my attitude and repeated my vow never to become a Catholic."[1]

ELLEN TARRY

1923. Although she entered the Catholic boarding school with a predetermination to avoid any Catholic influence from the nuns, gradually Ellen Tarry became impressed with the religion. Before graduation and with her mother's consent, she embraced the Roman Catholic faith. "The day before the graduates went home I slipped away for a last visit to the chapel where I had come to know my Prisoner of Love. Afterward, I found a door open that should have been locked and walked through to the still classrooms where so many hard days had been spent. I ran my fingers over the top of my worn desk and hugged the memory of the hours with Sister Timothy and Sister Robert. I could see a face for every seat and I wondered if any of us would ever meet again. I went downstairs to the music rooms where Sister Letitia had stood over me those last weeks as I played 'Papillon Roses' or 'Underneath the Leaves' on the piano in preparation for the homecoming when Nannie would say, 'Let us hear you play something.' The big door outside the music room slammed on me and I knew an important part of my life had come to an end."[1]

Summer, 1923. "Mama had made arrangements for me to enter State Normal, but I was anxious to get a job and earn some money before it was time to go to school again. Cousin Mabel, who was using her vacation from teaching to conduct a survey for a Negro insurance company, solved this problem by hiring me as her helper. I made $15 the first week and bought a complete new outfit. I also bought some reducing pills. Fortunately, I stopped taking the pills before they did any good or any harm. Without the fig newtons and Lorna Doones the excess fat melted away.

"I was glad when the time came for me to go to State Normal at Montgomery. . . . The last half of the summer session started the day after my arrival. The old campus at the corner of Thurmond, Jackson, and Tuscaloosa Streets boasted a modern girls' dormitory, a frame administration building, and one or two other wooden structures. . . .

"Montgomery, known as the 'Cradle of the Confederacy,' was little different from Birmingham. Most of the Negroes that I knew or would have occasion to know were teachers, doctors, dentists, nurses, postal workers, or preachers. Here and there one met a successful dressmaker, barber, or a merchant like Victor Tulane, who had been a trustee at Tuskegee Institute and a friend of Booker T. Washington's as well as a good friend of Papa's. There were one or two other merchants but I remember 'Daddy' Tulane best, because he used to come to the campus and bring ice cream and fruit for my friends and me. Many of the Negroes I never met worked as domestics in the homes of the wealthy whites or eked out a living as manual laborers. Montgomery had a larger rural Negro population on its outskirts than Birmingham and I met many boys and girls—teachers-in-training—from 'out in the country.'

"The news that I had become a Catholic had preceded me and I soon found that sides had already been taken. The day I enrolled someone elected to tell me that the Birmingham Board of Education would never appoint a Catholic. At the time I had no way of knowing that this was a rumor based on one anti-Catholic principal's statement. Regular Protestant devotional services were held on the campus and another self-elected informant told me that I would not be allowed to go out to attend Mass. President Trenholm soon cleared up the latter point, but some time passed before I was to learn that the first warning was without foundation."[1]

When Ellen Tarry returned to Birmingham she found that prejudice had not changed. After not receiving an appointment to teach in the public schools, she was forced to do substitute teaching and to teach evening classes for adults. "During months of substitute teaching, I worked in schools throughout Birmingham and its suburbs. There were many mornings when I left a trolley car and walked past a spacious brick building which served as an elementary school for whites. My school was usually an unpainted frame building where I would find forty or fifty little brown boys and girls packed in a room. Sometimes two classes shared one room and, with rare exceptions, toilet facilities for pupils and teachers alike were outdoors. So was the water fountain. Rooms were heated by old pot-bellied coal stoves. Lunches were brought from home in brown paper bags, although a few of the principals arranged for selling sandwiches, milk, and candies during the time I was teaching. Few of the children I taught had any conception of the world beyond the mountains which hemmed us in, but Mother Nature and youth combined to give them a joyousness of laughter and the spirit of adventure which has to suffer multiple wounds before it dies.

"The pupils in my evening classes were elderly men and women who were illiterate. The only signature that any of them could put on the enrollment card was an X. Most of them were domestic servants whose shoulders and hands showed their years of hard labor. There was always an air of expectancy in the classroom which blotted out the odors of the kitchens in which they cooked, or the yards they tended. The children I taught by day came to school because they were sent; my adult pupils came because they wanted to learn to read and write. Their gratitude was often overwhelming and each time I was confronted with a truant youngster I thought of the old man who kissed my hand and cried the night he learned to recognize and shape the first letter of the alphabet."[1]

Finally Ellen Tarry's religious affiliations were overlooked and she was given a fourth grade class at her alma mater, Slater School. "So I was going to teach in the elementary school I had attended as a child! Later, I was told it had been the general opinion that my association with white teachers at Rock Castle had disqualified me for work in the Birmingham schools.

"'Now that I know who your parents are,' my interviewer declared, 'all I can say is if you are half the woman your mother is and if you possess the sterling qualities your father possessed, then I will be proud to think I appointed you.'

"'Remember,' he reminded me, 'you did not create the race problem and neither did I. But it is here, and it is here to stay. I want you to go back to Slater School and teach those little Negro boys and girls how to stay in their places and grow up to be good useful citizens. If you ever need a friend, don't hesitate to come to me.'

"As I looked into a pair of the bluest eyes I had ever seen, I knew the man spoke in sincerity. Neither of us was responsible for the chasm between but for a few moments we were united in the act of meeting our respective destinies. Though I have never spoken to him since, in my thoughts, he has always been my friend.

"At the beginning of the next school year I was assigned to a fifth grade. . . . During the first few days when they were still being eased back into classroom routine, I discovered that I had a group of exceptionally bright youngsters. Though they had little more conception of the world beyond than had the others, I heard a group of small girls talking about what they wanted to do when they grew up, and that was a step in the right direction. It was the boys who seemed less sure of themselves. I worried about them.

"Among the Negroes I knew, there was an unwritten law which said girls had to be educated. Boys from large families were allowed to go to work after finishing high school. I knew of cases where these working brothers helped send their sisters through college. I also knew that this custom had produced a widening circle of young professional women who were perforce thrown in the company of unskilled laborers, and that many unstable marriages had resulted. It was frightening to think that the bright-eyed boys whose classroom lives were in my keeping might one day add to the human waste which was all around.

"In search of a window through which my boys and girls might snatch glimpses of the world beyond Red Mountain, I scanned magazines, newspapers, and books for mention of any and all achievements by members of our race. I pinpointed distant cities where Negroes had migrated to enjoy broader economic and cultural opportunities, and shared with my children whatever knowledge I had of a given community. I led my young charges afield by easy stages from the known to the unknown. A member of an old Birmingham family had become a soloist in one of Boston's largest white churches. A young woman from another well-known family had become a member of the Williams Jubilee Singers. To tour the country with a musical group and to sing in a big, white church in Boston seemed wonderful accomplishments to children who had never been outside Alabama."[1]

Late 1920's. At the end of the school year, Tarry returned to her first ambition—to become a writer. "During this period personal affairs occupied much of my time but I was still searching for a way to make my seventh grade teacher's prediction come true, that I would be a writer. I wanted to communicate with the world—to cry out against the outrage of racial discrimination and its attendant ills. But I knew it meant taking up another cross, and I hesitated. I reread Booker T. Washington, and studied everything by and about James Weldon Johnson, Du Bois, and Brawley that I could find in our humble library. One of my chief sources of inspiration, I remember, was the folksy articles by Bruce Barton which appeared in Sunday supplements around the latter part of the 1920's.

"The study of journalism, I thought, might be a stepping-stone, with books to come later. I dreamed of going to New York and enrolling at Columbia University's Pulitzer School of Journalism. But I had to start somewhere and a correspondence course was the first step. Then I went to a local editor and showed him the sketches I had written for my pupils.

"Guillermo Talliferro, who edited *The Birmingham Truth,* read my stories and hired me. The *Truth* served as an organ for the Knights of Pythias and the Court of Calanthes; with an assured source of revenue, Tally, as we called the editor, could afford to experiment. From week to week my assignments grew and I became a combination reporter-columnist-editorial writer. Tally pushed me until I finally managed to sell ads, too."[1]

1929. Tarry wrote editorials attempting to advance the Negro cause. These were radical considering the times. "Bit by bit the small reforms I advocated in the *Truth* came to pass. A cemetery where the older Negro families buried their dead and which had been allowed to reach a horrible stage of neglect was cleaned up. My clubs scheduled more book reviews, and more attention was given to Negro history. With each little victory, I became more aware of what I might be doing if only I were better prepared. I argued with myself; I prayed and thought of all that needed to be done. I could see and feel the lethargy which enslaved my people just as much as the unfair laws which gave them second-class citizenship. Even after I had sent for a catalogue and knew I could meet the requirements for admission to Columbia's Pulitzer School of Journalism, I was not sure how I would live if I left home. My only asset was a diamond ring which I could pawn, and I had a fear of being alone and hungry in a strange city.

"The night I made the decision to leave Birmingham I was sitting on the front porch looking out over the lights of the city in the valley below. The moon was full and all the stars were out. The radio, just inside the window, was playing and Rudy Vallee was singing;

> '. . . Look down, look down
> that lonely road
> Before you travel on. . . .' "[1]

August 11, 1929. Moved to New York City in order to advance her journalistic vocation. ". . . Nothing in New York seemed familiar. In Alabama we had already begun to feel the pinch of tight money, which we always expected during a Republican administration. In New York everybody seemed to be enjoying prosperity. . . . The contempt with which so many New Yorkers spoke of Alabama worried me and I became angry when people complimented me on a dress and said, 'Don't tell me you got *that* in Alabama. I didn't know they sold dresses like that down there.'

"I accepted the fact that I had an accent, since everybody talked or laughed about it. But it was more than the accent that got me into trouble at the corner grocery store. The clerks said they did not know I wanted white bread when I asked for 'light bread.' . . . After overcoming these petty irritations, the two New York customs I found hardest to accept were the pew rent boxes at the doors of Catholic churches where a coin was dropped before entering and the men who remained seated on public vehicles while women stood. Years later I conceded that both were logical and practical.

"I had never looked for a job before in my life and now that I was actually on my own the prospects were bewildering. I spoke to the people with whom I lived and to a classmate who lived upstairs in the same apartment building and they suggested that I look in the help-wanted ads. But most of the ads for young women wanted young white women and the others were for 'settled or mature Negro' women to cook, nurse, or keep house. I saw one or two for a 'light colored girl to keep a small bachelor apartment. Work pleasant,' but my friends said I would not like that kind of job. Wherever I went people laughed at my accent and I began to wonder why I ever had come to New York. The prospect of going to school was not enough to cancel out my disappointment."[1]

Ellen Tarry was forced to take a job as a waitress in a department store. "Only Negro waitresses were employed in the restaurant where I worked. I was the youngest in the group and they knew all the tricks of getting the best stations and the best customers. The lunch hour, when the surrounding buildings dumped many of their occupants into our store, was the busiest time. Though my 'Yes, ma'am,' and 'No, sir,' made most of the customers laugh, my speech was also a mark of distinction. Within a few weeks I had built up a following of the more leisurely customers—all male. Even so, I never felt comfortable when they called me 'Honey Chile' or greeted me with 'How're yo'all today?' "[1]

October, 1929. The stock market crashed, plunging the country into a Depression and Ellen Tarry lost her job. "When I received the notice of dismissal I was not too sad because I knew I needed a new job and new interests. And I never worried too much until the last dollar was broken."[1]

1930. Among the ranks of the unemployed, Tarry found brief jobs as a governess and as an attendant in a nightclub. "Jobs came and jobs went as the depression wore on. I followed rainbow after rainbow, but the pot of gold always vanished before I arrived. When I had to choose between staying at home and being hungry, or going to a party with someone I did not like and getting a good meal and enough sherry to make me forget who I was and why I had come to New York, I chose the party. I had learned to keep my mouth shut and if a prospective employer did not ask about my race I did not tell him. No party was too gay, however, to prevent me from arguing with the man or woman who made unwarranted or unfounded charges about the South. I was especially resentful of smug Northerners who advanced the theory that any Negro who was dumb enough to stay in the South should expect to be mistreated. With trembling fingers I could only cling to my belief in God and the hope that one day I would have the opportunity to write again and answer my friends who thought of Alabama as a land of savagery and ignorance."[1]

1933. "I had gone through a succession of jobs, sometimes holding two poorly paid ones at the same time, and working extra wherever I could. I had managed to get an apartment in a swanky building on St. Nicholas Place and enough flashy clothes . . . to [be dubbed] 'the Mae West of Sugar Hill.' I met a whole generation of men and women who, like myself, had matured during a depression. Layer after layer of sophistication was piled on to hide the accumulation of disappointment and shattered dreams.''[1]

1936. Held a job as a writer-researcher on the Federal Writers' Project. ''Work on the Federal Writers' Project, where we were gathering material for a book on the history of the Negro in New York, opened many new avenues of research to me. If I learned nothing else, I learned to make intelligent use of available library resources. My assignment was the Underground Railroad and I spent long hours in the labyrinthine stone building at 42nd Street and uptown in the Schomburg Collection, which was housed in the 135th Street branch. As I waded through documents which recorded the deeds of my favorite heroine, Harriet Tubman, my old interest in the life of the Underground Railroad's most daring conductor was revived. Lives of men like Frederick Douglass, David Ruggles, Isaac T. Hopper, Elijah Lovejoy, and the other brave abolitionists, writers, and statesmen who cried out against the evils of slavery and risked their lives to cheat the heartless men who trafficked in human flesh, became my daily fare.''[1]

1936-39. Studied under Lucy Sprague Mitchell in the Writers' Laboratory at Bank Street College, New York City.

December, 1939. ''On Christmas Eve I received my first check for *Janie Belle,* the foundling story that became my first book. It was scheduled for a late summer publication date. *Janie Belle* had come through just in time to play Santa Claus to a group of my most cherished story-hour children and I fought my way in and out of Macy's toy department that day to be sure that my boys and girls would be happy on the next.

''As Hitler's war machine continued to roll across Europe talk of the approaching conflict dominated most of the conversations.''[1]

1940. *Janie Belle,* Ellen Tarry's first book, published. She was one of the first authors to use blacks as main characters in her children's books. ''The hours I had spent in research while working on the Federal Writers' Project had left me a renewed interest in folk tales. In retrospect, I examined the stories I had heard from my mother and my grandmother and I knew that through many of these anecdotes they had passed along to me a part of the history of my people. It was in this manner that I first learned that among my ancestors had been 'rebs, slaves, and Cherokee Indians.' It was disturbing to realize that much of the unwritten history of the Negro in America would be lost when 'the old heads' died, and I felt the urge to start southward and talk with some of these old people. Concord, North Carolina, was my first stop.

''Concord, which is in the heart of the textile district, was different from most of the Southern towns I had visited before but it was hard for me to put the difference into words. I knew that there was less hostility between the races than in Alabama, but it crept out in odd places. There was less pretense at sophistication among the Negroes I had met and caste lines were not as evident as in towns farther south where mulattoes were conspicuous by their absence.''[1]

1942. ''. . . I went to Viking, where I met May Massee, who had a wide reputation for publishing worthwhile juvenile

books. So I became a Viking author. May Massee also understood my desire to have a Negro illustrate the little story of Hezekiah and the red automobile and was patient with my search for an artist whose sketches would meet her approval. We were both happy to select Oliver Harrington, whose cartoon, Bootsie, appearing in the Negro press, is an all-time favorite.''[1]

Became employed by a New York newspaper, *Amsterdam News.* ''It was like a dream come true for me to have the opportunity to write all day and get paid for it, too, and I knew I could trust Dan [Burley; the managing editor] because his wife was a friend of mine.

''My flair for attracting complicated situations was demonstrated the first morning I went to the newspaper office. Dan put a batch of assignments on my typewriter and the first one I picked up was on birth control. My story was to be built around a news release sent out by one of the advocating agencies, but knowing the attitude of the [Catholic] Church on this practice I did not want the story on my conscience or under my by-line. I saved the first assignment for last and then solved the problem by putting it in the waste basket. That was one of my lucky days. Dan never asked for the story on birth control.

''The following months were a time of ferment and decision, but I was happy in my work. Dan was a considerate 'boss' and an expert at waving the scent of a story under my nose. He knew I would never come back to the office until I had all of the facts, and he became resigned to the knowledge that regardless of the assignment he gave me it would be a feature with pictures attached by the time I put it in the wire basket on his desk.''[1]

That same year Ellen Tarry's second book, *Hezekiah Horton,* was published.

Reluctantly left the newspaper office to become a co-director for a Friendship House on the South Side of Chicago. ''The last thing I wanted to do, at that time, was leave New York. Writing satisfied me, as jewels and fine clothes satisfy many women. Writing for a newspaper gave me the opportunity to project many of my interests and quieted that old urge to do something about the plight of my people. I felt as if I had found my niche in life at last.

''There were many days at the Chicago Friendship House when I felt like a lone voice crying in the middle of the Loop. The worst part of our venture was past history. Never again would we have to pull tacks, scrub floors, or throw out dirty chicken coops. I wanted desperately to enjoy the fruits of our labor, but that little voice which speaks so loudly kept telling me that the South Side had taken Friendship House into its big heart and I was no longer needed. I felt I had served my purpose and that it was time for me to move on.''[1]

1943-1944. Worked with the U.S.O. during World War II.

1944. Returned to New York. Began work on another juvenile, *My Dog Rinty.*

November, 1944. Married a soldier and gave birth to a baby girl. ''The anguish caused by the housing shortage was forgotten when the child I had expected for Christmas came in November. Instead of the son I had prayed for, God sent me a daughter and my mother arrived one day before the little girl. One of Mama's friends who had comforted me during

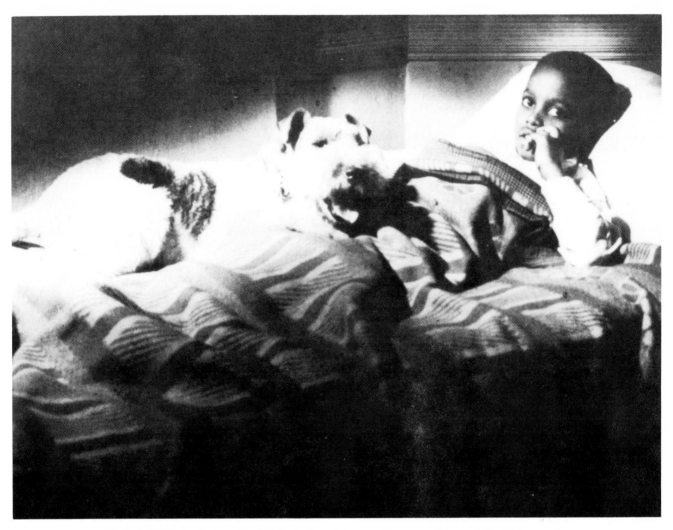

That night Rinty slept on David's bed, though he wasn't supposed to, and David lay awake thinking what could he do to make money so he could keep Rinty. ■ (From *My Dog Rinty* by Ellen Tarry and Marie Hall Ets. Illustrated by Alexander and Alexandra Alland.)

the months of waiting summed up the boy vs. girl situation in a most practical manner.

"'God knows what He's doing. A little girl will be much cheaper. You can always sleep with her and save on room rent.'

"... It was only after I was alone with the baby that I recognized the scope of the responsibility I had undertaken. Looking at the fat little girl wrapped in pink blankets as she slept in her bassinet, I questioned my right to condemn an innocent child to the heritage that comes to each Negro in America at birth.

"During war years, nights are always long and lonely for womenfolk who are alone with their children, and I had ample time to remember the wishes I had made for myself that had not come true. Already a galaxy of prayers as countless as the stars had been offered up for the girl-child God had entrusted to my care. I smiled at my own childishness when I felt the familiar words form on my lips.

       'Wish I will, wish I might;
       New moon, I make this wish tonight!'

"It was no new coin I showed my old friend this time. Proudly, I held high the young flesh of my flesh and blood of my blood. Silently, I asked the moon and its Creator that this new life might be useful, fruitful, and normal—in spite of the handicaps I knew lay in wait.

"During the following months Elizabeth passed through various stages of change. Fair at birth, her skin tone deepened into a smooth brown-like caramel candy. The dark mass of curls took on a reddish-brown hue and coarsened in texture. This, I hoped, would make life less complicated for her than it had been for her mother.

"Except for colic, brought on by my dogged insistence in following a fixed feeding schedule as I had been instructed, Elizabeth was a healthy, happy baby. Fortunately, her colic struck at night. During the day, after bottles were washed, formula mixed, and clothes were on the line, I was with Marie Ets working at all the business which goes into making a book. The story was written, but we had to find a 'typical' family and get permission to take pictures. Though it was hard finding a family to fit our needs, getting permission to take pictures in homes, places of business, public service centers, and churches in Harlem was an enormous task. My people's understandable suspicion of the white man and anything connected with the white man's world created situations which would have defeated the purpose of the book if I had not presumed upon many friendships. By the time Alexander and Alexandra Alland had taken the last picture for the book, I was immune to insult."[1]

August, 1945. "I went to work for local National Catholic Community Service as supervisor of the Harlem Area. NCCS had offices in the Harlem Servicemen's Center and, for the first time, I had the opportunity of working with men from all branches of the Armed Forces. I was especially impressed by the spirit of co-operation demonstrated by the Navy personnel. When I complimented one of the sailors on the manner in which they always assisted the staff, he said: 'On the ship there's nowhere to go. So you learn how to pull together. That's all there is to it.' The boys in blue were younger than most of the soldiers who came to the Center and much less sophisticated.

"Talk of peace was in the air. . . .

"On August 14 [1945], I left the Center at a few minutes past six and went to the YWCA for dinner. I had eaten and was standing at the information desk talking with a friend when we heard cries of joy coming from all parts of the building. My friend turned on the nearest radio and we heard the last part of the announcement that our war with Japan had come to an end. It was 7:01 P.M. by the clock on the wall. V-J Day had come at last."[1]

1947. "In 1947 Jackie Robinson was signed to play with the Brooklyn Dodgers and became the first Negro to play on a major baseball team. We got an apartment in Riverton, a middle-income housing development opened by the Metropolitan [Life] Insurance Company, and for the first time I had a comfortable home for my daughter. That winter New York was blanketed by a series of snowstorms, but for the first time in years I was warm and did not have to keep Elizabeth wrapped in blankets and sweaters. My good friends, the Handmaids of Mary, accepted her in their nursery school and we both entered another phase of development."[1]

1951. "In the latter part of 1951 I was appointed director of community relations for the St. Charles [Borromeo] School and Community Center Fund, which was conducting a campaign to erect a parochial school and community center in overcrowded Harlem under the leadership of Monsignor Cornelius J. Drew. Catholic, Protestant, and Jewish leaders, Negroes and whites, combined their efforts to build a new St. Charles, a better Harlem, and a stronger America. There were many times when I closed my eyes and thought back to the predictions of ignominious downfall which my townsmen had made when they learned of my conversion to 'that new religion.' As skills in public relations developed, I was grateful for the opportunity to work toward the fulfillment of my old dream of a community center.

"Many spiritual benefits resulted from my association with St. Charles. It was a privilege to work under the same roof with the Blessed Sacrament and to be able to share my sorrows and joys with Him. The St. Charles school is conducted by the Sisters of the Blessed Sacrament and it was thrilling, day by day, to see these nuns in familiar habits, to know that I was 'their child' and that they were pleased with the application of my talents which might never have developed if they had not guided me well during the crucial years of my adolescence."[1]

1954. On May 17th, the Supreme Court unanimously ruled that racial segregation in public schools is a violation of the constitution. "I know that time must still pass, hearts must be changed, and minds freed of fear, greed, and bigotry before the signs 'colored' and 'white' will be torn down and relegated to the trash cans of the New South and the history books written about the Old South. Southerners are slow to act but the ultimate change must come from within.

"The New South will welcome the talents of gifted Negro citizens, and prophets will be received with honor in their own land. As the yoke of ignorance and oppression is cast aside, a new era of prosperity will begin and the South will no longer be a poor relation. Her towns and cities, her parishes and villages will once more become a symbol for 'gracious living,' but this time 'with dignity for all.'"[1]

Throughout the 1950's and the 1960's Ellen Tarry continued to write books about famous Blacks and juvenile books with Black boys and girls as main characters. "In the juvenile field, when I started my teaching career, there were almost no books for young readers which showed the Negro as other than *Uncle Remus* or *Little Black Sambo.* Though *Uncle Remus* must be reckoned as an outstanding contribution to the folklore of the world and *Sambo* is universal, as a steady, exclusive reading diet such books would have given children a stereotyped idea of the Negro. Today, there are many beautifully illustrated juvenile books on library shelves which show Negroes in all walks of life. To have had a small part in adding to this list has been a privilege. Of such intangibles are the riches of an eventful life.

"It has been high adventure, during this past quarter century when wars, inventions, and daring achievements have wrought revolutionary changes throughout the world, to watch the pendulum swing across the dial of American history. It has been rewarding, if at times difficult, to hold on to the belief that 'things will be different someday.' Though that day is only dawning, tomorrow will come! Descended from slaves, rebels, and a vanquished people, I have lived to write boldly 'American' beside my name; to know that my child is, in fact, free. I salute my ancestors, my parents, and my friends who worked and prayed for this day. I rejoice for those who helped me to hold my head high, then joined our Creator before their faith was justified. . . .

"One day soon all who are concerned with a legacy for our children will join hands. If hostile forces contrive to separate us we will find ways to reach out to each other, regardless of race, just as my ancestors of another century found ways to 'steal away to Jesus.' The old North Star, which once led countless Negroes to freedom, still shines in God's Heaven. Then, when we are united, there will be no door in America marked 'colored' and no door marked 'white.' Instead there will be the third door—free from racial designations—through which all Americans, all of God's children, will walk in peace and dignity. So ends my song of hope for tomorrow. *Deo Gratias!*"[1]

FOR MORE INFORMATION SEE: Ellen Tarry, *The Third Door: The Autobiography of an American Negro Woman,* McKay, 1955, reissued, Negro Universities Press, 1971; Lee Bennett Hopkins, *Books Are by People,* Citation, 1969.

THOMPSON, Kay 1912-

PERSONAL: Born November 9, 1912 (or 1913, according to some sources), in St. Louis, Mo.; daughter of a jeweler.

CAREER: Debuted as a pianist with the St. Louis Symphony, 1928; featured vocalist with a St. Louis dance band, 1928; moved to California, 1929, and was first employed as a diving instructor; vocalist with the Mills Brothers on radio; singer and arranger for Fred Waring's Band, New York, N.Y.; producer, with Jim Backus, of radio show on CBS network, "Kay Thompson and Company"; Metro-Goldwyn-Mayer, Hollywood, Calif., arranger and composer, 1942-46; nightclub performer with the Williams Brothers, 1947-53; star of one-woman show, New York, N.Y., 1954; appeared in the motion pictures, "Funny Face," 1956, "Tell Me That You Love Me Junie Moon," 1970, and on television; has also composed songs; author.

WRITINGS: Eloise: A Book for Precocious Grown Ups (illustrated by Hilary Knight), Simon & Schuster, 1955; *Eloise in Paris* (illustrated by H. Knight), Simon & Schuster, 1957; *Eloise at Christmastime* (illustrated by Knight), Random House, 1958; *Eloise in Moscow* (illustrated by Knight), Simon & Schuster, 1959; *Kay Thompson's Miss Pooky Peckinpaugh and Her Secret Private Boyfriends Complete with Telephone Numbers* (illustrated by Joe Eula), Harper, 1970.

SIDELIGHTS: Kay Thompson possesses diverse talents. Besides writing her *Eloise* series, she is a successful singer, arranger, pianist, composer, choreographer, actress, creator of nightclub acts and television shows.

Eloise, the character in her books, was born sometime during her nightclub act with the Williams Brothers. In apologizing for being late for a rehearsal, Thompson responded in a high, childish voice that her name was Eloise and she was six. The other performers each invented a juvenile identity and joined the game. One day a friend urged her to put *Eloise* into book form and arranged an interview with Hilary Knight. "I went over . . . carrying my own ashtray. This girl doesn't smoke and hates dirt. When I arrived, my friend said, 'I'll call Hilary from across the hall.' A Princetonian young man, shy, gentle and soft-spoken, came in. He seemed terribly impressed with me, which naturally impressed me terribly with him. I noticed his hands, which were slim and artistic, and thought that was a step in the right direction. So I wrote twelve lines on a piece of paper and handed it to him. 'I'm going to write this book,' I said. 'I'll leave this with you. If you're interested, get in touch with me.' Then I spoke a few words of Eloisiana and left.

"That Christmas I received a card from Knight. It was an interesting, beautifully executed and highly stylized picture of an angel and Santa Claus, streaking through the sky on a Christmas tree. On the end of the tree, grinning a lovely grin, her wild hair standing on end, was Eloise. It was immediate recognition on my part. There she was. In person. I knew at once Hilary Knight had to illustrate the book. I knew also that I'd have to write it first. So I took three months off and wrote it.

"I holed in at the Plaza and we went to work. I just knew I had to get this done. Eloise was trying to get out. I've never known such stimulation. This girl had complete control of me. Ideas came from everywhere. Hilary and I had immediate understanding. Eloise was a little girl who lived at the Plaza, and she was a very special kind of little girl. We

KAY THOMPSON

wrote, edited, laughed, outlined, cut, pasted, laughed again, read out loud, laughed and suddenly we had a book. We took *Eloise* to Jack Goodman at Simon and Schuster and he recognized and understood Eloise immediately. We all became close friends, and the book went into print—only a thousand copies the first time, just to see how it went. It went. The avalanche started and hasn't stopped—we're in the sixth printing with no sign of a letup." [Cynthia Lindsay, "McCall's Visits Kay Thompson," *McCall's,* January, 1957."[1]]

The first Eloise book had sold over 150,000 copies at the time its sequel was published two years later.

"Here's what I'm interested in. Everything. Here's what I like to do. Everything. Here's what I want to do. Find out if there is something that I can still find out how to do."[1]

"Fatigue is a stranger to me. It's caused by monotony and a lack of interest in things. It has no place in a creative mind. People with nothing to do and nowhere to go bore me. Cary Grant in a hotel lobby after a long trip is like four showers and a glass of shampoo to me. Whenever I'm tired, I just think about the glorious colors of butterfly wings. It's refreshing. I mean, butterflies never get tired—or if they do, we never hear about it. Enthusiasm and imagination can carry you anywhere you want to go without Vuitton luggage." [Rex Reed, "You've Never Seen Anything Like Her," *Harper's Bazaar,* November, 1972.[2]]

Her energy probably springs from her personal diet. "I go along with a low-sugar diet, which means nibbling a lot of times during the day. In the a.m., an egg and a piece of orange. Two hours later, two ounces of Gorgonzola cheese and some cold roast beef with maybe a chunk of grapefruit. Two hours after that, a small portion of beautiful fish with watercress and lemon. Everything in tiny portions. I never eat much after 9 p.m. Maybe a peach before bed. Nothing heavy before sleep, unless you want to dream about dock strikes. An occasional B-12 shot if I feel tired, which isn't often."[2]

When asked if she considered her diversity an unique attribute she replied: "If artistically you are able to do one thing, you are more than likely able to do them all."[1]

I have my own room. It has a coat rack which is as large as me. ■ (From *Eloise* by Kay Thompson. Illustrated by Hilary Knight.)

At the height of her popularity Eloise became identified with the Plaza Hotel. Her portrait hung in a place of honor, and a room was named after her, with all the furnishings and decor taken directly from book illustrations. For a time, the hotel received calls from little girls wanting to talk to Eloise. Thompson spoke with many of the callers when she was there until she realized that Eloise's calls outnumbered her own.

I am Eloise
I am six
■ (From *Eloise* by Kay Thompson. Illustrated by Hilary Knight.)

Kay Thompson also founded Eloise Ltd., which produced records and post cards among other Eloise-related items. The character has also inspired a line of children's fashions, as well as dolls and hotel kits.

FOR MORE INFORMATION SEE: C. Lindsay, "Mc-Call's Visits Kay Thompson," *McCall's*, January, 1957; *Current Biography Yearbook*, H. W. Wilson, 1960; "Authors and Editors," *Publishers Weekly*, May 12, 1969; Rex Reed, "Rex Reed on Kay Thompson: You've Never Seen Anything Like Her," *Harper's Bazaar*, November, 1972.

TRAPP, Maria (Augusta) von   1905-

PERSONAL: Born January 26, 1905, in Vienna, Austria; emigrated to the United States in 1939, naturalized a citizen, 1948; daughter of Karl (an engineer) and Augusta (Ranier) Kutschera; married Baron Georg von Trapp (a World War I submarine commander), November 26, 1927 (died May 30, 1947); children: Rosemarie, Eleanor (Mrs. Hugh Campbell), Johannes; stepchildren: Rupert, Agatha, Maria, Werner, Hedwig (deceased), Johanna (Mrs. Ernst I. Winter), Martina (Mrs. Jean Dupire; deceased). *Education:* Graduated from the State Teachers College of Progressive Education, Vienna, Austria; entered the Nonnberg Benedictine Convent, Salzburg, Austria, as a novice, 1924-26. *Religion:* Roman Catholic. *Residence:* Stowe, Vt. 05672.

CAREER: Member of the Trapp Family Singers, performing in Europe, South and Central America, Canada, the United States, Hawaii, Australia, and New Zealand, 1938-56; founder and teacher of the Trapp Family Music Camp, Stowe, Vt., 1951-56, and the Trapp Family Austrian Relief, Inc., 1947; manager of the Trapp Family Lodge, Stowe, Vt., until 1967; author. *Member:* Catholic Women's Club of Stowe, Zonta Club. *Awards, honors:* Bene Merenti medal (Papal decoration), 1949; Catholic Writers Guild St. Francis de Sales Golden Book Award as best nonfiction, 1950, for *The Story of the Trapp Family Singers;* nominated Lady of Holy Sepulchre, 1951; National Catholic Conference of Family Life Catholic Mother of the Year Award, 1956; Honorary Cross First Class for Science and Art from the Austrian government, 1967; LL.D., St. Mary's College, 1957, D. Music, St. Anselme's College, 1966.

WRITINGS: The Story of the Trapp Family Singers, Lippincott, 1949, a later edition published as *The Sound of Music: The Story of the Trapp Family Singers*, White Lion, 1976; *Yesterday, Today, and Forever*, Lippincott, 1952, reissued, New Leaf, 1975; *Around the Year with the Trapp Family* (illustrated by Rosemarie Trapp and Nikolaus E. Wolff), Pantheon, 1955; (with Ruth T. Murdoch) *A Family on Wheels*, Lippincott, 1959; *Maria* (autobiographical), Creation House, 1972; *When the King Was Carpenter*, New Leaf, 1976.

SIDELIGHTS: **January 26, 1905.** Born in Vienna, Austria. "I was an only child and an orphan, and I had a most unhappy childhood.

"In the night before the 26th of January—before midnight!—I was born on the train. The train was almost empty. The conductor, having nine children of his own, knew all about everything and assisted my mother most professionally. But then he was stuck. He tried all his power of persuasion to get the young lady out of the train and into a hospital bed, which she refused sternly.

"'I promised my husband to arrive on this train, and he will be waiting for me at the station in Vienna. And there I will arrive' was her answer.

"And so it happened, to my chagrin, that when my mother appeared with the finished product and I was taken by her anxious husband to the General Hospital in Vienna—'just in case'—they wrote on my baptism certificate that I was born on January 26 in Vienna instead of 'on the train in Tirol on January 25.'

"As much as I could find out, my mother and father were very happy together and I grew up into a healthy youngster.

"I had walked very early and was running around fast as a weasel, but I hadn't said a single word yet and I was already two years old when my anxious parents took me to a doctor. He took one good look at me, shook his head, and said, 'Don't worry. She will make up for this later.' (Once in a while I have been reminded of this prediction.)

"And then disaster struck. . . . My young mother caught pneumonia and, this being before the time of antibiotics, no doctor could help her. I was told that my father thought that if he held her upright, leaning against his shoulder, she simply could not die. And so she died, leaning on his heart.

". . . The poor man was left with a helpless little child. In his own arms he brought me to the same cousin who had brought up my brother and who was in her sixties by now. But she took me in most willingly and lovingly.

"My first memories go back to the little house on the outskirts of Vienna, a section which had just been incorporated into the big city but was really still a village with its long main village street. There the farmhouses, low stone buildings with just a ground floor, were strung together by big tall wooden gates through which the hay wagons passed. Soon I would be 'big' enough to go to one farmer for the daily milk and to another one to get the potatoes, and a third one for vegetables; and so I came to know them all. Every farm and every house had its own well from which the people had drunk . . . since time immemorial; but since our village was now part of Vienna, we were told not to use well water for drinking anymore, only for cooking or washing. Therefore, every day at 5 P.M. I was sent to the city spring to bring home two milk pitchers full of water from the Vienna Woods. This section of Vienna borders the Marchfeld, a wide stretched-out plain, very flat, but full of historic memories. There I spent my early childhood.

"My foster mother was very kind, as was my foster father who died when I was very young; I remember his funeral only dimly.

"The only family I knew as a child were my foster parents, two grown-up sons, Alfred and Pepi, and two grown-up daughters, Anni and Kathy. . . .

"Unfortunately it was not the custom that I go visiting to other homes with children or that I would be allowed to invite children to our home. It was so very much a home of grownups set in their ways; they obviously didn't want to be disturbed by the noise of children, but I'm sure there was no hard feelings. It simply wasn't done, but the fact is that I grew up a very lonesome child. Kathy accompanied me every day to school and picked me up again afterward, so even there I didn't have the company of the other girls chatting and playing with each other.

MARIA von TRAPP

"And so it happened that out of necessity I began to invent company for myself. I imagined that I was living with a large family named Paultraxl; there were a mother, father and eleven children. Mr. Paultraxl was a well-to-do farmer, and through him I learned the most minute details of what was going on in the barn and in the field. It didn't matter that I had actually read all his books; in my make-believe life I was being told these things by Paultraxl. His wife was a loving soul, jolly, full of fun, hugging and kissing me, and all their children were lots of fun. Once in a great while Mrs. Paultraxl's sister, Frau Irbinger, came visiting with her clan. My, was that an ado. It so happened that this took place when my own family was out visiting, which was very rarely, because I needed all the space to accommodate my guests. If my foster family came home unexpectedly, they found all the chairs which we owned from all the rooms grouped around in a circle, as I had to take care of all my company. They would find me happily chatting, going from chair to chair, offering make-believe food and drink. Many a time I was scolded harshly for all that nonsense and my otherwise–kind foster mother would say, 'Don't you ever let me see that again.'

"So I was pushed back with my whole world of make believe into the distant corners of the garden. There I had made up practically an entire bakery with my little tin cake forms and the sand pile providing *Gugelhupf,* and all kinds of lush Viennese cakes like *Linzertorte, Apfelstrudel* and *Sachertorte.* I had them all lined up, preparing food for the 'next visit.'

"In these first years of my childhood, God entered my life for the first time in a very gentle and loving way. My foster mother was a deeply religious person, truly pious. Every morning she would go to church, many times taking me with her, and I remember how I often looked at her rather than at the altar. Her face radiated kindliness and the love of God.

"My foster mother told me the basic truths: That God is everywhere and sees me always; I can't hide from Him. Even if human eyes don't see that I do something wrong, He sees it.

"That Mary was my loving mother, especially as my true mother had left me too early, and I should always turn to her if I was in trouble.

"So I was finally one of the white-clad little girls who made their first communion in the third grade. I resolved on that day that I would never, but really never, again offend God, to whom I wanted to belong till I died." [Maria von Trapp, *Maria*, Creation House, 1972.[1]]

1910-1912. Maria saw her natural father infrequently. Their meetings were unpleasant and she hated being forced by her father to travel to foreign places with him. "My father had several ways of making a little girl unhappy. Besides Latin and French grammar, there was his wish to break his daughter into traveling around the globe—beginning early. And so he conceived the awful idea of grabbing me from my foster mother's lap, putting me in a coat and hat, and more or less dragging me along with a satchel in my hand to some railroad station to show me some of the most interesting places in beautiful Austria. The only problem was, I couldn't care less.

"Maybe it was because I had always lived so sheltered a life with such a small group of people that I was now so attached to them that even having to be away for more than half a day plunged me into deepest distress of homesickness. Being haunted by a most vivid imagination, I saw them in all kinds of peril and often in danger of death. Needless to say, it made me utterly unhappy. Such shyness existed between me and my father that I couldn't express my feelings in words. I only, from time to time, quietly cried and then noisily blew my nose, which again made him roaringly impatient. There we were in Zell am See, looking toward the majestic glaciers. But instead of breaking out in appropriate oh's and ah's, I sobbed, 'I am sure they are all sick back home.'

"I couldn't have displeased him more, and that happened every time we took a trip."[1]

1914. ". . . When I was nine years old, my father was found dead in his easy chair. He had slipped away during a nap.

"That was the end of my childhood.

"After Father's death, fear entered my life. . . . My Uncle Franz, my new guardian, made it clear to me that I had to come home from school nonstop, with no fooling around on the way. He said that he had his way of finding out everything, so I shouldn't try to hide anything or ever dare to lie to him.

"From the beginning I tried to oblige him. Many a day when I came home my uncle stood in the doorway with a stick in hand, telling me he 'knew all about it.' Then he turned me over his knee and spanked me hard.

"And when I remonstrated, 'But, Uncle Franz, I came home right away! I didn't even stop a single time,' he slapped me across the mouth and said, 'Don't lie! I know everything.'

"This threat was hanging over me every day throughout those years. However desperately I might plead my innocence, nothing helped. My old foster mother cried bitter tears when she saw what was happening, and her daughter, my uncle's wife, joined her. She must have had a sad fate because I could hear her low crying behind closed doors almost daily.

"Many years later, the poor man was taken to an insane asylum where he died, which explains everything. But at the time we didn't know that he was already sick. We only suffered under his cruel injustice, being punished for things we hadn't done.

"So passed my eleventh and twelfth years."[1]

1918. The discussion of religion was forbidden in Uncle Franz's house. He had adopted the atheistic attitude of post war socialistic Austria. So Maria von Trapp passed into womanhood without religion. "All the Bible stories which I had loved so dearly in my childhood were now branded as silly old legends with not a word of truth.

"This was the daily conversation during dinner. Involuntarily I lapped it up with a big spoon. It was different all right. Suddenly God was out of my life. But even at such an early age I felt an emptiness. How I envied my classmates for their warm friendship with God—while I was out in the cold.

"How I went through high school successfully, I really don't understand, for I became accustomed to playing hooky and 'enjoying life,' which meant that I was already going for long hikes through the wheat fields and strips of woodland located next to the last houses of Kagran.

". . . I was a good student and somehow learned fast. Toward the end of each semester I led a very secluded life with my books, so I always 'made it.'

"The Austrian report card used to have two words at its top. One word was *Betragen*, meaning behavior or conduct, and the second was *Fleiss*, meaning the degree of diligence the pupil showed in his work habits. After that came the twelve names of subjects for which he received grades. Unfortunately my impudence, my impetuousness, and my wrongly applied sense of humor constantly got me into trouble, so my first and second marks always caused an extra-hard spanking. But I deserved this. I was the horror and fright of my teachers. They couldn't possibly punish me enough; my imagination could always invent worse and juicier things of mischief. I remember how one teacher in my last school year, when I was fourteen years old, once called me out in front of the class, looked at me sternly, and said, 'And I wish on you a daughter exactly like yourself. Sit down.'"[1]

Maria von Trapp attended the State Teachers' College of Progressive Education in Vienna for four years. While at school, the young cynic looked down on the girls at the school who were practicing Catholics. "Some of the girls were practicing Catholics, and there was even a chapel in our school building where a daily mass was held. Very soon I had my own gang of which I was the undisputed leader.

"'Look at those Catholics,' I used to say. 'Isn't it ridiculous what they need to lead a decent life—seven sacraments, holy water, holy pictures, prayer books, Bibles, indulgences and whatnot. Well, we shall show them how we can get along without all those crutches, but we really have to be tops.'

(Maria von Trapp with Mary Martin, the star of "The Sound of Music," the play based on Baroness von Trapp's autobiography.)

"Sad to say, my gang widened in membership. Finally we were the majority, trying to prove to ourselves and everybody else that a decent life can be lived without God and all those props."[1]

However, during her graduation year, Maria von Trapp was influenced by a Jesuit priest who rekindled her Catholic faith. After graduation she entered a strict Benedictine convent. "Graduation came and went. After graduation classes, some of the class made an excursion into the high Alps. We had a whole week of hiking a distance of between 2,000 and 3,000 meters (6,000 to 9,000 feet) across the ice fields and glaciers, enjoying the most unforgettable scenery, especially the sunset. One has to have experienced the sunset on a glacier to realize how deep it impresses one's soul. Because I had had a little experience in mountain climbing, I was singled out by our guide to be the last one and to take the rope off and wind it up. So it happened that I was the last to stand there and watch the sinking sun turning to pink and red and casting shadows on the snow.

"Suddenly I had to spread my arms wide and shout, 'Thank you, God, for this great wonderful creation of Yours. What could I give You back for it?'

"At that moment it crossed my mind that the greatest thing I could give to Him was this very thing I was so greatly enjoying. In other words, give up mountain climbing, give up hiking, give up living out in nature, and bury myself in a convent which, to my recollection, was a dark place of medieval character.

"With the generosity of my young heart I said, 'Yes, Lord, here it is.'

"There at the abbey started two momentous years of my life.

"But as I look back on those two precious years I have to add hastily that they were by no means all hardships and trouble. I had never known a real warmth of homelife. Our noviciate was the first place where I really felt at home, secure and loved. Our Mistress of Novices (after a few months I was taken in with the others) understood beautifully how to make us love each other in word, in song, in deed. She showed that we cannot love God whom we do not see if we do not love our neighbor whom we do see—even if our neighbor had a terrible habit of clicking her rosary all the time, or if she got on your nerves by saying, 'But, but,' and looking reproachfully at you most of the time."[1]

1927. The convent sent Maria to the home of Baron Georg von Trapp, a widower with seven children. She was to tutor his daughter who had scarlet fever and had to drop out of school. "And now—to make a long story short—I fell in love! For the first time in my life. I fell in love with those wonderful children. There they were—from age four to fourteen—two boys and five girls. I don't know exactly how it happened, but in no time we were just one heart and soul."[1]

November 26, 1927. Maria married Baron Georg von Trapp. "Christ had given me, His bride, to the baron! I was furious and I had to tell Him so the very next day. I had asked my new husband to postpone our honeymoon because one of the boys, Werner, had a high fever and I wouldn't feel comfortable away from the children. I had even suggested that he go ahead on our honeymoon, which he politely declined, telling me we could go later. Around noon I stalked into our little parish church, right up front to the communion rail. I did not make a genuflection, with which we Catholics acknowledge the true presence of God in the Eucharist kept in the tabernacle.

"I stood there, stiff and blazing mad, and said, 'If any human man had done this to his bride—namely, arranged for her to marry another man while she thought he was as much in love with her as she was with him—I wouldn't think much of him. You have done just that! And You knew that I only wanted *You*. All right. You didn't want me. Now I don't want You anymore.' I turned around and stalked out.

"It happened to be the beginning of the time of Advent, the preparation for Christmas. I didn't want to go to church, so on the first Sunday I developed a terrific headache. On the second Sunday I was writhing in bed with sudden stomach cramps. And so I mysteriously fell sick every Saturday night in order to be quite well again for the beginning of the next week, when I suddenly discovered something. For a few nights in a row I noticed that the little ones, after our official night prayer was over, did not rise from their knees but covered their little faces with their hands and prayed on for a little while most fervently. Finally I learned that they were asking God to make their mother well enough so she could go to midnight mass with them.

"From that Christmas on, life was altogether different. I understood more and better my husband's love, and by and by I learned to love him more than I have ever loved before or after. For the rest of all our years together we always celebrated our wedding anniversary on Christmas Day."[1]

1928-1938. The family lived on their estate in the Tyrolean Alps. "'And they lived happily ever after,' one could almost say as the years went by.

"We had two hobbies in our family. One was to hike together and the other was to sing together. Both would prove very important one day for the Trapp family.

"The people were used to seeing us come out of our house dressed for mountain climbing with big knapsacks on our backs and mountain boots, walking around our garden fence to the little station where the local trains stopped that took us into the Alps.

"The people were also used to hearing us sing together by the hour on summer evenings. Sometimes we could sing those many beautiful Austrian folksongs nonstop for two hours without repeating.

"On our estate we had a chapel, and one day the bishop sent a new priest to say mass for us. That was the turning point in our life because Father Wasner was a musical genius. When he heard us sing he was quite enthusiastic that there would be a choir made up of our whole family. . . .

"Father Wasner acquainted us with the glory of the a cappella music of the sixteenth, seventeenth and eighteenth centuries. For the sheer joy of singing we continued sometimes for four or five hours. The word *amateur* comes from the Latin *amare*, 'to love.' We started out as true amateurs; but having such a great musician as our director, we slowly turned into professionals without knowing it. We were truly 'discovered' by the great opera singer, Lotte Lehman, who heard us behind the screen of hemlock trees in our park, and through her persuasion, finally got my husband's permission for us to give a concert during the Salzburg Festival. He shuddered at the mere thought of having his family on stage. Being an Imperial Navy officer and a member of the aristocracy, that just wasn't done. But Lotte Lehman, a great artist and a great lady, finally convinced him there was nothing undignified in it, so 'just for this one time' he allowed it. A new chapter in our lives began that very same day.

"During the festival, managers from all over the globe assembled in Salzburg. After this one performance we were offered contracts from every country outside the Iron Curtain, even from the United States. The captain bought a scrapbook and we pasted these contracts in as souvenirs. Little did we know that this very scrapbook would be our most precious possession, in fact our life line, in the black days ahead."[1]

March, 1938. "Then it happened. We were all sitting in our library listening to the voice of Chancellor Schuschnigg bidding farewell to Austria which was giving way to force. The very next thing was the German anthem and the tremendous roar of 'Heil Hitler!' It was the night of the 12th to 13th of March, 1938, a date we shall never forget. Austria was wiped off the map and incorporated into the 'Third Reich.'

"The door of the library opened and our butler came in, went over to my husband, and said, 'Captain, I have been an illegal member of the party for several years,' and he showed us his swastika.

"This was all so overpowering and so overwhelming that it left one numb.

"The very next day going into town—what a change. From every house hung a swastika flag. People on the street greeted each other with outstretched right arm, 'Heil Hitler!' and one felt absolutely like one was in a foreign country.

"At first we waited for the storm to blow over. My husband did not allow the swastika around the house or the new greeting or the new anthem to ever be heard. The pressure mounted and our lives were threatened by the Nazis."[1]

September, 1938. Abandoned their home, leaving everything except the $10 each was permitted to take out of the country. "So half a year passed, and then came the moment when my husband called the family together and said, 'Now we have to find out what is the will of God. Do we want to keep our material goods, our house, our estate, our friends—or do we want to keep our spiritual goods, our faith and honor? We cannot have both any longer.'

(From the movie "The Sound of Music" starring Julie Andrews, Twentieth Century-Fox, 1965.)

"Then he looked at his children and said, 'Listen, you can have money today and lose it tomorrow. The very same day you can start all over again, and that can happen more than once to you in your lifetime. But once you have lost your honor or your faith, then you are lost.'

"There was no real question what God wanted. As a family it was decided that we wanted to keep *Him*.

"We understood that this meant we had to get out.

"Overnight we had become really poor; we had become refugees. A refugee not only has no country, he also has no rights. He is a displaced person. At times he feels like a parcel which has been mailed and is moved from place to place.

"The first burning question for us was: 'How do we keep going?' After all, there were two parents and nine and a half children—yes, the tenth was on the way. The only thing we could do well together was sing, so we had to turn a hobby into a way of making a living.

"In the beginning we sang for just anything—a birthday party, a wedding, a devotion in church—until answers came back from the managers we had written, the men whose contracts were pasted in our scrapbook.

"Soon things began to happen. We were invited to sing in Milan which, we learned afterward, is the gateway to the music world of Italy. As this concert was most enthusiastically received, other engagements followed in Turin, Florence and finally Rome.

"Then real tragedy struck. People began to talk, pointing at us, and saying, 'This Trapp family! They are not Jewish! They didn't have to leave Austria. Just *why* did they leave?'

"To our untold horror, we noticed that people began to distrust us because they thought we might be spies for Hitler. Nobody seemed to be able to believe that one would voluntarily leave everything behind only and solely for one's conviction. And, sure enough, Italy told us to get out.

"Since we couldn't go back home, we had to go on. And so it happened all over Europe—from Italy we went to France. . . .

"No country wanted us for more than a couple of months at the most. So we went from France to Belgium, to Holland, to Denmark, to Sweden and to Norway, always singing and saving every penny for the last contract in our precious scrapbook: the USA. And we finally made it.

"In Oslo, Norway, we boarded a ship which must have been a first cousin of Noah's ark. We went down to its very belly, where we were surrounded by fellow refugees. But the main thing was, the ship was heading for New York. It took twenty-two days to get there, but finally we passed the Statue of Liberty and went ashore. My husband could barely stop me from kneeling down and kissing the ground of America, the promised land.

"In the moment of great joy in having arrived in the USA, I got us all into trouble. As I came to the immigration officer, he asked the usual question, 'How long do you intend to stay in the United States?' Instead of saying 'Three months,' as our visitor's visa read, I blurted out, 'I hope forever.' That was bad. Immediately it put us with the 'suspects' who were marched off to Ellis Island where we spent three days and three nights, full of anxiety. But after three days of being examined and interviewed, the authorities must have finally realized we were not spies because we were released.

"This was the rather dramatic beginning of the Trapp Family Singers. We have a proverb in German, 'Allen Anfang is schwer,' which means: 'Every new beginning is hard.' This was very true, for the next months were hard in America.

"Not the least of my personal problems was how I could possibly conceal that our tenth baby was on the way. Thank God, back home I had a very shrewd little seamstress. When I had told her my misgivings, she said consolingly, 'Oh, there's really nothing to it. All you have to do is make sure you are always a little fuller above than below.'

"'But Mimi,' I said helplessly, 'how in the world can I do that? I know me; I always get enormous.'

"'Let me do it for you,' Mimi said. And then she went to town and bought three different sizes of dresses and did something to them. When she handed them to me finally, she said, 'Now, listen. Every morning you step in front of a tall mirror and hold a book, and when it is flush, take the next size.'

"And this is exactly what I did—and it worked!"[1]

1939. "And so the months passed. The first concert tour was over and so was our visa, and the Trapp Family Singers were reminded to leave the country.

"There we were with a six-week-old baby in the middle of March. We had three invitations to do concerts in the Scandinavian countries and so, on the power of these contracts, we received a visa for Denmark, Sweden and Norway—for one concert each.

"We weren't even worried; we knew that this was the only thing for us to do, and God would provide. And He did! These three concerts finally turned into fifty-six performances throughout the Scandinavian countries—until September 30, 1939, when the war broke out.

"Then our American manager sent us tickets for our next crossing so that we were able to fulfill our contract with him. Thank God, during the war, America did not expel anybody.

"After the second concert tour we were able to pay back our initial debts, and lo and behold, there was a thousand dollars left! The other day I asked a banker, 'How much would a thousand dollars in 1939 be worth today?'

"He wasn't quite sure, but he thought it might be close to ten thousand dollars.

"It was a lot of money for us. Now came the question, should we walk in our national costume into Macy's or Wannamakers or Marshall Field's and come out in what we call civilian clothes? We felt so sorry to waste this hard-earned money on clothing, but at the same time we were so sick and tired of the constant traveling from hotel to hotel, with packing and unpacking, with the baby in the bus, that we decided in unison to continue wearing our Austrian outfits a little longer and buy a place of our own. So it was that we finally bought a farm in northern Vermont in the beautiful ski village of Stowe.

(From the New York stage production of "The Sound of Music," starring Mary Martin and Theodore Bikel, which opened on Broadway in 1960.)

"Then came the next hardship. The war was not over in half a year as everybody hoped and expected; it went on and on. Our two oldest sons, Rupert and Werner, were drafted. They chose the mountain ski troops."[1]

1945. Founded the Trapp Music Camp on their farm in Vermont. "The years passed. Along came the Trapp Family Music Camp where we sang our own program with hundreds and hundreds of Americans, trying to introduce music to the families of America.

"Then the war was over and both boys came home safe and sound. According to old Catholic tradition, they had made a vow: If they would come home safely from the war, they would build a chapel to 'Our Lady of Peace' on the highest point of our property. And so it happened, and the chapel is now visited every year by hundreds of our guests.

"Everything was looking up. The Trapp Family Singers had made a name for themselves from coast to coast, not only in America but also in Canada. The new house, a spacious Salzburger chalet, was finished. It has a porch on every floor and hundreds of window boxes which were full of flowers in the summer.

"The boys were back home and had begun to settle in their new lives. Rupert, the older, went on to medical school to repeat his examinations for his M.D., which he had received in Innsbruck shortly before we left Austria. Werner had started to get interested in running the farm."[1]

May 30, 1947. Husband, Baron Georg von Trapp, died. "Then the day came—on such a day one doesn't have to ask, 'What is the will of God?' All one can do, all one must do, is say, 'Thy will be done.'

"It was the day when God called our father.

"The bishop in Burlington gave permission for us to have our own 'God's Acre,' the German word for cemetery, near the house under the trees, and from there the captain is still running the ship."[1]

1948. Underwent an operation for a brain tumor. "In the year after my husband's death it was discovered that I had a brain tumor which had to be operated on; the doctor told me I had a fifty-fifty chance. I was a little bit worried. In case I didn't come back from the hospital, what were my poor children who had just lost their father to do? With both me and him missing, the concertizing would most likely not be continued. How could I provide for the future?

"Our very close friend, 'Uncle Craig,' the man to whom we turned in all troubles and who helped us solve problems and answer questions, advised us to add another wing to the house.

"'There is always snow in Stowe, you know,' he said smilingly. 'There will always be winter business here, and you can't go wrong in adding a few more beds.'

"That started the additions because, when it happened that I came back from the hospital safe and sound, the place soon proved to be still not big enough, so we added another wing. A few years later Johannes proved with pencil and paper that if we had twenty more rooms we could get out of the red in the winter, and the result was the so-called 'Lower Lodge.'"[1]

That same year Maria von Trapp became a United States citizen.

1949. Wrote her first book, *The Story of the Trapp Family Singers.* Later the book was adapted into the famous musical, ''The Sound of Music.'' ''When my first book appeared in 1949 it didn't set the world on fire. As one reviewer said later, 'The book has one mistake, the wrong title.'

"For that reason *The Story of the Trapp Family Singers* was placed in the music section of the bookstores and the libraries, and it took many years for the people to catch on that it was our life story.

"Once there came a little stir from Hollywood when one of the film companies wanted to buy the book. But they immediately said, 'We buy only the title; we make our own story to fit it.'

"This I couldn't do, so I had to give up the fame of Hollywood.

"Years passed. The book had been translated into different languages, including German. In Germany it made a much greater impact.

"The book was quite a few years old, however, when one day an agent for a German film producer arrived to say his client was interested in buying the film rights from the book.

"I am still proud of myself that I thought and even said, 'Let me ask our lawyer.'

"Therefore, I presented the contract which the German firm had left with us to our lawyer. In this contract it said that the film company wanted to buy the book for $10,000, whereupon my lawyer advised me to ask for royalties.

"The next time I was in New York I met the agent at the hotel and told him that we would like to receive $10,000 down payment and 'X' percent of royalties.

"I remember this situation as if it had happened yesterday. He looked at me long and thoughtfully and then said, 'Permit me to call Germany. This I cannot decide on my own.'

"I was still so European that I was deeply impressed that somebody would, just like drinking a glass of water, place a long-distance call across the Atlantic Ocean.

"In an incredibly short time he was back with a very sad face.

"'I am sorry, I have to inform you that there is a law in existence which forbids a German film company from paying royalties to foreigners.'

"For a moment I felt funny to be called a foreigner. Then I realized that I was now an American citizen and therefore qualified as a foreigner to a German film company.

"Unfortunately I took this information on face value instead of referring it to my lawyer to have it checked. I signed the contract.

"In the contract the payment was due within a year. A few weeks after signing the contract I was called by the agency, who said if I agreed to take off 10 percent I would have the $9,000 immediately. He didn't even give me time to ask the family or the lawyer.

"Well, we never—but really never—had any cash available. But we always had unpaid bills stacked up, so with a deep sigh I agreed. Two days later I received the check for $9,000.

"Little did I know that with this I had signed away all film rights for the book. To put it in modern English, I had been taken.''[1]

The Story of the Trapp Family Singers has been translated into nineteen foreign languages.

1950. ''Again, time was rolling on.... the Trapp Family Singers were asked to sing in several foreign countries, beginning in Mexico, going through Central America and almost every country of Latin America, and finally back to Europe on a concert tour. By that time we had become American citizens.

"When we had secretly left Austria we could tell only a very few chosen friends and relatives of our intentions, and they were all up in arms against it.

"Now twelve years later, we went back on that European concert tour which took us into Austria. There were the same cousins and friends who had lost everything, and most of them had also lost their sons for Hitler. With very few words they admitted that we had done the right thing. That was a solemn moment in our lives.

"Soon after the European concert tour, our children started to marry. Grandchildren started arriving, and we all knew that this was the beginning of the end of our singing group.

"For twenty blissful years we had traveled the world together, bringing music to people and experiencing at every concert what a great peacemaker music is.''[1]

1956. Toured Australia, New Zealand and the South Pacific. ''And after our last concert in Sydney, Australia, when we thought that our work had come to an end, we began to see a new beginning.

"In Sydney after our last concert we accepted an invitation to the home of Archbishop Carboni, who was the representative from Rome for all the mission stations in the South Pacific.... After sharing these experiences with us, he faced us and simply asked, 'When you are finished someday with your concert work, couldn't some of you come to the islands and start a lay missionary work among the people?'

"A year later we answered his invitation. The first to go were three of my children, Maria, Rose Mary and Johannes. Archbishop Carboni wanted our priest friend and conductor, Father Wasner, and myself to travel for a year throughout the many islands to find out just exactly what was going on and what could be done about it.''[1]

1957. Spent a year as a missionary in New Guinea. "I arrived in New Guinea with the largest suitcase permitted on a train or plane. Since we were stopping in Australia and had to be prepared for winter, I had brought a lot of warm clothing. And for New Guinea there were my summer things, plus various books, a little jewelry, and all kinds of everyday necessities without which we of the twentieth century think we can't exist.

"Then I made this wide trip throughout many centuries back into the stone age. Every time I was invited to a chief's house I brought presents. First my winter things. Then all kinds of little boxes in which I stored my paraphernalia. My huge suitcase got lighter and lighter and emptier and emptier. When there were only two light summer dresses and a little underwear left besides my Bible and a big red hankerchief, I decided to fold my belongings right into the handkerchief, which I knotted and fastened to a stick, while I gave my suitcase to Chief Iad in exchange for a dagger made of a human thigh bone with the joint as a handle.

"'Muchly used,' assured the chief.

"Then he added quickly, 'By my ancestors.'

"His much-beloved baby was playing around his legs when suddenly he grabbed him, put him in the suitcase, closed it, and sat on it. I had the hardest time to get him off it before the baby suffocated. Quickly I tore the lid off and took it with me, again to exchange it in the next village for a breast-plate made with stone tools out of mother of pearl.

"These last weeks, when I owned only the bare essentials, belonged to the happiest time of my life.

"And then our year of exploration had come to an end.

"Monsignor Wasner had become so entranced with the great need and the great possibilities of mission work that he accepted the invitation of the Bishop of Fiji to become a missionary in Naiserelangi. For seven years he did outstanding and very difficult work between the two ethnic groups, Fijians and Indians, before his health gave way. Soon afterward he was called to Rome and made a Papal Prelate. Now he is heading the House of Studies at the German Parish in The Eternal City.

"For twenty years he had been our musical director and our most faithful friend and helper. When my husband and I in 1938 had told our bishop in Salzburg of our intention to leave our home in order to get away from Hitler's tyranny, the bishop had advised Father Wasner right then and there to join us on this journey into the unknown.

"I can remember how the old gentleman looked thoughtfully through his window over to the cupola of the cathedral and said, 'It will prove one day to be of great importance that Father Wasner is leaving now.'

"That was a real prophecy, because without Father Wasner we never could have become the Trapp Family Singers who, after the war, collected daily, from every concert, anything that the kind-hearted Americans wanted to give for the poor people in Austria. It finally became possible for the Trapp Family Austrian Relief, Inc., to send over 275,000 pounds of goods into little war-torn Austria.

"And so the time finally came when a small party, just Father Wasner and ourselves, was sitting for the last time around the family table. It was good-bye and Godspeed before Father Wasner left for Fiji."[1]

November 16, 1959. "The Sound of Music," a play based on her book, opened on Broadway and was a tremendous success. "As the opening day came close, one day I received a huge package from Sak's Fifth Avenue. It was Mary [Martin's] personal present to me, a beautiful pale green gown with matching pale green slippers, to be worn during opening night and afterward at a party. How very typical of this very lovely person.

"Then came the opening night. What excitement! There had been enough publicity, let alone the illustrious names of Mary Martin, Rogers and Hammerstein, Lindsey and Kraus to arouse the curiosity of everybody.

". . . Mary Martin really portrayed me in all that young impetuousness. I was deeply touched, and I was the first one to jump to my feet. Then the whole house rose to a standing ovation for Mary Martin.

"Backstage we were both congratulated and photographed together and asked for autographs, and quite a bit of time had passed before we left the theater.

"The only thing I hadn't been quite happy about in the Broadway play was the portrayal of my husband, who had been made into a very strict disciplinarian, ruling his seven motherless children like a sea captain would his crew, while in fact he was the gentlest and kindest of fathers. That he called his children with a boatman's whistle was really because of practical reasons. Every one of us, myself included, had his own signal, and the shrilling of that whistle could be heard for miles; so when we were in different sections of our big estate, the whistle would always find us."[1]

1965. "The Sound of Music," Twentieth Century-Fox's film version of the broadway play, was released and became an equal success. "When I am asked (and that's many times a year), 'And how do you like the film the "Sound of Music?"' I still answer with that same old relief of that first viewing, 'I really like it very much, especially the beginning where you can see beautiful Austria photographed from a helicopter. The pictures were taken from the air around Salzburg, and I could see this view every morning at breakfast.'

"Thinking back on the opening night of the Broadway musical, I must have taken it for granted that I would be present at the first official showing of the premier of the film. When I didn't hear anything about it and no invitation arrived, I really humbled myself to go and ask the producer whether I would be allowed to come. He said he was very sorry, indeed, but there was no seat left.

"And that's the way it was, and that's the way it is. All the information I receive about the film is usually gotten from friends who send me clippings from newspapers, as I myself hardly ever read a newspaper. Somehow I feel sorry it is that way.

"One thing turned into a kind of hardship. That was when the newspapers reported the film's phenomenal financial success which finally turned into a box-office record, even leaving behind 'Gone with the Wind.' Unfortunately the people, not only in America but also in the rest of the world (the film has been shown literally all over the globe—to the last and newest African nation, to faraway South Sea Island

(From the movie "The Sound of Music" starring Julie Andrews sond Christopher Plummer, Twentieth Century-Fox, 1965.)

tribes—just everywhere), simply think that we are rolling in the millions, and this accounts for the stacks of begging letters which I receive. Requests to build this, that and the other thing. The latest was to build a cemetery. I didn't know that a person could build a cemetery.

"But, let me add quickly, that while we didn't become millionaires and all of us have always had to work hard for a living, 'Sound of Music' has brought other blessings far beyond the reach of money!"[1]

1967. Relinquished her managerial position at the Trapp Family Lodge in Stowe, Vermont. Her son, Johannes, became manager and is credited with popularizing cross-country skiing in the United States. "Then came the glorious winter when Johannes, who had already taken over the management of the Trapp Family Lodge, started a completely new program in skiing—cross-country skiing. Cross-country skiing was next to unknown. It had been tried here and there in Vermont, but never on a big scale. Johannes had the vision that the future of skiing was there, so he started with one Norwegian ski teacher, a tiny little workshop built into our garage, and about fifty pairs of rental skis and shoes in all sizes. Then on a very small scale, he advertised. And—lo and behold—the people came from all sides! At the end of the season he had five hundred people skiing on the trail he had laid out the previous fall with his Norwegian ski instructor friend, Per Soerli.

"Right after Christmas I joined the ranks."[1]

1976. *When the King Was Carpenter* was published. A grandmother for twenty-seven children and a great-grandmother, as well, Maria von Trapp values family life highly. "For more than twenty years I had been a grandmother. But I was not a 'practicing grandmother,' partly because I was really extremely busy, but partly for another reason. As my children got married I made up my mind never to be a *mother-in-law* in the proverbial sense of the word. Too long I had been accused of having been a domineering mother, so it was my iron resolution that this would not continue into the next generation. Unfortunately, with my tendency to exaggerate, I practically didn't go near the young couples in order to 'leave them alone.' I just left them alone too much. Children were born and suddenly began to go to school, and I hardly knew them. The last week in June is 'Family Week,' which now is the time for me to find out 'how much they have grown.'

"As I look back over my life I see two great obvious mistakes. First, I tried so desperately hard never to give my husband's children the impression that I was their stepmother that I hardly dared to take care of my own babies as they came along. I left them mostly to their older sisters while depriving them of a true mother's love. Years later I made the same mistake all over again with the grandchildren. Now I hope I have awakened in time."[1]

Maria von Trapp believes firmly in the "will of God" and has held tenaciously to this faith throughout her life. "There are those occasions when you don't have to go out and look for the will of God. You must remain still, in a state of silence, and say, 'Thy will be done.' When my husband and two daughters died, I had to repeat this to myself over and over again. Their deaths were terrible shocks to me. I felt numb. But with my whole being I said, 'Thy will be done.' When we say this, it is true that we are sad down to the very core of our beings, but we are also at peace with ourselves. Each one of us has many disappointments which occur in his

life. We all have our goals, ambitions, dreams and expectations, some of which happen less than we want them to or do not happen at all. But these disappointments must not be allowed to be obstacles within your inner soul when you say to God, 'Thy will be done.' In this way your peace will never be disturbed at all. This is the strong core of peace inside of you while the various storms which exist in life rage all around you." [From an article entitled, "The Problem of Maria Solved, Almost," by Frederick John Pratson, *The Saturday Evening Post*, April, 1978.[2]]

For those who have seen either the musical play or the motion picture of *The Sound of Music*, the story of Maria Trapp and her family is well-known. Mary Martin saw a German-made movie of the Trapp family and decided that it must become a Broadway musical. Howard Lindsay and Russel Crouse wrote the story based on Maria Trapp's book, and with lyrics by Oscar Hammerstein II and music by Richard Rodgers, the play opened on Broadway on November 16, 1959, and was a blockbuster success. Starring Mary Martin and Theodore Bikel, its run was 1,443 performances, winning six Antoinette Perry awards including best musical of the season. The play toured for two and a half years, playing to capacity houses everywhere. Over three million copies of the original cast album were sold.

Twentieth Century-Fox's film version was an equal success. Released in 1965, and starring Julie Andrews and Christopher Plummer, the motion picture grossed over $180,000,000 and won five Academy Awards, including best picture of the year. Its original soundtrack recording sold over eight million copies.

The sparse royalties that Maria von Trapp has received from the stage, film, and recorded versions of *The Sound of Music* have been used for Catholic missionary work, in which she is deeply involved.

HOBBIES AND OTHER INTERESTS: Swimming, hiking, horseback riding, cross-country skiing.

FOR MORE INFORMATION SEE: T. E. Murphy, "Lively Trapp Family," *Reader's Digest*, January, 1948; Maria Trapp, *The Story of the Trapp Family Singers*, Lippincott, 1949, a later edition published as *The Sound of Music: The Story of the Trapp Family Singers*, White Lion, 1976; *San Francisco Chronicle*, December 1, 1949; Matthew Hoehn, editor, *Catholic Authors*, Volume 2, St. Mary's Abbey, 1952; M. Trapp and Ruth T. Murdoch, *Family on Wheels: Further Adventures of the Trapp Family Singers*, Lippincott, 1959; R. Harrity, "Musical Family Musical," *Cosmopolitan*, December, 1959; J. S. Wilson, "The Trapps—After The Sound of Music," *New York Times Magazine*, December 13, 1959; *Current Biography*, H. W. Wilson, 1969; M. Trapp, *Maria*, Creation House, 1972; M. Trapp, "The Sound of Music," *TV Guide*, February 28, 1976.

VO-DINH, Mai 1933-

PERSONAL: Born November 14, 1933, in Hue, Vietnam; came to United States, 1960; naturalized U.S. citizen, 1976; son of Thang (a civil servant) and Do-Thi (Hanh) Vo-Dinh; married Helen Coutant Webb (a teacher), August 17, 1964; children: Katherine, Hannah. *Education:* Attended University of Lyon, Academie de la Grande Chaumiere, and Ecole Nationale Superieure des Beaux-Arts, Paris, 1959. *Home:* Stonevale, RFD #1, Burkittsville, Md. 21718.

"Then I am right!" Liên exclaimed, sitting up, sure now that her grandmother's dying had something to do with the first snowfall. ▪ (From *First Snow* by Helen Coutant. Illustrated by Mai Vo-Dinh.)

CAREER: Artist and author. Artist-in-Residence, Synechia Arts Center, 1974. *Member:* International Association of Artists, Artists Equity Association of New York. *Awards, honors:* Christopher Foundation Award, 1975.

WRITINGS: (And illustrator) *The Toad Is the Emperor's Uncle,* Doubleday, 1970; (and illustrator) *The Jade Song,* Chelsea House, 1970; (lecture) *Views of a Vietnamese Artist,* Southern Illinois University Press, 1972.

Portfolios: *Unicorn Broadsheet #4,* Unicorn Press, 1969; *Let's Stand Beside Each Other,* Fellowship Publications, 1969; *Recent Works by Vo-Dinh,* Suzuki Graphics, 1972; *The Woodcuts of Vo-Dinh,* Hoa-Binh Press, 1974.

Illustrator: Basho Issa, *Birds, Frogs, and Moonlight* (collection of Japanese poetry), translation by Sylvia Cassedy and Kunihiro Suetake, Doubleday, 1967; Nhat Hanh, *The Cry of Vietnam,* Unicorn Press, 1968; (and translator) Doan-Quoc-Sy, *The Stranded Fish,* Sang-Tao Press, 1971; (and translator) Nhat Hanh, *The Path of Return Continues the Journey,* Hoa-Binh Press, 1972; James Kirkup, *The Magic Drum,* Knopf, 1973; Helen Coutant, *First Snow,* Knopf, 1974; Nhat Hanh and Daniel Berrigan, *The Raft Is Not the Shore,* Beacon Press, 1975; (poetry) Nhat Hanh, *ZEN Poems,* Unicorn Press, 1976; Nhat Hanh, *The Miracle of Mindfulness,* Beacon Press, 1976; Ross Roy, *One Thousand Pails of Water,* Knopf, 1978.

WORK IN PROGRESS: Translator of a collection of short stories by leading contemporary Vietnamese writers; author of a collection of short stories in English.

SIDELIGHTS: "I am primarily a painter, and secondly, a printmaker (woodcut). However, I always accept an illustration assignment from publishers with delight if the book in question interests me. I believe that good illustrations can enrich the mind of a reader, young or old, if they go beyond the routine and the conventional. I especially love to illustrate with ink, or with pencil in combination with elements of my own woodblock prints.

"I was back in Vietnam during the war, in 1974—for Americans the war had ended, but it was still going on for Vietnamese. If anything, it was more murderous than ever.

"Naturally, the war affected me, an artist, profoundly as it did, in other ways, all Vietnamese. An entire generation grew up, lived, and died with it. Yet, my work cannot, except for occasional flarings of outrage and sorrow, be called violent or pessimistic. If anything, the war between Vietnamese and between Vietnamese and Americans has reinforced my faith in the miracle of life. It is a faith beyond hope or despair.

"I had many teachers at school, but those who have influenced me most were: Old Chinese masters, Picasso, Matisse, and before these two painters, Van Gogh and Rembrandt. Also the sculpture of Egypt. . . .

"What artists do I admire most? Surprisingly enough, the paintings that I, born and bred in Vietnam, am most fond of are by two Britishers, Francis Bacon, because of his searing portraits of modern man/woman, and Graham Sutherland, because he offers a way out for them. I also like Georgia O'Keefe, an American, a great American lady, very much.

MAI VO-DINH

"My opinion of modern art? I hope it counts! Modern art is but a reflection of modern life. Do you know the story from that Buddish text: A man gallops by on his horse. Someone shouts at him, 'Where are you going?' The man hollers back, 'Don't know! Ask the horse!'"

HOBBIES AND OTHER INTERESTS: Sports, growing vegetables, cooking.

WALDRON, Ann Wood 1924-

PERSONAL: Born December 14, 1924, in Birmingham, Ala.; daughter of Earl Watson (a bookkeeper) and Elizabeth (Roberts) Wood; married Martin O. Waldron, Jr. (a newspaper reporter), October 18, 1947; children: Peter, Laura, Thomas William, Martin III. *Education:* University of Alabama, A.B., 1945. *Politics:* Democrat. *Religion:* Presbyterian. *Home:* 409 South Main St., Hightstown, N.J. 08520.

CAREER: Free-lance writer. Atlanta *Constitution,* Atlanta, Ga., reporter, 1945-47; Tampa *Tribune,* Tampa, Fla., reporter, 1957-60; St. Petersburg *Times,* St. Petersburg, Fla., reporter, 1960-65; Houston *Chronicle,* Houston, Tex., book editor, 1970-75. *Member:* Theta Sigma Phi, Alpha Delta Pi.

WRITINGS: (With Allen Morris) *Your Florida Government* (adult), University of Florida Press, 1965; *The House on Pendleton Block* (juvenile), Hastings, 1975; *The Integration of Mary-Larkin Thornhill* (juvenile), Dutton, 1975; *The Luckie Star* (juvenile), Dutton, 1977; *Scaredy Cat* (juvenile), Dutton, 1978.

Here was an attic that surpassed all the attics in books. ■ (From *The House on Pendleton Block* by Ann Waldron. Illustrated by Sonia O. Lisker.)

SIDELIGHTS: "I have been a writer all my adult life. I have written for magazines and newspapers and now I write books. I like to write books for children best of all. I even like to read children's books.

"All my own books have grown out of my own family's experiences. *The House on Pendleton Block* is about a little girl whose family moves from Georgia to Texas and rents a mansion on an old street in a big city. Our family moved from north Florida to Houston, and some of the incidents in the book are based on things that happened to us.

"*The Integration of Mary-Larkin Thornhill* is about a white girl who attended a black junior high school. Our two younger boys both attended a black junior high in Houston. (The school in the book is not nearly as interesting as the school in real life.) *Luckie Star* is about a little girl who wanted to be a scientist and the summer she spent with her

family at the beach in north Florida. Our youngest son wants to be a scientist and, like the Luckie family, we often don't understand what he's talking about. Some of our best vacations have been spent at the beach in North Florida and I wanted to write a book about that wonderful sun-drenched area. And *Scaredy Cat* is about a little girl in Birmingham during the Depression—and I was a little girl in Birmingham during the Depression.

"My children have been of inestimable help to me in my writing children's books. Lolly helped me immensely with Chrissie in *The House on Pendleton Block*. She would say things like, 'Cut that—it's phony,' and I would realize that she was right. Both the younger boys helped me with *Mary-Larkin*. Martin, our youngest, was invaluable with *Luckie Star*—he had to tell me all the scientific bits."

FOR MORE INFORMATION SEE: Horn Book, April, 1976.

ANN WOOD WALDRON

WHEATLEY, Arabelle   1921-

PERSONAL: Born March 28, 1921, in Washington, Pa.; daughter of Samuel Larimer (a glass worker) and Nellie Bly (Headley) Wheatley; married Robert Lomas Buckbee (a credit manager), February 21, 1956. *Education:* Attended Washington Seminary, Washington, Pa., two years; Art Institute of Pittsburgh, two years. *Home:* (Summer) P.O. Box 66, Wind Ridge, Pa. 15380; (Winter) 27 Iowa Avenue, Arcadia, Fla. 33821.

CAREER: Illustrator. Venereal Disease Education Institute, Raleigh, N.C., illustrator, 1943-44; Contempo Studio, New York, N.Y., illustrator, 1944-47; free-lance illustrator, 1947—.

ILLUSTRATOR: Millicent Selsam, *Questions and Answers About Ants,* Four Winds, 1967; (co-illustrator with author) Ilka List, *Questions and Answers About Seashore Life,* Four Winds, 1970; Bernice Kohn, *The Beachcomber's Book,* Viking, 1970; Helen Hoke, *Ants: A First Book,* Watts, 1970; Ennis Rees (editor), *Riddles, Riddles Everywhere,* Scholastic, 1972; Elizabeth Shepherd, *Tracks Between the Tides,* Lothrop, 1972; Cathleen Fitzgerald, *Let's Find Out About Bees,* Watts, 1973; Sigmund Kalina, *Your Nerves and Their Messages,* Lothrop, 1973; Sigmund Kalina, *Your Blood and Its Cargo,* Lothrop, 1974; David Webster, *Let's Find Out About Mosquitoes,* Watts, 1974; Seymour Simon, *Life in the Dark,* Watts, 1974; Wilda Ross, *Cracks and Crannies, What Lives There,* Coward, 1975; Lili Ronai, *Let's Read and Find Out About Corals,* Crowell, 1976; Dorothy Hogner, *Endangered Plants,* Crowell, 1977; Seymour Simon, *Exploring Fields and Lots,* Garrard, 1978; Joan Lexau, *A Spider Makes a Web,* Scholastic Magazine, 1979. Contributing illustrator to *The Life of Sea Islands* (McGraw). Illustrations have appeared in *Encyclopedia International, The New Book of Knowledge* and *Americana Encyclopedia,* all published by Grolier.

SIDELIGHTS: "Have loved drawing since childhood. Had no money to continue college so borrowed a small amount to attend a commercial art school in Pittsburgh, thirty miles away, and I commuted by train. My motivation was to learn to earn a living doing something I liked.

"I developed a particular interest in line drawing or line plus color. Depending on the subject, I like to use pen and ink for fine detailed things, a dragged brush line for bolder effect. I prefer some degree of stylization to utter realism, for which I think the camera does a better job.

"I liked to work up drawings for things the camera can't provide—ecological relationships (for example, who eats whom in a pond), anatomical information, etc. I enjoy work which calls for a humorous approach.

"I lived in New York City's Greenwich Village until 1967, working on advertising—1967 to the present—book and magazine illustration in natural science subjects which I find much more satisfying than advertising, if much less remunerative. Enjoy very much doing the research necessary.

"Became particularly interested in nature subjects while doing all the animal and plant drawings for the *Encyclopedia International* (high school level) which took nearly two years in the early 60's. I continued with many illustrations for *The New Book of Knowledge* and *Americana Encyclopedia.*

"Living in the middle of New York was not such a bad place as one might think for learning about animals and plants. The American Museum of Natural History field trips started us on botany (my husband became as interested as I). New

ARABELLE WHEATLEY

No matter where you are, you can be sure a small plant or animal has a home. How many of these homes can you find in the cracks and crannies around you? ■ (From *Cracks and Crannies—What Lives There* by Wilda Ross. Illustrated by Arabelle Wheatley.)

York Entomological Society membership stimulated our special interest in insects.

"It became (and still is) our main entertainment to wander natural areas looking and photographing and trying to understand what lives there. We bought an old farm of 109 acres in the western Pennsylvania hills and since moving from the New York area, have spent our summers renovating the old house—marvelous place to work—marvelous place to watch allegheny mound ants, wildflowers, the natural plant succession which has been undisturbed for the last thirty years.

"Winters are spent in Florida prairie country. It provides opportunity to botanize all year, and inspect the mountains, swamps and other wonders in between."

HOBBIES AND OTHER INTERESTS: Baroque and earlier music, gardening, cooking, collecting fossils.

WHITE, William, Jr. 1934-
(Spinossimus)

PERSONAL: Born June 8, 1934, in Philadelphia, Pa.; adopted son of William (an accountant and auditor) and Ruth (McCaughan) White; married Sara Jane Shute (a nurse), September 8, 1956; children: Rebecca, Sara, William III,

James M., Elizabeth, Margaret. *Education:* Haverford College, B.S., 1956; Westminster Theological Seminary, M.Div., 1961, Th.M., 1963; Dropsie University for Hebrew and Cognate Learning, Ph.D., 1968. *Politics:* Christian-Social democrat (pacifist). *Religion:* Presbyterian (Reformed). *Home:* 2272 Patty Lane, Warrington, Pa. *Office:* Box 638, Warrington, Pa. 18976.

CAREER: Employed during his early career as mailman, hospital orderly, gas pumper, and mill hand; pastor of Reformed Church; U.S. Civil Service in Glenside, Pa., 1956-63; Temple University, Philadelphia, Pa., instructor in ancient history, 1964-68; Ellen Cushing College, Bryn Mawr, Pa., assistant professor of biology and physics, 1966-68; East Carolina University, Greenville, N.C., assistant professor of history, 1968-70; Philadelphia College of Textiles and Science, Philadelphia, Pa., professor of history, 1970-71; North American Publishing Co., Philadelphia, Pa., editorial director, 1971-72; consultant to Auerbach Corporation, Data Communications, senior medical writer, Emergency Care Research Institute, 1972-74; Gellman Associates, editor, 1975; free-lance writer, editor, translator, 1973—; Franklin Institute Press, Franklin Institute Research Laboratory, Philadelphia, Pa., publisher, 1976—.

MEMBER: American Association for the Advancement of Science, American Historical Association, Mensa, Intertel, Tyndale House (Oxford, England). *Awards, honors:* National Endowment for the Humanities grant for study in Israel, 1968; fellow of International Committee for Chemical Research (Japan), 1969-70.

WRITINGS—Adult: (Translator) *A Babylonian Anthology,* Morris Press, 1966; (contributor) Stephen Benko and John J. O'Rourke, *The Catacombs and the Colosseum,* Judson, 1970; (editor, contributor) *Reference Encyclopedia of Women's Liberation,* North American Publishing, 1972; (editor, contributor) *Reference Encyclopedia of Drugs and Drug Abuse,* North American Publishing, 1972; (editor, contributor) *Reference Encyclopedia of Ecology and Pollution,* North American Publishing, 1972; (contributor) *The Law and the Prophets,* Presbyterian and Reformed Publishing Co., 1973; (contributor) *The New Zondervan Pictorial Bible Encyclopedia* (5 volumes), Zondervan, 1975; (co-author with D. Estrada) *The First New Testament,* Nelson, 1978; *Cornelius Van Til* (biography), Nelson, 1979; (contributor) *The Moody Old Testament Word Book,* Moody Press, 1979; (contributor) *The Tyndale Family Bible Encyclopedia,* Tyndale Publishing Co., 1980; *A History of Western Thought.*

Juveniles—All self-illustrated; all published by Sterling: *A Frog is Born,* 1972, *A Turtle is Born,* 1973, *The Guppy: Its Life Cycle,* 1974, *The Siamese Fighting Fish: Its Life Cycle,* 1975, *An Earthworm is Born,* 1975, *The Edge of the Pond,* 1976, *Forest and Garden,* 1976, (with Sara Jane White) *The Terrarium in Your Home,* 1976, *The American Chameleon,* 1977, *The Cycle of the Seasons,* 1977, *The Edge of the Ocean,* 1977, *The Mosquito: Its Life Cycle,* 1978, *The Housefly: Its Life Cycle,* 1978, *The Spider: Its Life Cycle,* 1978, *A Snail is Born,* 1979. Writer for radio and television. Contributor of more than one thousand articles to periodicals, including *Vanguard of Canada, Christian Scholar's Review,*

WILLIAM WHITE, JR.

Westminster Theological Journal, Industrial Photography, Industrial Research, Microskopion. Contributor of fifty articles for the *Zondervan Dictionary of Biblical Archaeology,* 1979.

WORK IN PROGRESS: Secret in Clay, 1980; *Das Narrenschiff,* a twentieth-century version of Sebastian Brandt's poem; *The Astronatus: Its Life Cycle; The Swordtail: Its Life Cycle; The Neon Tetra: Its Life Cycle; The Soil Animals; Brightleaf,* a novel.

SIDELIGHTS: "As a boy I kept many pets and made notes on what I discovered about them. During summer vacations I read all of the biology and natural history books that I could find. I learned Latin and Greek before my sixteenth birthday so that I could pursue my two main interests: zoology with its scientific names in those two ancient languages and Bible. I received a great deal of help and encouragement in my interest in cold-blooded vertebrates from Dr. William T. Innes, the author of many books on fishes, and Dr. Henry W. Fowler of the Academy of Natural Sciences in Philadelphia. Although both men were in their eighties, they gave me many valuable hours of advice and experience.

"All of my books are family affairs. My wife and each of my six children have helped with the field and laboratory work needed for such details about the life cycles and behavior of organisms. We have spent whole days sifting mud, scouring creek beds and crawling on hands and knees in ponds to find and photograph microscopic life.

"My usual practice is to keep and observe the organism in or out of my home for several years before writing a book about the creature. This has resulted in our home having several large lizards, a few snakes, dozens of turtles and thousands of spiders all running loose in and about. Careful notes and accurate measurements are kept and all the material along with the photographs are sorted and filed to make up the data for a book.

"Each book requires special cages, aquaria or terraria to be constructed and special lighting and photographic equipment to be designed and built, I and my two sons have become very adept mechanics and amateur biological engineers doing this work. Wherever possible, I use the latest type of surgical optical equipment. I seek to provide for the juvenile reader the most up to date information in biology, physiology and ethology, written in a style that will delight the reader with the wonders of creation and the vast beauty of the living world.

"I enjoy letters about my books from school children and learn a great deal about organisms and better methods of writing about them from my readers."

HOBBIES AND OTHER INTERESTS: Literature, particularly Japanese and Russian; microbiology of the cold-blooded vertebrates.

WILDSMITH, Brian 1930-

PERSONAL: Born January 22, 1930, in Penistone, Yorkshire, England; son of Paul and Annie Elizabeth (Oxley) Wildsmith; married Aurelie Janet Craigie Ithurbide, 1955; children: Claire, Rebecca, Anne, Simon. *Education:* Attended Barnsley School of Art and the Slade School of Fine Art, University College, London, 1949-52. *Home:* 11 Castellaras, 06370 Mouans-Sartoux, France.

CAREER: Selhurst Grammar School for Boys, art teacher, 1954-57; freelance artist and illustrator of books for children, 1957—. *Military service:* Served in the National Service, 1952-54. *Awards, honors:* Kate Greenaway medal, 1962, for *Brian Wildsmith's ABC,* runner-up in 1964 and 1967; *Brian Wildsmith's ABC* received the Brooklyn Art Books for Children Citation, 1973; *Brian Wildsmith's Birds* was listed among the *New York Times* Choice of Best Illustrated Children's Books of the Year in 1967.

WRITINGS—All illustrated by the author: *A Brian Wildsmith Portfolio,* Watts, 1962-66; *Brian Wildsmith's ABC* (ALA Notable Book), Oxford University Press, 1962, Watts, 1963; *Brian Wildsmith's Mother Goose,* Watts, 1964; *Brian Wildsmith's 1, 2, 3's,* Watts, 1965; *Brian Wildsmith's Wild Animals,* Watts, 1967; *Brian Wildsmith's Birds* (ALA Notable Book), Watts, 1967; *Brian Wildsmith's Fishes* (ALA Notable Book), Watts, 1968; *Brian Wildsmith's Circus,* Watts, 1970; *Brian Wildsmith's Puzzles,* Oxford University Press, 1970, Watts, 1971; *The Owl and the Woodpecker,* Oxford University Press, 1971, Watts, 1972; *The Twelve Days of Christmas,* Watts, 1972; *The Little Wood Duck,* Oxford University Press, 1972, Watts, 1973; *The Lazy Bear,* Oxford University Press, 1973, Watts, 1974; *Brian Wildsmith's Squirrels,* Oxford University Press, 1974, Watts, 1975; *Python's Party,* Oxford University Press, 1974, Watts, 1975; *Maurice Maeterlinck's Blue Bird,* Watts, 1976; *The True Cross,* Watts, 1978.

Illustrator: Eileen O'Faolain, *High Sang the Sword,* Oxford University Press, 1959; Rene Guillot, *Prince of the Jungle,* S. G. Phillips, 1959, reissued, Oxford University Press, 1968; Frederick Grice, *The Bonny Pit Laddy,* Oxford University Press, 1960, published in America as *Out of the Mines,* Watts, 1961; Nan Chauncy, *The Secret Friends,* Oxford University Press, 1960, Watts, 1962; Eleanor Graham, *The Story of Jesus,* Hodder, Stoughton, 1960; N. Chauncy, *Tangara,* Oxford University Press, 1960; Madeleine Polland, *The Town across the Water,* Constable, 1961; Veronique Day, *Landslide!,* Bodley Head, 1961; Arabian Nights, *Tales from the Arabian Nights,* Oxford University Press, 1961, Watts, 1962; Roger L. Green, *Myths of the Norsemen,* Bodley Head, 1962.

Jean de La Fontaine, *The Lion and the Rat: A Fable,* Watts, 1963; Geoffrey Trease, *Follow My Black Plume,* Macmillan, 1963; Edward Blishen, editor, *Oxford Book of Poetry for Children,* Watts, 1963; Charlotte Morrow, *The Watchers,* Hutchinson, 1963; G. Trease, *A Thousand for Sicily,* Macmillan, 1964; Mother Goose, *Nursery Rhymes,* Oxford University Press, 1964; J. de La Fontaine, *The North Wind and the Sun* (ALA Notable Book), Watts, 1964; Kevin Crossley-Holland, *Havelok the Dane,* Macmillan, 1964, Dutton, 1965; J. de La Fontaine, *The Rich Man and the Shoemaker,* Watts, 1965; Charles Dickens, *Barnaby Rudge,* Ginn, 1966; Robert L. Stevenson, *A Child's Garden of Verses,* Watts, 1966; J. de La Fontaine, *The Hare and the Tortoise,* Watts, 1967; Philip Turner, *Brian Wildsmith's Illustrated Bible Stories,* Watts, 1968; J. de La Fontaine, *The Miller, the Boy, and the Donkey,* Watts, 1969.

ADAPTATION—Filmstrips, all produced by Weston Woods: "Brian Wildsmith's Wild Animals," "Brian Wildsmith's Fishes," "Brian Wildsmith's Circus," "Brian Wildsmith's Birds," and "Puzzles."

SIDELIGHTS: **January 22, 1930.** Born and raised in Penistone, a small mining village near Sheffield, Yorkshire, England. "I grew up in a Yorkshire mill town where everything was a perpetual gray and black with smuts dropping out of the sky." [From an article entitled, "You Plant a Way of Looking . . . ," by Pamela Marsh, *Christian Science Monitor,* November 6, 1969.[1]]

Wildsmith recalled that his native village, Penistone was ". . . a strict mining village environ in Yorkshire, England, totally without culture. I was the oldest of four children and had a free life with very few restrictions from my parents. I was not at all interested in art; I never even saw any. I was very interested in sports and music, being a passionate piano player and cricketer—cricket is one of the most popular sports in England and one that remains a mystery to all but Englishmen! I had decided to become a research chemist, but at the last moment some strange intuition guided me away from it. Thank God!" [Lee Bennett Hopkins, *Books Are By People,* Citation Press, 1969.[2]]

1940. At the age of ten, Wildsmith received a scholarship to attend a school in Sheffield where chemistry was his main interest. "I never questioned the fact that I was going to be a chemist. One day I was on my way to a science lesson, and I can remember standing in the corridor and thinking, 'I want to create.'

"I told the headmaster, 'I am leaving,' and I left the next day."[1]

A new world opened and he soon transferred to Barnsley Art School. There he received a scholarship to the Slade School of Fine Arts.

1949-1952. Studied art at the Slade School, University College, London, England. "Sheer ignorance carried me through. If I had known the pitfalls I wouldn't have had the nerve."[1]

Wildsmith, nevertheless, received a fine training as a painter from the school. "I developed a love, a great love of all kinds and all periods of art. I feel that I received a firm structural base on what art is rather than just how to deal it."[2]

1952-1954. Served two years in the military school. "Then came the Army. I taught maths at a military school of music. That year they had the greatest number of maths failures in the history of the British Army!"[1]

If he failed as a math teacher, Wildsmith, however, felt a close relationship to math and the sciences as an artist. "As a matter of fact, I am quite good at maths. After all, painting is one of the most exacting things you can undertake. It is very like mathematics in its use of symbols. But in painting you are creating the images.

"There is a close communication between artists and philosophers and research scientists, seeking different truths expressed in different ways. There are artists who could have been any of these things. But I am not sure whether a mathematician could be an artist because somehow in the artistic process a little miracle happens, and how it is done nobody knows—not even while the job is being done. Somehow a painting must express the soul of a thing—whatever it is that makes the thing what it is."[1]

1954-1957. Worked as an art teacher at the Selhurst Grammar School (equivalent to a United States high school) for Boys.

BRIAN WILDSMITH

1955. Married Aurelie Janet Craigie Ithurbide. After the couple had four children, Wildsmith became interested in illustrating books for children. "I realized just what an appalling gulf there was between what I knew to be good and fine in painting and illustrating and the awful damage being done to children's minds via children's books. I decided to commit myself fully to doing books for boys and girls. I believe in the Jesuit saying, 'Give me a child under seven years and he is mine forever.' How often have we left all that is good and free in our culture to be brought before the child too late, when his taste had already been formed, maltreated, or warped. By attracting a child to stories in pictures, consciously or subconsciously the shapes and colors seep into his artistic digestive system, and he is aroused and stimulated by them.

"I often try out material on my children, and I observe their every reaction intently. Children are fascinated with color and form, and there is no missing a child's spontaneous outburst. I adore children's writings, paintings, and often wish I could do as well."[2]

"I have four children. I have three girls and a little boy. The oldest girl is called Clare, then Rebecca, and then Anna, who is very cheeky. Then my son is Simon, and he is cheekier still. . . . They all like looking at books, and they all help me with my picture books. What happens is, I'm working in my little house in the garden . . . and they come running home from school, open the door, and they say, 'Let's have a look at it, Daddy.' So, they come in and they look at the painting I've done. I say, 'Well, do you like it?' They might say, 'Well, it's all right.' Then I know it isn't because they are not really excited about it. Then I think, 'Oh, you children, you just don't know.' So, I just pin it up on my board, and I look at it for about three days, and I think, 'Well, perhaps they're right, you know. It's not really very good.' So then I start again. They come again, and this time if they get excited and say 'Oh, I do like that,' then I know it's all right. Then I can go on to the next picture. This is how I can judge, you see, if they are right for young children. . . ." [Cornelia Jones and Olivia R. Way, *British Children's Authors,* American Library Association, 1976.[3]]

1957. Began his career as an illustrator for children's books. It was Mabel George, former children's book editor at Oxford University Press, who first recognized his ability and gave Wildsmith his start in illustrating books for children. "Books have always fascinated me, but the book publishing field seemed like a very closed shop, and I wondered how I might get a start making pictures for books. Then I read somewhere that in England 29,000 titles, on an average, are published every year. Well, it seemed that the thing to do was to design book wrappers. I reasoned out that the cost of making books must be quite expensive. The prices of illustrations and printing them would be so expensive that the publisher would be unwilling to stake this amount of money on someone without experience, such as I. I reasoned that book wrappers would be the thing because it's one picture rather than thirty or forty pictures for a book. This worked and in the end, after three years, I gave up teaching because I could make a living out of book wrappers—not a very good living, but enough. I did a reasonable amount of work for Oxford University Press. I had shown them my paintings earlier. In later years they did tell me that what they were waiting for was the right time to launch out in color books."[3]

1960. "[Oxford University Press] . . . asked me to make fourteen color plates for *The Arabian Nights.* The pictures received severe negative criticism from the *Times Literary Supplement* in London, and I felt sure that Oxford University Press, publishers of the book, would no longer be interested in my work."[3] One review began, "But the descent is steep to Brian Wildsmith's attack on the Arabian Nights. The seemingly aimless scribbles are splashed lavishly and untidily with bright smudges of paint." [From an article entitled "A Young British Illustrator Interviews Himself," by Brian Wildsmith, *Library Journal,* November 15, 1965.[4]]

"'Well,' I thought, 'that's the end of you, Wildsmith.' But I hadn't reckoned on Oxford. I think most publishers would have said 'Go away,' but Oxford really are publishers. They make a decision and they stick to it, and they back their decisions. I will be eternally grateful to them for it. They showed courage as well, and we've had a wonderful relationship. In a sense we trust each other. They trust my judgment and I trust theirs. So we're very happy partners.

"After that they asked me for my ideas on ABC's. That really was the start. The *ABC* seemed to break the barrier, and from then on we've never looked back."[3]

1962. Received the Kate Greenaway Medal for the outstanding picture book of the year, *Brian Wildsmith's ABC.* This book was the turning point in his career and was considered innovative for children's literature. Wildsmith relied strongly on visual ideas in his books. "What we try to produce is a book which a child who cannot read can enjoy—he won't need a parent or a teacher to help him—a book which can be enjoyed in many different ways on many different levels. The idea of a book without words is new. When the *ABC* was sent to America, the customs taxed it as a toy because it had no text. But of course it was communicating ideas.

"These books have been very successful with backward readers and subnormal children."[1]

1963. The Jean de La Fontaine fable, *The Lion and the Rat: A Fable,* illustrated by Wildsmith, was published. Wildsmith explained how and why he illustrated the La Fontaine fables. "The trouble about printing these lovely full-color picture books is the enormous cost involved. You need a fantastic amount of capital. There is a kind of saturation point, particularly in England, for the sale of some of these color books. Ideally you need international publishing among American and a few European countries.

"Then you get the question of idea. What is right for one country may not be right for another country. So you need an international idea. We hit upon this idea of the La Fontaine fables which had never been illustrated in the form of a picture book before. They are timeless stories, with a beginning, middle, and end within a very few lines. They are wonderful ideas, compactly expressed. They fitted our need beautifully.

"Then it was up to me. I spent a long time looking through La Fontaine, and I thought, 'My goodness, there is nothing here,' because some are a bit ribald, you know, and they are mostly political. I think in the end, from several hundred, I sorted out five or six that could be made into picture books for children."[3]

1964. *Brian Wildsmith's Mother Goose* was published. "Some kinds of books are more difficult to illustrate than others. Mother Goose presented a few problems—one in particular, for example:

"Oh, where, oh, where has my little dog gone?
Oh, where, oh, where, can he be?
With his ears cut short and his tail cut long,
Oh, where, oh, where can he be?

"I had to solve that problem. I had to solve the rhyme before I could make a picture of it. If you look in [my] Mother Goose, you'll see how it's been solved. There is that sort of problem with poetry sometimes, too.

"I've always had the opinion that illustrating books should be rather like playing the piano. You don't interpret Bach in the same way you play Chopin. To each you give a different interpretation, and each book should have its own appearance which is different from any other book. The difficulty is to make the two things, the book and the picture, absolutely one. To make them so right that there is no other way it can be done."[3]

1965. *Brian Wildsmith's 1-2-3's,* one of his favorites, was published. "I like it because it's a complete book for me. It is beautifully printed, and despite most of the pundits' outcries, it has more than justified itself commercially. In *1-2-3's* I have taken the basic abstract forms—the rectangle, the triangle, and the circle—and related them to numbers. The book progresses through these basic shapes; it builds up into recognizable forms to give the child an understanding of the beauty and fascination of figures and also makes him aware that the world around us is, broadly speaking, built up around basic shapes."[2]

Late 1960's. Bought a home in Dulwich, London complete with a garden studio for Wildsmith. His favorite possession was his Blüthner grand piano. "I saved up my money for twelve years to buy the piano! I love having people come to

Nine drummers drumming... ■ (From *The Twelve Days of Christmas*, adapted and illustrated by Brian Wildsmith.)

(From *Brian Wildsmith's ABC*. Illustrated by the author.)

my house, and I love to travel. If I didn't have a family, I would walk around the world. I love to play cricket and squash, a game that combines elements of tennis and handball.''[2]

Wildsmith has traveled extensively. His family often summered in Gerona, Spain where Wildsmith did a great deal of his illustrations. ''Most people think of England as a rather misty, mysterious sort of place, the colors not very bright; but really it's a very colorful place. We get the fog and the rain, but when that clears and the sun comes through, the color of the countryside is absolutely intense. Whereas, if you go abroad into the hot countries where the colors are supposed to be absolutely vibrant, it's so hot that you can't see the colors. There is sort of a heat mist and everything becomes faint; the colors fade out. But in England, the half-light brings out the intense color. I think they are very English—my books.''[3]

1975. Commissioned to design the sets and costumes for the musical film, ''The Blue Bird.'' Wildsmith has illustrated well over thirty children's books and is considered one of Britain's most famous contemporary illustrators. He is probably best known for his vibrant colors. ''Brilliant colors do appeal to me, and I think they definitely appeal to children. I don't think they are necessarily more beautiful than the subdued colors. I think a professional artist should be able to

work in whatever scale he feels is right for what he is doing. It is like a composer. He has to be able to pick the right key for what it is he is expressing. He's got to be able to work in the whole range and scale. Although I do think that the brilliant range in the color scale does have an attraction for children, I can work equally as well as in the lower scale, but somehow, my subject seems to demand the brighter scale. A lot of picture book artists are throwing a lot of bright color together, expecting this to look beautiful. This does not necessarily happen. For example, you can have a red and a green, and they can be absolutely revolting because they act against each other, the two colors. Yet you can do it again in such a way that the amount of red and the amount of green somehow become absolutely glorious together, and they sing, one against the other. This is one of the dangers of color work.

''There are some very fine artists working in picture books today, but very few very lovely picture books are being made. There is a demand for beautiful picture books, because many believe that only the very finest should be offered to young children. It's no good waiting until they are twelve before they are given a little culture. They should be brought up with it, so they can distinguish between the quality books and the mediocre, pseudo-quality books. Unfortunately, we are getting too many mediocre pseudo-quality books; they clog the market. They're coming out in thousands. The people in authority can't wade through all those books. They must rely on the reviewers. The reviews in England are in most cases very, very poor because the people who review, in my opinion, just don't know. Consequently, I think perhaps some of the worthwhile books get left behind.

"There are two kinds of illustration. There is the factual, diagrammatic type of illustration which is fine in its own right. It does its own particular job. Then there is the creative illustration. In the past few years certain artists have begun to really create for children, and their creative illustrations have caused a minor revolution in books for children."[3]

Wildsmith believes in an uncompromising excellence in children's books. "This business of what we give to children is very, very important. Our books must build within them a sense of quality—an ability to distinguish between the good and the indifferent. For children are as intelligent as we are, but they lack the experience."[1]

"Even if children don't react immediately to my books, somehow, I hope that I may sow a cultural germ in their artistic digestive systems which will one day flower and bear fruit."[3]

Brian Wildsmith's kaleidoscopic-like drawings have delighted children for nearly two decades. Wildsmith, who works mostly in full color, has thought of the relationship of the illustration and the printed text to be similar to a marriage—they complement one another, but can also exist separately.

FOR MORE INFORMATION SEE: M. Crouch, "Kate Greenaway Medal," *Library Association Record,* May, 1963; *Horn Book,* June, 1963, April, 1965, April and October, 1967, February, 1971, February and December, 1972, June, 1973, December, 1974, October, 1975, April, 1976; *New York Herald Tribune Books,* May 12, 1963; *Library Journal,* November 15, 1965; Brian Doyle, editor, *Who's Who of Children's Literature,* Schocken Books, 1968; Lee Kingman and others, compilers, *Illustrators of Children's Books, 1957-1966,* Horn Book, 1968; *Christian Science Monitor,* November 6, 1969; Lee Bennett Hopkins, *Books Are By People,* Citation Press, 1969; Diana Klemin, *The Illustrated Book,* Clarkson Potter, 1970; Doris de Montreville and Donna Hill, editors, *Third Book of Junior Authors,* H. W. Wilson, 1972; *Publishers Weekly,* August 16, 1976; Cornelia Jones and Olivia R. Way, *British Children's Authors,* American Library Association, 1976.

WILSON, Dorothy Clarke 1904-

PERSONAL: Born May 9, 1904, in Gardiner, Me.; daughter of Lewis H. (a minister) and Flora (Cross) Clarke; married Elwin L. Wilson (a minister), August 31, 1925; children: Joan, Harold E. *Education:* Bates College, A.B., 1925. *Politics:* Democrat. *Religion:* Methodist. *Home:* 114 Forest Ave., Orono, Me. 04473.

CAREER: Writer. Taught course on writing religious drama in workshops in Mexico City and Alexandria, Egypt, 1959, 1960; lectured in England and Scotland, 1960. *Member:* American Association of University Women, League of Women Voters, Phi Beta Kappa. *Awards, honors:* Bates College, Litt.D., 1947; Westminster award for religious fiction, for *Prince of Egypt,* 1949; Alpha Delta Kappa, Woman

of Distinction, 1971; New England United Methodist Award for excellence in social action, 1975.

WRITINGS: Twelve Months of Drama, Baker, 1934; *The Brother,* Westminster, 1944; *The Herdsman,* Westminster, 1946; *Prince of Egypt,* Westminster, 1949; *House of Earth,* Westminster, 1952; *Jezebel,* McGraw, 1955; *The Gifts,* McGraw, 1957; *Dr. Ida: The Story of Dr. Ida Scudder of Vellore,* McGraw, 1959; *The Journey* (juvenile), Abingdon, 1962; *Take My Hands: The Story of Dr. Mary Verghese,* McGraw, 1963; *The Three Gifts* (juvenile), Abingdon, 1963; *Ten Fingers for God* (biography of Paul Brand), McGraw, 1965; *Handicap Race: The Inspiring Story of Roger Arnett,* McGraw, 1967; *Palace of Healing,* McGraw, 1968; *Lone Woman: The Story of Elizabeth Blackwell—the World's First Woman Doctor,* Little, Brown, 1970; *The Big-Little World of Doc Pritham,* McGraw, 1971; *Hilary: The Brave World of Hilary Pole,* McGraw, 1973; *Bright Eyes: The Story of Susette la Flesche, an Omaha Indian,* McGraw, 1974; *Stranger and Traveler,* Little, Brown, 1975; *Granny Brand: Her Story,* Christian Herald Books, 1976; *Twelve Who Cared* (autobiographical), Christian Herald Books, 1977. Author of about seventy religious plays. Contributor of articles, short stories and plays to religious publications. Condensations in *Reader's Digest.*

FOR MORE INFORMATION SEE: Boston Post Magazine, March 27, 1949; *Portland Sunday Telegram,* Portland, Me., October 30, 1949; *Presbyterian Life,* November 12, 1949; *Wilson Library Bulletin,* June, 1951; *Lewiston Journal Magazine,* Lewiston, Me., January 10, 1953, October 17, 1959; *Christian Science Monitor,* March 4, 1955.

ZINDEL, Paul 1936-

PERSONAL: Born May 15, 1936, in Staten Island, N.Y.; son of Paul (a policeman) and Betty (Frank) Zindel; married Bonnie Hildebrand (a screenwriter), October 25, 1973; children: David Jack, Elizabeth Claire. *Education:* Wagner College, B.S., 1958, M.Sc., 1959. *Home:* 60 East 8th St., New York, N.Y. 10003. *Office:* c/o Harper & Row, 10 East 53rd St., New York, N.Y. 10022.

CAREER: Tottenville High School, Staten Island, N.Y., chemistry teacher, 1959-69; playwright and author of children's books, 1969—. *Member:* Actors Studio. *Awards, honors:* Received numerous awards for "The Effect of Gamma Rays on Man-in-the-Moon Marigolds" including Obie Award, 1970, Pulitzer Prize in Drama, 1971, New York Critics Award, 1971, and Drama Desk Award, 1971; honorary doctorate of humanities, Wagner College, 1971.

WRITINGS—Juvenile: The Pigman, Harper, 1968; *My Darling, My Hamburger,* Harper, 1969; *I Never Loved Your Mind,* Harper, 1970; *Pardon Me, You're Stepping on My Eyeball,* Harper, 1974; *I Love My Mother,* Harper, 1975; *Confessions of a Teenage Baboon,* Harper, 1977; *The Undertaker's Gone Bananas!,* Harper, 1979.

Plays: "Dimensions of Peacocks," first produced in New York, 1950; "Euthanasia and the Endless Hearts," first produced in New York, 1960; "A Dream of Swallows," first produced Off-Broadway, April, 1962; *The Effects of Gamma Rays on Man-in-the-Moon Marigolds* (first produced in Houston at Alley Theatre, 1964; produced Off-Broadway at Mercer-O'Casey Theatre, April 7, 1970), Harper, 1971; "And Miss Reardon Drinks a Little," first produced on Broadway at Morosco Theatre, February 25, 1971;

"The Secret Affairs of Mildred Wild," first produced in New York City, 1972; "Ladies at the Alamo," first produced at Actor's Studio, 1975; produced on Broadway at Martin Beck Theatre, April 7, 1977; _Let Me Hear You Whisper: A Play,_ Harper, 1974.

Screen and television plays include: "The Effect of Gamma Rays on Man-in-the-Moon Marigolds," produced by National Educational Television (NET), 1966, and Twentieth Century-Fox, 1973; "Let Me Hear You Whisper," produced by National Educational Television, 1966; "Up the Sandbox," 1972; "Mama," 1973. Also author of "The Pigman" (adapted from his novel), "Mrs. Beneker" (screenplay), and "Farewell to a Mouse Named Mars" (children's teleplay). Contributor of articles to newspapers and periodicals.

WORK IN PROGRESS: A play entitled "Destiny on Half Moon Street."

SIDELIGHTS: **May 15, 1936.** Born in Staten Island, New York. When Zindel was still young his father abandoned him, his mother, and sister. "I remember most of my life from the different places we lived in, because my family moved on the average of once or twice a year. That meant a constant changing of friends, it meant the family unit getting very close, and the animal friends being very dear—when they left, it was a great loss. Their departure was often timed with the moving, because we were going somewhere where the landlady would not permit pets.

"Number one, I know that I came from a very, very poor, broken home. My life didn't seem out of the ordinary at the time, but I was poor without knowing it.

"I also feel very close to minority groups. I grew right up in the midst of some, and sometimes sharing a home with them, on Staten Island. Of course, I never thought of them as 'minority groups.' I know that during World War II, when food was getting scarce, the black family next door to us had chickens. One of the things I'll never forget is my mother putting some corn out in the back yard to lure one of the chickens into our house. Now, my mother could never kill a chicken, so it was good thing that we were living with this Italian family at the moment. The mother in that family would wring a chicken's neck as easily as wring a washcloth.

**She kisses me before I dream
and turns on the light when the gorilla grabs.**
■ (From *I Love My Mother* by Paul Zindel. Illustrated by John Melo.)

"Staten Island is a very special place. It has about 25 distinct communities. Travis, for example, is Polish. That means that stores have the kielbasy sausages hanging in the window, and it means you have the women with the babushkas walking down the street—it's really like being in Poland. When you come in as an outsider, you *are* an outsider. That's why our family and the one black family in town would be friends—aside from the fact that they raised good chickens.

". . . One of our devices for survival in the war years was to raise collie dogs. Once, when they weren't selling, we ended up with 25.

"Animals at one time or another have eaten us out of house and home. They have ruined entire houses. And they were always somehow disappearing. When things would get really rough, foodwise or moneywise, or the dog would maybe bite one of the kids, I'd always come home from school and ask, 'Where's the dog?' And my mother would say, 'Well, the dog has gone on a little trip.' Animals were always being welcomed into our house with the greatest joy, but somehow their exits were horrible!" [From an article entitled, "Voice Talks With Paul Zindel," *Scholastic Voice*, April 27, 1970.[1]]

Zindel attended Port Richmond High School until a bout with tuberculosis forced him to interrupt his studies. "In high school the one important event was my getting tuberculosis. I had to leave school and go to Saranac Lake, New York, to a sanatorium called Stony Wold. I was there for a year and a half—the only kid, all the others were adults. I was 15 to 16½, and those are crucial years for a kid. I know they are. Being the only kid in an adult world has done things to me I don't even know about.

"It's not that the experience was horrible. It wasn't a concentration camp—it was the most beautiful place in the world. It was Tudor in style, and there were parts that looked like a Swiss chalet. It was bright and cheerful; the

PAUL ZINDEL

snow was fabulous on the mountains and the lake. I learned to play bridge and chess—and even a little piano.

"I returned for one visit to Port Richmond High School for the senior prom. I was escorting a 22-year-old girl from that sanatorium. There, ages begin to disappear from notice. And when I walked in with a 22-year-old woman, there were some pretty startled faces, let me tell you! I have a photograph of the prom, and the children in the background are aghast, while I'm not quite aware of what's going on—.

"I finally went back to high school, graduated a year later than I should have, and went on to Wagner College on Staten Island, majoring in chemistry."[1]

1958. Received a B.S. degree from Wagner College in New York. "Then I went to work as a technical writer for a chemical company. I had my little office, I had my little secretary—and I didn't know anything! My boss would call me in in the morning and get me in a corner and tell me about his part in the war (he was stationed in Washington), and send me back to research diethylamid, and I found that I didn't like the job. I also realized that they were a very wonderful company, and you couldn't do anything to get fired. That was the one advantage; the disadvantage was that they didn't pay very much.

"One day I found myself working very hard for an hour in the library, and then going to a movie in the afternoon. I knew then it was time to quit. Because work is the most

important thing in life, and unless that works out you're miserable.

"Riding to Manhattan on the ferry every morning, I used to see the same people, so I began identifying each one with a number—they all became characters. On the day I quit my job, I remember standing on the back of the ferry as it was pulling out. Here I am, with No. 1 over there, and No. 4 there, and everybody lined up, the whole cast of characters. And as the boat is pulling out of the slip, and the skyline comes more and more into view, the tears start running down my face like something incredible. It was just the fact that I would no longer be commuting to Manhattan—I had decided to become a teacher."[1]

1959. Received his M.Sc. degree from Wagner College.

1959-1969. Worked as a high school chemistry teacher. "I was a chemistry teacher for ten years at Tottenville High School on Staten Island. I have a B.S. in Chemistry and M.S. in education, and Wagner College, my alma mater, gave me a doctorate." [From an article entitled, "Of Life, Love, Death, Kids, and Inhalation Therapy: An Interview With Paul Zindel," *Top of the News,* Winter, 1978.[2]]

1966. Took a year's absence from teaching after receiving a Ford Grant. "A playwright today can very easily live on the income generated by his work. And there are so many grants. I only accepted one when I needed it: a Ford Foundation Grant for about $6,000 . . . to take a year off from teaching chemistry and to observe at the Alley Theater in Houston."[2]

Zindel's first play, "The Effects of Gamma Rays on Man-in-the-Moon Marigolds" was produced by National Educational Television that same year. "When Harper & Row saw 'Gamma Rays' they asked me if I would write some young people's books. I had never thought of writing for kids before. I began looking through all the teenage books that were floating around, and I said, 'Uh-uh. They're not doing it.' I realized right away that there was no competition. There were only two books that most kids ever read, *Catcher in the Rye* and *Lord of the Flies. Catcher* was the only book they really enjoyed reading, and the boys only read it because their girl friends made them. What kids like is that the characters talk the way kids actually talk.

"I wanted to write for teenagers as well as I could. I couldn't have them think I was 'writing down' to them, or that I wanted my book to be lifted out of their world and run as a big hit in the adult world. I wanted to do something honestly for that age group."[1]

1968. First book, *The Pigman,* was published. "I researched the form and drew upon my years of teaching high school and came up with *The Pigman.* After I turn in a draft of a book, Charlotte [Zolotow; vice-president of Harper & Row] comes up with many suggestions. It's usually always catching me in my major fault: showing only one side of a character, usually the dark side. Charlotte helps me stop and think about what the light side is, which tends to make the characters three-dimensional instead of two. I have been collecting material for an adult novel and will do one during the next couple of years.

"In my young adult novels I'm trying to say: 'Hey, kids, I recognize how boring Shakespeare and other brilliant writers can be when you're so young and not ready to plumb the great passions of Life as such writers have dished them up.

Beatrice: The Rabbit is in your room. I want you to bury it in the morning.
■ (From *The Effect of Gamma Rays on Man-in-the-Moon Marigolds* by Paul Zindel. Illustrated by Dong Kingman.)

Instead, if you're not ready for that I don't blame you because when I was your age I wasn't either and I learned to hate books. I've talked with many of you—terrific, smart kids—and I recognize that you enjoy certain things because they're closer to you. I'm writing novels for you that are (a), for the most part, school-oriented because school is important to you, it's a big thing in your lives; (b) I'm minimizing the role of parents because you get enough of them at home and you want them cast in small walk-ons; you're interested in the secret adventures between yourselves, the things you don't feel like including your parents in, not because you don't like them but because it's not as much fun; (c) I know you like first-person narratives, or at least narration techniques which keep the story seen through the teenagers' eyes; (d) I know you like interesting language and yet I know it must be lasting language—not slang, which will perish in a year or two, but rich, humorous, and sometimes wicked language because that's how you yourselves speak and it's a pleasure to talk to you; (e) I know you like romantic involvements, awkward kids who want to show affection for each other but know how difficult it is. I know you're worried about how you look, talk, and walk; (f) I know you like teenage protagonists who call a spade a spade because teenagers aren't phony as a rule. If anything, they tell the truth with a vengeance, but there's a reason for that, too; (g) I recognize that you like *mischief,* because mischief is one technique by which you remind the adult world that it can sometimes be a bit stuffy; (h) I know you like transitions of short chapters and an occasional funny diagram like something you'd write on a desk or blackboard because it relieves the dreary shape of a solid page of type; (i) I know you like fast pacing and ac-

tion because you're very active and love adventure and suspense; (j) and although I haven't been coming through for you lately on this count, I recognize that you really like very short books so you can fulfill book reports, and I apologize to you kids that I can't get a serious underlying point across to you in less than 50,000 words.' I think that's what I'm trying to tell the kids on one level.

"On a second level I'm trying to tell the kids something else. I ask them, 'Why do people hate?' I ask them, 'What is the process by which kids are made to feel inferior? Is it your parents? Is it a peer? A teacher? Strangers? Yourself? Who isn't encouraging you to feel good about yourself? Who is your evil mirror that prevents you from being happy and loving yourself and the world? Who puts you in positions of feeling powerless and that you're not up to snuff? What is the process by which this ends up creating in you a dislike for yourself and a fear of the world, which in turn finally emerges as hostility in you, or helplessness, or frustration?' I'm trying to tell the kids to examine self-hate and any feelings of inadequacy and to act to stop the process. I'm telling the kids that I loved the underdog and sympathize with his struggle because that's what I was and am in many ways still. I want my kids to feel worthy, to search for hope against all odds as they travel the plots of my books. I'm trying to tell all kids that they don't have to consider themselves misfits, that they deserve hopes and dreams and the technique and patience to make those dreams reality. I tell the kids that my books have a secret—a very useful secret—and to read them to find the lessons they teach, or to examine the problems they pose. I ask the kids to provoke discussion among themselves, to share the books with their teachers and librarians and parents and see that there is a beautiful tomorrow for them. I tell the kids that tomorrow becomes today through self-inspection and action and belief, that their minds come equiped by God or Nature with the spirit and means to be joyful and intimate with their fellow human beings. I tell them life can be sort of fun, but it isn't easy. I tell them in my novels to take good care of themselves, to be selfish if they must in order that their souls stay intact and their hearts never lie."[2]

Zindel also wrote the screenplay for *Pigman*. ". . . I took to screenwriting like a fish to water. You go to movies, and you think about them, you see the shots, and they build up in you. I was scared out of my wits at first, when I got the commission to do *Pigman*. I sat down and I wrote: 'Fade in.' Then I stopped.

"But I found a book on film writing that told you in plain English what was to be done. So I think I'm going to have a movie career.

"I loved writing the movie of *Pigman,* and I was able to clarify a whole lot of things that I hadn't understood fully when I was writing the novel.

"In the book there's a scene where John, Lorraine, and the Pigman visit the zoo together. They're awkward about talking, and that's about as deep as it goes. But in the movie I made the zoo scene accomplish something—Lorraine comes to accept the Pigman as a friend.

"Then comes the store scene, and I had to make sure that it accomplished something different. Lorraine is now a little concerned that she and John may be abusing the Pigman and she almost wants to take his side. This scene has to involve a deepening of the relationship between all three. They must not only understand and enjoy each other, they must care for each other.

"But it's hard. The Pigman wants to buy Lorraine the stockings. She doesn't want them for herself, but she takes them because she knows he'll be pleased. She also has to understand John a little better, because John is far readier than she is to accept presents from the Pigman.

"Kids always do things for a number of reasons, some selfish, some to be kind. It's always a mixed feeling for the teenager, it's never a pure action. There are always at least things going on, and it's a painful process.

"So the main deepening of the characters has to take place at the major part of the scene, when they're purchasing the roller skates. I realized, when I was doing the movie script, that I had left something out of the book at this point. I hadn't made Lorraine and John's need for each other strong enough. In the movie I do.

"The Pigman wants to buy them the skates. Lorraine doesn't want them, she's gotten the stockings, she doesn't want the old man to spend the money—she wants out. But now it's John who has the need. He needs to do something crazy, wild, and he needs somebody to do it with. But Lorraine is split—she doesn't want the Pigman to spend the money but, more important, she sees that John needs her.

"The major point of this scene is to bring Lorraine and John into a close relationship. This means that Lorraine has to drop some of her bashfulness and be able to participate with him in something kooky.

"So I do something very careful in the movie. My three characters are all together, at the peak of their relationship for the entire story. As they're zooming out of the sporting-goods department, the camera shoots by them, and you have the three monkeys in the pet shop across the way—pathetic, sad, and holding together for warmth. Visually, this tells what has been accomplished. The three monkeys represent the three friends. It's all—orchestrated."[2]

1971. Won the Pulitzer Prize in drama. "It was breathtaking to win the Pulitzer Prize in 1971 mainly because I didn't know what it was. I was watching 'King Kong' on television when the news came in, and all I knew was that whatever this prize was, it was going to make me have more friends and maybe bring love into my life because I was a very unhappy person. I also suspected it would give me more projects—and indeed I was immediately whisked out to Hollywood to work with Paul Newman and Barbra Streisand. It was all very preposterous, exciting, and corrupt—and fun and damning and useful. That prize brings with it many curses and many blessings."[2]

1973. Married Bonnie Hildebrand. The couple have two children, David Jack and Elizabeth Claire. "I was married rather late in life—age 37—to an exquisite little number named Bonnie Hildebrand. I met her in Cleveland, Ohio, where she was publicity director for the Cleveland Playhouse. Although she was then married to a psychologist who was involved with a suicide clinic, I soon took care of that, deciding that any girl who could do publicity as well as Bonnie deserved a truly fine husband like myself. I have since made her life a joy on earth with our two perfect children. David . . . and Elizabeth . . . the only hitch in her joy being that once in a while David tries to steal Elizabeth's toys and to knock her off, but Elizabeth is usually too busy dancing with her fur boa to notice.

"As I observe my son and daughter as infants I see great differences. Our home is unisex. I am open to anything my kids want to do, including choice of career. My initial observation, however, as a sort of new parent is that David will be more qualified to unload refrigerators at a G.E. factory than Elizabeth."[2]

1978. Zindel has written several teenage novels, most recent of which are *Confessions of a Teenage Baboon* and *The Undertaker's Gone Bananas*. "*Confessions of a Teenage Baboon* is a story so close to me that I almost had a nervous breakdown writing it. I pushed myself too close to the inner demons which drive me, and it leads naturally to my next book, *The Undertaker's Gone Bananas,* in which I will explore through teenage characters my feelings about death set against a thriller background. I can feel already that the theme of it is Death against Love, and Love is going to win hands-down. Love, unexpected, kind and exciting, has saved so many people, don't you think?"[2]

Although Zindel writes novels which are extremely popular with teenagers, he considers himself primarily a playwright. "Writing for the theater, or writing a novel, or giving a speech, or doing a lesson plan all have something in common. Basically they involve the imparting of a story which leads an audience through a series of conflicts to the learning of a lesson. A person is born with a disposition for one type of expression. For me, it was playwriting. Each form has a pure form, a classic form, and it's this form that interests

(From the stage production of "The Effect of Gamma Rays on Man-in-the-Moon Marigolds,"
starring Joan Blondell and Jennifer Harmon.)

me—not the sensational, lopsided, experimental flashes which sometimes divert, like fashion. I had to face up to the fact that my basic talent was in placing actors in one set and putting them in conflict, and hope that some insight into self and humanity would come out of it all. The novel and screenplay were very hard for me to work with because of the greater freedom of time and space they allow. To this day I keep in front of me when writing a novel a rule which states 'Any Portion of a Novel That Sounds Unbelievable in Action Should Be Transposed Into Narration.' The example sentence which follows is: 'The Reverend Kendall had an argument with his wife that night, left his home in a rage, went to a neighborhood bar, and proceeded to get drunk.' The playwright in me would stage the entire scene, write all the dialogue. The novel and screenplay don't require that; in fact, such indulgence renders the young adult novel tedious and any movie, boring. I fight desperately to embrace the delights and freedoms and demands of each medium.''[2]

Paul Zindel has always been a writer of plays about women, and has provided actresses with some of the best roles since Tennessee Williams, a writer with whom *Variety* compared him after the opening of "The Effects of Gamma Rays on Man-in-the-Moon Marigolds."

In a recent television interview Zindel explained that he liked to write about "what's happening," and the fact that his plays are about women does indeed mean that he thinks women are what's happening today. The women, however, are not always very nice. In fact, they are usually women in distress. This has been a central theme in his plays.

"I am virtually desperate for some sign, for any bit of hope, or reason, to make being a human sensible. In each of my plays, there is an attempt to find some grain of truth, something to hang onto. In 'Marigolds' it's this: One is composed of matter that's been around for millions of years, matter that comes from other worlds, other galaxies. That's a little thrilling, to be part of that infinity that is so vast and so marvelous that our minds cannot really grasp it.''

About his work, Zindel commented: "Whatever I do becomes summarized in my writing. When I have gained a certain quantity of experience which begins to shape itself into something secret and interesting, I feel I must tell others about it. So I sit around and daydream about how I'm going to tell it, and when I find a way of condensing it interestingly to myself, and I have a suspicion of a vision those characters will have toward the end of the play, then the excitement and the necessity of wanting to clarify that vision gives me the energy to work indefatigably. I can write a play in a week in those conditions.''

Zindel claims that people have told him he is a born playwright, and that he comes at a time when he is most needed, when "the Theatre is dying." His response to this was to describe the unique path which led to his profession. "I evolved into a writer of plays by never having gone near a theatre until I was in my twenties. The fact that I had written two plays by that time makes me believe that the seeds of theatre are born inside us.''

FOR MORE INFORMATION SEE: Village Voice, April 16, 1970; *New York Times,* April 19, 1970, July 26, 1970, March 8, 1971, February 26, 1971, April 8, 1977; *Time,* April 20, 1970; *Horn Book,* April, 1970, June, 1971, October, 1976; *Scholastic Voice,* April 27, 1970; *Washington Post,* January 27, 1971; *Boston Globe,* January, 1971; *Top of the News,* Winter, 1978.

SOMETHING ABOUT THE AUTHOR

CUMULATIVE INDEXES, VOLUMES 1-16
Illustrations and Authors

ILLUSTRATIONS INDEX

(In the following index, the number of the volume in which an illustrator's work appears is given *before* the colon, and the page on which it appears is given *after* the colon. For example, a drawing by Adams, Adrienne appears in Volume 2 on page 6, another drawing by her appears in Volume 3 on page 80, another drawing in Volume 8 on page 1, and another drawing in Volume 15 on page 107.)

Illustrations Index

AUTHOR INDEX

(In the following index, the number of the volume in which an author's sketch appears is given *before* the colon, and the page on which it appears is given *after* the colon. For example, the sketch of Aardema, Verna, appears in Volume 4 on page 1). This index includes references to *Yesterday's Authors of Books for Children.*

Aardema, Verna, *4:* 1
Aaron, Chester, *9:* 1
Abbott, Alice. *See* Borland,
    Kathryn Kilby, *16:* 54
Abbott, Alice. *See* Speicher,
    Helen Ross (Smith), *8:* 194
Abdul, Raoul, *12:* 1
Abel, Raymond, *12:* 2
Abell, Kathleen, *9:* 1
Abercrombie, Barbara (Mattes),
    16: 1
Abernethy, Robert G., *5:* 1
Abisch, Roslyn Kroop, *9:* 3
Abisch, Roz. *See* Abisch, Roslyn
    Kroop, *9:* 3
Abrahall, C. H. *See* Hoskyns-
    Abrahall, Clare, *13:* 105
Abrahall, Clare Hoskyns. *See*
    Hoskyns-Abrahall, Clare,
    13: 105
Abrahams, Robert D(avid), *4:* 3
Abrams, Joy, *16:* 2
Ackerman, Eugene, *10:* 1
Adair, Margaret Weeks, *10:* 1
Adams, Adrienne, *8:* 1
Adams, Andy, *YABC 1:* 1
Adams, Harriet S(tratemeyer), *1:* 1
Adams, Hazard, *6:* 1
Adams, Richard, *7:* 1
Adams, Ruth Joyce, *14:* 1
Adamson, Graham. *See* Groom,
    Arthur William, *10:* 53
Adamson, Joy, *11:* 1
Addona, Angelo F., *14:* 1
Addy, Ted. *See* Winterbotham,
    R(ussell) R(obert), *10:* 198
Adelberg, Doris. *See* Orgel,
    Doris, *7:* 173
Adelson, Leone, *11:* 2
Adkins, Jan, *8:* 2
Adler, David A., *14:* 2
Adler, Irene. *See* Storr, Catherine
    (Cole), *9:* 181

Adler, Irving, *1:* 2
Adler, Ruth, *1:* 4
Adoff, Arnold, *5:* 1
Adorjan, Carol, *10:* 1
Adshead, Gladys L., *3:* 1
Agapida, Fray Antonio. *See*
    Irving, Washington,
    YABC 2: 164
Agle, Nan Hayden, *3:* 2
Agnew, Edith J(osephine), *11:* 3
Ahern, Margaret McCrohan, *10:* 2
Aichinger, Helga, *4:* 4
Aiken, Clarissa (Lorenz), *12:* 4
Aiken, Conrad, *3:* 3
Aiken, Joan, *2:* 1
Ainsworth, Norma, *9:* 4
Ainsworth, Ruth, *7:* 1
Aistrop, Jack, *14:* 3
Aitken, Dorothy, *10:* 2
Alberts, Frances Jacobs, *14:* 4
Albrecht, Lillie (Vanderveer), *12:* 5
Alcott, Louisa May, *YABC 1:* 7
Alden, Isabella (Macdonald),
    YABC 2: 1
Alderman, Clifford Lindsey, *3:* 6
Aldis, Dorothy (Keeley), *2:* 2
Aldon, Adair. *See* Meigs,
    Cornelia, *6:* 167
Aldridge, Josephine Haskell, *14:* 5
Alegria, Ricardo E., *6:* 1
Alexander, Anna Cooke, *1:* 4
Alexander, Frances, *4:* 6
Alexander, Linda, *2:* 3
Alexander, Lloyd, *3:* 7
Alexander, Martha, *11:* 4
Alexander, Sue, *12:* 5
Alexeieff, Alexandre A., *14:* 5
Alger, Horatio, Jr., *16:* 3
Alger, Leclaire (Gowans), *15:* 1
Aliki. *See* Brandenberg, Aliki, *2:* 36
Alkema, Chester Jay, *12:* 7
Allamand, Pascale, *12:* 8
Allan, Mabel Esther, *5:* 2

Allen, Adam [Joint pseudonym].
    See Epstein, Beryl and
    Samuel, *1:* 85
Allen, Allyn. *See* Eberle,
    Irmengarde, *2:* 97
Allen, Betsy. *See* Cavanna, Betty,
    1: 54
Allen, Gertrude E(lizabeth), *9:* 5
Allen, Leroy, *11:* 7
Allen, Samuel (Washington), *9:* 6
Allerton, Mary. *See* Govan,
    Christine Noble, *9:* 80
Allison, Bob, *14:* 7
Allred, Gordon T., *10:* 3
Almedingen, Martha Edith von.
    See Almedingen, E. M., *3:* 9
Almedingen, E. M., *3:* 9
Almquist, Don, *11:* 8
Alsop, Mary O'Hara, *2:* 4
Alter, Robert Edmond, *9:* 8
Altsheler, Joseph A(lexander),
    YABC 1: 20
Ambrus, Victor G(tozo), *1:* 6
Amerman, Lockhart, *3:* 11
Ames, Evelyn, *13:* 1
Ames, Gerald, *11:* 9
Ames, Lee J., *3:* 11
Amon, Aline, *9:* 8
Amoss, Berthe, *5:* 4
Anckarsvard, Karin, *6:* 2
Ancona, George, *12:* 10
Andersen, Hans Christian,
    YABC 1: 23
Anderson, C(larence) W(illiam),
    11: 9
Anderson, Ella. *See* MacLeod,
    Ellen Jane (Anderson), *14:* 129
Anderson, Eloise Adell, *9:* 9
Anderson, George. *See* Groom,
    Arthur William, *10:* 53
Anderson, J(ohn) R(ichard)
    L(ane), *15:* 3
Anderson, Joy, *1:* 8

Kelly, Eric P(hilbrook),
  YABC 1: 165
Kelly, Ralph. *See* Geis, Darlene,
  7: 101
Kelly, Regina Z., 5: 94
Kelsey, Alice Geer, 1: 129
Kempner, Mary Jean, 10: 67
Kempton, Jean Welch, 10: 67
Kendall, Carol (Seeger), 11: 148
Kendall, Lace. *See* Stoutenburg,
  Adrien, 3: 217
Kennedy, John Fitzgerald, 11: 150
Kennedy, Joseph, 14: 104
Kennedy, X. J. *See* Kennedy,
  Joseph, 14: 104
Kennell, Ruth E., 6: 127
Kenny, Herbert A(ndrew), 13: 117
Kent, Margaret, 2: 161
Kent, Rockwell, 6: 128
Kenworthy, Leonard S., 6: 131
Kenyon, Ley, 6: 131
Kepes, Juliet A(ppleby), 13: 118
Kerigan, Florence, 12: 117
Kerr, Jessica, 13: 119
Kerry, Frances. *See* Kerigan,
  Florence, 12: 117
Kerry, Lois. *See* Arquette, Lois
  S., 1: 13
Kessler, Leonard P., 14: 106
Kesteven, G. R. *See* Crosher,
  G(eoffry) R(obins), 14: 51
Kettelkamp, Larry, 2: 163
Key, Alexander (Hill), 8: 98
Khanshendel, Chiron. *See* Rose,
  Wendy, 12: 180
Kherdian, David, 16: 175
Kiddell, John, 3: 93
Killilea, Marie (Lyons), 2: 165
Kilreon, Beth. *See* Walker,
  Barbara K., 4: 219
Kimbrough, Emily, 2: 166
Kimmel, Eric A., 13: 120
Kindred, Wendy, 7: 150
Kines, Pat Decker, 12: 118
King, Arthur. *See* Cain, Arthur
  H., 3: 33
King, Billie Jean, 12: 119
King, Cynthia, 7: 152
King, Martin. *See* Marks,
  Stan(ley), 14: 136
King, Martin Luther, Jr., 14: 108
King, Reefe. *See* Barker, Albert
  W., 8: 3
King, Stephen, 9: 126
Kingman, (Mary) Lee, 1: 133
Kingsland, Leslie William, 13: 121
Kingsley, Charles, *YABC 2:* 179
Kinney, C. Cle, 6: 132
Kinney, Harrison, 13: 122
Kinney, Jean Stout, 12: 120
Kinsey, Elizabeth. *See* Clymer,
  Eleanor, 9: 37
Kipling, (Joseph) Rudyard,
  YABC 2: 193
Kirk, Ruth (Kratz), 5: 95
Kirkup, James, 12: 120

Kirtland, G. B. *See* Joslin, Sesyle,
  2: 158
Kishida, Eriko, 12: 123
Kisinger, Grace Gelvin, 10: 68
Kissin, Eva H., 10: 68
Klass, Morton, 11: 152
Kleberger, Ilse, 5: 96
Klein, H. Arthur, 8: 99
Klein, Leonore, 6: 132
Klein, Mina C(ooper), 8: 100
Klein, Norma, 7: 152
Klimowicz, Barbara, 10: 69
Knickerbocker, Diedrich. *See*
  Irving, Washington,
  YABC 2: 164
Knight, Damon, 9: 126
Knight, David C(arpenter), 14: 111
Knight, Francis Edgar, 14: 112
Knight, Frank. *See* Knight,
  Francis Edgar, 14: 112
Knight, Hilary, 15: 157
Knight, Mallory T. *See* Hurwood,
  Bernhardt J., 12: 107
Knott, Bill. *See* Knott, William
  Cecil, Jr., 3: 94
Knott, William Cecil, Jr., 3: 94
Knowles, John, 8: 101
Knox, Calvin. *See* Silverberg,
  Robert, 13: 206
Knudson, R. R. *See* Knudson,
  Rozanne, 7: 154
Knudson, Rozanne, 7: 154
Koch, Dorothy Clarke, 6: 133
Kohn, Bernice (Herstein), 4: 136
Kohner, Frederick, 10: 70
Komisar, Lucy, 9: 127
Komoda, Kiyo, 9: 127
Komroff, Manuel, 2: 168
Konigsburg, E(laine) L(obl), 4: 137
Koning, Hans. *See* Koningsberger,
  Hans, 5: 97
Koningsberger, Hans, 5: 97
Konkle, Janet Everest, 12: 124
Korach, Mimi, 9: 128
Koren, Edward, 5: 98
Korinetz, Yuri (Iosifovich), 9: 129
Korty, Carol, 15: 159
Kossin, Sandy (Sanford), 10: 71
Koutoukas, H. M.. *See* Rivoli,
  Mario, 10: 129
Kouts, Anne, 8: 103
Krantz, Hazel (Newman), 12: 126
Krasilovsky, Phyllis, 1: 134
Kraus, Robert, 4: 139
Krauss, Ruth, 1: 135
Krautter, Elisa. *See* Bialk, Elisa,
  1: 25
Kristof, Jane, 8: 104
Kroeber, Theodora (Kracaw),
  1: 136
Kroll, Francis Lynde, 10: 72
Krumgold, Joseph, 1: 136
Krüss, James, 8: 104
Kumin, Maxine (Winokur), 12: 127
Künstler, Morton, 10: 73
Kuratomi, Chizuko, 12: 128

Kurelek, William, 8: 106
Kurland, Gerald, 13: 123
Kuskin, Karla (Seidman), 2: 169
Kvale, Velma R(uth), 8: 108
Kyle, Elisabeth. *See* Dunlop,
  Agnes M. R., 3: 62

Lacy, Leslie Alexander, 6: 135
Lader, Lawrence, 6: 135
Lady of Quality, A. *See* Bagnold,
  Enid, 1: 17
La Farge, Phyllis, 14: 113
Lagerlöf, Selma, 15: 160
Laimgruber, Monika, 11: 153
Laklan, Carli, 5: 100
Lamb, G(eoffrey) F(rederick),
  10: 74
Lamb, Lynton, 10: 75
Lamb, Robert (Boyden), 13: 123
Lamburn, Richmal Crompton,
  5: 101
Lampman, Evelyn Sibley, 4: 140
Lamprey, Louise, *YABC 2:* 221
Lancaster, Bruce, 9: 130
Land, Barbara (Neblett), 16: 177
Land, Jane [Joint pseudonym]. *See*
  Borland, Kathryn Kilby,
  16: 54. *See* Speicher, Helen
  Ross (Smith), 8: 194
Land, Myrick (Ebben), 15: 174
Land, Ross [Joint pseudonym].
  See Borland, Kathryn Kilby,
  16: 54. *See* Speicher, Helen
  Ross (Smith), 8: 194
Landau, Elaine, 10: 75
Landeck, Beatrice, 15: 175
Landin, Les(lie), 2: 171
Landshoff, Ursula, 13: 124
Lane, Carolyn, 10: 76
Lane, John, 15: 175
Lanes, Selma G., 3: 96
Lang, Andrew, 16: 178
Lange, John. *See* Crichton, (J.)
  Michael, 9:
Lange, Suzanne, 5: 103
Langner, Nola, 8: 110
Langstaff, John, 6: 135
Langstaff, Launcelot. *See* Irving,
  Washington, *YABC 2:* 164
Langton, Jane, 3: 97
Larrick, Nancy G., 4: 141
Larsen, Egon, 14: 115
Larson, Eve. *See* St. John, Wylly
  Folk, 10: 132
Larson, William H., 10: 77
Lasher, Faith B., 12: 129
Lasker, Joe, 9: 131
Lasky, Kathryn, 13: 124
Lassalle, C. E. *See* Ellis, Edward
  S(ylvester), *YABC 1:* 116
Latham, Barbara, 16: 187
Latham, Frank B., 6: 137
Latham, Jean Lee, 2: 171
Latham, Mavis. *See* Clark, Mavis
  Thorpe, 8: 27